Anonymous

History of Northumberland, Pennsylvania

Anonymous

History of Northumberland, Pennsylvania

ISBN/EAN: 9783337372965

Printed in Europe, USA, Canada, Australia, Japan

Cover: Foto ©ninafisch / pixelio.de

More available books at **www.hansebooks.com**

1751

HISTORY

OF

NORTHUMBERLAND CO.,

PENNSYLVANIA,

With Illustrations

DESCRIPTIVE OF ITS SCENERY,

Palatial Residences,

Public Buildings, Fine Blocks, and Important Manufactories,

FROM ORIGINAL SKETCHES BY ARTISTS OF THE HIGHEST ABILITY.

PHILADELPHIA:
EVERTS & STEWART,
716 FILBERT STREET.

1876

CONTENTS.

INTRODUCTORY.

ILLUSTRATIONS.

PORTRAITS.

BIOGRAPHICAL SKETCHES.

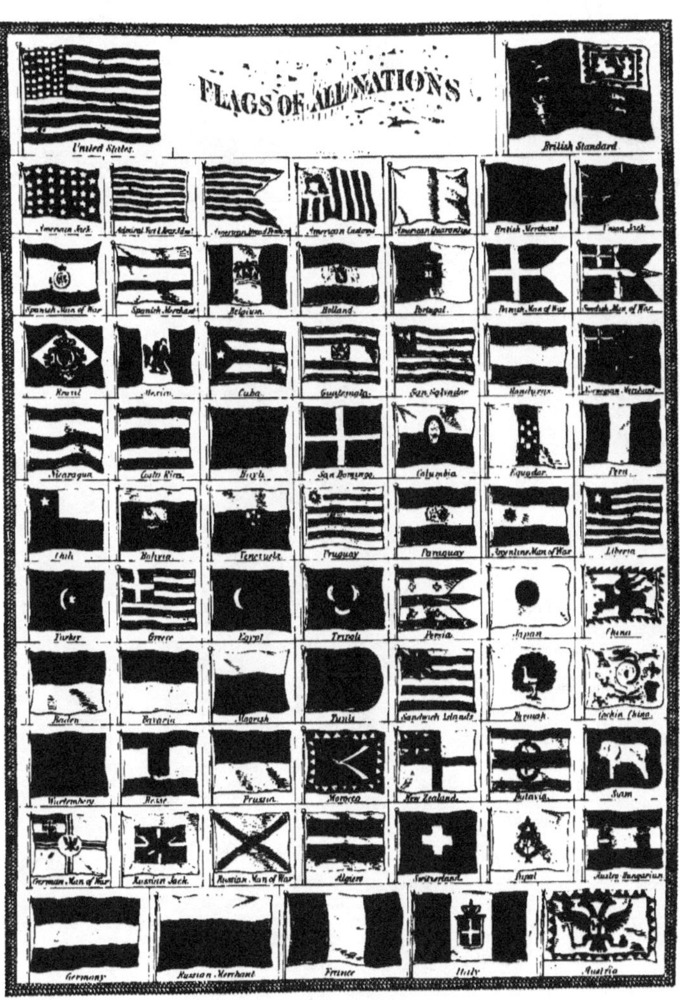
FLAGS OF ALL NATIONS
United States.
British Standard
British Merchant
Spanish Man of War
Spanish Merchant
Belgium.
Holland.
Portugal.
Danish Man of War
Swedish Man of War.
Cuba.
Guatemala.
San Salvador
Honduras.
Nicaragua
Costa Rica
San Domingo.
Columbia
Equador.
Peru.
Paraguay
Liberia
Turkey
Greece
Egypt
Tripoli
Persia
Japan
China
Baden
Bavaria
Moorish
Tunis
Sandwich Islands
Cochin China
Hesse
Prussia
Morocco
New Zealand
Batavia
Siam
German Man of War
Russian Jack
Russian Man of War
Algiers
Switzerland
Austro Hungarian
Germany
Russian Merchant
France
Italy
Austria

SEALS OF THE STATES OF THE UNITED STATES OF AMERICA.

SEALS OF THE STATES, (Continued.)

LOUISIANA.

TEXAS.

ARKANSAS.

TENNESSEE.

KENTUCKY.

OHIO.

MICHIGAN.

INDIANA.

ILLINOIS.

MISSOURI.

IOWA.

WISCONSIN.

MINNESOTA.

KANSAS.

CALIFORNIA.

OREGON.

NEBRASKA.

NEVADA.

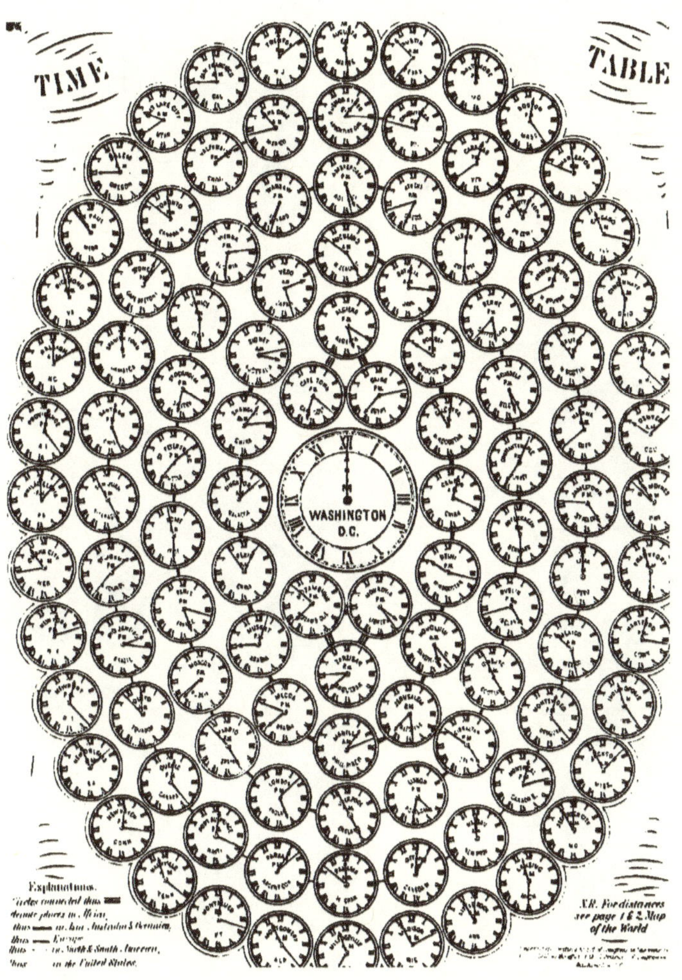
TIME
TABLE
WASHINGTON
D.C.
Explanations.
Circles connected thus denote places in Africa,
thus in Asia, Australia & Oceanica,
thus Europe
thus in North & South America,
thus in the United States.
N.B. For distances see page 1 & 2, Map of the World

HISTORY

OF

NORTHUMBERLAND COUNTY, PENNSYLVANIA.

CHAPTER I.

INTRODUCTORY.

THE object sought to be attained in writing a history of Northumberland County, in this the Centennial year of our experience in self-government, and the one hundred and fourth of our existence as a County, is not to provide an intellectual treat in classical literature, nor by the verboseness of our diction, to inflict upon our readers a voluminous compound of nothing new; but to provide a compendium, which shall, in as succinct a manner as possible, connect the living present with the extinct past; that the experiences of those, who in the certain past struggled against adverse storms, until finally overcome and sepulchred within the dark veil of oblivion, with which the progressive present so readily enshrouds unpleasant memories, may guide us in the possible future. History will do this—plain unvarnished history—that alone keeps alive the burning embers, that fill with an intense heat, the hearts of patriots of every age! American history possesses an interest for Americans, but little appreciated by the denizens of the old nations of the earth. But a few generations have come and gone, since this fair land was unknown, save to the Indians; so that every stroke of the axe, that by its ceaseless blows has disembowered the millions of acres that now blossom with the fruits of the husbandman's toil, possesses an interest to every child of America. The steady march of civilization that commenced its weary pilgrimage at Plymouth Rock, can be traced at each successive step, as it wends its way toward the setting sun. So recently have we commenced our history as a people, that the echoes of the joyful songs of praise, that burst from the throats of the storm-bound mariners, as they landed upon the dreary rock, have scarcely ceased to be heard. Every event of the struggle for existence, that followed, is fraught with interest to the descendants of those hardy and conscientious pioneers; and it is the province of the historian to preserve them fresh in the minds of our people, as a stimulus to more earnest effort in the struggles of the future. Many years have passed since the first feeble attempt was made to establish homes for the persecuted on these shores. Two and a half centuries have made their impress upon the face of time, and now, as we stand upon the pinnacle, which a hundred years' labor as a nation has erected, and view the past, our hearts should swell with pride at the thought of what has been accomplished in so short a period. On every hand are seen evidences of wealth and prosperity, unparalleled among any other people on earth; from the weakest, we have strengthened until our claim as the strongest nation is undisputed; and all this has been accomplished in less than fifteen generations of man. We must not stop here; profiting by the experiences of the past, as held up to view by the faithful historian, we have but to stride on, our steps becoming longer and stronger as we progress. Such is the province and duty of the writer of history; show what has been done, and there will be no limit to man's achievements in the future. Without the light afforded by history, every step in advance would be experimental; without the knowledge of what *has been*, the courage to try what *is to be*, would be wanting. The difficulties encountered here; the trials and sufferings of those who, one hundred and twenty-five years ago, let the light of civilization into the wilds of Northumberland County, are analogous to the experiences of the pioneers of every hamlet on the Western Continent. It is to give the full meed of credit to those hardy, self-sacrificing men and women, whose labors have accomplished so much for future generations, to secure for ourselves and those coming after, all the advantages gained by the lessons their self-denial and heroism have taught us, that we enter upon the pleasing, but arduous task of resurrecting from the sepulchre of oblivion, a faithful record of the acts of those modest but truly great, who were well content to retire behind the veil, so that others should enjoy the fruits of their labor. We, to-day, are living in the peaceful enjoyment of everything that a bountiful nature can provide; but do we reflect, that every *foot* of land that we now occupy, ere it could be made to yield its fruits, was moistened by the sweat, and in many instances, the blood of our ancestors! Northumberland County was the theater in which were enacted many trying scenes: probably no territory of like extent is richer in thrilling events; no section has cost a greater expenditure of muscle and blood. It is not expected to faithfully portray every event of interest; to give to each and all the full credit to which they are justly entitled; but it is expected to furnish as faithful a chronical of the leading men and incidents as can be obtained. Many generations have passed since the first settler penetrated the unbroken wilderness that prevailed here. Many matters that would be profitable for us to know, have been long since forgotten. The principal actors, after faithfully performing their part here, have gone to receive their reward, rendering it impossible to be as faithful in portraying the past as its importance demands; but an earnest effort will be made to make our history truly represent the most important facts, from the time when the good Conrad Weiser preached glad tidings to *Shikelimo* and his dusky followers, to the present. If we shall awaken in the mind of any future writer, a desire to penetrate deeper into the labyrinthian past; if we shall arouse in our people of to-day, an interest in their own local history; we shall have accomplished all that is expected, and shall leave it for the future historian to take up the work where we have left it, and complete what has been so imperfectly begun.

CHAPTER II.

BOUNDARIES OF NORTHUMBERLAND—DESCRIPTION—GEOGRAPHICAL—GEOLOGICAL—ETC.

An Act for erecting a part of the counties of Lancaster, Cumberland, Berks, Northampton and Bedford, into a separate County: Be it enacted, that all and singularly, the lands lying and being with the boundaries following: that is to say, beginning at the mouth of Mahantongo Creek, on the west side of the river Susquehanna; thence up the south side of said creek, by the several courses thereof, to the head at Robert Metur's spring; thence west by north to the top of Turey's Mountain; thence south-westerly along the summit of the mountain to little Juniata; thence up the north-easterly side of the main branch of little Juniata to the head thereof; thence north to the line of Berks County; thence north-west along said line, to the extremity of the province; thence east, along the north boundary, to that part thereof which is due north from the northern part of the Great Swamp; thence south to the most northern part of the Swamp aforesaid; thence with a straight line to the head of the Lehigh, or Middle Creek, thence down said creek so far, that a line run west-south-west, will strike the forks of Mahantongo Creek, where Pine Creek falls into the same, at the place called Spread Eagle, on the east side of Susquehanna; thence down and across the river to the place of beginning; shall be and the same is hereby erected into a County, henceforth to be called Northumberland.

The following acts conferred upon the people of the newly erected County, like privileges and guarantees as those possessed by residents of other counties. The Act was passed March 21st, 1772. As will be observed, Northumberland County originally comprised a large extent of territory, being most of that acquired) by purchase of the Indians by the Susquehanna Company, at Albany, in April 1754, and by the Proprietaries at Fort Stanwix, 1768. September 25th, 1786, a portion from the northern part was cut off, from which Luzerne County was organized. April 13th, 1795, Lycoming County was erected. September 19th, 1789, Mifflin was taken off; and February 13th, 1800, Centre was organized.

Union and Columbia were erected March 22d, 1813, from Northumberland. By Act of the General Assembly, approved February 21st, 1815, the townships of Turbut and Chillisquaque were taken from Columbia and annexed to Northumberland County, leaving the boundaries as now.

Northumberland formerly comprised a large extent of territory, out of which a large number of counties have been erected, as the needs of population and business required. The different counties organized within the territory originally embraced in Northumberland, were as follows:

Luzerne organized September 25th, 1786; Mifflin organized September 19th, 1789; Lycoming organized April 13th, 1795; Centre organized February 13th, 1800; Clearfield organized March 26th, 1804; Columbia and Union organized March 22d, 1813. Nearly all of these have been subdivided, so that out of Northumberland, twenty-six counties have been erected. As will be observed from above statistics, until 1786, all settlers in the northwest territory were compelled to come to Sunbury to attend to the legal business of the County. The expense and trouble were largely augmented by the difficulty of communicating with the settlements. Officials were compelled to journey a distance of fifty or one hundred miles to serve a suit, or summons a jury; these jury-men, to travel the distance often on foot to attend the sittings of the Court. All of these hardships, as they were, by no means were the only difficulties encountered by our ancestors, a narration of which it is the purpose of this work to faithfully portray. The following bill of items exhibits the cost of defining the County boundaries:

SUNBURY 1st JUNE 1796

The County of Northumberland Dr.

To Philip Myer John Eckman & John Reese the Commissioners for Running & Marking the Lines Dividing the Countys of Berks Northumberland Northampton & Luzern.

	L	s	d
To Expene of Chain Carriers Markers &c from Mahantongo & pine Creek to the Northampton County Line	59	16	1½
From Northampton County Line to the Lehi and up the same to Luzer C For Expene of Chain Carriers Markers pack horses &c	63	13	9
Expene of provitions and other Necessaries To Luzern County Line	49	16	10
To Philip Myar on Duty 40 Days a 8 Dolls pr Day the one half Being 4 Dolls pr Day To Do going to and Returning from the Lines	6	00	0
To Jno Eckman on Duty as above	60	00	0
To Do going to and Returning from the Lines	8	00	0
To John Reese on Duty on the Lines as above	60	00	0
To Do going to and Returning from the Lines	6	00	0
To Traveling Expence to Mr Rees the one half	1	18	1
	L367	4	9½

PHILIP MYER
JOHN ECKMAN
JNO. REES
} Commissioners for Running the Lines as aforesaid

It has been remarked by a celebrated historian, "that in the infancy of society, men are occupied with the business of the present, forgetful of the past and regardless of the future;" and the experiences of all ages and countries furnish abundant testimony to the truth of this declaration. There are few territories, the early settlement of which afford a more forcible exemplification of the truth of this, than that embraced within the confines of Northumberland County. The natural obstacles everywhere met; the dangers from foes without; the character of the people who constituted largely the pioneers into this then rugged and mountainous country, all tended to a condition of the mind of utter forgetfulness of all but the important present; and indeed the advance guards of civilization, in their trials, had abundant opportunity to realize the force of Longfellow's immortal stanza. "Life is real, Life is earnest," content to "Let the dead past bury the dead," and avoid speculation as to the grave being the final resting place of the soul.

"In the world's broad field of battle,
In the bivouac of life,
They were not dumb driven cattle,
They were heroes in the strife."

The strife was one continued effort to implant themselves upon the lands of their less fortunate fellows.

This County is peculiarly situated, describing in its boundary a figure never yet known to the geometrician. As originally defined, it embraced an extent of territory never well understood, but certainly much larger than many states. The County as now defined, would form the nucleus of a small solar system; the counties erected from old Northumberland, the planets extending far in all directions but the south, which, twenty-six in number, learned their first lessons in local self-government, from the parent. Geographically, it presents the shape of an old-fashioned chair, the back leaning a little forward at the top. The general appearance of the surface is hilly, and not altogether inviting; rocks forming precipitous cliffs are seen in all directions, in that portion lying south of the north branch of the river Susquehanna. Hills contending with each other for supremacy in altitude, dot the entire surface, forming the confines of innumerable vales, fertile and very productive, but limited in extent. Little rivulets are met in every direction, tergiversations of which equal the twisting course of Mother Eve's mortal enemy, but affording a scenery and water-power, unrivalled in the world. North of the East branch of the river, a different country is found. Montour's ridge, the dividing line between Northumberland and Montour County, separates the broken hilly south from the rich alluvial plains that lie to the north. The four northernmost townships present a surface of far different nature. From Montour's Ridge to Muncy hills the soil is fertile, the surface generally but moderately rolling. This entire country is densely populated by a class of people, whose reliance is upon the tillage of the soil. The western boundary is washed its entire length by the west branch and the main river Susquehanna. The flat lands along its borders extend back in some places to a considerable distance, and the entire distance from where the river crosses the southern boundary of Lycoming County, to its confluence with the east branch at Northumberland, farm houses and towns make up a pleasing picture. South of this point, the hills or bluffs rise abruptly at places near the water's edge, leaving but a narrow passage way between their base and the river. The river, one branch of which rises in the central part of Clearfield County, and by a circuitous route around the mountains, finds its way to Northumberland, meeting there the north branch which rises in Otsego Lake, New York, and by an equally tortuous course, meets and joins forces with the Otzinachson, is appropriately named Susquehanna, or Crooked River. For commerce, this stream is useless, except so far as its waters are made available for feeding canals, and furnishing power for manufacturing purposes. Its tergiversations are innumerable, in many places within a distance of 8 or 10 miles, flowing towards every point of compass. By the Indians, it was sometimes called "shallow stream," which they claimed was the true interpretation of the term Susquehanna. This also would be quite appropriate, as there are not two consecutive miles of river navigation, from Harris Ferry to the head of either branch, aside from that provided by artificial means, for a flat-boat. The bed of the stream is uneven, and very rocky, at places, the entire width being occupied by high bowlders, that rear their heads as a warning to the venturesome lumberman, who would seek among them a passage for his products to a market. The scenery borders on the grand, offering every variety, from the beautiful little islets that form a pleasing landscape, to the rocky cliffs that perpendicularly shoot heavenward, as if contending in majesty with the clouds. What a home for the red man was here found! Isolated from all that interrupted his enjoyment on earth, what ecstatic emotions must have enraptured his soul as he gazed upon the wondrous works of the God he adored, manifesting in the compilation, strength and wisdom, far beyond his crude imagination! It is easy for the dreamer to see a reproduction of the scenes, that a hundred and twenty years ago were daily enacted here. The dusky hunter, scaling the cliffs, paddling o'er the bosom of the crooked river in quest of his game, rambling with the freedom of a child of nature, as he was, wherever inclination prompted. The dark hued maid, with step as lithe and limb as free as the beautiful gazelle, bounding over ravines, through the forest, or chanting her love songs to the roving hunter. All these are reproduced, as the eye wanders over the magnificent scenery, more grand, because art has never been able to deface the rugged lines traced by the finger of God. The consonance of the scenery, with the aboriginal inhabitants, is striking; impressing the mind with somewhat too exalted opinion of those, who, by reason of being too susceptible, have imbibed many habits of their more enlightened brethren, and now are ready to be numbered with the things and people that were. The progress of civilization was very slow in this County, until the opening up of the great arteries of wealth—the coal veins of the Mahanoy and Shamokin region. For centuries, there had been accumulating in the bowels of the earth, far removed from the sight of man, a substance, which was to revolutionize the manufacturing and commercial interests of the world. The time was long coming when the value of Anthracite coal could be fully appreciated. The land was covered with dense forests, that must be removed ere the rich soil that they covered could be utilized; timber for all purposes was a useless article, that there was but little demand for; hence its use for heating, driving manufactories, etc., was but the operation of that Divine economy that so wisely pre-arranges all matters for man's enjoyment and prosperity. In the course of time, avenues of travel to the great plains of the west, opened up to occupancy and cultivation, myriads of acres of the finest of farming lands; thus dispensing with the necessity of cleaning the forests of the east; and man learned that timber was valuable for other purposes than heat; and the experience of others taught us that its greatest value consisted in its effect upon temperature. Then it was that God discovered to man the great coal beds, that for all time he had been storing up in its great store-house, against the day of want. At once, steam was utilized for thousands of purposes, never dreamed of, when the only means of vaporizing water was in the use of wood, that owing to its great bulk, could not be used in many places. Northumberland County, prior to that, was but sparsely settled and poorly cultivated; the farmers eked out a poor and scanty livelihood, with no markets for surplus, and nought to encourage enterprise; but with the opening of the coal fields, towns sprung up as by magic; the black diamonds possessed more attractive power than any other mineral, because the public-spirited saw in its use, a means for developing wealth in many directions. The coal of Northumberland is of superior quality, and is found in unlimited quantities. Iron also is found in many localities, and is of superior quality. Another great source of wealth is the immense beds of Limestone, found particularly in the southern part of the County, along Stone Valley Creek; thousand of kilns are now in operation, producing immense quantities of lime, that is very extensively sold throughout the region for fertilizing purposes.

Geologically, Northumberland takes rank with any County of the State, for variety and extent of its resources.

The Climate of this County is as varied as its surface, or its resources. The extremes follow each other in rapid succession, as changeable as the mind of a country belle. The following lines, copied in Mr. Meginnis's "Otzinachson," perhaps more faithfully portray the climate and its effects upon human nature, than aught else that has been published.

"Beneath the temperate zone this vale doth lie,
Where heat and cold a grateful change supply;
To fifteen hours extends the longest day,
When Sol, incenser paints his fervid ray;
Yet here the winter season is severe,
And summer's heat is difficult to bear;
But western winds oft cool the scorching ray,
And southern breezes warm the winter's day.
Yet oft tho' warm and fair the day began,
Cold storms arise before the setting sun;
Nay oft so quick the change, so great its power,
As summer's heat, and winter, in an hour!"

CHAPTER III.

INCIDENTS IN THE ORGANIZATION OF THE COUNTY—FIRST COURT—ETC.

THE Act erecting Northumberland County into one of the integral parts of the Commonwealth, was approved March 21st, 1772; and on the 24th day of the same month, William Plunket, Turbit Francis, Samuel Hunter, James Potter, William Maclay (some years subsequently United States Senator,) Caleb Grayson, Benjamin Allison, Robert Moodie, John Louden, Thomas Lemon, Ellis Hughes and Benjamin Weiser, Judges by appointment, convened at Sunbury to hold, for the new County, the first Court of General Quarter Sessions of the peace and gaol delivery. Edward Burd was appointed to prosecute for the Crown, which at that date exercised dominion over the Colonies. The business done was unimportant, as the labor to be accomplished, was providing for the future. No offences against the dignity of the province could be tried at this Court, as only three days before, the territory had been within the limits of some other County. James Wilson, Robert Magau, Edward Burd, George North, Christian Husk, James Potts, Andrew Robinson and Charles Stedman, were admitted to practice as Attorneys, being the first licensed to the Bar in the County. At the May term of the same year, Richard Malone, Henry Dougherty, Robert Martin, Marcus Hulings and John Alexander, of Turbut township, William Wilson, Francis Yarnall and Samuel Weiser, of Augusta township, were licensed to keep houses of entertainment, and sell spirituous or malt liquors. This action turned loose his Satanic Majesty, and henceforth the Magistrates would have abundant opportunity to exercise their functions as peace-makers; the Sheriff could turn his attention from the plow, or the axe, as all the powers of his body and mind would be necessary to restrain the lawless, and protect the innocent. The tax-gatherer had now his time employed in scraping together the hard earnings of the weak pioneers, to support the indigent and prosecute the criminals. With free rum, came free fights, freedom from legal restraint, and disorder generally. For four years after the close of the first Pennamite war in Wyoming, there was not an officer of the law in the valley. The absence of rum, rendered unnecessary the presence of all the paraphernalia of criminal courts. But the moment whiskey begins to run free, that moment idleness, vice and criminality begin to fill the pauper houses and jails. For six months the County existed, and not a Grand Jury had been summoned. But the Devil soon gave evidence of his presence, and at the August term for 1772, George Neagle, Sheriff of the County, returned the *writ of venire*, to him directed, with the following names of individuals who were sworn on the Grand Inquest for our Sovereign Lord the King, for the body of the County: John Brady, foreman; George Overmeyer, John Rhurick, Leonard Peter, Gerhard Freeland, John Jost, William Grey, Lodowick Derr, George Raw, Andrew Heller, George Wolf, William Cook, John Kelly, James Polk and John Walker. These gentlemen constituted the first Grand Jury for the County of Northumberland. What a sense of the great responsibility of their position, must have pervaded the minds of the men composing this Jury, as they viewed the field it was necessary for them to occupy! At this time, there were no public buildings, roads or bridges; everything was to be done, and but little to do with. Wisely has the great Creator modeled the natural man, that the necessities never exceed his ability to gratify them. If there was a slim exchequer, there was no necessity for large expenditure; hence it is reasonable to apprehend, that this first Grand Jury acquitted themselves about as satisfactorily as any of their four hundred successors have done. The names of nearly all composing the first Court and Jury, are names that have been handed down from generation to generation, as worthy of perpetuation, and so they are. Nearly every one immortalized himself in the trying struggles that followed in after years; and now it is the pride of nearly every inhabitant of the County to trace some connection with these old heroes. For the first few years, there was but little to break the monotony of the proceedings of the Court, beyond the trial of those charged with assault and battery, and fornication—a class of criminals that in those days were judged with a greater degree of leniency than the nature of the offences would seem to justify. There was but little to engage the time of our primitive Judges. Courts are usually but the exponents of public sentiment; and if offences, that now would shock the moral sensibilities of the most dissolute, were then wholly ignored, or at the worst, punished with trivial fine, and perhaps an admonishment "to go and sin no more," it would be manifestly unjust to charge the Courts with having been too lax in the execution of the law against those who had outraged decency; as the unsettled state of society, and the free intermingling of every discordant element, tended to the formation of a sentiment certainly not strict in its exactions or enforcement of moral obligations. At the May session for 1776, Daniel Pettit was accused of having altered a five dollar bill. He was arraigned, proven guilty, and sentenced to stand in the pillory one hour, and be confined in the County Jail one month. At the November session for 1778, Charles Bignell was arraigned for having given liberty to two negroes that had been committed to jail in his charge. Bignell was convicted and adjudged to pay a fine of five pounds, and give security for future good conduct. The first of these, a thief and forger, was sentenced to less punishment than the humane Bignell, who had but exercised the instincts of a charitable nature. People in those days of supposed purity, entertained as little respect for the requirements of government, and evaded laws with as great impunity as the members of the notorious Whiskey Rings of to-day. At one session of the Court, in the infancy of the County, true bills were found against fifty-seven different individuals, for selling whiskey without the sanction of a license. This indicated a disregard for the sanctity of the law, somewhat appalling. Fifty-seven criminals among one class, in a County containing a voting population that would scarcely fill a regiment. Think of this, ye aged moralists, who are wont to draw comparisons between the past and present, unfavorable to the present generation. If one of these law-breakers ever suffered a depletion of his pocket or restrainment of his liberty, it doth not appear. Every generation has its representative characters. The extreme moralist, whose face is set like flint against every form of vice; the devoted churchman, who studies naught but the creed and prayer-book; and the hardened criminal, hunted, harassed and punished until the joys of earth become turned to the bitterness of gall—whose hand is set against every man, and every man's against his. Of the last, Joseph Disbury was undoubtedly entitled to the palm, as being the most irrepressible wag and incorrigible loafer and thief of his day. The name of Disbury became the synonym of every thing bad. Joseph's propensities led him to the accumulation of property, oftener by illegitimate means than otherwise. He would steal anything that came in his way, and when confronted by his accusers, assumed an air of *sang froid*, that utterly nonplussed his enemies. He was frequently under arrest, and on one occasion, for appropriating a neighbor's cow, he left jail, minus his ears. At the August session of 1798, he was arraigned and tried on three indictments for burglary. He was found guilty and sentenced to seven years' hard labor on each, thus affording him boarding and lodging, at the expense of the State, for twenty-one years. It is said, that he outlived his long imprisonment, and at its expiration quitted Northumberland County for pastures new if not green. At the April session for 1804, John Beitzel, was tried for bigamy, the offense proven and the bigamist sentenced to six months' confinement in the jail. It would hardly be profitable to call in question the wisdom of those, whose duty it was to pass sentence in these two cases, for reasons before stated, but it is difficult to avoid speculation as to the sentiment of a society that demanded the incarceration of Disbury twenty-one years, and excused the bigamist who had polluted the home of his neighbor, and disgraced for all time himself, his co-criminals and the community in which he lived, with a six months' deprivation of liberty. Circumstances have full as much to do in forming society as men, and society forms its sentiment, influenced largely by those circumstances, hence the injustice of judging society by our own standard of excellence. Beitzel was tried, and his case passed upon in 1778. At the August session of 1792, fourteen years afterwards, William Armstrong was convicted of the crime of rape, and sentenced to be hung. From this it would appear that public sentiment had undergone somewhat of a change, indicating a healthier condition morally, and auguring well for the future. In the infancy of society, but little thought can be given to conventionalities, the absorbing question being the devising of means for self-preservation. People, at such times, being disposed to construe the Bible teachings literally, and take their neighbors as they find them. As the country improves, necessities of life are supplemented by luxuries, respite from arduous toil, that staring want made an every day necessity, gave relaxation to the mind, and permitted a more careful consideration of the moral and mental capacities and wants of mankind. Opportunity for thought and study developed tastes that could be satisfied only in the society of congenial spirits. This, in time, resulted in the establishment of caste, and the formation of grades in society, a feature as absolutely necessary, in every community, to the enjoyment of all, as a rigid enforcement of law is to its safety.

—

CHAPTER IV.

THE ABORIGINALS OF NORTHUMBERLAND COUNTY.

As much as has been written regarding the original inhabitants of this country, and as many speculations as have been indulged in by writers of almost every age, but little is definitely known of their history. It is thought by many, and with considerable show of reason, that a nation or race of people, superior to the Indians in intelligence, preceded them, and for ages plied their vocation, which were doubtless but little in advance of their successors, and have left some evidences of a civilization, not possessed by any Indian tribes known. The *Delaware* Indians had a tradition, which appears to have been generally believed among them, that they originally lived on the western shores of North America, and in journeying eastward, in quest of a more inviting country, found the valley of the Mississippi in possession of a powerful and warlike race, who were somewhat schooled in the arts of war, and lived in strongly fortified towns. These people, the *Alligewe*, refused the *Delawares* a free transit through their domains, and a fierce battle ensued, in which the intruders were successful, driving the *Alligewe* from their homes down the river. According to this tradition, a portion of the *Delawares* remained in possession of the conquered territory, another portion continued their journey eastward, and took possession of the country extending from the Hudson to the Potomac. While there may be nothing in the history of the *Delaware* Tribe, as it has been handed down to us, to confirm such a tradition, there is nothing to disprove it, and it is as well to furnish it for its worth, without groundless speculation; attending to what is definitely known, regarding our predecessors. In the early part of the 17th century, probably about 1610 or '12, a fierce war was, for a long time, waged between the *Iroquois* on one side, and the *Huron* and *Erie* Indians on the other; the result was, the total subjugation of the *Eries*, who left their old homes, adjacent to the lake, which still bears their name, and journeyed southward, settling in Georgia and Florida. The particular tribe emigrating south was the *Shawanese*; here they resided for many years, until, finally, becoming involved in war with the Spaniards and *Southern* Indians, they emigrated northward, and located at the confluence of the Wabash and Ohio rivers. Governor Cass, in writing of the *Shawanese*, says their history is involved in much obscurity. "Their language is *Algonquin*, and closely allied to the *Kickapoo*, and other dialects spoken by tribes, who have lived for ages north of the Ohio. But they are known to have recently emigrated from the south, where they were surrounded by a family, of tribes—*Creeks, Cherokees, Choctaws*, etc., with whose language they had no affinity. Their traditions assign to them a foreign origin, and a wild story has come down to them, of a solemn procession through the ocean, and of a miraculous passage through the great deep. That they were closely connected with the *Kickapoos*, the actual identity of language affords irrefragable proof, and the incidents of the separation yet live in the oral history of each tribe. We are strongly inclined to believe, that not long after the arrival of the French upon these great lakes, the *Kickapoos* and *Shawanese* composed the tribe known as the *Eries*; living on the eastern shore of the lake, to which they gave their name. It is said that this tribe was exterminated by the *Iroquois*; but it is more probable that a series of disasters divided them into two parts; one of which, under the name of *Kickapoos*, sought refuge from their enemies in the immense prairies between the Illinois and the Mississippi; and the other, under the name *Shawanese*, fled into the *Cherokee* country, and thence further south." Governor Cass does not materially differ from our own version of the origin of the *Shawanese* tribe, who at one day, inhabited this country. The fame of William Penn had penetrated the western homes of the *Shawanese*, who sought permission to locate among the *Delawares*. This tribe had been, for some time, on unfriendly terms with the *Six Nations*, and being desirous of accumulating a force against them, readily granted the permission asked. Accordingly, a portion of the *Shawanese* moved eastward, and settled in the forks of the Delaware. They brought with them, the war-like spirit which made them such unpleasant neighbors in the south, and disturbances arose, which became of so turbulent a character, as to necessitate the removal of the *Shawanese*. Their next move was to the banks of the Susquehanna, which presented an open field, as the *Monseys*, who for years had occupied the valley, had concentrated around Minsink, on the Delaware. The *Shawanese* found themselves sole masters of the valley; no enemy to annoy them; and they built a town, near the lower end of Wyoming Valley, which still bears the name of *Shawanese flats*. Their settlement extended low down, probably as far as the forks of the two branches. One of the kings, or chiefs of this tribe, was *Paxinos*, whose exploits are commemorated by giving his name to a little town on Shamokin Creek, in this County. Here, for many years, the *Shawanese* dwelt in peace; their wanderings up and down the earth terminated for a time. The women cultivated their little patches of grain; the hunter traversed the hills and forests in quest of game; the papooses gamboled in the sunshine, utterly regardless of all but the blissful present. But not long was this peaceful scene to continue. A cloud, that for fifty years was forming, appeared in the east, to cast a shadow over the happy homes of the hunted *Shawanese*. William Penn arrived in North America, in 1682, and, although a lowly Christian himself, had followers, who, having not the fear of God before their eyes, did not hesitate to excite the cupidity of the unsophisticated children of the forest, and by any and all means, take advantage. Penn formed many treaties, and concluded many purchases, no one of which, however, were well defined. Some of the deeds of purchase called for as much territory as a horse could run around, within a given time, or a man could walk around. One of these bounds, only, was ever settled in the noted Friend's day, and that by himself, in company with some chiefs and friends, when they made a day's journey, halting frequently to converse, smoke, and eat, making but about thirty miles in the allotted time. After his death, a copy of one of these walk-deeds, was found by Thomas and John Penn, who, at a council in 1733, fifty years after it had been drawn up, presented it to the Indians, and received from them an acknowledgement of its validity, and under this, an arrangement was made for a walk of one day and a half, to settle the boundaries. The Penns, although strict Quakers, did not shrink from using means, about the honesty of which there could be some question, and advertised far and near for the fastest walkers; offering five hundred acres of land, and five pounds in money, to the man who should walk the greatest distance in the allotted time. Every facility was furnished them; a direct line was run, underbrush cleared away, refreshments placed at convenient distances, that there might be no delay. During the month of September, 1737, Edward Marshall, James Yates, and Solomon Jennings, with three Indians, started at sunrise from a stipulated spot, and commenced the trial. At the end of two hours, Jennings and two Indians gave out; near Easton, the third Indian succumbed; the next day, Yates fell fainting, and Marshall proceeded on alone. At noon of the second day, he stopped, eighty-six miles from the starting point. This purchase took in all the good land, and, as a consequence, great dissatisfaction was felt, and manifested by the Indians. In their natural simplicity, they had trusted the whites many times, only to find themselves duped and intrigued. This had been repeated on so many occasions, that Indian nature could no longer submit, and the *Delawares* very properly refused to give up their rich hunting grounds, for which they had received no adequate remuneration. The Penns, determined to complete the robbery, dispatched a messenger to the *Six Nations*, who then claimed to hold the *Delawares* in subjugation, informing them of the circumstances, and urging a convention of chiefs, to settle the disputed claim. Accordingly, in the summer of 1742, the principal men of this powerful band, to the number of two hundred and thirty, repaired to Philadelphia, to meet the Chiefs of the *Delawares*, and a general council was opened. The Governor of the province opened the conference, after having judiciously distributed a large amount, as presents, among the *Iroquois* warriors, setting forth that the Proprietaries had made purchases in good faith, and asked the Chiefs of the *Six Nations* to see them established in their rightful territory. Here was a formidable assemblage. On the one side, the Governor, skilled in all the intrigue which Christianized people only practice; and the powerful *Iroquois*, with brain fired by the Governor's rum—their blankets stuffed with useless trinkets, from the same source; on the other, the handful of *Delawares*, wronged, cheated, decried and abused by their own race, because they possessed some little knowledge of the duplicity of the whites. There was but one result to such harangue. The representatives of the *Six Nations*, decided that the purchase had been made in a fair and legitimate way; that the *Delawares* had received full consideration for the land, claimed to have been purchased, and that they must leave. The decision was delivered by *Cannassatego*, a venerable Chief, who took occasion to deliver himself of a speech, which for hauteur, withering, burning sarcasm, has no equal in this, or any other language. He arose in the name of all the deputies, and, addressing himself to the Governor, said: "They saw the *Delawares* had been an unruly people, and were altogether in the wrong, and they had concluded to remove them." Then, turning to the *Delawares* in a violent manner, he said: "You deserve to be taken by the hair of your heads, and shaken till you recover your senses and become sober. We have seen a deed, signed by nine of your chiefs, above fifty years ago, for this very land. (The deed was the one made to William Penn in 1688, which his successors had resurrected from forgetfulness.) But how came you to take upon yourself to sell lands at all? We conquered you, we made women of you; you know you are women, and can no more sell lands than women. Nor is it fit that you should have the power to sell lands, since you would abuse it. You have been furnished with clothes, meat and drink, by the goods paid you for it, and now you want it again like children as you are. But what makes you sell lands in the dark? Did you ever tell us you had sold this land? Did we ever receive any part, even the value of pipe-shank for it? You have told us a blind story, that you sent a messenger to inform us of the sale; but he never came amongst us; nor have we ever heard anything about it. But well nd you are none of our blood; you act a dishonest part not only in this, but other matters. Your ears are ever open to slanderous reports about your brethren. For all these reasons, we charge you to remove instantly; we don't give you liberty to think about it. You are women; take the advice of a wise man and remove instantly. You may return to the other side of the Delaware where you came from, but we do not known whether, considering how you have demeaned yourself, you will be permitted to live there, or whether you have not already swallowed that land down your throats, as well as the land on this side. We, therefore, assign you two places to go to, either to *Wyoming* or *Shamokin*. You may go to either of these places, and then we shall have you men under our eye and shall see how you behave. Don't deliberate, but remove away and take this belt of wampum." The *Delawares* immediately left the disputed territory; some settling at Shamokin, and others at Wyoming; others still scattered along the river between the two places. It is easily to be conceived that the *Delawares* carried with them no very tender recollection of the English; the real cause of all their loss of home and its association, and what was a still greater source of chagrin—the withering contempt with which they had been treated by their masters, the *Iroquois*. They found their former allies and neighbors already in possession of the territory, but as the *Delawares* had moved, subject to orders of the Chiefs of the *Six Nations*, the *Shawanese*, who were also in subjection, interposed no obstacles to a peaceful settlement of their unfortunate and crest-fallen neighbors. Thus, through a succession of events, which were brought about after many years, did it occur that these two tribes came to occupy the fairy land of Northumberland. For many years did these two tribes dwell together undisturbed by foes without, or internecine strife within, with nought but the Susquehanna to divide their territories. But an event occurred, insignificant in itself, fraught with direful consequences to many a dusky warrior, that dissevered the friendly relations, and necessitated the establishment of a more formidable barrier between the two tribes. While the warriors of the *Delawares* were hunting among the mountains, a number of their squaws, were gathering wild fruits, along the margin of the river, below town, where they found some *Shawanese* squaws, who had crossed the river in their canoes, upon the same errand. A papoose, belonging to the *Shawanese*, having taken a large grasshopper, a quarrel arose among the children for possession, in which the mothers took part. A sanguinary battle ensued, in which a number were killed, and the *Shawanese* finally forced across the river. Upon the return of the warriors, both tribes prepared for battle, to avenge the wrongs sustained by their wives. The *Shawanese* crossed over and engaged the *Delawares*. After a bloody fight, in which many hundred were killed, the *Shawanese* were driven back to their own side of the river, shortly after which they left their country and removed to the Ohio. The *Delawares* were now left in undisturbed possession of the entire valley, their numbers being rapidly augmented by the liberal circulation of the story of their achievements over the *Shawanese*.

The *Delawares* arrived in this valley, in 1740, during the reign of the humane and noble *Shikilemo*, the far-famed chief of the subsidiary tribes or detachments, that have been settled here by order of the *Six Nations*. Notwithstanding the wrongs inflicted upon his people by the whites, and the Penn government in particular—of which the many instances of deception and chicanery, afforded the most irrefragable proof—he was ready to receive, with open arms, the humble disciples of Christ, who as early as 1746, found their way here, to dispense the doctrine of charity and fair dealing. How it must have tested the credulity of these upright heathen, to have given full credence to the words of his teachers. Often had his people trusted implicitly their more enlightened fellow beings, and as often had found themselves the dupes of avaricious, unprincipled tricksters. It is not claimed that the speculator of to-day is entitled to greater immunity from the charge of dishonesty, than the Penns, whose fame for uprightness had been heralded far and wide in advance; but it is claimed, that the rascals have not all lived in the 18th century. We have only to examine some of the records their own time has made, to have our pride for the Proprietaries hopelessly dashed. Look, for instance, at the following, showing the consummation of a robbery, without parallel, except in the machinations of a Tweed, who, to-day is a fugitive from home, not daring to let himself be known among civilized men. The Indenture reads as follows: "We, (here is given the unpronounceable names of thirteen Indian Chiefs,) right owners of all lands, *Quigquingus*, called Duck Creek, into Upland, called Chester Creek, all along by the west side of the river Delaware, and so between the said creeks, *as far as a man can ride with a horse in two days*; for and in consideration of these following goods, to us in hand paid, and secured to be paid by WILLIAM PENN, Proprietary and Governor of the Province of Pennsylvania, and territories thereof, viz.: 20 guns, 20 fathoms of match-coat, 2 fathoms of Stroudwater, 20 blankets, 20 kettles, 20 pounds of powder, 100 pounds of lead, 40 tomahawks, 100 knives, 40 pairs of stockings, 1 barrel of beer, 20 pounds of red lead, 100 fathoms of wampum, 30 glass bottles, 30 pewter spoons, 100 awl blades, 300 tobacco pipes, 100 hands of tobacco, 20 tobacco tongs, 20 steels, 300 flints, 30 pairs of scissors, 30 combs, 60 looking-glasses, 200 needles, one skipple of salt, 30 pounds of sugar, 5 gallons of molasses, 20 tobacco boxes, 100 *jews-harps*, 20 hoes, 30 gimlets, 30 wooden screw boxes, 100 strings of beads, do hereby acknowledge, etc.; given at New Castle, second day of the eighth month, 1685." This was one of Mr. Penn's first purchases, and, as will be observed by those familiar with the geography of Eastern Pennsylvania, it included nearly all of the valuable lands of Delaware, Chester and Bucks Counties. The object sought here, is not to cast any blot upon the fame which, whether justly or unjustly, has been given to Penn; but that those who had been ascribing to the Indians, attributes of beasts, may be enabled to judge Indian character a little more leniently.

Shikilemo nevertheless remained the true friend of the missionaries, and during the time of his reign, which lasted until his death in 1749, the whites had naught to complain of, in the treatment received by them from the red men. Whether this happy condition of things was attributable to the mercy of the Heathen King; to the guarded conduct of the whites, or to some other cause; it is not worth while to inquire. The fact is palpable, that so long as the whites dealt justly with the Indians, so long were they treated with great consideration and respect by the untutored children of nature. The superior intelligence of the Europeans, coupled with the known skill in utilizing all means, devised by the sciences and arts, for the advancement of the race, undoubtedly won the admiration of the Aborigines; and had this superior intelligence been given direction by wisdom, moderated by love, the end of time would have found the red and white men dwelling together in harmony, with mutual advantage to each. The Christianizing influences exerted by Zinzendorf, Mack and others, made an impression upon the Indian character, that was not wholly effaced for many years. They were taught faith in Divine promises, and clung to it with a tenacity, that threatened death itself could not weaken. Mark the reply of the Christian Indians to the demands of the *Six Nations*, delivered through *Paxinos*, the King of the *Shawanese*. A settlement had been formed at Gnadenhutten, now Mauch Chunk, of Indians who had, under the teachings of the Moravians, embraced religion. It was desired, for some purpose, to remove the families of these Indians to the Susquehanna. *Paxinos*, with twenty-three of his followers, and three ambassadors of the *Iroquois*, visited the settlement, and preferred the demand of their masters, that they remove at once. This demand they refused to comply with. Several responded with true heroism, "What can the Chiefs of the *Six Nations* give me in exchange for my soul?" said one. "God, who made and saved me, can protect me," replied another. "I am not afraid of the wrath of man, for not one hair of my head can fall to the ground without His will." "If even one of them should lift his hatchet and say, depart from the Lord and the Brethren, I would not do it," replied another. Some of these taunting replies savored of disloyalty to the *Great Head*, as the Council at Onondaga styled itself, and exhibited a spirit not encouraged by Paul, in his exortations obedience to magistrates; but they nevertheless manifested a strong faith in the God they had learned to love, and a love of religion, seldom found at the present day. Thus has the history of the Aboriginals of this valley been traced, with an earnest effort as possible to exhibit their true character. It is found, that there is much to condemn; but who can be found, with Christ's test of purity, to cast stones at the poor deluded creatures, who, for untold ages, have lived in moral darkness.

From the pen of J. F. Wolfinger, Esq., of Milton, in this County, we append a short sketch of the location and character of the Indian towns in this locality. In addition to the towns named by our authority above, there are to be found indisputable evidences of Georgetown having been the site of a town of considerable extent.

"Old Northumberland County contained numerous Indian towns, long before any white men saw this region of country. Let us, so far as we have been able to gather a knowledge of them, look at those that stood on the north branch of the Susquehanna River, between our present towns of Northumberland and Nescopeck, in Luzerne County.

"Nishmekkachlo. This town stood on the south side of Montour's Ridge, and somewhere about midway between our present towns of Northumberland and Danville—exact spot unknown to the writer of this sketch. I am inclined to think it was the residence of *Manawyhickon*, a distinguished *Delaware* Chief who ruled over the Indians of these parts before the great *Shikellamy* and *Sassoonan* Chiefs made their appearance at *Shahomokin* or *Shamokking*, the old Indian town on the present site of Sunbury, since our old writer informs us that *Manawyhickon* lived somewhere on the north branch, not far from *Shamokking*.

"Mahoning. This town stood near the mouth of Mahoning Creek, on its west side, a little below where the public bridge crosses the said creek, and about a mile below the present town of Danville in Montour County.

"Montour's Ridge, a pretty high and beautifully formed elevation of earth, runs north-eastward from a point near Northumberland, but leaves a nice valley of beautiful land between its base and the north branch of the Susquehanna River. This valley, as we approach Danville from Northumberland, gets narrower, until it ends in what is called "the narrow grounds"—just wide enough for the public road to pass conveniently along the foot of the ridge. And it was the eastern end of this 'Narrows,' where the old Indian town of Mahoning stood. Montour's Ridge at this point presents to the eye of the beholder, a high, bold, imposing appearance, and becomes more and more so, until it, just on the north side of Danville, terminates very suddenly, with a high wall-like face, towards the east; and then sweeping sharply around, it runs north for several miles, with the same high wall-like face on the west side of the small and narrow but beautiful valley of Mahoning, and its creek of the same name. Every traveler who visits Danville, looks with admiration upon this high, bluffy and picturesque termination of Montour's Ridge, and is delighted with the rich and beautiful dark green foliage of its thickly grown evergreen, pine and spruce trees, that crown its top and sides, (excepting a cleared or bare spot on its top just north of Danville) and towards the close of every sunny day, throw a dark, rich shade over the snug little valley at its base. Its scenery looks wild and romantic, even in our day, but must have been far wilder and grander, when the Indians roamed over the ridge in pursuit of wild turkeys and deer, and of the fish that swam in the waters close by.

"Montour's Ridge, at Danville, looks as if Noah's deluge, or some other great commotion of our earth's waters, had burst a passage way through the ridge at this point, and so made this valley, for the ridge itself reappears quickly again, with a sloping, but nearly an equally elevated face on the east side of Danville, and then runs on eastward to and beyond the town of Bloomsburg, in Columbia County, where it gradually slopes down and disappears. Mahoning was, therefore, a choice spot for an Indian town, of more than common note among the Indians.

"Toby's Town. This town, so called after a large and powerful Indian by the name of 'Toby,' stood on 'Toby's Run' a little above the Insane Asylum, about two miles above Danville. But whether it stood on the banks of the Susquehanna River, near the mouth of Toby's Run, or on top of the high ridge of earth there, along the river, I am not able to say. I passed along there in my boyhood days, on my road to and from Reading, and heard various stories about Toby and his town, but I can give no satisfactory account of them.

"Classawango. This town stood still farther up the river, but on the south side of the river, and about half way between Danville and the town of Catawissa, but I cannot state where it stood. Who can?

"Catawissa. This town stood at the mouth of Catawissa Creek, where the town of Catawissa, in Columbia County, now stands. This is evident from the fact that many Indian arrow heads, flint stones, smoke pipes, etc., have been plowed up there, and some are still found there in the fields around the town. The mountains, along whose sides the Catawissa railroad now runs, must have formed fine hunting grounds for these Indians.

"Oskohary. This town stood still farther up the north branch of our Susquehanna River, somewhere this side of the old Indian town of *Nishiberkon*, now the town of Nescopeck, in Luzerne County, but I am unable to fix the site of Oskohary. Who can do that?

"This sketch of Nishmekkachlo, Mahoning, Toby's Town, Classawango, Catawissa and Oskohary, is imperfect in many respects, and I have written it just to draw attention to these old Indian towns, and get some of our citizens to give us what traditional accounts they have had, as to the exact spots where said towns stood, and what Indian tribe or tribes dwelled there, and what were the names of their Chiefs, and also what the names of these Indian towns signified; since Indian names generally have some peculiar meaning, just as the Jewish names of olden times had among the Jews—as we learn from the Bible. And so I, in common with others, would be pleased to see our newspaper editors publish this sketch, and add to it such fragmentary information as they are able to gather up, concerning these ancient habitations of the red men on the north branch of the Susquehanna River. There certainly must be some traditional accounts, still existing in and around each of these neighborhoods, as it regards the said towns, and that, whatever it may be, would be very interesting in fixing the exact spots where they stood, and the like. My father lived in Northumberland when I was a boy and often took me along up to Danville in a sulky or buggy, to see an uncle of mine who then resided on a farm on the banks of the river above Danville; and in passing up and down between these towns, I often heard from my father and other persons, interesting stories about the Indians who once lived along Montour's Ridge; but I am unable to recall any particulars worthy of note. And so I must now leave my sketch to be corrected and completed by others who have better knowledge of these matters than I have. But I cannot close my remarks, without asking the reader to look at and admire the beauty of our Indian names, for we have no words in any of our languages—Greek, Latin, English or German—that are more beautiful than *Nishmekkachlo, Mahoning, Classawango, Catawissa and Oskohary*;—and our Indians acquired the knowledge of all these significant and beautiful words, without the aid of books, or any school, academy, or college. What do our *literati*, in this boastful age of schools think of that? How does it harmonize with their theories—that we must have books and schools to learn languages?"

CHAPTER V.

CIVIL WARS OF 1769—1784.

WAR, the arrangement of creatures of God's perfect skill in opposition, for the purpose of destruction of their own species, would seem to be the perfection of Satan's machinations for the destruction of the human race, and the peopling of his domains. War, when waged between nations and people of different races, for the redress of some real evil that every other means have failed to remedy, can scarcely receive the sanction of the really good; but when the scene of strife is brought to the fireside, the home of the defenseless; when the contestants are brethren, often of the same blood, and women and children became the hapless victims, to the vengeance of neighbors, then it is that we see it in all its hideous, horrid forms. No horrors can equal those of civil war, when brethren wrought up to the superlative of fiendishness, ruthlessly and maliciously seek the blood of their own kind, devastate the homes of those with whom they have dwelt on amicable terms. Man suddenly becomes transformed to a beast; feelings of friendship are turned to hatred; love to bitterness of gaul, and the thirst for blood is insatiable. Few of the people of the fair vales of the Susquehanna, realize that here, about their homes, one hundred years ago, was the scene of a strife, which, for unprovoked cruelty and true fiendishness in its details, has no parallel in the history of the world. Fewer still are able to clearly understand the cause. To enter fully into an examination of all the causes, and follow them up to a conclusion, would occupy much time and space; more than the reader of to-day would feel warranted in devoting to an examination of a matter, in which, although their ancestors were deeply interested; happily now the effects have all been removed, and the gulf bridged over, that for years divided the dwellers within the little community designated on the maps as Wyoming Valley.

Wyoming, until 1786, was embraced within the limits of Northumberland County. After 1772, all civil writs against the invaders from Connecticut were issued and executed by the civil officers of this County. The last military expedition of any magnitude against Wyoming, under the sanction of the Proprietaries, was commanded by Col. William Plunket, and rendezvoused at Fort Augusta. Many of the ancestors of those now living here, marched with the intrepid Plunket, and doubtless the blood of some dyed the soil of the valley, on that memorable occasion, when, in mid-winter, an effort was made to dislodge the Yankees. Hence it is, that a narration of some of the events of this war, will possess an interest to those descendants of the Pennamites who dwell in this County. (For information of this war, we are largely indebted to Pierce's History of Wyoming, in which we find the results of many months' arduous and earnest research. Undoubtedly some portions may be slightly tinged with prejudice, but as a whole, the record furnished is as impartial as it is possible to obtain.)

To arrive at a satisfactory understanding of the grounds of differences between the Colonies of Connecticut and Pennsylvania, which resulted in the civil wars, styled by some, the Pennamite and Yankee wars, it will be necessary to view the deeds made by the king, and the bounds of the territory conveyed by each. One great source of evil was the imperfect knowledge of those vast possessions, on the part of those claiming the right to convey by charter, title to lands here. In 1620, King James I. granted to the Plymouth Company, a Charter for the ruling and governing of New England, in America. In 1628, the Plymouth Company granted to the Massachusetts Colony their territory. In 1631, the President of the Plymouth Company, granted a large tract to Lord Say and Seal, to Lord Brook, and others, which was purchased by the Connecticut Colony. Those Charters or grants made the South Sea their western boundary. The location of the South Sea, or Pacific Ocean, was of course unknown at that time. April 20th, 1662, King Charles II. renewed and confirmed this Charter to the Connecticut Colony, and distinctly recognized it as a part and parcel of the old grant of 1620, by James I. to the Plymouth Company. Nineteen years after, in 1681, March 4th, this same king, granted by his letters patent to William Penn, in consideration for a debt due his father, Admiral Penn, his heirs and assigns, all that tract of land lying between a point on the south, twelve miles north of New Castle, and a line on the north, dividing the 42d and 43d degrees of north Latitude, and extending westward five degrees of Longitude from the Delaware River. Thus a tract of country, extending from north to south a whole degree of latitude, and from east to west five degrees of longitude, was granted to the Connecticut Colony in 1662, and to William Penn in 1681. Of course, both grantees claimed the land under their Charters, and with the exception of a difference in dates, each with equally strong grounds. But by the direction of the Crown, and in accordance with a custom long established, two other requisites were essential to secure the validity of a title—purchase from rightful owners, the Indians, and occupancy. William Penn and his successors, purchased various tracts of land from the Indians, and obtained deeds for the same. November 5th 1768, the Proprietaries procured from the *Six Nations* at Fort Stanwix, a deed for all the lands not previously sold to them, lying within the province of Pennsylvania; this purchase included the controverted land. In January, 1769, Stewart, Ogden and Jennings, on behalf of the Proprietary Government, took possession of the Susquehanna lands. Thus the three essentials—a Charter, purchase and settlements—were perfected on the part of the Pennsylvania government. Connecticut based her claim on a Charter, obtained in 1662, nineteen years before the date of Penn's Charter—a purchase made by the Susquehanna Company, at Albany, July 11th, 1754, and occupancy, established by the settlement of Jenkins, Buck and others, in August, 1762. Houses were erected, grain sown, but owing to the difficulty of obtaining supplies, these settlers were compelled to return to Connecticut during the severe weather of winter. In the spring of 1763, they returned to Wyoming and erected other buildings; but on the 15th of October, many of them were murdered and the rest driven off, probably by the *Six Nations*, encouraged by the Pennsylvania authorities. Thus it will appear, that the Connecticut people had made good their claim by complying with the three pre-requisites, viz: charter, purchase and settlement, in advance of the Proprietaries. The Charter of the former pre-dated the latter by nineteen years; the purchase by fourteen years; and the settlement by seven years; so that unless custom and law should go for naught, the Connecticut claim was founded on right, and could not be controverted by the Pennsylvanians. Other circumstances, however, would seem to favor a different view. On the 30th of November 1664, his Majesty's Commission appointed "to decide boundaries betwixt the Duke of York, and Connecticut Charter," with the approbation and assent of the agents of the Connecticut Colony, fixed a line east of the Hudson River, to be the western bounds of said colony. Again, in 1683, the Commissioners of Connecticut, with the Governor of New York, fixed upon a new line, which constitutes the present limits between the two States, and it was declared that the line fixed upon, "shall be the western bounds of the said Colony of Connecticut." This would appear to settle the question of right to any lands west of the line agreed upon, but the invincible Yankees were not to be thus thwarted in their design upon the fair vale of Wyoming and its surroundings, and claimed, that by virtue of their Charter, they overleaped the province of New York, and that the agreement made in 1683, did not invalidate their claim to what was beyond. This construction of the Charter, led to the unhappy differences that resulted so disastrously to hundreds of poor pioneers, who ventured their all, and life itself, in their eagerness to possess themselves of some portion of the valuable territory. The ablest men of England and America were drawn into the controversy. The question was viewed and discussed in every possible light, but no solution could be determined upon that would satisfy the contestants. At last, five Commissioners were appointed by Congress, who in 1782, met at Trenton, and for forty-one days, patiently listened to arguments *pro* and *con*. On the 30th day of December, 1782, after a careful investigation, the Commission delivered their decision in these words: "We are unanimously of the opinion, that Connecticut has no right to the land in controversy. We are also unanimously of the opinion, that the jurisdiction and pre-emption of all the territory lying within the Charter of Pennsylvania, and now claimed by the State of Connecticut, do of right belong to the State of Pennsylvania."

This settled the question of jurisdiction and pre-emption, and it would appear, to one not conversant with the ways that were dark, of the land speculators of Pennsylvania, that the way was clear for those who had settled under the auspices of the Susquehanna Company, to transfer their allegiance to the acknowledged authority, Pennsylvania, and continue on in their work of pioneer life. But not so, as it will appear from a further examination of this subject. After the massacre of the Yankees in October, 1763, His Majesty inhibited any further attempts at settlement within the prescribed limits, until the troubles with the Indians should become quieted. The Treaty at Fort Stanwix settled the difficulties, and immediately the Susquehanna Company perfected arrangements for re-inhabiting the lands formerly occupied by their agents. In pursuance of this design, it was resolved to lay out five townships, of five miles square, and that there should be granted to two hundred settlers, who were required to occupy and hold them against intruders. The Proprietary Government commissioned Charles Stewart, Capt. Amos Ogden and John Jennings, to lay out two manors, one on the west side of the river to be called the "Manor of Sunbury;" one on the east to be called the "Manor of Stoke." These parties were given a loan of one hundred acres of land each for seven years, on condition that they established an Indian trading-house and held the land against intruders. These men took possession of the houses that had been erected by the murdered Connecticut settlers and of course the way was open for a quarrel of the greatest magnitude when the Connecticut people should return, which they did in the month following the advent of Stewart, Ogden and Jennings. Finding their houses and improvements occupied by the Pennamites, they erected a block-house, and resolved to drive away the Pennsylvania party. They surrounded Ogden's block-house and demanded the surrender of its inmates. The wiley Ogden requested a conference, which was readily granted, when Sheriff Jennings immediately arrested the whole party, and carried them off to Easton jail. Here was an evidence of loyalty it is refreshing to contemplate. The Connecticut people to the number of forty, all determined men, bent on the destruction of the Pennsylvanians, in a moment of time, when confronted with the Majesty of civil law, surrendering themselves to one man and submitting to be marched off to jail! The prisoners were released at once on bail and returned to complete the work they had commenced. Ogden returned and arrested thirty-three and took them to jail, from whence they were at once released on bail, only to renew the struggle over the prize. In the spring of 1770, the Connecticut people were reinforced by one hundred and sixty of their friends, all of whom set to work erecting houses and clearing land. On the 24th of May, Ogden and Jennings returned, but finding the opposition too strong, proceeded to Easton and reported the condition of things to the Governor. The Susquehanna people desirous of peace, attempted to open negotiations looking to a peaceful settlement of the difficulties and in furtherance of this sent Col. Dyer and Major Elderkin with full powers to Philadelphia, to adjust all matters in dispute relative to Wyoming lands. This effort proved abortive and in the month following Col. Francis with an armed force, appeared in the valley and demanded the surrender of the Connecticut men, but the settlers being strongly fortified no attention was paid to the Colonel's demand. In September, Sheriff Jennings appeared with a force of two hundred, when the settlers surrendered. Articles of capitulation were drawn up, and it was stipulated that four of the number should be delivered up as prisoners, that seventeen of their number should be permitted to remain to gather the crops of grain, that all other men, women and children should depart for Connecticut, and that all private property should be respected. The sufferings of these poor people, forced from their homes, just as the inclement season was coming upon them, were terrible. One mother, it is said, roasted the body of her dead child and fed the flesh to her surviving children, to keep them from starving.

Ogden, to his disgrace as a man and soldier, violated the stipulations and entered upon the property of the fugitives, capturing everything salable and disposing of it for himself and followers. He seized everything worth moving so that the seventeen men left to gather the grain, having no means of subsistence for the winter, were forced to follow their friends to Connecticut. Ogden, well satisfied with his success, left a few men in charge of the fortifications, and moved with his force to the country below the Blue Ridge and disbanded, supposing he had effectually stopped any settlement in Wyoming by the Connecticut people. For four months the territory which had been the subject of such bitter disputes, remained in the possession of the Pennamites. But in the spring of 1770, a band of rangers from Paxton, who had become dissatisfied with the Proprietary Government, under the leadership of Lazarus Stewart, of Lancaster County, affected an arrangement with the Susquehanna Company, and proceeding to the valley took possession. Ogden, who had been recruiting at Philadelphia from the effects of his arduous labors, in driving defenseless women and children to the forest to perish, was greatly astonished at the turn of events, and hastily collecting a body of men returned to Wyoming. Major Durkee, who had been captured by Ogden the fall before and imprisoned, had in the meantime returned and united with Stewart. The result was a capture of Ogden and his men, all of whom except six, who were left to care for the Pennamites' property, departed. The Yankees were as forgetful of plighted pledges as the Pennamites, and ejected the six men, taking possession of their effects.

An application was made to General Gage, by the Proprietary Government for assistance to dispel the Yankees, but without effect. In May of 1770, Col. Zebulon Butler with a number of followers arrived from Connecticut greatly augmenting the force. Peace now for a time reigned. The people applied themselves assiduously to the work of building houses, sowing grain and making preparation for winter. But the enemy that was to scatter desolation where all was peace and plenty, was near at hand. In September Ogden, with a large force, entered the valley and captured several settlers in the field at work. The people in the fort were thrown into the greatest consternation, at the sudden appearance of so strong a force, and became easy victims to the impetuous Ogden. The Yankees were all captured, some confined at Easton, others in Philadelphia. Ogden again retired from Wyoming leaving twenty men to hold possession, but he had scarcely disappeared beyond the mountains ere Captain Lazarus Stewart, at the head of thirty men, broke into the fort in the night, drove the half-awaked, half-naked garrison out and took possession.

The year 1771 opened with another vigorous effort on the part of the Proprietaries to regain possession of the valley. Ogden, with one hundred men, reappeared, accompanied by Sheriff Hacklein of Northampton County, who bore a warrant for the apprehension of Stewart. To the Sheriff's demand for a surrender, Stewart returned an emphatic refusal. An attack was made by Ogden, which was repulsed with the loss of one killed. The night following, Stewart, with twenty-six men, left Fort Durkee. He felt conscious of having irritated the Pennsylvania Government to such an extent that his life would doubtless be in jeopardy if captured, and chose to put distance between himself and the civil officers. The garrison surrendered and again Ogden held possession of the disputed lands. He had so often accomplished the same result, hoping that it had been final, and leaving, found his hopes dispelled by the ubiquitous Yankees, that he resolved to remain and hold possession. For two months, he was undisturbed, but soon his illusive dream of peace vanished, and he found himself, in April of 1771, closely besieged in Fort Wyoming, by Captains Butler and Stewart. So closely was he pressed that no opportunity was afforded for obtaining water or food, and it soon became evident that without some succor, they must again fall into the hands of Butler. The man's energy and bravery were equal to the emergency, however, and during the night he entered the river and floated down beyond the sentinels and escaped to Philadelphia. Great excitement prevailed on his arrival in the city of Brotherly Love, and prompt measures were taken, and soon a strong force, with provisions, under command of Captains Dick and Morris, were on the way to the relief of the beleagured garrison. But the Yankees were not asleep. Intimation of the approach of the Pennsylvanians reached these vigilant officials, and measures were taken to intercept Ogden. An ambush was laid, the pack-horses with all the provisions were captured, while the men were left to escape to the fort, where the garrison was on the verge of starvation. In this condition their final subjugation was only a matter of time. They capitulated and Butler and Stewart, more merciful than their prisoner, observed the terms of capitulation and left them to pursue their way unmolested. The valley was now in possession of the Yankees. The fortunes of war had been varied, resulting in success to one party to-day, the next disaster, and so continuing for the two years that it had been prosecuted, and naught but the unquenchable enthusiasm of such men as Ogden on one side, and Lazarus Stewart on the other withstood the varied, and very questionable success that attended their exploits. Happily, the war was ended for a time at least, and the people began to direct their attention to more peaceful pursuits, and to developing the latent resources of this truly inviting spot. Up to this time there had been no form of government or established discipline in Wyoming. [The society, composed almost entirely of men who had lost the culture, noticeable in men who are daily thrown in contact with the softer sex, was rough and uncouth. One thing observable in the settlers along the Susquehanna, was the absence of a certain disturbing element, found in most frontier settlements, the idle and shiftless, who follow after pioneers and are but drones in the busy life. Every man appeared to be imbued with a determination to make the most of circumstances, and recover the prestige lost during the struggle for possession between the contending factions. Almost the first thing to which the attention of our forefathers was directed, the moment they had emerged from the clouds of war, was the establishment of schools and churches, for the better support of which permanent arrangements were perfected. The original settlers were composed of Presbyterians and Baptists almost exclusively, two societies that at that day could readily and easily fraternize, thus securing unity of action in the great work to be performed. The Presbyterians were generally of Scotch-Irish origin; the Baptist emigrated from the New England Colonies,—thus bringing together for the advancement of the race the energies of two classes of people, more liberally endowed with all the attributes of true moral and physical manhood, than any other people, probably in the civilized world. What a source of regret that anything should occur to mar the harmony here prevailing! Who could estimate the good this combined effort might have accomplished, if permitted to develop its full strength. But Satan was lurking about this Eden, in the form of the avaricious speculator, and was even then infusing his poisoning jealousy into the minds of some. A further account of this civil strife will be reserved for another chapter.

PLATE II.

LAW. BUILDING,
SUNBURY, NORTHUMBERLAND CO., PA.
PROPERTY OF S. P. WOLVERTON.

CHAPTER VI.

THE CIVIL WAR OF 1769–84, CONTINUED.

Our fathers crossed the ocean's wave
To seek this shore;
They left behind the coward slave
To welter in his living grave;—
With hearts unbent, and spirits brave,
They sternly bore
Such toils as meaner souls had quelled;
But souls like these, such toils impelled
To soar.—*Percival.*

As early as 1771, says Pearce, two townships on the West Branch were settled by emissaries of the Susquehanna Company, and named Charleston and Judea, to which a few settlers were enticed, and formed a nucleus, about which, in 1774, people to the number of about one hundred gather. By Act of the Connecticut Assembly, approved in January, 1774, the Wyoming territory, was erected into a town to be called Westmoreland. The towns of Charleston and Judea were included within the limits of this town, as was nearly all the territory of Northumberland, which was annexed to Litchfield County. This act of Connecticut aroused the energies of the proprietaries to make another attempt to wrest the territory from the Yankees. Accordingly, in September of 1775, Col. William Plunket, at the head of five hundred Northumberland militia, moved up to the West Branch of the river from Sunbury, and exhibited his bravery by utterly breaking up the infant settlement, killing one man and taking the rest prisoners, confining them in Sunbury jail. Col. Plunket, flushed with his victory over the settlement at Muncy, where with five hundred soldiers he captured a few men and put to flight a number of women and children, determined, with the sanction of the Proprietary government, to move up the North Branch and destroy the settlements at Wyoming. So greatly was he elated with his brilliant success, that he was utterly forgetful of the ordinary dictates of prudence and collected together seven hundred men in mid-winter and started out on the rash expedition. He found the Yankees on the alert, who under the command of Captains Butler and Stewart, soon cooled Plunket's military ardor. The prestige of his former success, availed not against a determined resistance on the part of two hundred determined men, and the crest-fallen tory retired down the river, having lost several killed and wounded. This military expedition was accompanied by William Cook, Esq., Sheriff of Northumberland County, who was armed with sundry writs for the arrest of certain offenders. But the worthy sheriff was not afforded an opportunity to serve his writs and he returned with Plunket. In the meantime Congress had been petitioned by the settlers for some redress. This body being then in Philadelphia, it was resolved, that the Assemblies be requested to take the most speedy means to prevent hostilities. This resolution produced but little effect on the government of Pennsylvania, as evidenced by its action in authorizing the expedition under Plunket, which resulted so disastrously. On the 20th of December Congress took further cognizance of the matter, and resolved upon the following: "WHEREAS a dispute subsists between the Colonies of Connecticut and Pennsylvania relative to lands on the Susquehanna River, which dispute it is apprehended if not suspended during the present troubles of the Colonies, will be productive of pernicious consequences, it is *Resolved*, That it is the opinion of this Congress, and it is accordingly recommended, that the contending parties immediately suspend all hostilities, and avoid every appearance of force until the dispute can be legally decided; That all property taken and detained be immediately restored to the original owners; That no interruption be given to either party to the free passing and repassing of persons, behaving themselves peaceably, through the disputed territory, as well by land as by water, without molestation of either persons or property; That all persons seized and detained on account of said dispute on either side, be dismissed and permitted to return to their respective homes, and that things being put in the same situation they were before the late unhappy contest, they continue to behave themselves peaceably on their respective possessions and improvements until a legal decision can be had on said dispute, or this Congress shall take further order thereon, and nothing herein done shall be construed in prejudice of either party." This resolution was passed before Plunket had progressed far in his contemplated movement against Wyoming, but it produced but little effect; no counter orders being sent to him by the authorities, he continued on his course, with the results already known. It is apparent that the Proprietary government from some cause, had an interest involved that might suffer if the dispute was left for settlement to a legal tribunal, and preferred, by the last resort of Revolutionists, to obtain forcible possession. And all propositions of the settlers, as well as the general government, were treated with contempt, by these exemplary descendents of William Penn. But a storm-cloud was arising in the east of such magnitude as to fill with apprehension the minds of all, and cause our Susquehanna people to forget for a time, their local differences, in the consideration of the momentous question of independence, beside which the troubles of the Yankees, dwindled into insignificance. From the attitude assumed by the Indians it became manifest, that the *Six Nations* had formed a coalition with the English to wage war upon the Colonists, and from the exposed position of the people of Northumberland County, it became necessary to devise some means of defense in case of molestation from their neighbors, whose territory they were occupying. In furtherance of this design, fortifications were erected at various places along the river, and every available means of defense was brought into requisition, to be ready for use in cases of emergency. In the busy preparation for war the people were not unmindful of the demands of posterity, and every facility within reach of their limited resources was provided for the education of the young, for putting the civil government in working order; and much progress was made during the six years that intervened from the date of Plunket's expedition until 1782, notwithstanding the entire valley had been devastated with the fire, sword and tomahawk. An examination of the conduct of some of the officers of the British Army during the struggle for Independence, exhibits a ferocity and fiendishness seldom paralleled, never exceeded elsewhere. But as inhuman as was their conduct, as devoid of all feeling of humanity as they appeared to be, their atrocity pales before the recital of the acts of the beast Butler and savage *Brandt*, at the massacre of Wyoming. It seems to be fitting that the atrocity of such fiends should be faithfully portrayed, that their conduct may be contrasted with the more despicable of every age, and enable the present generation to see to what extent man can debase himself when under the power of the Devil, even when surrounded with the moral and healthful atmosphere that pervaded the entire Christian world during the eighteenth century.

THE MASSACRE ON THE SUSQUEHANNA.

As early as the 8th of February, 1778, General Schuyler wrote to Congress: "There is too much reason to believe that an expedition will be formed, by the Indians, against the western frontiers of New York, Virginia and Pennsylvania." The next month he informed them, "A number of the *Mohawks* and many of the *Onondugas*, *Cayugas*, and *Senecas*, will commence hostilities against us as soon as they can; it would be prudent therefore to take measures to carry the war into their country—it would require no greater body of troops to destroy their towns, than to protect the frontier inhabitants." No effective measure being taken to repress the hostile spirit of the Indians, numbers joined the tory refugees, and with this commenced their horrid depredations and hostilities upon the back settlers, being headed by Colonel Butler, and *Brandt*, an half-blooded Indian, of desperate courage, ferocious and cruel beyond example. Their expeditions were carried on to great advantage by the exact knowledge which the refugees had of every object of their enterprise, and the immediate intelligence they received from their friends on the spot. The weight of their hostilities fell upon the fine new settlement of Wyoming, situated on the eastern branch of the Susquehanna, in a most beautiful country and delightful climate. It was settled and cultivated by a number of people from Connecticut, who claimed the territory as included in the original grant to the Connecticut Colony from Charles II. The settlement consisted of eight townships, each five miles square, beautifully placed on each side of the river. It had so increased by a rapid emigration, that the settlers sent a thousand men to serve in the Continental army. To provide against the dangers of their remote situation, four forts were erected to cover them from the incursions of the Indians. But it was their misfortune to have a considerable mixture of royalists among them; and the two parties were actuated by sentiments of the most violent animosity, which was not confined to particular families or places; but permenting every spot where least expected, served equally to poison the sources of domestic security and happiness, and to cancel the laws of nature and humanity.

The warnings to the fated settlement were frequent; spies in every garb appeared among the settlers and their suspicions were aroused. The Indians by no means being novices in the art of deception, small parties would frequently appear, making every manifestation of sincerest friendship, and lulling the inhabitants into a fancied state of security, and, at the same time, keeping the enemies of their dupes fully advised of all that it was essential to the accomplishment of their nefarious schemes. The settlers, however, soon took the alarm; Colonel Butler had several times written letters to Congress and General Washington, acquainting them with the dangers to which the people were exposed, and requested assistance; but the letters never reached their destination, having been intercepted by the tories. A little before the main attack, some small parties made sudden irruptions, and committed several robberies and murders; and from ignorance, or a contempt of all ties whatever, massacred the wife and five children of a settler sent for trial to Connecticut, in their own cause. On the third of July, the enemy suddenly appeared in full force on the Susquehanna, headed by Colonel Butler, a Connecticut tory, and cousin to Zebulon Butler, the second in command in the settlement. He was assisted by most of those leaders, who had made themselves terrible in the frontier war. Their force was about sixteen hundred strong, one-fourth of which was composed of Indians, lead by their own chiefs. The whites were so disguised as to be hardly distinguishable from the Indians. One of the smaller forts, garrisoned mainly by tories, was given up. Another was carried by assault, and all, except the women and children, massacred in the most inhuman manner. Colonel Zebulon Butler, leaving a small number to garrison Fort Wilkesborough, crossed the river with about four hundred men to Fort Kingston, whither the women, children, and all non-combatants, crowded for protection. He suffered himself to be enticed from his fortress by his cousin, and agreed to march out and hold a conference with the enemy in the open field, at so great a distance from the fort, as to be beyond all protection from it. Upon their withdrawing, according to their own proposition, in order to hold a parley for the conclusion of a treaty, he marched out about four hundred armed men, nearly the whole strength of the garrison—so great was his distrust of the enemy—to guard him to the place for holding the parley. On his arrival, he found nobody to treat with, and advanced toward the foot of the mountain in pursuit of a flag, to show the enemy his desire to comply with all that they could ask. Suddenly he was freed from his delusion, by being surrounded and fiercely attacked from all sides. He fought with bravery, notwithstanding the surprise, and at the end of three-quarters of an hour, evidently was becoming master of the situation, when a soldier, under a misapprehension of orders, or overcome by fear for personal safety, cried aloud, "the Colonel has ordered a retreat." This exhibition of poltroonery decided the fate of the heroic band. In the state of confusion that ensued, an unresisted slaughter commenced, while the enemy broke in on all sides unobstructed. Colonel Zebulon Butler, and about seventy of his men escaped; the men got across the river to Fort Wilkesborough; the Colonel made his way to Fort Kingston, which was invested the next day on the land-side. The enemy, in a spirit of heartless barbarity, sent the bloody scalps of one hundred and ninety-six of their late comrades into the fort, to dispirit the already demoralized garrison. In the evening, the Colonel quitted the fort with his family, and went down the river, being probably the only officer that escaped. Colonel Nathan Dennison, who succeeded to the command, seeing the impossibility of an effectual resistance, went with a flag to Colonel Butler, to know what terms he would grant on a surrender; to which application, Butler responded, with a savageness that would have shamed the most inhuman of his savage followers —*the hatchet*. Dennison having defended the fort, till most of the garrison were killed or disabled, surrendered at discretion. Some of the unhappy persons were carried away alive; but the most were shut up in houses and barracks, and consumed; while their less than savage conquerors danced around in hellish glee. The savages then crossed the river to the only remaining fort, Wilkesborough, the inmates of which, in hopes of mercy, surrendered without demanding any conditions. Here were stationed about seventy Continental soldiers, who had been engaged in the defense of the frontiers; these were butchered in the most inhuman manner; the butchers using every ingenuity to aggravate and prolong the tortures of their victims. The remaining men, women and children, were confined in houses, and suffered death by being burned together.

A general scene of devastation was now spread through all the townships. Fire, sword, and other instruments of destruction alternating, until every settlement, except those occupied by tories, was destroyed, and the inhabitants butchered or driven from their homes. The barbarities of the inhuman monster Butler, extended to the stock of the wretched people; many were slaughtered; others, with tongues cut out, were left to die the death of starvation. Some cases of especial cruelty were practiced. Among others, Captain Bedlock was stripped, his body filled with splinters and set on fire; Captains Kersey and Durger, were thrown alive into flames, and held in place with pitch-forks, until death relieved their sufferings. The carnage ceased only for want of victims. A few women and children were fortunate enough to escape to the woods, and became fugitives from their now desolate homes. The sufferings endured by these helpless wanderers, many of whom perished in their flight, will only be known when the final pages of this atrocious scene are unfolded to view at the bar of judgment. These scenes were enacted within the limits of Northumberland County, in an age when the refining influences of Christianity had softened the heart of mankind toward its fellows, and taught us that the principle virtue of the truly good was charity.

We may search in vain among the annals of the days of the Spanish Inquisition, for a parallel to the inhumanity exhibited by the monster Butler, in his ruthless destruction of the defenseless of his own race, and, in some cases his own blood. Hunt the records of the dark ages through for a more unfeeling, beastly sentiment, than that of his reply to the brave Dennison, when seeking some mitigation of cruelty for his followers, he asked for the terms of surrender; "*the hatchet*" was the only response of this blood-stained wretch. Volumes have been written, of the sufferings of the people of Wyoming, but never can American people rightly appreciate Butler, and his banditti, or the nation that fostered and sustained him in his horrid work. Over two hundred settlers of the Susquehanna met with violent deaths at the time of this massacre, and many were killed by the Indians, who, at various times, stealthily sought isolated settlements, and with fire and hatchet destroyed every vestige of civilization. No sooner had the little settlement partially recovered from this shock, than they found themselves again arrayed against the whole power of the Pennsylvanian government. Connecticut had withdrawn all claim to jurisdiction after the decree of the commission at Trenton and left the weak Colonists to contend with their old enemies. No community of equal extent in the country had responded so nobly to the call for troops during the war as the little territory of Northumberland County. Many of her best citizens had perished in the struggle for Independence. Many widows and orphans had been left hopelessly dependent upon the charity of those little more fortunate than themselves. As a consequence, the ability of the people to defend themselves was much less than formerly; and it would seem that after all the bitter experiences of the past that any sacrifice would have been made rather than renew the internecine strife. But human nature is very much alike, whether found among the Yankees and Pennamites of Northumberland in 1780, or more civilized localities in this the Centennial year, and each party was thoroughly imbued with a consciousness of the rectitude of their conduct. The petition of the settlers to Congress for redress at this time, presents to view a condition of things that it would seem should melt the strongest heart, and prompt those having the necessary power to the perfection of some measure for relief. The petition was worded as follows: "We have settled a country which in its original state of but little value, but now cultivated by your memorialists, is of the greatest importance to them, being their all. We are yet alive, but the richest blood of our neighbors and friends, parents, children and husbands, has been spilt in the general cause of our country, and we have suffered everything this side of death. We supplied the Continental army with many valuable officers and soldiers, and left ourselves weak and unguarded against the attack of the savages, and others more savage by nature. Our houses are desolate, many mothers are childless, widows and orphans are multiplied, our habitations are destroyed and many of our neighbors reduced to beggary." But all this availed nothing against the cupidity of innumerable speculators who infested the Proprietaries, to use force in dispelling the Connecticut people. The General Assembly appointed a commission, consisting of Joseph and William Montgomery and Joseph McLean, with instructions to repair to Wyoming and compromise the dispute between the settlers and the Commonwealth. This committee recommended that the settlers be allowed land in the western part of the State as consideration for their improvements, provided they would enter into contracts to relinquish all claims, and remove immediately. Such a foul wrong as this report contemplated to inflict upon the intended victims would, of course, arouse the indignation of any one with the least atom of manhood; but unjust and outrageously unfair as it was it received the sanction of the self-righteous Friends who claimed the soil of Pennsylvania, and of all their emissaries. Among the latter was one Patterson, who had been in the employ of the Penns for many years, and at this time held the appointment of justice of the peace in Northumberland County. He, with his associates, backed by a military force, commenced a system of contemptible and cowardly annoyances upon the Yankees, by quartering the soldiers upon the inhabitants, arresting people and confining them under guard within the fort, and inflicting upon them every indignity that would suggest itself to a depraved and cowardly spirit like his. Old men suffering with disease, men who had spent years fighting the British foe, and had just returned to their homes, were hurried off to a loathsome prison, destitute of even a floor, and there compelled to lie down, the guard being instructed to shoot any who attempted to rise. The men secure in prison, Patterson turned the women and children out of doors and put his followers in possession of their homes. Petitions were sent to Congress, to the Assemblies of Pennsylvania and Connecticut, but without avail. On the 13th and 14th days of May, 1784—days that will be ever memorable on the Susquehanna River, for the consummation of the most fiendish deeds ever perpetrated by mortal man—Patterson's soldiers dispossessed one hundred and fifty families, and forced five hundred men, women and children to march through the wilderness to the Delaware, sixty miles distant. "Several children died from starvation and exposure; women just ready for confinement were compelled to wade swollen streams, and the sufferings of the entire impoverished throng were beyond the possibility of pen or tongue to describe. Cripples on crutches, babes in the mother's arms, the helpless conveyed on litters, were driven along at the point of the bayonet, through a dreary, uninhabited wilderness." Patterson overreached himself by his wanton cruelty, and drew forth the indignation of all good men, and by none was his unauthorized and outrageous course denounced more strongly than by the people of this County. The settlers were powerless to help themselves, and they could only appeal to the authorities for redress. The next move on the part of the Pennsylvania Government, was the appointment of Colonel Armstrong and Hon. John Boyd, with full power to restore peace to Wyoming. In August, 1784, the commissioners arrived in the valley, with three hundred infantry and fifteen cavalry. They issued their proclamation declaring peace and good order, and demanding a cessation of hostilities. The Yankees accepted his promises and were immediately arrested; some were sent to Easton to jail, forty-two others to Sunbury. Of those sent to Sunbury, ten escaped on the morning of the 25th of August, when the rest were forced into a dirty dungeon and treated with the utmost rigor until finally released on bail. Those confined at Easton, overcame their keeper and released themselves. The perfidious Armstrong was removed, but shortly afterward was promoted to the rank of general, and returned to the valley on the 17th of August, in command of one hundred men. An engagement ensued in which Armstrong was defeated. The next day Armstrong sent thirty men to gather buckwheat on the flats, but they were surrounded by the Yankees, and the grain captured. At this junction, the Assembly of Pennsylvania passed an Act, restoring the dispossessed Yankees to their lands and homes, a conciliatory measure of but temporary relief however. The settlers at once commenced devising measures for protection, organized the militia, with Franklin for colonel, and appointed committees to prepare some form of government. An effort was made by Franklin to erect a new State, out of the precincts of Pennsylvania. The authorities at Philadelphia saw at once that the infamous policy pursued by Pennsylvania was fast leading to a dismemberment of the State, and that it became necessary to adopt other and prompt measures. Timothy Pickering, a lawyer of distinguished ability was requested to repair to Wyoming, and examine into the condition of things there. This he did in the months of August and September, 1786, and returned to Philadelphia, reporting that "Yankees were entirely satisfied with the constitution of Pennsylvania, and were ready to submit to its government, provided they could be quieted in the possession of their farms." September 25th, of the same year, Luzerne County was organized, and Pickering, Hollenback and others, were commissioned justices of the peace. On the 27th of December, notice was served on the electors of Luzerne, through Pickering, Butler and Franklin, that an election would be held, on the first day of February, 1787, for the election of one supreme Councillor, one member of the House of Representatives, and high Sheriff. This was an exquisite strategic movement, intended to divide the Yankees—and succeeded. Franklin was elected to the General Assembly, but he failed to be caught in the cunningly spread net, and stubbornly adhered to his former position, refusing to take a seat in the Assembly. On the 28th of March, following the election, the Pennsylvania authorities, seeing the utter failure to gain any vantage ground by the futilous course, so long pursued, passed what was known as the "confirming law," and appointed Pickering, Montgomery and Muhlenberg a commission, to sit at Wilkesbarre and decide upon contestant claims. So often had the plighted faith of the agents of the government been broken, that the Yankees watched with great distrust the action of the commissioners. Pickering had long been known as a man of unswerving rectitude, and strictly honorable in all his dealings; he pledged his honor as security for the good faith of Pennsylvania, but still he was distrusted. A public meeting was called, which was addressed by the friends of each party. Franklin delivered a most sarcastic and withering speech, in which he denounced the conduct of Pennsylvania as well as his former friends, who had been estranged from their common cause, and now took sides with Pickering. The long pent-up emotions of the excited multitude could not be restrained, and the convention broke up in a row, in which fists and clubs were freely used. Order was finally restored and a vote taken, which resulted in an acceptance of the privileges guaranteed in the Confirming Act. Franklin in vain attempted to unite the people again, in which effort he was seconded by General Ethan Allen; the people had tired of disorder, and eagerly accepted any compromise that would tend to quiet the disturbing elements of their society. His fierce nature knew no submission—he harangued the people daily, denouncing the authorities and demanding the repeal of the confirming law, which was mainly brought about by two clergymen of the place. Franklin was arrested and carried off to Philadelphia, and the wild, turbulent Yankees finally subdued, through the consummate tact and ability of Colonel Pickering.

The Legislature of Pennsylvania, finally, in 1799, passed the compromise law, under which Pennsylvania claimants were compensated. Commissioners appointed under this law, examined the nature of different claims, and if it appeared that a Connecticut claimant was an actual settler before the Trenton decree, certificates were issued confirming the title by the payment of a small consideration. This restored peace to the community, which, for a period of thirty years, had been distracted by a bitter strife, in which passion and selfishness had predominated, and the voice of reason been unheeded. No more striking instance of the ungovernableness of man, when blinded by passion, and controlled wholly by selfishness, is afforded in the annals of history, than that found in the history of the civil wars on the Susquehanna. The Connecticut party justly deemed themselves the victims of harsh usage, and partial legislation; and being of the same blood as those who, in Boston harbor, gave the British government so distinctly to understand that they would submit to no wrong, it is not surprising that they obstinately resisted the arbitrary proceedings of Pennsylvania. The conduct of the government of the Penns, and after their retirement, of the Commonwealth, was without excuse. The vacillating legislation exposed her to the severest criticism. The General Assembly was undoubtedly corruptly influenced in the repeal of wholesome measures, that would have allayed unpleasant feeling, and at any time, restored quiet. The attitude assumed by Pennsylvania, and the injustice perpetrated upon the claimants on the Susquehanna, by reason of her unwise legislation, is graphically set forth in a report made by the High Court of Censors—a body that convened once in seven years, and to which was preferred the complaints of the wronged settlers.

After a careful investigation, this tribunal reported as follows: "It is the opinion of this Council that the decision made at Trenton early in 1783, between the State of Connecticut and this Commonwealth, concerning the territorial rights of both, was favorable to Pennsylvania. It likewise promised the happiest consequences to the confederacy, as an example was thereby set of two contending sovereignties adjusting their differences in a court of justice, instead of involving themselves, and perhaps their confederates, in war and bloodshed. It is much to be regretted, that this happy event was not improved on the part of this State as it might have been. That the persons claiming lands, at and near Wyoming, occupied by emigrants from Connecticut, now become subjects of Pennsylvania, were not left to prosecute their claims in the proper course without the intervention of the legislature. That a body of troops was enlisted, after the Indian war had ceased and the Civil government had been established, and placed at Wyoming—for no other apparent purpose than that of promoting the interests of the claimants under the former grants of Pennsylvania. That these troops were kept up and continued there, without the license of Congress, in violation of the Confederation. That they were suffered, without restraint, to injure and oppress the neighboring inhabitants, during the course of the winter. That the injuries done to these people excited the compassion and interposition of the State of Connecticut, who, thereupon, demanded of Congress another hearing, in order to investigate the private claims of the settlers at Wyoming, formerly inhabitants of New England, who from this instance of partiality in our rulers, have been led to distrust the Justice of the State; when in the mean time, numbers of soldiers, and other disorderly persons, in a most riotous and inhuman manner, expelled the New England settlers before mentioned, from their habitations, and drove them towards the Delaware, through unsettled and almost impassable ways, leaving these unhappy outcasts to suffer every species of misery and distress. That this armed force stationed, as aforesaid, at Wyoming, as far as we can see, without any public advantage in view, has cost the Commonwealth the sum of £4,460, and upwards, for the base levying, providing and paying of them, besides other expenditures of public monies. That the authority for embodying these troops was given privately, and unknown to the good people of Pennsylvania; the same being directed by a mere resolve of the House of Assembly, brought in and read the first time on Monday, the 22d of September, 1788, when on motion, and by special order, the same was read a second time and adopted. That the putting this resolve on the secret Journal of the House, and concealing it from the people, after the war with the savages had ceased, and the inhabitants of Wyoming had submitted to the government of the State, sufficiently marks and fixes the clandestine and partial interest of the arrangement, no such condition having been thought necessary in the defense of the northern and western frontiers during the late war. And lastly, we regret the fatal example which this transaction has set of private persons, at least equally able with their opponents to maintain there own cause, procuring the interest of the Commonwealth in their behalf, and the aid of the public treasury. The opprobrium, which from hence has resulted to this State, and the dissatisfaction and prospect of dissention, now existing with one of our sister States, the violation of the confederation, and the injury hereby done to such of the Pennsylvania claimants of land at Wyoming, occupied as aforesaid, as have given no countenance to, but on the contrary have disavowed these extravagant proceedings. In short we lament that our government has in this business manifested little wisdom or foresight; nor have acted as guardians of the rights of the people committed to their care. Impressed with the multiplied evils which have sprung from the imprudent management of this business, *we hold it up to public censure*, to prevent, if possible, further instances of bad government, which might convulse and distract our new-formed nation."

CHAPTER VII.

THE CENTENNIAL OF CHEMISTRY—DR. PRIESTLY.

The first day of August, 1874, was a memorable one to the denizens of the quiet little borough of Northumberland. At an early hour, it was evident that something was about to occur, sufficiently apart from the usual routine of the humdrum of life, of the quiet, contented people of this secluded nook, to arouse from their lethargy those who, for a generation, had floated along the current without an effort to change its course. Years had passed, stirring events had followed each other in rapid succession, changing society, revolutionizing science, destroying nations, establishing others from the ruins, since the earth had closed over the wearied form of him who was the principal actor in the wonderful event, that the unusual assemblage at Northumberland had convened to commemorate. One hundred years before, Dr. Joseph Priestly, in the investigation of his beloved science, had made the all important discovery of oxygen gas. To those uninformed as to the influence of this single element upon all animated life, it would probably seem that a feeling had been aroused wholly unproportioned to the magnitude of the event; but to those who had devoted valuable lives to the investigation of the abstruse science, the interest manifested was hardly commensurate with the importance of the discovery to the *genus homo*. The purpose of the multitude was made manifest in the address of Col. David Taggart, who welcomed the assembled scientists of the nation in words which adequately explained the object of the convention.

"I have been chosen by my fellow-citizens to offer to the learned and distinguished men and women, who have gathered here to commemorate a grand discovery and to honor a great name, a brief but earnest welcome. We cannot follow you through the wide realms of science, nor explore very deeply the mysteries of nature, for we know more about oxen than oxygen, and a great deal more about the whey of milk than the Milky Way, but we can move with equal step in paying tribute of respect and reverence to the illustrious man, who, eighty years ago, found among "the rude forefathers" of this hamlet, a quiet home, and, seventy years ago, an honored grave.

"While in the lapse of everlasting time, all human names must be forgotten, many ages will have come and gone and left their silent footmarks on the earth, before that of Priestly will pass from the memories and the records of his fellow-men. He has written it in letters of light and glory, upon the highest and broadest pillar of the universe. By right of genius and labor, he takes rank with "the dead but sceptered sovereigns who still rule our spirits from their urns."

"Like the eagle, he built his eyrie upon the mountain top, inaccessible to vulgar intrusions. In that pure atmosphere he dwelt not above human spite, jealousy, and detraction—for it is easier to get below than above them, —but above their annoyances. The shafts of bigots and fools were aimed at him, but they could not penetrate the triple armor, which Philosophy, Enthusiasm, and Truth had thrown around him. Like you, gentlemen, he made science his mistress, and with a pure heart and an untiring mind he worshipped, her "Through long days of labor, and nights devoid of ease," and to-day he stands with Galileo, Newton, Harvey, Franklin, Faraday and Humboldt, grand, colossal, and enduring, one of the great high-priests in the boundless and beautiful Temple of Nature.

"A brutal English mob could burn his dwelling, and in an hour of political madness and religious frenzy, destroy the work of years, but it could not stay the indomitable energy of his genius, nor dim the lustre of his well-earned renown. While the miserable wretches who composed that mob have long ago given back to the great element which he discovered, seventy-five per cent. of their worthless carcasses, more than eighty years afterward, his great name is a talisman to draw to this quiet village, many of the most renowned knowledge-gatherers of the nation—besides several from New Jersey, and Canada,—an aristocracy of learning and intellect that can afford to look down from its high citadels of thought and achievement, with pity, if not contempt, upon the mere vulgar aristocracy of blind accident, the painted caterpillars of pretentious, illiterate wealth.

"As I am not vain enough to suppose that any one cares to listen to me, when such illustrious names are upon the bills, I will merely reiterate to you, men and women of sense and science, in behalf of *all* my neighbors, a very sincere and unfeigned welcome, to our homes and to our hearts. And let me assure you most earnestly, that we are not only willing, but anxious, to do all things possible to make you remember with pleasure your well-timed pilgrimage to the home and grave of the greatest discoverer of his time."

The people of the present and future have a deep interest in the events that made up the life of the truly great Priestly. A history of his life and acts, forms an essential feature in the history of the community in which he dwelt and labored. The discoveries made by him, here, in the home of his adoption, sufficiently indicate the character of the man, when judged from a scientific standpoint. His writings on politics and kindred subjects, indicate his standing as a politician and man of letters. His free way of thinking, and free style of writing, were somewhat at variance with the strict Federalist sentiments of the dominant party of his day, which brought him into a controversy with the factionists that affected his popularity with the masses; otherwise, he could easily have been the leading politician of his time. His logic was potent, but sometimes a little rough. His manner of expression, piquant; which led doubtless to a greater degree of asperity among his reviewers, than was deserved. His friends were numerous, his confidants but few. His compositions would fill volumes, which written for the public eye and expressive of the views of a liberal-minded man, who lived many years in advance of the age, were not the true tests of his real character. His honest convictions are best exhibited in his private correspondence. One of his letters written to a prominent member of Congress, between whom and Priestly there was an affinity of feeling on all questions of real moment, is here published, as best illustrative, perhaps, of his political status:

NORTHUMBERLAND, Jan. 7, 1799.

"DEAR SIR: As you do not complain of the liberty I have taken, I shall trouble you pretty often in the same way. As my son has probably sailed before this time, I wish you would tell Mr. Gales that he agreed with Mr. Kennedy, the printer in this town, about the printing of my "Comparison of the Institution of Moses," &c., and undertook to buy a quantity of type for the work, and that I have seen the paper maker; so that if, as he writes to Mr. Degruchy, he has made any agreement with Mr. Gales about the printing of the same work, he must have forgotten what was done here, and that I think myself bound by. If he has agreed with him about the printing of the Church History, it is very well, and part of the copy shall be sent to Mr. Gales whenever he chooses.

"You say you wish I were as zealous a friend of America as Mr. Hone is of France. Both Mr. Hone and myself, as well as Dr. Price, and many others, were as zealous in the cause of America as he now is in that of France. If I had not been so, I should not have come hither, nor am I changed at all. I like the country and the Constitution of your Government as much as ever. The change, dear sir, is in you. It is clear to me that you have violated your Constitution in several essential articles, and act upon maxims by which you may defeat the whole object of it. Mr. Adams openly disapproves the most fundamental article of it, viz: the election of the Executive. But as you say, we cannot see our own prejudices, and cherish them as truths.

"I may be doing wrong in writing so freely, and I have been desired to be cautious with respect to what I write to you. But I am not used to secrecy and caution, and I cannot adopt a new system of conduct now. There is no person in this country to whom I write on the subject of politics besides yourself, nor do I recollect what I have written, but I do not care who sees what I write, or knows what I think on any subject. You may if you please show all my letters to Mr. Adams himself. I like his address on the opening of the Congress, and I much approve of his conduct in several respects. I like him better than your late President. He is more undisguised. We easily know what he thinks and what he would do, but I think his answers to several of the addresses, are mere intemperate railing, unworthy of a statesman.

"My general maxims of policy are, I believe, peculiar to myself. When I mentioned them to Mr. Adams he was pleased to say that "if any nation could govern itself by them it would command the world." Of this I am fully persuaded; but he has departed very far from them. All that I can expect is the fate of the poet Lee, who when he was confined in a mad-house and was asked by some stranger why he was sent thither, replied "I said the world was mad and the world said I was mad, and they outvoted me." My plan would prevent all war and almost all taxes. But if the calamities of war, heavy taxation, the pestilence, or any other evil, be required for the discipline of nations, as I believe that in the present state of things they are, they will be introduced from some cause or other. This country, as well as others, wants a scourge and you are preparing one for yourselves.

"With every good wish to you and your country, I am dear Sir, (though an alien) yours sincerely,

J. Priestly."

The growth of science is most clearly shown in the sketch of Priestly's life, which is extracted from an address delivered by Professor Henry H. Croft, at the Centennial Anniversary of Chemistry. "Priestly's life may be said to have been two-fold or manifold. He was an ardent investigator of scientific truths; he was also an earnest, honest, free-thinking politician." So multitudinous are his works on these and many other subjects; so versatile seem his talents to have been, that as, Dumas remarks, we feel almost inclined to believe there must have been two or more Priestly's, just as some have imagined there must have been *two* bearing the name of Raymond Lullius. Few writers have been more voluminous; but Brougham remarks, few are now less read.

Born at Fieldhead, near Leeds, in 1733, of very strict Calvinistic parents, Joseph Priestly, at a very early age, acquired strong religious tendencies; but, although at first a Calvinist, he soon began to entertain ideas for himself, and got into a state of doubt, becoming somewhat of a convert to Arminianism. At this time we find him devoting himself to the study of not only the ancient languages, such as Latin and Greek, together with the modern ones, but also in aid of his biblical studies, of Hebrew, Arabic, Chaldee and Syriac. His power of acquiring languages, and his memory generally, seem to have been enormous, and rendered him in future years a most formidable antagonist in all those polemical discussions, in which he was so prone to engage. His religious opinions were what, at that time, was considered peculiar and heterodox; and, on attempting to enter the ministry, he was rejected on account of his views with regard to the original sin, the atonement, and eternal damnation, views, which resulting from his own fervent convictions, he maintained openly and fearlessly, and subsequently, although acting as a preacher at Needham, he failed to become popular, partly on account of an impediment in his speech, but more from his known tendency to Arianism and to Socinianism. To the latter sect, better known under the name of Unitarians, he finally belonged. Brougham sarcastically remarks, that the people of Needham probably thought their privilege of hell-torments to be rudely invaded by their preacher. His disbelief also in the Trinity being notorious, he very soon—at the early age of twenty-five, got into a disagreeable controversy with many parties, and had to leave Needham. At Nantwich he succeeded better, established a school, and commenced his scientific studies, for which however, he had had very little preliminary preparation. These he continued afterwards at Warrington, whither he removed in 1761.

An acquaintance with Benjamin Franklin, led him to turn his attention to electricity, and within the year he produced his "History of Electricity," a work which, although thought much of at that time as a useful compilation, does not seem to have added greatly to his reputation; the same may be said, to a greater extent with regard to his "History of Vision," both works being too rapidly and carelessly written, a common fault with all of Priestly's writings. He made a number of experiments on electricity, which, although not adding much to the science, rendered his name so well known, that he was elected member of the Royal Society. About this time, there was an opportunity of his being appointed chaplain on Captain Cook's second voyage, but here his unfortunate religious opinions came in his way, and he was rejected by the admiralty on account of his heterodoxy. While at Warrington, 1761–1768, his pen was most prolific, and among his writings may be mentioned, "A Theory of Languages," books on "Oratory and Criticism," on "History and General Policy," on the "Constitution and Laws of England," on "Education," "A Chart of Biography," "A Chart of History." In 1767, he removed to Leeds, and became minister of Millhill Chapel, and wrote many controversial books and pamphlets. In after times he wrote "Letters to a Philosophical Institution," "An Answer to Gibbon," "Disquisitions on Matter and Spirit," "Corruption of Chemistry," "Early Opinions on Christ," "Familiar Letters to the Inhabitants of Birmingham," "Two Different Histories of the Christian church," and a large number of other works. Sufficient have been named to show his great industry and the versatility of his mind. In 1773, he entered the service of Lord Shelburne, afterwards Marquis of Landsdown, as chaplain, and remained with him seven years, leaving with a pension of £150 per annum, and no ill feeling on either side, but probably from the openness with which he expressed, and the pertinacity with which he maintained his views on religious and political subjects. In Lord Shelburne's company, he visited Paris, and various parts of the continent, and at Paris was present at a discussion between two chemists as to the nature of *red percipitate*, now known as "mercuric oxide." It is not improbable that what he heard that day led to his future experiments, and hence to this meeting.

Leaving Lord Shelburne, in 1780, he settled in Birmingham, and continued his scientific and theological studies and writings for several years. Unfortunately he entered into a violent controversy with members of the Established Church, and, as he had no hesitation in expressing his views very freely, and did not confine himself to polemical discussion with the above named sect, but equally with Calvinists, Arminians, Arians, Presbyterians, Methodists, Roman Catholics and Swedenborgians, it is not to be wondered at that he got into some disrepute. It was not sufficient for any one to agree with him partially, he must agree entirely; a deviation of a thousandth of an inch, either one way or the other, constituted an antagonism. Indeed, it is doubtful whether any one ever entertained Dr. Priestly's belief, except Dr. Priestly himself.

Whatever amount of toleration in religious matters there may be in England now, there was much less a century ago. The Established Church looked upon all Dissenters with suspicion and dislike; and the government of the day, fearing the introduction of reform and liberal opinions, emanating generally from the dissenting portion of the community, took much the same view. So powerful a writer on religion and politics, was an eye-sore to a Tory government. Burke's paper on the French Revolution had been answered by Priestly in such a manner as to arouse the indignation of that statesman, and to cause him to attack Priestly with great virulence, even in the House of Commons. Priestly had rendered himself obnoxious to the church by his so-called heterodox ideas on religious matters; to the government, by his bold advocacy of liberal opinions; to the people of England, generally, by his openly expressed admiration of the French Republic. The popular feeling was at that time very *strong* against *France*; and the fact of a minister of religion expressing his admiration of a system, which only three weeks before had been instrumental in causing those atrocious butcheries which disgraced the French Republic, naturally created a feeling against Priestly, for which, however, he was not in the least accountable, any more than the British nation was guilty of the unwarrantable treatment to which he was shortly submitted, at the hands of a mob, and some prejudicial parties.

On a celebration of the storming of the Bastile, held at Birmingham, at which, however, Priestly was not present, popular feeling rose to such a hight, that the church and house of Priestly, and those of many of his friends, were destroyed by the mob. We know what an unreasoning thing a mob is. You, in the United States, are not entirely unacquainted with it. On a recent visit to England, I went to Nottingham and saw the castle, one of the most magnificent edifices of England, in ruins, from some absurd popular outbreak, I believe the Chartists. Priestly, not sure of his life in Birmingham, went to London, and here found the feeling still strongly against him; a feeling for which I shall not attempt to apologize, as it is something which at this time we can scarcely conceive. He had the greatest difficulty in obtaining lodging, the landlord being afraid of his house being burned down. He was shunned by the members of the Royal Society. His life was embittered, and he left England for a land where he was sure his religious and political opinions might be freely promulgated, without interference or complaint. He was somewhat wrong; the same odium, which attached to him in the old country, accompanied him here to a slighter extent. Clergymen of any other sect looked on him as a heathen, though, when they came to know him, acknowledged their transgressions. His political principles found no favor with the Adam's administration, and I am told he was threatened with expulsion from the country. Under Jefferson's reign, Priestly was at peace, and ended his days, after a continued writing on religious and scientific subjects, here, where we are assembled to-day.

CHAPTER VIII.

HORSE-RACING—BEAR SHOW—FOOT-RACING—EARLY MANUFACTURES—FOURTH OF JULY CELEBRATION—FRANKLIN'S LETTERS—DOMESTIC TRAGEDY—SHAMOKIN AND MAHANOY—EARLY TIMES' SCHOOLMASTER—SUNBURY COURT—ETC.

A FEW incidents, amusing and otherwise, have been collected together illustrative of the men and times of years ago. The amusements catered into show the tastes of our forefathers. The extract from the proceedings of a 4th of July celebration, the patriotic ardor that pervaded the minds of those who so recently had come into possession of the inheritance of a free government; the schoolmaster's letter, the standard of excellence of pedagogism; the difficulties encountered by Mr. Montgomery, the feeling regarding the innovations of machinery; the letters from Franklin and others; all show the character of the people composing the pioneer settlements of our county.

HORSE-RACING.

Much time was spent in the early days of our county, by our fast *old men*, in horse-racing, cock-fighting and fox-chasing. Fox-chasing was the favorite amusement, and whenever the condition of the ground would admit of it, many of the gentlemen of the day would be seen flying over the hills and ravines on their blooded hunters, preceded by a band of forty or fifty hounds in search of poor Reynard. The first at the death won the brush, and was entitled to all the whiskey that could be consumed and five public suppers. Horse-racing also had its devotees, among others one Mr. Grant, who resided above Sunbury, and who was the owner of a fast beast recognized by the name of Crooked-tail. On one occasion Mr. Grant arranged for a trial of speed between his favorite and a celebrated horse from Lancaster, and staked $1000 on the race. So greatly was he excited over the approaching race, that three days before the trial he was prostrated with fever, which terminated fatally a few hours after it was announced to him that his horse was beaten.

BEAR SHOW.

Many years ago, there appeared at the hostelry of Mr. Prince, who, at that time, kept the once famous hotel where the Court House now stands in Sunbury, a tall, lank, cadaverous-looking individual, whose twang and garb at once proclaimed him a native of Plymouth Rock, or some spot contiguous thereto, leading an enormous black bear. The bear was fastened in the stable, and handbills put up, announcing that for the small sum of six-and-a-quarter cents, the citizens of Sunbury could examine a specimen of the Zoological kingdom *yclept* a bear. Many visited and admired old Bruin, and, among others, Thomas Robins, a rough, harsh spoken, and harsher appearing individual, who was the owner of a large bull-dog which he offered at once to pit against the bear for a fight. The Yankee accepted at once, and put up five dollars as a wager, which was covered by Robins, the fight to come off the next day but one. At the time appointed, a large number of people paid their fip-and-a-bit and entered the stable to witness the set-to. Robins, confident of winning the stakes, came forth with his mastiff, and, at the word, the canine made a spring for the bear's nose. A blow, administered with lightning quickness by the sleepy-looking child of the forest, a fierce yell from the dog, and the fight ended. The dog was seen to fly through the air with the rapidity of light, struck the side of the barn with a loud thud, fell back, and disappeared like a shot from a rifle through the door. Robins, crest-fallen, handed over the stakes, and left swearing vengeance against the timorous dog.

EARLY AMUSEMENTS.

John Cowden and David Taggart, two of the early settlers from Ireland, became involved in a dispute as to speed and bottom on a foot-race, and it was decided to determine the vexed question by a race. The distance was measured off. Taggart to run over one-half of the course, and carry Johnny Deutlar, a pursy little subject with a breath of beam equalling or exceeding his keel. Taggart lost, as he claimed, because Deutlar could not ride well. The race excited a good deal of interest, and served to amuse the people and afford a topic of conversation for sometime.

EARLY MANUFACTURES.

In an article published in the *Republican Argus* of date August 17th, 1808, William Montgomery, a public-spirited citizen of the county, labored hard to convince the people of the utility of machinery adapted to manufacture cloth from wool. His scheme to organize a stock company, the capital of which should be $2,000, divided into one hundred shares, for the purpose of establishing at Danville a woolen factory, met with strong opposition from the fogy element, who argued that the labor of converting the wool into cloth for domestic purposes, was the especial duty of the wives and daughters, and that the introduction of machinery for that purpose would take from women a very important and useful work, resulting in a neglect of a very essential part of young women's education. This argument, weak as it was, could not be met by the astute reformer, who appeared in some doubt as to the probability of finding other fields of usefulness for women. Mr. Montgomery astounded the people by the prediction that the carding and weaving of wool by machinery would be followed by machinery to manipulate crude cotton in the same manner. Could this truly philanthropic man have moved aside the veil that hid from view the developments of a few decades of years in advance, he might well have wondered at the accomplishments of the "rising genius of America." The "rising genius" has ever been equal to the emergency, and not a field of usefulness has been monopolized by the fruits of the inventive genius, but that others have been opened, more compatible with the tastes and wants of those whose labor appeared at a discount. Well can it be remembered when the work on the spinning-wheel and loom formed a very important part of the domestic economy, when it was the pride of American girls to equal their mothers in their adeptness at the spinners' and weavers' art; but those days have passed, and other and far more important duties have been found for our daughters. They are not the drones our ancestors feared they must become, owing to the progress of improvements which drove them from the wheel and loom, and relieved them from a bondage worse than serfdom. The true status of womanhood, has never been adequately determined, but when a comparison of the present, is made with their position during the dark ages, much can be seen to excite gratitude to an Omnipotent, who endowed woman with just those elements of character that so eminently fit her for the exalted field of usefulness she now enjoys. After repeated efforts, the scheme to establish a woolen factory at Danville, was successful. The plan was somewhat on the co-operative principle, furnishing facilities for the wool producers, to have the crude article manufactured into cloth for home consumption. How many years elapsed before the primitive factory was superceded by others on a more enlarged scale, does not appear. But the old establishment was in operation long enough to gain for its operators the confidence of the people, and pave the way to more extended operations, not only in the manufacture of wool, but every other article required by man; and yet there is room for women, and ample opportunities for the employment of all her talents and energies, in fields much more suited to her tastes and organism than the old tread-mills, that our ancestors deemed so essential to the proper development of the muscle and brain of our daughters.

4TH OF JULY, 1808.

In this, the Centennial year of our existence as a nation, it may be interesting to know something of the feelings that prompted those who lived seventy years ago—for the 4th of July, was then, as now, a national holiday—a day to call forth the patriotic sentiment of the country—a day on which the people could commingle together and duly commemorate the natire day, sending the interchange of good fellowship, re-affirm their adherence to the truths enunciated by the glorious old patriots, who on the 4th of July, 1776, proclaimed the United Colonies, free and independent.

On the 4th day of July, 1808, the good people of Northumberland assembled themselves together, and proclaimed to the world the following sentiments, being embodied in seventeen toasts:

First. The sovereign people—nature never made a slave. Six cheers.

Second. The day—and all true patriots and philanthrophists who honor it. Six cheers.

Third. The National Government of the United States—may it be as lasting as time, and its administration always pure and upright. Nine cheers; tune, Hail Columbia.

Fourth. The Democrats of Pennsylvania, and their brethren in the sister States—may vigilance and firmness be their motto; virtue their guide, and the public weal their object; Six cheers that indicated the political sentiment of the assembly.

Sixth. The memory of Franklin and Washington, and other departed heroes and sages, whose councils and military virtues contributed so ably to the establishment of our Independence—may every true American shed a tear over their hallowed tombs. A solemn pause; tune Roslin Castle.

Seventh. The right of suffrage, and the purity of elections may they never be impaired or infringed.

Eighth. Public and private schools—the diffusion of knowledge promotes general happiness.

Tenth. The liberty of the press, and freedom of speech on public men, and public measures.

Twelfth. Commerce untrammeled by the tyrants of the ocean—until then we hail the embargo. Tune, Yankee Doodle.

Thirteenth. The respective States of the Union—may they preserve their respective sovereignties, sufficiently to secure the people's rights.

Fourteenth. The President and Vice-president of the United States, and the heads of departments, who have, with effect, opposed European annoyance and tyranny. Twelve cheers; tune, Jefferson's March.

Seventeenth. The American ladies—may we duly appreciate the virtuous matron and modest virgin, who prefer their homespun attire, to imported gewgaws. Twenty-four cheers; tune, in praise of the fair.

The sovereign people of the United States—may they bear in mind, that they are the only legitimate source of power, and always be prepared to humble the arrogant, who affect to despise them.

The Government of the United States—may it be confined to national purposes only. State government—the best for local purposes.

American manufactories—may it be the pride of every American citizen to appear dressed in homespun.

INCIDENTS.

[Copies of letters addressed to Major Lawrence Keene, Prothonotary of Northumberland County, then residing in Sunbury, Pa. 1784.]

[DR. BENJAMIN RUSH TO MAJOR KEENE.]

PHILADELPHIA, September 6th, 1784.

"DEAR SIR:—I take pleasure in recommending to your good offices, Dr. Andrew Ross, a gentleman of excellent character, extensive learning and great eminence in the profession of physic. He was introduced to my acquaintance by a letter from Dr. Franklin, the original of which I send you. He intends to settle in Sunbury, if he finds the place agreeable. His views are not only to practice physic and surgery, but to improve his fortune by purchasing lands. I need not suggest to you how great an acquisition such a man will be to a village, or a county. Indeed, I conjure the whole State as enriched by such a citizen. May I beg the favor of you to mention his name, and show Dr. Franklin's letter to all your friends. He will require your advice in procuring lodgings. I hope my good friend, Mrs. Keene, will afford her aid to detain him in your woods. I am sure she and your family will derive great benefit from him in case you should be visited again with billions, or any other kind of fevers. The doctor will entertain her in return for her kindness, with stories of Gentoo, Turkish and Egyptian ladies, for he has not only seen, but resided several years in Constantinople, Egypt, and the West Indies.

"Please to present my compliments to Mr. Joseph Wallis, and tell him that I would have written to him in favor of Dr. Ross, but I hope he will consider this letter as addressed to him as well as yourself.

"With compliments to my good friend, Mrs. Keene, I am, dear sir, with great regard, your sincere friend and humble servant,

BENJAMIN RUSH."

[FRANKLIN'S LETTER TO RUSH.]

——PASSY, March 12, 1784.

"DEAR FRIEND:—This will be delivered to you by Dr. Ross, who is strongly recommended to me by persons of distinction in England, and who, after travelling over a great part of the world, wishes to fix himself for the rest of his life in America. You will find him a very ingenious, sensible man, and be pleased with his conversation; and you will therefore excuse my requesting for him those civilities which you have a pleasure in showing to strangers of merit, and such counsels as from his unacquaintedness with our country may be useful to him. With great esteem, I answer, my dear friend,

yours, most affectionately,

B. FRANKLIN."

[DR. RUSH TO MAJOR KEENE.]

PHILADELPHIA, September 24, 1784.

"DEAR SIR:—Ever desirous to contribute as much as lies in my power to the growth and reputation of Sunbury, the capitol of our County, I have encouraged Mr. Ralph Bouie, a lawyer of excellent character, from Scotland, to settle in your village. May I beg your particular attention to him? He means to invite a body of emigrants from Scotland to settle in Northumberland, if he likes the country.

"Please to tell Mr. Jos. Jacob Wallis, I shall send him the three warrants he wrote for in a few days. I readily assert to being connected with him in them upon the terms he mentions. With compliments to Mrs. Keene, I am dear sir, yours sincerely,

BENJAMIN RUSH."

AN EARLY TIMES SCHOOLMASTER.

Mr. James Tickman being desirous of immolating himself on the altar of public duty, offered his services to the people of Augusta, to train the youthful mind "in the ways that are rough"—in other words to give them a good classical education. He winds up an earnest appeal to those he solicited as patrons, in a euphonious P. S. "You will also send books and paper and pens and a pennife, as I always larne skolars to make their own pens, but, you need not send pens to them that you don't want to rite, nor books to them you don't want to reed, which they can do without them. I need not tell in the words of the poet,"

Tis edokation forms the youthful minds,
Just as the twig's inclined
The tree will bend.

DOMESTIC TRAGEDIES.

A domestic tragedy, of a character, at the present day to excite but little comment, but then in the fall of 1848, of such a nature as to shock the whole community, occurred in the quiet, Teutonic settlement of Upper Mahanoy, at the time mentioned. Mr. Daniel Snyder, wife and family, resided here, where for many years they had been in the quiet and peaceful enjoyment of the fruits of their honest toil, and where they looked forward to a life of comfort, with their family about them. For some time, Mrs. Snyder had been laboring under an apparent aberration of the mind, and had spent some time in the asylum, from which she had returned home cured. One morning, shortly after her return, she arose from her bed, leaving her husband sleeping, went to the yard, procured an axe, and by two well-directed blows, ended the mortal existence of him, who a few minutes before had been lying by her side all unconscious of the terrible fate so soon to be his. Mrs. Snyder attempted to throw herself in the well, but she was prevented by her son, who by this time was aroused. She then returned into the house, seized a razor, and nearly severing her head from her body, fell dead besides her husband's body.

In 1862, there resided in Shamokin, about three miles south of Snydertown, a Mrs. L. C. Chamberlain, who unfortunately had a step-daughter married to a Mr. E. B. Rhoades. Rhoades joined the army in 1861, but returned after the expiration of one year, stopping on his way home to his friends, with Mr. E. T. Drumheller, landlord at Sunbury, and registered his name on the hotel register, November 6th, 1862. This act, simple and common-place as it was, led to his conviction on the first trial for the murder of his mother-in-law. Rhoades arriving home, accused Mrs. Chamberlain of having wronged his wife, her step-daughter, out of fifty dollars, for which he could get no satisfaction. Of the controversy between the two—the slayer and the slain—nothing is known, but that through some means he enticed her into the woods, two hundred yards from her house, and then shot her dead. He was arrested, tried by an impartial jury, and pronounced guilty; his plea of being at the time of the murder, in the army, being controverted by Mr. Drumheller's hotel register. A new trial was granted, and Rhoades was cleared. It would hardly do to impugn the honesty of twelve jurymen; men who, in this country of unexampled freedom and purity, often settle issues involving lives, and thousands of dollars, and frequently themselves unable to read; but it is claimed that Mr. Rhoades' old father was poorer by some twenty thousand dollars, after his son's acquittal.

ELEVEN HUNDRED JUDGES.

Many years ago, there resided about eight miles east of Sunbury, a farmer and hotel keeper, who was noted far and wide for the good cheer dispensed at his table and counter, and who could appreciate a good joke with the best. Approaching his hostelry one warm summer day, came a neighboring farmer, earnestly debating in his mind, how he should obtain a drink of bonnyface's brandy, without producing an equivalent in coin. He was returning from court at Sunbury, and at last a happy idea entered his cranium. He entered the hotel, and after passing the compliments of the day, commenced in strong terms a denunciation of the court. Upon being interrogated as to the cause of his asperity, he replied that there were eleven hundred judges on the bench, and still it was the weakest court ever seen in Sunbury. Bets being made, and an explanation asked for, he proved it as follows. Judge Jordan, occupies a seat on the bench—he is 1; Judge —— sits beside him—he is 1; Judge —— sits on the other side—he is 0; I occupied a seat for a few minutes beside him, another 0; making 1100. The thirsty farmer was declared winner by the multitude, whose acquaintance with the judges, enabled them to appreciate the joke.

CHAPTER IX.

WAR OF THE REBELLION—MUSTER ROLLS—CAPTAINS JAMES TAGGART, WELLS, AND SLATER—SANITARY COMMISSION, ETC.

By far the most important event in the history of this country, since its advent as an independent nationality among the nations of the earth, was the war which commenced in 1861, and ended in 1865, overthrowing the oligarchy that had been attempted in one section, and proclaiming us at once the free and independent people, that we had only been in name to that date. As to the issues growing out of the attempt to establish a separate nationality in one part of the United States, and the results of the struggle for national life, we, as local historians, have nothing to do, except in so far as the events of the war affected localities and local interests. It is our purpose and duty to speak only of the part borne by, and the effect produced upon Northumberland County and its people, leaving to others the discussion of the intricate questions involved, and a settlement of the issues brought out. The spirit manifested by the leaders of the South, engendered in the breasts of the people of the North a strong feeling, that became intensified in bitterness, at every progressive step. It was not sectional, but was participated in by every man and woman who had an ancestry to honor, and a future to provide for. So general was this feeling, that at the first attempt to throttle the infant—that had hardly as yet thrown off its swaddling clothes—a universal cry of alarm and distress was heard, throughout the entire land, emanating from every patriotic heart in the country. The enormity of the crime sought to be committed against our institutions, was not fully comprehended, until the clash of arms, in the hands of contending hosts, began to resound from the scene of strife. For a moment the liberty-loving sank down, as if palsied with fear, but the reaction brought to the front millions eager to avenge the country's wrongs. With the scenes that followed to many of us were familiar. With the gloom, that like a funeral pall overhung our beloved land the first thirty months of the struggle, came the feeling of despondency, reaching almost to despair, that wrenched from the hearts of all a wail of sorrow and woe. The dark cloud, like the canopy of night, that at Fort Sumpter was scarcely larger than a man's hand, extended its ebony hue, until the entire horizon had been overcast, and bade fair to wrap in its mantle, the institutions that a hundred years of arduous labor had scarcely established; but intensified the love of country that pervaded every breast, and aroused to action, the lovers of liberty everywhere. The calls for help were responded to, all over the loyal North, and legions proffered aid to repel the advances of those who sought the nation's life. It would be invidious to particularize, when all exhibited so much enthusiasm, and hence it only becomes us, to treat upon the part enacted by our own soldiers, in the bloody contest. As has been elsewhere stated, the inhabitants of Northumberland are composed largely of the descendents of the Scotch-Irish, —than whom a more determined and fearless people never lived—of English whose love of freedom prompted them to a settlement in a country presuming little else then a life of hardship and deprivation of all that had made home attractive—and of hardy, brave, Germans, whose love of quietude and wealth, never vitiates their love of country. Among the descendents of such an ancestry, the call for help to save liberty to the future, was not in vain. From town and hamlet; from hillside and vale; from the farm and shop, in countless numbers, the sons of Northumberland moved in solid phalanx to the front, and on many a hard-contested field, shed the blood of the bravest and best, in defense of universal liberty. How well they responded; and the fate that befell many, will be shown in the final statements accompanying the muster rolls of Northumberland soldiers. A strong and persistent effort has been made to do full justice to the brave men of this County, who staked life itself on the issue between the South and General Government. Officers have been appealed to, and every source followed up, but all to no avail. We had hoped to perpetuate in local history, scenes and incidents of the last war, that in a few years will pass into the realms of forgetfulness; to record here the deeds of daring participated in by our soldiers; to preserve for posterity, by narration of events, the names and deeds of heroes, whose bones now lie mouldering in Southern graves, and whose names will soon be forgotten. To this end, the co-operation of all officers and relatives has been solicited, but in no case, except by Colonel Taggart, of Northumberland, and Dr. John, of Shamokin, has a favorable response been made. The muster rolls are doubtless imperfect, as some names have been omitted, and some added of soldiers from other counties. Such as it is, we append it, trusting to be instrumental in this wise of perpetuating the memory of a few of the brave of Northumberland County.

EIGHTH REGIMENT.*

Company A.

Captain, Cyrus Strouse; 1st Lieutenant, W. J. Allen; 2d Lieutenant, G. B. Cadwalder; 1st Sergeant, John Harris; 2d Sergeant, Andrew Kreiger; 3d Sergeant, J. B. Snyder; 4th Sergeant, F. Rhoads.

1st Corporal, Jacob Rhoads; 2d Corporal, Jacob Muchler; 3d Corporal, Israel Stambach; 4th Corporal, J. B. Getter.

Musicians—W. P. Caldwell, and Henry Starchal.

Privates—Lewis L. Bevno, William Booth, John Brennan, Ziba Bird, William Bower, George Blanksley Hugh Boyd, Benjamin F. Culp, William Culp, Patrick Colyer, William Colyer, Thomas Caldwell, Alexander Caldwell, Charles Conrad, George Cramer, John Downey, Frederick Dibner, Jacob Dindorf, J. B. Eaton, David Ephlin, J. E. Eisenhart, E. P. Fulk, Darius S. Gilger, C. L. V. Haas, James H. Haas, Thomas Harris, Henry Holshoe, Joel Holshoe, John M. Heilner, John Hancock, James Hollister, Henry Irich, Jacob W. Irich, J. M. John, Thos. R. Jones, Charles Kreiger, Geo. W. Klase, John K. Lake, Michael Mireberger, Jeremiah Maize, Charles Medarn, John Meehan, John Nelfer, W. B. Osmund, Jacob Peifer, J. W. Philipop, Josiah Raup, George Raup, Michael Ragan, James Sterrit, Godfried Sherman, William Shuck, Michael Salter, Jacob Shield, August Shaunl, W. Stilwagoner, D. S. Shipp, Wesley Van Gasken, Peter Wentz, John Weir, D. J. Woodley, G. W. Weaver, Thos. R. Williams, J. B. Zheuder.

11TH REGIMENT.†

Company F.

Captain, C. J. Bruner; 1st Lieutenant, J. P. S. Gobin; 2d Lieutenant, J. H. McCarty; 1st Sergeant, J. E. McCarty; 2d Sergeant, C. P. Pleasant; 3d Sergeant, S. H. Helper; 4th Sergeant, Jacob Rohrbach.

1st Corporal, S. B. Bright; 2d Corporal, C. D. Wharton; 3d Corporal, Daniel Oyster; 4th Coporal, William Byers.

Musicians—H. D. Wharton, and Jacob Weiser.

Privates—Henry Alwiser, Julius Arbiter, Jared Brosious, Henry Bucher, Robert Brooks, Samuel Bartscher, W. M. Brisban, Joseph Bright, Alfred Beckley, B. F. Bright, Francis Carr, W. J. Covert, William Christ, Henry Drisel, Lewis Dome, David Druckamiller, Joseph Drieslinger, William Edze, Samuel Eyster, Jacob Feight, Stephen Golding, B. W. Giddes, P. S. Gusslers, W. D. Huss, Joseph Hildebrand, Charles Harp, Harris Hopper, Albert Haas, Allen Hunter, Elias Hedding, Jared C. Irwin, George Keihl, Daniel Michael, Charles McFarland, Sylvester Meyers, William Martin, John Messner, Wm. H. Millhouse, Mahlon Myers, P. C. Newbaker, George Oyster, Frederick Pill, Henry Quitschilber, Albert Robins, Reuben Ramsey, A. Roderigue, L. T. Rohrbach, Eugene Reiser, F. Schrank, Hugh Smith, John Snyder, C. W. Stewart, J. E. Seidel, Joseph Smith, E. Starkloff, C. Schall, W. Stedman, Charles Swoop, Geo. Tucker, William Volke, Lot B. Wertzel, George Weyman.

34TH REGIMENT.‡

(Unless otherwise given, the date of muster in each case was June 21st, 1861.)

Company B.

Captains—James Taggart; killed at Charles City Cross Roads, June 20th, '62. Charles Wells; promoted from Sergeant to 2d Lieutenant, September 26th, '61; to 1st Lieutenant, December 16th, '61; to Captain, July 1st, '62; killed at Fredericksburg, December 13th, '62. James D. Slater; promoted from Sergeant to 2d Lieutenant, December 16th, '61; to 1st Lieutenant, July 1st, '62; to Captain, December 13th, '62; transferred to Veteran Reserve Corps, September 1st, '63. John A. Maus; promoted from Sergeant to 2d Lieutenant, September 8th, '62; to 1st Lieutenant, March 5th, '63; to Captain, January 1st, '64; to Brevet Major, March 13, '65; mustered out with company, June 11th, '64.

1st Lieutenants—Henry A. Colt; resigned November 9th, '61. James A. Keefer; promoted from Sergeant to 2d Lieutenant, March 5th, '63; to 1st Lieutenant, January 1, '64; dismissed March 3, '64. Peter Vandling; promoted from 2d to 1st Lieutenant, April 2d, '64; mustered out with company, June 11th, '64. Charles C. Jones; 2d Lieutenant, resigned October 8th, '61.

---

* Three months' service. Mustered in April 22d, 1861.

† Recruited at Sunbury, Northumberland County. Mustered in April 24th, 1861. Three months' service.

‡ Recruited in Northumberland County.

PLATE III

ST EDWARD'S CATHOLIC CHURCH AND PAROCHIAL RESIDENCE, *SHAMOKIN, NORTHUMBERLAND CO. PA.*

ERECTED BY FATHER KOCH, PASTOR

1st Sergeants—Josiah Newbery, mustered out with company, June 11th, '64. Joseph Hogan, wounded, and prisoner at New Market Cross Roads, June 30th, '62; died at Richmond, Va. Sergeants—J. G. Dieffenbacher, discharged on Surgeon's certificate, August 2, '61. Saul K. Kreeger, transferred to 191st Regiment, P. Vols., June 6th, '64; veteran. J. C. Newbury, transferred to 191st Regiment, P. Vols., June 6th, '64; veteran. Joseph Martin, transferred from Veteran Reserve Corps; mustered out with company, June 11th, '64.

Corporals—W. H. Morgan, mustered out with company, June 11th, '64. G. W. Fisher, captured at Gettysburg, July 2d, '63; absent at camp parole, at muster out. J. M. Scout, mustered out with company, June 11th, '64. David Hawk, transferred from Veteran Reserve Corps; mustered out with company, June 11th, '64. James Throp, transferred from Veteran Reserve Corps; mustered out with company, June 11th, '64. L. Vandling, discharged November 10th, '62, for wounds received at New Market Cross Roads. J. C. Curson, discharged November 10th, '62, for wounds received at New Market Cross Roads. W. B. Wallis, transferred to 191st Regiment, P. Vols., June 6th, '64; vet. William Young, August 12th, '62; transferred to 191st Regiment, P. Vols., June 6th, '64. J. C. Voris, July 25th, '61; killed at Fredericksburg, December 13th, '62.

Musicians—H. C. Standish, dishonorably discharged, December 10th, '61. George Birkindine, discharged on Surgeon's certificate, April 10th, '63.

Privates—H. J. Angle, July 25th, '61; transferred to regular army, November 27th, '62. William Black, mustered out with company, June 11th, '64. D. O. Beddoes, discharged on Surgeon's certificate, October 24th, 26.' William Beidleman, transferred to regular army, November 27th, '62. Jesse Barnhart, January 22d, '64; transferred to 191st Regiment, P. Vols., June 6th, '64. Ed. Barnhart, January 22, '64; transferred to 191st Regiment, P. Vols., June 6th, '64. B. F. Bashore, January 22d, '64; transferred to 191st Regiment, P. Vols., June 6th, '64. J. H. Brautigan, killed at Fredericksburg, December 13th, '62. J. W. Dennet, killed at Gaines' Mill, June 27th, '62. J. F. Bashore, February 3d, '64; killed at Spottsylvania Court House, May 10th, '64 Samuel Clark, transferred from Veteran Reserve Corps; mustered out with company, June 11th, '64. William Cutler, missed in action at Spottsylvania Court House, May 10th, '64. Henry Croop, discharged on Surgeon's certificate, August 7th, '61. John Campbell, transferred to regular army, December 6th, '62. Alonzo Copp, transferred to 191st Regiment, P. Vols., June 6th, '64; vet. Jacob Cole, July 25th, '61; transferred to 191st Regiment, P. Vols., June 6th, '64. Z. Chapple, February 3d, '64; transferred to 191st Regiment, P. Vols., June 6th, '64. William Cample, died at Camp Pierpont, Va., December 10th, '61. James Duffy, discharged on Surgeon's certificate, August 7th, '61. George Danuth, transferred to 191st Regiment, P. Vols., June 6th, '64; vet. Henry Dale, died at Camp Pierpont, Va., December 10th, '61. Henry Erlston, October 9th, '61; discharged on Surgeon's certificate, October 29th, '61. Willard Eckert, transferred to 191st Regiment, P. Vols., June 6th, '64; vet. Beujamiu Evert, July 25th, '61; transferred to 191st Regiment, P. Vols., June 6th, '64; vet. Albert Fisher, discharged on Surgeon's certificate, July 13th, '61. John Fleegle, August 8th, '61; transferred to 191st Regiment, P. Vols., June 6th, '64; vet. Isaac S. Fleegle, February 9th, '64; transferred to 191st Regiment, P. Vols., June 6th, '64; vet. Amos Garmon, discharged on Surgeon's certificate, October 28th, '62. John H. Gibbons, discharged on Surgeon's certificate, January 29th, '63. Simon Gibbons, October 9th, '61; died at Camp Pierpont, Va., December 11th, '61. John Goranflo, August 8th, '61; died at Baltimore, November 26th, '62. Joseph Gibbons, deserted August 21st, '62. E. D. Hughes, mustered out with company, June 11th, '64. Julius Hurlinger, discharged on Surgeon's certificate, August 7th, '61. George Hawthorne, discharged on Surgeon's certificate, October 24th, '62. Foster Henry, discharged on Surgeon's certificate, September 22d, '63. Charles T. Hood, February 3d, '64; transferred to 191st Regiment, P. Vols., June 6th, '64. Charles Johnson, October 9th, '61; discharged on Surgeon's certificate, December 14th, '61. Samuel Johnson, October 9th, '61; discharged on Surgeon's certificate, November 2d, '62. William Jarrett, discharged on Surgeon's certificate, November 28th, '62. J. H. Johnson, July 21st, '61; promoted to hospital steward, October 31st, '63. William Kieffer, discharged on Surgeon's certificate, December 26th, '61. Daniel Killbride, transferred to regular army, November 27th, '62. Edward N. Kline, transferred to regular army, December 29th, '62. Isaac Kremer, discharged on Surgeon's certificate, March 12th, '63. Amos E. Knapp, July 25th, '61; died at Camp Pierpont, Va., December 7th, '61. James K. Little, mustered out with company, June 11th, '64. John C. Lloyd, discharged on Surgeon's certificate, August 7th, '61. William Lyons, discharged on Surgeon's certificate, September 28th, '61. James E. Morgan, July 25th, '61; transferred to 191st Regiment, P. Vols., June 6th, '64; vet. John C. Morgan, transferred to 191st Regiment, P. Vols., June 6th, '64; vet. John Marriot, died at Philadelphia, August 22d, '62. Fred. B. Murray, August 2d, '61; deserted, June 1st, '63. James M'Fall, mustered out with company, June 11th, '64. M. M'Pherson, transferred to 191st P. Vols., June 6th, '64; vet. John M'Nier, transferred to 191st Regiment, P. Vols., June 6th, '64; vet. John M'Elrath, July 25th, '61; transferred to 191st Regiment, P. Vols., June 6th, '64; vet. Aug. Newbury, July 25th, '61; transferred from Veteran Reserve Corps; mustered out with company, June 11th, '64. Brooks Newbury, July 25th, '61; transferred to 191st P. Vols., June 6th, '64; vet. Joseph Newcomer, February 9th, '64; transferred to 191st P. Vols., June 6th, '64; vet. Albion Newbury, died at Cumberland, Md., July 11th, '61; Nicholas Peifer, transferred to 191st P. Vols., June 6th, '64; vet. J. M. Phillips, July 25th, '61; deserted; date unknown. David Rake, discharged on Surgeon's certificate, May 22d, '63. Jacob Renner, transferred to 191st P. Vols., June 6th, '64; vet. Evan Renner, transferred to 191st P. Vols., June 6th, '64; vet. George Rake. transferred to 191st P. Vols., June 6th, '64; vet. Alexander Rake, died at Alexandria, February 29th, '64. G. H. Kipple, July 25th, '61; mustered out with company, June 11th, '64. J. F. Scholrin, mustered out with company, June 11th, '64. W. Starrick, transferred from Veteran Reserve Corps; mustered out with company, June 11th, '64. Tilghman Sums, discharged on Surgeon's certificate, August 7th, '61. C. W. Scout, discharged on Surgeon's certificate, August 7th, '61. J. Steinhelper, transferred to U. S. Regular Army, December 29th, '62. W. Smith, discharged on Surgeon's certificate, February 7th, '63. John Snyder, transferred to 191st P. Vols., June 6th, '64; vet. T. Strawser, February 3d, 64; transferred to 191st P. Vols., June 6th, '64; vet. C. Starrick, October 9th, '61; killed at Fredericksburg, December 1Sth, '62. George A. Silfer, deserted; date unknown. J. Trumphore, mustered out with company, June 11th, '64. F. Trumbower, transferred to regular army, December 6th, '62. L. L. Travis, August 8th, '61; transferred to 191st Regiment, P. Vols., June 6th, '64; vet. D. B. Van Kirk, transferred to regular army, November 27th, '62. David Vincent, February 12th, '64; transferred to 151st P. Vols., June 6th, '64. John G. Wing, discharged on Surgeon's certificate, July 14th, '62. Joseph Wallace, July 25th, '61; discharged on Surgeon's certificate, November 8th, '62. Wm. Weltheiss, transferred to regular army, November 27th, '62. F. Winkelman, July 25th, '61; transferred to 191st P. Vols., June 6th, '64; vet. John Williams, July 25th, '61; transferred to 191st P. Vols., June 6th, '64; vet. Joseph Williams, August 8th, '61; transferred to 191st P. Vols., June 6th, '64; vet. Sol. Williard, October 9th, '61; transferred to 191st Regiment, P. Vols., June 6th, '64.

46TH REGIMENT.*

(Unless otherwise given, the date of muster in each case is September 8th, 1861.)

Company K.

Captains—Cyrus Strouse, captured at Middletown, Va., May 24th, '62; promoted to Major, November 1st, '62; killed at Chancellorsville, Va., May 2d, 1863. Alex. Caldwell, promoted to 2d Lieutenant, November 1st, '61; to 1st Lieutenant, August 9th, '62; to Captain, November 1st, '62; mustered out with company, July 6th, '65.

1st Lieutenants—G. B. Cadwalader, August 30th, '61; promoted to Quarter-master, September 17th, '61; promoted to Assistant Quarter-master, U. S. Vols., July 8th, '63. W. P. Caldwell, killed at Cedar Mountain, Va., August 9th, '62. Darius S. Gilger, promoted to 1st Sergeant, October 1st, '61; to 2d Lieutenant, August 9th, '62; to 1st Lieutenant, November 1st, '62; discharged, December 18th, '63, for wounds received at Gettysburg, July 3d, '63. Jacob B. Getter, promoted to 2d Lieutenant, November 1st, '62; to 1st Lieutenant, March 21st, '64; discharged September 1st, '64, for wounds received at Dallas, May 25th, '64; vet. Thomas Alderson, promoted to 2d Lieutenant, April 18th, '65; to 1st Lieutenant, May 23d, '65; mustered out, July 16th, '65; vet. 2d Lieutenants—J. W. Phillips, March 21st, '64; killed near Dallas, Ga., May 25th, '64; vet. August Shensel, promoted to 2d Lieutenant, July 5th, '65; mustered out with company, July 16th, '65.

1st Sergeant, George Blanksby, January 13th, '64; promoted to 1st Sergeant, July 5th, '65; mustered out July 16th, '65; vet. Sergeants—Daniel Dubb, January 13th, '64; promoted to Sergeant, April 1st, '64; mustered out July 16th, '65; vet. D. M. Snyder, January 13th, '64; promoted to

* Recruited in Northumberland County.

Sergeant, January 1st, '61; mustered out July 16th, '65; vet. John Neuert, January 13th, '64; promoted to Sergeant, July 5th, '65; mustered out July 16th, '65. J. B. Zehnder, discharged on Surgeon's certificate, July 1st, '64. John McCleese, discharged, December 6th, '62, for wounds received at Cedar Mountain, Va., August 9th, '62. Thomas Caldwell, discharged on Surgeon's certificate, October 9th, '63. W. S. Farrow, prisoner from April 14th to April 29th, '65; discharged by General Order, June 5th, '65; vet. J. H. Haas, killed at Cedar Mountain, Va., August 2d, '62. Joseph Long, killed at Peach Tree Creek, Ga., July 20th, '64; vet.

Corporals—J. Hottshoe, January 13th, '64; promoted to Corporal, November 1st, '62; mustered out with company, July 16th, '65; vet. J. J. Tribley, January 13th, '64; promoted to Corporal, July 20th, '64; mustered out with company; vet. E. Hottshoe, January 13th, '64; promoted to Corporal, January 1st, '65; mustered out with company. J. H. Duttery, March 10th, '64; promoted to Corporal, May 31st, '65; mustered out with company. S. A. Bird, March 15th, '64; promoted to Corporal, May 31st, '65; mustered out with company. D. B. Eisenhart, February 29th, '64; promoted to Corporal, July 5th, '65; mustered out with company. A. J. Hine, March 16th, '64; promoted to Corporal, July 5th, '65; mustered out with company. T. V. Peusyl, July 13th, '64; promoted to Corporal, April 1st, '65; mustered out with company. J. A. Shipp, discharged, January 19th, '63, for wounds received at Cedar Mountain, Va., August 9th, '62. J. N. Young, September 12th, '61; discharged, December 30th, '62, for wounds received at Cedar Mountain, Va., August 9th, '62. J. E. Eisenhart, discharged on Surgeon's certificate, April 23d, '63. C. H. Young, September 12th, '61; discharged on Surgeon's certificate, December 6th, '62. William Shurk, wounded at Cedar Mountain, Va., August 9th, '62; died September 19th, '62; buried at Alexandria, Va. John Raup, March 16th, '64; killed near Dallas, Ga., May 25th, '64; vet.

Musicians.—B. D. Walker, February 26th, '64; mustered out with company, July 16th, '65. C. L. V. Haas, discharged on Surgeon's certificate, October 10th, '62. C. Zimmerman, promoted to Drum-major, August 31st, '64; mustered out with regiment, July 16th, '65; vet.

Privates—Thomas Armstrong, July 30th, '63; substitute; mustered out with company, July 16th, '65. J. A. Armstrong, July 30th, '63; substitute; mustered out with company, July 16th, '65. Franklin Arter, September 12th, '61; died of wounds received at Cedar Mountain, Va., August 9th, '62; buried at Culpepper Court House, Va. Samuel Allard, missing in action at Winchester, Va., May 25th, '62. C. J. Dittenbender, February 27th, '64; mustered out with company, July 16th, '65. Charles Burch, September 14th, '63; substitute; mustered out with company. A. Bennington, July 4th, '63; drafted; mustered out with company. Falon Brady, January 13th, '64; wounded in action, July 20th, '64; absent at muster out. William Bass, March 15th, '65; absent; sick at muster out. Edward Brown, discharged on Surgeon's certificate, December 6th, '62. William B. Bird, mustered out September 16th, '64; expiration of term. Frank Barmoski, discharged for wounds received at Cedar Mountain, August 9th, '62. Charles Brandt, wounded at Winchester, Va., May 25th, '62; died October 4th, '62, of wounds received at Antietam, September 17th, '62. Samuel Baker, June 26th, '63; substitute; killed near Atlanta, Ga., July 20th, '64. John Brooks, missing in action at Winchester, May 25th, '62. W. Brocious, deserted, June 1st, '62. George Blain, deserted, June 1st, '62. C. H. Conrad, February 29th, '64; mustered out with company, July 16th, '65. Samuel Clayberger, March 19th, '64; mustered out with company, July 16th, '65. F. A. Clark, January 4th, '64; discharged on Surgeon's certificate, May 23d, '65; vet. John A. Coder, February 29th, '62; died September 19th, '62, of wounds received at Cedar Mountain, Va. Samuel Clark, July 11th, '63; drafted; died January 18th, '64; buried at Stone River. J. J. Cunningham, missing in action at Cedar Mountain, August 9th, '62. Thomas Collier, deserted, January 14th, '63. William M. Cook, September 11th, '62; substitute; deserted, date unknown. J. T. Crandall, substitute; deserted, June 22d, '65. Charles H. Duttery, January 13th, '64; mustered out with company, July 16th, '65. Thos. Dunlap, July 10th, '63; drafted; mustered out with company. Aaron Dreper, February 22d, '65; mustered out with company. C. Dougherty, March 15th, '65; mustered out with company. C. H. Dunkleber, January 13th, '64; absent on furlough at muster out. Patrick Donovan, discharged, December 26th, '62, for wounds received at Cedar Mountain, Va., August 9th, '62. John Dailey, July 28th, '63; drafted; killed near Atlanta, Ga., July 20th, '64. John Duncan, January 27th, '63; died at Indianapolis, Ind. Percival Dark, February 25th, '64; prisoner from April 14th to April 29th, '65; discharged by Gen. Order, May 18th, '65. Valentine Epler, January 13th, '64; mustered out with company, July 16th, '65; vet. J. Eheohart, March 10th, '64; mustered out with company, July 16th, '65; vet. John Epler, September 12th, '61; discharged January 20th, '63, for wounds received at Antietam, September 17th, '62. J. Enrfeltz, killed at Cedar Mountain, August 9th, '62. John Fox, March 7th, '64; mustered out with company, July 16th, '65. George Flowers, July 11th, '63; drafted; mustered out with company. George Frederick, February 29th, '64; absent; sick at muster out. W. A. Funkhouser, July 29th, '63; substitute; discharged on Surgeon's certificate, May 23d, '65. Charles Ginther, January 13th, '64; mustered out with company, July 16th, '65; vet. J. A. Gilger, March 16th, '64; mustered out with company, July 16th, '65; vet. Jesse Gensel, March 15th, '64; mustered out with company, July 16th, '65; vet. George Grove, July 13th, '63; substitute; mustered out with company. A. H. Graham, July 11th, '63; drafted; mustered out with company. J. T. Getter, February 27th, '64; mustered out with company. David Goss, February 27th, '64; mustered out with company, July 16th, '65. William Grim, July 5th, '63; substitute; absent, sick at muster out. Patrick Gohlen, discharged on Surgeon's certificate, January 20th, '62. John Gillinger, died August 15th, '62, of wounds received at Cedar Mountain, August 9th, '62; buried at Alexandria. Edward Hame, January 13th, '64; mustered out with company, July 16th, '65. D. J. Hine, February 27th, '64; mustered out with company, July 15th, '65. Joel Houpt, February 25th, '64; mustered out with company, July 16th, '65. Charles M. Harp, March 4th, '64; mustered out with company, July 16th, '65. G. H. Hubbert, February 7th, '65; mustered out with company, July 16th, '65. William F. Haas, February 23d, '65; mustered out with company, July 16th, '65. Michael Hume, discharged on Surgeon's certificate, September 20th, '62. F. D. Heckert, mustered out September 16th, '64; expiration of term. J. W. Hesson, July 27th, '63; drafted; discharged at New Albany, May 16th, '64. William Hoffmann, deserted, August 29th, '62. L. L. Haas, not on muster-out roll. Michael Jacobs, January 13th, '64; mustered out with company, July 16th, '65. William Jeallison, July 14th, '63; substitute; mustered out with company, July 16th, '65. Robert M. Jones, February 9th, '64; mustered out with company, July 16th, '65. John Johnson, mustered out September 16th, '64; expiration of term. William H. Jones, February 27th, '64; killed near Marietta, Ga., July 22d, '64. Joseph Jaggers, July 13th, '63; drafted; killed accidentally at Savannah, Ga., January 1st, '65. David Jones, missing in action at Cedar Mountain, August 9th, '63. John A. Kable, February 26th, '64; mustered out with company, July 16th, '65. Abraham Keiper, February 23d, '65; mustered out with company, July 16th, '65. John Knipe, September 12th, '61; discharged, December 6th, '62, for wounds received at Cedar Mountain, August 9th, '62. Nicholas Kern, September 12th, '61; discharged on Surgeon's certificate, December 6th, '62. W. H. Kerlin, March 9th, '64; killed at Atlanta, Ga., July 20th, '64. Francis M. Lott, July 10th, 64; mustered out with company, July 16th, '65; vet. Joseph Lever, mustered out September 16th, '64; expiration of term. W. H. Lott, prisoner from April 14th to April 29th, 65; discharged on General Order, May 18th, '65; vet. W. C. Leibig, March 14th, '64; died August 19th, '64, of wounds received at Allentown. John London, deserted, September 1st, '62. Ephraim P. Mets, January 13th, '64; mustered out with company, July 16th, '65. Paul Martin, February 22d, '64; mustered out with company, July 16th, '65. James Martin, February 24th, '64; mustered out with company, July 16th, '65. Charles Morgan, discharged on Surgeon's certificate, October 31st, '62. Arthur Mooney, September 14th, '61; discharged on Surgeon's certificate, January 19th, '63. Reuben Mullen, September 12th, '61; mustered out September 16th, '64; expiration of term. Elias Maurer, March 4th, '64; discharged, October 26th, '64, for wounds received at Dallas, May 26th, '64. C. W. Mottler, February 25th, '64; died at Dechert, Tenn., April 10th, '64. John Medlicott, January 13th, '64; died October 27th, '64, of wounds received at Peach Tree Court, Ga., July 20th, '64. Joseph McCarty, August 29th, '62; promoted to Adjutant, August 12th, '64; mustered out with regiment, July 16th, '65. John E. McCarty, August 29th, '62; promoted to Sergeant, Company I, April 1st, '64; discharged, by General Order, June 8th, '65. W. J. McDowell, July 11th, '63; substitute; died September 7th, '64; buried at Chattanooga. Guy McCauly, deserted, September 1st, '62. C. Neiswanter, January 13th, '64; mustered out with company, July 16th, '65. Amos Neiswanter, January 13th, '64; mustered out with company, July 15th, '65. James H. Patton, July 31st, '63; drafted; mustered out with company, July 16th, '65. Daniel S. Peifer, discharged on Surgeon's certificate, June 20th, '62. Lewis Paul, discharged, October 25th, '62, for wounds received at Cedar Mountain, Va. Joseph Perry, deserted, September 1, '62. Moses

Reed, January 13th, '64; mustered out with company, July 16th, '65; vet. Paul Roth, March 8th, '64; mustered out with company, July 16th, '65; vet. William Roth, discharged, December 8th, '62, for wounds received at Cedar Mountain, Va. Isaiah Roderuel, discharged on Surgeon's certificate, September 25th, '63. Joseph W. Ruse, March 1st, '62; mustered out, March 25th, '65; expiration of term. I. N. Robinson, July 27th, '63; substitute; died at Philadelphia, Pa., date unknown. William Reynolds, March 15th, '65; drafted; deserted, June 22d, '65. J. Simmers, July 13th, '64; mustered out with company, July 16th, '65; vet. Enoch Shuda, July 13th, '64; mustered out with company, July 16th, '65; vet. S. A. Startzell, July 13th, '64; mustered out with company, July 16th, '65; vet. Nicholas Steiben, September 4th, '63; substitute; mustered out with company, July 16th, '65. Thomas Smith, July 11th, '63; drafted; mustered out with company, July 16th, '65. Henry Startzell, February 24th, '64; drafted; mustered out with company, July 16th, '65; John Stevenson, discharged on Surgeon's certificate, October 25th, '62. Henry Salters, mustered out September 13th, '64; expiration of term. W. H. Snyder, January 13th, '64; discharged by General Order, May 27th, '65; vet. Henry Shaffer, February 29th, '64; transferred to Veteran Reserve Corps, March 15th, '65. Philip Stambach, January 13th, '64; transferred to Veteran Reserve Corps, March 15th, '65. D. G. Startzell, died December 8th, '61, at Alexandria, Va. W. H. Slenker, died, February 26th, '62, at Hancock, Md. William Simmers, September 12th, '61; killed at Winchester, May 25th, '62. Augustus Snyder, deserted, June 1, '62. George A. Thomas, July 13th, '64; mustered out with company, July 16th, '65; vet. Robert Tooley, March 10th, '64; mustered out with company, July 16th, '65; vet. Jacob Treibley, March 8th, '64; mustered out with company, July 16th, '65; T. B. Tannery, February 7th, '65; mustered out with company, July 16th, '65. J. N. Tittsworth, discharged on Surgeon's certificate, February 13th, '63. William C. Thorp, discharged December 8th, '62, for wounds received at Cedar Mountain. William Taylor, discharged on Surgeon's certificate, April 23, '63. John Taney, February, 25th, '64; prisoner from April 14th to April 29th, '65; discharged May 18th, '65, by General Order. Alfred Tittsworth, killed at Cedar Mountain, August 9th, '62. D. J. Woodley, January 13th, '64; mustered out with company, July 10th, '65. John L. Walton, April 13th, '65; substitute; discharged by General Order, July 13th, '65. R. G. Wilson, July 31st, '63; substitute; prisoner from February 15th to April 2d, '65; discharged June 12th, '65, by General Order. Walter Williams, March 7th, '64; captured; died October 8th, '64, at Andersonville; Georgia grave, 10,521. M. Worzkoski, died of wounds received at Cedar Mountain, Va., August 9th, '62. P. J. Zimmerman, died December 20th, '61, at Frederick, Md.; buried at Antietam. Alexander Zancollar, February 25th, '64; killed at Marrietta, Georgia, July 20th, '64.

47TH REGIMENT.*

(Unless otherwise given, the date of muster in each case is Sept. 2d, 1861.)

Company C.

Captains—J. P. S. Gobin, promoted to Major, July 24th, '64; to Lieut.-Colonel, November 4th, '64; to Colonel, January 3d, '65; mustered out with regiment, December 25th, '65. Daniel Eyster, promoted to 2d Lieutenant, December 13th, '62; to 1st Lieutenant, April 16th, '64; to Captain, September 1st, '64; wounded at Berryville, September 5th, '64, and Cedar Creek, October 19th, '64.

1st Lieutenants—James Van Dyke, resigned, January 10th, '62. Wm. Reese, promoted from 2d to 1st Lieutenant, January 14th, '64; discharged, April 14th, '64. W. M. Hendricks, promoted to 1st Lieutenant, September 1st, '64; resigned, May 9th, '65. 2d Lieutenant C. S. Beard, promoted to 2d Lieutenant, September 1st, '64; to 1st Lieutenant, July 5th, '65; mustered out with company, December 25th, '65; vet.

1st Sergeants—S. Y. Haupt, wounded at Pocotaligo, S. C., October 22d, '62; promoted to Sergeant, November 1st, '64; mustered out with company. Wm. Fry, promoted to Sergeant, September 1st, '64; prisoner from October 19th, '64, to March 4th, '65; died at Sunbury, March 28th, '65. Sergeants.—Samuel Eyster, promoted to Sergeant, December 1st, '64; mustered out with company. W. F. Finck, wounded at Cedar Creek, Va., October 19th, '64; promoted to Sergeant, April 1st, '65; mustered out with company, J. W. Switeman, promoted to Corporal, November 1st, '64; to Sergeant, July 10th, '65; mustered out with company. B. F. Miller, Sergeant, August 1st, '65; mustered out with company. Peter Smelser, discharged on Surgeon's certificate, June 17th, '64. Wm. Pyers, wounded at Pleasant Hill, La., April 9th, '64; killed at Cedar Creek, Va., October 19th, '64. Peter Haupt, September 17th, '61; died of wounds received at Pocotaligo, November 15th, '62. John Barthow, September 1st, '61; Sergeant, September 1st, '64; killed at Cedar Creek, October 19th, '64.

Corporals—Timothy Snyder, September 1st, '64; mustered out with company. David Sloan, December 1st, '64; wounded at Berryville, Va., September 5th, '64; mustered out with company. Michael Dersing, promoted April 22d, '65; mustered out with company. Henry Seneff, promoted April 22d, '62; mustered out with company. George R. Good, promoted July 1st, '65; mustered out with company. Stewart Kirk, promoted July 1st, '65; mustered out with company. L. G. John, February 23d, '64; promoted August 1st, '65; mustered out with company. J. H. Heim, mustered out September 18th, '64; expiration of term. David Snyder, October 6th, '64; promoted to Corporal, August 1st, '65; mustered out, October 5th, '65. G. K. Hebler, wounded at Cedar Creek, October 19th, '64; deserted, June 1st, '65. Mark Shipman, April 1st, '65; deserted, June 2d, '65.

Musicians—Samuel Pyers, March 27th, '63; mustered out with company December 25th, '65. J. H. Schmdey, January 9th, '62; discharged by order of War Department, April 9th, '63. H. D. Wharton, promoted to Commissary-Sergeant, July 1st, '65; discharged, October 12th, '65. J. Bolton Young, died at Washington, D. C., October 17th, '61.

Privates—James G. Allen, December 25th, '62; deserted, April 15th, '63. Henry Brown, mustered out with company, December 25th, '65. John Berry, February 24th, '64; mustered out with company, December 25th, '65. J. W. Bricker, March 8th, '65; mustered out with company, December 25th, '65. Jared Brooks, mustered out with company, December 25th, '65. W. H. Brookins, discharged on Surgeon's certificate, August 27th, '62; discharged on Surgeon's certificate, July --, '63. D. S. Beidler, mustered out, September 18th, '64; expiration of term. G. P. Blain, November 28th, '63; wounded at Cedar Creek, October 19th, '64; mustered out, May 10th, '65. G. K. Beaver, October 6th, '64; mustered out, October 6th, '65; expiration of term. Daniel Beaver, October 6th, '64; mustered out, October 6th, '65; expiration of term. Matthias Beaver, October 6th, '64; mustered out, October 6th, '65; expiration of term. Geo. W. Bertle, died at Washington, D. C., August 8th, '64. James Brown, killed at Cedar Creek, October 19th, '64. M. M. Berger, captured at Cedar Creek, October 19th, '64; died at Landisburg, N. C., January 6th, '65. Emanuel Beaver, October 6th, '64; died at Winchester, December 21st, '64. Edgar Baker, July 29th, '63; deserted, July, '63. Joseph Baker, July 29th, '63; deserted, July, '63. Zachariah Brown, October 9th, '63; deserted, January 16th, '64. William Brennan, deserted, June 15th, '65. James Bullard, June 22d, '64; deserted, July, '64. Perry Colvin, wounded at Cedar Creek, October 19th, '64; absent in hospital at muster out. Augustus Calvin, February 15th, '65; mustered out with company. John D. Calvin, September 12th, '61; promoted to Signal Corps, October 13th, '63. R. W. Druckmiller, September 13th, '61; mustered out September 18th, '64; expiration of term. Seth Deibert, October 2d, '62; killed at Pocotaligo, October 22d, '62. David T. Evans, February 22d, '64; mustered out with company. Charles Ehrie, October 2d, '62; mustered out October 2, '65; expiration of term. A. J. Finck, November 20, '63; mustered out with company, December 25th, '65. John W. Firth, mustered out with company, December 25th, '65; vet. Reuben L. Fish, November 28th, '63; mustered out with company; vet. George Fritz, discharged on Surgeon's certificate, July 7th, '64. J. Gensemer, mustered out with company, December 25th, '65; vet. William Good, November 20th, '63; mustered out with company, December 26th, '65; vet. Wm. Gehring, November, 26, '64; mustered out with company, December 25th, '65; vet. Jos. R. Gray, February 23d, '64; mustered out with company, December 25th, '65; vet. Jesse O. Green, December 18th, '63; wounded at Cedar Creek, Va., October 19th, '64; discharged on Surgeon's certificate, February 14th, '65. J. B. Gardner, killed at Cedar Creek, Va., October 19th, '64. J. C. Grubb, died, November 2d, '64; of wounds received at Cedar Creek, Va. Alex. Given, February 25th, '64; died, December '64, of wounds received at Cedar Creek, Va. Jeremiah Gardner, March 28th, '64; died at Philadelphia, April 11th, '64. Alfred Hunter, mustered out with company, December 25th, '65. H. W. Haas, November 27th, '63; mustered out with company, December 25th, '65. Charles Harp, mustered out, September, 18th, '64; expiration of term. Conrad Holman, wounded at Pocotaligo, October 22d, '64; prisoner from April 8th to July 22d, '64; mustered out, September 18th, '64; expiration of term. Robert Harrel, February 24th, '64; discharged on Surgeon's certificate, April 13th, '65. Richard Hill, September 13th, '64;

* Recruited at Sunbury.

transfer from company E, 14th Cav., February 20th, '65; mustered out, September 17th, '65; expiration of term. Freeman Haupt, discharged by General Order, December 21st, '63. C. K. Herb, November 20th, '63; transferred to Veteran Reserve Corps, March 12th, '64. George Hauer, killed at Pocotaligo, October 22d, 62. Jeremiah Haas, wounded at Pocotaligo, October 22d, '62; killed at Sabine Cross Roads, La., August 5th, '54. J. S. Hart, died at New Orleans, La., August 5th, '64. Jared C. Irvin, February 21st, '65; mustered out with company, December 25th, '65. Samuel Jones, January 22d, '64; mustered out with company, December 25th, '65. G. D. John, February 23d, '64; wounded at Cedar Creek, Va., October 19th, '64; mustered out, July 6th, '65. Cornelius Kramer, wounded at Pleasant Hill, La., April 9th, '64; mustered out with company, December 16th, '65; vet. Lorenzo Kramer, February 23d, '65; mustered out with company, December 25, '65. E. H. Leiser, November 27th '63; mustered out with company, December 25th, '65. Isaac Kemble, mustered out, September 18th, '64; expiration of term. D. W. Kemble, mustered out, September 18th, '64; expiration of term. Isaac Kramer, November 23d, '63; wounded at Cedar Creek, Va., October 19th, '64; discharged on Surgeon's certificate, August 8th, '65; vet. James Kennedy, died, April 27th, '64, of wounds received at Pleasant Hill, La., April 9th, '64; vet. Theodore Kiehl, killed at Cedar Creek, Va., October 19th, '64. Geo. W. Keiser, February 20th, '64; killed at Cedar Creek, Va., October 19th, '64. George Kramer, November 20th, '63; died on board of United States transport, "Mississippi," August 27th, '64. Wm. Logan, February 21st, '65; mustered out with company, December 25th, '65. L. K. Landon; discharged on Surgeon's certificate, March 3d, '62. Charles Leffer, October 2d, '62; wounded at Pocotaligo, October 22d, '62; mustered out, June 14th, '65. M. Larkins, October 2d, '62; wounded at Pocotaligo, October 22d, '62; mustered out, October 1st, '65; expiration term. Wm. Leinberger, October 2d, '62; transferred to company A, 21st Regiment Veteran Reserved Corps, April 28th, '65. Thos. Lothard, wounded at Pocotaligo, October 22d, '62, and Sabine Cross Roads, La., April 8th, '64; deserted, July 5th, '65; vet. Eli Miller, absent, without leave at muster out. Samuel Miller, prisoner from April 8th to July 22d, '64; mustered out with company. John Munsch, mustered out with company, December 25th, '65. J. W. McLane, November 27th, '63; mustered out with company, December 25th, '65. Alex. McCullough, February 24th, '64; mustered out with company, December 25th, '65. Adam Maul, prisoner from May 2d to July 22d, '64; on detached duty at muster out. Robert C. McNeal, mustered out with company. J. W. McNew, wounded and prisoner at Pleasant Hill, La., April 9th to July 22d, '64; mustered out with company. William McNew, mustered out with company. Samuel McNew, November 28th, '63; mustered out with company. John McGraw, mustered out with company. Warren McEwen, discharged on Surgeon's certificate, December 7th, '62. George Miller, wounded at Pleasant Hill, La., April 9th, '64; mustered out, September 8th, '64; expiration term. William Michael, January 23d, '64; wounded at Cedar Creek, Va., October 19th, '64; mustered out, May 20th, '65. Edward Matthews, October 2d, '62; prisoner from April 8th to July 22d, '64; mustered out, October 8th, '65; expiration term. George Malick, deserted, June 1st, '65. F. H. McNeal, deserted, June 15th, '65. Benj. McPhilipps, mustered out, December 25th, '65. Thomas Nipple, wounded at Sabine Cross Roads, La., April 8th, '64; mustered out with company. Dav. Naylor, discharged on Surgeon's certificate, April 13th, '65; vet. Jno. S. Oyster, November 20th, '63; mustered out with company. Rich'd. O'Rouke, wounded at Cedar Creek, Va., October 19th, '64; mustered out with company. John B. Otto, mustered out with company, December 25th, '65. Wm. Plant, mustered out September, '64; expiration of term. Wm. Pfeil, September 8th, '61; mustered out September, '64; expiration of term. Raphael Perez, May 20th, '63; discharged; date unknown. J. R. Rhine, mustered out with company, December 25th, '65. H. B. Rodrigue, November 27th, '63; mustered out with company, December 25th, '65. Jacob Reim, February 21st, '65; mustered out with company, December 25th, '65, P. M. Randall, mustered out with company, December 25th, '65. Alexander Ruffner, mustered out with company, December 25th, '65. H. B. Robinson, November 28th, '63; discharged by order of War Department, January 24th, '65; minor. Joseph Rish, October 6th, '61; mustered out October 6th, '64; expiration of term. S. M. Reigle, discharged on Surgeon's certificate, October 9th, '65. John Sanker, wounded at Cedar Creek, Va., October 19th, '64; mustered out with company, December 25th, '65. John W. Smith, mustered out with company, December 25th, '65. Adam Strong, February 24th, '64; absent, sick, at muster out. Zach. Seaman, February 24th, '65; mustered out with company. H. C. Seasholtz, February 23d, '65; mustered out with company. Ira Seasholtz, February 23d, '65; mustered out with company. Christian Schall, mustered out September 18th, '64; expiration of term. Isaac Snyder, mustered out September 18th, '64; expiration of term. Charles F. Stewart, prisoner from October 19th, '64, to March 4th, '65; mustered out, May 29th, '65; vet. H. A. Shilfin, November 27th, '63; wounded at Cedar Creek, October 19th, '64; transferred to V. R. C., February, '65. Joseph Smith, killed at Cedar Creek, October 19th, '64. Peter Sweinhart, November 20th, '63; died, December 1st, '64, of wounds received at Cedar Creek, Va., October 19th, '64. John C. Sterner, killed at Pleasant Hill, La., April 9th, '65. Ephraim Thatcher, mustered out, September, '64; expiration of term. Noah Ulrich, mustered out, October 5th, '65; expiration of term. Robert W. Vincent, February 26th, '64; mustered out with company, December 25th, '65. Frederick Vaun, February 24th, '64; transferred to Company G., Dec. 16th, '64; mustered out with company. David Werkle, wounded at Cedar Creek, October 19th '64; absent, sick, at muster out. Joseph Walters, wounded at Cedar Creek, October 19th, '64; mustered out with company. Samuel Walters, November 28th, '63; mustered out with company. Henry W. Wolf, mustered out, September 18th, '64; expiration of term. Theo. Woodbridge, mustered out, September 18th, '64; expiration of term. James Whistler, mustered out, September 18th, '64; expiration of term. Benjamin Walls, wounded at Pleasant Hill, La., April 9, '64; mustered out, September 18th, '64; expiration of term. Samuel Whistler, mustered out, September 18th, '84; expiration of term. Charles Wenrick, November 26, '63; mustered out, June 6th, '65. Solomon Wetzel, October 17th, '64; mustered out, October 16, '65; expiration of term. George C. Watson, died at Key West, Fla., August 26th, '62. Peter Wolf, killed at Pocotaligo, October 22d, '62. John E. Will, killed at Cedar Creek, October 19th, '64. E. B. Walters, November 28th, '63; died at Charleston, August 20th, '65; vet. J. W. Walton, deserted, June 2d, '65; vet. James Wolf, deserted, Feb. 6th, '63.

53D REGIMENT.

(Unless otherwise given, the date of muster in each case, is Oct. 2d, 1861.)

Company H.

Captains—McCurdy Tate, discharged, August 28th, '62. P. H. Schreyer, October 10th, 61; promoted to Captain, August 28th, '62; commissioned Major, September, 18, '67; not mustered; mustered out, October 8th, '64; expiration of term. James D. Marsh, promoted to Captain, November, 2d, '64; mustered out with company.

1st Lieutenants—Lawrence Huff, promoted to 1st Lieutenant, March 1st, '63; commissioned Captain, September 28th, '64; not mustered; mustered out, October 8th, '64; expiration of term. W. W. Deatler, promoted to Commissary-Sergeant, December 22d, '63; to 2d Lieutenant, December 8th, '64; to 1st Lieutenant, January 18th, '65; mustered out with company, June 30th, 1865. 2d Lieutenants—S. T. Platt, promoted to 2d Lieutenant, August 22d, '63; dismissed, April 13th, '64. M. Thornton, promoted to 2d Lieutenant, January 24th, '65; mustered out with company.

1st Sergeants—Alfred Hays, promoted to 1st Sergeant, March 28th, '65; mustered out with company. Charles Allen, promoted to 1st Sergeant; died at Annapolis, March 28th, '65. Sergeants—H. S. Geiger, promoted to Sergeant; mustered out with company. J. F. Albright, promoted to Sergeant, January 24th, '65; mustered out with company. S. Robenold, promoted to Sergeant, February 27th, '65; absent, sick; mustered out. J. F. Ryan, promoted to Sergeant, March 28th, '65; mustered out with company. James Geist, promoted to Sergeant; prisoner from June 10th to November 25th, '64; discharged, by General Order, same date. John C. Irwin, February 11th, '64; captured; died at Millen, Ga., October 14th, '64. S. D. Haughenback, killed in action, June 16th, '64. Wm. Harrison, died, July 2d, '64, of wounds received in action.

Corporals—Levi A. Leferm, promoted to Corporal; mustered out with company. Amandus Gold, January 30th, 64; promoted to Corporal; prisoner from August 25th to September 25th, '64; mustered out with company. J. M. Confer, promoted to Corporal; prisoner from June 1st to September 13th, '62; mustered out with company, June 30th, '65. James Rodermel, January 30th, '64; promoted to Corporal, February 22d, 65; mustered out with company. A. D. Galutia, April 4th, '64; promoted to Corporal February 23d, '65; absent, sick; mustered out. Theodore Scott, wounded in action, June 17th, '64; absent at muster out. D. P. Waltman, promoted to Corporal, May 25th, '68; mustered out with company. W. J. Bickford, August 30th, '63; drafted; promoted to Corporal, December 11th, '64; absent, sick, at muster out. Jacob Carey, August 30th; drafted; promoted to Cor-

ST JOSEPH'S CATHOLIC CHURCH, ERECTED BY REV JOSEPH KOCH, PASTOR, LOCUST GAP, NORTHD CO, PA.

ST PATRICK'S CATHOLIC CHURCH, REV. FATHER KOCH, PASTOR, TREVORTON, NORTHUMBERLAND CO, PA.

poral, January 1st, '65; absent, sick, at muster out. Lionel Stanley, promoted to Corporal; prisoner from October 14th, '63, to November 9th, '64; discharged, by General Order, same date. John Showers, October 1st, '64; drafted; discharged, by General Order, May 31st, '65. James Ossenan, March 22d, '64; discharged, by General Order, June 16th, '65. C. F. Hobobow, October, 22d, '63; discharged, by General Order, June 16th, '65. R. P. Strine, October 22d, '63; died, May 12th, '64, of wounds received in action. Henry Kohler, October 22d, '63; not on muster-out roll. H. W. Hagenback, October 22d, '63; not on muster-out roll. M. L. Everhart, October 22d, '63; not on muster-out roll. J. M. Hougendobler, October 22d, '63; not on muster-out roll. Wm. C. Best, October 22d, '65; not on muster-out roll. Joseph Black, October 22d, '65; not on muster-out roll.

Musicians—Wm. Langmacker, February 25th, '64; mustered out with company. James McCleary, February 26th, '65; mustered out with company. John Caldwell, promoted to pl. musician, November 1st, '61; vet. John Dally, not on muster-out roll.

Privates—Seth Andrews, August 19th, '63; drafted; absent, sick, at muster out. W. J. Ameigh, September 26th, '64; drafted; died, April 13th, '65, of wounds received in action. S. W. E. Byers, March 24th, '64; absent, sick, at muster out. D. Buchanan, October 26th, '64; substitute; mustered out with company, June 30th, '65. Samuel Bittner, June 3d, '64; drafted; discharged on Surgeon's certificate, December 3d '64. Perry C. Brown, September 27th, '64; drafted; discharged by General Order, May 31st, '65. J. D. Barber, September 28th, '64; discharged, by General Order, May 31st, 65. John Boal, October 1st, '64; discharged, by General Order, May 31st, '65. Benjamin Bittner, October 1st, '64; drafted; discharged, by General Order, May 31st, '65. John D. Burd, April 4th, '64; captured; died at Florence, October 14th, '64. J. N. H. Bell, April 4th, '64; died, June 10th, '64, of wounds received in action. M. Bumbaugh, August 29th, '62; drafted; deserted, March 5th, '65. J. H. Brubaker, August 28th, '63; drafted; deserted February 10th, '65. G. W. Bowers; not on muster-out roll. Charles Britton, not on muster-out roll. W. W. Barrows, not on muster-out roll. Nicholas Becker, not on muster-out roll. R. P. Bratton, not on muster-out roll. Thomas Bird, not on muster-out roll. J. B. Culbertson, August 21st, '63; drafted; deserted October 9th, '64; returned, November 1st, '64; mustered out with company. Francis Cannovan, October 18th, '64; substitute; absent, sick, at muster out. N. D. Clutter, April 12th, '64; mustered out with company. Peter Q. Cerlough, August 29th, '63; drafted; absent, sick, at muster out. Thomas Collins, November 1st, '64; substitute; discharged by General Order, June 8th, '65. Frederick Carver, October 1st, '64; drafted; discharged by General Order, May 13th, '65. John M. Coist, January 19th, '63; died, August 13th, '64, of wounds received in action. W. L. Coster, April 4th, '64; died at City Point, Va., July 8th, '64. Christopher Corwin, April 4th, '64; killed in action, March 31st, '64. Friend Cook, March 5th, '64; discharged by General Order, May 13th, '65. William C. Coyle, not on muster-out roll. Walter Cowden, not on muster-out roll. L. W. Divelbiss, August 19th, '63; drafted; mustered out with company, June 30th, '65. Jacob Divelbiss, August 27th, '63; drafted; absent, sick, at muster out. Charles N. Dunbar, April 4th, '64; discharged by General Order, May 31st, '65. David Dougherty, October 4th, '64; drafted; discharged by General Order, June 16th, '65. Ira Downs, April 4th, '64; captured; died at Salisbury, N. C., November 30th, '64. William Dix, October 24th, '64; substitute; deserted April 20th, '65. William Deetz, not on muster-out roll. G. W. Deer, not on muster-out roll. W. H. Dobbs, March 25th, '64; deserted March 27th, '64. Oscar E. Erway, April 4th, '64; deserted July 15th, 64; returned December 26th, '64; discharged by General Order, July 8th, '65. George Eaton, February 3d, '64; absent, sick, at muster out. J. L. Evans, September 17th, '63; drafted; absent, sick, at muster out. John Eveland, not on muster-out roll. Peter Fowler, April 22d, '64; not on muster-out roll. Charles A. Fisher, September 17th, '63; drafted; absent, sick, at muster out. John Fisher, November 29th '62; mustered out with company, June 3d, '65. Samuel Fisher, June 4th, '64; discharged by General Order, June 19th, '65. Hugh Fisher, not on muster-out roll. Aaron Fox, not on muster-out roll. John B. Grumm, April 4th, '64; mustered out with company, June 30th, '65. Timothy Galutia, April 4th, '64; absent, sick, at muster out. W. J. Grover, April 4th, '64; mustered out with company, June 30th, '65. Jeremiah Garris, March 3d, '64; missing in action, May 12th, '64. G. W. Gutes, September 27th, '64; drafted; discharged by General Order, May 31st, '65. Charles Gummo, September 27th, '64; drafted; discharged by General Order, May 31st, '65. Robert Hall, March 24th, '64; wounded in action, April 2d, '65; absent at muster out. John High, mustered out with company, June 30th, 65; vet. D. Hendrickson, April 4th, '64; wounded at Cold Harbor, June 3d, '64; absent at muster out. Daniel Harvey, March 31, '64; wounded at Spottsylvania Court House, May 12th, '64; absent at muster out. Levi Hamilton, March 28th, '64; mustered out with company, June 30th, '65. D. S. Hopkins, February 29th, '64; discharged by General Order, July 7th, '65. M. V. Huffinaster, August 28th, '63; drafted; mustered out with company. Thomas Hughes, February 26th, '64; discharged by General Order, June 5th, '65. Henry Houtz, October 1st, '64; drafted; discharged by General Order, May 31st, '65. George House; discharged on Surgeon's certificate, February 20th, '65. John Henry, November 1st, '64; substitute; killed in action, March 31st, '65. Hall Henry, captured; died at Florence, S. C., October 20th, '64. A. S. Hutch, April 4th, '64; died July 2d, '64, of wounds received in action. S. W. Hopkins, April 4th, 64; discharged by General Order, May 15th, '65. Joseph Harris, not on muster-out roll. Alexander Hazlett, not on muster-out roll. George Jones, February 27th, '64, mustered out with company, June 30th, '65. Nelson Johnston, September 30th, '64; drafted; discharged by General Order, May 31st, '65. James A. Koony, March 22d, '64; mustered out with company, June 30th, '65. Daniel King, March 22d, '64; mustered out with company, June 30th, '65. William Keener, March 24th, '64; mustered out with company, June 30th, '65. Samuel Kelly, April 4th, '64; discharged by General Order, June 16th, '65. John F. Kain, October 14th, '63; substitute; deserted April 28th, '64; Milton Kirkwood, February 2d, '64; discharged by General Order, July 19th, '65. Daniel Knittle, not on muster-out roll. James Knittle, not on muster-out roll. Levi E. Kistler, not on muster-out roll. John Langer, February 11th, '64; mustered out with company, June 30th, '65. J. L. Lyman, August 27th, '63; drafted; deserted July 1st, '64. W. A. Lewis, not on muster-out roll. William Long, not on muster-out roll. Bernard Leform, not on muster-out roll. Cyrenius Murray, mustered out with company, June 30th, '65. Joseph Mauck, January 31st, '64; mustered out with company, June 30th, '65; John Murphy, October 28th, '64; substitute; deserted June 17th, '65. A. Middlesworth, October 22d, '64; substitute; mustered out with company. Francis Myers, October 22d, '64; substitute; discharged by General Order, July 8th, '65. William Morrison, March 31st, '64, absent, sick at muster out. Gabriel Miller, February 26th, '64; missing in action June 22d, '64. Jacob Martial, March 23, '63; substitute; mustered out with company, June 30th, '65. Leonard Messimer, March 8th, '64; mustered out with company. Lyman Miller, February 26th, '64; mustered out with company. John Mauck, discharged on Surgeon's certificate, February 21st, '65. Andrew Mallory, October 4th, '64; drafted; discharged on General Order, June 16th, '65. Laurin Matson, September 28th, '64; drafted; discharged on General Order, May 31st, '65. E. D. Martin, February 29th, '64; discharged by General Order, June 20th, '65. Michael Many, captured; died at Florence, S. C., November 30th, '64; vet. And. Marshall, April 5th, '64; deserted November 30th, '64. John Moyer, not on muster-out roll. John Mayer, not on muster-out roll. James L. Miller, not on muster-out roll. Martin Miller, not on muster-out roll. William Moffit, not on muster-out roll. James M'Namee, not on muster-out roll. Ashbel Norton, October 20th, '64; substitute; discharged by General Order, June 5th, '65. Adam Nearhood, March 9th, '64; mustered out with company, June 30th, '65. David Noble, October 24th, '64; substitute; discharged by General Order, June 7th, '65. John Ohler, June 23d, '64; drafted; deserted July 21st, '64; returned October 25th, '64; mustered out with company. William Purdy, February 22d, '64; missing in action, May 12th, '64. S. L. Potter, August 28th, '63; drafted; absent, sick, at muster out. William Parker, October 7th, '64; drafted; discharged by General Order, June 16th, '65. W. H. Plowman, September 28th, '64; drafted; died, February 2d, '65, at City Point, Va. Robert Patterson, not on muster-out roll. Michael Powers, not on muster-out roll. John Quinn, December 29th, '63; mustered out with company, June 30th, '65. Joseph Reed, October 29th, '61; mustered out with company, June 30th, '65. George T. Rodermel, October 29th, '61; mustered out with company, June 30th, '65. Lemuel Rauck, January 30th, '64; mustered out with company, June 30th, '64. John H. Rich, October 21st, '64; substitute; mustered out with company. John Rich, October 28th, '64; substitute; mustered out with company. Lindsley Roop, March 26th, '64; absent, sick, at muster out. Henry Roop, March 26th, '64; mustered out with company. William Roop, April 7th, '64; absent, sick, at muster out. Alexander Robinson, February 29th, '64; absent, sick, at muster out. Henry Robinold, February 25th, '64; wounded, with loss of arm; discharged November 30th, '64. A. M. Richardson, October 4th, '64; drafted; discharged by General Order, June 9th, '65. John C. Reifsnyder, August 28th, '63; drafted; discharged by General

Order, May 31st, '65. Zach. Robinold, not on muster-out roll. David C. Secor, April 4th, '64; wounded at Spottsylvania Court House, May 10th, '64; absent at muster out. Philo Stonemets, April 4th, '64; mustered out with company. John Scutchall, July 5th, '64; drafted; deserted July 24th, '64; returned; mustered out with company. Edward Short, October 28th, '64; substitute, mustered out with company. Lafayette Steffy, April 4th, '64; discharged by General Order, May 15th, '65. A. W. Standish, February 8th, '65; mustered out with company. Joseph Shirey, August 20th, '63; drafted; mustered out with company. Chas. J. Smith, October 19th, '63; substitute; mustered out with company. Jacob Stull, August 19th, '63; substitute; absent, wounded at muster out. Joseph Shirk, March 12th, '64; absent, sick, at muster out. Peter Swisher, March 19th, '64; mustered out with company. Wm. Suttle, March 22d, '64; absent, sick, at muster out. Simon Strunan, August 28th, '61; absent, sick, at muster out. John Swart, February 24th, '64; absent, sick, at muster out. George Sweeny, March 1st, '64; mustered out with company. Thos. Smith, mustered out November 8th, '64; expiration term. John Seibert, discharged March 23d, '65; for wounds received in action. Reuben Snyder, January 30th, '64; discharged on Surgeon's certificate, February 9th, '64. Joseph Smith, February 9th, '64; transferred to Veteran Reserved Corps, October 1st, '64. John Steinbacker, April 14th, '64; died June 1st, '64, of wounds received in action. O. C. Sherman, August 20th, '63; drafted, deserted April 30th, '64. William Stanley, not on muster-out roll. Wm. P. Shutt, not on muster-out roll. David Stiber, died at Harrison's Landing, date unknown. Simon Springer, not on muster-out roll. Wm. H. Swenzell, not on muster-out roll. Michael Shaffer, April 22d, '64; not on muster-out roll. Dennis Tobin, November 1st, '64; substitute; mustered out with company. James Thurston, April 14th, '64; captured; died at Andersonville, September 10th, '64. John Taylor, not on muster-out roll. Geo. Vandling, mustered out November 8th, '64; expiration term. W. H. Vannetta, not on muster-out roll. John Vannetta, not on muster-out roll. Geo. E. Williams, August 28th, '63; drafted; mustered out with company. Samuel Wingard, October 1st, '64; drafted; discharged by General Order, May 31st, '65. Wm. Wherry, March 24th, '63; discharged by General Order, June 2d, '65. Levi F. Webb, not on muster-out roll. Joseph Wetzel, not on muster-out roll. Henry H. Wilson, wounded at Fair Oaks, May 31st, '62; discharged on Surgeon's certificate; date unknown. John Yelton, March 29th, '64; absent; sick, at muster out.

74TH REGIMENT.

(Unless otherwise given, the date of muster in each case, is March 17th, 1865.)

Company C.

Captains—Elias P. Rohrbach, March 3d, '65; promoted to Major, May 2d, '65; mustered out with regiment, August 29th, '65. John H. Lewis, March 4th, '65; promoted from Adjutant, July 9th, '65; mustered out with company.

1st Lieutenant—S. S. Hendricks, February 20th, '65; discharged by Special Order, May 12th, '65. 2d Lieutenants—C. D. Rohrbach, March 29th, '65; discharged by Special Order, May 21st, '65. B. F. Bright, promoted to 2d Lieutenant, July 2d, '65; mustered out with company, August 29th, '65.

1st Sergeant—Earnest Starkloff, mustered out with company, August 29th, '65. Sergeants—H. B. Longsdorf, mustered out with company, August 29th, '65. W. H. Row, March 9th, '65; mustered out with company, August 29th, '65. P. S. Gussler, mustered out with company, August 29th, '65. J. G. Young, promoted to Sergeant, July 2d, '65; mustered out with company.

Corporals—A. H. Boyer, mustered out with company, August 29th, '65. Jacob Fetter, mustered out with company, August 29th, '65. Perry Jarrett, March 9th, '65; mustered out with company, August 29th, '65. Uriah Foulk, mustered out with company, August 29th, '65. Alexander Cassatt, mustered out with company, August 29th, '65. W. B. Longsdorf, mustered out with company, August 29th, '65. J. R. Bright, March 7th, '65; promoted to Corporal, July 2d, '65; mustered out with company. Philip Keefer, March 18th, '65; mustered out with company.

Musicians—Henry Cassatt, March 8th, '65; mustered out with company. P. F. Zimmerman, mustered out with company.

Privates—Philip Arrison, March 23d, '65; mustered out with company. Pharos Adams, March 8th, '65; mustered out with company. Henry Billman, March 8th, '65; mustered out with company. Jacob W. Bright, mustered out with company. Chas. H. Bucher, mustered out with company. H. W. Bucher, absent on furlough on muster-out. John Bell, mustered out with company, August 29th, '65. John T. Brower, mustered out with company, August 29th, '65. Absalom Beaver, March 29th, '65; mustered out with company, August 29th, '65. Henry Boyer, deserted, June 9th, '65. D. K. Conrad, mustered out with company, August 29th, '65. Jacob Cassatt, mustered out with company, August 29th, '65. Peter H. Coble, deserted, July 9th, '65. Leonard Dole, March 27th, '65; mustered out with company, August 29th, '65. Landis Fry, mustered out with company, August 29th, '65. J. P. Griggs, March 8th, '65; mustered out with company, August 29th, '65. Wm. Gurringer, March 8th, '65; mustered out with company, August 29th, '65. Monroe Gessey, mustered out with company, August 29th, '65. Geo. B. Genther, mustered out with company, August 29th, '65. W. J. Harp, mustered out with company, August 29th, '65. F. J. Haughton, mustered out with company, August 29th, '65. J. W. Hopper, mustered out with company, August 29th, '65. Thomas Menninger, mustered out with company, August 29th, '65. B. A. Hopper, mustered out with company, August 29th, '65. Galen Holshue, mustered out with company, August 29th, '65. Fred. Herman, mustered out with company, August 29th, '65. Aaron Hummel, March 9th, '65; absent on furlough at muster-out. M. K. Herman, March 8th, '65; deserted, July 9th, '65. Edward Israel, mustered out with company, August 29th, '65. Daniel Jarett, March 13th, '65; mustered out with company, August 29th, '65. M. S. Kaufman, March 8th, '65; mustered out with company, August 29th, '65. Henry Kemble, mustered out with company, August 29th, '65. Eli Kerlin, mustered out with company, August 29th, '65. John Lesser, March 23d, '65; mustered out with company, August 29th, '65. J. W. Lyon, mustered out with company, August 29th, '65. John J. Landaw, mustered out with company, August 29th, '65. Gideon Landaw, mustered out with company, August 29th, '65. Frank Leader, mustered out with company, August 29th, '65. Wm. Leeman, mustered out with company, August 29th, '65. Solomon Lesser, April 5th, '65; mustered out with company, August 29th, '65. Martin Mills, March 13th, '65; mustered out with company, August 29th, '65. John S. Messner, mustered out with company, August 29th, '65. Samuel Milkof, March 9th, '65; mustered out with company, August 29th, '65. Thomas E. Metzgar, April 6th, '65; mustered out with company, August 29th, '65. J. W. Meyers, deserted, July 9th, '65. James McPherson, March 13th, '65; mustered out with company, August 29th, '65. Robert B. McCay, March 13th, '65; mustered out with company, August 29th, '65. James P. McKenney, March 13th, '65; mustered out with company, August 29th, '65. A. J. McKain, April 5th, '65; mustered out with company, Aug. 29th, '65. W. C. Otto, mustered out with company, Aug. 29th, '65. Albert Robins, March 7th, '65; mustered out with company, Aug. 29th, '65. John Baker, absent on furlough at muster-out. W. H. Rohrbach, mustered out with company, Aug. 29th, '65. Julius Ray, mustered out with company, Aug. 29th, '65. G. A. Reeser, mustered out with company, Aug. 29th, '65. Wm. Ritter, March 8th, '65; mustered out with company, August 29th, '65. John Ritter, March 9th, '65; mustered out with company, August 29th, '65. L. Renninger, March 29th, '65; mustered out with company, Aug. 29th, '65. P. M. Snyder, March 28th, '65; mustered out with company, Aug 29th, '65. John M. Shire, March 24th, '65; mustered out with company, August 29th, '65. Noah Stettler, March 13th, '65; discharged by General Order, July 9th, '65. John Stettler, March 13th, '65; deserted, June 25th, '65. Peter Stepp, deserted, July 9th, '65. John Shuyler, March 8th; deserted July 1st, '65. Henry Upslinger, March 9th, '65; mustered out with company, August 29th, '65. John Wilver, March 23d, '65; mustered out with company, August 29th, '65. John Zimmerman, March 9th, 65; mustered out with company, August 29th, '65. Henry Zerbe, mustered out with company, August 29th, '65.

Company E.

(Date of muster, February 28th, 1865.)

Captain, W. H. Wolfe, mustered out with company, August 29th, '65.

1st Lieutenant, H. M. Spayd, mustered out with company, August 29th, '65. 2d Lieutenant, J. T. M'Gregor, discharged, June 21st, '65.

1st Sergeant, H. S. Thomas, mustered out with company, August 29th, '65. Sergeants—C. H. Seaman, mustered out with company, August 29th, '65. Thomas Sutterson, mustered out with company, August 29th, '65. Adam Ratdorf, mustered out with company, August 29th, '65. James Murphy, mustered out with company, August 29th, '65. W. Irvin, mustered out with company, August 29th, '65.

Corporals—Joseph Middleton, promoted to Corporal, June 15th, '65; mustered out with company. Jacob Haus, mustered out with company, August 29th, '65. Hiram Dye, mustered out with company, August 29th,

'65. Thomas Brooks, mustered out with company, August 29th, '65. Owen Nagle, mustered out with company, August 29th, '65. L. B. Wetzel, mustered out with company, August 29th, '65. J. S. Middleton, mustered out with company, August 29th, '65. S. J. Irvin, discharged by General Order, May 15th, '65.

Musicians—John Marshall, mustered out with company, August 29th, '65. S. B. Morgan, mustered out with company, August 29th, '65.

Privates—George W. Askine, discharged by General Order, June 19th, '65. Alexander W. Blair, mustered out with company, August 29th, '65. James Buoy, mustered out with company, August 29th, '65. Charles C. Bright, discharged by General Order, July 9th, '65. W. H. Blind, mustered out with company, August 29th, '65. Nathan Burkhart, mustered out with company, August 29th, '65. Amos H. Barrett, mustered out with company, August 29th, '65. G. F. Baker, discharged by General Order, August 29th, '65. Joseph Burk, discharged by General Order, August 1st, '65. C. W. Coleman, mustered out with company, August 29th, '65. R. C. Creitzer, mustered out with company, August 29th, '65. William Coup, mustered out with company, August 29th, '65. Daniel W. Cox, mustered out with company, August 29th, '65. J. Dateman, mustered out with company, August 29th, '65. E. Diefenderfer, mustered out with company, August 20th, '65. James Dixon, mustered out with company, August 29th, '65. John Divel, mustered out with company, August 29th, '65. W. H. H. Diehl, mustered out with company, August 29th, '65. S. B. Dodge, mustered out with company, August 29th, '65. Geo. R. Detwiler, discharged by General Order, June 29th, '65. W. S. Eckert, mustered out with company, August 29th, '65. J. H. Ernst, discharged by General Order, August 1st, '65. Michael Fix, mustered out with company, August 29th, '65. William H. Freed, mustered out with company, August 29th, '65. William D. Freymire, discharged by General Order, June 30th, '65. J. J. Gehrig, mustered out with company, August 29th, '65. J. D. Gehrig, mustered out with company, August 29th, '65; W. J. Garkins, mustered out with company, August 29th, '65. Charles M. Goodman, mustered out with company, August 29th, '65. Edwin F. Gold, mustered out with company, August 29th, '65. W. Y. Gray, mustered out with company, August 29th, '65. William F. Gressler, discharged by General Order, June 29th, '65. J. B. Gehrig, discharged by General Order, August 1st, '65. S. Hoagland, mustered out with company, August 29th, '65. James Hoagland, mustered out with company, August 29th '65. William Hull, mustered out with company, August 29th, '65. John Hilbourn, mustered out with company, August 29th, '65. Reese S. Harris, mustered out with company, August 29th, '65. W. H. Huth, discharged by General Order, June 30th, '65. J. R. Housel, discharged by General Order, July 9th, '65. Isaac Harline, discharged by General Order, August 1st, '65. W. A. Imbody, mustered out with company, August 29th, '65. George Imbody, mustered out with company, August 29th, '65. S. J. James, deserted, March 10th, '65. Arthur L. Kline, mustered out with company, August 29th, '65. John D. Kline, mustered out with company, August 29th, '65. Henry Kissinger, mustered out with company, August 29th, '65. O. P. Kaufman, mustered out with company, August 29th, '65. Stephen Kendrick, mustered out with company, August 29th, '65. Benjamin Klingfelter, discharged by General Order, July 9th, '65. D. H. Keifer, discharged by General Order, August 1st, '65. W. H. Miller, mustered out with company, August 29th, '65. Henry Montague, mustered out with company, August 29th, '65. Benjamin Miller, mustered out with company, August 29th, '65. L. A. Mathias, mustered out with company, August 29th, '65. John Martin, discharged by General Order, June 30th, '65. G. W. Overpeck, discharged by General Order, August 1st, '65. John Peeler, Jr., mustered out with company, August 29th, '65. Henry C. Paul, mustered out with company, August 29th, '65. William Penny, mustered out with company, August 29th, '65. Israel Philipps, mustered out with company, August 29th, '65. Jacob H. Rishel, mustered out with company, August 29th, '65. Samuel W. Riddel, mustered out with company, August 29th, '65. Heyman Reynolds, mustered out with company, August 29th, '65. E. H. Reese, died, June 20th, '65. William Stutzman, mustered out with company, August 29th, '65. George P. Swarts, mustered out with company, August 29th, '65. David L. Starrick, mustered out with company, August 29th, '65. Charles H. Smith, mustered out with company, August 29th, '65. T. J. Sticker, mustered out with company, August 29th, '65. G. P. Straub, mustered out with company, August 29th, '65. W. B. Sladden, mustered out with company, August 29th, '65. J. D. Swarts, discharged by General Order, June 30th, '65. Benjamin Snyder, discharged by General Order, August 14th, '65. Albert Tregs, mustered out with company, August 29th, '65. F. M. Vandergrift, mustered out with company, August 29th, '65. Peter Werts, mustered out with company, August 29th, '65. Joseph Werts, mustered out with company, August 29th, '65. William Weimar, mustered out with company, August 29th, '65. John Yount, mustered out with company, August 29th, '65.

CAPTAIN JAMES TAGGART.

James Taggart, who recruited and first commanded Company "B," Fifth Pennsylvania Reserves, was the third son of John and Hannah Taggart. He was born in Northumberland, February 4th, 1827. His maternal grandfather was Matthew Huston, who, more than seventy years ago, represented the County of Philadelphia in the Assembly, and was afterwards chief clerk of that body, when Lancaster was the seat of government. His paternal grand-father, David Taggart, was the sole escort of Simon Snyder, when he left his home in Northumberland County, to be inaugurated Governor of the State. They made the whole journey on horse-back with no baggage, but their saddle-bags, and got a good ducking in Middle Creek, which they attempted to ford without knowing the way. Traveling expenses were light in those days—whisky only three cents a drink, and pure rye at that! What unfortunate worshipper of Bacchus does not envy his grand-father! There is no modern improvement to balance the degeneracy and the high price of whisky.

When the war began, Captain Taggart was a merchant in his native village—a widower with two children—under seven years of age. He was so well esteemed, that when it was known that he would accept command of the company, the ranks were soon filled with men and boys, whose ages ranged from seventeen to fifty-three. The oldest was Albin Newberry—the youngest, John Brantijam. Henry A. Colt, was First, and Charles C. Jones, Second Lieutenant; and James D. Slater, First Sergeant.

They left for Camp Curtin, in May, 1861, and immediately after the first battle of Bull Run, marched to the front.

On the 30th of June, 1862, at the battle of Glendale, the last of the seven days' fight, Captain Taggart fell in the same volley with the brave and beloved commander of his regiment, Colonel Seneca G. Simmons, and Major Henry J. Biddle, General M'Call's, Chief of Staff. His remains were never found, but still mingle with the soil of the battle-field. His monument, at Northumberland, bears this fitting inscription:

> "They never fall, who die
> In a great cause; the block may soak their gore;
> Their heads may sodden in the sun; their limbs
> Be strung to city gates and castle walls;
> But still their *spirit* walks abroad. Though years
> Elapse, and others share as dark a doom,
> They but augment the deep and sweeping thoughts,
> Which overpower all others, and conduct
> *The world at last to freedom.*"

In a family of nine, his was the first death in thirty years. His father still lives in his eighty-first year, and three brothers and an only sister yet survive.

CAPTAIN CHARLES WELLS.

Captain Taggart was succeeded by his First Lieutenant, Charles G. Wells, a gallant and capable officer, also a native of Northumberland. He was a man of wit, as well as of patriotism and courage. He was a carpenter by trade, and in politics an intense Native American. On one occasion, he was making a huge pine grave-box for an Irishman. It was so big, that Charley remarked: "The devil will think he has brought his shanty with him." He was killed in the thickest of the fight at Chancellorsville.

CAPTAIN JAMES D. SLATER.

The next captain was James D. Slater, a scarred veteran of the Mexican war, a blunt, brave man, who never feared to fight for his country, or his opinions. On election days, he was a tower of strength to his party, and his bold logical utterances made him a formidable opponent. His political adversaries gave him a wide berth, for he had a rough way of calling wrong things by their right names. He escaped the perils of two bloody wars to die peacefully at home. On three Decoration Days the flowers have been heaped upon his grave.

No company in the service has been commanded by three better, braver, truer men, and it was worthy of them.

Captain Taggart's son and daughter still live in Northumberland. Wells died childless, and Slater never married.

THE SANITARY COMMISSION OF NORTHUMBERLAND COUNTY.

Poets have sung of the courage and heroism of the women of Sparta, whose self-sacrifice, in defence of their beloved city, has become known to the civilized world. The respect and esteem, in which women are held in all Christendom, has been greatly increased by the admiration of mankind, for the bravery exhibited by the women of old, whose enthusiasm inspired the fathers, husbands, sons and brothers, with more than mortal courage, and expelled the invaders from their ancient citadels. The day has passed, when it was necessary for the weaker part of mankind, to cut off their flowing locks, to weave strings for the bows of the archers, and to throw their frail bodies into the breach, to inspire with greater courage, their natural defenders; but the opportunity for the exhibition of a fervor, unparalleled in the annals of the world's history, was presented during the trying scenes that filled our land with sorrowing lament, in the progress of the last war. Prior to 1861, the women of America were characterized the world over, as effeminate, and for the performance of any of the sterner duties of life, incompetent by reason of their delicacy. In every thing of a refining nature, in the drawing man out of self, building up the finer part of his nature, and giving lustre to a character that would be otherwise filled with dross and all manner of uncleanliness, the women of America take rank far above their sisters of the Old World, who have never fully removed the veil that the dark ages left over them, dwarfing the growth of the best part of their natures. Here, women stand on a pedestal far above the aspirations of man, occupying the middle ground, between Heaven and earth, constituting a happy medium between Divinity and finiteness. They had gradually assumed the role apparently best suited to them, and none dreamed them possessed of the elements of true heroism, which the opportunities occasioned by the last war so strikingly developed. Man buckled on his armor, and went forth to combat with the enemies of his country, nerved to the work, by the remembrance that the home sheltering his trembling, delicate wife or sister, was threatened with desecration, unthinking that he had left behind him, a spirit that when aroused, would exhibit more true moral courage, than the strongest soldiers in the ranks, but such was proven. The moment a wail of distress came up from the wounded friend, women sprang to the rescue, and performed feats of courage, self-sacrifice and endurance, in comparison with which the accomplishments of the women of Sparta, sinks into insignificance. The citizens of every locality in the North, have just reason to feel proud of the achievements of their women. Everywhere was the one response to the cry for help, the heartiness of which buoyed the drooping spirits of the sick and wounded, and saved from the stranger grave, thousands of the country's brave defenders. Through the favor of the worthy Secretary of the Sanitary Commission for Sunbury, we are made familiar with the work performed by the women of the County, and can form some conception of the labor and good accomplished.

The people of Sunbury began their good work for the soldiers, April 18th 1861. A company of volunteers from Sunbury, went to Harrisburg on Saturday morning, April 19th, and by Monday morning, every man was furnished with a new flannel shirt and a needle-book. These were made by the women of Sunbury, from material purchased by the citizens of the town. On Monday, April 21st, the companies from the upper counties, and from Western New York, began to pass through the town by railway. They were very hungry, and were fed by the people. This led to the habit of keeping ham, bread and coffee, in readiness, to use immediately. During the war, at least forty thousand soldiers were furnished with meals. At one time, the "Bucktail" Regiment of one thousand men, commanded by Colonel Kane, was furnished with two meals, and lodged for twenty-four hours. Sometimes, when the soldiers left the town, there was not a loaf of bread in it; as the people, with but few exceptions, were unfailing in their liberality. Boxes were sent from time to time to the army, and stockings were knit by a society formed for that purpose. They met every Tuesday evening, at the houses of the members. During May, 1863, several circulars from the United States Sanitary Commission were received. A meeting was called at the house of Mrs. William Wilson, May 30th, 1863, and the "Sanitary Aid Society of Sunbury, Pennsylvania," was organized. Mrs. Charles Pleasants, was elected President, and served until the society closed. Vice-Presidents: Mrs. W. Wilson, Mrs. Alexander Jordan, Mrs. John B. Packer, Mrs. William J. Greenough, Mrs. James Boyd and Miss Maria E. Fisher. Treasurer: Mrs. Beulah A. Clement. Secretary: Mrs. E. Donnel. Committees were appointed, and every one set to work in good earnest. Mr. Charles Pleasants gave the use of a room in his building, and the hours of meeting were fixed for Thursday afternoon in summer, and Thursday evening in winter.

The box was sent to the commission, 1309 Chestnut street, June 14th, 1863. During the months of August and September, a battalion of the provost guard, was stationed here. The society took charge of the sick soldiers, and the ladies of the society took turns in furnishing the meals for them. The upper rooms of the old Court House, were used as a hospital. On New Year's day, 1864, a supper was given by the society, and in August a tableaux. Donations of money and material were liberally bestowed. January 1st, 1865, there were eighty-nine members on the roll of the society. After a battle, there was generally an extra meeting and extra supplies were sent. The contributions to the Sanitary Fair were very liberal. Extras were published by the *Gazette* during the battle of the Wilderness and sold for the benefit of the society. June 25th, 1865, the society provided supper for the 150th and 151st, Regiment of New York Vols., numbering twenty-five hundred men, who were returning from the army. This closed the active duties of the "Sanitary Aid Society." November 1865, "Society closed."

E. DONNEL, *Secretary*.

Volumes have been written of the achievements of our soldiers during the four years' struggle; thousands have been expended in erecting monuments, commemorating some notable feat or bloody field; but here, four years' labor, filled with a self-sacrifice and devotion, to which the world's history furnishes no parallel, and it was but an infinitesimal portion of the work done by the Sanitary Commission, are ended with this brief motive, "Society closed." The ever memorable words, "It is finished," uttered by the Savior of mankind, suspended upon the ignominious cross, proclaimed to the world, that the work he came to perform was completed. But who of finiteness can form any estimate of the work this true sentence announced as ended. For years there had been a struggle between Divinity as represented in him and humanity; Divinity at all times maintaining the ascendency. Four years, the women of Northumberland County had toiled almost ceaselessly, with aching brain and anxious hearts for the alleviation of their suffering heroes. How many anxious sighs and tearful prayers, were interwoven in the meshes of the delicate fabrics, so skillfully prepared—not time, but eternity, will discover. What sacrifices were made in behalf of the loved ones far away, the recipients will never know. All we know is, that silently and lovingly was the work done, and when no longer occasion required the offerings, as silently the "Society closed." Side by side with the names of the country's brave defenders, should be inscribed in letters imperishable, those of the noble women, whose noble sacrifices made possible the success of our soldiers.

At the first meeting of the regular Sanitary Commission, held in Sunbury, June 4th, 1863, there were present:

Mrs. A. Jordan, Mrs. C. Pleasants, Mrs. William Willson, Mrs. J. B. Packer, Mrs. Henry Billington, Mrs. George Walker, Mrs. W. L. Dewart, Mrs. William Rockefeller, Mrs. Jordan Rockefeller, Mrs. Thomas D. Grant. Mrs. Andrew N. Brier, Mrs. George Smith, Mrs. John Buyers, Mrs. George Hill, Mrs. George Wren, Miss Maria A. Fisher, Miss Mamela Covert, Miss Lizzie Lazarus, Miss Mary Lazarus, Miss Malinda Weiser, Miss Sallie Fry, Miss Sarah Engle, Miss Louisa Hendricks, Miss Mary E. Masser, Miss Emma Painter, Miss Maggie Donnell, Miss Amelia Keihl, Miss Louisa Weaver, Miss Rachel McCarty, Miss F. M. F. Donnell, Mrs. Samuel Gobin, Mrs. Horatio Wolverton, Mrs. William Reed, Mrs. Lewis W. Gibson.

Mrs. Charles Pleasants, President; Miss Beulah A. Colement, Treasurer; Miss Elizabeth Donnel, Secretary. For two years and six months, they met together week after week for the noble purposes of their mission. Their members were added to at different times, until at its close there were ninety-two names on the rolls. The value of the supplies forwarded to the camps and hospital, during that time, was upwards of fifteen hundred dollars, embracing every article that could alleviate suffering and increase the comfort of the sick and wounded.

The society has closed, but the remembrance of the good accomplished will remain fresh in the hearts of all, so long as time shall last.

PLATE V

EV-LUTHERAN CHURCH,
MILTON, NORTHUMBERLAND CO., PA.

ST JOHN'S CHURCH OF EVANGELICAL ASSOCIATION,
REV. W. A. LEOPOLD, PASTOR,
SUNBURY ST. SHAMOKIN, NORTHUMBERLAND CO. PA.

FIRST PRESBYTERIAN CHURCH,
REV A. C. CLARKE, PASTOR.
SUNBURY ST. SHAMOKIN NORTHUMBERLAND CO. PA.

CHAPTER X.

CHURCHES.

THE GERMAN REFORMED CHURCH.

A CELEBRATED writer has said, that the "History of the World is little else than a History of Eminent Men." This sagacious remark is eminently true of Church History. It is little else than a record of the feelings and acts under Divine inspiration, of men whose education and circumstances have fitted and marked them for the great work of reforming a lost people.

Ulrich Zwingle, the great reformer of Switzerland, the father and founder of the German Reform Church, commenced his work twelve months before the great Luther from the centre of Europe, hurled forth his powerful darts that spread such consternation among the ranks of the emissaries of the Pope. Zwingle was born January 1st, 1487, took charge of a church at the age of eighteen, and at twenty-nine began to preach boldly in opposition to the tenants of the Catholic Church. At the early age of forty-four, this bright light was extinguished, but the rays that emanated from his fertile and powerful mind, have penetrated to the furthermost confines of the earth, carrying joy to the hearts of millions that now worship in accordance with the creed that he promulgated. To the efforts of the pastor of this church in Milton, we are indebted for a full History of the German Church in our country and Northumberland County.

The great reformation of the sixteenth century, which commenced in Central Europe, but gradually spread over the whole of that continent, divided itself at an early day into two distinct branches, the Reformed and Lutheran. The Reformed movement was inaugurated by Ulrich Zwingle, in Switzerland, in 1516, one year before Luther commenced his reformation in Wittenburg. The chief theological difference between Zwingle and Luther had reference to the Lord's Supper. Luther held to the real presence of Christ in the Eucharist, in such a sense that the communicant actually receives the body and blood of Christ, "in, with and under," the form of the bread and wine; whilst Zwingle taught the Holy Communion to be simply a commemorative ordinance. The system of Zwingle was afterwards somewhat modified, and more fully developed by John Calvin, who, in contrast with Zwingle's notion of mere commemoration in the Holy Supper, maintained the real spiritual presence of Christ in that sacrament in such a sense that the worthy communicant only is made a partaker of Christ by faith under the operation of the Holy Ghost.

Our branch of the Holy Catholic Church is a part of this general Reformed movement in Europe in the sixteenth century. We, however, properly date our establishment as a specific German Reformed Church from the year 1562, in which the Elector Frederick, the Third, surnamed the Pious, of the Palatinate in Germany, employed two Calvanistic divines, Zacharius Ursinus and Casper Olevianus, to draw up the Heidelberg Catechism, which ever since that time has been the only acknowledged confession of faith in our church. The object of the Elector Frederick in having this Catechism drawn up at that time was, if possible, to have it serve the purpose of harmonizing the Reformed and Lutheran parties in his dominions. Hence the catechism was made to combine the moderate spirit of Melancthon, a Lutheran, with the general doctrinal system of Calvin. It is this peculiarity of our confession of faith that gives us our distinctive character as a denomination, especially in the United States, where our ministers generally have more strongly emphasized the Melancthonian than the Calvanistic elements in the catechism. I cannot now speak of our confessional symbol further than to say, that immediately upon its appearance in print it was introduced into all the Reformed Churches of the Palatinate, as well as many other parts of Europe.

You will now please call to mind what was said in my Centennial discourse two weeks ago, in reference to the sufferings, privations and persecutions endured by our German Reformed ancestors in this part of Germany, the Palatinate on the Rhine, as early as 1689. Roman Catholic fanaticism then drove our forefathers out of their houses in mid-winter, their dwellings were burned, their crops destroyed, and men, women and children left without shelter and food. In 1719, they were forbidden to use the Heidelberg Catechism, their confessional standard, and prevented from worshipping in the Church of the Holy Ghost, in Heidelberg. Thus persecuted and oppressed at home, these German Reformed people turned their eyes towards this new world, and came hither in search of a home, where they might have freedom to worship God according to their own faith, customs and usages.

As early as the middle of the seventeenth century, a company of Germans had already found a home and religious toleration in America. Before William Penn arrived, in 1682, Germantown, now a suburb of Philadelphia, was founded by the Germans. In 1711, nearly seven thousand Germans arrived in America, from the Palatinate. At first they settled in Schoharie County, New York, but the following year, 1712, they constructed for themselves rafts, upon which they floated down the Susquehanna, and took up their abode in what is now Berks County, this State. From them, it is supposed, the greater part of the German Reformed population in Berks and Lebanon counties, are descended.

During the following ten years, large numbers of Reformed people settled in Pennsylvania, and in 1731, their number here was no less than 15,000. It must be remembered, however, that at that time they were not as yet an organized church.

These people were generally supplied with bibles, catechisms, prayer-books, which they brought with them from the fatherland, and often were accompanied by pious school-masters, who, after their arrival here, gathered the people together on the Lord's day, and read to them an appropriate sermon. But there is no account of any regularly ordained Minister being among them, and preaching to them, until 1727. In this year, the Classis of the Palatinate sent over to America the Rev. George Weiss, with about 400 people of the Palatinate. Mr. Weiss settled in Montgomery County, Pa., and there organized a congregation and consistory. He also, a few years later, established another church in Philadelphia.

Before Mr. Weiss arrived in America, however, Rev. John Boehm, a native of the Palatinate, had preached in the vicinity of the present Boehm's church, in Montgomery County. It appears he was not at first licensed to preach the Gospel, but the necessities of the times were such, that his action, though irregular, was approved of by the proper authorities. He afterwards labored very successfully in different congregations in the vicinity of Philadelphia.

In 1746, Rev. Michael Schlatter was sent to America by the Synod of Holland, for the purpose of organizing the Reformed people here into congregations, place pastors over them, and in a general way superintend the affairs of the German Reformed church in this country.

In September, 1749, the first Synod of our church, or Cœtus, as it was then called, assembled in Philadelphia. There were present at that meeting five ministers and twenty-six elders, representing forty-six congregations, and a communicant membership of about eight thousand souls.

Through the instrumentality of Mr. Schlatter, a number of Reformed clergymen were subsequently induced to come over from Europe to take charge of the congregations in Pennsylvania, and the ranks of our ministry continued to be supplied from that source for many years.

In 1751, we had twelve ministers, forty-six congregations, and a communicant membership of ten thousand. In 1776, one hundred years ago, twenty-three ministers, sixty-five congregations, and thirteen thousand members. In 1801, thirty ministers, one hundred congregations, and a membership of twenty thousand. In 1828, one hundred ministers, four hundred congregations, and thirty-five thousand members. In 1851, two hundred and five ministers, seven hundred and ten congregations, and a membership of sixty-six thousand; and at the present time, 1876, six hundred and fifty ministers, one thousand three hundred and fifty congregations, and a communicant membership of one hundred and forty-five thousand. In 1776, twenty-three ministers; in 1876, six hundred and fifty! In 1776, sixty-five congregations; to-day, one thousand three hundred and fifty! During the past twenty-five years, our ministry has increased from two hundred and eighty-five to six hundred and fifty, and our membership from sixty-six thousand to one hundred and forty-five thousand, notwithstanding the unhappy controversy that has been waged in our midst during this time.

Our first theological school was organized in 1825, at Carlisle, in this State. It was removed to York, in 1829; to Mercersburg, in 1835; and to Lancaster, in 1871. The Theological Seminary, at Tiffin, Ohio, was established in 1850. A few years later, another divinity school was founded at Sheboygan, Wisconsin. Ursinus College and Theological School, at Collegeville, near Philadelphia, were established in 1869.

Our first church paper was a German one, established in 1827. The first English paper was published in 1828; and the first church periodical published in the west, was established in 1848.

To-day, we have ten academic and collegiate institutions; five theological schools; five missionary societies; three educational societies, to aid indigent young men in preparing for the ministry; two orphans' homes; sixteen church periodicals, in the English and German languages; one thousand five hundred consistories; forty-four classes; six District Synods; and one General Synod.

Until 1825, our ministers conducted all religious services in the German language. And much opposition was waged against the introduction of the English language into our church services; and it was attended, moreover, with great disturbances. To this fact must, doubtless, be attributed our slow growth, in this country, for a long time, as compared with other churches around us. We were on the ground earlier than many of the denominations now existing here, but we clung too tenaciously to the German language, and so failed to reach the English-speaking people, and, unfortunately, we awoke to the fact a little too late.

Our forefathers brought with them from Europe, and used in connection with their baptismal, confirmation and communion services, and on all special occasions, the Liturgy of the Palatinate. A new Liturgy was prepared by Rev. Dr. Mayer, and adopted in 1840. In 1847, another book of worship, known as the "Provisional Liturgy," was prepared and recommended to the churches for trial. That book was again referred to a committee for revision, which reported in 1866, what is now known as the "Order of Worship," or Eastern Liturgy. In 1868, the western portion of the church prepared another Order of Worship, known as the Western Liturgy, for the use of those who were opposed to the doctrinal system, and responsive service of the Eastern Order of Worship.

From this hasty sketch, it will appear that our growth as a church, especially during the last twenty-five years, has been remarkably rapid, and the outlook for our future is full of hope and promise. The Heidelberg Catechism, which the Roman Catholic Church sought so strenuously to crush out of existence in the Palatinate, in 1689, was brought by our fathers to these western wilds, and here, as at home by the Rhine, they taught it to their children, and have bequeathed it to us, their descendants, as a precious legacy.

I now turn to the history of this congregation, and ask you with me to "remember the days of old," of the Reformed church in Milton.

The few Reformed families living in and around Milton, were, as nearly as can now be ascertained, occasionally supplied with preaching by Reformed clergymen who came this way, as early as 1805, in a log school-house on lower Market street, built in 1796. That school-house was occupied about the same time by the Lutheran, Methodist, and Presbyterian people of this place. About the year 1807, the Germans residing here, being desirous of having their children taught in their own language, bought of Mr. David Bridge, a small log building, which he had previously erected for himself as a private dwelling-house, situated on Mahoning street, on a small space of ground now lying between the residences of Mr. Bower and Mr. Critzer. In that small building, then used by the Germans as a school-house during the winter season, the Reformed people continued to be more or less frequently supplied with preaching until 1812, in which year the Rev. Justus Henry Fries, becoming pastor of the Paradise congregation, commenced supplying them with divine services as often as his other labors permitted. Father Fries preached in that log house on Mahoning street until 1817. In this year, the Reformed people united with the Lutheran and Presbyterian congregations of Milton, in erecting a church edifice on the hill, at the east end of Mahoning street, known as the "Harmony Church." It was through the instrumentality of Mr. Daniel Bright, a store-keeper, and a member of the Reformed party, that the services of Conrad Henry, a master builder, residing in Reading, and quite celebrated in his day as a workman, were secured in erecting the proposed church building. I have been told that great extravagance characterized the building of that church—that as much material was consumed in its construction as would have been required to erect almost two such houses. It must be remembered, however, that buildings of all kinds were more substantially constructed fifty years ago than at the present time.

On Sunday, October 5th, 1817, the corner-stone of the new church was laid, in which various documents, as is usual, were deposited, and the building afterwards progressed more or less rapidly, until its completion in 1819. On the 25th of April, 1819, an election was held by the Reformed people for two church officers, which resulted in the choice of Christian Markle, as elder, and Joseph Rhoads as deacon. These two persons were properly ordained and installed into office by the Rev. Father Fries. Previous to this time, it appears, there did not exist any regularly established consistory, and hence April 25th, 1819, must be regarded as the time of the organization proper of this congregation.

On Sunday and Monday, the 23d and 24th of May, 1819, the new church edifice being completed was solemnly dedicated to the service of the Triune God, in the midst of appropriate German and English services. The Reformed pastor, Father Fries, was assisted on that occasion by the Rev. Martin Bruner, of Sunbury.

Three years later, in 1822, the harmony previously existing between the congregations worshipping in the hill church, became seriously disturbed, and it is said, the state of feeling soon became such, that Discord would have been a far more appropriate name for the church than Harmony. In this same year, 1822, a lottery, known as the Harmony Lottery, was established by the congregrations occupying that building, for the purpose of raising funds to liquidate a debt resting upon their church. The price of a ticket was three dollars. There was a drawing on the 10th of June, another on the 18th of July, and ten succeeding ones. During the month of June or July, of the same year, a stroke of lightning from an almost cloudless sky, only a small black cloud being visible in the heavens, passed down the steeple of the church, and entering the building behind the pulpit, passed out at the door. This was regarded by many persons as a clear token of God's sore displeasure at the method that was employed to secure funds for the church.

Great dissensions existed from this time forward in the Hill church. In 1827, the two German congregations, the Reformed and Lutheran, instituted a law-suit against the Presbyterian people, and obtained judgment against them in the sum of $1262.00, and the Sheriff of this County on the 27th of January 1831, sold out the interest of that congregation in the church building for the sum of $800.00. The German congregations afterwards offered to re-convey to the Presbyterians the half of the church property for $1000.00, or to rent the building to them for $40.00 per annum. Neither of these proposals, however, were accepted by them, and in 1832, they abandoned that church. The Reformed and Lutheran congregations now continued to occupy the building conjointly until 1850, when the Lutherans sold out their interest to the Reformed, who were now left in sole possession of the Harmony church property.

I have not allowed myself in this sketch to omit or suppress any fact that has come to my knowledge in reference to the history of the Hill church. It is the duty of the historian to record truthfully alike both the evil and the good—the good that we may imitate and follow it—the evil that we may avoid and shun it. We all rejoice to-day at the friendly and harmonious feeling existing between the different churches of our town. But I am certain no such feeling would exist among us if we all worshipped in one house, and owned it in common. The Reformed church has learned the lesson, from frequent sad experiences in the past, and that lesson is confirmed by the history of the so-called "Harmony Church," that it is not a very easy matter, for two or more different congregations to own and occupy the same house of worship conjointly, and get along harmoniously very long. It is much better, in all cases, where it is possible for every denomination to have its own church building, and carry on its work in its own way, whilst yet, in a general way, all can labor harmoniously together for the advancement of the common cause of our common Lord.

The Reformed people remained in the Hill church until that building was removed in 1850. This congregation then worshipped in the Reformed Presbyterian Church, on Walnut street, until the lecture room of this building was ready for occupancy.

I have already spoken of the pastorate of the Rev. Father Fries. He is to be regarded as the founder of this congregation, on the 25th of April, 1819, at which time he may also be said properly to have become its pastor. His pastoral labors ceased here in 1823, in which year he closed his labors in all the congregations he had served east of the Susquehanna River. Father Fries, is said to have been favored with a strong physical constitution, and have possessed a very retentive memory. He generally rode on horseback, was never known to miss an engagement, and was invariably punctual almost to the minute.

At the time when he resigned the congregations on this side of the river, Father Fries had under his instruction, two young men who were preparing themselves for the work of the ministry, viz.: Daniel Weiser, who died recently, and Samuel Gutelius, the latter of whom Father Fries recommended to this, and the other congregations he had served, as his successor. Accordingly, Mr. Gutelius was elected and installed pastor in 1824. During his pastorate, Rev. Martin Bruner frequently came up from Sunbury, and preached for him, and in that way helped to further the interests of this congregation. Mr. Gutelius retired from the pastorate in 1817.

His successor was the Rev. Henry Wagner, who was installed pastor in 1827, and resigned in 1835, after having served this charge for a period of eight years.

The next pastor was the Rev. Daniel Gring, who was installed in 1835. In 1840, Rev. Ephraim Kieffer, of Mifflinburg, became Mr. Gring's colleague, to preach for him in the English language. This arrangement with Mr. Kieffer ceased in 1844. In December of the same year, Rev. Henry Harbaugh, of Lewisburg, associated himself with Mr. Gring, to preach exclusively in the English language, and Mr. Gring having resigned in 1846, Mr. Harbaugh, in 1847, accepted a call from this congregation to preach in both languages. He resigned in 1849.

After Mr. Harbaugh's resignation, the congregation extended a call to the Rev. E. M. Long, which he accepted. He was installed pastor in 1849, and resigned in 1852.

His successor was the Rev. A. G. Dole, now located at Huntingdon, Pa. Mr. Dole was installed and entered upon his labors in April, 1854, and resigned the pastorate in October, 1865, after having faithfully served the congregation twelve-and-a-half years.

The Rev. Samuel H. Reid was the next minister in charge. He was elected pastor on the 6th of January, 1866, and resigned and retired from the duties of the pastorate on the 1st of April, 1873, after having done the congregation good service for seven years.

My own election as your pastor took place on the 13th of July, 1873. I preached here as a Licentiate in July, and again in August. On the 1st of September, I permanently located in your midst, preaching afterwards regularly, and discharging all duties pertaining to the pastoral office, with the exception of the administration of the Holy Sacrament. On the 27th of October, I was publicly ordained to the ministry, and formally installed as your pastor, by East Susquehanna Classis, at a special meeting held in this church for that purpose.

The foregoing is a correct list of all the ministers who have served this congregation since its organization. The whole number is ten, of which number, only four are at present living. The rest have fallen asleep.

The corner-stone of the building in which we worship to-day, was laid on the 17th of May, 1866. The Rev. John W. Steinmetz, then of Danville, preached the sermon on that occasion. On the 18th of November of the same year, this house was consecrated to the worship of God under the name of St. John's Reformed Church of Milton. The dedicatory sermon was preached by the Rev. W. C. Cremer, then of Sunbury.

From what has now been said, it will appear that this congregation has a history extending over a period of fifty-seven years. It would have been exceedingly interesting to me, and doubtless to you also, if I could have ascertained and inserted in this sketch the names of all the persons who have served this congregation as elders and deacons since the first church officers were elected in 1819. Unfortunately, however, either no record of the church was kept during the greater part of this time, or if kept has been lost; so that I have been obliged to spend several weeks in gathering the material for this sketch. I have gone from place to place in search of facts and dates, and have sought out aged persons whom I supposed might possess such information as I needed, and yet it was not until a few days ago that I saw my way clear to prepare the latter part of this discourse. The thought that in the absence, to a great extent, of the original records, I have succeeded in preparing an accurate history of this congregation as I believe this to be, is indeed a sufficient reward for what time and labor I may have expended in gathering the facts of which it consists. But I desire here to urge upon you the importance of promptly recording, and carefully preserving in permanent form, such facts connected with your history as a church as you may think of interest to those who shall come after you. It is a very easy matter for you who are now in the congregation, and conversant with its history, to place on record, events as they transpire, and have them handed down to your children and children's children. But if you fail to do this it will, as I now know from experience, be a very difficult task for those who may constitute the congregation one hundred years hence, to acquaint themselves with its history during your life time. "Remember the days of old, consider the years of many generations; ask thy Father and He will shew thee; thy Elders and they will tell thee."

From a mere handful of men, women and children, residing here as early as 1805, this congregation has increased to its present membership of two hundred and twenty-five souls. From worshipping first in a log school-house on lower Market street, and later in a log building on Mahoning street, this congregation to-day occupies a house of worship, second to no other Reformed church in this County. From being supplied with preaching at first, probably only every six months, then every three months, and later every four weeks, and from being connected with other neighboring congregations in a pastoral charge, you now are a separate charge, and are provided with religious services generally twice every Lord's day, with frequent additional services during the week.

Let the goodness of God displayed in His dealings with this church in the past, move you to a faithful discharge of all the duties devolving upon you, as those who now have its affairs in hand. Let the fathers who have fallen asleep, and are now surrounding you as a great cloud of witnesses, looking down upon you from the heavenly world, animate you with new energy and zeal in your efforts to carry forward the good work they inaugurated when they established this congregation. Be faithful to your church, and labor for its prosperity, so that when you shall rest with your Father, the generations who shall rise up and take your places, may have as much occasion for rejoicing in tracing the history of this church in your time, as we have had abundant cause for encouragement and devout thanksgiving to-day, in calling to remembrance its days of old.

LUTHERAN CHURCH.

The German Reformed and Lutheran societies embrace a large proportion of the church-going people of Northumberland County. The membership is made up largely of Germans, who predominate in the lower townships, and whose zeal and taste have supplied numberless places of worship, neat, commodious, and attractive, in all parts of the County. Probably in no other part of the United States, of equal population, can there be found so great a number of beautiful country churches, as the enterprise of the members of these two societies have provided in the precincts of our County. The German Reformed, because the most numerous, has doubtless the most. The Lutherans rank next. Elsewhere will be found a carefully prepared history of the first of these societies, and it seems fitting that some account of the origin and purposes of the Lutheran church be furnished in these pages. The cardinal principles of the church are supposed to be based upon the creed promulgated by the great reformer, Luther, about three hundred and seventy years ago, who commenced life at Eisleben, November 10th, 1483, four years before the birth of Ulrich Zwingle, the father of the German Reformed church. The earnest zeal and simplicity that characterized Luther's every word and act, seems to have become incorporated in the church that bears his name. Earnest opposition to the Church of Rome, was the strong propelling power that urged him irresistably onward, with a force that the whole power of the Pope could not stay. Kings and potentates were arrayed against him, only to be brushed aside by the logic of the simple monk. Well might the poet ask: "What was Luther's power? What was the rock on which he stood, that seemed of adamant?" Beautifully, as if by the pen of inspiration, has this interrogatory been answered:

"'Twas simple 'faith in God.' He had espoused
The cause of truth—eternal, holy truth;
And He, whose attributes are infinite,
Vouchsafed his blessing.'

'Twas simple faith that enabled Luther to wrest the sceptre from the hands of the power at Rome, bring nobility to his feet, and plunge the whole of Europe into a condition of excitement that, for a time, bade fair to dismember the church. Luther was a preacher, and here are his ideas of a good preacher: "He should preach orderly. He should have a ready wit. He should be eloquent. He should have a good vein. He should have a good memory. He should know when to make and end. He should be sure of what he advances." He also gives his ideas of the requirements of a preacher who would please the world: "He must be learned. He must have a fine delivery. He must have neat and quaint words. He must be a proper person, whom the women fancy. He must not take, but give money. He must preach such things as the people willingly hear." There is nothing in the creed of Lutheranism, as taught by Martin Luther, to distinguish one branch of the Christian church of to-day, that may have adopted his name, from all others of orthodox faith; hence a treatise on the peculiar tenets of the Lutheran church would be as unprofitable as uninteresting to the general reader. The great reformer directed the labors of his life towards a dissemination of the truths of the Gospel, as they emanated from the hearts of the inspired writers, in all their simple and original purity, untrammeled, himself, by any particular creed. Scores of different denominations have been organized, all based upon the same principles, all laboring for a common purpose, none of which, however, can lay any particular claim to being the original Lutheran church. The one which has perpetuated the name of Luther, was first established in this country about 1621, at New York. The Rev. Jacob Fabricius, was the first preacher in America. After 1860, the German emigration to the Province of Pennsylvania became very great; each year thousands were added, and the churches representing their peculiar faith were soon established. The first churches built in this County, were by the Lutheran Society, the membership of which increased very rapidly, and soon became strong in numbers and wealth. Latterly, this church appears to have been loosing ground; as the English language was more generally introduced, the great similarity of this to the Methodist, and other denominations, was discovered, and the distinctive features of the Lutheran church were lost, or became merged into others. There are, however, a goodly number of those who still cling to the good old Lutheran doctrine, as it was in its primitive purity, and houses of worship are found in every town of consequence, and throughout the County, in those rural districts mostly peopled by the descendants of those from Luther's home, and the field of his early labors.

H. E. HAITHCOX, PASTOR.

TRINITY EV. LUTHERAN CHURCH, SUNBURY ST. SHAMOKIN, NORTH'D CO., PA.
REV. H. G. HAITHDOS, PASTOR, ERECTED 1869.

HISTORY

OF THE

TOWNSHIPS, BOROUGHS AND VILLAGES,

OF

NORTHUMBERLAND COUNTY.

EARLY HISTORY OF SUNBURY.

Before the discovery of America by Columbus, an Indian town existed where Sunbury now stands. It was the oldest and most important of all the towns in this region, inhabited by the *Six Nations*. It was called, in the Indian language, *Sha-ho-mo-king*. This name was subsequently written *Shaumokin*, and now it is Shamokin, and is the name of a town in the eastern part of Northumberland County.

Shamokin (Sunbury) was written *Schaumoki* by the *Delawares*. In very early times, the place was called *Schachamoki, the place of eels*, and the creek *Schachamekhan, eel stream*. It was next called *Schachkhenamendi*, signifying *the place where gun-barrels are straightened*, in allusion to the smithy built at Sunbury, in July, 1747, by Joseph Powell and John Hagen, of Bethlehem, where the blacksmiths, Schmid, Wess and Keffer, wrought in iron, until October, 1755.

From its central position, near the confluence of the two branches of the Susquehanna, Shamokin was a place of great note among the Indians, and was the headquarters of distinguished chiefs who presided over the *Six Nations*. It was also the Council Ground of all those Indians who resided between this place and the Potomac; also of those up the Juniata, up the west branch to its headwaters, and north and east to the headwaters of the north branch and the Delaware.

It was here that the dignitaries of many tribes, with their feathers and their paint, their wampum and their war-gear, met to join the wisdom of their councils; to make their sad decrees of war, or to send up cumulative vapors from the calumet of peace.

When Shamokin—now Sunbury—first became known to the white settlers, it was presided over by *Shickelemy*, a *Cayuga* chief, and father of the greatly wronged *Logan*, who afterwards figured so prominently in the Indian history of Pennsylvania. *Alumappees*, one of the chiefs of the *Delawares*, also lived here. He was the keeper of the public treasure of the *Six Nations*, and would occasionally get intoxicated, and spend the beads and wampum for rum, and finally became a defaulter to the Indian government.

The earliest available record that relates to this Indian town, dates back to 1728. Gov. Gordon lays down certain instructions to Smith and Petty, who were about to make a journey to Shamokin. In this letter of instructions, the Governor particularly requests them to call upon his Indian friends, *Alumappees*, *Opekasset*, *Shackalawlin* and *Shickelemy*, and give them his particular regards.

At this time, Sunbury was somewhat scattered, but, in the main, covered the ground now occupied by Market Square, and the blocks lying north of it, between the railroad and river. There were then upwards of fifty wigwams and houses in the town and its vicinity, with about three hundred inhabitants, averaging about six inmates to each wigwam.

Sunbury was also a point from which their war-paths radiated, or to which their highways centred. One main path went up the river by the mouth of Warrior Run to Muncy, and thence into Sullivan and the Towanda region. Another passed up the ravine in Blue Hill, a few rods below the end of the Northumberland bridge, thence up Turtle Creek into Buffalo Valley, and on to Kittanning and the west. There was also a main path down the river, about on the line of Fourth street, by the grave-yard, crossing Shamokin Creek near the little white house, and ascending the hill southward, about on the line of the present path in that locality. This went to the Harris Landing, now Harrisburg, with branches to the Juniata, Cumberland and Lancaster regions. Another path went up the ravine at Bacher's brewery, around Bake-oven Hill, and thence in the direction of Shamokin Creek to the Wyoming Valley, and to the headwaters of the Schuylkill.

In 1729, *Shickelemy*, the great and good chief, who resided at Sunbury, lost one of his sons, and Gov. Gordon wrote a letter of condolence, sending a shroud in which to bury him.

In 1730, John Hartt and John Fisher were living in Sunbury as traders, and Hartt was shot while burning a ring for deer.

In 1744, *Shickelemy* lost another of his sons, called *Unhappy Jake*, who was killed in a war then going on between the *Six Nations* and the *Catawbas*. Six other Indians of the *Six Nations* from here, were also killed at the same time. *Shickelemy* took the death of his son, as Weiser says, "very hard," and the Governor sent him up some small presents to "wipe off the old man's tears and comfort his heart."

In the Spring of 1744, the first aggravated case of murder occurred on the Juniata, when John Armstrong, an Indian trader, and his two servants, James Smith and Woodworth Arnold, were inhumanly and barbarously murdered by an Indian of the *Delaware* tribe, named *Musemeelin*. The atrocity of this murder was so aggravating, that a Provincial Council was held to take the matter into consideration, and it was finally resolved that Conrad Weiser should be sent to Shamokin to make demands, in the name of the Governor, for those concerned in the affair. Mr. Weiser arrived at Shamokin on the second day of May, 1744, and delivered the Governor's message to *Alumappees*, the *Delaware* chief, and the rest of the *Delaware* Indians, in presence of *Shickelemy* and a few more of the *Six Nations*. *Alumappees* replied that it was true that the evil spirit had influenced some of his tribe to commit the murder, and that he was very sorry it had occurred; they had taken the murderer and delivered him to the friends of the deceased, to be dealt with according to the nature of the deed. After the conclusion of the address by *Alumappees*, *Shickelemy* arose and entered into a full account of the unhappy affair, which is very long and interesting. When the conference with the Indians was ended, a feast was prepared, to which the Governor's messengers were invited. Mr. Weiser states that there were about one hundred persons present, to whom, after they had in great silence devoured a fat bear, the eldest of the chiefs made a speech.

FIRST RELIGIOUS SERVICE—MORAVIAN MISSION.

The first religious service in Sunbury, other than that which the Indians gave to the Great Spirit, was held by Moravian missionaries. Loskiel, in his history of Moravian missions, states that on the 28th of September, 1742, Count Zinzendorf, accompanied by Conrad Weiser, Martin Mack and his wife, and two Indians named Joshua and David, after a long and tedious journey through the wilderness, arrived at the town of Shamokin—now Sunbury. The chief *Shickelemy*, stepped out and gave them a hearty welcome. Zinzendorf immediately announced himself as a messenger of the living God, come to preach unto them grace and salvation. *Shickelemy* replied that he was happy to receive and entertain an ambassador from the Great Spirit, and would afford him all the assistance in his power. As a proof of his integrity, it is stated that on one occasion, when these pious missionaries were about going to prayers, the Indians making a terrible noise with drums and singing, the Count sent word to *Shickelemy*, who immediately ordered silence.

The Indians, at that time, lived upon wild meat, fish, corn and vegetables, and as the curious crowd which gathered around these missionaries were surveying them, one of their number stepped forward and presented the Count with a fine watermelon. The Count was so much pleased with this act of friendship that he took his fur cap from his head and presented it to the Indian in return.

Rev. David Brainerd visited Shamokin in 1745, for the first time. He endured much suffering, being in delicate health. He was kindly received and entertained in true Indian style, but had little satisfaction on account of the heathenish dance that occurred in the hut where he was obliged to lodge. Rev. Brainerd had started to come here the preceding year, but while passing from Easton, through what he terms "the vast howling wilderness," his horse broke his legs in the rocks and he was compelled to kill it and return. He says, in 1746, that there were three languages spoken by the Indians in Sunbury; that they were very immoral, and many of them addicted to intemperance.

In this same year, says Loskiel, Mack and wife again visited Shamokin, where they staid two months. During this time they not only suffered much illness and troubles of various kinds, but frequently were eye-witnesses to the most diabolical abomination, practiced by the savages more in this place than any other. Several times they were in danger of being murdered by drunken Indians, yet their fervent desire to gain souls for Christ, inspired them with such consolation that, according to Mack's own statement, their hard fare in an Indian cottage, afforded them more real pleasure than all the luxuries of the most sumptuous palace could have done. They spent a part of their time in assisting the Indians to cultivate their corn. In 1748, Shamokin was visited by Bishop Camerhoff and the pious Zeisberger, who came for the purpose of establishing a Moravian mission. The Moravian mission was kept open till Braddock's defeat, 1755, when the alarming aspect of affairs caused the brethren to abandon it and fly to Bethlehem. What success they had among the Indians is nowhere positively stated, but it is presumed that they succeeded in accomplishing considerable good.

THE FIRST HOUSE.

The first house constructed on the English plan, that was erected within the limits of what is now Sunbury, was built in September, 1744, by Conrad Weiser, for the Indian chief *Shickelemy*. In a letter to James Logan, dated September 29th, 1744, Mr. Weiser says:

"*Sir*:—The day before yesterday I came back from Shamokin, where I have been with eight young men of my country people, whom *Shickelemy* hired to make a locke house for him, and I went with them to direct them. We finished the house in seventeen days; it is forty-nine and one-half feet long, and seventeen and one-half feet wide, and covered with singels."

This structure was doubtless built of rough logs notched together, and the shingles with which it was covered, were probably heavy split boards, and at the present day would perhaps be called clapboards.

For what purpose such a building was designed by *Shickelemy* is not stated, further than it was a "*locke house*," from which it may be inferred that he intended to incarcerate therein some of his refractory subjects.

During the building of this house, the fever was very bad among the Indians, and five or six died. *Alumoppees*, the *Delaware* king, and Indian treasurer, was also very sick, but recovered.

The second house was built after the English custom, in the year 1747, by John Hagen and Joseph Powell, of the Moravian mission. The structure was used as a residence by Martin Mack and wife, by whom the first settlement at Shamokin—now Sunbury—was made.

THE FIRST BLACKSMITH.

As Shamokin (Sunbury) was an important point for the Indians, and used as a depot, or tarrying-place, for their war parties against the *Catawbas* of the south, they were very anxious to have a blacksmith to save them the trouble of long journeys to Tulpehocken or Philadelphia, to get their implements of war repaired. On application to the Provincial Government, their request was granted on condition that he should remain with them no longer than they proved friendly to the English. As all was peace and harmony among the two nations at that time, of course they assented to the proposition, and a gentleman named Anthony Schmidt, from the mission at Bethlehem, had the honor of being the first representative of Vulcan at Shamokin. This was about the year 1746. Shortly after this,—probably the next year, —John Hagen and Joseph Powell, of Bethlehem, Pa., came to Shamokin and erected a smithy. Hagen died soon after his arrival.

Shamokin was considered a dangerous place of residence for a European, the air being unwholesome, not to mention the extravagance in drinking and its dangerous conquences.

AN EARLY BLACKSMITH.

As early as 1790, Paul Baldy, a Revolutionary soldier, opened a shop on the site of the present Presbyterian church. It was built partly of hewn and partly of unhewn logs.

FIRST CHURCH EDIFICE.

The first church edifice was erected in 1792, and was a log structure. It stood on the site of the present Lutheran church. The second church, also of logs, was built a year or two later, by the Presbyterian and Reformed denominations combined, and occupied the site of the present Reformed church edifice. The

FIRST ENGLISH PREACHER

in Sunbury was Rev. Mr. Morrison, of the Presbyterian persuasion. He used to officiate in this second log church.

FIRST GRIST-MILL.

The first grist-mill was built by Maclay as early as 1785. It was constructed of logs, and for a long time was the only one in this section of the country. In 1820, there was a log house and grist-mill on the Haas farm, east of town.

THE FIRST DRUGGIST.

The first druggist was Dr. Solomon Markley, who came from Dauphin County and commenced that business as early as 1795. He died about 1814, and his wife continued the business until 1821. The building occupied was situated on Market street, near where the office of Wm. I. Greenough now stands.

In 1774, in the month of September, it was very sickly in Sunbury. The old chief *Shickelemy*, his wife, and many other Indians, had the "fever and ago," as they expressed it, very much, and *Alumoppees*, the old defaulting treasurer, who wasted the lands and the wampum, actually shook himself to death! One of the Moravian missionaries, probably one of the Mack family, died here in the same year. In July, Conrad Weiser gave *Shickelemy* and his sons, all the wheat meal they could bring from Tulpehocken on their horses, amounting to nine bushels, which was probably the largest cargo of breadstuffs ever brought into Sunbury up to that date.

A REMINISCENCE.

In one of his letters, dated at Tulpehocken, October 15th, 1747, Conrad Weiser thus writes to Richard Peters, Secretary of the Province of Pennsylvania:

"I must at the conclusion of this, recommend *Shickelemy* as a proper object of charity. He is extremely poor—in his sickness the horses have eaten his corn; his clothes he gave to the Indian doctors to cure him and his family—but all in vain. He has nobody to hunt for him; and I cannot see how the poor old man can live. He has been a true servant to the government, and may perhaps still be, if he lives to do well again. As the winter is coming on, I think it would not be amiss to send a few blankets or match-coats, and a little powder and lead. If the government would be pleased to do it, and you could send it soon, I would send my sons with it to Shamokin before the cold weather comes."

In the early part of November, 1747, the following goods were brought for *Shickelemy*:

Five strowd match-coats at seven pounds; one-fourth cask of gun-powder, two pounds, fifteen shillings; one-half cut bar of lead, one pound; fifteen yards of blue half thicks, two pounds, seven shillings, and six pence; one dozen best buck-hefted knives, nine shillings; four Duffel match-coats, three pounds; amounting to sixteen pounds, eleven shillings, and six pence.

DEATH OF SHICKELEMY.

In the month of April, 1749, occurred, at his residence in Sunbury, the death of the *Cayuga* chief, *Shickelemy*. He was truly an excellent, and good man, possessed of many noble qualities of mind, that would do honor to many white men, laying claims to refinement and intelligence. He was possessed of great dignity, sobriety, and prudence, and was particularly noted for his extreme kindness to the whites and missionaries. He was the most intimate and valued friend of Conrad Weiser, who entertained great respect for him. On several important occasions, he attended the sittings of the Provincial Council, at Philadelphia, and performed embassies between the Government of Pennsylvania and the *Six Nations*. Conrad Weiser visited him frequently at his house, in Shamokin, on business for the Government, and was in turn visited by him, at Tulpehocken. He had several sons, one of which was *Logan*, the *Mingo* chief, and another, named *Taghneghdoarus*, who was the eldest, and who assumed the duties of chief after the death of his father.

In the decease of this Indian chief, the whites lost the best and truest friend they ever had among the tawny sons of the forest. Loskiel, who knew him well, thus speaks of him: "Being the first magistrate, and head chief of all the *Iroquois* Indians living on the banks of the Susquehanna, as far as Onondaga, he thought it incumbent upon him to be very circumspect in his dealings with the white people. He mistrusted the brethren at first, but, upon discovering their sincerity, became their firm and real friend. Being much engaged in political affairs, he had learned the art of concealing his sentiments, and, therefore, never contradicted those who endeavored to prejudice his mind against the missionaries, though he always suspected their motives. In the last years of his life, he became less reserved, and received those brethren, who came to Shamokin, into his house. He assisted them in building, and defended them against the insults of the drunken Indians; being himself never addicted to drinking, because, as he expressed it, he never wished to become a fool. He had built his house upon pillars, for safety, in which he always shut himself up when any drunken frolic was going on in the village. In this house, Bishop Johannas Von Watterville, and his company, visited and preached the Gospel to him. It was then that the Lord opened his heart; he listened with great attention; and, at last, with tears, respected the doctrine of a crucified Jesus, and received it in faith. During his visit in Bethlehem, a remarkable change took place in his heart, which he could not conceal. He found comfort, peace and joy, by faith in his Redeemer, and the brethren considered him a candidate for baptism; but hearing that he had been already baptized by a Roman Catholic priest, in Canada, they only endeavored to impress his mind with a proper idea of his sacramental ordinance, upon which he destroyed a small idol that he wore about his neck. After his return to Shamokin, the grace of God bestowed upon him was truly manifested, and his behavior was remarkably peaceable and contented. In this state of mind he was taken ill, was attended by Rev. David Zeisberger, and in his presence, fell happy asleep in the Lord, in full assurance of obtaining eternal life, through the merits of Jesus Christ."

He was buried in the Indian burying-ground, above town, where his dust still sleeps, if it has not been washed away by the inroads of the river upon the bank. A slight transposition of the words of Longfellow seem to breathe the sadness of the good man's absence:

"Many moons and many winters
Have gone by since he departed,
But the Master of Life had called him
To the realms of light and morning.
On this shore stood *Shickelemy*,
Turned and waved his hand at parting,
Moved into the purple sunset,
By the Blue Hill, up the West Branch;
And the Indians gazing after,
Watched him floating, rising, sinking,
Said, 'Farewell, Oh! *Shickelemy*!'
And the melancholy forest,
Moved through all its depth of darkness,
Whispering, 'Farewell, *Shickelemy*!'
And the waves upon the pebbles,
Rising, rippling on Cake's margin,
Said, 'Farewell, oh! *Shickelemy*!'
Thus this Christian chief departed
From the presence of his people,
To the islands of the blessed,
To the kingdoms of Ponemah."

Upon the death of *Shickelemy*, Governor Hamilton sent Conrad Weiser to Shamokin to let the children and grand-children of the deceased chief know that the Governor of Pennsylvania and his council, condoled with them for the death of their father, and to give them a small present in order to wipe off their tears, according to the custom of the Indians. The present consisted of six strowd match-coats and seven shirts with a string of wampum. Another string of wampum was also given to *Taghneghdoarus*, *Shickelemy's* eldest son.

Shickelemy's death was the beginning of evil days. His son was made chief, but was unable to restrain his people.

In 1755, the French formed an alliance with the Indians, promising to recover and give them back their lands upon the Susquehanna. Large bodies of French and Indians had crossed the Allegheny mountains, for the purpose of murdering, scalping and burning. It was the intention of the French to overrun this portion of the country and erect fortifications at different points, making Shamokin their headquarters. This fact was reported to the Provincial Government, by Andrew Montour, with a recommendation, that a fort be immediately erected at Shamokin, for defence.

Soon after, in the autumn of 1755, the inhabitants on Penn's Creek were attacked, many of them killed, and twenty-five taken prisoners. Their houses were burned and crops destroyed. This was the

FIRST INDIAN MASSACRE IN PENNSYLVANIA.

Forty-six of the settlers fled to Sunbury for protection, but the behavior of the Indians here was so suspicious, that they left on the following day, and were fired upon by Indians in ambush below Sunbury, having four more of their number killed.

Shortly after the massacre on Penn's Creek, the Moravian mission at Shamokin was broken up, and the settlers fled to Bethlehem. This they were compelled to do in order to save their lives, as the Indians were very rude, and probably would have murdered them if they had remained much longer.

Still later in the autumn, the Indians again appeared in considerable numbers around the Shamokin region, and during the following month committed several barbarous murders upon the remaining whites. No particulars, however, are preserved.

SHAMOKIN DESTROYED.

About this time the Indians abandoned the town of Shamokin, probably on account of fear of the English, who were expected there in a considerable force, to erect a fort and make preparation for the defence of the frontier. On the 3d of June, 1756, a scout, consisting of George Allen, Abe Loverhill, James Crupton, John Gallaher, John Murrah, and Robert Eyer, were sent up the river to reconnoitre the enemy at Shamokin. They reported that they arrived there on Saturday night, and, not observing any enemy, went to the place where the town had been, but found all the houses consumed, and no trace of it left. They remained there till ten o'clock the next day, but observed no signs of Indians.

Thus was the ancient town of Shamokin destroyed by its own inhabitants. It seemed that they were anxious to obliterate all trace of their settlement at this point, when they found that the whites were encroaching so rapidly upon their lands. Like the Russians, they were determined to leave nothing behind that could be of any benefit to the enemy. Shamokin, in having been such an important point among them, from time immemorial, was left, no doubt, with regret; and the dusky warrior, as he turned into the forest, could not refrain from looking back at the spot he loved so well, that was to be abandoned forever. The flames of the burning wigwams lighted up the gloom of the surrounding wilderness; the little pappooses clung closer to their mothers, and looked wistfully around. This closes the first act in the drama.

ERECTION OF FORT AUGUSTA.

It being fully determined by the Provincial Government to erect a fort at Shamokin, instructions were issued to Col. Wm. Clapham, by Governor Morris, in June, 1756, as follows:

"Herewith you will also receive two Plans of Forts, the one a Pentagon, the other a Square with one Ravelin to Protect the Curtain where the gate is, with a ditch, covered way, and Glacis. But as it is impossible to give any explicit directions, the Particular form of a fort, without viewing and Considering the ground on which it is to stand, I must leave it to you to build it in such form as will best answer for its own Defence, the command of the river and of the Country in its neighbourhood, and the Plans herewith will serve to show the Proportion that the Different parts of the works should bear to Each other.

"As to the place upon which this fort is to be erected, that must be in a great measure left to your Judgment; but it is necessary to inform you that it must be on the East side of the Susquehana, the Lands on the West at ye forks & between the branches not being Purchased from the Indians, besides which it would be impossible to relieve and support a garrison on that side in the winter time. From all the Information I have been able to Collect, the Land on ye south side of the east branch, opposite the middle of the Island, is the highest of any of the low land thereabout, and the best place for a fort, as the Guns you have will form a Rampart of a moderate highth, command the main river; but as those Informations come from persons not acquainted with the nature of such things, I am fearfull they are not much to be depended on, and your own Judgment must therefore direct you.

"When you have completed the fort you will cause the ground to be cleard about it, so to a convenient distance and openings to be made to the river, and you will Erect such buildings within the fort and place them in such a manner as you shall Judge best.

"Without the fort, at a convenient distance, under the command of the Guns, it will be necessary to build some log houses for Indians, that they may have places to Lodge in without being in the fort where numbers of them, however friendly, should not be admitted but in a formal manner, and the guard turned out, this will be esteemed a compliment by our friends, and if enemies should at any time be concealed under that name, it will give them proper notions of our vigilance and prevent them from attempting to surprise it.

"As soon as you are in Possession of the Ground at Shamokin, you will secure your self by a breast work in the best manner you can, so that your men may work in safety, and you will inform me of your arrival there, and let me know what you will have occasion for that I may apply to the Commissioners to supply it."

This extract embraces the principal part of the instructions relating to this point, and may be found at length in the Archives of the State, pages 667 and 668.

When Col. Clapham received these instructions he was at Fort Halifax, at the mouth of Armstrong's Creek, thirty-two miles below Shamokin, with a body of several hundred men. He had a number of mechanics also engaged in building boats for the transportation of their provisions and munitions of war. These boats were pushed against the current. Navigating the river at that time, and in such a manner, was very laborious as well as dangerous; for the savages were constantly on the lookout to surprise them. He also manufactured carriages at this place for his cannon, but the number is not given. It is inferred, however, from letters, that he had a number of pieces.

It appears that the Colonel had some difficulty with his men here, on account of pay already due them. Not being able to pay them, on account of the scarcity of funds, some of the soldiers, and the bateau-men, became very obstreperous, and refused to perform their duty. The latter were Dutchmen, according to his account, and twenty-six in number. They were arrested and confined for mutiny.

The following extract is from a memorandum made in 1802, by Colonel Samuel Miles, of the Revolutionary army:

"We crossed the Susquehanna and marched on the west side thereof, until we came opposite where the town of Sunbury now stands, where we crossed over in batteaux, and I had the honor of being the first man who put his foot on shore at landing. In building the Fort at Shamokin, Capt. Levi Trump and myself had the charge of the workmen, and after it was finished our battalion remained there as garrison until the year 1758."

In July, 1756, Col. Clapham arrived at Shamokin, with a command of about four hundred men. Temporary breastworks were hastily thrown up for their better protection, and preparations made to build a fort without delay. The men, however, were much dissatisfied about their pay, and it was with great difficulty that they could be restrained from returning. Matters finally assumed such a serious aspect, that on the 13th of July a council was held in the camp, to take into consideration what was best to be done. As it shows clearly the troubles encountered by the commander, and forms an important feature in the history of Fort Augusta, we copy it entire, as follows:

"Present—all the officers of Col. Clapham's Regiment, except Capt. Miles, who Commands the Garrison at Fort Halifax.

"The Subalterns complain, that after expectation given them by several Gentlemen, Commissioners, of receiving seven Shillings Six Pence each Lieut., & five Shillings & Six Pence each Ensign per day, the Commissary has received Instructions to pay a Lieut. but five shillings and six pence, and an Ensign four Shillings.

"Capt. Salter affirms, that the Gentlemen Commissioners assur'd him that the Subalterns pay was Augmented from five Shillings to the sums mention'd above.

"Lieut. Davies reports, that Mr. Fox assured him that the pay of a Lieut. in this Regiment would be Established at seven Shillings & six Pence per Day, and that Mr. Peters, the Provincial Secretary, told the same as a thing concluded upon, but hinted at the same time that he might expect but five shillings and six pence per Day, before he came into the Regiment.

"Lieut. Garraway says, that Mr. Hamilton told him at Dinner, at Mr. Cunninghams, that the Pay of a Captain in this Regiment was to be ten Shillings, a Lieutenants seven Shillings and six pence, & an Ensign five Shillings & Sixpence.

"Capt. Lloyd says, that Mr. Hughs, one of the Gentlemen Commissioners told him the same thing.

"The Gentlemen Officers beg leave to Appeal to his Honor, the Governor, as an Evidence that that Opinion Universally Prevailed thro'out the Regiment, and thinking themselves unjustly dealt with by the Gentlemen Commisers., are Unanimously Determined not to Honor their most hearty and sincere thanks for the Favours received, the grateful impression of which they shall never forget, and at the same time request a permission from your Honor to Resign on the Twentieth day of Augst next, desiring to be relieved accordingly.

"[Signed] Levi Trump, Patrick Davis, Daniel Clark, Chas. Garraway, Asher Clayton, Wm. Anderson, John Hambright, William Plunket, Sam. Jno. Atlee, Chas. Brodhead, Wm. Patterson, Joseph Scott, John Morgan, Samuel Miles, James Bryan, Pat. Allison."

From this document, which may be found on page 700 of the Pennsylvania Archives, volume first, it will be perceived that considerable difficulty existed between the government and the officers, which threatened seriously to impair the harmony that should exist between them.

James Young, who appears to have been a paymaster in the service of the government, visited Shamokin about this time, and found great confusion and dissatisfaction existing among the officers. On the 18th of July, 1756, he wrote a long letter to Gov. Morris, detailing the troubles in the camp. Col. Clapham, he states, was much displeased, on account of there not being a sufficiency of money forwarded to pay the troops. He complained loudly, of what he termed his ill usage, and went so far as to threaten to leave the service, and join the Indians, if something was not done soon.

Young, it appears, did not pay any of the officers, on account of their claiming more than he was instructed to allow them. All of them, with the exception of three or four, had been under arrest by order of the Colonel, and released at his pleasure without trial. *He* much doubted the propriety of building a fort at this point, as there was great danger of it being deserted by the men, and given up to the enemy.

On the same day, Colonel Clapham and James Burd, wrote a long letter to Gov. Morris, setting forth their grievances as follows:

SHAMOKIN, July 18th, 1756.

"*Sir:* I am desir'd herewith to Transmit to your Honor the result of a Council held at the Camp at Shamokin, July the 13th, in consequence of a disappointment in the Pay of ye Subalterns, from wch it will appear to your Honor that they think themselves ill treated by the Gentlemen Commissioners, whose Honor they rely'd on and several of whose promises they recite in Regard to their Pay, and that they are unanimously determined to resign their Commissions on the 20th day of August next if the respective Promises and Assurances of the Gentlemen Commissioners on that Head are not fully Comply'd with before that time.

"I further beg leave to address your Honor with a Complaint in behalf of myself, and the other Captains and Officers of this Regiment. I had the honor to receive from you, Sr., a Commission as Captain in the Regiment under my command, dated March the 29th, for which the Gentlemen Commissioners, notwithstanding it was represented to them, have been pleased to withhold my pay and Assign'd as a Reason that a man can execute but one Office at a time, and ought to devote his whole service to it, which is not only an unjust remark, but affronting to all Gentlemen who have the Honor to hold directly from his Majesty's officers more than one Commission at the same time, by supposing them deficient in some part of their Duty, and is virtually an invective against the Government of Great Britain itself. They have likewise been pleased to deal with Mayor Burd upon the same principles and have paid him only as a Captain, which must be confessed is a very concise method of reducing without the Sentence or even the Sanction of a Court Martial.

"The several Captains think themselves affronted by the Commissrs Instructions to the Commissary to pay but two Sergeants and forty-eight Private Men in each Company, notwithstanding two Corporals and one Drummer were appointed in each Company by your Honor's express Command, this instruction appears to them also as a contempt of your Honor's Orders, and have accordingly paid these non-commissioned officers out of their own Pockets.

STEVENS SCHOOL BUILDING, THIRD ST. SHAMOKIN, NORTH^D CO. PA.

PENROSE SCHOOL BUILDING, FRANKLIN ST. SHAMOKIN. NORTH^D CO. PA.

ACADEMY BUILDING,
COR. ARCH & EIGHTH STS., SHAMOKIN, NORTH^D COUNTY, PA.

CENTRAL SCHOOL BUILDING, SUNBURY ST. SHAMOKIN, NORTH^D CO. PA.

"I entered into this service at the Solicitation of some of the Gentlemen Commissioners, in Dependence on Promises, which they have never performed, and have acted ever since not only in two Capacities but in twenty, having besides the Duties of my Commissions as Col. & Captain been obliged to discharge those of an Engineer and Overseer at the same time, and undergone in the Service incredible Fatigues without Materials and without thanks. But as I am to be paid only as a Col. I intend while I remain in this Service only to fulfill the Duties of that Commission, which never was yet supposed to include building forts and ten thousand other Services which I have performed, so that the Gentlemen Commissioners have only to send Engineers, Pioneers and other Laborers, with the necessary Teams and Utensils, while I, as Col. preside over the Works, see that your Honor's orders are punctually executed, & only Defend the Persons engaged in the Execution of them. In pursuance of a resolution of your Honor and the Gentlemen Commissioners to allow me an Aid-De-Camp who was to be paid as a Supernumerary Capt. in the Regiment; I according appointed Capt. Lloyd as my Aid-De-Camp on April 2d, 1756, who has ever since acted as such in the most Fatiguing and disagreeable Service on Earth, and received only Captain's Pay.

"Your Honor was pleased to appoint Lieut. Clayton Adjutant to the Regiment under my command by a Commission, bearing date the 24th day of May, 1756, but the Gentlemen Commissrs have, in Defiance of all known rules, resolved that an Officer can Discharge but one Duty in a day, and have paid him only as a Lieutenant. Impowered by your Honor's orders, and in Compliance with the Exigencies of the Services, I hir'd a number of Battoe men at 2-6 per day, as will appear by the return made herewith to your Honor, and upon demanding from the Paymaster General money for the Payment of the respective Ballances due to them, was surprized to find that the Commissy had by their instrdctions restraing him from Paying any incidental Charges whatever, as thinking them properly Cognizable only by themselves.

"'Tis extremely Cruel, Sr, and unjust to the last degree That men who cheerfully ventured their lives in the most dangerous and Fatiguing services of their Country, who have numerous Families dependant on their labor, and who have many of them while they were engaged in that service, suffered more from the neglect of their Farms and Crops at home than the Value of their whole pay. In short, whose Affairs are ruined by the Services done their Country should some of them receive no pay at all for these services, if this is the case I plainly perceive that all Service is at an end, foresee that whoever has the command of this Garrison will inevitably be Obliged to Abandon his Post very shortly for want of a Suply of Provisions. Your Honor will not be surprized to hear that in a government where its Servants are so well rewarded I have but one Team of Draught Horses, which, according to the Commissioners remark, can but do the Business of one Team in a day from whence you will easily Judge that the Works must proceed very slowly and the Expence in the end be proportionable.

"Permit me, Sr, in the most grateful manner to thank your Honor for the Favour conferred on me and on the Regiment under my command which I am sensible were meant as well in Friendship to the Province as myself. I have executed the trust Reposed in me with all Possible Fidelity and to the best of my Knowledge, but my endeavors as well as those of every other Officer in the Service have met with so ungenerous a Return so contracted a Reward that we can no longer serve with any Pleasure on such terms. And if we are not for the Future to receive from your Honor our Orders, our Supplys and our Pay beg Leave unanimously to resign on the Twentieth of August next, & will abandon the Post accordingly at that time, in which Case I would recommend it to the Gentlemen Commissioners to take great Care to prevent that universal Desertion of the men which will otherwise certainly ensue.

"Thus much I thought it necessary to say in my own Vindication, and I am besides by the rest of the Gentlemen requested to add, that they have still further cause of Complaint from a Quarter where they little expected it, & are conscious to themselves they never deserved it, esteeming much higher their treatment from the other Gentlemen Commissioners in regard to their Pay than the ungenerous Reflections of one of those Gentlemen on the Conduct of an Expedition which it too plainly appears it was never his Study to Promote, and will appeal to their Country and to your Honor for ye Justice of their Conduct in the present Step.

"'Tis with utmost concern and Reluctance that the Gentlemen of this Regiment see themselves reduced to the necessity of this Declaration and assure your Honor that nothing but such a Continued series of Discouragements could have ever extorted it from those who hope that they have not used any Expressions inconsistent with that high Regard they have for your Honor, and beg leave with me to Subscribe themselves

"Your Honor's

Most obedient humble Servant,

WILL'M CLAPHAM,
JAMES BURD."

Notwithstanding these complaints, the government was slow to supply the wants of the soldiers, occasioned no doubt by the scarcity of funds and provisions. The command of Colonel Clapham still remained at Shamokin, and on the 14th of August, 1756, he again writes to Governor Morris that their wants were still unsupplied, and that they only had about half a pound of powder to each man, and none for the cannon. Their stock of provisions was also low—winter was approaching, and the prospect of famine stared them in the face, unless a supply was laid in. Boats had been despatched to Harris' for flour, but they encountered so much danger in passing down to Halifax, that their safe return was almost despaired of.

In this same letter the Colonel informs the Governor that he was obliged to put Lieutenant Plunkett under arrest for mutiny, and only awaited the arrival of the Judge Advocate, to have him tried by court-martial.

Notwithstanding the difficulties that existed in the command of Colonel Clapham, and the threats of the officers, that they would throw up their commissions, and abandon the post by the 20th of August, if they were not paid, it nowhere appears that any of them carried this threat into execution. The commanding officer, no doubt, on more deliberate and calm reflection, came to the conclusion that they had a savage and wiley enemy to contend with, and that it was absolutely necessary for their own preservation, that defences should speedily be erected, to guard the frontier against their incursions. In view of this, and the more patriotic feelings that triumphed over the minor considerations of personal bickerings, the work of erecting Fort Augusta steadily progressed. In September they received some supplies from below, which tended to revive their drooping spirits. Previous to this, the men were placed upon short allowances of flour.

Peter Burd writes to Governor Morris, September 14th, 1756, and states, "that the fort is now almost finished, and a fine one it is; we want a large flag to grace it." They had labored, it appears, indefatigably, for some six weeks, upon the works. The commanding officer was in a better humor, and about this time, informs Benjamin Franklin, that, in his opinion, this post is of the utmost consequence to the Province, and that it is defensible against all the power of musketry. From its position, however, he feared that it was more exposed to a descent on the West Branch, and recommended that it be made stronger.

It may be interesting to the people of Sunbury, to know what kind of provisions, the quantity, and the materials of war, were possessed by the garrison of Fort Augusta, one hundred years ago. In view of this, I transcribe the first report of the Commissary, Peter Burd, made in September, 1756, as follows:

Provisions in Store, September ye 1st.

46 bbs. beef and pork.	5 do. of peas.
9 do. of flour.	1 Bullock.

Brought up September ye 1st.

3 cwt. powder.	11 frying pans.
6 do. of Lead.	1 Stock Lock.
92 pair shoes.	A Lump of Chalk.
4 Lanthorns.	27 bags flour about 5,000 cwt.
1,301 Grape shot.	4 Iron Squares.
46 hand granades.	12 Carpenter's Compasses.
58 Cannon ball.	1 ream writing paper.
50 blankets.	4 quires Cartridge Do.
4 brass kettles.	Some match rope very ordinary.
6 falling axes.	33 head of Cattle.

About this time, William Denny was appointed Governor of the Province of Pennsylvania. Colonel Clapham wrote him a long letter, stating the condition of the garrison, and the amount of pay due them. Many of the soldiers left families that had become very destitute, and the government should do something to alleviate their wants. The Colonel stated that he had advanced all the money he could raise, besides borrowing, and now was without a single farthing in his pocket. His men frequently deserted, and no wonder. At this time he had three hundred and twenty under his command, which was an inadequate number to protect the frontier, and carry on the work on the fort at the same time. One hundred men were constantly employed in transporting provisions for the rest; and yet, owing to the difficulties they had to encounter, they never were able to get much of a supply ahead; and it was very necessary that a stock of provisions to last six months should be on hand.

A short time after this, in another letter to Governor Denny, Colonel Clapham says, in conclusion:

"'Two bushels of Blue Grass Seed are necessary wherewith to sow the Slopes of the Parapet & Glacis, and the Banks of the River—in eight or ten Days more the Ditch will be carried quite round the Parapet, the Barrier Gates finished and Erected, and the Pickets of the Glacis completed—after which I shall do myself the Honor to attend your command in person."

In due course of time Fort Augusta was completed, and was one of the strongest, as well as most important, of all the frontier forts built at that gloomy period of our history. The following description of it is taken from the original drawing in London, a copy of which may be found in the State Library at Harrisburg, and is undoubtedly correct in every respect:

"Fort Augusta stands at about forty yards from the river on a bank twenty-four feet from the surface of the water. The side which fronts the river is a strong palisade, the bases of the logs being sunk four feet into the earth, the top hollowed and spiked into strong ribbond which run transversely and are morticed into several logs at twelve feet distance from each other, which are larger and higher than the rest, the joints between each palisade with five logs well fitted on the inside and supported by the platform—the other three sides are composed of logs laid horizontally, neatly dovetailed and trunnelled down, they are squared; some of the lower end three feet in diameter, the least from two feet and a half to eighteen inches diameter, and are mostly white oak."

Doubtless the action of the water has considerably worn away the banks from what they were at that day, for it is less than "forty yards" from the spot where the fort stood to the bank of the river.

In 1757 or 1758, Major James Burd succeeded Colonel Clapham, in the command of Fort Augusta. At this time they had the fort placed in a good condition, to resist the attack of an enemy. Below I annex a copy of the report of military stores, made December 6, 1758, by Adam Henry:

"12 Pieces of Cannon in good order.
2 Swivels in good order.
4 Blunderbusses in good order.
700 Rounds of cannon balls.
123 Bags of grape shot.
383 Cartridges of powder, made for cannon.
112 Cartridges of powder, made for swivels.
12 Barrels of powder.
46 Hand granades.
29 Rounds of cut shot."

With this amount of *material* of war on hand, there is no doubt but the garrison would have made a formidable show of resistance.

Time passed on. Nothing very remarkable occurred at Fort Augusta for several years. We have accounts of various Indian meetings being held here, however; speeches being made by the chiefs, and other business transacted.

Captain Gordon, who acted in the capacity of Engineer, recommended that a substantial magazine be erected in one of the bastions of the fort. His description of the manner in which it should be constructed is very precise, and as it is in a tolerably good state of preservation, we copy his specifications as follows:

"A Magazine ought to be built in the South Bastion, 12 by 20 feet in the clear, also a Labratory of the same dimensions in the East Bastion. The Wall of the Magazine to be 2½ Foot thick, with three Buttresses, 2 Foot thick at the bottom, levelling to 9 inches at Top, in each side. The breadth of Buttresses, 3½ Feet. The Magazine to have an arch of 2½ Brick thick, and to be under ground within 1½ Foot of the Top of the Arch. The Walls seven foot high from the Level of the Floor, and to have a Foundation 2 Foot below the Floor; great care taken to lay the Joists, and to fill up between with Rubble Stone and Gravel, rammed; the Joists to be covered with Plank 2½ inch thick. An Air Hole, 1 foot Square to be practised in the Gavel end, opposite the Door. The Passage to the Magazine to have a zigzag, and over the Arch some Fine Plaister laid, then covered with Fine Gravel, and 4 foot of Earth a Top.

"The Laboratory likewise to be arched, but with 1½ brick and without Buttresses.

"A Fraise ought to be completed round the Fort, to be introduced upon the Horizontal Line at 20 Degrees of Elevation, or as much as will be sufficient to discover it underneath from the Flanks. This Fraise to be 2½ feet in the Ground, 3½ without, not to exceed 5 inches in Thickness, the Breadth from 4 to 7; a number of these Fraises ought, before set in the Wall, to be tunnelled on a Peice of Slab or Plank, of 5 inches broad, within 6 inches of the ends, which gives an inch at the end clear of the Slab; the distance from one to another 2½. After made fast to this Slab, to be introduced in the Wall and the Earth ramm'd well between. When the Earth is well fixed and the whole set round, or a considerable way, another Peice of 8 inches broad and 2 thick, should be nailed al along close to the wall, which will bind the whole very fast together."

This document bears date, May 6th, 1758. It is rendered more interesting at the present day, as the magazine can yet be seen. It will probably last for many years to come.

In July following, a small reinforcement arrived at the fort. The total number of available men, including officers, in the garrison, at this time, amounted to but one hundred and eighty-nine. They were pretty well supplied, however, with munitions of war, and could have made a formidable stand against superior numbers.

The commanding officers received instructions to confine all the French deserters, that had been enlisted as soldiers, and send them under guard to Lancaster Jail. This was to prevent them from again joining the French, on their expedition from *Chingle-clamoos*. About this time a new flag-staff, seventy feet in height, was erected, but unfortunately their old colors were entirely worn out, and they had to wait some time for the arrival of new ones.

John Shickelemy, who, during the French and Indian war, had become estranged from the English, appears again about Shamokin, in 1759 or 1760. The Governor, it seems, sent him a string of wampum and solicited his attendance at a council to be held at the fort. He also extended to him his hand, thanked him sincerely, and greeted him as a friend. This was to gain his esteem, for *Shickelemy* had been a little treacherous; he attended the conference, and after it was over, requested some provisions to last him home. They gave him a hundred weight of flour and some meat, and he started in fine spirits. Nothing further of any importance is reported to have transpired about the fort, until July 12th, 1762, when quite an excitement was raised on a report of liquor being furnished the Indians. The Indian Agent informed Lieutenant Graydon, who had command in the absence of Colonel Burd, that he had detected his (Colonel Burd's) store-keeper in selling liquor to them, and had sufficient proof to convict him. He demanded of the Lieutenant that the liquor be seized, and as the instructions from the Governor were strict, he was obliged to do it. The store-keeper, however, denied the fact. It appeared that Mr. Holland, Colonel Burd's good friend, had been posted at a "peep-hole," made in the wall in the adjacent house, from whence he could see in the Colonel's store; and the proof was that he saw some squaws in the house with the store-keeper—that one of them asked for rum, and showed a dollar, on which the door was closed, and the rum delivered to her. Lieutenant Graydon was accused of being in the store at the same time. He was very much incensed about it, and admitted having been there, but saw no liquor sold to them. He forthwith informed Colonel Burd of the accusation, who wrote from Lancaster, under date of July 18th, 1762, as follows:

"I am pestered with that fellow, Nathaniel Holland, Clerk to the Indian Store, at Fort Augusta. He has accused Mr. Dennis McCormick, my clerk, for Issuing Provisions at that place, with having carried on a trade with the Indians, in consequence of which he has seized all the Rum in Store, and he further says that this Clandestine Trade is carried on by my Particular orders. Mr. Holland has sent an Express to Philadelphia, and Mr. McCormick has come down to me here, and in order that this letter may come to your hand soon and safe, I have sent him with it to you.

"Inclosed is Mr. McCormick's Deposition, which was taken here, as I intended to have sent him back to Augusta, if I could have forwarded my letters by a safe hand to Philadelphia, but failing of this, I am under the necessity of sending himself.

"Now, Sir, as to a trade being carried on with the Indians By me, for me, by my Clerk, by the Officers, or Garrison of Fort Augusta, or in any manner, or in any way whatsoever, at Fort Augusta, to my knowledge, I hereby declare to be absolutely False, & to the truth of this I am ready & willing to take my oath in any words that the Commissioners, or even that Scoundrell Holland would commit to paper, and further, I can procure if Necessary the oaths of the Officers and Garrison of Augusta to the same purpose, & of every person living on the Susquehanna, from Harris's to Augusta, that I never brought a skin, or any other Indian Commodity whatever to their knowledge from Augusta.

"You will observe by the Deposition that Mr. McCormick did want of an Indian Squa, a thin Indian dressed winter Skin to line a pair of plush britches for himself, which he was getting; if this is the ground of the Complaint, it must appear to his Hon'r the Gov'r & Commisers to be intirely malitious in Holland, & not from a well grounded zeal of serving his Country.

"It Really vexes me much to be eternally plagued in this manner by Holland, and the more so that it is an accusation of the highest breatch of trust for me to break a well known Law of that Government whose bread I daily eat.

"I must, therefore, beg your friendly offers in laying the state of the case clearly before the Governor, if Necessary; and if this affair is represented to my disadvantage, that you would represent it as it really is, & you are fully at liberty to show this letter to any Person whatsoever, as I shall support it in every particular, etc."

From the tone of this letter, it will readily be inferred that Colonel Burd was not in the best humor when he wrote. How the matter was finally adjusted, or whether anything further grew out of it, does not appear upon record. At a conference with the Indians, held at Lancaster, on Monday, the 23d of August, 1762, Governor Hamilton presiding, *Thomas King*, one of the chiefs and representatives of the *Six Nations*, rose and said:

"Now all the different tribes of us present, desire that you will call your soldiers away from Shamokin, for we have concluded a peace, and are as one brother, having one head and one heart.

"If you take away your soldiers, we desire you would keep your trading house there, and have some *honest* man in it, because our cousins follow their hunting there, and will want a trade. This is the way for us to live peaceably together.

"Brother Onas (the name for Penn:) I must tell you again, these soldiers *must* go away from Shamokin Fort. I desire it, and let there only be traders living there; you know who are the *honest* people; we desire that only *honest* people may live there, and that you will not be too hard with us, when they may buy our skins and furs, and such things as we may have to sell. This will be the way for us to live peaceably together; but for you to keep soldiers there, is not the way to live peaceable. Your soldiers are very often unruly, and our warriors are often unruly; and when such get together, they do not agree, for, as you have now made peace with all our nations, there is no occasion for soldiers to live there any longer."

There is no doubt that the Indians would have been much gratified to have had the garrison removed from Shamokin, as it was a cherished spot where they loved to dwell, and where reposed the mouldering bones of their ancestors. The proposition to place an "*honest*" man there to keep a store, is a scathing commentary upon the probity of the whites, in their dealings with these dusky children of the forest. Judging from the manner in which they dealt with them, it is doubtful whether a man could have been found who would have conducted business in accordance with this old Indian's idea of "*honesty*." It seemed that they were destined to be cheated on every occasion, and in the most shameful manner, too.

The soldiers were not removed from Fort Augusta. Such a course would have proved very bad policy, for the cup of the Indian's destiny was not full, and bloody scenes were yet to be enacted, before he turned his face for the last time upon the blue hills of Shamokin. In 1765, a number of men from Cumberland, in the neighborhood of Carlisle, went up to Shamokin, for the purpose of murdering what Indians they might find there. On the alarm being given, they hastily collected their families together and fled. They came to Shamokin and appeared on the opposite side of the river, next the Blue Hill. Three of them, says Lieutenant Graydon, came over to the fort, and reported that they were from Cumberland County, and that there were fifty of them in company. They alleged that their object was to look at the land on the river, and at the Great Island, where some of them proposed to go and settle. Some of the party returned before they got that far; others went on to the Great Island. Some of them settled where Lock Haven now stands.

"We cannot conjecture," continues the Lieutenant, "what these people's intentions were, but they seemed very inquisitive about Indians, which made us suspect that they had a design against those who were about us."

The names of the three men that came over to the fort, were: John Woods, James McMein, and James Dickey. About this time, a number of Indian families intended settling on the Great Island, and erecting cabins. Whether they went is not definitely known, but it is supposed they did. William Maclay seems to have been the next commander of Fort Augusta, and Colonel Hunter succeeded him. The time when Colonel Hunter assumed the command is not stated, but it was probably about 1770.

Colonel Hunter had command of Fort Augusta during the time of the Revolution, when it was the great point to which all the settlers of both branches converged, when compelled to abandon their homes in the wilderness by the attacks of the savages. All the forts erected along the west branch, were under his supervision, and the duties that devolved upon him were great. He may be considered the watchful guardian of the frontier. Scenes of the most thrilling character were enacted at that period. A fine brick mansion now stands on the identical spot formerly occupied by the fort. It was subsequently owned by Miss Hunter, a lineal descendant of the old colonel. It is now owned by Col. J. W. Cake. Truly, it is built on sacred ground.

Early in the war of the Revolution, the *Seneca* and *Monsey* tribes were in considerable force, and Pine and Lycoming Creeks were almost navigable to the State line for canoes. Fort Augusta at that time was garrisoned by about fifty men, under Colonel Hunter. They were called "a fearless few."

Captain John Brady, at this time, suggested to his friends at Fort Augusta, the propriety of making a treaty with the *Seneca* and *Monsey* tribes, knowing them to be at variance with the *Delawares*. By doing so, it was thought that their friendship and assistance might be secured against the *Delawares*, should they commence any inroads upon the settlements. His proposition was approved of, and petitions were sent to the Council praying the commissioners might be appointed, and Fort Augusta designated as the place of holding the conference. The request was granted, and commissioners were appointed. Notice was given to the two tribes, by Brady and two others selected for the purpose.

They met the chiefs and laid before them the proposition. They appeared to be delighted, and listened to the proposal with pleasure. After smoking the pipe of peace and promising to attend at Fort Augusta on the appointed day, they led them out of the camp, shook hands with them cordially, and parted in seeming friendship.

Brady was very shrewd, feared to trust the friendship so warmly expressed, and took a different route in returning with his company, to guard against being waylaid and surprised.

On the day appointed for holding the treaty, the Indians appeared with their wives and children. The warriors numbered about one hundred, and were dressed in their war costume. Care had been taken to make the fort look as fierce as possible, and every man was at his post.

In former treaties, the Indians had received large presents, and were expecting them here; but finding the fort too poor to give anything of value, (and an Indian never trusts,) all efforts to form a treaty with them proved abortive. They left the fort, however, apparently in good humor, and well satisfied with their treatment, and taking to their canoes, proceeded homeward. The remainder of the day was chiefly spent by the officers and people of the fort in advising means of protection against anticipated attacks of the Indians. Late in the day, Brady thought of Derr's trading-house, and foreboding evil from that point, mounted a small mare he had at the fort, and crossing the north branch, rode with all possible speed. On his arrival, he saw the canoes of the Indians on the bank of the river near Derr's. When near enough to observe, he saw the squaws exerting themselves to the utmost at their paddles to work to his side of the river; and that when they landed they made for thickets of sumach, which grew in abundance on his land to the heighth of a man's head, and very thick upon the ground. He was not slow in conjecturing the cause. He rode on to where the squaws were landing, and saw that they were conveying rifles, tomahawks and knives, into the sumach thickets, and hiding them. He immediately jumped into a canoe and crossed to Derr's trading-house, where he found the Indians brutally drunk. He saw a barrel of rum standing on end before Derr's door, the head out. He instantly overset it, and spilled the rum, saying to Derr, "My God, Frederick, what have you done?" Derr replied: *Dey dells me you gif um no dreet town on the fort, so dinks as I gif one here, als he go home in bease!"*

Next day the Indians started off. They did not soon attack the settlements, but carried arms for their allies, the English, in other parts.

As the Revolution had become general, the most active preparations were made to devise means of defence. Companies of volunteers were raised, and every laudable effort used to induce the patriots of that period to march to the defence of their country. A central committee of safety was established at Philadelphia, and committees in the various counties were organized and under the control of the central committee. The subordinate committees were in correspondence with the central one, and kept it posted up in every movement in their respective districts. A committee of safety for Northumberland County was appointed. They held regular meetings, and kept a record of their proceedings in a large book, kept for the purpose. This book was given to Joseph G. Wallace, of Lewisburg, (deceased,) many years ago, by his uncle, Captain Gray, a Revolutionary hero. It contained the names of the principle men of the County, the business transacted at their meetings, etc., which was very interesting. This book, it is to be regretted, has been carried off and probably lost.

Sherman Day examined the book some fifteen years ago, when he was collecting his Historical Collections of Pennsylvania, and made a few extracts from it. He was compelled to be as brief as possible, as the limits of his work would not permit of lengthy extracts. To him, then, are we indebted for all that has been taken from that interesting, as well as official document.

From it we learn that on the 8th of February, 1776, the following gentlemen, being previously nominated by their respective townships as they then existed, to serve in the committee for the space of six months, met at the house of Richard Malone, at the mouth of Chillisquaque Creek: For Augusta township, John Weitzel, Esq., Alexander Hunter, Esq., Thomas Ball; Mahoning township, William Cook, Esq., Benjamin Allison, Esq., Mr. Thomas Hewet; Turbut township, Captain John Hambright, William McKnight, William Shaw; Muncy township, Robert Robb, Esq., William Watson, John Bucknlew; Bald Eagle township, William Dunn, Thomas Hughes, Alexander Hamilton; Buffalo township, Mr. Walter Clark, William Irwin, Joseph Green; White Deer township, Walter Clarke, Matthew Brown, Marcus Huling.

Captain John Hambrigh was elected chairman, and Thomas Ball, clerk. The field-officers of the battalion of the lower division of the county, were Samuel Hunter, Colonel; William Cook, Lieutenant-Colonel; Casper Weitzel, First Major; Mr. John Lee, Second Major. Those of the upper battalion appear to have been William Plunket, Colonel; James Murray, Lieutenant-Colonel; Mr. John Brady, First Major; Mr. Cookson Long, Second Major.

Each captain was ordered to return at least forty privates. Each battalion consisted of six companies. The captains of the lower battalion were Nicolas Miller, Charles Gillespie, Hugh White, William Scull, James McMahon, William Clarke, and afterwards Captain John Simpson; and of the upper or Colonel Plunket's battalion, Henry Antes, Esq., Samuel Wallis, John Robb, William Murray, William McAlhatton, Simon Cool, David Berry.

THE FIRST PHYSICIAN.

The first physician on the territory of Sunbury was probably Dr. William Plunket. He was related to Samuel Plunket, High Chancellor of Ireland, and was very wealthy. While under the influence of liquor, he, in company with some others, assassinated an English nobleman, and fleeing from justice was smuggled, it is said, on shipboard, from England, in a barrel. Before he left Europe, he was one day in a nail factory, and attracted the attention and sarcasm of a nobleman, in another part of the establishment, who made a bet with one of his comrades that Plunket could not tell the time of day, and sent a servant with his watch to settle the question. Plunket quietly put the watch in his own pocket and told the servant to tell his master to call for it in person, and he would give him the time of day until he was satisfied. The nobleman never came for it, and the Doctor kept it as his life-long companion. He settled at what was then called Harris' Ferry, now the site of Harrisburg. He married a daughter of John Harris, Sr., father of John Harris, who assisted in laying out the city of Harrisburg. Dr. Plunket was a Tory. He and his son-in-law could never agree on the question of American independence. One of his daughters married Samuel Maclay, who was the brother of William Maclay, who was the maternal grand-father of Dr. Awl, now one of the oldest citizens of Sunbury. Another daughter married Mr. —— Richardson; and another a Mr. Bell, both of whom became prominent men and members of Congress. The reason why Doctor Plunket maintained loyalty to the old country was, doubtless, because he bore the title of Baron Fingal, which he would have instantly forfeited by espousing the American cause. Dr. Plunket was a judge and surveyor, as well as a physician. His office was that of the late Ebenezer Greenough, on Front street, adjoining the Episcopal church, now occupied by the venerable David Rockefeller. Dr. Plunket was very tyrannical and cruel in his treatment of offenders. Before the whipping-post was erected, he used to put the heads of criminals through a rail-fence, and thus satisfy the offended law by executing the sentence of the court.

One of the most striking events of Plunket's life, was his daring raid against the squatters, who, claiming the land under the old Penn purchase, had begun settlements in the vicinity of Wyoming. Threats of invasion were sent and returned, until finally Plunket raised a company, marched up towards Wyoming and met the settlers.

The following account of the result is obtained from Dr. Wm. M. Awl, of Columbus, Ohio, (now in his seventy-eighth year,) who remembers hearing the same related to his father, Samuel Awl, by Samuel Harris, who was a participant in the transaction:

As the parties approached each other, William Maclay, a Lieutenant of Captain Plunket's company, raised his gun and was about to shoot a desperate character known as Simon Gurty, for whose head, it is understood, a reward had been offered. Gurty at once took in the situation, and saw that he could save himself, if at all, only by strategy, and instantly cried out—"Is Sam. Harris in this company?" This question had its desired effect and caused a few seconds delay, which Gurty instantly embraced, and "by a nimble use of his legs soon put himself beyond the reach of any ordinary shooting-iron."

Scarcely had Gurty escaped, when a great commotion began in the crowd, and it was discovered that Capt. Plunket was dashing around among the so-called intruders, crying out, "Surrender, you rebels," or words to that effect, at the same time brandishing a large sword and threatening instant annihilation to all who might dare to make any show of resistance. It was a very daring feat, but was quickly and most efficiently performed. The result was that Capt. Plunket and his company captured the enemy, and both parties came down to Chillisquaque, and "most of them got on a drunk," when Wm. Maclay and a servant man by the name of John Ray packed the guns into a canoe and brought them down to Sunbury, after night.

After the death of his wife, Dr. Plunket employed Betty Wyley as housekeeper during the remaining years of his life.

He died in Sunbury, in 1801, having been blind for several years previous, during which time he had ropes stretched around his yard for a guide and support. His remains were interred in the old Sunbury burying-ground.

BLOODY SPRING.

The following extract from a memorandum made in 1802, by Colonel Samuel Miles, of the Revolutionary army, explains the circumstance from which this spring received its name:

"In the summer of 1756, I was nearly taken prisoner by the Indians. At about half-a-mile distant from the fort stood a large tree that bore excellent plums, in an open piece of ground, near what is now called the 'Bloody Spring.' Lieut. S. Atlee (Samuel John Atlee, Col. of Musketry Battalion, and taken prisoner at Long Island) and myself, one day took a walk to this tree to gather plums. While we were there a party of Indians lay a short distance from us concealed in the thicket, and had nearly gotten between us and the fort, when a soldier belonging to a bullock guard not far from us came to the spring to drink. The Indians were thereby in danger of being discovered, and in consequence thereof, fired at and killed the soldier, by which means we got off and returned to the Fort in much less time than we were coming out."

It is said that the blood of this unfortunate man ran down into the spring, and colored its waters a crimson hue, and it was named the "Bloody Spring," in commemoration of this tragical event. The name is preserved to this day, and many curious legends are related concerning it. It is on the original Grant farm, now owned by Mrs. William I. Greenough. The peculiar rocks around the spring have been disturbed in building the railroad, and much of its romantic beauty is lost.

Whether there was more than this one man murdered here, there is no account upon record. This single murder is well authenticated, however, and it is supposed that *it* alone gave rise to the name. The following beautiful legend is perhaps worth preserving:

THE LEGEND OF THE BLOODY SPRING.

Bright sunset lingers on the western hills,
A flood of golden light the valley fills,
The Susquehanna's radiant waters throw
Back to the sky in joy, its crimson glow.
Dim grow the shadows in the woodland deep,
Where the wild pigeon seeks his place of sleep;
Soft steals the Sun's last slant and fading rays
Through the grape arbor's tangled leafy maze
That shades, with many a graceful thick festoon,
The limpid fountain from the heats of noon,
As bubbling up amid the moss so green
Its sparkling waters shine like silver sheen;
And dashing on in many a bright cascade,
Fills its sweet music in the leafy glade.
An Indian warrior, wearied with the chase,
In the cool fountain laves his sun-burnt face,
His arrows casts aside his bow unstrings,
And on the flowery bank himself he flings.
The streamlet's music, in its ceaseless play,
His charmed senses steals in sleep away,
While through his slumber its wild voices seem
Like the strange melody of some sweet dream—
Enchanted notes of a seraphic band
Borne on a zephyr from the spirit land.
Beside him kneels, with all a wife's fond pride,
Lanawileah, his dark, but beauteous bride,
Whom, scarce six moons ago, in desperate war,
He stole from the defeated Delaware,
Braiding a wampum, her loved brave to grace;
And smiling, as she gazes on his face,
To mark the varied changes there express'd,
As blissful dreams float through his peaceful rest.
With wild emotions, her young bosom thrills,
As in a whisper, sweet as 'mid the hills,
Echo the wood notes of the faithful doves,
He faintly breathes the name of her he loves.
Softly she bends to kiss the lips that frame
The liquid syllables of her own name.
But scarce an instant had she lingered there,
When twanged a bow-string on the startled air.
Too surely aimed, the arrow's stony dart
Pierced through her own into the warrior's heart.
And in each other's embrace, closely wound,
Lifeless they lie upon the blood-stained ground.
Their life-blood gushing to the water's side,
Mingles its crimson with the crystal tide,
Until the fount, so clear and bright before,
Seems to well up a flood of purple gore.
Forth from his ambush in the laurel brake,
Hideous in war-paint, springs the Spotted Snake,
A moment stands, and on his fallen foe,
With all the malice, rage and hate can throw
Into his fiend-like eyes, he fiercely glares;
Then from the lifeless head the scalp he tears,
His work of death and vengeance is complete,
Down the deep dell he flies with footsteps fleet;
Night draws her sable mantle round the wood,
And darkness covers up the scene of blood.
Often, as o'er the summer's sky is spread
The sunset's glorious canopy of red,
Old hunter's say, this spring's pure waters vie
With the deep crimson of the western sky;
And oft, as twilight, from the mountain tops,
Her misty veil into the valley drops,
Two dark and shadowy forms may still be seen
Reclining on its bank of mossy green.

JOHN MULLEN. M. L. BITTENBENDER.

SHAMOKIN IRON WORKS.

JOHN MULLEN & CO., PROPRIETORS.

CORNER FRANKLIN AND INDEPENDENCE STS, SHAMOKIN, NORTHUMBERLAND CO, PA.

THE INDIAN BURYING-GROUND.

An extensive Indian burying-ground was located at the upper end of Sunbury, where it seems that hundreds, and for aught we know, thousands of Indians had been consigned to the grave from time immemorial. Years after the white settlers came. They found large quantities of Indian relics and implements of war, consisting of stone-hatchets, pipes, wampum, etc., that were displaced by the spring freshets in the river, which washed away the banks. Skeletons, too, in an upright position were thus exhumed in great numbers.

The spot was doubtless chosen because of its adaptation to their religious belief, and in that light was full of meaning and highly romantic. The fact that it was on a neck of land around which the waters formed a semi-circle, the farthest to the west, made it seem like a favored point, from which their spirits could sail to their fancied hunting-grounds, in the regions of the setting sun. Standing there, they could imagine the spirits of their loved ones passing away, over the river, until the shadows of Blue Hill and the overhanging sycamores of the west branch, hid them everlastingly from human view.

EXCAVATIONS AROUND SUNBURY.

The hills around Shamokin in various places bear marks of having been excavated, but for what purpose it is now impossible to divine, and nothing is left but vague conjecture. It is alleged by some, that the Indians were possessed of the knowledge of the existence of some kind of mineral which they used in considerable quantities.

P. B. Masser, Esq., of Sunbury, describes the remains of what appeared to have been a small furnace, covered by a mound, that was discovered near the bloody spring. It was examined by him in 1854. The bed appeared to have been about six feet square and constructed of stone. It bore every trace of having been subjected to the action of an intense fire, as the sand was baked and blacked in such a manner as not to be mistaken. On giving it a careful examination, several particles of gold was discovered, which he still retains in his possession. A tradition is preserved, that three Englishmen, at a very early period, came here and erected the furnace.

MANORS.

The first surveys made for the Proprietaries were called Manors, in accordance with the custom established by William Penn, and continued by his sons, till the close of the Proprietary Government.

THE FIRST SURVEY.

The first survey ever made in this region was the Manor of Pomfret, including the land on which Sunbury now stands. It was surveyed on the 10th day of December, 1768, and contained 4,766 acres and allowance. The line started at the mouth of Stillhouse Run; thence southward 280 rods; thence over the Catawissa hills, eastward 844 rods; thence southward across the Shamokin creek, 400 rods; thence a little south of the creek, westward to the river, and then up the river to the place of beginning, including all the land from the mouth of Shamokin Creek to Stillhouse Run, and eastward about two-and-three-fourth miles.

SUNBURY LAID OUT.

The town of Sunbury was laid out by John Lukens, Surveyor-General of Pennsylvania, on the second, third, and fourth days of July, 1772, on the level plain a mile south of Fort Augusta. The first house in this new town was erected that same year by Mr. Lukens, and was a frame structure, situated on the north-west corner of Market square. Soon afterwards, another house was built by William Maclay, of stone, which is still standing and is in a good state of repair. It is located on the north side of Arch street, fronting that street and the river. It is now occupied by S. P. Wolverton, Esq.

The third house was built of logs on the south side of Market street, between Third and Fourth streets. The lot is now the property of Maclay Gearhart. At that time, Mungo Reed resided on what was then called Shamokin Island, near the confluence of the two rivers, a few yards above the fort. Thomas Grant, and Colonel Hunter, commander of the fort, lived on farms which they had taken up close by. Robert Murdock, also, had a farm here. These are considered among the first *bona fide* settlers at this point, who formed the nucleus around which the other emigrants clustered.

SUNBURY IN 1772.

In 1772, according to the best and most reliable information obtainable, there was but one house where Sunbury now stands; one at Fort Augusta; one at the Grant farms; one at Shamokin Island; one at Northumberland; and but four between that point and where Milton now stands, where there was one. Between Milton and Muncy hills there were six families, and not more than eight or ten on the river above.

The following correspondence explains itself and may be of interest.

HARRIS'S FERRY, December 25th, 1772.

"*Sir*:—As the six months allowed for patenting the lots in Sunbury are very near expired, I have enclosed a list of all the persons who have taken lots since my last letter to you on the same subject. I have likewise determined not to grant any more until I receive further instructions from you. All the tickets which I have signed are dated 3d July last, and should I continue to grant more, unless I altered the date, there would be a manifest inconsistence in them with regard to the time of patenting.

"As there are not yet any instructions for selling of the Island nor laying out of the out-lots, I would be very well pleased to have liberty to clear out an old Indian field above and adjoining the Gut, which goes out of the east branch. This field is a mile-and-a-half from Sunbury, and as there is nothing but underwood grows in it at present, the cleaning of it would not be destructive of timber. It is true Captain Hunter would readily give me all the leave I could desire, as it will not by any means interfere with him; but I think it best not to meddle with it without at least acquainting you of it. I have enclosed the fees of entrance which I received from the persons mentioned in the list.

"As to the affair of dividing your land on Chillisquaque, I never intended to make any charge respecting it; nor will I. I am very sensible of more important services which you have rendered me, and am only sorry that the land fell so very far short of your own and every other person's expectations respecting it. I am sir, with real respect,

Your most humble servant,

Mr. Tilgham. WM. MACLAY."

FORT AUGUSTA, June 5th, 1773.

"*Sir*:—I sometime ago mentioned to you in one of my letters my desire of having the right of pre-emption of a mill-seat on Shamokin Creek, about a mile-and-three-quarters from Sunbury. I am since informed that sundry others have applied for it, and one man has been declaring his intention of settling and building without any leave. The mill would be of very great service to the town. Jacob Haverling, a mill-carpenter, has offered to be my partner and undertake the building, and as I now have some money which I could spare, I am strongly inclined to join him if the mill-seat could be procured. I must question whether it will be in your favor to give me the answer which would be most agreeable relating to this matter, and indeed would not have troubled you with this, had it not been at the pressing instance of the person who proposes the partnership. I apprehend fifty acres would answer the purpose, including the mill-seat, and if such a thing would be agreed on as to let me have it, I would send down the price of it to Mr. Physick immediately. But as the burthen of advancing the money will be entirely on myself, I would have the grant only to myself. If convenient, I would be glad of a line from you, or a message by the bearer.

"A considerable number of people are very urgent to get lots in Sunbury, and some of them are here with their families who would build immediately. I have prevented some of them from going down by telling them that I would, by this opportunity, write down for leave to grant any of those lots which have never heretofore been granted. A great number of houses are building, and many more would if workmen could be got.

"Vast numbers of people are daily crowding up, and we are happy in the pleasing prospect of having our valleys filled with inhabitants. This is remarkably the case with prospect to the west branch. But alas! we have an east branch, too, which throws a damp over all our expectations. This, however, cannot always last. I am in haste and with the utmost respect,

Your much obliged and humble servant,

James Tilgham, Esq. WM. MACLAY."

THE FIRST STORE

In Sunbury, was opened by William Dewart, in 1775, in a log building, on Chestnut street, between Second street and Center alley, on the site of the present residence of Miss Ann Billington. He afterwards purchased a lot on Market street, where he erected a store and residence.

Mr. Dewart was born in Ireland, in 1740, and emigrated to this country in 1705. He died in 1814.

THE FIRST WEAVER

Was also William Dewart, who had his loom in one corner of the above-named store.

THE FIRST HOTEL

Was kept by Judge Shaffer, who opened a public house as early as 1793, on the corner of Front and Spruce streets, near the old ferry. The building was a two-story log structure, and contained four or five rooms.

THE FIRST WATCHMAKER

Was John Beitzel, who came from Chambersburg and opened the business on what is now Front street, somewhere down town. He afterwards carried on the business in the county jail, where he was put for bigamy.

THE FIRST COURT.

The first court within the present limits of Sunbury, was held at Fort Augusta, April 9th, 1772, before Judge William Plunket and his associate justices. This was the "Court of the Private Sessions of the Peace," and was held under the auspices of the English government. It was called in the twelfth year of the reign, and by the authority of George the Third, by the grace of God, King of Great Britian, France, and Ireland, defender of the faith, etc.

Twelve judges were appointed to hold court, but only six of them, to wit: William Plunket, Samuel Hunter, Caleb Graydon, Thomas Lemon, Robert Moodie, and Benjamin Weiser, then appeared, and were sworn in and took their seats as judges. Eight lawyers were at the same time sworn in as attorneys of said court, to wit: James Wilson, Robert Magraw, Edward Burd, George Noarth, Christian Hooke, James Potts, Andrew Robeson, and Chas. Steculman—the three last named having been first examined in the usual form, touching their fitness to practice law as attorneys of said court. Edward Burd was the first Prosecuting Attorney, and William Maclay the first Prothonotory of the County. The judges were equal to each other in authority, but William Plunket, the first one named in their commission, acted as the President of the Court. George Nagel, then high sheriff of Berks County, acted as the sheriff of Northumberland County, until his place was supplied by William Cook, who was the first regular sheriff of our County. John Brady was the foreman of the first Grand Jury, which sat at Fort Augusta, in August, 1772.

The vault of the old fort was used as a jail. The first suit was James Patton *vs.* James Gally; Magaw, for plaintiff, and Wilson and Noarth, for defendant.

The first jury trial was William Simpson *vs.* Cornelius Atkinson, verdict for defendant in ejectment.

Among the early suitors, were Christian Gundy, ancestor of the late Superintendent of Schools, in Union County *vs.* Lodwick Derr, owner of a farm where Lewisburg now stands, afterwards called Deerstown, then Lewisburg.

The first deed was recorded June 8th, 1772, in Deed Book A, page 1. William Lee to S. Young and William Giffin, for 300 acres of land of Penn's Creek. It was acknowledged before Esquire Hunter, at Fort Augusta. The deeds recorded since have filled 63 volumes.

The first mortgage was recorded August 31st, in Deed Book A, page 7. William Scull to Edward Biddle and others, covering 154½ acres where Northumberland now stands.

The first letters of administration were granted to Magdalena Weiant, on the estate of her husband, Michael Weiant, dec'd., on the 18th day of December, 1772.

The first will recorded was on the 4th day of August, 1774, by Joseph Rotten. The witnesses to this will, were James McCoy and Samuel Mather. Mr. Rotten gave his eldest daughter a bed and a black cow.

The first motion made in Sunbury court was to divide Northumberland County into townships. In pursuance of which, it was divided into Penn, Augusta, Turbut, Buffalo, Bald Eagle, Muncy, and Wyoming. Out of these seven townships have since been taken twenty-six of the counties of the State. The first constable in Augusta township, then including Sunbury, was Alexander Grant.

The first road petition was for a highway leading from here to Muncy. The first licenses for the sale of intoxicating drink were granted in 1776—nine in number. The first Commonwealth suit brought in Sunbury court, was the King *vs.* Thomas Williams, *alias* Thomas Adams, for larceny. The second and third suits were against the same man for the same offence. He plead *not guilty*, but the jury thought he was mistaken, and he was sentenced in each case to return the stolen property, to pay a fine of five pounds, and receive over his bare back at the commons whipping-post twenty-one lashes, and stand committed in the magazine of the fort until the sentence was complied with. The whippings were ordered for the 30th of September, and the 1st and 2d of October, 1772. This was a prescription on the cumulative plan, and might have been very unpleasant for Thomas, had he not managed to break jail.

The first Prothonotary, Register and Recorder, (then one office,) was William McClay. He was also the first representative in Congress from Northumberland County. The first Sheriff was William Cook. The first Treasurer was Alexander Hunter. The first District Attorney was Edward Burd. Hunter was also the first representative in the Legislature of Pennsylvania.

In 1778, the massacre at Williamsport occurred, and the people came pouring into Sunbury from all the regions above. Men were shot or tomahawked, women scalped alive, and children killed or carried into the wilderness. The Sunbury people received those who escaped, and provided for them as best they could. Colonel Broadhead, with one hundred and forty men came to their relief.

On the 8th of August, 1778, James Brady, son of Captain John Brady, was brought to his mother's house in Sunbury, having been scalped below Williamsport, by an Indian whose name he gave. His brother afterwards killed the Indian on the Allegheny. In the same or the following year, Robert Lyon was sent with a canoe loaded with stores up to Wyoming. There were some very pretty daughters of a Mr. Fisher, living at Fishing Creek, and Robert, forgetting that he was captain of the first grand inland and international line of communication up the north branch, left his boat and cargo at the water's edge, and went to see the girls! In this way many a young man has got himself into trouble, and Robert was not an exception, for the Indians came and took him to Erie and made him run the gauntlet. He there fell into the hands of a British officer who proved to be a long-lost brother, and was released. On the 28th of July, 1779, one hundred British Regulars and two hundred Indians took Fort Freeland, under John Lyttle. Captain Boon, with the Chillisquaque Rangers, went to their relief and were captured, and every post north of Sunbury fell into the enemy's hands. The excitement here was great, and tales of butchery and horror came from every settlement.

PUNISHMENT OF CRIMINALS.

The following extract from the Sessions Docket of August, 1784, will be of interest.

RESPUBLICA *vs.* JOS. DISBERRY.	Indictment for Felony. Defendant arraigned, plead *not guilty*. A jury of the country being called, same to wit:

Peter Hosterman, Adam Grove, Geo. Shaffer, Philip Frick, John Harrison, Michael Grove, William Clark, Adam Christ, Robert Irwin, Paul Baldy, John Shaffer and Alexander M. Grady, who, being duly elected, tried and sworn upon their oaths, respectively do say that Joseph Disbury is guilty of the Felony whereof he stands indicted.

Judgment—that the said Joseph Disberry receive thirty-nine lashes between the hours of eight and six o'clock, to-morrow; to stand in the pillory one hour; to have his ears cut off and nailed to the post; to return the property stolen or the value thereof; remain in prison three months; pay a fine of thirty pounds to the Honorable the President of this State for the support of the government, and stand committed until fine and fees are paid.

At February Sessions, 1785, Patrick Quinn was sentenced to receive "twenty-one lashes on his bare back at the common whipping-post, on Friday the 20th day of February, 1780, at nine o'clock in the morning, for stealing a tow linen shirt of the value of ten shillings."

In 1781, the Lee family were scalped and tomahawked in Dry Valley. Lee was brought to Sunbury in a dying condition. Two soldiers from the fort while acting as carriers in bearing his remains to the grave, commenced quarreling and finally began to kick each other under the coffin. Colonel Hunter quelled the disturbance by seizing a whip and lashing them over the shoulders.

The last white man killed near here by the Indians was a Mr. Taylor, on Shamokin Creek.

THE FIRST FERRY.

The following is a copy of petition filed in the Archives at Harrisburg:

To the Honorable the Representation of the Freemen of the State of Pennsylvania, in General Assembly met at Philadelphia the twenty-second day of October, A. D. 1787.

The petition of the subscriber, an inhabitant of the town of Sunbury, in the county of Northumberland, and State of Pennsylvania, most humbly showeth,

That there was a grant made by the Honourable Thomas Penn and Richard Penn, Esqs., unto Robert King his executors, administrators and assigns by their patent, bearing date the 14th of August, 1772, for the keeping a ferry over the main river of Susquehanna, at the town of Sunbury, in said county, and the said patent being conveyed by Robert King to Adam Haverling, on the 30th of November, A. D. 1773, and by the said Adam Haverling conveyed unto Stophel Getting, on the 17th day of April, 1775, and by the said Stophel Getting conveyed unto Abraham Dewitt, on the 9th day of October, 1779, and by Eleanor Dewitt (Alias Coldern), administratrix of Abraham Dewitt, deceased, conveyed unto your petitioner, on the 25th day of October, 17—, and as he hath water craft made on purpose for said ferry before there was any on Sunbury side, and now hath sufficient craft in good order, and having the rights as transferred by sundry recitals, and is in peaceable possession, therefore humbly requests of your honorable body to grant him the privilege of keeping said ferry upon the terms your honors shall think just and reasonable for a term of years, and your petitioner as in duty bound, will pray.

JOHN LYONS.

We, the under-named subscribers do certify that the above petitioner, John Lyon, hath had said ferry some time in possession, and that he hath attended to the same regularly, and hath kept his water craft in good order.

We therefore request of your honors to grant his request, and you will oblige, gentlemen, your most obedient humble servants:

Jas. Crawford,	Daniel Montgomery,
Wm. Bonham,	Samuel Wallis,
Benjamin Lyon,	James McCune,
Jos. Buchanan,	Abraham McKinney,
Daniel Reese,	Enoch Skeer,
James Davidson,	Jacob Anderson,
Wm. D. Brady,	John Kidd,
Robert Wilson,	John Mead,
Benjamin Lewis,	Henry Lebo,
John Harrison,	Augustus Stouer,
Wm. Adam,	John Bell,
Daniel Sheedley,	John Black,
Chas. Gobin,	Geo. Wolff,
Wm. Geary,	Jack Robins,
Wm. Murdock,	John Young,
Joseph Wallis,	Jacob Keberling,
John Watson,	Daniel Beatty,
Henry Landerslice,	Robert Coldern,

John Dickinson.

EARLY STAGES.

The early stages to Harrisburg crossed the river here by ferry, went down the west side to Montgomery's Ferry, two-and-one-half miles below Liverpool, and there re-crossed. After the completion of the Centre turnpike, the stages went over the town hill to Reading and Philadelphia, being just a week on the round trip to Philadelphia and return. The semi-annual meeting of the Board of Directors of this old pike is still kept up, and a little of that convival business so important to the inspiration of old memories and good fellowship, is still transacted.

The following advertisement from an old paper refers to one of the first stage lines:

MAIL STAGE.

DANIEL LEBO,

BEGS leave to inform the public, that after the first day of October next, his Stage will leave Reading every Wednesday afternoon, and arrive in Hamburgh, alias Carter'stown, the same evening; from whence it will proceed on Thursday morning, and arrive in Sunbury, on Friday at 12 o'clock. On the Saturday, following, it will return to Reading, to arrive there on Sunday afternoon.

Passengers going to Philadelphia, are requested to take notice, that Mr. Coleman's Stage will leave Reading every Monday morning for that city.

September 23, [illegible].

THE OLD IRON CANNON.

From the best information obtainable, it seems that this piece of ordnance was brought from Fort Harris, (now Harrisburg,) and placed upon the ramparts of Fort Augusta, in the year 1772. From there it was taken to Fort Muncy, where it remained until 1774, when it was brought back to Augusta. In the year 1775, when Colonel Hunter was ordered, with his command, to report at Harris Ferry, the cannon was ordered to be spiked and thrown into the river, which was done, when the fort was evacuated. In 1798, it was taken from the river by George and Jacob Mantz, Samuel Hann, and Henry Shoop. Several cords of hickory wood were burned in taking the temper out of the file, with which it was spiked, so that it could be drilled out. In 1824, it was stolen from the river bank, at Sunbury, by citizens of Selinsgrove, then Union County, and hidden away in Mr. Becker's cellar, and in 1825, George Weiser, Esq., of Sunbury, having business in Selinsgrove, by some means discovered where it was hidden, bribed the maid, who was also from Sunbury, to have the cellar door unlocked, and the dog removed from the premises, when a company from Sunbury, consisting of George Hileman, John Epley, John Weaver, John Pickering, James McCormick, Jacob Diehl, and others, went to Selinsgrove on the night of the 3d of July, with a good wagon, and a fast team of horses, took the cannon from the cellar, and started for Sunbury; and when a short distance above the Penn's Creek bridge, they fired a few rounds, thus raising the alarm in Selinsgrove; and, as they expected to be pursued, they hurried up in double quick time, crossed the river in a flat that was in readiness, hurried up to the hotel, then kept by John Weaver, at the corner of Third and Market streets, in the stone building now owned by Wm. H. Miller, carried it up to the attic, placed a bed over it, on which Joseph Eisely, then a boy fourteen years of age, who was bar-keeper at the hotel, slept until morning, when it was brought down and used at the celebration that day (July 4th.) Dr. Morris composed an appropriate poem on the subject, which was sung at the celebration, and was afterwards published in one of the papers. It was said that Mr. Becker killed his dog the next morning, when he discovered the loss of the cannon. In 1830, it was stolen by citizens of New Berlin, then Union County, named Charles Awl, Samuel Keeler, Charles Baum, Elias Hammel, Michael Kleckner, Thomas Hallabush, Samuel Winter, and Thomas Getgen. After some time, George and Ezekiel Follmer, and Jacob Keefer, went to that place to recover it. They returned without accomplishing anything, save the spraining of Keefer's back, by the breaking and falling of the platform on which the cannon was placed. The next fall, a party of men headed by George Prince, went over and captured the trophy. In 1833, some persons from Selinsgrove, pretending to have a claim, came and captured it. It remained in that place until July 4th, 1834, when Dr. R. H. Awl, Charles Rinehart, H. A. Simpson, Edward Lyon, George Mahan, Peter Zimmerman, Thomas McEwen, Jerry Mantz, Jacob and John Rheichtine, and Weiser Zeigler, laid a plan to re-capture it.

Two of the boys were sent to Selinsgrove in disguise, to find where the cannon was hid, at night, which they found no difficulty in doing. They all met at the red bridge that night, stole a horse from Mrs. Rhinehart, and a wagon from Hugh Bellas, loaded the cannon, stole the ferry-flat, crossed the river, and started on their way to Sunbury. One of the boys stole a keg of powder, and at daybreak, on the 5th of July, opened fire, on the river bank, in front of Esquire Levy's residence. Mr. Levy became very enthusiastic over the victory; so much so, that at evening, when there was danger of being attacked by Union County, he came out with musket and drawn sword, and offered to command the defense, but the assaulting party failed to appear. In 1849, about thirty young men from Danville, undertook to capture it.

Jerry Hall, of Sunbury, who was then clerk in the Danville post-office, learning the plot of the Danville boys, confiscated a horse belonging to Dr. Updegraff, and a saddle of G. M. Shoop, the Danville post-master, and prevailed upon Clinton Fisher to go to Sunbury, in haste, bearing a letter from said Hall to H. D. Wharton, notifying him of the plot. Mr. Wharton notified Captain C. J. Bruner, who was commander of the forces, which numbered some half-dozen men. The Sunbury people rallied their forces, and placed pickets on duty. The cannon was in the cellar of the house adjoining the old ferry-house, then occupied by Benjamin Krohn. Wm. B. Martin had the post of honor, being in front of the house. When the Danville party presented their appearance, they were surprised to find that they had been outgeneraled. They were advised to retire, and get out of town as soon as possible, otherwise some of them might return feet foremost. Mrs. Krohn and several other ladies, had their weapons in good condition—said weapons consisting of several kettles of boiling water.

SUNBURY IN 1794.

There were, in 1794, three stores in Sunbury. One kept by Wm. Dewart, grand-father of Hon. Wm. L. Dewart, on the spot now occupied by the coal-office of James Boyd & Co.; another by John Buyers, grand-father of Capt. John Buyers, on the lot south of the three-story McCarty building; and the third by James Black, grand-father of Hon. John B. Packer, two lots further north. The house in which I. T. Clements now lives, was built for a hotel in 1796, by James Smith, grand-father of the present post-master, John J. Smith. There had been a building in the same place two years earlier, but in the attempt to burn shavings in the cellar, the flames done a little extra labor on their own account, and the house went up in smoke.

At that time, there were no buildings on the south side of Market square, and a foot-path went across lots from our present court house to the old depot. The land around the gas factory and northward was covered with birch, knarled-oaks and grape-vines, with occasional pools of water full of pheasants, ducks, etc. The basin lots were full of bushes, logs, bogs and frogs.

The well at Neff's Hotel was dug in 1794, five years before the death of Washington. The Donnel House was once a hotel, where "news much older than their ale went round," and where John G. Youngman, father of the present editor of the *Gazette*, put up when he first came to Sunbury. There was once a still-house where Dr. Haupt's house now stands. A tan-yard where the old Markle House stands. Mr. Daniel Hager, lived in a log-house where John Haas now resides, and had a pottery on the next lot east of his dwelling. An old hotel, afterwards the old barracks, stood near the south-west corner of Chestnut and Front streets. The old Pleasant's House was once a jail, with plank up-ended behind it for a jail-yard.

There were in those days spirit-knockings, or spooks, and people enough who believed that hobgoblins were a necessary part of God's economy. Old Becca Gorman lived in a haunted house near the William Penn House, and was herself regarded as the incarnation of things mysterious. The old whipping-post stood in front of the old court house, near the market house, which was a structure about eighty feet long, and twenty wide, standing upon pillars of brick. The old stone-house of Miss Weitzell was the hotel at which the Supreme Judges stopped. Drumheller's old hotel was built in 1796, at which time they raised the sign of a buck. The first camp-meeting was held in Chillisquaque in 1806, which Judge Jordan attended when a little boy. A man named Jones was once hung on the gallows erected between the dam and the old ferry, for murdering a man named Lary, at Cattawissa. Another man named Armstrong, was hung about a year later at the same place for felony. They were buried near two linden-trees, and a Sunbury doctor stole their bones. The gallows rotted away, these being the only cases of capital punishment in the County.

SUNBURY INCORPORATED.

The following is the first section of the Act of Incorporation, of the Borough of Sunbury, passed March 24th, 1797:

"SECTION I. *Be it enacted by the Senate and House of Representatives of the Commonwealth of Pennsylvania, in General Assembly met, and it is hereby enacted by the authority of the same*, That the town of Sunbury shall be, and the same is hereby erected into a borough, which shall be called "the Borough of Sunbury," forever; the extent of which said borough is and shall be comprised within the following boundaries, to wit: Beginning at the mouth of Shamokin Creek, where it empties into the river Susquehanna, at low water-mark; thence up the said creek, on the north side thereof, to the mouth of the gut; thence up the same, on the west side thereof, to the line of Samuel Scott's land; and by the same to the river aforesaid, at low water-mark; thence down the same river, at low water-mark, to the place of beginning."

COUNTY BUILDINGS.

Between 1794 and 1800, the first county buildings (now torn down,) viz: The old Court House, Prothonotary's office, Commissioners' office, and Register and Recorder's offices, were built. They were very substantial and neat two-story brick buildings for their day. The three offices just named were all under one and the same roof, and occupied the whole front or northern part of the present spacious court house ground. The old court house stood in the center of the public square, immediately in front and north of our old county offices. It was built about the year 1797. All the records that refer to it are lost, except some orders for money in compensation for services, signed by John Weitzel. There is a book containing the records of orders, which are continued from the minute-book, but said minute-book cannot be found, neither contract for building. So that we are unable to present anything farther on the subject. It was here, in those old departed brick structures, that the distinguished departed lawyers, Bradford, Hall Bellas, Greenough, Hepburn, Packer, Donnell, and others displayed an industry, learning, and eloquence that made them famous not only at home but abroad.

THE PRESENT COURT HOUSE.

The contract for building this edifice was allotted to D. S. Risel, January 5th, 1865, in the sum of $97,000. From said contract we obtain the following: The building is one hundred and sixteen feet eleven inches long by sixty feet wide, with projecting corners of three feet each way, making the entire length one hundred and twenty-two feet eleven inches and the width sixty-six feet two inches; it is two stories high with a cellar underneath. The outer walls of the four angles are of hard brick, and are two feet nine inches thick, and the intermediate walls, also of brick, two feet six inches thick. The walls of the cellar are of a good quality of quarry building-stone; it is eight feet deep in the clear, and contains three heaters for heating the whole building; they are from the manufactory of Matzinger & Bros., Philadelphia. It also contains coal rooms, etc. The first story is twelve feet from floor to floor, and contains the offices of Prothonotary, Register and Recorder, Treasurer, County Commissioners, Sheriff, and an arbitration room, each of which, with the exception of the Sheriff's office, contains a fire-proof vault in which the records and valuable documents are kept. On the second floor is the court room, which is twenty-eight feet high in the clear. The bar and seat of justice are finely finished in ash and walnut, and the other portions of the room in an imitation of oak. The work is neatly done and reflects credit upon its builder. There is also upon this floor, jury-rooms, witness-rooms, etc. The tower upon the north-west corner is about one hundred and twenty-five feet high. It contains a clock of the best manufacture, which has four dials.

THE FIRST REGULAR JAIL.

On the 21st of March, 1772, the Colonial Legislature provided for the erection of Northumberland County, with judges, courts, etc., for the government of its own internal affairs. The fifth section of this act declared that the said "courts shall, from and after the publication of this act, sit and be held for the said County of Northumberland, on the fourth Tuesday in the months of May, August, November and February, in every year, at Fort Augusta, until a court house shall be built; and when the same is built and erected in the county aforesaid, the said several courts shall then be holden and kept at the said court house on the days before mentioned."

The same act also declared that William Maclay, Samuel Hunter, John Louden, Joseph Wallis, and Robert Moodie, or any three of them should have authority to view the grounds and fix on a site for the building of a court house and jail, in and for Northumberland County, and purchase the said ground or grounds subject to the approval of the Governor of Pennsylvania. (Section 1, Smith's Laws, 367-9.)

1773, April 2.—William Maclay, who was the first Prothonotary and Register and Recorder of our Northumberland County courts, in a letter of this date written from Fort Augusta to James Tilghman, of Philadelphia, in regard to a jail for our County, says: "Sir, I enclose to you a letter from three of the Trustees for the public buildings of this County respecting some measures which we have lately fallen on to rescue us from the scandal of living entirely *without* any place of confinement or punishment for villains. Captain Samuel Hunter had address enough to render abortive every attempt that was made last summer (1772) for keeping a regular jail, even after I had been at considerable expense in fitting up *this magazine* (at Fort Augusta) *under which there is a small but complete dungeon*. I am sorry to inform you that he has given our present measures the most obstinate resistance in his power and impeded us with every embarrassment in the compass of his invention. We know nothing of the footing (authority) on which Captain Hunter has possession of these buildings, and only beg that the County may be accommodated with this old magazine *with the addition* proposed to be made to it, and with the house in which I now live to hold our court in, I have repaired the house in which I now live, but expect to have an house ready to remove to in Sunbury before our November court. As the present repairs are done entirely by subscription you will readily guess that Captain Hunter is not among the number of subscribers. As there are many pieces of old iron, etc., which formerly belonged to the fort, not of any use at present, the Trustees propose using any of them which can be converted to any advantage for grates, etc., for our temporary Goal, unless they receive contrary directions from Philadelphia."—(See Penn'a Archives, vol. 4, pages 462-3.)

The James Tilghman here noticed, was then Secretary of the Colony or Province of Pennsylvania, and so the proper person for William Maclay to write to touching this "old Magazine's Dungeon," and "the additions proposed to be made to it," as "a place of confinement for villains."

As there appears nothing in the Pennsylvania Archives, or in the Colonial Records denying this request of Prothonotary Maclay, and his two associate trustees, it may be inferred that he and they, by leave of the Provincial Council of Pennsylvania, made additions to the magazine of Fort Augusta to answer the purposes of a temporary county jail.

On July 23d, 1774, the Colonial Legislature now passed "An Act for lending the sum of £800 to the County of Northumberland for building a Court House and Prison in said County." (See 10 Col. Rec. 197-8 and 1 Smith's Laws XIV.) We have already seen that Capt. S. Hunter was one of the trustees appointed by the Provincial Council at Philadelphia for purchasing ground and erecting a court house and jail for Northumberland County; but Capt. Hunter was also in 1772, and for some years afterwards, the com-

RES. OF WILLIAM BROWN, COR. ARCH & LINCOLN STS. FRONTING MARKET. SHAMOKIN, NORTH'D CO. PA.

INDUSTRIAL IRON WORKS, WM BROWN, PROPRIETOR INDEPENDENCE ST.

"STIRLING COLLIERY," FULTON & KENDRICKS, PROPRIETORS. COAL TP., NORTH'D CO., PA.
PHILADELPHIA OFFICE, 113 WALNUT ST. NEW YORK OFFICE, TRINITY BUILDING.

mander of Fort Augusta, and for some reason unknown to us, resisted Maclay and his colleagues in making use of the Fort's magazine and dungeons as a place for confining and punishing criminals. But in 1775 and 1776, he, Hunter, united with Maclay in building the first regular jail of Northumberland County.

For in March, 1775, Samuel Hunter, William Maclay, and Robert Moodie, commenced the building of "a new jail in Sunbury," as their orders upon Alexander Hunter, the first Treasurer of Northumberland County, for the payment of materials furnished, and work done, clearly show. And these same orders, or vouchers, also show that the said Hunter, Maclay, and Moodie, among other things, employed James Chisnall to quarry the stone for said jail; John Lee, to furnish the lime; John Harris, Sen., Paxton, (now Harrisburg,) to furnish the iron; Frederick Weyman, to supply the hinges, hooks, rivets, etc.; Joseph McCarrell, Zachariah Robins, and Conrad Platner, to haul the stone, lime, scaffold-poles, etc.; Henry Crawford and Robert Lenet, to do the stone-mason work; Wilton Atkinson, to do the blacksmith work; and John Buyers and John Maclay, to do the carpenter work of said jail, which seems to have been furnished in 1778.

It was a stone and brick structure, one part being used for a court house, and the other for a prison. It was subsequently used, a portion of it, for a printing-office, and still later, the building served the purpose of a store and dwelling.

Though much modified in appearance, the old structure is still standing, and can be seen on the south side of Market street, corner of Centre alley. It is owned by Mrs. Dr. Leisenweaver, only surviving child of Charles Pleasant. For many years it has been known as the "Pleasant House." Its original cost was about four thousand dollars.

THE SECOND JAIL.

On March 10th, 1801, John Frick, Abraham M'Kinney, and Flavel Roan, the then Commissioners of Northumberland County, now met, and paid Evan R. Evans, a Sunbury lawyer of some note, four hundred and fifty dollars, for Sunbury town lots Nos. 149 and 150, as the site for the building of a county jail, being the ground where the new and third jail is in process of erection. These county commissioners, at the same time, made a contract with Frederick Hawger and Mathias App, for two thousand bushels of lime; with Zacharias Robins, for five hundred perch of stone; and with George Deitz, to do all the mason work; and with Andrew Grove and Jacob Dorst, to do all the smith work on the jail, at ten cents per pound. This done, they authorized John Frick, of their own body, to superintend the whole business of building the sandstone jail and its yard-walls.

On the 2d of November, 1802, the county commissioners agreed to allow the said John Frick six per cent. of all the monies that passed through his hands in said business, as a compensation for his time and services therein.

On April 25th, 1803, the commissioners paid John Frick, for the building of said jail and its yard walls, as allowed by John Buyers, Daniel Montgomery, and Evan R. Evans, the auditors of his accounts, the sum of $6,850.30; percentage on same, 323.90; to which said auditors, on the 1st of August, 1804, added for stone not previously allowed said Frick, the further sum of 94.00. Total, $7,274.20.

To the foregoing, if we add the cost of the lots, which was four hundred and fifty dollars, and allow about two hundred and seventy-five dollars for incidentals, it will bring the cost of the second jail up to eight thousand dollars, which is probably not far from being correct.

THE NEW JAIL.

In the Spring of 1876, the structure that constituted the second jail was torn down, and a new one (third) commenced, on the same site, on Second street, corner of Mulberry alley.

The contract for its erection was awarded to Ira T. Clement, of Sunbury, in the amount of ninety-one thousand, six hundred and thirty-six dollars. This is exclusive of the iron and water-pipes, which will probably cost some forty thousand dollars additional. It is estimated that the building, when completed, will stand to the County in the amount of one hundred and forty thousand dollars.

GENERAL DESCRIPTION.

The building to be two stories, with basement under entire building. A tower in front of centre. All of the exterior walls and those of the prison wings and internal to be built of stone. The front of building to be relieved with dressed-stone trimmings.

The first floor to be elevated above the pavement grade five feet seven inches.

The steps to the entrance and to the basement and the base of building to be of select stone, patent hammer dressed.

The front of building to be of select stone, first-class rock work, laid in Ashler courses.

The guard wall, which is to enclose the entire balance of lot; facing on Second street two hundred and thirty (230), and one hundred and seventy-two feet (172) on Arch street, one hundred and seventy-two (172) on alley, and two hundred and thirty (230) in rear, leaving an eight (8) foot alley on line of lot.

The main building fronting on Second street on centre of lot.

The main entrance opens into a vestibule four feet by twelve (4x12), from thence into a hall ten feet (10) wide. On the one side is the warden's office, stair-hall, committee and turnkey's rooms.

The other side fitted up for family use—a parlor stair-hall to second floor, dining-room and kitchen.

On the second floor, three rooms on either side of hall, store-rooms, bath and water-closet, and stairs to third floor, and tank-room, which is to contain two tanks of three thousand (3,000) gallons each, to receive the water from the steam-pump. The tanks supply the building throughout, including a hose outlet on each floor.

The hall on first floor extends back to an angular hall, from which opens the vestibule entrance to the corridors of the prison-wings, extending back ninety-six (96) feet, and fifteen (15) feet wide, with cells on either side.

The corridor to be laid with flag-stone. The second tier of cells having iron platforms three (3) feet wide, with stairs of iron at each end. There are to be twenty-three (23) cells on each floor of each wing. A laboratory, and six (6) large rooms for work-rooms, and one for sick-room or hospital, all supplied with water and water-closets.

One wing to be fitted with extra cells for penitentiary and solitary confinement, and work-shops. The entire building arranged for summer and winter ventilation. To be heated by steam, by indirect radiation, from the boiler which is located in rear of the centre of building for that purpose; also, the pump, with all the steam arrangements and supplies, coal, etc.

Basement under entire building, the part under centre building to be fitted up for kitchen, bake-room, and laundry, with sink, oven, range, and boiler, and sad-iron heaters, etc., to be thoroughly drained to the river.

The entire building to be fitted with all the most modern improved arrangements for prison purposes.

FLOODS.

In the year 1744, occurred the first great flood of the Susquehanna, of which there is any record. Another took place in 1756, and one in 1772. Another called the "great pumpkin flood," took place in the fall of 1786, when a great invoice of pumpkins went down to Port Deposit. The spring of 1800, witnessed another flood; also the 6th of August, 1814. Another in 1847, and one again in 1865, of which some citizens may have some faint recollection, when the pigs "rummaged through the attics," and Sunbury wore the aspect of Venice with its gondolas.

Again, in March, 1875, occurred a flood almost equal to the one in 1865. In it the bridge connecting Sunbury with Lyon's Island was swept away.

RAILROADS.

There are five lines of railroads centering in Sunbury, viz: the Philadelphia and Erie, the Northern Central, Shamokin Division Northern Central, Sunbury and Lewistown, and Danville, Hazleton and Wilkesbarre railroads. These roads give unusual facilities for the shipment of goods in every directions, and give Sunbury great advantages as a manufacturing center.

Philadelphia and Erie Railroad.—This road is leased and operated by the Pennsylvania Railroad Company. It is two hundred and eighty-eight miles long, extending from Erie to Sunbury. It connects at Erie with the Lake Shore road for all points in the West; at Sunbury with the Northern Central Railway for Baltimore, Philadelphia and New York, also for the Shamokin coal regions; and with the Danville, Hazleton and Wilkesbarre Railroad for all points on the Lehigh; at Corry with the Oil Creek and Allegheny Valley Railroad and Atlantic and Great Western Railway; at Irvington with the Warren and Franklin Railroad; at Emporium with the Buffalo, New York and Philadelphia Railroad; at Driftwood with the Low Grade Division of the Allegheny Valley Railroad; at Williamsport with the Northern Central Railway, and with the Catawissa Railroad (P. & R. R. R. Lessee); at Milton with the Catawissa Railroad; at Lewisburg Junction with the Lewisburg Centre and Spruce Creek Railroad; and at Northumberland with the Lackawanna and Bloomsburg Railroad.

The officers of the company at Sunbury are: Jacob Shipman, passenger agent; H. F. Mann, freight agent; N. F. Martz, baggage-master; Capt. Roach, depot-master.

Northern Central Railway.—This road extends from Sunbury to Baltimore, a distance of one hundred and thirty-eight miles. It connects with railroads diverging from Baltimore as follows: at Relay with the Western Maryland Railroad; at Hanover Junction with the Hanover Branch; at York with the York Branch of the Pennsylvania Railroad; at Harrisburg with the Cumberland Valley, Pennsylvania and Lebanon Valley Railroads; at Dauphin with the Schuylkill and Susquehanna Railroad; at Millersburg with the Lyken's Valley Coal Railroad; at Treverton Junction with the Mahoney and Shamokin Branch of the Philadelphia and Reading Railroad; at Sunbury with the Philadelphia and Erie and Danville, Hazleton and Wilkesbarre Railroad, the Sunbury Division of the Northern Central Railway.

The officers of this railway at Sunbury are: Jacob Shipman, ticket agent; H. F. Mann, freight agent; N. F. Martz, baggage-master.

Sunbury and Lewistown Railroad.—This road is a branch of the Pennsylvania railroad, and is operated by that company. It extends from Sunbury to Lewistown, a distance of fifty miles.

Danville, Hazleton and Wilkesbarre Railroad.—This road, owned and operated by the Pennsylvania railroad, extends from Sunbury to Tombicken, where it connects with the Lehigh Valley railroad. The officers are the same as the Philadelphia and Erie. The road is a new one, but promises to become an important link in the railroad system of the State. E. B. Westfall is superintendent of the Sunbury Division, embracing the D., H. and W. and the Shamokin Branch.

THE PASSENGER DEPOT.

Is used by all the railroads centering in Sunbury. It is an elegant brick structure, located at Third and Arch streets, and was completed June 1, 1872, at a cost of thirty-five thousand dollars. The first floor contains the ladies' and gentlemen's waiting-rooms, ticket-offices, telegraph-offices, baggage, mail, and express-rooms, station-master's and train-men's rooms, etc.

The second floor is occupied by E. B. Westfall, superintendent of the Sunbury Division, and by other officials who have their headquarters at this point.

THE RAILROAD SHOPS AT SUNBURY.

The railroad repair-shops located at Sunbury were constructed by the Sunbury and Erie Railroad Company, in 1864–5. They consist of machine-shop, car-shop, blacksmith-shop, boiler, and tin-shop, and round-house The Sunbury and Erie Company passing under the control of the Pennsylvania Railroad Company, they were occupied by this company in January, 1866, and became the headquarters of the motive-power department of the Eastern Division, Philadelphia and Erie Railroad. Frank Thompson, now general manager of P. R. R., was then Division-superintendent, and Thomas J. Hamer, master-mechanic. Since then considerable change has been made. In 1872, the D., H. and W. R. R., and in 1873, the N. C. R. R. passed under the control of the P. R. R., and their shops at Sunbury and Shamokin were transferred here. They are now the motive-power headquarters of the Eastern Division of the Susquehanna, with Thomas Gucker, of Williamsport, superintendent; and of the Sunbury Division, with E. B. Westfall, of Sunbury, superintendent, and are under the supervision of W. F. Beardsley, master-mechanic. The number of men employed in the different departments centering here, is as follows: Master-mechanic, one; foremen, four; road-foremen of engines, two; stationary-engineers, one; laborers on coal-platform, nine; car-inspectors, twenty-two; car-cleaners, two; watchmen, four; store-keeper, one; clerks, three; engine-preparers, ten; engine cleaners, eleven; engineers, seventy-one; firemen, seventy-four; machinists, twenty-three; machinists' helpers, ten; machinists' apprentices, thirteen; blacksmiths, fifteen; blacksmiths' helpers, seventeen; blacksmiths' apprentices, two; boiler-makers, ten; boiler-makers' helpers, eight; boiler-makers' apprentices, one; tin-smiths, one; tin-smiths' helpers, one; tin-smiths' apprentices, one; copper-smiths, one; copper-smiths' apprentices, one; carpenters, forty-three; car-laborers, forty-three; painters, five; painters' apprentices, one; laborers, twenty; telegraph-operators, one. From the foregoing list it will be seen that there are now employed, four hundred and three men in the various departments centering at the railroad shops.

SUNBURY BOROUGH OFFICERS.

Chief burgess—John Bourne; second burgess—W. I. Greenough; assistant burgesses—W. H. Miller, John Bowen, J. A. Boyd, W. T. Grant; councilmen—James Kirchner, Andrew Hoover, G. B. Cadwallader, H. F. Meagus, W. C. Packer, Charles Garinger, Charles Seusenbach, W. W. Moody; town clerk—George Bucher; borough collector—Solomon Weaver; borough treasurer—N. S. Engel; assessors—S. Faust, Sr., Thomas G. Cooper; street-commissioners—John Leeser, Samuel Savidge, M. A. Keefer, Jeremiah Savidge.

The regular meetings of the Borough Council are held at the council chamber, over the engine-house on Chestnut street, near Third, on the first Tuesday evening of each month.

THE POST-OFFICE

at Sunbury, Pa., is located on Third street, between Market and Chestnut streets. The building is of brick, three stories in height, twenty-one feet front, forty-three feet in depth and is lighted by gas. The interior design was executed by the Yale Lock Manufacturing Company, of Stamford, Conn., and cost two thousand one hundred dollars. It is one of the most convenient and ornamental structures of the kind in central Pennsylvania. The general delivery is in front, four feet in width. The delivery cases extend back six feet on an angle, and are covered with stained glass, from whence two rows of boxes extend back nineteen feet. The space between is six feet; the space between the boxes and walls on each side is five feet. On the left side is the money-order delivery. The number of boxes is eight hundred and eighty-eight, as follows: Seven hundred and sixty-eight lock-boxes, twenty-four lock-drawers, and ninety-six call-boxes. The boxes are the patent metallic Yale box with gilt fronts. The wood-work is pine inlaid with walnut. The distance from the front door to delivery is ten feet. The entrance to the back office is on the right. The distribution table is made of walnut inlaid with oak, and is constructed on the circular plan. It has a capacity for twelve No. 1 mail-pouches at one time. Ten pouches of mail matter are received at the office daily for delivery and distribution, and the same number are sent out daily. About one thousand letters are cancelled daily at this office. The money-order system was commenced here August 10th, 1872. About one thousand orders are issued per year, and about the same number paid. The number of letters registered is about four hundred per year. Since 1870, the business of the office has increased about twenty per cent. J. J. Smith is the present post-master, and G. W. Young, deputy.

UNION PARK AND AGRICULTURAL ASSOCIATION

Was organized March 24th, 1873. The officers were: Solomon Malick, President; Isaac Campbell, Vice President; George B. Cadwallader, Treasurer; P. H. Moore, Recording Secretary; Lemuel Shipman, Corresponding Secretary; William A. Sober, Librarian; and an executive committee of thirty persons. This association has for its object, the improvement of live-stock and the advancement of agriculture, horticulture, and the domestic and mechanical arts and sciences in Northumberland County. The present officers are: President, Emanuel Wilvert; Vice President, Jacob M. Follmer; Treasurer, P. H. Moore; Recording Secretary, Thomas M. Pursel; Corresponding Secretary, John Klase; Librarian, W. C. Packer.

HOTELS.

Sunbury is well supplied with houses of entertainment, of which the following are the principal ones:

City Hotel.—Some three-fourths of a century since, there stood on the south-east corner of what is now Market and Fourth streets, an old tavern, familiarly known as "The Buck," which was one of the oldest tavern-stands in Sunbury, it having been built in 1796. It was first kept by Jonas Weaver, and next by D. Gibson, who was succeeded by Charles Weaver. In 1863, the present proprietor, E. T. Drumheller, took possession, and in 1871, the old structure was torn down and a new one erected. The present City Hotel is sixty by one hundred and eleven feet, and three stories high. It was designed by Mr. Wetzel, of Danville, and built by Messrs. Haines & Co., of Sunbury. It cost thirty-five thousand dollars, and contains forty-seven sleeping-rooms, besides parlors, sample-rooms, etc.

Washington House.—This hotel is situated on the corner of Market and Second streets, opposite the court house. The present proprietor, C. Neff, assumed control in 1866. It is located in one of the most quiet parts of the borough.

Central Hotel.—This public house is located on the north-east corner of Market square. The corner part of the building was erected fifty years ago or more, by Martin Weaver. In 1859, additions were made to the building by James Van Dyke, who opened it as a hotel. In 1865, it was purchased by Henry Haas, the present popular proprietor, who also remodeled the building somewhat. It is supplied with the modern conveniences, and from its "central" location is a desirable stopping place. William K. Dunham, is the polite clerk.

Clement House.—This house of entertainment was built by Messrs. Moore and Dissinger, and was opened to the public on March 13th, 1871. It was named in honor of Ira T. Clement, Esq., of Sunbury. It was occupied by different landlords till January, 1875, when the present proprietor, Peter Burrell, assumed charge.

The hotel is furnished with all the modern appliances of convenience and comfort. It contains the largest rooms of any hotel in the borough, is heated by furnaces and has gas in every apartment. It is also supplied with hot and cold water, and has a bath-room for the accommodation of guests. There is also in the building a hair-dressing saloon.

The Clement House is the only hotel in the place that is furnished with the conveniences just enumerated. In addition to these, it has also the other essentials of sample-room, reading-room, parlor, etc. It is enjoying a deserved popularity under the efficient management of the accommodating proprietor, Peter Burrell, and the polite attentions of the gentlemanly clerk, Nat. Ford.

The drug-store of Dr. C. M. Martin & Co., and the grocery-house of Samuel Byerly occupy a portion of the ground-floor of this hotel.

EDUCATIONAL.

The common school law of Pennsylvania was adopted by the borough of Sunbury immediately after its passage in 1834, and the public schools of the place have since been conducted under its provisions. The first public school edifice was erected in 1835, on what is now the west side of Third street, between Market and Chestnut. It was a brick structure, two stories high, and contained four school-rooms. This building furnished all the school accommodations in the borough till 1866. Caketown was laid out in this year, but a school-house was erected there in 1865. It was a one-story brick, and cost about five hundred dollars. In 1866, were erected the north-east and south-west ward buildings, and in 1868, the north-west and south-east edifices. They are all of the same style of architecture, and cost some four thousand dollars apiece. In 1875, the school-board purchased the old frame Baptist church, adjacent to the south-east ward building, and the same is now occupied as a school-house. The board are about to dispose of the Caketown school-house, and purpose to erect on a lot in the vicinity, a two-story brick edifice that shall contain two rooms. In 1870, a system of grading was introduced into the Sunbury public schools, which system continues to the present time. In August, 1871, a high-school department was established, and Mr. G. G. Miller became principal of the same. This school was first held in what was known as the Bartholomew building, on the west side of Fourth street, between Market and Arch streets. In 1866, the number of pupils enrolled in the borough was about four hundred; in 1876, it was eight hundred and twenty-three. The present superintendent of schools is Professor Block, and the corps of teachers numbers thirteen. The following constitute the present board of education: W. S. Rhoads, president; J. R. Cressinger, secretary; M. P. Scupham, treasurer; Jacob Fetter, John De Haven and F. L. Haupt.

FOUNDRY AND MACHINE-SHOP.

This establishment was commenced in 1839, by Messrs. Rohrbach & Brothers, as a foundry. It then employed three men. The shops are located on Chestnut street, near the Pennsylvania railroad track. In 1856, it was enlarged. In 1859, the firm was changed to C. D. and J. Rohrbach, by whom it was conducted until 1861. It was then changed to Rohrbach & Cooper, who continued the business until 1866, when George Rohrbach and Son became proprietors. In 1867, it was again enlarged and a machine-shop added. In 1870, the firm was changed to George Rohrbach & Sons, who still continue the business. The buildings cover about six thousand square feet, and are two stories high. The foundry does a general foundry and machine-shop business.

SUNBURY STEAM FLOURING-MILLS.

The mills are owned by Messrs. Moore, Campbell & Co., and are situated on Walnut street; they are enclosed by a brick building thirty-five by forty feet, and four stories high. They were originally built in 1855, but have since been extended and improved, so that now the mill is provided with four runs of burrs, and complete machinery of all kinds. It is run by a thirty-horse-power steam-engine, and gives employment to four men.

WASHINGTON INDEPENDENT STEAM FIRE COMPANY.

The history of the Washington Independent Steam Fire Company, of Sunbury, dates back to 1837, as near as we can learn, and up to 1876, is as follows: The Good Will Fire Company was in existence in 1837. How much earlier the company was organized cannot be ascertained. The engine was owned by Northumberland County, and the membership of the company was made up of old citizens, many of whom are dead, and a few still living. The following are the names of all the old members ascertainable at this date, June, 1876: Peter Lazarus, John Young, George Young, John Bogar, Samuel Gossler, Henry Yoxtheimer, Jacob Painter, Jacob Weimer, Gideon Markle, David Haupt, George Weiser, (Judge) David Druckemiller, Jacob Young, Henry Petery, Sebastian Haupt, Charles Gossler, Charles Dering, William N. Robins, David Robins, Daniel Haas, Benjamin Hendricks, James H. Husted, William H. Miller, George Sarles, R. A. Fisher, John Eisley, A. Jordan, George Bright.

The members still living are, Peter Lazarus, A. Jordan, George Bright, David Haupt, Daniel Druckemiller, Daniel Haas, Benjamin Hendricks. The average age of these men is about seventy-five years. There were other members, of whom there is no record. At that time their dues were six-and-a-quarter cents per month, and the following is a receipt for money paid to the treasurer of the company:

"Received, Dec. 1st, 1837, of Geo. Bright, the sum of Eighteen ¾ cents for the use of Sunbury Fire Company. JAS. H. HUSTED."

In 1843, the county commissioners purchased an Agnew hand-engine, called the Washington, and the company was merged into the Washington Fire Company, and continued until the breaking out of the Rebellion in 1861, when it was disbanded, as many of its members went into the army. The old Good Will engine is now in use in the borough of Northumberland.

The company was reorganized July 17, 1873, and a gift enterprise started to raise money with which to purchase a new steamer, which was done in the beginning of the year 1875. In the same year, the company built the engine-house they now occupy, on Third street, at a cost of nearly six thousand dollars. The engine, hose-carriages, hose, etc., cost the company about seven thousand two hundred dollars.

The membership amounts to about one hundred men in good standing. The present officers are, Solomon Stroh, President; George M. Renn, Vice President; J. M. Campbell, Secretary; T. D. Reed, Financial Secretary; William H. Miller, Treasurer; S. F. Nevin, Foreman.

The following are the charter members: Solomon Stroh, P. M. Shindel, John C. Miller, William H. Miller, T. S. Shannon, B. F. Bright, John Muckert, D. C. Dissinger, J. K. Keefer, A. A. Youngman, A. Lentzer, S. F. Nevin, G. M. Renn, H. J. Waltz, William D. Haupt, Levi Seasholtz (deceased), Amos Steel, M. C. Gearhart, I. S. Gossler.

THE SUNBURY ORCHESTRA.

On the 5th day of January, 1870, there was a petition presented to the Honorable Judges of the Court of Common Pleas of Northumberland County, for a charter for an organization, to be known as "The Sunbury Orchestra," which was granted. The following are the names of the petitioners: Thomas M. Pursel, Jacob Shipman, F. K. Hill, William H. Bucher, David Fry, John W. Bucher, Charles D. Wharton, R. F. Bucher, P. P. Smith, and J. R. Cressinger. The following were elected as officers: Director, J. R. Cressinger; Assistant Director, Ferd. K. Hill; Treasurer, Jacob Shipman; Secretary, Ferd. K. Hill. The present officers are, Charles D. Wharton, President; Jacob Shipman, Treasurer; Thomas M. Pursel, Secretary; Thomas D. Grant, Musical Director. There are eight members belonging to the organization, as follows: Thomas M. Pursel, Jacob Shipman, F. K. Hill, J. Weiser Bucher, Charles D. Wharton, P. Pursel Smith, Harry D. Wharton, and Thomas D. Grant.

The Sunbury Orchestra purchased fifteen cornet instruments, which they offered to loan to any persons that would organize a band in Sunbury. They are now used by the Sunbury Silver Cornet Band.

THE SUNBURY SILVER CORNET BAND

Was organized in December, 1872. The officers were, President, George H. Gibson; Secretary, Philip H. Renn; Treasurer, Charles Peterman; Teacher, John Clymer. In 1874, the band decided to change teachers, and employed Carl Kirchner. At present there are sixteen members. The officers are as follows: President, Martin Strattiff; Vice President, John Zimmerman; Treasurer, Frederick Zeiser; Secretary, Silas Thurston.

SUNBURY GAS COMPANY.

The Sunbury Gas Company was chartered in 1870, and the gas was first furnished for public consumption in November, 1871. The present officers are, S. P. Wolverton, President; T. H. Purdy, Secretary and Treasurer; Hiram Levy, Ira Hile, S. P. Wolverton, Directors; Ira Hile, Superintendent. The works are located near Market street, and employ two men. The company has laid down nearly two-and-a-half miles of main-pipe. Their gas is manufactured from petroleum oil by a new process. The price to consumers is one cent per hour for each ordinary burner, equivalent to two dollars per thousand feet for coal-gas. The company supply forty-two street gas-lamps, for which the borough pays three dollars for each lamp per month, including gas attendance and repairs. The office of the company is at the office of T. H. Purdy, on Market street.

POMFRET MANOR CEMETERY

Derives its name from the Manor of Pomfret, which William Penn gave to this section of country in honor of John Pomfret, an English poet. It is a very beautiful place, twenty acres in extent, and is situated on the hill south of the borough. It was laid out in 1871. It is managed by an association, of which J. W. Cake is President, Lloyd T. Rhorbach, Secretary, and J. A. Cake, Treasurer.

SUSQUEHANNA COFFIN WORKS.

This institution commenced business in October, 1874, on a small scale, employing only three men. It has since been enlarged so that now it employs twenty-four men, and manufactures over three hundred coffins per month. It is owned by Messrs. Fryling, Bowen & Engel.

SUNBURY COFFIN AND CASKET WORKS.

This establishment commenced business in July, 1875, and the factory is connected with the planing-mill on Third and Arch streets. The finishing-room and wareroom are on Front street, below the Shamokin Railroad. The capacity of the works is one hundred and twenty-five coffins and caskets per week. It manufactures six styles of each, and gives employment to twenty-five hands. Ira T. Clement is proprietor, and J. D. James, superintendent.

FORT AUGUSTA BUILDING AND LOAN ASSOCIATION.

This association was incorporated in 1869; L. T. Rohrbach, President; J. M. Fox, Vice President; Jacob Shipman, Secretary; Henry Clement, Treasurer; Directors—L. T. Rohrbach, D. Attick, H. F. Mann, N. F. Martz, Joseph Eyster, N. F. Lightoner, G. C. Brandon, J. A. Middleton, W. S. Rhoads, W. H. H. Offenbach; Solicitor, C. A. Reimensnyder.

Present Board—N. F. Martz, President; D. C. Dessinger, Vice President; Jacob Shipman, Secretary; Henry Clement, Treasurer; Solomon Malick, Solicitor; Directors—Ira T. Clement, A. Hoover, Hunter Newberry, William Simpson, Jacob Shipman, N. F. Martz, Emanuel Wilvert, W. H. Miller, V. Deitz, P. H. Moore.

Office, corner of Third and Market streets. Meets the fourth Thursday of each month. The object of this association is to accumulate a fund and invest the same, so as to enable members to purchase real estate, erect buildings, pay off encumbrances, and for other similar purposes. Members are enabled to buy homes with payments no heavier than the ordinary yearly rent paid by men with families.

THE ACCOMMODATION LOAN AND SAVING FUND.

Incorporated, 1870. S. Faust, Sr., President; J. Shipman, Secretary; H. Clement, Treasurer; S. B. Boyer, Solicitor; John Shissler, N. F. Martz, H. Y. Fryling, P. H. Moore, Ira T. Clement, Directors. Meets every fourth Monday, for the purpose of loaning money to stockholders in sums of fifty dollars and upwards, upon approved security. Object (see Fort Augusta Association.)

KNIGHTS OF PYTHIAS.

Eastern Star Lodge, No. 148, K. of P., was instituted March 24th, 1869, with the following charter members: S. B. Boyer, G. W. Renn, J. Hine, T. S. Shannon, W. A. Fetter, John E. Smick, C. D. Bucher, John Clark, J. M. Bostian, D. Attick, A. N. Brice, Henry Clement, David Fry, Emanuel Wilvert, J. Weiser Bucher, and C. A. Reimensnyder. Present Officers—P. C., William Simpson; C. C., John Mantz; V. C., Thomas J. Lyon; Pre., John Simpson; M. at A., Daniel C. Lyon; K. of R., S. R. Wynn; M. of F., George W. Snyder; M. of E., John Clark; I. G., E. M. Ness; O. G., Joseph Yarnall. This is a mutual aid society, allowing any sick member five dollars per week. Meetings every Wednesday evening, at Bright's Hall, corner Third and Market streets.

MASONRY.

Lodge No. 22, Ancient York Masons, held at Sunbury, received their charter on the 4th of October, 1779, from the "Provincial Grand Lodge," held at Philadelphia, which lodge was itself, at that time, under the jurisdiction of the "Grand Lodge of England," which was revived by his royal highness, Prince Edwin, in the year of our Lord, 926. The officers of No. 22, in 1779, were: Stephen Chambers, Worshipful Master; Henry Starrett, Senior Warden; and John Chatham, Junior Warden. The officers of the Provincial Grand Lodge, were: William Ball, Esq., Grand Master; William Shute, Grand Senior Warden; and John Howard, Grand Junior Warden. On the 25th day of September, 1786, the Provincial Grand Lodge became independent from the Grand Lodge of England, under the name of the "Grand Lodge of Pennsylvania," and the first officers were: William Adcock, Esq., Grand Master; Joseph Dean, Grand Senoir Warden; and George Ord, Grand Junior Warden. On the 20th day of March, 1787, this Grand Lodge renewed the charter of Lodge, No. 22, whose officers then were: William Wilson, Worshipful Master; Richard Martin, Senior Warden; and Samuel Gardner, Junior Warden. Up to this time (July 4th, 1876,) about five hundred members belonged to this lodge, of which number, one hundred and twenty-two still remain active members. The present officers (for the year 1876,) are: James H. McDevitt, W. M.; John M. Campbell, S. W.; John W. Stevenson, J. W.; Joseph Eisely, Secretary; and Mark P. Scupham, Treasurer. The Past Masters, are: Mark P. Scupham, William T. Grant, Edward C. Hauha, Benjamin Zeidemoyer, John B. Lenker, John Haas, Harvey K. Goodrich, Maclay C. Gearhart, John K. Clement, and James Farra. This lodge sustained its good standing, and continued its regular monthly meetings throughout all the anti-Masonic persecutions without interruption.

CAKE'S ADDITION TO SUNBURY.

This was laid out in 1866, by J. W. Cake, and consists of four hundred acres of level land. It extends along the river from the old borough line two hundred rods, then back from the river about a mile to the road leading from Sunbury to Catawissa. This land was a part of the Manor of Pomfret. Upon this was located Fort Augusta, a prominent station during the French and Indian war. The magazine of this fort is still in a perfect state of preservation, and is one hundred and twenty years old, having been built in 1756. Upon this tract of land is also located the shops of the Philadelphia and Erie Railroad Company, whose track crosses it at a distance of about one thousand feet east of the river.

PURDY'S ADDITION,

Or Purdytown, as it is generally known, was laid out by T. H. Purdy, Esq. It is well built up, and contains some fine residences.

SUNBURY BANKS.

First National Bank.—This bank was incorporated as a State bank, April 1st, 1831, under the corporate title of the "Bank of Northumberland," and was located in the borough of Northumberland, Pa., with a capital stock of two hundred thousand dollars, and commenced business on Monday, September 26th, 1831.

The first election of directors was held at the house of James Lee, in the borough of Northumberland, on Thursday, August 4th, 1831, when the following gentlemen were chosen, viz.: John Cowden, John B. Boyd, James Merrill, A. B. Cummings, John Taggart, Joseph Wallis, Abbot Green, James Hepburn, Daniel Brautigan, Henry Frick, William Clyde, Alexander Jordan, and Dr. David Petriken. James Hepburn was elected President, August 8th, 1831, and served until April 23d, 1840, when he resigned. John Taggart was elected President of the bank, April 30th, 1840, who served until November 20th, 1863, when he was succeeded by William Cameron. William Cameron resigned the presidency, June 25th, 1867, and on the same day, J. B. Packer was elected in his place, who has been the president of the institution ever since.

Joseph R. Priestley was elected the cashier, August 8th, 1831, and served in that capacity until his death, which occurred on Tuesday, November 10th, 1863. November 19th, 1863, S. J. Packer was elected to fill the place of Mr. Priestley, and he has been acting in that capacity from that date to the present time.

The original stock of the bank was subscribed by one hundred and fourteen different persons. The present number of stockholders is ninety-five.

PLATE XI

W. R. KUTZNER & CO.,
DRUGS AND HARDWARE,
SHAMOKIN, PA.

The notes of the Bank of Northumberland were redeemed at par, in gold, in the city of Philadelphia, while the notes of a large number of the banks of the State were at a discount of one-fourth to one-half of one per cent. The bank always retained the confidence of the public, and was justly considered one of the best in the State. The total amount of dividends paid to shareholders, since the organization, is seven hundred and thirty-four thousand dollars.

By virtue of an Act of Assembly, passed April 16th, 1864, the bank was removed from Northumberland to Sunbury, July 25th, 1864. It existed as a State bank, until July 1st, 1865, when it surrendered its State charter, and was organized as a National bank, under the title of the "First National Bank of Sunbury, Pa."

At a meeting of the stockholders of this bank, held January 25th, 1876, the following directors were elected for the ensuing year: John B. Packer, James K. Davis, Henry C. Eyer, William H. Waples, Simon Cameron, William I. Greenough, John Haas, William M. Rockefeller, William Cameron, Alexander Jordan, George Smuller, George Schnure, and George F. Miller. The present officers are: J. B. Packer, President; S. J. Packer, Cashier; John E. Torrington, Book-keeper; Thomas D. Grant, Teller; Samuel R. Snyder, Clerk; George Follmer, Messenger.

Augusta Bank.—This institution was organized, and a charter obtained, in 1873. The bank building is situated on Packer street, near the corner of Front. It is a neat and well-arranged edifice, twenty-five by thirty-four feet, and cost eight thousand dollars. The authorized capital of the bank is one hundred thousand dollars, fifty thousand of which have been paid in. Its present officers are: J. A. Cake, President; M. L. Snyder, Cashier; J. W. Cake, John S. Snyder, J. H. Jenkins, J. Adam Cake, J. R. Kauffman, M. L. Snyder, H. L. Cake, and W. W. Moody, Directors.

CHURCHES.

Presbyterian Church.—The precise period when the Presbyterian Church, in Sunbury, was organized, cannot be determined. There is no record evidenced of it, and no member of the church is now living, who lived at the time of her organization. It existed before 1787, for in the month of May, in that year, the Rev. Hugh Morrison, a probationer from the Presbytery of Root, in Ireland, was called as pastor to the congregations of Buffalo, Northumberland, and Sunbury. He officiated as pastor in the Sunbury congregation until his death, which took place in 1804. He was buried in the burial-ground, in Sunbury. His wife died soon after, and was buried near him. Where the congregation worshipped, when the church was organised, is not known. About the year 1794, the Presbyterian congregation, and the German Reformed congregation, united in erecting a log church on the corner of Second and Chestnut streets, then the corner of Blackberry and River streets. In this building these two congregations worshipped in great peace and harmony, until about the year 1841, when they separated. The Presbyterians sold their interest in the church and church property to the Reformed congregation, purchased a lot on the corner of Third and Chestnut streets, then Blackberry and Deer streets, and on it erected a small one-story brick church, in which they worshipped until within the last four years. The congregation sold this building, and purchased a lot on the north side of Market street, and erected a very handsome brick church, two stories high, with a beautiful steeple, one hundred and thirty feet high. It is very much admired for its just proportions, convenience, beautiful finish, and situation. Its style is Romanesque. The Rev. Isaac Grier, after an interval of about two years, was installed pastor of the church, and continued as such until his death, on the 23d of August, 1814. He was buried in Northumberland, where he lived at the time of his death. Robert Fisher Nash Smith, of Virginia, succeeded Mr. Grier, and William R. Ashmead succeeded Mr. Smith. Mr. Ashmead was succeeded by William Richmond Smith, a cousin of Robert F. N. Smith. Wheelock S. Stone succeeded William R. Smith. After Mr. Stone left, William R. Smith, who had resigned his charge, and removed to Ohio, was invited to return. He accepted the invitation, and thus succeeded, as also preceded, Mr. Stone. He was pastor of the Sunbury and Northumberland congregations at the time of his death. William Simonton succeeded Mr. Smith, and after dissolution of the pastoral relation, James D. Reardon accepted a call, and was installed pastor. Samuel W. Reigert, of Lancaster, succeeded Mr. Reardon. Mr. Simonton, Mr. Reardon, and Mr. Reigert, are still living. Mr. Lawson, now in Oxford, Chester County, succeeded Mr. Reigert, and Rev. Samuel J. Milliken, now laboring near Philadelphia, succeeded Mr. Lawson. Martin Luther Ross succeeded Mr. Milliken, and is now the pastor of the church.

The church was often without a pastor, but the pulpit was occupied by supplies. Mr. Gray of Ireland, Mr. Millick, Jonah Henry Young, and others, whose names cannot now be determined, are well remembered as supplies.

The church at present has a membership of 268. The members of this session, are John Eckman, Philip Hylis, William W. Moody, George W. Hacket, and Alexander Jordan.

The Sabbath-school connected with the church averages 150 children. There are twenty teachers, one superintendent, one assistant superintendent, and two librarians.

The first elders, according to the tradition of the church, were John Buyers, and William McAdam. Alexander Jordan was ordained elder, in August, 1832. He acted as such until the present time. Peter Pursel, Lewis Dewart, William Gulick, Charles Gobin, Robert Mateer, and Andrew N. Brice, were elders, at different periods. Messrs. McAdam, Buyers, Pursel, Dewart, and Gulick, are dead.

Methodist Episcopal Church.—Some time about the year 1790, a Methodist preacher from the Wyoming region traveled through the lower north branch, and up the west branch country, on what we may call a "religious exploration." The result of the same was, that in 1791, two preachers were sent, viz.: Richard Parriott and Lewis Browning. These men formed a circuit, called "*Northumberland,*" commencing at Briar Creek, or Berwick, in what is now Columbia County; westward to White Deer Valley; thence by the left bank of the west branch across Loyalsock, Lycoming and Pine Creeks, to the Bald Eagle Creek; up the same to the neighborhood of now Unionville, Centre County; thence by Bellefonte and Spring Creek to Penn's Valley; from that point by Shamokin Creek and ridges to the Nescopec Creek; from thence to the place of beginning. This circuit was traveled once in four weeks, with preaching every day but one. Sunbury was included in this charge.

In 1793, the pioneer Bishop of American Methodism—Francis Ashbury, visited the country. He came to Northumberland, and found there a small society. He was entertained at the house of Mrs. Taggart in that place. The Bishop preached a number of times both in Northumberland and in Sunbury. As far as known, this is the first mention of preaching by a Methodist in Sunbury, though it is presumable that Parriott, Browning, or James Campbell, William Colbert and James Paynter, who followed them in 1792 and 1793, may have preceded the Bishop.

In Sunbury, the inhabitants were mostly German, and the Methodist preachers consequently had but few hearers at most. This fact may also have prevented the organizing of a society or the gaining of a membership. We learn that perhaps twenty years later there was but one Methodist family in Sunbury, viz.: William Search and wife, living on Arch street. This couple, with a few others, for years would walk to Northumberland to meet with the society there, and hear preaching.

The year the first class was formed in Sunbury cannot precisely be ascertained. The class, however, consisted of some ten or twelve persons. The first leader was Jacob Heller, who also was a local preacher. In that class, were William Search and wife, Solomon Shafer and wife, a young man named Jacob Dawson, Eli Deemer and wife, (his first wife), and Mrs. Nancy Follmer, (now Grandmother Yoxtheimer), the, perhaps, only surviving member.

The class met in a small house that stood on Front street, below Chestnut street, at 2 o'clock on Tuesday afternoon. All the members were punctual in their attendance at that hour. It is related of the members, that at the hour of class, whatever work they were engaged in at once ceased, and in the working-dress of the laborer or house-keeper, "sun-bonnet," etc., they would repair to the place of worship. The preachers would frequently, as was the custom in that day, meet the class. The house on Front street was occupied by Solomon Shafer. Afterwards, for a time, the class met in a house near the corner of Chestnut and Fourth streets.

The first preaching-place for the Methodists was in the grand jury room in the old "State House," which stood where the court house now is. Sometimes, on special occasions, they would occupy the court-room in the old court house.

In the years 1837 and 1838, Rev. H. G. Dill was on the circuit embracing Sunbury. He held a successful revival meeting in the grand jury room, in the fall of 1837. When Mr. Dill took charge, there were, perhaps, twenty members in the society. At the protracted meeting there were thirty united. This so encouraged the society, that they resolved on the erection of a church edifice; although there were troublesome times in the progress of Methodism in Sunbury—the work being opposed by the then resident ministers of other churches.

The church was commenced in 1838. When Mr. Dill closed his term, and left in the Spring of 1839, the church was under roof and enclosed with the doors and windows, and also the floor laid, and no debt so far as they had gone. The building was completed in the fall of 1839, and Mr. Dill, who came to the dedication, preached the first sermon in the new church on Saturday morning, and the Rev. John Miller, presiding elder, preached the dedicatory sermon on the first Sunday in December, 1838, from the text, "I will glorify the house of my glory." (Isaiah LX. 7.)

The building is the same now occupied by the Catholics on Arch street. The cost of lot and building cannot now be given. Eli Dremer and James Husted were on the board of trustees and building committee.

The Methodist Society, numbering about ninety, were placed in a separate charge in 1868. They sold their property to the Catholics, and bought the corner of Arch and Second streets, where they commenced the erection of a building in 1869. It is built of brick, ninety-five feet deep, and fifty-five feet wide, two stories high. The corner-stone was laid by Bishop Simpson in the Fall of 1869, and the basement was dedicated by Bishop Ames in March, 1870. The audience room was completed, and in October, 1873, was dedicated by Rev. B. Ives, Dr. Simms, and others. The church is not, as yet, completed—the tower, etc., unfinished. The cost of the building and lot may possibly reach thirty-eight thousand dollars. The present membership numbers about two hundred and seventy-five.

The preachers who successively preached in Sunbury are, taking the list as it stands for Northumberland circuit: 1791, R. Parriott, S. Browning; 1792, James Campbell, William Colbert; 1793, James Campbell, James Paynter; 1794, Robert Manley, John Brodhead; 1795, James Ward, S. Timmons; 1796, John Seward, R. Sneath; 1797, John Lacky, Daniel Higby; 1798, J. Sackey, John Leach; 1799, James Moore, Benjamin Bidlack, Daniel Stevens; 1800, Ephraim Chambers, Edward Larkins, Asa Smith; 1801, Johnson Dunham, Gil Carpenter; 1802, Anning Owen, James Aikens; 1803, Daniel Ryan, James Ridgway; 1804, T. Adams, Gideon Draper; 1805, Christopher Frey, James Saunders.

In 1800, Lycoming circuit was cut off from the Northumberland circuit, and perhaps from this date, there may have been regular preaching in Sunbury. It is doubtful whether there was more than occasional preaching previous to this time.

In 1806, Robert Burch, John Swartswelder; 1807, Nicholas Willis, Joel Smith; 1808, Thomas Curren, John Rhodes; 1809, Timothy Lee, Loring Grant; 1810, Abraham Dawson, Isaac Puffer; 1811, B. G. Peddock, J. H. Baker, R. Lanning.

In 1812, "*Shamokin*" circuit was formed, embracing all the territory east of the north branch to the Broad Mountain, and from Nescopec Creek on the north to the Dauphin County line on the Susquehanna. Sunbury was in this charge.

The preachers on this new charge were, in 1822, James H. Baker, J. Hickox; 1813, A. Dawson, Nathaniel Reeder; 1814, Marmaduke Pearce; 1815–16, B. Ridlack; 1817, A. Dawson; 1818, Israel Cook; 1819, Elisha Bibins; 1820, M. Pearce; 1821–22, John Rhodes; 1823, David Steel; 1824. John Tanneyhill; 1827, Jonas Munroe; 1828, Henry Tarring; 1829, E. E. Allen.

In 1830, the name of the circuit was changed to that of "*Sunbury.*"

The preachers were, in 1830, Josiah Forrest; 1831, O. Ege, J. H. Brown; 1832, W. Howe, J. Clerk; 1833, T. Tanneyhill, J. R, Tulcutyre; 1834, T. Tanneyhill, John Guyer; 1835, O. Ege, J. Anderson; 1836, O. Ege, G. C. Gibbons.

In 1837, Luzerne mission was cut off embracing all north of Catawissa.

In 1837, the preachers were H. G. Dill, Charles E. Brown; 1838, H. G. Dill, John Hall; 1839, J. Rhodes, Wm. Hirst; 1840, J. Rhodes, John Ball; 1841, S. Ball, G. H. Day.

During the term of Messrs. Ball and Day, the first Sunday-school in connection with the Methodist Church in Sunbury was organized: James Husted was appointed superintendent, and Solomon Shafer, secretary. George Bucher and Miss Elizabeth Dremer, (now Mrs. Elizabeth Bucher,) were teachers in the school. At the present time, (1876), they are still teachers. The lines between the churches were very closely drawn, and the Methodist Sunday-school numbered but a small party. There were twenty-one dollars in money collected in town for a Sunday-school library, to which was added some fifteen dollars more from the country appointments.

In 1842, the preachers were George Berkstresser, W. S. Baird; 1843, A. Brittain, J. Montgomery; 1844, A. Brittain, J. W. Tongue; 1845, J. W. Haughawout, J. S. McMurray; 1846, J. W. Haughawout, T. Barnhart; 1847, P. McEnally, B. Huffman; 1848, James Ewing, J. P. Simpson; 1849, J. Ewing, Wm. Gwynn; 1850, John Stine, W. Gwynn; 1851, J. Stine, A. Hartman; 1852, J. A. Ross, T. M. Goodfellow.

The territory north of Northumberland County was cut off, and Catawissa circuit formed.

In 1853, J. A. Ross was the preacher; 1854, J. G. McKechan, J. Burns; 1855, J. G. McKechan, B. P. King; 1856, T. Tanneyhill, N. W. Colburn; 1857, T. Tanneyhill, M. L. Drum; 1858–59, George Warren, F. B. Riddle; 1860, E. Butler, J. P. Swanger; 1861, E. Butler, J. A. Dixon; 1862, A. M. Creighton, B. F. Stevens.

In 1863, Shamokin and Trevorton were separated from the circuit.

The preachers in 1863, were A. M. Creighton, E. T. Swartz; 1864, B. P. King, J. M. Akers; 1865, B. P. King, W. H. Norcross; 1866, J. Anderson, E. Shoemaker; 1867, J. Anderson, W. Fritz. J. Anderson died this year.

In 1868, Sunbury was made a station—that is, all the country appointments were separated from the town.

The preachers since, were 1868–69–70, W. W. Evans; 1871, J. C. Clarke; 1872–73, G. D. Pennepacker; 1874–75–76, J. A. DeMoyer, the present pastor.

The Sunday-school of the M. E. Church organized as stated above, continues to the present time, and has sent forth two off-shoots in the shape of mission-schools; the one in the Purdytown addition, and the other in the Caketown addition to Sunbury.

The Sunday-school in Sunbury, at the formation of the society into a station in 1868, was placed in the hands of the pastor as superintendent. Each pastor in turn, up to the present year, served as such. The present year the pastor declining, George Follmer (a grandson of the Mr. Follmer, a member of the first-class), was elected. The statistics for the past year are as follows: Officers and teachers, twenty-nine; number of scholars, one hundred and eighty-one; volumes in library, three hundred and twenty; expenses of school, past year, about seventy-five dollars.

The mission Sunday-school in Caketown was organized in 1869, by the election of Henry Y. Fryling, as superintendent. Philip Arrison is the present incumbent. The statistics for the past year are as follows: Officers and teachers, eleven; number of scholars, sixty; volumes in library, one hundred; expenses of the school, the past year, about fifteen dollars.

The mission Sundy-school in Purdytown was organized in 1869, by the election of E. Z. Shipe, as superintendent. He is the present superintendent. The statistics are as follows: Officers and teachers, eighteen; number of scholars, eighty-nine; volumes in library, two hundred and fifty; expenses the past year, thirty dollars.

The total statistics of the M. E. Sunday-schools of Sunbury, are: Officers and teachers, fifty-eight; number of scholars, three hundred and thirty; volumes in library, six hundred and eighty; expenses for the year, one hundred and twenty dollars; collections for mission purposes in the Sunday-school for the year, one hundred and eight dollars and forty-two cents.

The society was incorporated by the county court, in 1858, and the present board of trustees consists of J. A. DeMoyer, president; W. D. Melick, secretary; W. R. F. Weimer, treasurer, and George Bucher, Wm. Murray, Isaac Furman, and Samuel Byerly, as members.

St. Matthew's Church.—The character of incorporation under which this parish was admitted into the Diocese of Pennsylvania, bears date of April 24, 1827, and at the diocesal convention of the same year the parish was received into the diocese.

The vestrymen at that time, were Charles Dering, John D. Hegins, Ebenezer Greenough, Charles G. Donnel, Jacob Painter, J. C. Robins, Jeremiah Shindel, and Wm. Dewart. These parties were the signers of the charter of incorporation.

The parish was organized by the Rev. James De Prue, who was the first rector. Previous to this, occasional service was held at different times by the Rev. Mr. Hopkins, and the Rev. Mr. Eldred.

In 1834, a church edifice was erected on the north-east corner of Broadway and Mulberry alley. It was a brick structure, and is still standing and used as a place of worship by the society. It has a seating capacity of about two hundred. It was consecrated in December, 1836. The Sunbury school of this society was organized in January, 1825, and was one of the earliest in the borough. It owns a fine library of choice reading.

The following parties have served the society as rectors, and in the order of their names: Rev. James De Prue, Rev Christian Wiltberger, Rev. Isaac W. Smith, Rev. Alfred Londerbach, Rev. William Sydney Walker, Rev. Joshua Weaver, Rev. B. Wistar Morris, now the Bishop of Oregon, Rev. William Musgrave, Rev. William White Montgomery, Rev. J. W. Gougler, Rev. Lewis W. Gibson, Rev. Charles Van Dyne, Rev. Gideon J. Burton, and Rev. Horatio H. Hewitt, the present rector. The present vestrymen, are George B. Youngman, William I. Greenough, William T. Grant, George W. Smith, Thomas D. Grant, William R. Dunham, and Henry B. Masser.

Baptist Church.—The first Baptists known to reside in Sunbury, were Joseph Richardson, and Ann, his wife, who were constituent members of Shamokin Baptist Church, constituted in 1794.

In 1815, Henry Clark, Rebecca, his wife, Ann Clark, Mary Clark, Lavina Frilling, and Miss D. Crosby, an English school-mistress, resided in the borough, making, with the Richardsons, eight members in all.

Of those early Baptists, the venerable Joseph Richardson was one of the church deacons. Henry Clark, was afterwards pastor of the Little Muncy and Loyalsock churches. None of these are now living, except Mary (Clark) Robins, in Upper Augusta, in her 80th year.

Excepting an occasional service by some itinerant, there was no Baptist preaching in Sunbury until Rev. Eugene Kincaid, of Milton, held frequent meetings, prior to his departure as Missionary to Burmah, in May, 1830.

The first Baptist church in Sunbury, was organized December 15th, 1842, with eighty-one constituent members, most of whom had been baptised by John H. Worrel, from Philadelphia, who became their first regular pastor.

Prior to this period, the few Sunbury members were connected with Shamokin churches. Their house of worship stood near Shamokin Creek, two miles above Snydertown. Here is the oldest grave-yard in that region of country. Rev. John Wolverton was their pastor from 1811 to 1822.

The Sunbury Baptist Church enrolls one hundred and ten members. They own a lot on the corner of Chestnut and Fourth streets, on which they purpose to erect a house of worship, and then to use their neat chapel, which is situated on a part of the lot, for a lecture and Sunday-school room.

The Reformed Church.—This church, organized in 1784, is one of the oldest organizations in Sunbury. It was incorporated in 1825. Number of communicants, one hundred and fifty. The church is a brick structure, and is located at the corner of Second and Chestnut streets. In the winter of 1871-2, the congregation erected a substantial brick parsonage at a cost of four thousand dollars. Rev. Calvin S. Gerhard, pastor.

Rev. Martin Bruner was one of the early pastors. Among the clergymen who have served this church, may be mentioned the names of Richard A. Fisher, who was pastor for some eighteen years. His successors were D. Y. Heysler, J. W. Steinmetz, W. C. Cremer, A. H. Dotterer, and the present incumbent, Calvin S. Gerhard, who came in 1870.

CENTENNIAL CELEBRATION IN SUNBURY.

On the Fourth of July, 1872, occurred the celebration of the one-hundredth anniversary of the existence of the borough of Sunbury.

Some days previous, the following card of invitation was issued by the Sunbury committee of arrangements, which explains itself:

"*To the Citizens of Northumberland County*:—Inasmuch as the citizens of the borough of Sunbury have now in hand the arrangements for the celebration of the "Centennial of the Borough," on the coming Fourth of July; and inasmuch, also, as the centennial of the County of Northumberland occurred on the twenty-first day of March last, at the suggestion of numerous citizens of the County, the committee of arrangements have concluded to include the entire County in their invitation to participate in the proceedings of that day, and therefore invite, most earnestly and cordially, all the borough and township officials to come in a body, and all the citizens thereof. The committee further suggest that each borough and township appoint its committee of organization and arrangements, to act with the Sunbury committee, of which Solomon Malick, Esq., is chairman. The committee hope to have a general good time, a general greeting of all the good people of the County; a time of rejoicing over our borough and County centennial, as well as the recurring anniversary of American Independence. Let all come.

By order of the Committee of Arrangements."

Northumberland's Greeting to Sunbury.—In response to an invitation from our borough authorities to the citizens of Northumberland to attend our Centennial Anniversary on the Fourth of July, the following reply has been received:

MAJ. WM. L. DEWART—

"*Dear Sir:* I have been appointed by the town council to return you their sincere thanks for your kind and generous invitation tendered to them, and through them to the citizens of Northumberland, to join the citizens of Sunbury in celebrating the centennial of the birth of your beautiful and prosperous town. The time seems not far distant when the two towns will join hands, and, with the bridge free to the public, we shall be one continuous city. The petty rivalry that formerly existed between the bully-rums and the pine-knots, has given way to a feeling of respect and admiration for each other, and a cordial and fraternal feeling exists between them, which will continue to strengthen. We accept your invitation as cordially as it was given, to participate in your festivities as a body, and with the sincere thanks for your generous hospitality, we are ever yours truly.

M. B. PRIESTLEY, Committee."

The initial ceremonies of the day were inaugurated by the ringing of bells and loud whistling of locomotives, and at the shops above and below town, at midnight. This was followed by the firing of cannon, the crashing of windows, and the shooting of fire-crackers. The dawn of day revealed a warm sun, and the arrival of the regular fourteen daily trains, together with a number of excursion trains, brought to the town crowds of people and visiting organizations, to participate in the work of the day. The streets and dwellings were neatly displayed with evergreens, portraits of the older citizens and fathers of the Revolution, and the stars and stripes, while a number of bands and a drum corps from Harrisburg enlivened the scene with cheering music.

It was found, very early in the morning, by the arrival of a number of fire companies from Harrisburg, Lock Haven and Selinsgrove, and of military companies from Williamsport, Lewisburg, Locust Gap, Excelsior and Shamokin, with a number of civic societies, that the occasion would be marked by a success more than anticipated.

The parade in the morning was one of the finest ever congregated in central Pennsylvania. It was the feature of the ceremonies, which in point of appearance, was most admired. In the procession, the main elements were the military and firemen.

The committee of arrangements, who actively engaged in the work for the celebration, were composed of Solomon Malick, Esq., Major D. Heim, W. H. Miller, A. N. Brice, Esq., Colonel George Wagenseller, H. Y. Friling, John Haas, Solomon Stroh, P. H. Moore, Christian Neff, W. I. Greenough, Esq., J. A. Cake, Esq., W. P. Roberts, General J. K. Clement, Valentine Dietz, J. M. Cadwallader, C. J. Fox, T. S. Shannon, T. H. Purdy, Jacob Seasenbach, and C. J. Bruner.

The chief marshal, of the day was Colonel George B. Cadwallader, and his assistants, Major W. Calder Kapp, of Northumberland, Captain Heber Painter, Captain Beech Ammon, of Dry Valley, Captain H. F. Mann, John J. Smith, E. M. Bucher, P. C. Oberdorf, and Philip Forrestor.

The procession started from Second and Market streets, at eleven o'clock, in the following order, headed by the Freeburg Band.

Carriages containing Judge Rockefeller, General Simon Cameron, Judge Jordan, and George Prince.

Then followed in order, carriages containing Hon. J. B. Packer, and other speakers.

Then carriages with chief burgess and town council, soldiers of 1812, and of the Mexican war.

Repas Brass Band, of Williamsport.

A section of artillery, two brass pieces from Lewisburg, drawn by horses, and accompanied by twenty-five men.

The battery was commanded by Lieutenant Myers, in the absence of the regular commander, Captain McCalla. The following were the military companies:

Williamsport Greys; Captain A. H. Stead, with fifty-five men, dressed in grey uniform and fully equipped.

Washington Rifles; Captain John McElicee, with eighty-two men, from Locust Gap, Northumberland County, sixty-one guns, five sergeants, and eight color guards.

Geary Bucktails; Captain F. D. Strausser, with sixty men, from Excelsior, Northumberland County.

The following were the civil societies:

Sunbury Lodge of Odd Fellows, No. 203, Isaac Kerns, marshal, with fifty men, and visiting members of other lodges.

Improved Order of Red Men, Shohomo Tribe, No. 69, of Sunbury, with —— men, under J. M. Bell, marshal.

Patriotic Sons of America, of Sunbury, Camp No. 19; E. J. Gibson, marshal, with sixty men.

Knights of Pythias, of Sunbury, No. 143, composed of members from Sunbury and Northumberland Lodges, Thomas Taubman, acting marshal, with seventy-five men.

United Order of American Mechanics, Bragy Council, No. 221, Sunbury, Martin Kinney, marshal. Hollowing Run Council, No. 285, E. C. Gobin, marshal. Millersburg Council, No. 99. Junior Council, O. U. A. M., of Sunbury, No. 131, Henry Grayville, marshal. In all, the American Mechanics numbered one hundred and twenty-five men, and with their red, white and blue regalia, looked well.

Next in order came the Conclaves of Sunbury, Council, No. 11, in bright uniform, white pantaloons, black coats, and neat caps, swords, and belts, under command of General John K. Clement. They numbered about thirty men.

Then came the Fire Department, headed by the Sunbury Silver Cornet Band, with fifteen men. Of this department, George Washington Smith, was chief marshal.

The first company in line was the Sunbury Steam Fire Engine Company, No. 1, with forty men. The steam fire engine was in line, drawn by a team of horses. The engine was handsomely trimmed with wreaths, tastefully prepared by ladies.

The visiting fire companies, eight in number, were the guests of the Sunbury Company. They were received by committees at the engine-house, where their "machines" were housed and cared for. The engine-house was also trimmed, and an arch thrown across the street in front. These decorations were also the work of the ladies. J. K. Davis, Esq., and T. G. Cooper, were active in the management of details.

Next in order of march came the Susquehanna Steam Fire Engine Company, of Selinsgrove, with forty men, Captain Mecker, marshal.

Williamsport Band, with seventeen men.

Hope Hose Company, No. 5, of Williamsport, sixty-eight men.

Lock Haven Band, sixteen men.

Dauntless Hook and Ladder Company, of Lock Haven, forty-four men. The boys had their carriage in line.

Caturnet Steam Fire Engine Company, Lock Haven, forty men in line with hose-carriage.

Good Will Fire Company, of Harrisburg, twenty-five men. The boys were in line with their steamer, named in honor of the Mayor of Harrisburg, William T. Verbeke.

Harrisburg Band, fifteen men.

Mt. Vernon Hook and Ladder Company, of Harrisburg, thirty-four men in line with carriage and ladders.

Washington Steam Fire Engine Company, of Williamsport, fifty-seven men, with steamer in line.

Drum Corps of Harrisburg, with eight men. They belonged to the "Hope" Fire Company, of that city.

Hope Steam Fire Company, No. 2, of Harrisburg, forty-six men. The boys had in line a large and beautiful four-wheeled hose-carriage, nicely trimmed, called "Jennie Cameron." The Hope boys were in mourning, on account of the sad death of a member, George Lower, who was struck by a bridge in looking out of the car window, at Dauphin, on their way up, and almost instantly killed.

Sunbury Boys in Blue, under Captain William Helm. These were young fellows of ages ranging from 12 to 16 years, fired with military ardor and a desire to do honor to the occasion, which they did.

Sunbury Boys in White, called the "Washington Guards," under Captain Robert Grant. These were still more juvenile in age and appearance. They marched like veterans, and with their improvised wooden-guns, presented a strong military resemblance.

The entire fire department of the parade looked well, and all behaved admirably. The utmost good order prevailed as well as good feeling among all the organizations.

The Line of March.—The route of procession was from Market square to Front street; up Front to Arch; out Arch to Fourth; down Fourth to Walnut; out Walnut to Front; up Front to Chestnut; out Chestnut to Fifth; up Fifth to Market; out Market to Market square, when at about twelve-and-a-half o'clock, the procession was dismissed for dinner. The procession numbered about one thousand men.

The Great Dinner.—The Sunbury Company provided dinner, through the Methodist congregation, at the new church, for visiting companies, where about four hundred men partook of a well-prepared meal.

It was estimated that there were not less than ten thousand strangers in town, but the liberality of the citizens was sufficient for the emergency. Among the most hospitable, was General Clement, who opened his house to dinner one hundred and fifty military and conclaves. Many others did likewise; among them Hon. J. B. Packer, Hon. Alexander Jordan, and others.

Afternoon Exercises.—At two o'clock, the time appointed, the afternoon exercises commenced. A stand twelve by thirty-two feet had been erected at the western end of Market square, and trimmed with spruce and flags. A large portrait of General Washington, loaned by H. B. Masser, Esq., adorned the center in front, while two large silk flags procured at Harrisburg, by A. N. Brice, Esq., hung from either end. The meeting was organized at the time named by calling Hon. William L. Dewart to the chair.

The following Vice Presidents, all of them over sixty-five years of age, were appointed:

Sebastian Boughner, Esq., Philip Renn, Col. Elisha Kline, Jacob Sensholtz, Jacob Eckman, Isaac Kline, Mr. Knouse, Samuel T. Brown, Peter Baldy, of Danville, John Moore, Hugh Teats, Esq., Dr. John Baker, John D. Conrad, Daniel Hileman, Mr. Strasser, Jacob Bloom, Benjamin Knouse (Trevorton), John Starner, John Taggart, Jesse Horton, William Forsyth, John Hileman, Francis Bucher, John Shive, Henry Billington, George Prince, William H. Muench, Mordecai Lawrence, Andrew C. Huston.

Of these old heroes of more than half-a-century, George Prince, was then eighty-four years of age. He kept many years ago the St. Lawrence Hotel, in Sunbury. He is now deceased. Sebastian Boughner was then seventy-four years of age. He was a soldier of 1812, and fought at the capture of Fort Erie, in 1814. Andrew C. Huston, an old printer, was then eighty-five years old. He now resides in Northumberland, where, some seventy years ago, he learned his trade with Andrew Kennedy, in the Northumberland *Gazette* office. All these old men labored actively in the early historic times of this neighborhood and County.

Secretaries:—Solomon Malick, Esq., A. F. Brice, Esq., of Sunbury; M. B. Priestly, of Northumberland; B. M. Bubb, of Georgetown; Frank John, of Shamokin, C. O. Bachman, of Watertown, and R. M. Frick, of Milton.

Major Dewart then called the meeting to order, and briefly addressed the crowd as follows:

"*Fellow Citizens:*—It is with pride and pleasure that I assume the duties assigned me by the committee and yourselves. This is a glorious day for old Sunbury—a glorious day for Solomon Malick, Esq., our worthy and most excellent Chief Burgess, who conceived this successful centennial celebration of our town. This is a great day, because it is the recurring anniversary of our National Independence, as well as the one-hundredth anniversary of our existence as a borough. We are here assembled to celebrate the centennial of our now wide-awake town. We will not all likely be present at the next hundredth anniversary. It is likely that I will be the only one present at that coming celebration. I was not here at the last celebration. I think my wife was sick, or I was cutting grass. But I will not take up time with these introductory remarks. I return to you, and all the organizations present, the heartfelt thanks of all our people for your participation in these ceremonies on this great occasion. I now have the honor of introducing to you, as the orator of the day, a gentleman who has lived among us for fifty-seven years—a gentleman of large judicial experience and ability—the HON. ALEXANDER JORDAN."

Judge Jordan occupied about thirty-five minutes in the delivery of his address. He said the meeting was called for three objects. First, to celebrate the centennial anniversary of the borough of Sunbury; second, to celebrate the anniversary of our National Independence, and third, to select a spot in the public square, on which to erect a monument to the memory of the brave men who fell in the great Rebellion. He referred to the probable condition of the place on which Sunbury is located, at the time of its location one hundred years ago, by whom the survey was made; the reason why its growth was not more rapid; its population in 1815; the number of brick and other buildings at that time; and its present population and improvements.

In speaking of the second object, he referred to the oppressive system of taxation adopted by the British Parliament in reference to the colonies; the otal disregard by the King and Parliament to the appeals made by the colonies for redress, and the determination of the colonies to be free. The adoption of the Declaration of Independence; the war and its glorious termination; our growth, prosperity, happy form of government, influence of our Republican principles in other nations, and how our government could be perpetuated.

In reference to the third object, he spoke of the propriety and duty of living to erect enduring monuments to the memory of the men who fell in battle during the late rebellion; of the loss of valuable life; of the strength of our Government; that it could not be destroyed by the unhallowed touch of treason, and of the final settlement of the momentous question of slavery, and the right of secession; and that we could now emphatically sing, "This is the land of the free and the home of the brave."

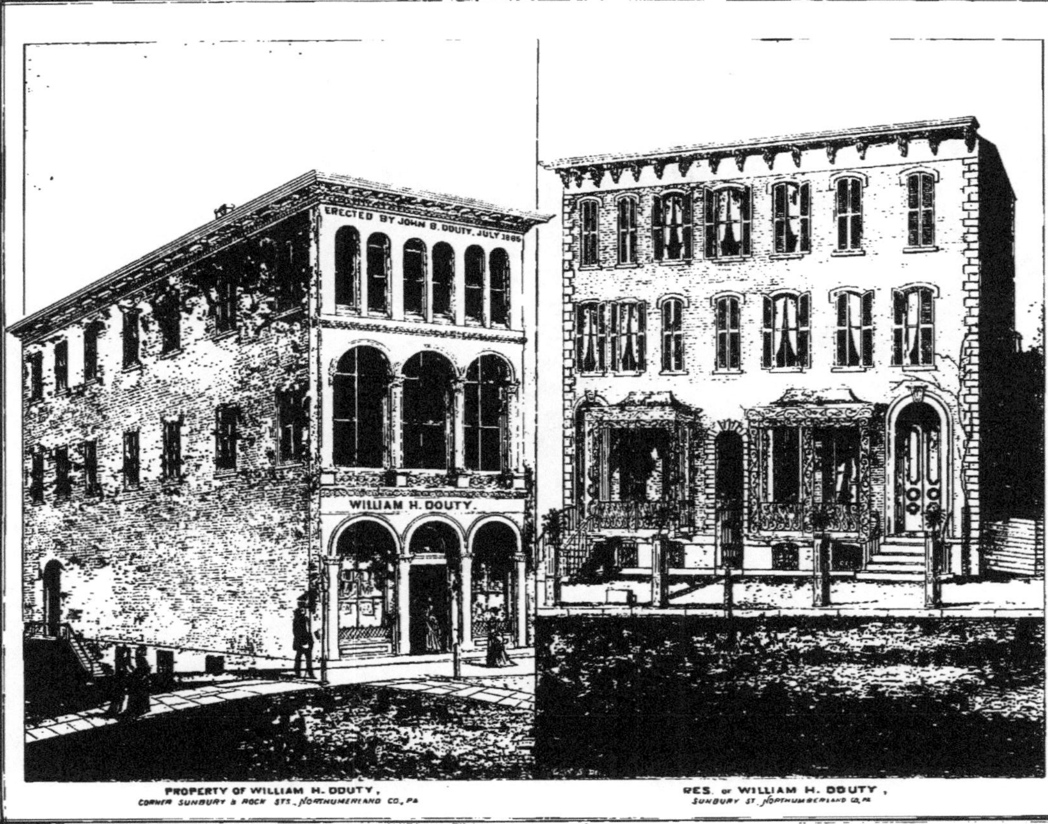

PROPERTY OF WILLIAM H. DOUTY,
CORNER SUNBURY & ROCK STS., NORTHUMBERLAND CO., PA.

RES. OF WILLIAM H. DOUTY,
SUNBURY ST. NORTHUMBERLAND CO. PA.

According to previous arrangement, Hon. A. Jordan and Hon. Simon Cameron then proceeded with axe, stakes, and tape-line, together with the soldier's committee, A. N. Brice, Heber Painter, General Clement, S. H. Knowles, and F. M. Bucher, to measure off the site for a County Soldiers' Monument to be erected in Market square. These gentlemen then measured off the ground for the base which will be fifteen feet square, and located nearly opposite the residence of S. J. Packer, Esq. After the measurement had been made, and stakes driven, General Cameron stepped to one side, and by invitation of the committee addressed a few remarks, in substance as follows:

"*My Friends of Old Northumberland County:*—I am proud to be among you to-day. Since my boyhood days, and since I left this portion of Pennsylvania, to enter more actively into the race of life, very many of the old familiar faces have disappeared. I take pleasure in visiting your town at least once in a year, and very frequently much oftener. I remember well the time when you did not have any railroads, and long before the time when the canal was dug on the other side of the river. At that time, I suggested that the canal should go on the eastern side of the Susquehanna, because of the coal which filled these mountains; but the projector of that enterprise hooted at the idea, and said the canal was intended to be used in transporting the produce of the rich farms beyond the western side of the river, and so it went there. I refer with pleasure to the fact that I presided at the first railroad meeting held in your old court house, to project the first railroad to your town. The untold wealth underlying the hills which surround you, as yet but little improved and delved, will gradually populate and improve the valley, until the Susquehanna Valley will be the richest and the most populous in the State. The time will come when Northumberland and Sunbury will form one city, a community of interests, and of population, all bent on one object—improvement. The time will come when the bridges between Sunbury and Northumberland will be thrown open to free travel, and other bridges will be erected across this river; and some of you may live to see the day when a large and growing town will be built over on the Blue Hill. These may seem like idle prophesies, but I have been accustomed to look forward to the future, and you may live to see more than this fully realized. When I left your midst, I thought for many years I would come back here and make this my home and my final resting-place, but that will not be so now. I remember how I went forth a poor boy, but I did not go without friends. Everybody in this County seemed friendly toward me, and took me kindly by the hand. And let me say here, that kind words given to a boy are worth tons of money in after life. In later years the friendliness of the people of your County has been warmly extended, by both Republicans and Democrats, and I have felt your generous words and acts of approval as you have said, go ahead, Simon. And so I say to you all, go ahead! and God bless you."

After the above remarks had been concluded, Judge Jordan and General Cameron went back to the stand.

A. N. Brice, Esq., Chairman of the Committee to raise funds for the Soldiers' Monument, then announced the following subscriptions to that object:

Colonel James Cameron Post,	$350 00
Hon. A. Jordan,	200 00
Hon. Simon Cameron,	200 00
Hon. J. B. Packer,	200 00
William I. Greenough, Esq.,	200 00
Hon. William M. Rockefeller,	100 00
Hon. William L. Dewart,	100 00
S. P. Wolverton, Esq.,	100 00
Colonel George Wagenseller,	50 00
Hollowing Run Council, No. 285, O. U. A. M.,	25 00

An account of the Soldiers' Monument Association will be found under its appropriate head.

The next speaker was T. H. Purdy, Esq., who delivered a historical oration, which was subsequently published. Before he was through, however, a heavy shower interrupted the proceedings, and the rain did not cease till five o'clock. Hon. J. B. Packer and Hon. Frank Bound were also to speak, but the rain prevented.

THE BALLOON ASCENSION.

Prof. Light's balloon "Aerial" which had been inflating during the day, was detained on account of the heavy fall of rain, but at 6 o'clock the Professor sailed out in his balloon into mid-air. He moved rapidly in a northeasterly direction. He landed about three miles from town near Charles Moore's farm, after an ascent of about half-an-hour. In descending, his fall was rapid and uncontrolable, and he injured his ankle. The Professor and his balloon were brought into town the same evening. The balloon ascension cost the committee about five hundred and seventy-five dollars.

A display of fire-works was had in the evening from a flat on the river, at a cost of one hundred and sixty-five dollars. Thus ended the festivities of the one-hundredth anniversary of the settlement of Sunbury.

CONCLUSION.

The same causes which made Sunbury an important Indian town, make it an important American city. It is a railroad and commercial centre—a city in its infancy, surrounded by all the elements of wealth and by nature's richest scenery. To be convinced of this, go to the grave of John Mason, upon Blue Hill, or up to the old prospect chestnut, upon Catawissa road, and feast your eyes upon the unmatched beauty of the scene. From out the misty distance come the creeping trains upon six lines of rail. The old canals unite their waters with the gentleness of age. The mighty rocks rise up as sentinels on either side. Two growing towns lift up their spires, and from their stacks send up the smoky ensign of a nation's toil. View next the green-clad islands, which seem to rise and slumber in the silvery sheen below, laved with the rippling waters from these mingling Susquehannas, coming, as they do, from Wyalusing and Wyoming on the north, to join the mists of Clearfield, and the silvery fountains of Emporium. What more could Nature add, unless it were the broad, blue mirror of Shamokin dam?

"These are stately Susquehannas, joining waters for the bay,
And on either side are looming mountain summits, grim and grey.
'Tis a master-piece of Nature, picture-like from Nature's hands,
And amidst it in its beauty, our old Indian city stands.
Queen of all these rolling rivers, rich in history sublime,
Crowned with glories undiminished, from the unremembered time.
Stored with relics rare and olden, relics which no charm outvies,
Reaching with their shadowy fingers back to sacred memories;
What the marvel, that such beauty breathes upon the heart a spell?
What the wonder, that such grandeur wakens enterprise as well?
Why should Nature not ennoble, linked with Art's enchanting chain,
Giving impulse to our labor, health and brilliancy to brain?
Yes, from out this regal city, sitting on its wave-washed throne,
Towers a standard for the people, for us all to gaze upon;
'Tis the standard of improvement, 'tis by freedom's hall upheld,
And the furnace-blast shall fan it, and out of nature's field
Shall come the coal and lumber, and the iron from earth's breast,
To reward us for our labor, and our sons may tell the rest,
When the moss-grown clock of ages, shall have tolled for you and me,
And have measured off the summers of another century!"

THE SUNBURY AMERICAN.

The first number of the *Sunbury American* was issued September 12th, 1840, by Messrs. H. B. Masser and Joseph Eisely, Mr. Masser being editor and proprietor, and Mr. Eisely, the publisher. It had a sudden and unexpected birth by virtue of the following circumstances: Northumberland County was at that time largely Democratic, and a nomination was almost equal to an election. A split occurred in the Democratic County Convention on the selection of a candidate for the Assembly, Jesse C. Horton, of Point, being the choice of the upper end, and C. W. Hegins, of Sunbury, that of the lower end of the County. The friends of Mr. Hegins, not satisfied with the action of the delegates, withdrew and recommended him as the candidate of the people.

There was, at that time, only one paper published in the lower part of the County—the *Sunbury Gazette*,—which, unexpectedly to the friends of Mr. Hegins, espoused the cause of Mr. Horton. Two other papers, the *Millenian* (Whig,) and *Ledger* (Democratic), were both published at Milton. As the latter also supported Mr. Horton, the Hegins party was left without an organ. This party embracing many of the most influential and intelligent citizens of the County, it was resolved, at once, to establish a new paper.

The result was, that, in a very few days, the *Sunbury American* made its appearance, under the management of H. B. Masser, and the late Hon. Chas. G. Donnel. Mr. Masser subsequently became sole conductor of the new journal, and the *American* soon became a fixed institution. It took, from its start, a firm stand for protective tariff.

In 1843, the "*Amerikaner*," a German paper, was started in the same office, and was continued till 1863, when it ceased to be published.

On the first of April, 1848, Mr. Eisely retired from the *American*, which was conducted by Mr. Masser, till September, 1864, when Mr. Emanuel Wilvert became a partner. In April, 1866, Mr. N. S. Engle was taken in as a partner, and the firm became Masser, Wilvert and Engle. In April, 1869, Messrs. Masser and Engle retired from the business, and the *American* has since been under the exclusive control of Mr. Wilvert, who has since enlarged the establishment, by the addition of steam and power-presses, and other essential materials.

In the latter part of President Buchanan's administration, the *American*, which was previously a Democratic journal, espoused the cause of the government, and vigorously supported the administration, through the terrible struggles of the late Civil War, and has continued a staunch Republican advocate.

NORTHUMBERLAND COUNTY DEMOCRAT.

The *Northumberland County Democrat*, published at Sunbury, was established March 8th, 1861, by T. H. Purdy and Cyrus O. Bachman. The *Sunbury Gazette* had, up to that time, been the recognized organ of the Democratic party, of Northumberland County, when it threw off its fealty to that party, and became a Republican paper; hence the establishing of the *Democrat*, which has since done unremitting service for the Democracy. Mr. Bachman retired several years after the paper was established, and left Mr. Purdy sole proprietor, who continued as such till January 1st, 1867, when J. E. Eichholtz and John J. Auten, took control. This firm continued in existence but six months, after which J. E. Eichholtz was sole proprietor, till July 1st, 1868, when Alvin Day became associated with him. This firm continued for three years, when Mr. Eichholtz again became, and still continues, as sole editor and proprietor.

SUNBURY DAILY.

The *Sunbury Daily* was established December 6th, 1872, and has been published ever since, except for a single month. J. E. Eichholtz was the projector of the enterprise, and has remained its proprietor, ever since. It has, however, been edited and published by various parties, and the editor and publisher, at present, is G. G. Frysinger. It is published in Mr. Eichholtz's *Democrat* office.

THE SUNBURY GAZETTE.

The establishment in which the *Gazette* is printed is one of the oldest in central Pennsylvania. It was established in 1812, by John G. Youngman, who, coming from Maryland, where he had been working as a journeyman printer, in Hagerstown, Frederick and Baltimore, started the publication of a German newspaper in Sunbury, with the title of the *Northwestern Post*, a name which was considered appropriate to this section of country at that time. It was Republican in politics, advocating the Jeffersonian principles. This name was continued until the building of the canals by the State, when it was changed to the *Canal Boat*, suiting the popular interest that then prevailed in regard to internal improvement.

About 1833, the publication of the German paper was discontinued, and an English paper was started, named the *Workingmen's Advocate*. This name was continued until 1839, when it was changed to the *Gazette*, by which title it has been known since. When the name *Gazette* was assumed, the original proprietor, John G. Youngman, connected his eldest son, George B. Youngman, in partnership, in its publication, and they continued it until 1855, when it went into the hands of its present proprietors, A. A. and John Youngman, with John Youngman as editor. The politics of the English publication (*Workingmen's Advocate* and *Gazette*) were Democratic until 1861, when the *Gazette* took sides with the Republican party, and still remains in connection with that political organization.

Its circulation is quite extensive in the County in which it is published, besides extending to neighboring counties and beyond the limits of the State. John G. Youngman, the original proprietor, died in September, 1871, at the advanced age of eighty-six years. He did work as a compositor in the office within a year previous to his death. George D. Youngman, who was connected with his father in the publication of the paper, engaged in agriculture in 1861, and has been quite successful in fruit-raising and wine-making.

SUNBURY MILITARY RECORD.

The following exhaustive record of Sunbury in the late Civil War, is from an oration delivered by A. N. Brice, Esq., on Decoration-day, May 29th, 1875.

On the morning of 15th of April, 1861, three days after the attack on Sumpter, word was received in Sunbury, that President Lincoln has issued a call for seventy-five thousand men to serve for three months, in putting down the Southern Rebellion.

The whole community at once became wild with excitement, and enlistments commenced under the auspices of Captain C. J. Bruner and Lieutenant J. P. S. Gobin. The following extracts from Mr. Brice's diary will bring in present review, the exciting scenes of that eventful time:

"April 19th, '61.—The excitement is growing intense. The people are wild with enthusiasm. The Star Spangled Banner has been raised aloft, and proudly waves from every prominent building. Party-lines and controversies have disappeared, and every heart beats to the call of country. Troops from all parts of the State are pouring in.

"Saturday, April 20th, '61.—Part of a company, numbering about thirty men, was raised in Sunbury, and started for Harrisburg.

"Sunday, April 21st, '61.—The remainder of the company, numbering between forty and fifty men, was raised, and in the afternoon, at the beating of the drum, the men met and drilled, and in the evening, marched to the Lutheran church, where Rev. Riser preached a sermon on the 'crisis.' The house was immensely crowded. The ladies were engaged all day in making shirts and necessary articles for the soldiers. Sunday turned into battalion-day for the protection of the flag! Long may it wave!

"Monday, April 22d, '61.—At an early hour the people began to assemble at the depot to bid farewell to the remainder of our volunteers. By the time the cars arrived, thousands had collected, and the scene was truly grand and inspiring. An immense train of soldiers came down. They were greeted with wild shouts by the multitude. Our boys were soon aboard the train. The silent tear was shed, the farewell given, and they were off, amid the rattling of drums and the shouts of the excited populace, for the war.

"Tuesday, April 23d, '61.—The excitement continues unabated and still increasing. Companies are passing through, and are greeted with wild cheers by the excited throng. The ladies of Sunbury are vieing with each other in their offices of benefaction and love. They are carrying armfuls of provision to the soldiers, who, in turn, cry, 'God bless the ladies of Sunbury, and three cheers!'

"Wednesday, April 24th, '61.—The quota of seventy-five thousand men is filled."

I desire to record here my tribute of praise to the noble women of the war. It is with a very large degree of pride, that I call to mind their self-sacrificing efforts for the relief and comfort of the troops as they passed through to the front. I doubt whether a town in the United States did more through its patriotic women than ours. While a member of the Army of the Potomac, and of the James, I frequently heard soldiers from different States speak in the highest terms of praise of the ladies of Sunbury. Many of those large-hearted women who took an active part then, who cheered and labored for the soldier, have gone also to their rest. Let the tear be shed for them as well. Let the heart beat for them. Let the evergreen be spread and the flower strewn upon their graves also, and the living we will remember till the last roll-call summons the last of us to the other land.

The man who deserves the honor of first leaving Sunbury for the war, was Isaac H. Dunkleberger, who afterwards rose to the rank of brevet-colonel in the regular army. He is now living in California.

THE FIRST SACRIFICE.

One of the first who left Sunbury was Col. James Cameron, commander of the celebrated New York Highlanders. He was in the first battle of Bull Run, in July '61, and was there killed. His name will be carved on our granite monument as the first soldier from Northumberland County who gave up his life in the war.

LONGEST IN THE WAR.

The soldier who served longest in the war was Samuel Miller, of Sunbury. He enlisted in company I, Fourteenth Pennsylvania Volunteers, for three months; served four years and four months in company C, Forty-seventh Pennsylvania Volunteers. He then remained at home about two months, and enlisted in company I, Thirteenth United States infantry; served a year in this, when it was consolidated with the Thirty-first United States infantry; served in the Thirty-first United States infantry two years. The Thirty-first and Twenty-second were then consolidated. He served three years in the Twenty-second regiment, and was then honorably discharged for disability arising from hard service, having served in the army over ten years. While in the Indian wars, after the close of the Rebellion, he shot and killed an Indian chief, thus saving the life of Dr. J. P. Wright, who, out of gratitude, gives Samuel a bounty of ten dollars per month. He was a brave, faithful soldier.

THE FIRST COMPANY.

The first company from Sunbury was lettered F, and made part of the 11th regiment under Col. P. Jarrett. It was mustered April 23d, '61. Their record is as follows:

Charles J. Bruner, captain; J. P. Shindel Gobin, 1st lieutenant; Joseph H. McCarty, 2d lieutenant; F. McCarty, 1st sergeant; Charles J. Pleasants, 2d sergeant; S. Herman Helper, 3d sergeant; Jacob Rhorbach, 4th sergeant; Samuel F. Bright, 1st corporal; Chas. D. Wharton, 2d corporal; Daniel Oyster, 3d corporal; William Byers, 4th corporal; Henry D. Wharton and Jacob Weiser, musicians.

Privates—Henry Aliviser, Julius Arbiter, Jared Brosious, Henry Bucher, Robert Brooks, Samuel Bartscher, William M. Brisbon, Joseph Bright, Alfred Beckley, Benjamin F. Bright, Francis Carr, Wilson J. Covert, William Christ, Henry Drisel, Lewis Donie, David Druckamiller, Joseph Driselinger, William Edge, Samuel Epler, Jacob Feight, Stephen Golding, Benjamin W. Giddis, Peter S. Gussler, William D. Haas, Joseph Hildebrand, Charles Harp, Harris Hopper, Albert Haas, Allen Hunter, Elias Heddings, Jared C. Irwin, George Keihl, Daniel Michael, Chas. McFarland, Sylvester Myers, William Martin, John McClusky, Ephraim Metz, Robert Martin, John Messner, Wm. H. Millhouse, Mahlon Myers, Philip C. Newbaker, George Oyster, Frederick Pill, Henry Quittchilber, Albert Robins, Reuben Ramsey, Aristides Roderigue, Lloyd T. Rohrbach, Eugene Reiser, Frederick Schrauck, Hugh Smith, John Snyder, Chas. W. Stewart, John E. Seidel, Joseph Smith, Earnest Starkloff, Christian Schall, William Stedman, Charles Swoop, George Tucker, William Volke, Lot B. Weitzel, George Weyman.

The Eleventh regiment was placed in the Sixth Brigade, under Colonel Abercombie. They did efficient service during their term of enlistment, and were engaged in battle at Falling Waters, Va., on the 2d of July, 1861. In this engagement, Christian Scall, of Captain Bruner's company, was wounded. Their term of service having nearly expired, and their places being unsupplied by other troops, Gen. Patterson made an earnest appeal for the men to remain a week or ten days over their time. At the command, "Shoulder arms," every musket went up with a will, to the great satisfaction of the General, who rode forward and exclaimed: "With you, my brave Blue Jackets, I can hold this place alone." In the special order No. 127, of Gen. Patterson, discharging this regiment, he uses these words: "It gives the Commanding General great satisfaction to say, that the conduct of the regiment has merited his highest approbation."

On the 7th of May, 1861, President Lincoln issued a second proclamation, calling for forty-two thousand volunteers, for three years; twenty-five thousand regulars, for five years; and eighteen thousand seamen, for five years.

On the 20th of August, 1861, a company, recruited for three years, left Sunbury for the front, under Captain J. P. S. Gobin, and were mustered in on the 2d of September, 1861. It was lettered C, and placed in the 47th Pennsylvania Volunteers, under the command of Colonel Tilghman H. Good. In making a record of this company, I have enumerated out of it only those who went from Sunbury and vicinity, as near as I have been able to designate them, noting first those who were promoted as field-officers, etc.:

J. P. Shindel Gobin, colonel, mustered into service September 2d, '61; promoted from captain, company C, to major, July 25th, '64; to lieutenant-colonel, November 4th, '64; to colonel, January 3d, '65; to brevet-brigadier general, March 13th, '65; mustered out December 25th, '65, with regiment.

James Vandyke, quarter-master, mustered in September 2d, '61; promoted from 1st lieutenant, company C, to quarter-master, September 24th, '61; resigned January 16th, '62.

William M. Hendricks, sergeant-major, promoted from company C September 17th, '61; discharged September 12th, '65; vet.

Henry D. Wharton, commissary-sergeant, promoted from company C, commissary-sergeant July 1st, '65; discharged October 12th, '65; vet.

The record of company C, Forty-Seventh Pennsylvania Volunteers, is as follows:

Daniel Oyster, captain, mustered in September 2d, '61; promoted to 2d lieutenant December 13th, '62; to 1st lieutenant April 18th, '64; to captain September 1st, '64; wounded at Berryville, Va., September 5th, '64; and Cedar Creek, Va., October 19th, '64; mustered out with company December 25th, '65.

William Reese, 1st lieutenant, mustered in September 2d, '61; promoted from 2d to 1st lieutenant January 14th, '62; discharged April 14th, '64.

William M. Hendricks, 1st lieutenant, mustered in September 2d, '61; promoted to 1st lieutenant September 1st, '64; resigned May 9th, '65.

Christian S. Beard, 1st lieutenant, mustered in September 2d, '61; promoted from sergeant to 2d lieutenant September 1st, '64; to 1st lieutenant July 5th, '65; mustered out with company December 25th, '65; vet.

Jacob K. Keefer, 2d lieutenant, mustered in September 2d, '61; promoted to 2d lieutenant July 5th, '65; mustered out with company December 20th, '65.

Samuel Y. Haupt, 1st sergeant, mustered in September 2d, '61; wounded at Pocotaligo, S. C., October 22d, '62; promoted to sergeant November 1st, '64; to 1st sergeant July 5th, '65; mustered out with company December 25th, '65; vet.

William Fry, 1st sergeant, mustered in September 2d, '61; promoted to 1st sergeant September 1st, '64; prisoner from October 19th, '64, to March 4th, '65; died at Sunbury, March 28th, '65; vet.

Samuel Eister, sergeant, mustered in September 2d, '61; promoted to sergeant December 1st, '64; mustered out with company December 25th, '65; vet.

William F. Finch, sergeant, mustered in September 2d, '61; wounded at Cedar Creek, Va., October 19th, '64; promoted to sergeant April 1st, '65; mustered out with company December 25th, '65; vet.

Benjamin F. Miller, sergeant, mustered in September 2d, '61; promoted to sergeant August 1st, '65; mustered out with company December 25th, '65.

Peter Smelser, sergeant, mustered in September 2d, '61; discharged on surgeon's certificate June 17th, '64; since died in Sunbury.

William Pyers, sergeant, mustered in September 2d, '61; wounded at Pleasant Hill, La., April 9th, '64; killed at Cedar Creek, Va., October 19th, '64; buried in National Cemetery, lot 9; vet.

Peter Haupt, sergeant, mustered in September 17th, '61; died at Hilton Head, November 16th, '62, of wounds received at Pocotaligo, S. C., October 22d, '62.

John Bartlow, sergeant, mustered in September 1st, '62; promoted to sergeant September 1st, '64; killed at Cedar Creek, Va., October 19th, '64; buried in National Cemetery, Winchester, lot 10; vet.

George B. Good, corporal, mustered in September 2d, '61; promoted to corporal July 1st, '65; mustered out with company December 25th, '65; vet.

John H. Heim, corporal, mustered in September 2d, '61; mustered out September 18th, '64; expiration of time.

Mark Shipman, corporal, mustered in September 2d, '61; promoted to corporal April 1st, '65; vet; since died.

Samuel Pyers, musician, mustered in March 27th, '63; mustered out with company December 25th, '65.

Henry D. Wharton, musician, mustered in September 2d, '61; promoted to commissary-sergeant July 1st, '65.

J. Bolton Young, musician, mustered in September 2d, '61; died at Washington, D. C., October 17th, '61.

Henry Brown, private, mustered in September 2d, '61; mustered out with company December 15th, '65.

J. Weiser Bucher, private, mustered in March 8th, '65; mustered out with company December 25th, '65.

Jared Brosius, private, mustered in September 2d, '61; mustered out with company December 25th, '65.

Samuel H. Billington, private, mustered in September 17th, '61; wounded at Pocotaligo, S. C., October 22d, '62; discharged on surgeon's certificate July, '63.

Martin M. Berger, private, mustered in September 1st, '61; captured at Cedar Creek, Va., October 19th, '64; died at Salisbury, N. C., January 6th, '65.

R. W. Druckemiller, private, mustered in September 13th, '61; mustered out September 18th, '64, expiration of time.

Abner J. Finch, private, mustered in November 20th, '63; mustered out with company December 25th, '65.

William Good, private, mustered in November 20th, '63; mustered out with company December 25th, '65.

William Gehring, private, mustered in November 20th, '64; mustered out with company December 25th, '65.

Alfred Hunter, private, mustered in September 2d, 1861; mustered out with company December 25th, '65.

Henry W. Haas, private, mustered in November 27th, '63; mustered out with company December 25th, '63.

Charles W. Harp, private, mustered in September 2d, '61; mustered out September 18th, '64; expiration of time.

Freeman Haupt, private, mustered in September 2d, '61; discharged by general order December 21st, '63; since died in Sunbury.

Jeremiah Haas, private, mustered in September 2d, '61; wounded at Pocotaligo, S. C., October 22d, '62; killed at Saline Cross Roads, La., April 8th '64.

Jared C. Irvin, private, mustered in February 21st, '65; mustered out with company December 25th, '65.

Cornelius Kramer, private, mustered in September 2d, '61; wounded at Pleasant Hill, April 9th, '64; mustered out December 25th, '65.

Lorenzo Kramer, private, mustered in February 23d, '65; mustered out with company December 25th, '65.

D. W. Kemble, private, mustered in September 2d, '61; mustered out September 18th, '64; expiration of time.

Theodore Kiehl, private, mustered in September 2d, '61; killed at Cedar Creek, Va., October 19th, '64; buried in the National Cemetery, Winchester, lot No. 10.

William Logan, private, mustered in February 21st, '65; mustered out with company December 25th, '65.

L. K. Landau, private, mustered in September 2d, '61; discharged on surgeon's certificate March 3d, '62; since died in Sunbury.

Eli Miller, private, mustered in September 2d, '61; absent at muster out.

Samuel Miller, private, mustered in September 2d, '61; prisoner from April 8th to July 22d, '62; mustered out with company December 25th, '65.

John Munsh, private, mustered in September 2d, '61; mustered out with company December 25th, '65.

Adam Maul, private, mustered in September 2d, '61; prisoner from May 3d to July 22d, '64; absent on detached duty at muster out.

Warren McEwen, private, mustered in September 2d, '61; discharged on surgeon's certificate, December 7th, '62.

John S. Opler, private, mustered in November 20th, '63; mustered out with company December 25th, '65.

John B. Otto, private, mustered in September 2d, '61; mustered out with company December 25th, '65.

Hugh B. Rodrigue, private, mustered in November 27th, '63; mustered out with company December 25th, '65.

Jacob Renn, private, mustered in February 21st, '65; mustered out with company December 25th, '65.

P. M. Randall, private, mustered in September 2d, '61; mustered out with company December 25th, '65.

Alexander Ruffaner, private, mustered in September 2d, '61; mustered out September 18th, '64; expiration of time; since killed by a fall in Sunbury.

Henry C. Seasholtz, private, mustered in February 23d, '65; mustered out with company December 25th, '65.

Ira Seasholtz, private, mustered in February 23d, '65; mustered out with company December 25th, '65.

Henry A. Shiffer, private, mustered in November 27th, '63; wounded at Cedar Creek, Va., October 19th, '64; transferred to Veteran Reserve Corps February, '65.

Joseph Smith, private, mustered in September 2d, '61; killed at Cedar Creek, Va., October 19th, '64; buried in National Cemetery, Winchester, lot No. 10.

Peter Swinehart, private, mustered in November 20th, '63; died December 1st, '64, of wounds received at Cedar Creek, Va., October 19th, '64.

John C. Sterner, private, mustered in September 2d, '61; killed at Pleasant Hill, La., April 9th, '64.

Robert W. Vincent, private, mustered in February 26th, '64; mustered out with company December 25th, '65.

David Weikle, private, mustered in September 2d, '61; wounded at Cedar Creek, Va., October 19th, '64; absent (sick) at muster out.

Henry W. Wolf, private, mustered in September 2d, '61: mustered out September 18th, '64, expiration of time.

Cornelius Wenrick, private, mustered in November 20th, '63; mustered out June 6th, '65.

George C. Watson, private, mustered in September 2d, '61; died at Key West, Fla., August 26th, '62.

In the same regiment, company H., E. Masser Bucher was mustered in February 25th, '65, and discharged December 25th, '65, with the company.

The Forty-seventh regiment was in eleven engagements, viz: First capture of Fort Finnegan, October 4th, '62; St. John's Bluff, Fla., October 5th, '62; Pocotaligo, S. C., October 22d, '62; Saline Cross Roads, La., April 23d, '64; Mansura, La., May 17th, '64; Berryville, Va., September 5th, '64; Winchester, Va., September 19th, '64; Fisher's Hill, Va., September 22d, '64; Cedar Creek, Va., October 19th, '64. It also took part in an expedition to St. John's Bluff, on St. John's River, Fla., in which an immense amount of stores were captured. In the campaign of 1864, the regiment marched upwards of one thousand miles. It was in five of the Southern States, and made nine voyages on sea. It was the only Pennsylvania regiment that participated in the Red River expedition. The men re-enlisted as veterans October 13th, 1863, and on the 9th of January, 1866, after a service of four years and four months, they were mustered out at Camp Cadwallader.

Colonel Gobin, in his incidents of the war, has this note in reference to a member of company C: "Benjamin F. Walls, of company C, was 65 years old when he enlisted; was a farmer of considerable means from Juniata County. When examined at Harrisburg the surgeon pronounced him too old for the service. 'By the Lord!' exclaimed the Squire, 'I have yet to learn that a man ever becomes too old to serve his country!' He was passed, was made color-sergeant, was wounded severely at Pleasant Hill, Louisiana, but afterwards returned to his regiment and served out his three years."

It is said of Martin Berger, of this company, that after his capture, and while a prisoner at Salisbury, North Carolina, he burrowed a hole in the ground to protect himself from the weather. He died, and was buried in that same hole.

George C. Watson, of the same company, died at Key West, Florida. He was cared for by the company and a monument worth seventy-five dollars was erected by them to his memory.

The next company from Sunbury was headed by Captain John Buyers. It was partly raised in Luzerne County, and was mustered into the Fifty-eighth Pennsylvania Volunteers, under Colonel J. Richter Jones, in January and February, 1862, as company I. A regimental organization was effected on the 13th of February, 1862. The regiment re-enlisted, and was finally mustered out January 24th, 1866. Moore, in his rebellion record, volume six, says of the Fifty-eighth, "There are thousands at the north who curse the army for inaction, who, if they knew half the brave things done by the men in the field, would be shamed to silence by their deeds of valor. Colonel Jones and his heroes of the Fifty-eighth Pennsylvania have done some splendid work, and by his vigilance has made the bushwhackers cry for quarter." The captain of company I, John Buyers, was a number-one man, and the commanding officer when it was mustered out, Captain Heber Painter, was as true a soldier as ever lived. I knew the men of this command while in service, and can say of them they were good soldiers and never dishonored the fair fame of our town in the annals of the war. Among its best soldiers who deserve honorable mention, were Sergeants William H. Blair and William B. Martin, Color-Corporal Robert Martin and others. To this company belongs the honor of first entering the rebel Capital after the surrender, and Robert Martin, of Sunbury, carried the first flag into the city of Richmond at the head of our victorious army.

The record of this company who belong to Sunbury and vicinity is as follows:

* * * * * * * * * *

John Buyers, captain, mustered in January 28th, '62; resigned May 30th, '63.

Heber Painter, 1st lieutenant, mustered in October 8th, '61; promoted from private to 1st sergeant November 26th '64; to 1st lieutenant March 1st, '65; commissioned captain January 23d, '66;—not mustered—mustered out with company, January 24th, '66.

Wm. H. Blair, 1st sergeant, mustered in November 20th, '61; promoted to corporal December 1st, '64; to 1st sergeant March 1st, '65; commissioned 1st lieutenant January 23d, '66;—not mustered—mustered out with company January 24th, '66.

Samuel Wolf, sergeant, mustered in October 8th '61; promoted to corporal October 1st, '64; 1st sergeant April 25th, '75; commissioned 2d lieutenant January 23d, '66;—not mustered—mustered out with company.

Wm. H. Gass, sergeant, mustered in October 8th, '61; promoted to corporal January 25th, '65; to sergeant April 25th, '65; mustered out with company.

Norman W. Haas, sergeant, mustered in October 8th, '61; promoted to corporal June 10th, '65; to sergeant June 26th, '65; mustered out with company.

George W. Klase, sergeant, mustered in January 23d, '62; died at Suffolk, Va., December 11th, '62.

Robert Martin, corporal, mustered in October 8th, '61; promoted to corporal; prisoner from September 20th to October 20th, '64; mustered out with company.

Hiram Fisher, corporal, mustered in December 30th, '61; promoted to corporal April 1st, '65; mustered out with company.

Samuel Taylor, corporal, mustered in October 8th, '61; promoted to corporal April 8th, '65; mustered out with company.

John Fisher, corporal, mustered in December 30th, '61; promoted to corporal April 24th, '65; mustered out with company.

H. Housewart, corporal, mustered in December 18th, '61; killed in action September 29th, '64.

Solomon Yordy, corporal, mustered in January 23d, '62; promoted to corporal December 18th, '62; mustered out January 25th, '65; expiration of time.

PLATE XIII

RESIDENCE OF A. A. HEIM, LINCOLN ST SHAMOKIN, NORTHUMBERLAND CO., PA.

Jos. Crist, corporal, mustered in October 8th, '61; promoted to corporal January 23d, '62; mustered out November 19th, '64; expiration of time.

Daniel Boughner, corporal, mustered in January 13th, '62; promoted to corporal October 27th, '62; transferred to Fourth U. S. artillery November 24th, '62.

John Mullen, musician, mustered in November 20th, '61; mustered out with company.

Samuel Bartsher, private, mustered in October 8th, '61; mustered out with company.

Martin L. Bloom, private, mustered in October 8th, '61; died in Northumberland County, December 7th, '64; vet.

Samuel Crist, private, mustered in November 28th, '61; mustered out with company.

Daniel Conrad, private, mustered in October 8th, '61; killed at Cold Harbor, June 3d, '64.

Benjamin F. Diehl, private, mustered in October 8th, '61; discharged on surgeon's certificate, June 20th, '65.

Philip Forester, private, mustered in October 28th, '61; mustered out January 24th, '65; to date October 28th, '64; expiration of time.

Solomon Fasold, private, mustered in January 23d, '62; transferred to Fourth U. S. artillery November 24th, '62.

Henry Gutschall, private, mustered in December 28th, '61; wounded in action September 29th, '64; absent at muster out.

John Groner, private, mustered in January 29th, '62; discharged October 10th, '65; for wounds received at Cold Harbor, June 3d, '64.

Emanuel Gutschall, private, mustered in March 23d, '62; drowned in Paradise Creek, Va., August 10th, '62.

Wm. Galagher, private, mustered in December 11th, '61; died June 13th, '64, of wounds received at Cold Harbor, June 3d, '64; buried at Alexandria, Va.

Harris A. Hopper, private, mustered in December 12th, '61; mustered out with company.

Samuel Heim, private, mustered in January 23d, '62; mustered out February 3d, '65; expiration of time.

James Hoey, private, mustered in October 8th, '61; died at Hagerstown, Md., January 11th, '65.

Wm. B. Martin, private, mustered in October 8th, '61; mustered out with company.

Henry Miller, private, mustered in January 23d, '62; discharged on surgeon's certificate May 10th, '62.

Charles A. Peal, private, mustered in January 23d, '62; died at Camp Suffolk, Va., December 2d, '61.

John Reed, private, mustered in December 12th, '61; wounded at Cold Harbor June 3d, '64; mustered out with company.

William Reeser, private, mustered in January 23d, '62; died at Washington, N. C., August 30th, '63.

Elias Baker, private, mustered in December 9th, '61; died at Fortress Monroe, Va., of wounds received at Chapin Farm, September 29th, '64; mustered out with company.

John G. Snyder, private, mustered in October 8th, '61; wounded at Fort Harrison, Va., September 29th, '64; mustered out with company.

Jacob Slough, private, mustered in October 8th, '61; mustered out with company.

Emanuel Stroh, private, mustered in October 8th, '61; died October 20th, '64; buried at Alexandria.

DeLaf S. Wynn, private, mustered in October 8th, '61; wounded in action September 20th, '64; absent at muster out.

Peter Zeliff, private, mustered in October 8th, '61; transferred to company H, January, '62.

In the summer of 1862, the President made a call for three hundred thousand more men, and some of those for nine months. Under this call, T. R. Jones, formerly of Snydertown, and A. N. Brice, of Sunbury, by authority from Gov. Curtin, at once recruited a company, commencing July 29th, 1862. In the evening of that day, a meeting was held in the old court house, which stood on Market square. It was largely attended, and was very enthusiastic. A strong speech was made by Hon. J. B. Packer in favor of the company. I cannot but refer in this public manner out of common gratitude to the kindness of this gentleman. When I most needed help he was ready with money and influence, and used both freely in my behalf. He deserves special mention in this particular, because his hand and heart were always open to perform some kind act. The public knew little of the numberless instances of his generosity. I was also indebted to Hon. Alexander Jordan, my preceptor, for sterling counsel and valuable aid. Although a Democrat, he was always as ready as any in counseling a patriotic course and in vindicating and maintaining the honor of an assailed country. Age has not dimmed his faculties, deadened his patriotism, nor lessened his friendship.

We started for Harrisburg, August 9th, 1862, and were mustered in the 14th of August, 1862, moving to the front on the 19th of August, as company C, One Hundred and Thirty-first Pennsylvania Volunteers, under Colonel P. H. Allabach. The regiment, after reaching Washington, D. C., was ordered over into Virginia. It remained there till September 14th, 1862, when it was ordered to move with the army of the Potomac to Antietam, engaging in that whole campaign. After Antietam, it marched through Warrenton to Fredericksburg, and participated in the battle at that place in December, 1862. The number of men lost there in killed, was twenty-one; wounded, one hundred and thirty-two; missing, twenty-four. Among the killed was Lieutenant, William A. Bruner, formerly of Sunbury, and among the wounded were Captain I. B. Davis, of Milton, and Lieutenant J. R. Irwin, of Watsontown. Among the men killed in my own company was Landis Sturner, of Sunbury, as brave a boy as ever went to war. The company also participated in the Burnside muddy march, and in the battle of Chancellorsville. It was highly complimented by General A. A. Humphreys when discharged.

At the time of our return home, May 25th, 1863, we were received very kindly by the citizens. A parade was formed of the town council, soldiers of 1812, committee of citizens, a band, discharged soldiers, and fire companies with their old engines of that day, and marched through the streets. A speech of welcome was delivered to us in the square by Hon. J. B. Packer, after which the company marched to the Central Hotel, where a committee of ladies, Mrs. William L. Dewart, Mrs. L. T. Rohrbach (then Miss Jennie Haas,) Mrs. C. H. Faust (then Miss Lilah Weiker,) Mrs. Captain Torrington (then Miss Mary Friling,) and Miss Amelia Kiehl, had prepared a most sumptuous supper. It was heartily eaten, and the boys separated for their homes.

The company record is as follows:

Thomas R. Jones, captain, mustered out with company May 23d, '63.

Joseph L. Reeder, 1st lieutenant, discharged November 29th, '62.

A. N. Brice, 1st lieutenant, promoted from 2d lieutenant, January 1st, '63; mustered out with company.

Owen M. Fowler, 2d lieutenant, promoted from sergeant March 1st, '63; mustered out with company.

David M. Nesbit, 1st sergeant, mustered out with company.

Lott B. Weitzel, sergeant, mustered out with company.

George M. Arnold, sergeant, promoted from corporal September 14th, '62; mustered out with company.

Ephraim Foulke, sergeant, promoted from corporal August 2d, '62; mustered out with company.

Lorenzo D. Robins, sergeant, promoted to hospital steward August 26th, '62.

Samuel Bower, corporal, mustered out with company.

Ira M. Rockefeller, corporal, mustered out with company.

Silas R. Snyder, corporal, mustered out with company.

Charles P. Seasholtz, corporal, wounded at Fredericksburg, Va., December 12th, '62; mustered out with company.

Solomon P. Klase, corporal, promoted to corporal September 14th, '62; mustered out with company.

John Ed. Eckman, corporal, promoted to corporal March 1st, '63; mustered out with company.

John A. Bucher, corporal, discharged on surgeon's certificate March 22d, '63.

John G. Blair, corporal, mustered out with company.

Samuel Swank, corporal, promoted to corporal September 14th, '62; wounded at Fredericksburg, Va., December 13th, '62; discharged on surgeon's certificate February 12th, '63.

James E. Forrester, musician, mustered out with company.

Kimber C. Farrow, musician, mustered out with company.

Jesse M. Auchmuty, private, mustered out with company.

Milton Bastress, private, mustered out with company.

Ed. L. Beck, private, mustered out with company.

William H. Beck, private, absent on detached service at muster out.

Benjamin F. Barnhart, private, mustered out with company.

Cyrus G. Bittenbender, private, mustered out with company.

Sylvanus A. Bird, private, wounded at Fredericksburg, Va., December 13th, '62; mustered out with company.

John R. Boughner, private, discharged on surgeon's certificate December 22d, '62.

Joseph Conrad, private, mustered out with company.

Charles H. Culp, private, mustered out with company.

John L. Cooper, private, mustered out with company.

Hiram Dill, private, mustered out with company.

John Dawson, private, discharged on surgeon's certificate February 16th, '63.

Wesley Ely, private, mustered out with company.

John Ernst, private, mustered out with company.

William Evert, private, mustered out with company.

George D. Irwin, private, mustered out with company.

John K. Erdman, private, discharged on surgeon's certificate February 15th, '63.

John Evert, private, killed at Fredericksburg, December 13th, '62.

John Fox, private, mustered out with company.

George Farley, private, discharged on surgeon's certificate February 7th, '63.

Peter Fisher, private, killed at Fredericksburg, Va., December 13th, '62.

William Good, private, mustered out with company.

Jacob T. Hepner, private, mustered out with company.

Elias Hoover, private, wounded at Fredericksburg, Va.; mustered out with company.

James Hunt, private, mustered out with company.

Samuel J. Hoey, private, mustered out with company.

Adam S. Haas, private, mustered out with company.

James Harris, private, mustered out with company.

Francis Hoover, private, mustered out with company.

John Hoffman, private, mustered out with company.

Frederick K. Hammer, private, mustered out with company.

John K. Haas, private, discharged on surgeon's certificate February 12th, '63.

Thomas Johnson, private, mustered out with company.

Abraham Culp, private, mustered out with company.

Moses Kulp, private, wounded at Fredericksburg, Va., December 13th, '62; mustered out with company.

James Kincaid, private, mustered out with company.

T. Koppenheffer, private, mustered out with company.

Joel Koppenheffer, private, mustered out with company.

Daniel M. Kerschner, private, mustered out with company.

Peter Kulp, private, wounded at Fredericksburg, Va., December 13th, '62; mustered out with company.

Jacob Keiser, private, discharged on surgeon's certificate March 6th, '63.

Jeremiah Koppenheffer, private, discharged on surgeon's certificate September 29th, '62.

George W. Lavan, private, killed at Fredericksburg, December 13th, '62.

James W. Lyon, private, mustered out with company.

William Maguire, private, mustered out with company.

Vandine Martz, private, mustered out with company.

Charles M. Mettler, private, mustered out with company.

Henry W. Moore, private, mustered out with company.

Sylvester Myers, private, mustered out with company.

George Mautz, private, discharged on surgeon's certificate December 26th, '62.

Jacob Mower, private, died at Sharpsburg, October 6th, '62, of wounds received accidentally; buried in National Cemetery, Antietam, section 26, lot B, grave 122.

Alonzo Oakum, private, mustered out with company.

Oliver Overdorf, private, died at Sharpsburg, Md., October 12th, '62.

Daniel S. Peiper, private, mustered out with company.

Henry K. Price, private, mustered out with company.

Samuel Ruch, private, mustered out with company.

Jesse J. Reed, private, mustered out with company.

Samuel Reed, private, mustered out with company.

Sirvetus O. Reed, private, wounded at Fredericksburg December 13th, '62; discharged on surgeon's certificate; mustered out with company.

John Smith, private, mustered out with company.

William Savidge, private, mustered out with company.

John L. Shipman, private, mustered out with company.

Saul Shipman, private, mustered out with company.

Henry R. Shipp, private, mustered out with company.

R. F. Stambach, private, mustered out with company.

Josiah Strausser, private, mustered out with company.

Francis M. Smith, private, discharged on surgeon's certificate January 6th, '63.

Isaac Sarvis, private, died at Washington, D. C., January 16th, '63, of wounds received at Fredericksburg, Va., December 13th, '62.

Charles A. Spratt, private, killed at Fredericksburg, Va., December 13th, '62.

Landis Starner, private, killed at Fredericksburg, Va., December 13th, '62.

George Y. Weimer, private, mustered out with company.

Peter Wentz, private, mustered out with company.

David Willet, private, discharged on surgeon's certificate April 13th, '62.

Samuel Welker, private, killed at Fredericksburg, Va., December 13th, '62.

Conrad Yeager, private, mustered out with company.

Solomon Yeager, private, mustered out with company.

William Yeager, private, wounded at Fredericksburg, Va., December 13th, '62; absent in hospital at muster out.

Adonijah Yocum, private, mustered out with company.

I have found, in my brief examination and inquiry into the history of those who enlisted in the war from Sunbury, that a considerable number went out in different regimental organizations, and have been very much scattered. I have done the best I could in hunting them all up, but feel conscious that some have been left out, although not purposely. At some future time the list may be perfected.

The following men went out to the Western Department, in '64, and joined company M, of the Seventh Pennsylvania cavalry:

George E. Beard, corporal, mustered in February 25th, '64; promoted to corporal March 1st, '64; mustered out with company August 23d, '65.

Edward L. Beck, corporal, mustered in February 23d, '64; died of wounds received at Dallas, Ga., May 27th, '64.

Robert M. Barthow, private, mustered in February 22d, '64; died at Louisville, Ky., August 12th, '65; buried in National Cemetery, section D, range —, grave 8.

Zebedee Bostian, private, mustered in February 23d, '64; mustered out with company August 23d, '65.

John B. Durst, private, mustered in February 23d, '64; mustered out with company August 23d, '65.

Charles D. Kiehl, private, mustered in February 19th, '64; mustered out with company.

Edward Lyon, private, mustered in February 19th, '64; mustered out with company August 23d, '65.

John Lyon, private, mustered in February 17th, '64; mustered out with company August 23d, '65.

Charles Landau, private, mustered in February 17th, '65; prisoner from October 1st, '64, to April 20th, '65; discharged June 12th, to date May 19th, '65.

Thomas Malone, private, mustered in February 17th, '64; prisoner from October 1st, '64, to April 20th, '65; discharged June 12th, to date May 19th, '65.

Edward Oyster, private, mustered in February 23d, '64; mustered out with company August 23d, '65.

Raphael Pereze, private, mustered in February 16th, '64; mustered out with company August 23d, '65.

James Shiffer, private, mustered in February 22d, '64; mustered out with company August 23d, '65.

William Stroh, private, mustered in February 16th, '64; transferred to Veteran Reserve Corps June 10th, '65; discharged by general order August 14th, '65.

The following entered the Fifth Pennsylvania cavalry, company H, in 1861–1864:

John J. Smith, private, mustered in November 1st, '61; discharged May 20th, '63, for wounds, with loss of leg, received at Williamsburg, Va., April 11th, '63; present post-master at Sunbury.

Silas R. Snyder, corporal, mustered in September 7th, '64; promoted to corporal February, '65; discharged by general order May 19th, '65.

Andrew N. Brice, private, mustered in September 7th, '64; discharged by general order May 19th, '65.

John N. Snyder, private, mustered in September 7th, '64; discharged by general order May 19th, '65.

Chambers S. Wynn, private, mustered in September 7th, '64; discharged by general order.

The following entered the One Hundred and Fifty-second regiment, or Third artillery, battery K:

Benjamin F. Laudan, private, mustered in February 25th, '64; mustered out with battery November 9th, '64.

Isaac Leeser, private, mustered in February 26th, '64; mustered out with battery November 9th, '64.

Joseph Richardson, private, mustered in February 26th, '64; discharged by special order October 17th, '65.

Company I, Eighty-fourth Pennsylvania Volunteers, received the following recruits, through the efforts of Lieutenant George S. Good, in September, 1862:

Edward Gibson, private, mustered in September 15th, '62; transferred to the Fifty-seventh Regiment, Pennsylvania Volunteers, company G; discharged by general order.

Charles Gearhart, private, mustered in November 6th, '62; discharged at Columbus, O.; since died.

Orlando Krigham, private, October 6th, '62; transferred to company G Fifty-seventh Regiment, Pennsylvania Volunteers, June 13th, '65; wounded and captured at Chancellorsville, May 3d, '62.

A. B. Lawrence, private, mustered in September 15th, '62; transferred to companies B and G, Fifty-seventh Pennsylvania Volunteers.

H. K. Lawrence, private, mustered in September 15th '62; transferred to company B.

John Shissler, private, mustered in September 15th, '62; discharged on surgeon's certificate—date unknown; since died.

Joseph H. McCarty entered company K, Forty-sixth Pennsylvania Volunteers August 29th, '62; promoted to adjutant August 12th, '64.

J. Ed. McCarty entered the same company at the same time; promoted to sergeant of company I, April 1st, '64.

John G. Blair, re-enlisted in company E, Forty-ninth Pennsylvania Volunteers October 28th, '63; substitute—captured—died at Andersonville, Ga., September 3d, '64—grave 7,747.

J. M. Bastian entered company B, One Hundred and Seventy-second Pennsylvania Volunteers November 3d, '62; mustered out August 1, '63.

Henry E. Martin enlisted in battery K, Second artillery; afterwards transferred, and probably killed.

Fred. Hammer re-enlisted in battery L, Second artillery March, '64; mustered out January 29th, '66.

Christian Martin entered battery L, Second artillery February, '64; mustered out January 29th, '66.

Sylvester Myers entered battery L, Second artillery March, '64; mustered out February 20th, '66.

Washington Harp, private, mustered in '62; wounded at Fredericksburg, Va., December 13th, '62; discharged—date unknown.

James Haas, private, mustered in October 6th, '62; wounded at Mine Run, Va., November 5th, '63; transferred to company G, Fifty-seventh regiment, P. V. June 13th, '65.

Jonathon Haas, private, mustered in September 15th, '62; transferred to company G, Fifty-seventh regiment, P. V.

Arthur Robins, private, mustered in September 15th, '62; company G, Fifty-seventh regiment, P. V.; discharged February 21st, '63.

Melancthon Brosius, enlisted in company F, Eighty-fourth P. V., and was killed in battle; date unknown.

The following soldiers enlisted in an independent cavalry company, under Capt. Murray, June 17th, '63; discharged August 11th, '63.

Richard F. Bucher, George E. Beard, Jacob Fieg, James W. Lyon, J. Cares Welker.

1st Lieutenant, William M. Thurston, Forty-third regiment, First artillery, battery F, was promoted to 1st lieutenant April 22d, '65; he was originally mustered in July 8th, '61; was mustered out June 9th, '65, with battery.

Lemuel Shipman, 2d lieutenant, was mustered in November 8th, '62; promoted from 1st sergeant June 5th, '64, to 2d lieutenant, in the One Hundred and Fifty-second regiment, Third artillery, battery D; mustered out with battery November 9th, '65.

Among the officers from Sunbury was General J. K. Clement, who served at the first battle of Bull Run. He afterwards served as provost-marshal of the district, with the rank of captain.

The following men enlisted in company G, One Hundred and Eighty-eighth Pennsylvania Volunteers, during the year 1864:

George D. Ervin, 1st lieutenant, mustered in February 26th, '64; promoted from sergeant September 10th, '65; commissioned 2d lieutenant November 26th, '62; mustered out with company December 14th, '64.

Henry D. Bright, private, mustered in February 24th, '64; discharged by general order June 28th, '65.

Solomon Cherry, private, mustered in March 5th, '64; discharged on surgeon's certificate June 24th, '65.

Charles J. Conrad, private, mustered in September 3d, '64; discharged by general order May 9th, '65.

John Dillman, private, mustered in February 9th, '64; mustered out with company December 14th, '64.

D. Druckemiller, private, mustered in February 25th, '64; mustered out with company December 14th, '65.

Frederick D. Kline, private, mustered in February 20th, '64; killed at Petersburg, Va., June 29th, '64.

George McNier, private, mustered in December 29th, '63; wounded at Fort Harrison, Va., September 29th, '64; mustered out with company December 14th, '65.

Frederick Shrank, private, mustered in February 26th, '64; mustered out with company December 14th, '65.

Richard F. Bucher, enlisted in company K, Eleventh Pennsylvania cavalry, February 25th, '64; captured at Ream's Station, Va., June 29th, '64—exchanged—now in the regular army.

William A. Fetter, enlisted in company D, Seventh Pennsylvania cavalry, October 31st, '61; mustered out October 3d, '64.

Philip Renn, enlisted in company B, Twelfth regiment, U. S. infantry, September 16th, '61; discharged September 16th, '64; re-enlisted in Hancock's V. R. Corps, February 28th, '65; died at Jarvis Hospital, Baltimore, October 20th, '65.

Lieutenant Charles Israel Pleasants entered the Eleventh U. S. infantry early in the war; he was probably killed in the battle of the Wilderness, under Grant; was never found; he was a brave, faithful officer.

Hunter P. Newberry, enlisted in company D, Third artillery, One Hundred and Fifty-second Pennsylvania Volunteers, February 27th, '64; mustered out November 9th, '65.

James C. Kerschner, was in company C., One Hundred and Fifty-second Pennsylvania Volunteers, Third artillery, February 29th, '64; mustered out November 9th, '65.

Harvey K. Goodrich, sergeant, company B, Third Pennsylvania cavalry; mustered in July 23d, '61; mustered out with company August 24th, '64.

After the disastrous movements of second Bull Run and the Peninsula, the Rebel army moved northward. On the 10th of September, 1862, Gov. Curtin called for fifty thousand men to defend the soil of Pennsylvania. These were called the "emergency men of 1862." In obedience to this call company D, Third regiment, was organized in Sunbury and hurried to the front, under Capt. C. J. Bruner. Col. Dorris, Jr., and Lieut.-Col. W. C. Lawson commanded the regiment. This company was never questioned for its bravery, but its reputation for a leaning towards hen-coops was unenviable. It was organized September 11–13, and discharged September 23–25, 1862:—

Company D.—Captain Charles J. Bruner; 1st lieutenant, A. J. Stroh; 2d lieutenant, Jacob Rohrbach; 1st sergeant, James B. Roney; sergeants—Jeremiah H. Zimmerman, Peter Gussler, Joseph Bright, Geo. W. Stroh; corporals—Jacob W. Covert, Henry Bucher, Geo. Oyster, William Grant, Jacob B. Messer, Fred. Kleine, Henry Milhouse, Albert Haas; musicians—John W. Bucher, D. J. Wharton—promoted to principal musician; privates—Philip Arison, Solomon B. Boyer, Thomas Baldy, Jacob Bell, John Bell, George Bloom, William Bowen, Peter Bright, George Bucher, Richard F. Bucher, Benjamin Brosious, Edward Bower, George Beard, Samuel H. Byers, Jonathan M. Bastian, Philip Clark, John Kay Clement, Ira T. Clement, Henry Clement, Abraham M. Covert, Franklin Dellbough, John Durst, Norman S. Engle, Henry K. Fagely, Jacob Fetter, George Fullmer, Henry Y. Friling, Landis Fry, Nevin W. Fisher, William Fisher, John Gering, Samuel Gerringer, James Griggs, George Genther, George W. Hileman, Jacob S. Hendricks, Martin L. Hendricks, Samuel Harrison, Alexander Haupt—died, date unknown—William Haupt, Washington Harp, Jackson Harp, Jacob Hoover, George W. Haupt, John Haas, 1st, John Haas, 2d, James Hileman, Franklin U. John, James Kerstner, George P. Krohn, Wm. Kiefer, Philip Kiefer, Orland Krichbaum, John Leeser, James Lyon, Edward Lyon, William Logan, Anthony Lentzer, Lewis Miller, Charles Martin, Alexander Muntz, Thomas McGaw, Hunter Newberry, John Oyster, Henry Peters, John B. Packer, Julius Ray, Wm. Rohrbach, Lloyd T. Rohrbach, Jacob Renn, Levi Seasholtz, Cornelius Smith, Ernest Starkloff, Henry Strauss, Silas E. Wiles, John Weaver, William E. Youngman, Jacob Youngman, George Zettlemoyer—94.

The disaster to our arms at Fredericksburg and at Chancellorsville, emboldened the Southern army to again attempt an invasion of the North, and accordingly a proclamation was issued by the President, calling for one hundred thousand men. On the 26th of June, 1863, Gov. Curtin called for sixty thousand men for State service for ninety days. Under this call, twenty-eight regiments were organized. A company was raised in Sunbury by Capt. S. P. Wolverton, letter F, and joined the Thiry-sixth regiment at Harrisburg, under Col. H. C. Alleman. It was mustered in July 4th, 1863—discharged August 11th, 1863. During the time of their service, Capt. Wolverton and his men were constantly on duty. Although the campaigns of these emergency companies were bloodless, their prompt response to the call of the country gave sure guarantee of their readiness for duty and of their patriotism.

Company F.—Captain, Simon P. Wolverton; 1st lieutenant, Andrew J. Stroh; 2d lieutenant, Jacob Rohrback; 1st sergeant, William C. Goodrich; Sergeants—Charles D. Wharton, George D. Bucher, Albert Haas, B. F. Bright; Corporals—Warren McEwen, Samuel P. Bright, Samuel Hoey, Martin L. Hendricks, Samuel Harrison, Charles Conrad, Isaac S. Kern, Robert B. Ammerman; Privates—Zebadee Bostian, George Bloom, Isaac Bair, John A Bucher, Edward L. Beck, Benjamin Bahner, Isaac Bubb, Henry D. Bucher, John Coogan, David Druckemiller, Conrad Detry, Andrew Detry, William Foulk, Landis Fry, George U. Folk, Peter Hileman, Luther Harrison, Thomas Henninger, John E. Heller, Andrew J. Heller, Jacob B. Hoover, William D. Haupt, Charles D. Kiehl, Martin S. Kauffmann, William Krighaum, Peter Krohn, Lorenzo Kramer, Michael Keefer, Isaac Leeser, John Lyon, Benjamin F. Landau, George Mantz, Isaac Miller, Mahlon Myers, Lewis Miller, Jacob A. Miller, John Oyster, Edward Oyster, Raphael Perez, Franklin Patrick, William H. Rohrback, Arthur Robins, Henry L. Renn, Simon Renn, Silas Renn, Julius Ray, William H. Shiffer, John Shuler, Andrew S. Speece, Henry C. Sensholtz, George A. Sterner, Jonas Trego, John Weaver, D. J. Wharton, Silas E. Wiles, John R. Walls, John Webber, William E. Youngman, Abraham Zimmerman—74.

In March, 1865, the Seventy-fourth Regiment Pennsylvania Volunteers, was recruited by the addition to it of seven new companies. Among them was Company C, from Sunbury, under command of captain E. P. Rohbach. It was mustered in during March, 1865, and discharged August 29th, 1865. Its record is as follows:

Elias P. Rohback, captain, mustered in March 3d, '65; promoted to major May 2d, '62.

John H. Lewis, captain, mustered in March 4th, '65; promoted from adjutant to captain July 8th, '65; mustered out with company August 29th, '65.

Samuel S. Hendricks, 1st lieutenant, mustered in February 20th, '65; discharged by special order May 12th, '65.

Clinton D. Rohrbach, 2d lieutenant, mustered in March 21st, '65; discharged by special order March 29th, '65.

Benjamin F. Bright, 2d lieutenant, mustered in March 17th, '65; promoted from sergeant to 2d lieutenant July 2d, '65; mustered out with company.

Earnest L. Starkloff, 1st sergeant, mustered in March 17th, '65; mustered out with company.

H. B. Longsdorf, sergeant, mustered in March 17th, '65; mustered out with company.

W. H. Row, sergeant, mustered in March 9th, '65; mustered out with company.

Peter S. Gunsler, sergeant, mustered in March 19th, '65; mustered out with company.

John G. Young, sergeant, mustered in March 17th, '65; promoted to sergeant July 2d, '65; mustered out with company.

A. H. Boyer, corporal, mustered in March 17th, '65; mustered out with company.

Jacob Fetter, corporal, mustered in March 17th, '65; mustered out with company.

Perry Jarret, corporal, mustered in March 9th, '65; mustered out with company.

Uriah Foulk, corporal, mustered in March 17th, '65; mustered out with company.

Alexander Cassatt, corporal, mustered in March 17th, '65; mustered out with company.

W. B. Longsdorf, corporal, mustered in March 17th, '65; mustered out with company.

Joseph R. Bright, corporal, mustered in March 7th, '65; promoted to corporal July 2d, '65; mustered out with company.

Philip Keefer, corporal, mustered in March 14th, '65; mustered out with company.

Henry Cassatt, musician, mustered in March 8th, '65; mustered out with company.

P. F. Zimmerman, musician, mustered in March 17th, '65; mustered out with company.

Philip Arrison, private, mustered in March 23d, '65; mustered out with company.

Jacob W. Bright, private, mustered in March 17th, '65; mustered out with company.

Charles H. Bucher, private, mustered in March 17th, '65; mustered out with company.

Henry W. Bucher, private, mustered in March 17th, '65; mustered out with company.

John Bell, private, mustered in March 17th, '65; mustered out with company.

Henry Boyer, private, mustered in March 29th, '65; mustered out with company.

Daniel K. Conrad, private, mustered in March 17, '65; mustered out with company.

Jacob Cassatt, private, mustered in March 17th, '65; mustered out with company.

Landis Fry, private, mustered in March 17th, '65; mustered out with company.

James P. Griggs, private, mustered in March 8th, '65; mustered out with company.

William Gaeringer, private, mustered in March 8th, '65; mustered out with company.

Monroe Gensy, private, mustered in March 17th, '65; mustered out with company.

George B. Genther, private, mustered in March 17th, '65; mustered out with company.

Jackson W. Harp, private, mustered in March 17th, '65; mustered out with company.

Flem. J. Haughton, private, mustered in March 17th, '65; mustered out with company.

John W. Hopper, private, mustered in March 17th, '65; mustered out with company.

Thomas Henninger, private, mustered in March 17th, '65; mustered out with company.

Bernard A. Hopper, private, mustered in March 17th, '65; mustered out with company.

Edward Israel, private, mustered in March 17th, '65; mustered out with company.

Eli Kerlin, private, mustered in March 17th, '65; mustered out with company.

John Leeser, private, mustered in March 23d, '65; mustered out with company.

James W. Lyon, private, mustered in March 17th, '65; mustered out with company.

John J. Landaw, private, mustered in March 17th, '65; mustered out with company.

Gideon Landaw, private, mustered in March 18th, '65; mustered out with company.

Frank Lender, private, mustered in March 17th, '65; mustered out with company.

Solomon Lesser, private, mustered in April 5th, '65; mustered out with company.

John J. Messner, private, mustered in March 17th, '65; mustered out with company.

Thomas E. Metzgar, private, mustered in April 6th, '65; mustered out with company.

Robert R. McCay, private, mustered in March 17th, '65; mustered out with company.

James P. McKenney, private, mustered in March 17th, '65; mustered out with company.

Albert Robbins, private, mustered in March 17th, '65; mustered out with company.

William H. Rohrbach, private, mustered in March 17th, '65; mustered out with company.

Julius Ray, private, mustered in March 17th, '65; mustered out with company.

George A. Reeser, private, mustered in March 17th, '65; mustered out company.

PROPERTY OF COL. J.W. CAKE, FRONT STREET, SUNBURY, NORTH'D CO., PA

Laferius Renninger, private, mustered in March 20th, '65; mustered out with company.

Peter M. Snyder, private, mustered in March 28th, '65; mustered out with company.

John Wilver, private, mustered in March 23d, '65; mustered out with company.

John Zimmerman, private, mustered in March 17th, '65; mustered out with company.

The Regimental Band of the Forty-fifth Pennsylvania Volunteers belonged to Sunbury, and went out September 14th, '61. They were discharged by general order September 27th, '62, the Government having reduced the number of bands for the service. The band was made up as follows: Thomas D. Grant, leader. Musicians, Edward M. Bucher, Samuel P. Bright, W. T. Blair, Jacob Feig, Charles D. Wharton, L. B. Howard, Jared C. Irwin, Jesse Metz, John C. Miller, Charles D. Snavely, Henry Stulin, James R. Strickland, Samuel Van Buskirk, George W. Weaver, Philip Whitmore, Jacob Weiser, George W. Walls.

I have estimated the number of arms-bearing population in Sunbury and suburbs during the war at about eight hundred. Of these, at least three hundred and twenty-five were in the volunteer service, many of them over four years. In addition, one hundred and sixty-eight were in the emergency service; making in all four hundred and ninety-three men, or more than one-half of those who were fit for duty in the army. Sunbury furnished one brevet brigadier-general, three colonels, one major, seven captains, eight 1st lieutenants, eight 2d lieutenants, and one adjutant.

The following is a list of the honored dead lying in our grave-yard. It is not complete, but is as correct as I am able to get it at this time:

William Fry, company C, Forty-seventh Pennsylvania Volunteers, died March 20th, '75.

Peter Haupt, company C, Forty-seventh Pennsylvania Volunteers, died November 14th, '62.

Isaac M. Wilkerson, died February 1st, '61.

Philip Renn, company B, Twelfth, wounded, died October 20th, '65.

Harris A. Hepper, company I, Fifty-seventh Pennsylvania Volunteers, died March 22d, '68.

William Landau, died June 29th, '65.

Landis P. Starner, company C, One Hundred and Thirty-first Pennsylvania Volunteers, died December 13th, '63.

Isaac N. Sarvis, company C, One Hundred and Thirty-first Pennsylvania Volunteers, died January 15th, '63

James Wilkerson.

Emanuel Gotshall, company I, Fifty-eighth Pennsylvania Volunteers.

George Miller, company C, Forty-seventh Pennsylvania Volunteers, died '66.

Frederick Kline, company G, One Hundred and Eighty-eighth Pennsylvania Volunteers, died June 30th, '64.

Mahlon Myers.

John B. Durst, company H, Seventh Pennsylvania cavalry, died January 17th, '68.

Joseph Crist, company I, Fifty-eighth Pennsylvania Volunteers, died December, 69.

Samuel Crist, company I, Fifty-eighth Pennsylvania Volunteers, died '73.

Franklin Houser, died '73.

Freeman Haupt, company C, Forty-seventh Pennsylvania Volunteers.

J. Bolton Young, company C, Forty-seventh Pennsylvania Volunteers, died October 17th, '61.

Peter Smelser, company C, Forty-seventh Pennsylvania Volunteers, died July 8th, '73.

John Shissler, company I, Eighty-fourth Pennsylvania Volunteers.

Isaac Lesser, company K, One Hundred and Fifty-second Pennsylvania Volunteers, died '74.

Lieutenant Charles Israel Pleasants, Eleventh U. S. infantry, killed in the Wilderness; never found, but a monument erected here to his memory.

James Hoey, company I, Fifty-eighth Pennsylvania Volunteers, died June 11th, '65.

Edward L. Beck, company C, One Hundred and Thirty-first Pennsylvania Volunteers, and company M, Seventy-fourth Pennsylvania cavalry, died June 8th, '64.

Samuel Butcher, company I, Fifty-eighth Pennsylvania Volunteers.

David W. Druckemiller, company G, One Hundred and Eighty-eighth Pennsylvania Volunteers.

Lafayette Landau, company C, Forty-seventh Pennsylvania Volunteers.

Robert Brooks, Third Pennsylvania artillery.

Ulrich Eisele, (German.)

Dr. Jacob B. Masser was a surgeon in 1862, at the patent-office general hospital, in Washington City, having tendered his services to the government at the second battle of Bull Run. He was commissioned, and sworn into the United States service.

The following soldiers of the war of 1812, are also buried in our grave-yard, whose names I enter in this sketch: Peter Hileman, John Hileman, Christian Bower, Frederick Lazarus, Jacob Bright, John Colcher, Jacob Martin, John Eisely, William M. Gray, Jacob Mantz, George Mantz, George A. Prince, John Heddings, Captain McCurdy.

The historian gives place to the following extracts from Mr. Brice's oration, already alluded to, for the reason that, although they do not properly belong to the department of history, they are, nevertheless, so beautifully appropriate to the subject, and find an echo in so many hearts, that the citizens of Northumberland County will indulge a laudable pride in having them preserved in this permanent form. Said Mr. Brice:

"To keep alive the memories of these heroic men, we propose erecting a monument of granite, yonder, in the public park. Its foundation, sure and strong, has been laid in solid stone and cement, and in faith that the work will be fully completed. The committee, composed of John J. Smith, Major George B. Cadwallader, General J. K. Clement, E. Masser Bucher, Solomon Malick, Esq., Lieutenant L. H. Kase, L. M. Yoder, Lieutenant D. C. Dissinger, Jared C. Irwin, Henry D. Wharton, H. F. Mann, P. H. Moore, and Lieutenant A. N. Brice, are anxiously waiting for the improvement of the times, that we may go forward. Rest assured, we mean to succeed in our project. The granite shaft will go up, and the monument stand as a reminder to those who come after us, that brave men and true, from old Northumberland County, fought and died in defense of the flag. Its voice will not be for war, but for peace.

"It is worthy of remark that the bitter feelings engendered by the war are rapidly passing away. It is only remembered among soldiers that we are all Americans!—that, although we of the North fought under the stars and stripes, and they of the South under the stars and bars—while we sang the Star Spangled Banner, and they the Bonnie Blue Flag—we are one now in sentiment, bound together by common ties in a sisterhood of States. Living as we do, in a country grand in its majestic rivers, forests, lakes; beautiful in scenery; lofty in mountain grandeur; magnificent in resources; boundless in territory; fertile in its soil; plenteous in its productions and energies; with malice towards none,—here we have full opportunity to exercise that charity which suffereth long and is kind. While some of our large religious bodies, from whom better things were expected, are standing aloof upon mere technical differences; the secular societies, bound by the mystic tie, have long since united in brotherly love; and the soldiers, forgetting the heat and storm of battle, are now strewing flowers upon the graves of Union and Confederate soldiers alike. The Union officers and soldiers, of the army of the Potomac, invite the officers and soldiers of the late Confederate army, of Northern Virginia, to participate with them in their annual re-union. The Confederates of the Western army, have tendered a similar invitation to those who fought for the Union, to join with them, in their annual meeting, at Memphis, Tennessee.

"The war and all before it is now history. The genuine heroes of that war are respected by each other for their bravery, no matter on which side of the line they fought. Reynolds, McPherson, Lyon, Sumner, Warren, Lander, Baker, Stonewall Jackson, Lee, Hill, Johnson, Zollicoffer, Cleburne, are all regarded as men of martial ability and courage. Brave men are always generous and magnanimous. We here reach out the hand and heart of friendship for all, whether of the blue or gray. If it be true that the war was an engine of Providence to carry out His purposes, why should men stand out in hostility? True it is, that sentiment is outrunning statesmanship, in binding up the breaches of the war. The time is here, when we can and will all join hand in hand, as citizens of a common country, baptised in blood.

"As we thus take part in these beautiful ceremonies, let us not forget the widow and the orphan. We have not outlived them. The armless sleeve and the crutch, are yet seen on our streets. Let these widows, and orphans, and men, not be forgotten. While no government in the world has made better provision for her pensioners than ours, there are other relations we bear to these wards of the Republic, that in solemn trust must not be denied. What we respectfully demand of the United States, is an equalized bounty bill. I believe that in justice this will yet come.

Thoughtfully, let us move among the mounds of the dead. The humblest of these men were martyrs in the cause of their country. They sleep their last sleep. They are not moved by the tread of friend or foe. Their quiet is undisturbed by our song and muffled strains of music. We will some day rest with them, and the country we served, side by side, will be left to our children and to strangers. In the language of the great Lincoln, as he stood by the dead on the field of Gettysburg:—"It is for us to be here dedicated to the great task remaining before us, that from these honored dead we take an increased devotion to that cause, for which they gave their full devotion; that we here highly resolve that these dead shall not have died in vain; that this nation, under God, shall have a new birth of freedom; and that government of the people, by the people, and for the people, shall not perish from the earth."

THE NORTHUMBERLAND COUNTY SOLDIERS' MONUMENT ASSOCIATION

Was organized in the borough of Sunbury, on the 25th of May, 1872, in pursuance of a call made on the 18th of May, 1872, signed by A. N. Brice, John J. Smith, Heber Painter, D. C. Dissinger, Charles J. Fox, S. H. Knowles, and J. E. Torrington. At the meeting of May 25th, 1872, an executive committee of fifteen was appointed, composed of A. N. Brice, P. H. Moore, Heber Painter, John Kay Clement, J. J. Smith, T. S. Simpson, L. M. Yoder, S. H. Knowles, G. B. Cadwallader, D. C. Dissinger, H. G. Thatcher, Charles J. Fox, E. M. Bucher, H. F. Mann, and L. H. Kase. John J. Smith, was made President; Heber Painter, Secretary; P. H. Moore, Treasurer. August 6th, 1873, H. D. Wharton was elected a member of the executive committee, in place of H. G. Thatcher, resigned. June 18th, 1873, Heber Painter resigned as Secretary, and A. N. Brice was elected in his place. On the 5th of August, 1873, the Common Pleas of Northumberland County granted a charter to the association. The site for the monument having been marked out on Market square, on the 4th day of July, 1872, by Hon. Alexander Jordan and Hon. Simon Cameron. On the 30th of May, 1874, at the time of the decoration of the soldiers' graves with flowers, the corner-stone was laid with Masonic ceremonies. The foundation was laid in cement and stone during the Summer of 1873. The panic of 1873, having set in, the work of completing the monument has been retarded, but the committee are hopeful that ere long, with the aid of subscriptions from our generous citizens, headed by Hon. Simon Cameron, Hon. J. B. Packer, Hon. A. Jordan, W. I. Greenough, Esq., S. P. Wolverton, Esq., Judge Rockefeller, W. L. Dewart, and others, the grand work will be completed.

TURBUT TOWNSHIP.

About midway between the southern and the northern extremities of that narrow neck of Northumberland County which extends from the north branch to the Lycoming line, lies the territory embraced in the present township of Turbut. It is about five miles in extent, from west to east, with an average width of little more than three miles, from north to south. Delaware and Lewis townships form the northern, and Chillisquaque the southern boundary line. Montour County joins it upon the east, while the right bank of the west branch is its western limit.

But when old Turbut township was first erected, by decree of the Northumberland County court, on the 10th of April, 1772, and so named in honor of Colonel Turbut Francis, who had large grants in it for military services, it embraced five times its present area, and the following are the recorded boundaries: "Beginning on the east side of the Susquehanna at Fort Augusta; thence up the easterly side of the north branch, to the old line, formerly run for a division between Berks and Northampton Counties; hence by the same line, north-east to the top of Muncy Hills; thence along the top of the same, westerly to the west branch of the Susquehanna, and crossing the same to the west side, and down the same to the junction of the branches, and crossing the Susquehanna, to the place of beginning, so as to include the Forks and Island." From this territory have since been partitioned: Chillisquaque township, in 1786; Delaware township, in 1843; and Lewis township, in 1843.

In natural beauty and in material advantages, it differs but little from what is found throughout the entire range of the west branch valley. There is the same winding river; the same diversity of hill and vale and woodland; the same "waving fields and pastures green"—as fertile and as favored as any the sun ever shone upon—and the same evidences of thrift and prosperity on every hand. Bubbling springs and clear streams are frequent, beautiful open groves and belts of thrifty timber are everywhere interspersed; while the handsome, substantial houses, the full barns and granaries, with "cattle upon a thousand hills," show how beautifully the generous limestone soil has rewarded the labor of the husbandman.

Its earliest history too, is similar to that of most of the settlements in the dark and bloody ground of the upper Susquehanna. It is the old romantic story of how stern resolute men, in the more sterile settlements of the East, hearing of the marvellous fruitfulness of the Otzinachson valley, resolved to profit by its bounty and its promise, though they *knew* that the tomahawk awaited them and their families, there—and how, through privation and watchings, captivity and torture, they toiled and fought and suffered on, till they won for their children's children, the peace and plenty which are there to-day.

Let us not forget that there was a time, when neither plenty nor peace were there—that

> "Havoc has been upon that peaceful plain,
> And blood has dropped there, like the drops of rain;
> And corn grows o'er the still graves of the slain."

Through these wilds, too, came the good missionaries: Brainerd, Zeisberger, Bishop von Watteville and others of scarcely less note; carrying their lives in their hands, and braving every hardship, in the effort to save the red men's souls. And they were rewarded with some measure of success; many Indians were converted by their teachings, though, it must be said, there were not a few who afterwards proved recreant to their professions. The great *Shickelemy* was one of those who received baptism, and who remained firm to the last. He died at Shamokin, in 1749, and of that event, Loskiel says: "He found comfort, peace, and joy, by faith in his Redeemer, and the brethren considered him as a candidate for baptism. * * * *

In this state of mind he was taken ill, was attended by Dr. David Zeisberger, and, in his presence, fell happy asleep in the Lord, in full assurance of obtaining eternal life through the merits of Jesus Christ."

But after the defeat of General Braddock in 1755, the vindictiveness and treachery of the Indians increased to such an extent, that even the brave missionaries could stay among them no longer; so they quietly but mournfully took their departure from the field of their labors, and left the Indian to his godlessness and cruelty.

And that it was only through the trials and virtues of the ancestors—their courage which never wavered; their labor which never ceased; their steadfastness and trust in God, which endured to the end—that we, their descendants, have come to this heritage.

Of the events occurring in the township territory prior to the year 1772, we have little more than a tradition. We know that the Shamokin war-path, passed directly through it—the Indian military road, if we may use the term—leading from the great central point of Shamokin to the upper lodges at Muncy, Great Island and Sinnemahoning, and even through to the lake and to Niagara. That over this path, the Indian war parties came and went, reddening every mile of the way with blood and butchery; of the chiefs who led these hordes, we know that nearly all were alike, cruel and treacherous; all of them, at same time, professing friendship to the pale-faces; but only to lull and betray them; sparing neither age nor sex, and laughing with savage glee at the bright scalp of the little child, hanging intertwined with the long hair of the mother, in the foul smoke of the wigwam. A few noble exceptions only proved this rule, and among the chief of these, were *Andrew Montour*, the *Seneca*, and *Shickelemy*, the *Cayuga* chief, who was justly called the white man's friend.

There is not, to-day, a living person who knows the name of the first white settler in Turbut, but nothing is more certain than that pioneers were there, very soon after 1750. They may have been, and they probably were, of that transitory class who are the foam which is pushed on in advance of the solid wave of immigration; but whatever they were, it is indeed a pity that their names, and their seniority of pioneership, are hidden in impenetrable oblivion.

Two years after the township organization (in 1774), it contained two hundred and thirty-seven tax-payers, as follows:

Blair, J.
Blue, F.
Blue, William
Biggar, J.
Bannart, M.
Brandon, J.
Bailey, S.
Batman, F.

Eason, John
Eason, Robert
Erwin, F.
Erwin, A.
Erwin, John
Fulerton, A.
Freeland, G.
Fitzsimmons, W.

Logue, H.
Lemmerson, C.
Levy, E.
Malone, R.
Montgomery, John
McKnight, W.
Miller, J.
McCallon, R.

Black, J.
Berry, G.
Bennet, G.
Boon, H.
Bright, M.
Bradley, D.
Brady, John
Byers, John
Broadly, M.
Boyd, John
Bailey, William
Bowman, Wm.
Calron, J.
Curry, John
Carscadden, James
Clark, A.
Curry, Robert
Clark, John
Coughran, J.
Clark, A.
Clark, William
Calturt, M.
Carson, Joseph
Clark, James
Camfort, J.
Chainy, John
Clark, John
Crawford, James
Carney, A.
Coughran, John
Camel, M.
Carson, D.
Coughran, C.
Cook, William
Caldwell, William
Carr, A.
Chambers, D.
Cunningham, M.
Cox, C.
Calhoun, G.
Clark, William
Chambers, J.
Chainy, J.
Crothers, John
Chattin, John
Callender, C.
Davis, R.
Denney, John
Dougherty, P.
Dougherty, H.
Dixton, John
Durham, James
Davis, N.
Donold, John
Davis, D.
Dunlap, John
Dowdle, M.
Duncan, M.
Davis, Wm.
Defance, John
Deen, John
Deen, A.
Dougherty, John
Espy, J.
Espy, James
Erwin, G.
Erwin, R.
Eagon, F.
Erison, John
Emmit, John
Emmons, A.

Farron, B.
Fulton, B.
Freeland, A.
Fulmore, J.
Foshean, E.
Foutz, C.
Fredrick, G.
Field, G.
Fisher, W.
Freeland, J.
Forster, W.
Frig, P.
Gillespy, William
Gillespy, J.
Gillilan, A.
Gibson, A.
Gray, John
Gaskin, T.
Gowdy, J.
Gordon, S.
Geddis, P.
Gillespy, C.
George, William
Ginning, F.
Gallaway, J.
Grant, A.
Galbraith, R.
Gray, John
Gilfillan, R.
Hains, R.
Hamilton, G.
Hews, T.
Harrison, J.
Hays, D.
Hood, John
Hufman, H.
Hullius, T.
Hamersly, J.
Hemrod, S.
Harrison, W.
Hays, James
Hendershoot, M.
Hatchenson, W.
Hembright, John
Hunter, James
Hunter, T.
Horton, K.
Ireland, D.
Jury, O.
Jones, B.
Johnston, William
Johnson, H.
Jurdon, T.
Jones, P.
Johnson, John
Jurden, B.
Kerney, P.
Kirk, M.
Kelly, D.
Kennedy, D.
King, R.
Kenersey, W.
Lytle, John
Love, R
Leighton, W.
Luckey, R.
Luckey, J.
Leach, J.
Loge, J.
Lemmon, T.
Lomax, C.

McWilliams, W.
Murray, William
McCandles, R.
McFarling, R.
McDrior, J.
Miller, J.
McHenry, I.
Martin, J.
McWilliams, I.
Murphy, J.
McWilliams, R.
McClanahon, J.
McWilliams, H.
Mehaffy, T.
Moody, R.
Murry, J.
Murry, J.
McCandles, G.
McCluny, J.
McClintock, J.
McMath, A.
McKnight, J.
McConnell, G.
Miller, I.
Menger, R.
McKee, G.
Mehaffy, J.
Mils, J.
Mead, D.
McMahan, J.
Murx, A.
Marshell, W.
McCully, P.
McKin, W.
Martin, P.
Martin, R.
McClaws, J.
Moore, J.
McCulloch, J.
Neilson, J.
Neel, T.
Oaks, S.
Ogdon, J.
Piper, William
Plunket, William
Parson, B.
Phillips, S.
Pedrick, R.
Physick, L.
Pollock, J.
Paterson, William
Paton, William
Purveyance, S.
Roudke, R.
Robinson, J.
Reed, E.
Rickey, J.
Rees, M.
Rendels, J.
Russel, R.
Reed, M.
Ross, William
Sterret, B.
Simpson, A.
Stedden, T.
Shaw, L.
Spear, S.
Spear, A.
Semple, J.
Simson, J.

FREELAND'S SETTLEMENT AND FORT.

In 1772, the same year in which Marcus Hulings, Sr., opened his tavern at Limestone Run, (now in the borough of Milton,) there came from Essex County, New Jersey, two families, whose names were to be prominently identified with the history of the County and of Turbut township—the family of Vincent, and that of Jacob Freeland.

The Vincents, Cornelius, John and Peter, chose a point on the river, a mile or so from the mouth of Warrior Run, and about three miles above Milton, but Jacob Freeland located some distance up from the river, near where Warrior Run Church now stands.

Being a man of much foresight, he had brought along with him, all the way over the tedious route from Jersey, the necessary iron work and gearings, for the building of a mill, for the knew it was a prime necessity, in a new settlement. In the succeeding winter, he cut his timber, and early in the Spring of 1773, he commenced the work, and pushed it vigorously through to completion. It had the inevitable effect of bringing prosperity to the settlement and to its founder; and during the nine years which intervened before the building of the first mill upon Limestone Run (now Milton), the latter place was much inferior in importance to Freeland's settlement. New immigrants came in, mostly from New Jersey, and among them in 1773, were Samuel Gould and his family, and Timothy Williams with a dozen children.

Freeland's mills* being now in prosperous operation, he justly regarding himself, in a manner, as the father and guardian of the settlement, bethought himself of a means of defense, in case of attack by the merciless and treacherous savage.

He resolved to build a stockade, sufficiently capacious to afford an asylum for the surrounding settlers from any sudden irruption of the Indians. It was a work of much labor, in the cutting, hauling, and planting of the logs, but in the Summer of 1775—while the fusillades were rattling along the declivities of Bunker Hill—it was completed. Nor was it finished much too soon!

It mounted no artillery, and had few of the appliances of scientific fortification; but it was pierced with loop-holes for musketry, and its friendly logs saved many a head from the scalping-knife, in the four years which preceded its final capture.

Freeland also enclosed a half-acre of ground around the fort. This enclosure was surrounded by a picket, far less strong than the main stockade, but it afterwards did excellent service to the families of many of those who had fled from their homes at the time of the great runaway.

Upon one occasion, in the latter part of the year 1778, a small party had left Freeland's fort for Northumberland town. There were six or eight men on foot, and with them were two women on horseback—Mrs. Durham and Mrs. McNight—each has an infant in her arms as she rode.

When they had reached a hollow not far from the Vincent settlement, the crack of the rifles of the savages told them too late that they had fallen into an ambuscade. The horse of Mrs. McNight became unmanageable, wheeled, and made for the fort. Her child was thrown from her arms, but she caught it by the foot, and so carried it, swinging by the side of her galloping horse, until mother and child were safe and sound within the shelter of the stockade.

Such were the frontier women of those days! Poor Mrs. Durham was less fortunate; her child was killed in her arms, and she herself thrown from the horse. An Indian tore the scalp from her head and left her, apparently lifeless. Two men named Williams and Gaffy,† soon passed where she lay, and they were amazed to see her partially rise and beg for water; she had been scalped, but was otherwise uninjured. She recovered and lived many years.

Some seven or eight years before, during an attack by Indians on the house of John Tate, near Northumberland, a girl named Catharine Storm, was similarly scalped. She, too, recovered and lived to an old age. Those were strange experiences; few, very few, have ever lost their scalp and yet lived to tell the tale!

The fort was captured in 1779, by a body of more than three hundred Indians and British, under command of Capt. McDonald of the English army. The people there had been warned that such a party was coming down the valley, and that it would be wise to abandon the fort, but they disregarded the warning, although, only a few days before, two young men—one a son of Jacob Freeland, and the other a Vincent—had been killed while at work in a field not a great way off.

More than fifty women and children were at Freeland, with only twenty-six fighting-men behind the log rampart, but they considered themselves a host, and felt secure in their bravery.

It was in the gray fog of early dawn, on the 28th of July, that the savage foe made his attack. Old Mr. James Watt, and two young men, had gone incautiously outside the fort. An Indian sprang from his concealment, and tomahawked Mr. Watt, and, at the same moment, one of the young men was shot through the head. The other, unhurt, leaped inside and closed the gate in an instant. The savages raised the war-whoop, and rushed to the attack, but Captain Lytle and his true men were ready for them, and promptly sent a bullet wherever an Indian's head was seen. The result, however, could not be doubtful, in a fight where the numbers were so unequal.

* He had both grist and saw-mills, as is shown by the tax list of 1774.

† The father of Andrew Guffy, Esq., now of McEwensville.

Captain McDonald was honestly desirous of preventing the massacre, which he knew must follow if the fort was taken by storm. He therefore summoned a surrender, with promise of safety to the women and children, and with half-an-hour allowed for decision. A council of war was held; resistance seemed hopeless, and so, at the end of the half hour, the fort surrendered.

The following is a *verbatim* transcript of the "Articles of capitulation entered into between Captain John McDonald, on His Majesty's part, and John Lytle, on the part of Congress:"

"*First.*—The men in the garrison to march out and ground their arms on the green, in front of the fort, which is to be taken possession of immediately by His Majesty's troops. *Agreed to.*

"*Second.*—All men bearing arms, are to surrender themselves prisoners of war, and to be sent to Niagara. *Agreed to.*

"The women and children are not to be stripped of their clothing, nor molested by Indians, and to be at liberty to move down the country where they please.

JOHN MCDONALD, *Captain Rangers.*
JOHN LYTLE, " "

To the honor of Captain McDonald, it must be recorded, that he kept his promise, and restrained his savage allies from butchery, though he found it almost impossible to do so.

The warriors and their squaws, (of whom there seems to have been a large number accompanying the expedition,) sacked the fort, and then set it on fire, after which they retired a short distance down the run, and commenced preparations for a feast, while some of the warriors spread themselves down the valley for further depredations.

At Muddy Run, Captain Hawkins Boon had heard the noise of the attack, and collecting thirty-two men, besides himself, he hurried to Lytle's relief. In his eagerness to succor his friends at the fort, he came up incautiously, and fell into the Indian ambuscade; for their runners had seen the rescuing party, and brought up the news of its coming. In a hollow, only a very short distance below the fort, the savage fire was poured in on them with fatal effect, but neither Boon nor his brave men were daunted, and their answering bullets did their errands *well.* The fight raged on hotly for some time, but when the white men were half slain, and the survivors at last saw their captain fall, they turned and fled. The Indians pursued with great determination, but only succeeded in capturing one man, and of him they made short work.

The killed of Boon's command were: Captain Hawkins Boon, Captain Samuel Dougherty, Jeremiah McGlaghlen, Nathaniel Smith, John Jones, Edward Costikan, Ezra Green, Samuel Neal, Math. McClintock, Hugh McGill, Andrew Woods, James Watts, John McClintock, William McClany, James Miles, Henry Gilfillen, and one unknown.

Captain Boon had been a surveyor and an expert woodsman, but had, a few years before, settled at the mouth of Muddy Run, where he had built a log mill, and a small, rude defensive work, which the settlers called Fort Boon. The Indians burned them both. The mill was probably at the site now occupied by Kemerer's mill, two miles above Milton.

Among those captured at the fort was Daniel Vincent, then nineteen years old, and just married. His young wife never heard from him during his captivity, and, after three years of fading hope, she at last fully believed herself a widow. At length, after the war, he returned, to find himself unrecognized! Was it strange? The three years, from nineteen to twenty-two, the unfamiliar beard, and the hardships of captivity, had wrought an effectual disguise; but the *voice* was unchanged, and when he called her Christian name, in the old tone, she fell on his neck, and thanked God for His mercy.

On the death of this man, many years after, we read as follows in the *Miltonian*, of February 3d, 1827:

"Daniel Vincent died January 26th, aged 67. The deceased was among the first settlers of this part of Pennsylvania. He was likewise one of those who bore an ample part in the privations and troubles consequent to a war for independence. He was one of the defenders of the infant settlement, and among the intrepid defenders of Freeland's fort, when it was yielded to an overpowering host of savages. He was then severed from his family, conducted to Canada, where he remained a captive until the close of the war."

Fort Swartz was built in 1774, at or near the old ferry, about a mile above Milton. It was a log structure, named in honor of Major Christian Godfried Swartz, of Col. Weltner's German (Penn'a.) Battalion, a detachment of which, under command of Swartz, garrisoned the fort, at the time of Freeland's capture, but we do not find that any attempt at assistance or rescue was made by them in emulation of the generous bravery of Captain Boon. Fort Miniger, at the mouth of Warrior Run, and Fort Rice, at Chillisquaque, were also log defences, and manned, in part, by Weltner's men. Fort Rice was the only defensive work above Augusta, which held out without abandonment or surrender, through the entire war. All these forts, during the time of their existence, were within Turbut township.

PARADISE AND FORT MONTGOMERY.

In 1767, a Mr. Patterson patented a tract of seven hundred acres of land, which now lies in the extreme southeastern part of Lewis township, but which, for seventy-one years, formed a part of Turbut. He named the tract "Paradise," and certainly it was not wholly a misnomer, judging from its appearance at this day. The country is gently rolling, and extremely fertile, though, perhaps, not more so than thousands upon thousands of acres all along the valley. But the feature in which it is especially marked, is the unusual beauty of its open groves of oak, and other hard woods so free from underbrush and decaying debris, that they have the appearance of well-kept parks.

From this patent, the general name of Paradise came to be applied to a large scope of territory, stretching in both directions, from Patterson's entry—the larger portion however, lying in Turbut township, where the two Paradise churches are located.

In 1771, Mr. Patterson removed to White Deer Creek, to reside there with his daughter, Mrs. Hunter, and sold his patented lands in Paradise, to John Montgomery, of Dauphin County, who at once established there his household goods, and built a small house of hickory logs, by a perennial spring, which then, as now formed the extreme head-waters of Muddy Run. With a wise precaution against the dangers of the times, he also built a strong log barrier, enclosing both cabin and spring, and this rude defence, gained from the surrounding settlers, the high-sounding name of "Fort Montgomery."

The "fort" may have sometimes had the effect to deter attacks of Indians; but at the time of Freeland's capture, it made no show of resistance. On that memorable morning, John Montgomery heard the volleys, away to the northward, and, mounting his boys, bade them reconnoitre cautiously towards Freeland's. They came in sight of that fort, and seeing it in possession of the Indians, rode swiftly back with the alarm. Everything which could be removed, was with headlong haste, packed in the wagons, with the women and children, and turning their faces southward, they did not look back till they halted in Dauphin County, whence they had removed eight years before.

After the troublous times were past, they returned to Paradise, but found only the charred ruins of house, barn, and fort. A small stone-house was at once erected, and afterwards a larger one, covering the spring. In the front wall of the older house, was a smooth stone which told the date of erection, "W. M. 1789," the letters standing for William Montgomery, the son of the original purchaser from Patterson.

In a still later stone-house, adjoining the others, was a tablet, upon which was cut "Tobias Eschbach, 1833." Both these stones, with their inscriptions, are now to be seen, laid in the foundation wall of the new house, which Philip Raup built, in 1873, within a few feet of the Montgomery spring; Mr. Raup having purchased the property of the heirs of John T. Montgomery, and, having demolished the oldest of the houses, for the building-stone contained in it. Of those three old houses, the one covering the spring, still remains in excellent preservation, and the spring itself, is flowing as bright and clear, as it did, when the hickory logs of Fort Montgomery enclosed it, a hundred years ago.

John Montgomery (who purchased of Patterson), died by the falling of a tree, November 8th, 1792, aged 58, and David, his son (born in Dauphin, in 1767), died, November 23d, 1859, aged 92. Father and son lie in the old church-yard, at Chillisquaque. Of his later descendants, the most distinguished, was Hon. John G., his grandson, born January 28th, 1805, who established in the practice of law, at Danville, was elected to Congress, in 1856, and died of disease contracted at the National Hotel, at Washington, in 1857. Some years before, his bride had met a tragical death, on the next morning after their marriage, at McEwensville. They were returning to their home, in Paradise, when, the horse taking fright, she was thrown from the sleigh, and instantly killed.

David B. Montgomery, another grandson, born November 28th, 1810, still lives near the old spring. He has served two terms in the lower house of the Pennsylvania Legislature, and one in the Senate, during the war of the Rebellion.

Still another grandson, William Montgomery died in 1875, of small-pox, at McEwensville.

PLATE XV

Res. of J. A. CAKE, Sunbury, Northumberland Co, Pa.

Farm Property of COL. J.W. CAKE, Front St. Sunbury, Northumberland Co, Pa.

Tower over Magazine of Fort Augusta.

The descendants of the first John Montgomery are very numerous, and are widely scattered over Northumberland, and adjoining counties.

Turbut township has very few industrial interests, except agriculture. In fact—excluding those manufacturing establishments, which lie just out of the borough line of Milton, but which are undeniably a part of the town—there are only the "Boonville" flour mills, of W. B. Kemerer, Esq., at Muddy Run. These mills are located where the railroad crosses the Run, and on, or very near, the very spot where Capt. Hawkins Boon's mill stood, a century ago. (The opinion seems to be quite general, that Boon had no mill there—only a fort, and a dwelling-house—but the letter of Col. Samuel Hunter to Col. Matthew Smith, under date of Sunbury, July 28th, 1779, which says—'this day, about about twelve o'clock, an express arrived from *Capt. Boon's mill*, informing us that Freeland's fort was surrounded by a party of Indians,' etc., absolutely decides this question.) The old mill was burnt in 1779. In 1840, Abraham Straub removed his mill from Milton island, to the place where Kemerer's mill now is. Straub afterwards sold to Moses Chamberlain and Daniel Bisel. Then Chamberlain sold to a Mr. Yager, leaving the firm Yager & Bisel. From them, John Ott became the purchaser, and he, in turn, sold, in 1861, to W. B. Kemerer, the present owner. The mill was burnt in March, 1874, and immediately replaced by the present excellent establishment. Its size is forty-five by fifty-five feet, with four run of burrs, driven by water and steam, and doing both merchant and custom work.

A lumber mill, owned by Messrs. Nagle and Eshach, also stood near there, upon the canal, but was recently burned, and has not been rebuilt.

A mill which was owned by William Follmer, in the southeastern corner of the township, on Limestone Run, was a few years ago moved to Pottsgrove, in Chillisquaque township, that being thought a more eligible location.

The Paradise Reformed Church.—Established as a congregation in 1804. For seven years their preaching was very irregular. During that time, the Rev. Mr. Ingold held occasional worship in the houses, and sometimes in the barns of members. Their first regular pastor was Rev. Jost Henry Fries, who came to them in 1811, and preached in the school-house at Paradise until 1823. Next came Rev. Samuel Gutelius, during whose pastorate a brick church building was erected in union with the Lutherans. The site was about five miles from Milton, on the Paradise road. It was dedicated in August, 1824. Succeeding Mr. Gutelius, were Revs. Henry Wagner, Daniel Gring, George Wolf, Lucien Cort, D. B. Albright, and Henry Mosser.

The present pastor, Rev. J. K. Millet, assumed the Paradise charge in 1873.

In 1859, the congregation having become large, their interest in the church building was sold to the Lutherans, and a new brick edifice was built by subscription. It is located on the Paradise road, near the old one, and its cost was five thousand dollars. The first records of this church, for a period of nearly forty years, were kept in German. The membership is two hundred and fifty. Sabbath-school attendance, sixty.

Paradise Lutheran Church.—The Lutherans at Paradise and vicinity became a congregation in 1824, their first pastor being the Rev. Mr. Sheets. In August of that year, they dedicated their house of worship—a brick church building—which they had erected in union with the Paradise Reformed congregation, and when, in 1859, the Reformed people withdrew from the union to build their new church, they sold their union interest to the Lutherans, who thus became sole owners of the edifice, in which they still hold their worship. Their present pastor is Rev. Jacob Wampole, of Turbutville. They have a small Sabbath-school.

The Follmer Church, (Lutheran.)—There is no authentic record of the *exact* date of its establishment, but Mr. David Eschbach, who resides in the Paradise section of Turbut township, and who is one of the oldest residents, as well as one of the best informed men of the County, in church affairs, places the date at 1800 or 1801. He well recollects the Rev. Mr. Stock, who was one of the earliest, though probably not the first of its pastors.

Their worship was held in an old log church, up to 1859, the time of the erection of their present brick church. Its location is in "Pleasant Valley," in the easterly part of Turbut township, on the Washingtonville road about four miles from Milton. Their pastor is the Rev. Mr. Bergner, and a flourishing Sabbath-school is connected with the church.

The public schools of the township are eleven in number, teaching the common and some of the higher branches, during five months of the year. These are, to some extent, supplemented by "pay" schools, for two or three months more. The school buildings are all of brick, and although small, are neat and comfortable structures, and the schools themselves are very creditable.

The school directors for the township, are David Eshbach, Peter Bastian, Henry Buss, John Mosteller, John Hoffa, John W. Huether.

The population of Turbut, in 1860, was one thousand seven hundred and sixty, and in 1870, was one thousand eight hundred and three.

The history of the old township of Turbut is virtually that of all the country lying between Northumberland and the Muncy hills, and so interwoven is its past, with that of the newer townships and boroughs which have been lopped off from it, that their history cannot be entirely eliminated without detriment, both to accuracy and symmetry. Nor can the opposite course be adopted, for if the histories of the boroughs were only to be taken up from the time of their erection, they would then be shorn of that preponderating interest which attaches to the ancient facts and incidents of their settlement, and earliest vicissitudes. They should therefore be intertwined in such a manner as, on the one hand, to preserve as much as possible the identity of each; and on the other, to do the least practicable violence to the rules of local and chronological arrangement.

DELAWARE TOWNSHIP

Was erected from Turbut, by order of the court, at the April term, in 1843. Its boundaries are, on the north, Lycoming County; east, Lewis township (which was erected from Turbut at the same time); south, Turbut township; and west, the Susquehanna River. The population in 1860, was one thousand nine hundred and three; and in 1870, it was one thousand eight hundred and seventy-nine.

As its erection is of so recent date, nearly all of its history is covered by that of old Turbut township (from which it was partitioned,) and by those of the boroughs of McEwensville and Watsontown, which lie within its territorial limits.

The Shamokin war-path lays through this township, and later—over nearly the same route—was laid the Northumberland and Muncy road, on which the weekly mail commenced to pass, on horseback, as early as 1804, and the mail stages of Cummings, and Hall, and Hulings, ran for many years after 1808. In the easterly direction, the old "Potash road" afforded a route of travel from the river, by Pine Grove (McEwen's,) to the farther part of Turbut. This road was opened in the early years of the century, by Mr. Harrison, to give egress to the river, for the product of the potash works, which he established for the conversion of the large quantities of wood and timber growing on his farm, six miles beyond John Quigley's plough-shop. The origin of the name of the road, is apparent. The designation is still applied to one of the streets in McEwensville.

This road, for a considerable distance from the river, passed up Warrior Run, upon which, were the "Vincent," and the "Truckenmiller" mills. The first Vincent mill, was of logs, built in 1773, by Daniel Vincent, who settled there from Essex County, New Jersey. This was replaced in 1792, by the stone structure. The establishment is now run by Mr. Yengler, and is known by his name.

The first mill upon the Truckenmiller site, was also a log building, erected by Shaw (precise date not known.) It was afterwards bought by the grandfather of Dr. Hunter, of Watsontown. By him, it was demolished, and a frame building erected in its place. Next, it was owned by the Truckenmillers, from whom it received its name, and now, after several intervening changes of ownership, it is again in the possession of one of the same family, and name.

Farther up the run, and to the northward of McEwensville, now stands David Gold's mill, occupying the site of the old Wilson mill, which was built as early as 1795 (ex-Sheriff Reader recollects well, that when not more than six or eight years old, he went with "grist" to this mill with his father.) This old mill gave place to another, which years after came into possession of Mr. Gold, who again rebuilt and remodeled it about twenty years ago. He sold out to one Bennett, who introduced steam as an auxiliary propelling-power, to be used in times of low water. This experiment was found unprofitable and abandoned, upon which Mr. Gold repurchased the property, and now operates it.

To the southward of the Potash road, towards Muddy Run, was Peter Jones' blacksmith shop, situated in the forks of the road, and a place of no little note in early times. Near there, was the farm of Alexander Guffy (grandfather of A. J. Guffy, Esq., of Watsontown,) who came from Scotland to this country before the revolution. He lived there long before 1800, and was at one time a distiller as well as farmer. In the year 1778, he was one of the party who were with Mrs. Durham, when she was scalped and left for dead, below Freeland's fort, and he brought water in his hat to her, to slake the agonizing thirst of her return to consciousness.

Still further to the southward, lived John Wilson, who in some way, came to be called by the settlers, "Gaily" Wilson.

The origin, as well as the orthography of the *sobriquet* is unknown, but it seems proper to spell it "Gaily," for certainly there was a good deal of the Troubadour in his composition. He was by trade a carpenter, but was also good at singing and dancing, particularly when his favorite beverage was abundant and easy of access. He was excellent too, at narration, and often gave thrilling accounts of his adventures with the Indians. One of the most exciting of these, was to the effect, that upon a certain morning in 1778, he, with seventeen others, started from Freeland's fort, in search of some stray horses, but had gone only a short distance, when a large party of Indians, in ambush, fired on them, killing all his seventeen companions, while he himself with his hair standing on end, fled like a deer back to the fort, and cleared the parapet at a single leap. He ran so swiftly, he said, that the skirts of the bright blue coat, which he wore that day, stood horizontally to the rear, and he was always fond of calling himself "Blue Jay" Wilson, from his fancied resemblance to that gaudy bird, upon the occasion of that memorable retreat.

He often worked at the houses of David Montgomery, Alexander Guffy, and many of the other settlers, and was always welcome, for he was both jovial and inoffensive. He died, sexton of Chillisquaque Church, and he sleeps in its enclosure, near the grave of his old patron David Montgomery.

Neil McCoy, a distiller, living farther north in the township, was another frolicsome spirit. Upon occasions of a public character, he was always present, with his sons, and their antics added greatly to the general hilarity. In father and sons, the flow of animal spirits was unfailing.

In national characteristics, Delaware is like the other parts of old Turbut. It is rolling, well-watered, healthy, and extremely fertile. Among the names of ancient residents, were those of Irwin, Craig, Brown, Wilson, Murray, Kerrigan, and Hogue, all as good farmers as any in the County.

The Village of Dewart, is of very recent date. Some time after the opening of the railroad, a small station was made there, principally for the accommodation of such business as might cross the bridge, at that point, from Uniontown, on the west side of the river. Afterwards, a post-office was established there, through the influence of Hon. William L. Dewart, of Sunbury, and both the station and the office were named Dewart, in his honor. The village is still very small. There are two hotels, and two general stores, but, as yet, no church, though the Methodists have taken down their old house at "Stony Batter," and commenced to re-erect it at Dewart. A short distance south of the village, are the enclosed grounds, which the Northumberland County Agricultural Society have leased for their annual fairs. This was only established there in 1875, having been removed from the lands of D. H. Driesbach, in Lewis township.

The river bridge, before mentioned, is owned by a bridge company, in Union County. It was built about twenty years ago, and carried away in the great flood of 1865, but soon re-built by the company.

About three miles east of Dewart, is the very small village of *Packersville* containing one store, and a post-office of the same name.

On the Philadelphia and Erie Railroad, about three miles north of Dewart, is the distillery of John Eyster, a frame building forty-five by sixty feet, built in 1866.

Near David Gold's mill, one-half mile north of McEwensville is a small tannery, once owned by Jacob Stitzel. It now does but little work. These, with the mills before mentioned, comprise all the manufacturing industries of Delaware.

Public Schools.—There are in Delaware township, thirteen brick school-houses, in which are taught fourteen schools. The house at Dewart, is called the "Academy," as one of the two schools taught there, is of a grade higher than the others of the township.

The free term lasts five months of the year, and from four to five months more tuition, is paid for by subscription. The teachers' salaries are thirty to sixty dollars per month.

Present Board of School Directors: President, John Eyster; Secretary, Josiah Keysher; Treasurer, Madison Tygart; Joseph Kerr, Dr. — Harley, D. P. Billman.

The Warrior Run Presbyterian Church, is one of the oldest in the County. As early as 1775, it had erected a house of worship. A beautiful little grove at the lower extremity of Watsontown, still marks the site, as also that of the old grave-yard, in which, one of the inscriptions records a death that occurred in 1787.

A second log building was erected in 1789, two-and-a-half miles north-east of the first site. Here, the people worshipped,—even in winter—without fire-place or floor. The first fire was upon a brick hearth, in front of the pulpit, where the burning charcoal scattered dust, and generated deadly gases as well as heat. And yet, while the people thus evidenced hardihood and self-denial, they were not, according to present standards, equally praiseworthy in all respects. They even petitioned the legislature to sanction a lottery, by which to secure money for religious purposes, and one of the important transactions upon record, is a collection of pew-rent by legal process!

The pulpit in the second log building was very high and narrow, and in front of it was a capacious desk, from which one or two persons led the service of singing.

Two sermons were preached, between which an intermission was allowed. This too often occasioned enough conversation upon the neighborhood news, or upon politics, or enough of giddiness, flirtation, and merriment among the young, to dissipate the impression made by the one service, and to unfit them for the other. Indeed, an old and intelligent citizen testifies, that at one time the fascination of a service at Warrior Run was very much like that of a grand party, so far as many were concerned. How many engagements, other than those matrimonial; how many scandals circulated, and witticisms perpetrated during those intermissions, must be left to the reader to conjecture.

The present commodious structure of brick was erected in 1835. The site is still a beautiful one, although the stumps of the trees, which have died, give evidence how much more shady was the grove in former times than now, even with the young evergreens which have sprung up, and which will, in time, supply the places of their deciduous predecessors.

The Rev. John Bryson was the first pastor. In this relation he remained for fifty-two years, embracing eleven of the last, and forty-one of the present century. In the possession of the Rev. J. P. Hudson, of Williamsport, is the original call for the services of Mr. Bryson, with the names of the original signers of Chillisquaque and Warrior Run, making a joint call, and promising as salary, one hundred and fifty pounds, Pennsylvania money, equal to four hundred dollars. With this small salary pledged, it can be realized how the one hundred and nine signers (heads of families, with few exceptions) had so divided their reponsibility that no one would be expected to give more than a few shillings, and would have enough left for daily rations of whisky to the family. For the first missionary describes his host, as "sometime boisterously orthodox, at other times, obviously supine, but always scrupulously sober on the Sabbath." And some of the citizens can yet recollect when at a funeral, the entire company were formed in line, and the bottle of cordial passed, very much as buckets were formerly passed from hand to hand, at a fire; but with this difference, that one was water, and the other as oil, upon the flames. After Mr. Bryson resigned, in 1841, Rev. S. S. Shedden was his successor till 1852, and since his retirement, the church, with but short vacancies, has been faithfully served by Rev. Henry M. Parsons, Rev. Edward D. Yeomans, Rev. Lorenzo Westcott, Rev. S. P. Herron, and by the present pastor, Rev. George Elliott.

The descendants of the Vincents, Kirks, and Durhams, of Fort Freeland renown, are still prominent in the membership of the Warrior Run Church. And, if the members venerate her dust, and attach sacredness, especially to the sleeping-places of her dead, it is because the glory of a former day is like that of the First Temple, which, in the estimation of the "Chief of the Fathers," no second temple could rival or supersede.

The Cemetery, at Warrior's Run, has a beautiful and romantic location, by the brick church, of 1835. It was chartered many years ago, and that fact was one of the moving causes towards the rupture in the church in 1841, which resulted in the establishment of the church at McEwensville, under the pastorate of Rev. J. P. Hudson. After the lapse of a quarter of a century, it is now hard to arrive at *all* the causes which led to those fierce bickerings, and induced the separation; but, it is *sure*, that the incorporation of this old burial-place, was *one* of them. The interments there have not been confined to Presbyterians, and, although this is by no means the oldest, it is, probably, more populous than any other house of the departed, in the upper portion of the County.

Union Baptist Church.—In 1839, there were, in Delaware township (then Turbut), six Baptists, who, though members of White Deer and Clinton Churches, occasionally enjoyed preaching in school-houses and groves in their own neighborhood, by Elder G. M. Spratt, D. D. The first ordinance of baptism was administered in the Susquehanna River, near the present site of the "Jack mill," May 31st, 1840, in presence of a large audience. The second baptism was in Delaware Run, September 1st, 1841.

By urgent request, a council was called, which met the same year at Watsontown school-house, and organized the "Union Baptist Church," consisting of twenty-one members (11 male and 10 female). Upon that occasion the sermon was preached by Elder D. C. Wait. Elder W. S. Hall was elected pastor of the new church, and Amos S. Anderson and Robert Everitt, deacons.

After having worshipped so long in school-houses and groves, they met upon one occasion, in the Fall of 1844, at Scott's school-house, but found the door locked against them. One of the brethren proposed forcing an entrance with a fence rail for a battering-ram, but Elder Hall forbade it, and preached from his seat in the saddle, a very telling sermon from the appropriate words—"*And the door was shut.*" This incident roused a determination to build for themselves a meeting-house; and on March 15th, 1845, Joseph Everitt and John Oyster were made a committee to purchase a lot upon which to rear it. The lot was purchased, on Delaware Run, and a brick house built thereon, which was dedicated, free of debt, June 5th, 1847. The sermon on that occasion was preached by Elder Joe Lee Bradley, of Lewisburg, now of Danville. Elder Hall's pastorate continued a year and a half, and after him came Elder Joseph R. Morris. On June 5th, 1843, Elder John Edminster became pastor, and remained till February 14th, 1848. Elder W. T. Bunker was their pastor from July 29th, 1849, till Christmas in 1853. After him, the pulpit was supplied by Elders Henry Essick, D. W. Walker, Dr. A. K. Bell, and George Frear, until February 1st, 1857, when Elder Joshua Kelley took charge and remained nearly two years. Then, for three years, Elders W. C. Moore and S. W. Zeigler preached regularly as supplies. August 17th, 1860, Elder J. G. Miles assumed the charge and preached till October 1st, 1863. Then, for three years, preaching was had by supplies, the last of whom was Elder S. K. Boyer, who left June, 1866. This was the last of the Union Baptist Church, for in that year (1866), the name was changed to "Watsontown Baptist Church," but the meetings continued to be held in the house at Delaware Run until 1871, when the new meeting-house in Watsontown was dedicated and occupied regularly.

Dewart M. E. Church.—The Dewart appointment was organized some years previous to that at Watsontown, and it has been connected with the same circuits. At present it belongs to the Watsontown Station, the members, for the most part, attending preaching at Watsontown. The old church building, which stood farther up in the township, has been taken down, and is in process of re-erection at Dewart. This, when completed, will be their place of worship.

St. John's Delaware Run Church, (Lutheran.)—Prior to 1818, the members of the Evangelical Lutheran congregation, residing in the north-western part of Delaware township, had held their meetings at the house of John Loss, under the charge of Rev. Jacob Repass; but in that year they united with the Reformed members, in the erection of a log church, near Delaware Run, and about two miles north of Dewart. This church was called "St. John's Union," or more generally the "River Church." Rev. Jacob Repass remained pastor until 1825, when he resigned, and was succeeded by Rev. Jared Sheets, who resigned in 1836. Rev. C. F. Stoever ministered to them from 1837 till 1845, and was succeeded by Rev. S. M. Boyer, in 1846. In 1859, Mr. Boyer resigned, and was succeeded by Rev. Jacob Albert, who remained in their service until 1865. The congregation was then without a pastor for more than two years, during which time the joint congregations demolished the old log building, and built, on nearly the same ground, a plain brick church, forty by fifty-five feet, and named it the "St. John's Delaware Run Union Church." On the completion of this, the Rev. Mr. Billheimer took the pastorate, and soon effected a connection of this with the Lutheran congregation in Watsontown, the two constituting a pastoral charge. They were served successively by Revs. J. B. Keller, P. S. Mack, and S. P. Orwig, the last named assuming charge in 1873, and being the present pastor. The number of communicants is now one hundred and twenty-five. They have a Union Sabbath-school of one hundred and forty scholars. This school is as old as the congregation, and, prior to the erection of the log church, it was taught in the school-house at Delaware Run.

SHAMOKIN TOWNSHIP.

This township was erected from Catawissa, at the August session of the court for Northumberland, 1788. The baptismal name of, Ralpho, was given to the territory, for what reason doth not clearly appear. The year following, the name was changed to Shamokin, by Act of Assembly. The name *Shamokin*, signifying eel creek, or pond, appeared to possess a peculiar charm for the whites, as well as the Indians, have given it to every natural, or unnatural division entitled to a name. (See annals of Shamokin City.)

The township is described, as follows, viz: "Beginning at the mouth of Roaring Creek; thence up said creek to the head thereof; thence on the Ridge to the south branch of Roaring Creek; from thence up said creek to Yarnall's path; thence a south-easterly course to the county line, which said line of division the court confirmed, and the court erect the upper division thereof into a township, separate and apart from Catawissa township, and order from henceforth that the said newly erected township shall be called and known as Ralpho." Nearly ninety years have passed, since the name Ralpho was applied to the large extent of territory, the boundaries of which are delineated above bringing with it innumerable changes to men and things, but, to few more than the confines of this, one of the largest sub-divisions of Northumberland County.

In 1813, a modicum of the territory was cut off, and christened Little Mahanoy. In 1819, Rush township was organized from Shamokin; in 1837, Coal; 1851, Cameron; 1853, Zerbe; and in 1854, Mt. Carmel, leaving the limits as shown on the maps to-day. A complete list of the resident tax-payers of Ralpho, or Shamokin township for 1788, will be found appended. By this can be determined the number of settlers at that day. The earliest settlements appear to have been made in the vicinity of what is now known by the euphonious name of *Snufftown*, on the main path or road leading from Fort Augusta to the coal fields and east. This town has but little aside from the antiquity of its origin, which is sufficiently apparent from the character of its improvements to recommend it to public notice. Not far from here, about equidistant from Snydertown, stands the beautiful edifice, erected in 1873, by the Baptists of Shamokin township, on the ground where, eighty years before, their ancestors chanted their anthems, and songs of praise, as they dedicated the first temple of worship in the wilds of Shamokin township.

This house stands in a secluded spot, with surroundings unadorned save as fashioned by the Divine architect, but in itself a fitting monument to the devoted spirit of a people who make the ground work of their religion, the declaration, "The obligation to glorify God, rests upon all created intelligence, because *it is right in itself.*"

A family by the name of Lewis, consisting of the old gentleman, wife, three sons, and two daughters, located on the creek, about two miles from Snydertown, before the war, on what is now known as the Saxton farm. The family were industrious, and soon established themselves a home, in which they hoped to pass their lives in the enjoyment of peace and plenty; but alas for the frailty of human expectations. The wily savage was lurking about, ready to change the scene to one of bloodshed and desolation. The home was attacked; the old gentleman and his wife killed and scalped; two sons were captured; the third escaped to Sunbury. The two captives were held by these captors until the restoration of peace, when they returned to their desolated home. One of the brothers shot an Indian, prompted by a thirst for revenge. He was arrested, and tried at Sunbury, for murder, but acquitted. On receiving his discharge, he exclaimed to the judge: "For God's sake keep Indians away from me, as I will kill all I see, out of revenge for the death of my father and mother."

John Reeder came into this locality some time before the Revolutionary war, and lived near the present town of Elysburg. He was driven out by the Indians, at the time of the general exodus, and remained away about seven years, after which he returned to Lycoming County, and lived for a time on Loyal Sock Creek. Afterwards, he lived near Shamokin, and at the Bear Gap, where Joseph Reeder was born; Joseph is still residing in Elysburg, at the ripe age of seventy-eight. Miss Kisiah Wilkinson, accompanied young Reeder on his retreat, and, returning with him, married a Mr. Wolverton, afterwards, Leonard Rothamel. She died about twenty years ago, at the age of, probably, ninety years.

Jacob and Casper Reed, were the first settlers, in the vicinity of what is now known as Reed's Station. They were here as early as 1774, and, like all others who thus early penetrated the interior, suffered from the depredations of the Indians. Reed's Station takes its name from this old family, and now is surrounded with finely-cultivated farms, which evidence thrift and abundance.

INDUSTRIES OF SHAMOKIN.

As early as 1774, a Mr. Hughes owned and operated, a grist and saw-mill, on Shamokin Creek, where now stands the extensive property of Mr. Shipman. At the time Mr. Hughes established himself here, the entire surrounding country was a wilderness, with here and there a squatter, who held their lives in their hands, being liable, at any hour, to hear their death-knell from the throat of some monster. With such surroundings, and such dismal prospects for paying custom, Mr. Hughes' judgment might well be questioned, for making, apparently, so rash an adventure. But time demonstrated the correctness of his reasoning. A few years elapsed, ere he erected a large stone-house, near his mill, which stands to-day, although one hundred years have left their impress; it is in good state of preservation, and habitable. A few years ago, Mr. Shipman purchased the property, and has improved until he has a perfect paradise in the wilderness. A large, fine brick-dwelling occupies the fore-ground, flanked by the wagon-barn, itself a beautiful building, the mill, back on the banks of the creek. Mr. Shipman has about perfected his mill, in which he takes commendable pride, and now grinds one hundred and twenty-five bushels of wheat per day, into the finest flour. His place is about two miles from the old red mill, which was an old-time industry.

A mill was erected about one mile from the present site of Paxinos, probably about 1780, where the old red mill now stands. Here, often, people came from a great distance, to get their grain converted into flour and meal.

The first settlement in this vicinity was made by Isaac and William Fichworth, probably soon after the Revolutionary War, certainly prior to 1790. A hotel was built at what is now Paxinos, at least ninety years ago by the brothers Fichworth, and the locality was called Fichworth for many years. The name was subsequently changed to Shamokin and finally to Paxinos. The name Paxinos, was given by Mr. Woods, Superintendent of the construction of the railroad at the time of the completion of same to the place, in honor of the celebrated Indian king or chief of the *Shawanese* tribe who at one time occupied this valley. Irish Valley was first settled by Samuel Lober, about 1795. Mr. Lober left a family of six children, three of whom are still living. The valley owes its name to a tragical event that occurred here many years ago, when an Irishman lost his life in the creek, which is now called Irish Creek. The old mill referred to, was originally built by Bernard Eyregood, and by him sold to Samuel Lober. After Mr. Lober's death the building was rebuilt by his heirs, and in 1831, sold to John Fisher. In 1873, John W. Reed purchased the property, by whom it is still owned, having been thoroughly renovated by him, it is now one of the best mills in the County. Mathias Persing came into Shamokin township, in 1795, and settled near Fichworth. His son, William Persing, is still living, and although at the advanced age of eighty-four years, he is as active as a man of thirty; in possession of his faculties. Jacob Leisering, a venerable patriarch of four score and four years, and to whom the writer is indebted for much of the information as to the early history of Shamokin township, is still living at "Bear Gap," vigorous and remarkably active, with a good memory. He is just the character that the searcher after historical information loves to meet. The old gentleman is keeping a temperance hotel at Bear Gap. This is a small place of a few families, having one flouring-mill, one saw-mill, one blacksmith shop and one store. Near the place is a noted cave, in which bears formerly hibernated. The town is located in a gap of the hills on the main traveled road; hence the name "Bear Gap."

The first school, when the English language was taught at Reed's station and probably in Shamokin township, was taught in the old log school-house, built at the site now occupied by the German Reformed Church. The school was presided over by Charles Stock.

William H. Muench, located at the place, in 1819, and took charge of the school, teaching both the German and English languages. He remained as teacher of the same school, for twenty-four years, to him came the young for many miles around. Some from the weigh scales, within two miles of where Shamokin is situated, a distance of five miles to the old school-house, to be instructed, walking back and forth each day. The little brick is now occupied by the free schools.

The German Reform Society, have erected at the same place, a handsome edifice, which is regularly occupied. To say that the architecture of the church is beautiful, hardly expresses the sensations when first viewing this temple, built in the woods, no dwellings near, the songs of the worshippers blends harmoniously with the music from the feathered songsters, in the forest surrounding. The following facts relative to this church have been obtained from Mr. Henry Muench, the venerable teacher to whom reference is elsewhere made. "The German Reformed Church was founded about 1812, by Mathias Kershner, Andrew and Jacob Fry, Abraham Arter, Solomon Kirk, Andrew and John Smith. The corner-stone of "Jacob's Church" as it was named, was laid on the 28th of August, 1814. Dedicated August 14th, 1816. The building was of brick, two stories high, gallery on three sides, and cost three thousand dollars. The size was thirty-six by fifty feet. In 1870, the house was re-built and enlarged, size being increased to forty by seventy feet, with basement for a Union Sabbath-school. The exterior of the building indicates great taste and liberality, on the part of the society. The total cost was seven thousand dollars. The officiating parties of the German Reformed Church since its organization, have been, Rev. Mr. Ingold, Mr. Adams, Martin Bruner, B. H. Knoeble, Richard A. Fisher, Henry Hoffman, Charles Rittenhouse, Mr. Hibshman, Leah D. McKelly and the present pastor, Rev. Mr. Reiter.

IRISH VALLEY

Is thickly populated with an industrious, thrifty class of people. Many of the original settler's descendants, Mr. Lober, are scattered along the stream that meanders among the hills. Near the south-west portion of the township, the Methodists have a fine chapel; a little further up, the Baptist Society have a church; still further, near the confluence with Shamokin Creek, the United Brethren have erected a creditable edifice for worship. Several school-houses, saw-mills, blacksmith and shoe shops, are located at convenient distances, all of which indicate public spirit, wealth, and intelligence among the people, and a desire to educate the moral man, as well as the physical and intellectual. The thrift observed in Irish Valley extends all over Shamokin township, as nowhere, outside of Lancaster County, probably, can be found such evidences of prosperity among farmers, as is observable among the farmers of Northumberland County, and particularly Shamokin township.

This township has been greatly reduced in size since its organization. Its present boundaries are as follows: On the north by Rush township and Columbia County; on the east by Columbia County, bordered by Roaring Creek; on the south by Coal and Zerbe townships; on the west by Upper and Lower Augusta townships. The surface is varied, and somewhat peculiarly formed. It is traversed in all directions by hills, which form many pleasant and fertile valleys. Irish Valley, on the south, is little more than a narrow defile, closed in by mountains. The township is well watered by Shamokin Creek, and its tributaries, which enter the township near the center of the southern line, runs almost directly north, to the northern boundary, and skirting the base of the hills, that border closely upon its margins, makes a nearly right angle, turning west, and flows into the river near Sunbury. Population, 1870, two thousand two hundred and eighty-two.

FREDERICK WILLIAM KAUMAN.

One of the most remarkable citizens of Shamokin township, and long known as the *oldest inhabitant*, was the above person. According to the record in the old family Bible, in his possession, he was born in Nasa, Germany, on the 8th of June, 1760. His death occurred on August 1st, 1867, in his one hundred and eighth year.

When he emigrated to this country, in 1772, he was sold for his passage to a George Sell, near Kutztown, Berks County, for seven years, for the debt of twelve pounds. At his death he held this agreement, which says—"the said George Sell was bound to give him his board, lodging, and apparel, and have him taught to read and write, and at the end of the term to give him two suits of clothes, one of which must be new, besides twelve pounds in money." Soon after the expiration of his indenture, he came to Shamokin township, and settled there. He was an excellent farmer, and his method of culture was looked upon as authority. He was eccentric in his habits, and by some was looked upon with superstition. The tradition is current among his neighbors to this day, that large sums of gold are buried near his late residence. During his life, he had some ten or twelve clocks in his home, all keeping the correct time, and he frequently told persons that after his death, when his personal effects should be sold, he would peep in at a certain window, and watch the transactions.

A few years before his death, he cradled, bound and shocked fourteen dozen of rye, in one day, without hat or shoes. Only one year before his death, he cultivated and dug his potato crop. He was the last link that connected the past with the present. His funeral sermon was preached from the following text, selected by himself: "Is not my help in me? and is wisdom quite driven from me?"—Job, 6:13. His descendants are quite numerous.

QUAKERS.

The only organized meeting of the Society of Friends, in Northumberland County, is in Shamokin township. The meeting was organized about 1844. They hold their meetings in a plain frame building, pleasantly situated on a public road, two miles north of Bear Gap. The congregation is small.

RESIDENCE OF DR. D.S. HOLLENBACH, COR. OF EIGHTH & ARCH STS, SHAMOKIN, NORTHD CO, PA.

RES. OF G.W. RAVER, COR. SHAMOKIN & SPURZHEIM STS SHAMOKIN, NORTHD CO., PA.

TAX-PAYERS OF RALPHO OR SHAMOKIN TOWNSHIP, NORTHUMBERLAND COUNTY, AS REPORTED BY JOHN WILTZER AND DANIEL MEAD, ASSESSORS, 1787:

Black, James
Buyers, John
Bell, Alexander
Baltz, Paul
Boyle, William
Baker, Aaron
Bower, Philip
Bartshar, H.
Burk, James
Black John
Cline, John
Clindinen, John
Culdrum, Robert
Conrad, J.
Clark, Uriah
Coldman Peter
Caufield, N.
Cameron, D.
Crooks, H.
Douty, H.
Dewart, W.
Doane, John
Delong, J.
Erter, J.
Ergood, Bernard
Epley, Martin
Eichinder, L.
Gettis, C.
Gray, W.
Goodhart, H.
Goss, J.
Gorman, R.
Geiger, M.
Groove, A.
Grant, Alexander
Gibson, Reuben
Green, Nilly
Gerlin, Peter
Goss, Martin
Goben, Charles
Gough, Widow
Gray, Jos.
Goodhart, W.
Gilger, Adam
Gilberson, Lewis
Goss, Ludarek
Gottig, C.
Grant, Thomas
Heyerlind, J.
Halloway, J.
Harris, Samuel
Hoglin, W.
Hawley, Daniel
Hites, Silas
Harrison, G.
Hall, George
Hunter, Widow
Harrison, John
Haas, Widow
Hurst, Stephen
Jones, Samuel
Keyser, G.
Kleiber, George
Keel, H.
Kuntz, D.
Kindis, M.
Kern, L.
Lions, J.
Laurence, J.
Lebo, Henry
Lonihon, C.
Loy, Adams
Lewis, Reuben
Ludwick, J.
Loop, Christian
Laycock, W.
Lang, Michael
Maclay, William
McKinney, Alex.
McKinney, Widow
Mantz, Nich
Miller, Adam
Murdock, William
McAdams, William
Mead, David
Mead, John
Melig, John
Melig, David
McBride, Robert
Martz, Jacob
Martz, David
McLaughlin, Samuel
Martz, Conrad
Moody, Samuel
McMahon, G.
McClout, August
Pontius, Mark
Patterson, Benjamin
Pearson, George
Hentzel, Conrad
Rickin, John
Rousher, N.
Rubental, Jacob
Renn, Adam
Reely, Widow
Robins, Z.
Riehm, N.
Rouneefer, Andrew
Renn, Bernard
Stoner, A.
Shreiner, N.
Schenk, S.
Schisler, C.
Simpson, John
Smith, Peter
Sharp, D.
Shenfield, N.
Sed, Abraham
Silverwood, James
Snyder, C.
Swarm, George
Tanner, George
Thompson, J.
Vanderslice, H.
Withington, N.
Welker, M.
Welsh, Jr., Jacob
Welsh, Sr., Jacob
Wietsel, M.
Wietsel, John
Wallis, Joseph
Yoner, Jacob
Yougham, Jones
Young, John
Zimmerman, George

POINT TOWNSHIP.

On petition of sundry inhabitants of the County, the court at the February term of 1786, divided Mahoning township, and named that portion lying between the two forks of the Susquehanna, "Point." The name is probably owing to its peculiar shape. It is described as follows: Beginning at the nine-mile track on the north branch, and extending westerly along Montour's Ridge to the fording at William Crook's mill, on the Chillisquaque Creek. The township is nearly surrounded by the north and west branches of the Susquehanna, and contains within its borders a great deal of fine bottom land. Montour Mountains extend along the northern boundary, dividing it from Chillisquaque township. Much of the surface is hilly, and poorly adapted to agriculture, and nowhere, except along the banks of the rivers, can the soil be cultivated with profit. The first officers were as follows: Joseph Corbett, constable; L. McCartney and Bernard Hubley, overseers of the poor; James Hepburn and James Jenkins, supervisors; Daniel Ruse and Daniel Kelly, viewers of fences.

EARLY SETTLERS OF POINT TOWNSHIP.

About 1756, Thomas Lemon settled on the old path between the forks of the river and Danville, at what was known as the Old-stone Halfway House. He kept tavern here many years, and reared a large family, whose experience in the harsh school of the pioneers developed powers, that eminently fitted them for the important role they were called upon to act after arriving at maturity. While living here in about 1760 or 1761, the *Delaware* Indians made a descent upon the settlement. James Lemon, a lad of fourteen years, was absent from the house when he discovered the Indians. He crept unobserved underneath a bridge, near his home, and remained until the departure of the Indians. It is easy to appreciate the young lad's sensations, while hiding from his would-be murderers. The house was too strong for the savages, and they retired without making any attack.

After the death of his father, James occupied the old homestead, where he raised several children, two of whom are yet living. James died the same year.

Of James Lemon's family, four boys died at the old homestead. Percival moved to Wyoming County, and for many years was Judge of the Court. He died about 1866. Of the two living, Martha married, in 1812, William Cook, son of the first Sheriff of Northumberland County. After his death, in 1825, she married General Jesse Horton, and now survives him, having attained the venerable age of eighty-two. General Horton died February 21st, 1873. Mrs. Horton still occupies the farm originally settled by her grandfather. To her and her son-in-law, we are indebted for the history of the Lemon family.

Mrs. Rebecca McWilliam, the other surviving child of James Lemon is now living in Montour County. Of the grandchildren of James Lemon, several are living in Northumberland County. Mrs. Simpson, wife of A. C. Simpson, Esq., of the town of Northumberland, and daughter of Martha Horton *nee* Lemon, and Miss Carrie Horton, still residing with her aged mother, near the same place, are the only ones in the immediate vicinity of the old home, which is still owned and occupied by members of the Lemon family.

The provinces of this and other townships of Northumberland County, north of the river, were composed of the hardy race, who have accomplished so much for the development of Pennsylvania, that emigrated from the north of Ireland, and were known as Scotch-Irish. These people were infused with characteristics that eminently fitted them for the lives of frontiersmen. Courageous, honest, unused to toil and hardships, they could cope successfully with difficulties that would retard the progress of any other people. It was this people that opened the pathway to the wilds of the Susquehanna, forced back the Indians, and made the settlement of these valleys possible. Very soon after the purchase of 1768, they began to flock in, and, as will be discovered by an examination of the first assessor's returns, occupied nearly all the territory in what is now known as Point township. After them came the Germans, who purchased the little improvements, and developed the agricultural resources of the country; hence a strong sprinkling of German names is now found on the tax-book of the County. The names of a few of the early settlers have been obtained, and such facts as to their settlement, as obtainable; will be embraced in this work.

James Hepburn and John Cowdon came from the north of Ireland probably some time before 1780. They settled in the vicinity of Northumberland, and became closely identified with the interests of the new county. Many of the prominent citizens of the county claim direct descent from these men.

Captains John Boyd and John Bull, officers of the Revolutionary war, came to the County soon after the war, and for many years lived in and near the forks of the river. They both are buried in the cemetery at Northumberland.

James Wallis, a somewhat noted character, was also an early pioneer, from Berks County. He died here at the age of one hundred and two years. His son, Joseph, died in 1866, at the age of eighty-four, and his grandson, James, is still living at the age of seventy.

John and Henry Shriner were also early settlers.

John Nixon, a grandson of the able financier and patriot, Robert Morris, settled on the north branch, five miles above Northumberland. He possessed many of those characteristics that marked his grandfather a man of distinction. His descendants are among the most respected in the township.

John McCalla, the father of a large family of daughters, was an inhabitant of the County some time before the close of the last century. His character, but not his name, is perpetuated in the lives of many of his family.

Thomas Taggart, of Scotch descent, was born in Ireland, in 1728. He came to Northumberland County, in 1772, bringing with him a numerous family, and much energy and great powers of endurance. His was a remarkable family, and while none have attained to any very great degree of eminence, many have evidenced ability far superior to that of some occupying high positions. William, a son, was born in August, 1773, about the first male child born in the County. During the war of 1812, he held the commission of major. He died at the age of eighty-four, and his descendants are found in nearly every part of the Union. Thomas, born 1762, was killed by the Indians, in 1780. David, the father of the venerable, John

Taggart, still living at the age of eighty-one, was born February, 1769. He succeeded Simon Snyder, as treasurer of the County, in 1809, which office he held for three years. At the time of the election of Mr. Snyder to the Gubernatorial chair, Mr. Taggart, accompanied him to Harrisburg. The journey had to be made on horseback, through woods, across streams, in one of which the distinguished party were involuntarily baptised. John Taggart, son of David, for many years, held the position of State Commissioner of Canals, which he resigned in 1838, and was succeeded by the great commoner, Thaddeus Stevens. Of John Taggart's family, there have been three sons, and one daughter. David has served in the counsels of the State, having been elected to the Senate, at the age of thirty-two. He was for one or more terms, speaker of the Senate. He joined the army in 1861, and served until 1873, and has now retired to private life, and having surrounded himself with an extensive and careful selected library, and innumerable pets, in the shape of fancy fowls of all descriptions, he is prepared to travel the downward road of life with the greatest possible amount of enjoyment. Colonel David Taggart, is one well fitted to direct and lead, in far more important positions than any he has yet held, and it is to be regretted that he is so well satisfied with his life, as to deprive his country of the services of a writer of his ability. Elsewhere, will be found a eulogy on the character of Lincoln, delivered by him, which has scarcely been surpassed, for simplicity of style, forcibleness of language, and true eloquence, by any writer, or speaker. James Taggart was killed at the battle of Glendale, before Richmond, June 30th, 1862. M. H. Taggart, now holds an important trust in the office of the Treasurer of the State. Mary, the only daughter of John Taggart, is married to Dr. Joseph Priestley, while her cousin and granddaughter of David Taggart, is married to M. B. Priestley, the only two living male descendants of the celebrated Joseph Priestley, whose biography will be found elsewhere.

As before stated, the Germans succeeded the Scotch-Irish in the settlement of the township, opening up every available spot, and establishing mills, etc. About 1790, a few English people, driven from their homes by the persecutions of their government, were attracted hither by the fertility of the soil, and desirable location, which formed the nucleus for the settlement of a highly intellectual and cultivated colony. Foremost among these men, the sons of Dr. Joseph Priestley, who purchased large tracts of land, with a view to encouraging others, like situated with themselves. Among others, came John Binns, who was charged, in England, with high treason, and saved his neck by making a hurried exit from the land of his nativity. Binns may have conducted himself in such a manner as to arouse the indignation of the British lion, but, personally, his character was above reproach. He left England much involved, settled in Point township, established a distillery which proved remunerative, and he liquidated every dollar of his indebtedness. Such an example of moral honesty is worthy of all commendation. Mr. Binns became a leading politician of the Democratic school, finally removed to Philadelphia, became an alderman, and died full of years, about 1860.

Robert J. Walker, whose fine physiognomy adorns the twenty-five cent fractional currency, and was Secretary of the Treasury during Buchanan's administration, spent his early youth and manhood in Point township; his father lies buried in the cemetery, at Northumberland.

Simon Cameron, the shrewdest politician of the age, was a poor boy in this County, many years ago. It was in Northumberland he received his first lessons in the "art preservative," and under the tutelage of the learned A. C. Huston, that he was inducted into the mysteries of type-setting.

Robert C. Grier, who retired from the bench of the Supreme Court of the United States, in 1874, on account of old age, was another of the residents of Point township, in his early days. He succeeded to the principalship of Northumberland High School, on the retirement of his father, the Rev. Isaac Grier.

Matthew Huston was a prominent citizen of the township. His settlement dates at an early period. He was, for two terms, a member of the legislature and clerk of the senate, while Lancaster was the capital of the State. Mr. Huston has been intimately associated with the development of the varied interests of the County, and his memory will be ever revered as having been a useful citizen. As would be expected, in a community where are nourished such talents, where the associations and surroundings are such as to develop all that make men true and great, due attention is given to schools and churches. Probably, nowhere in central Pennsylvania do these institutions receive greater encouragement, than in the little nook denominated Point township.

CHILLISQUAQUE TOWNSHIP.

This was erected from Turbut and Mahoning townships, in May, 1786, and described and bounded as follows: "Beginning at the corner of Point township, on the top of Montour's Hill, nearly opposite to the nine mile tree, and extending from thence to Joseph Wilson's, on the north side of Chillisquaque Creek; from thence to the top of Limestone Ridge, to the house occupied by Neal Davis, on Colonel Francis' land; from thence, a straight course to the west branch of Susquehanna."

The first constable was John Cheney. Overseers of the Poor—John Murray and John Gillespy. Supervisors—Thomas Strawbridge and James Stedman.

THE FOLLOWING IS A LIST OF THE ORIGINAL TAX-PAYERS OF THE TOWNSHIP—WILLIAM GRAY AND P. HERTERMAN, ASSESSORS:

Alexander, John	Fisher, William	Murray, John
Allen, William	Francis, Turbit	McMehin, James
Bates, Daniel	Finney, Robert	McWilliams, Robert
Blare, Jr., John	Gillespy, John	McBride, Hugh
Blare, Sr., John	Gillespy, Widow	Miller, Alex.
Biggart, Jos.	Gaddis, P.	Murray, James
Cheney, Johnston	Galloway, John	Oliver, Stephen
Clark, Abram	Gray, John	Oakes, Samuel
Clark, John	Hunter, John	Palmer, Thomas
Carscadon, Sr., James	Horn, Stephen	Rodgers, Thomas
Carscadon, Jr., James	Hempleman, A.	Rees, Martin
Carscadon, William	Hewitt, Thomas	Robinson, James
Caughran, Charles	Hustus, F.	Reed, William
Caughran, James	Harrimer, Thomas	Randles, David
Caughran, John	Harper, Samuel	Randles, James
Chuny, John	Irwin, George	Randles, Robert
Campbell, William	Irwin, Samuel	Sweeny, Archie
Cuny, John	Kelly, Laurence	Suly, John
Dunlap, James	McMullar, Neal	Scott, David
Donaldson, John	McLay, Charles	Stedman, David
Davidson, James	Milligan, W.	Shaw, John
Davidson, Thomas	Mchue, Richard	Stedman, James
Donaldson, James	Murray, William	Shaddon, James
Davis, Andrew	McKitch, Patrick	Strawbridge, Thos.
Elliot, Benjamin	Martin, John	Shipman, James
Funston, John	Morison, Job	Teeple, George
Funston, James	McMehin, John	

Chillisquaque is sufficiently timbered, well-watered and generally healthy. The surface is rolling, and in many parts may be called rough. Agriculturally, it is much inferior to the other portions of the original township of Turbut. But what it lacks in this particular, may be overbalanced four-fold, by the wealth hidden beneath the surface.

Iron ore is there in profusion, the stratum and the quality being identical with that which is found at Bloomsburg, at Danville, and at Turtle Creek, in Union County. This result is obtained from tests of the ore-beds upon lands of Hezekiah Parks, two miles from Montandon, and at other points.

Lime of the very best quality may be manufactured in most parts of the township. There are, within a mile of Montandon, ten kilns in continual blast, and have a constant demand for their product, for shipment to distant points.

All along the western part of the township, from the northern bound to Chillisquaque Creek, the soil is sand, which the farmer, from his point of view, despises. This layer of sand is twenty feet thick, and so clear, that it requires no screening for masonry or plaster. It is shipped by railroad and canal to Danville, Mifflinburg, and other places, and so favorably is it known there, that contracts for the erection of buildings and other structures are often so drawn as to oblige the contractors to procure Montandon sand for the work.

Immediately after the grants of land upon the river had been made, in 1769, to Colonel Hunter, Colonel Francis, and other officers, for military services, many speculators, as well as pioneer settlers, appeared in the country about Shamokin, and in Northumberland. From thence, they pushed on, and, of course, soon invaded the territory which is now embraced in this township. The mouth of Chillisquaque Creek was a point which would naturally offer attractions to prospectors, and we find that Richard Malone, had located himself there immediately after 1770. He was a prominent man through the struggle for independence—a member of the Committee of Safety, and a delegate to the Constitutional Convention. Colonel Turbut Francis was also a resident in this part of the township which bore his (Christian) name, and Alexander Miller and John Alexander were there—men of mark, and of some wealth.

Before the township was partitioned from Turbut, Thomas Strawbridge had established a tannery; Archibald Sweeney, Jesse Funston, and William Allen, had each a distillery, and Thomas Palmer a grist and saw-mill (probably the predecessor of the old "Wilson Mill").

During the Indian wars, their irruptions and massacres were chiefly confined to localities further up the river, and Chillisquaque escaped most of these horrors. Fort Rice was located at Chillisquaque Creek, and was the only one, of all the forts above Shamokin, which held out through all the war. Probably the protecting shade of Fort Augusta had much to do with its immunity from Indian attack, and there is also little doubt that the near proximity of that stronghold, caused Rice's defenders to remain, with more confidence than they would have felt, had they occupied the more remote posts.

It was garrisoned by a detachment of Weltner's (Pennsylvania) German Battalion, who can hardly be said to have shown as much eagerness to aid Fort Freeland in its extremity, as did the brave and devoted Hawkins Boon and his gallant men, when they marched to its succor, on that fatal Summer morning, in 1779.

But if the location of these settlements saved them from many of the horrors of that bloody time, still the brave men who lived there, did all their duty in the struggle. John Brady was a settler there, upon the river opposite Lewisburg, and near the present village of Montandon. He lost his life by the savages, near Muncy, and a favorite son was killed and scalped by them above the Loyalsock; while another son, the redoubtable Captain Samuel Brady, made his name a terror to red-skins of every degree, from Shamokin to the Ohio River; slaying them early and late, not from love of slaughter, nor yet even for revenge, (though he had reason enough for it,) but as a matter of conscientious duty, to save those of his own race—innocent women and children—from the scalping-knife and the torture.

The war of 1812 was, of course, unfelt as to any effect produced by it here. A few, fond of adventure, entered the service, but this agricultural community moved on, in its usual pursuits, just as it always has, in times of profound peace.

The mails from Northumberland to Williamsport passed through the township on horseback, from 1804, and the mail stages, after 1809—also a line across, from Lewisburg to Danville and the eastern towns.

Those great public improvements—canal and railroad—both across the entire township (the Philadelphia and Erie road from north to south, and the Philadelphia and Reading from east to west).

Great expectations were indulged in of benefits to accrue from the canal, but it is hard to find where they have ever been realized. After its completion, produce went, and merchandise came by the canal, instead of the river or the land route, as before; but no towns have been built in Chillisquaque, nor any additional business brought here, as the result of its opening.

Still greater hopes were laid on the coming of the locomotive, and they have hardly been better realized in the meagre results at Pottsgrove and Montandon.

The Lewisburg bridge was built about sixty years ago, by a company of Union County stockholders. It was carried away (as were nearly all the bridges on the river) in the great flood of 1865. In due time it was rebuilt, and is now used, both for the public travel and for the passage of trains on the branch railroad, from the Philadelphia and Erie road to Lewisburg. On the completion of the Sunbury and Erie railroad through the township, a station was established opposite the head of this bridge, for the accommodation of travel crossing it, to and from Lewisburg. And the planting of this bridge brought into existence the village and post-office of Montandon, which contains one public house, one general store and one drug-store. It has also one attorney at law, Robert M. Cummings, Esq., and two physicians, Drs. Purdy and James. As late as 1868, there was but a small cluster of houses and a very small store—kept in the railroad company's warehouse; one physician, Dr. Purdy, and no church. There are now two, (Baptist and Methodist,) and a cemetery of about six acres, lying a half-mile east of the village. It is enclosed by an ordinary wooden fence, and has, as yet, but few embellishments; but further improvements are in contemplation, and it will doubtless soon be made a very handsome ground.

Pottsgrove is a small village of something more than a hundred inhabitants, lying in the north-eastern part of the township, and a short distance south of the Philadelphia and Reading Railroad. It has a post-office, tannery, mill, two stores (one belonging to Grangers,) and no church.

Sodom is a very small group of houses, less than a mile east of Montandon, where the road from Milton to Northumberland crosses that leading from Lewisburg to Danville. Once there was a tavern at these cross-roads—a stopping-place for the mail stages of both lines. One of the first proprietors of this inn was Lot Carson, from whom came the name Sodom, the place where Lot lived. Poor Carson came to a sad end, being drowned in a well, into which he had fallen while under the influence of liquor, of which he was much too fond.

Chillisquaque post-office is in the south-eastern part of the township, near where Richard Malone lived a hundred years ago. There is no village there.

MILLS AND INDUSTRIES.

The flour-mill of D. Heiser & Co. is on Chillisquaque Creek, near the Philadelphia and Erie Railroad. It occupies the site of the old "Wilson mill" of sixty years ago, and also probably that of Thomas Palmer's, which was built by him as early as 1778.

Palmer's was a log structure; the Wilson mill was of stone, and its successor, Heiser's present mill, is a frame building. It does good work and prospers.

Steam Flour-mill at Pottsgrove.—This mill was first erected on Limestone Run, in Turbut township, by William Follmer. It was there operated both by water and steam-power. Becoming unprofitable in that location, it was removed, and re-erected at Pottsgrove, about 1872, by William Follmer, Michael Rissel, and James Smith. It is now doing a good business, under the management of Rissel, Smith & Co.

The steam lumber-mill of Chester Butler, is an establishment of moderate capacity, built in 1870. Its location is about one-and-a-half miles south of Montandon, between the canal and the river. A natural basin existed there, which saved a very considerable expense in the formation of the "log pool." In prosperous times! its business is good.

Saw-mill of A. E. Kuff & Co.—This stands on Chillisquaque Creek, near Heiser's flour-mill. It has been long out of operation, and is not in repair.

The Montandon planing-mill, manufactures doors, sashes, shutters, frames, siding, flooring, and all work usual in planing-mills. The location is a short distance from the village, on the road to the river. It was built before the opening of the railroad, by John Dieffenderfer and Driesbach. Afterwards, Joseph Nesbit acquired an interest, and the works and business were extended. The operating firm is now Nesbit, Dieffenderfer & Co.

Public Schools.—There are ten public schools in the township, two of which are graded. There are ten school-houses, of which nine are of brick and one of stone. The term of free tuition extends five months in the year, and short terms, in addition to this, are taught by subscription. The present, (1876,) Board of School Directors, is as follows: President, S. B. Walter; Secretary, William M. Auten; Treasurer, Joseph Negley; John C. McWilliams, William Fetzer, Isaiah C. Rishel.

Baptist Church, Montandon.—The Baptist house of worship, at Montandon, was dedicated in 1860. There is no church organization, but there has been a congregation of fifteen or twenty Baptists in Montandon and vicinity, for more than ten years before the erection of the church building. They met sometimes in the school-house, and when forbidden or locked out from that shelter, they obtained the use of the railroad depot, or met in private houses. Their preaching is, and has always been, supplied by the theological students of Lewisburg. Meetings are held in the school-house at Chillisquaque (P. O.) by the Baptist residents of the vicinity. The services there are conducted by students from Lewisburg, and by itinerant preachers.

Evangelical Church.—About two years ago, the Methodist congregation, wishing to transfer their place of meeting from Sodom—where the church-building was located—to Montandon, decided to sell the old edifice and to build a new, at the latter place. It was purchased for the use of the Evangelical congregation, and was taken down and re-erected at a point in the township, about two miles north from Montandon, and near the house of William Bartholomew. Services are now regularly held there by the pastor of the Evangelical Church of Milton, in whose charge it is.

Montandon Methodist Church.—This church organization was effected in 1834. The first pastor was Rev. Marmaduke Pierce. After him, the pastorate has been successively held by Revs. Henry Taring, George Gyre, John Bowen, John Moorehead, Frank Gerhard, George Warren, Henry Wilson, —— King, —— Haughawout, J. W. Olewine, A. P. Wharton, —— Tunnyhill, and John Vrooman. For twenty-six years after organization, their worship was held in school houses, and in private residences, but in 1860, their first church edifice was completed at the cross roads, known as Sodom. In 1870, wishing to remove to Montandon, they sold the old church to the Evangelical association, for removal and re-erection. It was not, however, till 1874, that they were enabled to complete their new edifice at Montandon. It is a good and commodious house, on the main street. Rev. John Vrooman, is the present pastor, and they have a small Sabbath-school.

Methodist Worship at Pottsgrove.—There is a small Methodist congregation, for whom services are held in the school-house, at Pottsgrove, by the Rev. Mr. Vrooman, of the Montandon circuit.

Near Chillisquaque Creek, and about a mile-and-a-half in a southerly direction from Montandon, is a property which the inhabitants of the township call the "Priest's Farm." It was once owned by Jacob Spring, a bachelor and a Catholic, who, at his death, some years ago, bequeathed it all (the farm, of a hundred acres or more, and a timber tract on Montour's Ridge,) to the Catholic Church, to be held by that organization for its own use and profit forever. The Priest at Milton, by virtue of his office, holds this property in charge for the church. Near this farm is a Catholic cemetery, which was laid out upon the farm of Michael McGee. But there is no church at either of these places.

We have seen how, in little more than ten years after the entrance of its first white settler, Chillisquaque had three distilleries, running in full blast, and this number was largely increased afterwards. About forty years ago, there were, in the township, thirteen taverns, besides smaller places, where whisky was dealt out to those who craved the poison.

To-day, it has not a single distillery, brewery, or tavern, (the Montandon House has no tavern license, and is merely a boarding-house,) nor is there a shop, saloon, or place of any kind, where ardent spirits or beer is sold within its boundaries!

Truly, in respect to sobriety and temperance, Chillisquaque is a banner township; and in this particular, at least, has accomplished a marvellous improvement since the days of poor Lot Carson.

The name *Chillisquaque*, was first given to the creek, and later, to the township. It is said that in the Indian dialect, the word means "frozen duck." It certainly sounds like it. But whether it was really a knowledge of the Indian tongue, or merely imaginative ingenuity, which first led to this interpretation, must remain a doubtful question.

The population of the township in 1860, was one thousand three hundred and forty-one; and in 1870, it was one thousand five hundred and ninety-seven.

RUSH TOWNSHIP

Was erected from Shamokin, at the August session, 1810, and described as follows: "Beginning at a white oak tree, at the head of Little Roaring, in the line of Columbia County, and thence the following courses and distances, viz.: South 78° west, one hundred and twenty perches, to a pine; south 74° west, one hundred and sixty-four perches, to a black oak; south 82° west, one hundred and ten perches; west, one hundred twenty-eight perches, to a chestnut oak; north 80° west, two hundred and twelve perches, to a post on Jacob Reed's field; north 84° west, six hundred and forty perches, to a chestnut oak; south 11° west, eighty perches, to a chestnut oak; south 85° west, sixty-four perches; north 82° west, eighteen perches, west, two hundred and forty perches, to a post; south 84° west, five hundred and seventy-six perches, a little north of Snydertown, and intersecting the Augusta township line on the south side of the ridge."

First Constable, Philip Andras. Overseers of the Poor—John Dewitt, John Hunt. Supervisors—John Kane, Peter Kane.

EARLY SETTLERS.

Jacob Gearhart, an officer of the Revolutionary war, came into what is now known as Rush township soon after the restoration of peace, and first lived in a little log-house on the bank of the river, immediately back of Rosenstein's hotel. His *entree* into this location, was probably about 1784. He found that he was not the first to detect the superior advantages of the location, as a family by the name of Carr had preceded him by several years. John Carr was located on lands where now (1876,) William Faux resides; Jacob, his brother, had located and improved the lands now covered by the beautiful residences that make up Riverside. Jacob Gearhart and his sons soon built them a log structure on the site, where, in about 1796, they erected a portion of the large frame structure, which is still standing in a very conspicuous position, attesting the good judgment of the early builders, in selecting a commanding view for their permanent home. Cotemporary with his settlement, was that of the Montgomery, of Revolutionary fame. General Daniel Montgomery located and improved the present site of Danville, which took its name from the Revolutionary hero. Mr. Gearhart reared at the old homestead, a family of twelve children, all of whom, with a single exception, remain about the old nest, and died almost within sight of the old home within which they had been born. Many branches of the old stock yet live in the vicinity, and have perpetuated, in an eminent degree, the sterling qualities of the venerable patriarch, Jacob.

About two miles below Riverside, near the bank of the river, a Mr. Robinson purchased of the original warrantees, a tract of three hundred and twenty acres of land, which is now occupied by J. C. Richard, Allan Sichler, and the heirs to the Carr estate. The consideration for this tract is thus stated: "Know ye, that we, Samuel Crooks and David Crooks, for and in consideration of one yoke of steers, one cow, one mulatto boy, and three hundred and seventy-five pounds specie, lawful money aforesaid, doth grant, etc., three hundred and twenty acres of land." These lands are of the finest along the river.

Harmon Snyder, who emigrated to this locality about the same time with Gearhart and others, became intimidated when looking over the high pines that grew in the rich alluvial lands along the river, and went back among the hills, where clearing land would not be attended with so much labor, and settled, where since has sprung up the wealthy and thriving agricultural district, now *yclept* Rushtown.

William Kase was one of the early pioneers of this township, and as early as 1784 or '85, settled among the hills, back from the river, and located a large tract of land, which, by hard work, he converted into attractive homes for his numerous descendants, who followed him on the stage of life. His son, William H. Kase, born August 21st, 1806, remained on the old farm, and spent many years in tilling the soil, thus laying the foundation for a life of usefulness. He reared a family of seven sons and two daughters, one of whom, J. Hudson, still resides at the home of his forefathers, a worthy and respected citizen.

William H. Kase became a man of considerable prominence, having been twice elected to the legislature, where he served his people with honesty and ability. He entered freely into the discussion of all questions of government polity, and won the confidence of his friends and constituents by his probity and earnest zeal for the improvement of his County and State. He died August 28th, 1871, at the age of sixty-five years. Modest to a fault, his record was one of which his descendants may well feel a considerable degree of pride.

Michael Weaver emigrated to Berks County from Germany, and about 1770, settled in what is now known as Rush township, on lands since known as belonging to Peter Haughawout's estate. He was driven from his home many times, and took refuge at Fort Augusta, from whence frequent sorties would be made by bands of the refugees, driving the Indians back, and enabling the settlers to gather in their crops. At the breaking out of the war of the Revolution, Mr. Weaver enlisted in the Continental army, and remained in the service seven years, and was mustered out at the close without a mark or scar received from the enemy. Leaving the army, he returned to his early home, about four miles from Riverside, and there lived until 1824, when he slept with his fathers, and was laid beside his wife, on the farm their own hands had redeemed from a state of native wildness. One of his grandsons, W. M. Weaver, was Sheriff of Northumberland County, from 1863 to 1866, and has been long known as proprietor of the National Hotel, at Shamokin.

Among the earlier settlers of this section was Alexander Moore, who, in 1788, moved from New Jersey, and located on Shamokin Hills, about one mile south of present site of the hamlet known as Rushtown. He and his young wife (Mr. Moore was but nineteen, and she some years younger) started out in life with an inheritance of good health, and plenty of energy. They were married at night in their old home in New Jersey, and before twelve hours of their honeymoon had passed, were on their way to the field of their future labors, in the wilds of Shamokin. Their course led them through where Pottsville now stands. In the heart of what is now a flourishing city, Moore killed a wild turkey. In course of time, and after much hardship, all of which was borne with true Spartan heroism by the girlish bride, they pitched their wigwams on Shamokin Hills. Here, for upwards of sixty years, they labored hand-in-hand, and by hard work and economy, surrounded themselves with a competency. They eminently fulfilled the law, which commanded that the population of the earth be multiplied, as they left eleven children, who have done considerable towards developing the country. Mr. Moore for fifty years held the responsible position of justice of the peace, with credit to himself and satisfaction to his neighbors. As an evidence of the prowess of many of the early settlers of this country, Mr. Moore's grandson, now a worthy citizen of Sunbury, relates that his grandfather had been known to lift a barrel of whisky from the ground and drink from the bung. But few of the present

RES. OF STEPHEN BITTENBENDER, ERECTED 1857, SHAMOKIN ST. SHAMOKIN, NORTH^D CO., PA.

RES. OF SAML. JOHN, COR. SHAMOKIN & SPURZEIN STS., SHAMOKIN, NORTH^D CO., PA.

generation, fond as our people are of the ardent, could accomplish such a feat. The labor necessary to clear away the forests and cultivate the soil in those days, developed the muscles essential to strength and endurance. Then want never stared in the face he who had health and strength. The strong arm alone could supply all wants, and in a large majority of instances, pave the way to opulence for those following after.

Kline Grove, a little post-town of Rush township, was first settled by the grandfather of John T. and F. A. Kline, from whom the locality derived its name. Nature reigned supreme when the pioneer first entered these wilds; the wolves, bears and Indians competed with Grandfather Kline for years for possession, but the strong arm of civilization forced submission, and to-day, his descendants are enjoying the fruits of the herculean labors, in the possession of homes that, for beauty and productiveness, are hardly surpassed in the County.

LEWIS TOWNSHIP

Was erected from Turbut, in 1843, by order of the court, at its April session. It is bounded, west by Delaware township; north by the Lycoming line on Muncy Hills; east by Montour County; and south by Turbut township.

Many of the most stirring events of Indian and Revolutionary warfare in Northumberland County, occurred within the present limits of this township, while it was yet a part of old Turbut, in which connection they have been recounted. Within the bounds of Lewis laid the Patterson patent of Paradise—the settlement and "fort" of the Montgomery's, as well as the renowned Fort Freeland, with the mills and farm of old Jacob, who first brought the name of Freeland from Jersey to Northumberland County. His original farm is now divided into three—the Tinbrook, the Driesbach, and the McFarland farms. The Tinbrooks were well known as scythe-makers, at that place, years ago. D. H. Driesbach is now, not only proprietor of one of these sub-divisions, but also of the Eagle Hotel, at Turbutville. John McFarland owns the flour-mills at Watsontown, a hotel, and other real estate at Dewart, as well as a part of the Freeland lands, and the historical mill site. Sixty years ago, all this property was known as the Hower farm and mill; one by that name being proprietor after Freeland, and being also the builder of the stone-basement structure now owned and run by McFarland. On "Let Run," in the northern part of the township, near Lycoming line, is a steam saw-mill of small capacity, carried on by John Harman. These are all the manufacturing establishments of the township.

Kieferstown is no unimportant hamlet, about two miles south-east from Turbutville.

Lewis Centre is a similar cluster of houses, two-and-a-half miles north of the borough. In 1873, a Methodist church (which had been but a short time completed) was destroyed there by fire. No one can be found who has any knowledge whatever of the circumstances of the burning. There is now no church at either of these places.

About 1825, and for some years thereafter, a part of the eastern section of the township, bore an unenviable reputation, as being the haunt of counterfeiters. Their headquarters were supposed to be at Abraham Hawes' tavern, just across the line, in Montour County, but Abraham's private residence was in Northumberland, and there he was finally captured by Sheriff Henry Reader. After serving his term in the State Prison, he returned to his crimes, and incurred another sentence. One Giltner, a confederate of Hawes', and a resident of Turbut, was also convicted, and underwent full punishment within the prison walls. But since the coining fraternity were hunted out, no part of the County has been more law-abiding than this.

The ancient grave-yard near Fort Freeland, is nearly, if not quite, a century old. The first interments there, were doubtless of those killed in the Indian fights and massacres of that bloody neighborhood, and these were added to, for some years after, by natural deaths among the settlers of the vicinity. It is now a long time since any have been buried there.

Schools.—There are nine public schools, and the same number of good brick school-houses in Lewis. The term of free teaching is five months in the year, and about two months' additional tuition is secured by subscription. The teachers' salaries are thirty-five dollars per month. The common English branches are taught, and the schools are good, for the grade.

The Board of School Directors for 1876 is, President, John Klapp; Anthony Gauger, C. L. Hackley, Levi Follmer, Jeremiah Leinbach, Daniel Hoy.

The population of Lewis township, in 1860, was one thousand two hundred and ninety-nine, and in 1870, one thousand two hundred and twenty-eight.

LOWER AUGUSTA TOWNSHIP.

Was formed by a division of Augusta township, which was effected November 4th, 1846.

The territory now embraced within Lower Augusta was of that first settled, and originally a part of old Augusta township, but in 1846 set up an individual organization. It is peopled largely by Germans, who early occupied the territory, and by whose industry and economy fine farms have been opened.

The surface is generally rough and hilly; the soil but moderately productive, except with careful husbandry. It is quite thickly populated, particularly in the vicinity of Seven Points, and along the valleys. Agriculture is the principal industry, as it is in most other localities where the German element predominates. Little Shamokin Creek traverses the township; other streams afford abundance of water for all purposes. The township is bordered on the east by Shamokin; south by Zerbe, Little Mahanoy and Jackson; west by the Susquehanna River; north by Upper Augusta. Population, in 1870, eighteen hundred and two.

William and Nicholas Shipman came into the locality, and settled along Boyles Run, in 1794. They brought families with them, and some of their descendants are still living in the township. They emigrated from New Jersey. Abraham, a grandson of William, is now living near the same place, and at the age of sixty-six, as free from chronic complaints as a boy of ten. Jacob Conrad settled on the Holland Run some time before the Shipmans came to the country. Casper Snyder settled on the same stream, near its mouth; the two last settled before the war. A grandson now lives on the farm improved by Mr. Snyder. The first mill built in the township was built on Holland Run, at a very early day, and is now owned by William W. Dewitt. John Weitzel located on Little Shamokin Creek, and built a mill about 1787, which is now owned and operated by his son, Joseph Weitzel. The early settlers endured many hardships, the extent of which can scarcely be conceived at the present day. The Conrads located under a big white-oak tree, and there remained until they had time to build houses.

CHURCHES.

The German Reformed Society established a church in the township in 1815, which is known as the "Stone Church." The Rev. Peter Shingle was the first Lutheran pastor. He preached altogether in German, and labored hard for his people to retain their native tongue. The German Reformed have three distinct church organizations now in the township.

The Methodist society organized a church many years ago, probably about 1830 or '35. They have now several different societies.

The Presbyterians were among the first to establish a church in the township. The Rev. John Bryson officiated for many years in barns, or wherever he could get an audience. The different societies were weak in those days. The members scattered over large areas of territory, rendering it difficult to concentrate interest in any particular locality, and consequently difficult to erect houses of worship. But the strong, fervent faith of our fathers stopped not at ordinary barriers; their earnest zeal carried them forward in every conscientious duty.

UPPER AUGUSTA TOWNSHIP.

This was a portion of one of the original townships of Northumberland County, and was organized at the first session of court for the County, held at Fort Augusta, April 19th, 1772. It was described as follows: "Beginning at the mouth of Mahantango Creek, on the west side of the Susquehanna river; thence with the County line, crossing the river to the Mahantango's mouth, on the east side; thence with the same County line up said creek to the Spread Eagle, in the forks of said stream; thence with the said County line east north-east, to the old line formerly run for a division between Berks and Northampton Counties; thence by the same old County line, north-west to the east branch of the Susquehanna; thence down the same to Fort Augusta; thence crossing the river and down the same to place of beginning." It will be observed that Augusta, at one time, embraced a large proportion of the County south of the north branch. It has since been sub-divided until reduced to its present size and shape, until from the largest it is now one of the smallest townships in the County. In 1808, for reasons set forth in a petition of the inhabitants of Sunbury, the latter place was organized into a separate township. In 1846, Lower Augusta was formed, which embraced a large extent of territory; subsequent to this date, the section known as Limestone Valley, was again attached to Upper Augusta, thereby increasing its extent and giving it very irregular boundaries. In 1785, Catawisa township was erected from Augusta, which was itself divided in 1788, and Shamokin organized. The first constable of Augusta was Alexander Grant, father of Thomas Grant, for many years a prominent man of the County. The surface is generally hilly and rough, but contains quantities of fine farming lands, particularly along Shamokin Creek, which traverses the township from east to west. The soil is usually good, and affords valuable returns to the industrious farmers who are occupying every available portion of it. It is bounded on the west by the Susquehanna; north by the north branch; east by Rush and Shamokin townships; and south by Lower Augusta.

Samuel Crooks settled near the Gravel Run, on the Susquehanna River. He located about 1772 or '73, and took up large quantities of lands. The farm is known as lying opposite Crooks' Riffles. John Moore settled on Shamokin Creek, near Snydertown, about the same date that Crooks settled at the Riffles. His descendants are still living in the same locality.

The first mill in Upper Augusta was built of logs by William Maclay, about one mile south-east of Sunbury, on Shamokin Creek. In 1833, the old log mill was purchased by McCarty & Davis, torn down, and its place occupied by a fine brick building, which is still standing, owned by John S. Haas, who took possession in the fall of 1830.

Appended will be found a correct list of the tax-payers of Augusta township, showing the personal property owned by each, subject to taxation at that time, 1773. This should be preserved for all time, and such comments as the descendants of these tax-payers may be able to make, as to incidents of early life among their ancestors, would form a basis of a full and reliable local history. It will be observed, that at this early day, one year after the organization of the County, there was considerable wealth among the people, and an accumulation of property of a kind that eminently distinguished the early settlers of Augusta, Shamokin and Mahanoy townships, from the shiftless, roving adventurers that generally succeed the Indians and wild beasts.

TAX-PAYERS OF AUGUSTA TOWNSHIP, 1774.

Boyle, William
Brosius, Bert
Clark, John
Conrad, Jacob
Conn, Robert
Conrad, Adam
Croninger, N.
Cover, Gasper
Clark, Uriah
Covil, Daniel
Crevous, Sebas
Cliver, George
Cliver, Henry
Clarke, William
Dunkleberger, F.
Durhes, Robert
Davis, William
Dunn, John
Eule, George
Eichinger, L.
Ebley, Martin
Everhart, Philip
Ellis, James
Fowler, David
Fisher, John
Forster, William
Ferst, Peter
Forest, Henry
Fricker, A.
Fox, David
Flowers, Samuel
Giger, Val.
Gerhart, P.
Garmont, Charles
Green, Solomon
Gettig, Stoper
Grant, Alex.
Gough, Charles
Hughes, Ellis
Harris, Samuel
Hunter, Samuel
Haines, Max
Haverling, Jacob
Hufty, Charles
Hyman, George
Harrison, John
Hawke, George
Haverling, A.
Hinkle, Anthony

Hughes, Thomas
Krookes, Samuel
Kovile, Henry
Kreil, Henry
Kovile, Peter
Keller, Henry
Ketterby, Andrew
Kowfrild, N.
Logan, James
Lyster, Martin
Leller, Godlip
Lewis, Eleinen
Lips, John
Maclay, William
McCarrall, Joseph
McBride, Robert
Moody, A.
Meades, D.
Martin, Jacob
Moll, John
Miller, John
McGahan, Thomas
McKinley, H.
McCormick, Patrick
McKinney, D.
Miller, Nicholas
Meades, Eli
McNeil, James
McClegg, James
McDonnel, James
Meyrs, Isaac
Moore, John
Murra, C.
McNear, D.
Murrer, John
Overmier, G.
Peiffer, John
Philips, John
Pearson, Samuel
Poor, James
Read, J.
Reely, Fred.
Robinson, Z.
Rowe, C.
Reigert, Henry
Ream, John
Redman, Michael
Randle, Robert
Runyon, Thomas

Ream, John
Rebock, V.
Reitz, Geo.
Ross, Gustave
Robinson, John
Shippen, Joseph
Stough, M.
Starr, James
Simpson, J.
Shakespear, D.
Scull, William
Snavely, Carp
Shakespear, Samuel
Sutton, Stephen
Streinbach, Thomas
Soper, John
Smith, Daniel
Suebler, Gasper
Shellam, George
Sheffer, Michael
Sheffer, John
Shuter, Nicholas
Smith, Peter
Stein, Abraham
Shirts, Jacob
Snider, Conrad
Spoon, John
Stophel, S.
Titsal, ——
Troy, Michael
Vaughn, G
Whitmore, P.
Weber, Samuel
Whitmore, S.
Woolfe, George
Weaver, Jonas
Weaver, M.
Weitzel, John
Weild, James
Wall, John
Wiggins, John
Yarnall, M.
Yarnall, F.
Younkman, Ellis
Youghans, Jonn.
Zartman, Jacob
Zartman, Henry
Zantzinger, N.

MAHANOY TOWNSHIP

Was erected from lower part of Augusta, at the February session of the court, year 1775, and described, as follows: "Beginning within water-mark on the west side of Susquehanna; thence crossing the same by a direct line to the top of Mahanoy Mountain; and along the same to the County line; thence by the County line to the Spread Eagle, to the mouth thereof; thence crossing the Susquehanna, and up the western shore of the same, to the place of beginning."

First Constable, Sebastian Brassius. Overseers of Poor—Samuel Weber and John Fisher. Supervisors—John Shaffer and Peter Almony.

From Mahanoy were formed: Point, 1786; Upper Mahanoy, 1806; Jackson, 1836; Jordan, 1852; Washington, 1856.

The old Mahanoy township here described, has long since ceased to exist as a territorial organization, but the name is perpetuated in those of three different townships of the County, which, with various qualifications, have received the name of Mahanoy.

UPPER MAHANOY TOWNSHIP.

Divided August session, 1806, into Mahanoy and Upper Mahanoy. Constable elected, Upper Mahanoy, John Latchu. Upper Mahanoy township presents about the only geometrical figure not yet described by the boundaries of the townships of Northumberland County. It lies along the border of Schuylkill County, by which it is bounded on the south; by Cameron township on the north; Washington and Jordan on the east. The surface is mountainous and susceptible of supporting but a sparse population. It is traversed in all directions by little streams, which wind among the hills, watering the little valleys, which alone appear sufficiently fertile to attract settlement. Population, eight hundred and seventy-eight.

The territory now forming Lower Mahanoy township was among the first settled outside of the immediate vicinity of Fort Augusta. It is claimed that the first settlement was made in the year 1777, and there appears nothing authentic to establish an earlier date; but there are traditions among the people of difficulties encountered with the Indians before the Revolutionary war, and of the exodus from this section of white settlers to escape the scalping-knife, from which, if true, it would appear that, some years before the date established by history, the adventurer had erected his cabin here. As early as 1778, a Mr. N. Brosius, whose descendants are yet numbered among the prominent of Mahanoy township, built a grist-mill on Stone Valley Creek. This mill has been renovated at divers times, but the foundation is still there, although a hundred years have elapsed since the laying of the corner-stone. This would be proof conclusive of the settlement of this country prior to the date fixed in the chart, as there must be a demand among the populace for public improvements, as no person at that day would venture largely on future prospects. The names of all the original settlers will be found appended hereto, showing the population of Mahanoy township in 1778 to have been considerable, and the improvements of no moderate pretensions for the day.

A preponderance of German names sufficiently indicates the character of the population. The fine farms, handsome residences, and a general appearance of comfort, evidence thrift and abundance seldom found so generally among any race, except the Germans. The similarity of the names of the present with those of one hundred years ago, furnish proof of the non-migratory habits of the people who first settled here. The township is hilly and rough, the surface being similar to that of most parts of Northumberland County, south of the north branch of the Susquehanna. The limestone, which is found underlaying a large proportion of the surface—itself a mine of wealth—and the thrifty habits of the inhabitants, have divested the country of most of its wildness, and now charming homes are found scattered over the entire township. It is bounded on the east by Jackson and Jordan townships; south by Dauphin County; west by the Susquehanna River. Population in 1870, one thousand seven hundred and ninety.

TAX-PAYERS OF MAHANOY TOWNSHIP, NORTHUMBERLAND COUNTY, RETURNED FOR THE YEAR 1778, BY WILLIAM CLARKE AND WILLIAM TURNIN, ASSESSORS:

Albert, Peter
Albert, Jacob
Almony, Peter
Buchart, M.
Brosius, B.
Brosius, N.

Kester, P.
Krigan, J.
Kistater, L.
Kitster, M.
Kull, P.
Kable, Casper

Riter, George
Shever, John
Shockenecut, H.
Smith, Peter
Sterly, B.
Sieslinger, N.

Bamgertner, H.
Bemlor, G.
Berwell, A.
Bridgr, V.
Biddle, E.
Brosius, N.
Calhoun, G.
Denner, G.
Deppy, C.
Foster, William
Foster, George
Foster, Peter
Foster, Jr., George
Fisher, Martin
Fisher, John
Grimiger, N.
Garrison, N.
Horton, John
Hain, M.
Hain, Henry
Herkert, John
Hoope, John
Hetotrick, N.
Hetrick, C.
Heim, Jr., G.
Heim, Sr., G.
Heil, M.
Heberling, J.
Hable, Abraham
Harter, John
Jagley, G.
Knell, J.
Keterly, A.
Kuhle, Henry
Kable, D.
Krails, H.
Kofman, C.
Kuller, H.
Kaimer, James
Kunkle, M.
Leobarte, M.
Lower, C.
Lefler, P.
Latshaw, H.
Lefler, C.
Loury, Henry
Miniam, Mary
Miner, Q.
Meyer, Isaac
McKee, Alexander
Markey, D.
Miller, Mary
Maier, Jacob
Maier, Widow
McKinley, ——
Noran, M
Osarighter, Jacob
Phiffer, J.
Philippe, Jon.
Peter, Richard
Pope, Nicholas
Right, George
Robuck, V.
Railen, H.
Railen M.
Reddy, P.
Stough, J.
Sheckengauft, Y.
Shever, Fritz
Striker, J.
Stinberger, D.
Sweyer, L.
Shultz, L.
Shop, John
Snider, A.
Stump, John
Snider, J.
Sheaver, M.
Sebastian, S.
Stump, Sr., C.
Stump, Jr., C.
Shever, John
Shaver, N.
Trootman, P.
Tupper, W.
Thom, M.
Thompson, W.
Wenser, Samuel
Whitman, P.
White, Joseph
Whitmore, C.
Wolf, John
Witman, J.
Weser, F.
Yoram, J.
Zartman, J.
Zartman, H.
Zartman, M.

LITTLE MAHANOY TOWNSHIP

Was erected from Augusta and Shamokin, at the April session, 1813, and bounded as follows: "Beginning at the top of the Mahanoy Mountain, near the river Susquehanna; thence along the line that was lately run, which divides the Mahanoy townships from Augusta and Shamokin townships, to the County line; thence the best course to the Stony Gap, at Shamokin Creek; thence along the mountain to the place of beginning."

This township was organized in 1813, and has been diminished in size, until but little is left of that which once was Little Mahanoy. What remains presents a very irregular appearance, and is but a little valley hemmed in on all sides by mountains, which form its boundaries. The population is small, being confined to the centre of the township, where considerable arable land is found. It is bordered on the north and west by Lower Augusta township, east by Zerbe and Cameron, south by Washington and Jackson. Population in 1870, two hundred and sixty-nine.

JACKSON TOWNSHIP

Was erected and formed a new township from Upper and Lower Mahanoy, at the January session, 1835, and bounded as follows, viz.: "Beginning at a large stone heap on the summit of the Line Mountain, in the line dividing Upper and Little Mahanoy townships; thence south 7° east, five hundred and sixteen perches, to a small maple on the eastern bank of Middle Creek; thence up the same, making said creek the line, the several courses thereof, five hundred and thirteen perches, to a small apple tree on the southwest bank of the west branch of the said creek; thence south 7° east, eight hundred and forty-five perches, to a white oak on the bank of Mahantango Creek; thence down said creek, the several courses thence, one thousand nine hundred and forty-four perches, to the western abutment of the bridge over said creek, near Snyder's mill; thence north 25° west, five hundred and twenty-four perches, to a double chestnut on the top of Fisher's Ridge; thence north 5° west, five hundred perches to Fidler's Run; thence down the same, making as it run the line, the several courses thereof, five hundred and ninety-two perches, to the eastern bank of the Susquehanna River; thence across said river north 70½° west, three hundred and fifty-one perches, to the opposite thereof, and the Union County line; thence up the same, the several courses thereof, one thousand one hundred and seventeen perches, to the line dividing the townships of Little Mahanoy and Augusta; thence along the same, and the dividing line of Upper and Little Mahanoy townships, one thousand nine hundred and eighty perches, to the place of beginning."

First Constable, M. Drumheller.

This township, with most other townships of the lower part of Northumberland, was originally settled by Germans, who emigrated here from Berks and Montgomery Counties, and at an early day, somewhat anterior to the Revolution, formed the nucleus of what has since become an important settlement. The Germans are, as a people, agriculturists, and here they have given their attention to tilling the soil. Much of the soil is heavy, and as a rule, non-productive, except Stone Valley, which extends back from the river twelve miles. The land here in this valley is reasonably productive, and is all underlaid with lime. Much attention is given here to burning lime, and in this valley it is estimated that upwards of one thousand lime-kilns are in operation, in a distance of ten or twelve miles.

The industries of the township were but few, besides farming and lime-burning, and for many years there was but one mill in all Jackson township. The mill owned by Weiser is on the site of the first mill built in the township. There are now three mills in Jackson; one owned by Keitz, in operation about fifteen years; Weiser's, and the third owned by David Boner, which has been in operation not less than seventy-five years.

But little attention was given to schools in Jackson, for many years after its first settlement. Occasionally, a term of one to three months would be held, where the German language was taught; but not until 1866, at which time free schools were started, did the people become very much interested in this all important work. Now schools are held in five different houses in the township, for from seven to nine months a year. If our German fellow-citizens were indifferent about schools, they did not neglect the much more important work of educating their moral natures. Near the east end of the township, the German Reformed and Lutheran people erected a log house, which was used for a great many years, and in about 1846 was torn down, and replaced by a fine brick edifice. An Evangelical Church has also been built in the township for the accommodation of people of the peculiar Evangelical creed.

These churches are well sustained, and regularly supplied with preaching, whatever their peculiar creed or faith. One thing is observable, the people who attend are eminently conscientious, industrious and respectable citizens.

Many years ago, there resided in Jackson township an old lady by the name of Xanders. She died in 1856, at the age of about ninety-five years. She made a home with Mr. Swartz, uncle of the Clerk of Commissioners' Court, for many years, and to the family with whom she resided she related many scenes of distress and hardship, through which she passed. On one occasion, her family was attacked by the Indians; all escaped but one sister, who was captured and carried away, but, after many years, returned. A young girl, with the fleeing refugees, was shot through the breast, and in falling, fortunately fell behind a log, and being hidden from the Indians, succeeded in staunching the flow of blood with her apron, and rejoined her companions.

Jacob Heberling settled on the Mahanoy Creek before 1776, and built a grist-mill which was patronized for many miles around. Mr. Heberling' family was frequently disturbed by the Indians, and often were forced to leave their homes for self-preservation. An old white-oak tree, which stood for many years after the country became thickly populated, was the receptacle for their valuables, whenever the people were compelled to leave. The mill has passed through several hands and been frequently remodeled. It is now owned by Mr. Holshoe.

Churches.—The German Reformed and Lutherans built a church in this township about 1800, which was attended by the early settlers for many miles around.

JORDAN TOWNSHIP

Was erected from Jackson and Upper Mahanoy townships, April 5th, 1852. It was named in honor of Judge Jordan, for many years law judge of Northumberland County. Its location is on the extreme southern bounds of the County, and has Dauphin County on its southern boundary; Lower Mahanoy township, west; Jackson and Washington north; and Upper Mahanoy east. The surface is rough and mountainous, Fisher's ridge traversing the township in a most direct line east and west through the centre. Scattered around among the little valleys, formed by almost innumerable peaks of mountains or hills, are settled a large number of farmers, who appear, despite their rough surroundings, to have dug out pleasant and attractive homes. The first parties in the new township, were Peter Schwartz and Benjamin Mackle; first Constable, D. Dehner. The Fishers, John and Martin, settled in what is now Jordan township, some time prior to 1776. The farm, improved by them, is now occupied by D. M. Swartz, commissioner's clerk at Sunbury.

The surface of this township is somewhat rough and hilly, and would be considered, in Illinois, a very undesirable place for farmers. Fortunately for this, and many other as little favorable localities, it was peopled by a race, whose industry and economy have become proverbial; and where many would scarcely dare to settle, this hardy people have built up fine homes and surrounded themselves with abundance. Farming is the principal business. The burning of lime, also occupies the attention of many, lime being extensively used by the farmers for fertilizing purposes. Industries are but little varied here, there being but one mill, which was originally built about 1810. The old mill, about 1840, was demolished and in its place erected one which is now owned by Granville Wirt. This mill is operated by water-power, and is capable of doing a great deal of work.

The schools of Jordan amounted to but little prior to the inauguration of the free-school system, which happy event occurred in 1866. There are now seven school-houses in the township, all well sustained, where both English and German languages are taught.

The German Reformed and Lutherans built a house of worship about 1852, or '53, near Irvin post-office.

About 1835, Peter Kopel started a tannery near Irvin, for the manufacture of leather. This tannery is still operated by the original proprietor, who, like his tannery, is growing rapidly infirm.

Irvin Post-office.—This town is located in Jordan township, and is a central location. The first business-house was started by Daniel Swartz, about 1840. He here kept a general assortment of merchandise, and, his situation being central, he soon gathered about him a goodly number of inhabitants, to whom he sold lots. He built and conducted a tavern. There are now in the town one hotel, one cigar-shop, one store, one blacksmith-shop, one carpenter-shop, one shoemaker, a post-office, and nine family residences, giving a population of about one hundred people.

CAMERON TOWNSHIP

Was erected from Coal township, by Act of Assembly approved February 10th, 1851, First Justices: Solomon B. Boyer and Solomon Dunkleberger. Constable, John Hein.

The township presents the form of an irregular parallelogram, having a length of about eight times its width. The Mahanoy Creek passes through the entire length of the township from east to west, forming along its banks the only eligible spots for settlement. It is very sparsely settled, being too rough and mountainous, except along the stream, to invite settlement. The population, in 1870, was six hundred and three.

Gowen City was laid out in 1870, by Mr. Helfenstein. Peter Weikle was the original proprietor. The place contains one hotel, one store and a few dwelling-houses.

ZERBE TOWNSHIP*

Was created, by Act of Assembly, March 11th, 1853, which reads as follows: "All that part of Coal township, lying west of a line beginning at the line between Coal and Cameron townships, at a point two thousand feet westward, or where the said line crosses the west boundary of a tract of land surveyed in the name of Alexander Hunter, the 27th day of October, one thousand seven hundred and ninety-four; thence north 4° west, to the line between the townships of Coal and Shamokin."

First officers: Justices, Daniel Beckley and John Metz. Constable, J. Pennepacker.

COAL TOWNSHIP*

Was erected out of Shamokin and Little Mahanoy, at November session, 1837. First Constable, Samuel Eisenhart. Overseers of the Poor, George Carteher and George Gutshal.

* For annals of the township, see Shamokin.

WASHINGTON TOWNSHIP

Was erected out of the eastern part of Jackson and western end of Mahanoy, January 14th, 1856. First Justices, Peter Reed and M. D. Huffman. Constable, Solomon Billman.

This township, boasting an ancient and honored name, is of modern origin, having been organized in 1856. The surface is traversed by the same ranges of hills, which rise up and confront advancement in every part of Lower Northumberland. It is bounded north by Little Mahanoy and Cameron townships; east by Upper Mahanoy; south by Jordan, and west by Jackson. Population, 1870, eight hundred and one.

MT. CARMEL TOWNSHIP*

Was erected November 14th, 1854, out of the eastern end of Coal township. First Justices, Felix Darich and John Yarnall. Constable, George A. Keibler.

SHAMOKIN BOROUGH.

Shamokin † is the largest, wealthiest, busiest, and most populous town in Northumberland County. The site chosen shows the wisdom of the founders, who, in the early period of the coal trade, foresaw the mighty business that would be developed in the future. They could not say, as William Penn did in laying out Philadelphia, that "it seemed appointed for a town, because of its coves, docks, springs and lofty lands," for the location was a dark and almost impenetrable swamp, thickly covered with pine, hemlock, laurel and rocks. It might at that time, with great propriety, have been called the "Shades of Death." A more dreary and forsaken spot could hardly have been found, and none but far-seeing business men would have ever thought of selecting the site for a town.

Shamokin is centrally situated in the great Shamokin Coal Basin, at the Gap in the Big Mountain, which opening is the principal outlet for shipment of coal to the Susquehanna from the Middle Coal Field. The location is regarded as a healthy one, being at an elevation of seven hundred and thirty feet above the level of the sea, but a better drainage would add to its salubrity.

The town lies in a narrow valley, in the centre of Coal township. The Big Mountain forms its northern boundary, while several spurs of ridges lie to its south, cut by the Shamokin Creek, which crosses the valley and town in a winding direction. The tributaries that unite with the creek at Shamokin, are Coal Run, from the east, and Carbon and Furnace Runs, from the south-west. The irregular course of the old creek channel, the uneven surface of ground, and the different plans of persons who laid out the different parts of the town, have greatly interfered with a regular arrangement of the streets.

Surrounded by mountains and hills that circumscribed its horizon and municipal bounds, cut up by spurs, ravines and tortuous streams that prevented the rectangular plan of town-building from being carried out, and possessed of a surface that was either a swamp or a pile of rocks, it presented such striking objections, that no ancient city-builder or modern town-lot speculator would then have taken the land for the taxes. But such men as General Daniel Montgomery, Burd Patterson, John C. Boyd, and Alexander Jordan of that date, and Kimber Cleaver, Judge Helfenstein and William H. Marshall of a later period, well knew the inherent worth of the locality, though many of these statements, at that time, were ridiculed.

The many reverses that befell Shamokin in its early history, did not shake their faith, and among the old residents, there were several who stubbornly maintained "that Shamokin would yet be a city." Their argument was "the coal is here; when it is wanted the town will improve." The result has shown that their logic was good. The vigorous growth of the place for the past few years, the springing up of numerous hamlets and villages in its vicinity, its favorable location in one of the richest coal basins of the State, and its excellent communication with all the great coal markets, indicate that Shamokin is destined to become one of the great mining centres of the

* For annals of the township, see Shamokin.

† The History of Shamokin, Trevorton and Mount Carmel has been prepared by Dr. J. J. John, of Shamokin, a long resident of that place. Its history is a part of his own experience in the battle of life he has so successfully fought.

PLATE XVIII.

RES. OF WM A. SOBER,
FRONT ST., SUNBURY, NORTHUMBERLAND CO., PA.

RES. OF CHAS M. MARTIN, M. D.
CHESTNUT ST., SUNBURY, NORTHUMBERLAND CO., PA.

RES. OF G. W. ZIEGLER,
COR. THIRD & ARCH STS., SUNBURY, NORTHUMBERLAND COUNTY, PA.

JACOB SHIPMAN,
SUNBURY, NORTHUMBERLAND COUNTY, PA.
FIRE, LIFE & ACCIDENT INSURANCE OFFICE, COR. THIRD & MARKET STS.

Commonwealth. The orthodox faith of the old residents has been confirmed by the great corporations of the day, three of which having purchased nearly all the coal lands in the Shamokin coal basin. By the Philadelphia and Reading Railroad and the Lehigh Valley Railroad on the east, and the Northern Central Railway on the west, it has direct access to the markets along our seaboard, and the great lakes of the north-west.

Shamokin has frequently been termed the Pottsville of Northumberland County, and it is well deserving of the name.

The following list of outlets and distances to markets, points out the value of its location: To New York, New Jersey Central Railroad, via Tapton, one hundred and seventy-six miles; to New York, Lehigh Valley Railroad, one hundred and eighty-four miles; to Philadelphia, Philadelphia and Reading Railroad, one hundred and twenty-six miles; to Baltimore, Northern Central Railway, one hundred and forty-seven miles; Havre de Grace, Pennsylvania Canal, one hundred and forty miles; to Erie and the lakes, Philadelphia and Erie Railroad, three hundred and seven miles; to Elmira, New York, Northern Central Railway, one hundred and thirty-seven miles.

ORIGIN OF THE NAME.

"There's a great deal in a name."

The word Shamokin is of Indian origin, and like most words from this source, possesses a very euphonious sound. Indeed, it is truly fortunate for the historical language of our State, that so many of our streams and localities have retained the beautiful names bestowed on them by the red men. What prettier words than Wyoming, Wyalusing, Catawissa, Shamokin, Popemetung, etc.?

Writers of poetry and romance have not failed to recognize this fact, and in legend and story have used many Indian names, thus adding charm and interest to their works of song and fiction.

The word Shamokin, in the language of the *Delawares*, (who, with a few *Shawnese*, occupied this part of the State,) signifies *Eel Creek*, or *Eel Pond*. The name was given to our creek on account of the great number found in it, at or near where it empties into the Susquehanna. The name was also applied to the famous Indian village that stood on the banks of the river, where Sunbury is now located. This was ever a favorite spot with the Susquehanna tribes, and no word was dearer to the ear of a *Delaware* than the word Shamokin. Our town then, and for a century afterwards, was a howling wilderness. Its dark, swampy forests were only inhabited by beasts of prey, and a lonely path along the mountain side, leading to the Tulpehocken region, was occasionally traveled by some roving Indian band. Not even the rude *Delawares* would build their wigwams here, in such a solitary wild, that is now the site of a great mining town.

The name Shamokin seems ever to have been a popular one. When the Moravians established a missionary post at Sunbury, in 1748, they omitted their usual custom of applying a scriptural name, and retained the Indian one. The name Shamokin soon extended itself to prominent points around. The great island in the river was termed the Shamokin Island; the valley extending eastward was called Shamokin Valley; and the long range of hills running parallel to it, was named the Shamokin Hills; after the formation of the County, the name was applied to one of the principal townships; next to what is now termed the Big Mountain; next to the First Baptist Church, in this part of the State, founded in 1794; next to a post-office, at Smithtown, and finally the name was bestowed on our town, and to one of its principal streets. So much for the name.

THE DANVILLE AND POTTSVILLE RAILROAD.

The completion of the Schuylkill Canal, in 1825, attracted the attention of business men in Philadelphia, and other parts of the State, to the importance and necessity of connecting the waters of the Delaware and the Susquehanna by means of this improvement. Rittenhouse, and others, of a much earlier period, had conceived the idea of joining the waters of these two great rivers by a canal, but the undertaking was too vast for the means at command at that day.

The honor and origin of this railroad may justly be given to General Daniel Montgomery, of Danville, one of the most enterprising and far-seeing business men of his time.

In 1826, the legislature of the State granted a charter for the Danville and Pottsville Railroad Company, with a capital of three hundred thousand dollars—the fourth one granted. Under this act nothing was done; but in April, 1828, a supplement was passed, increasing the stock to one million dollars, and authorizing branches to Sunbury and Catawissa, so as to catch all the trade of both branches of the Susquehanna.

The following were among the commissioners appointed: Burd Patterson, Benjamin Pott, of Pottsville; Joseph Paxson, of Catawissa; General Montgomery, of Danville; John C. Boyd, Joseph R. Priestley, and John Taggart, of Northumberland; and Judge Jordan, Hugh Bellas, and E. Greenough, of Sunbury, etc.

The leading men in this enterprise were Stephen Girard, of Philadelphia, who owned large tracts of coal land in the Mahanoy region; Burd Patterson, of Pottsville, one of the ablest and most far-seeing business men that ever resided in the State; and General Montgomery, of Danville, father-in-law to John C. Boyd, the founder of Shamokin.

At this time, General Montgomery, who was one of the Canal Commissioners of the Commonwealth, procured the services of Moncure Robinson, Esq., one of the most famous civil engineers of our County, and during that Summer explored the woods and waters between Sunbury and Pottsville, in running experimental lines, to ascertain if a railroad could be constructed over a route, probably one of the most unfavorable in the County. In 1831, Mr. Robinson submitted his report, stating that a railroad was practicable, and could be made for six hundred and seventy-five thousand dollars. This included the grading of a road bed for a double track, the laying of a single track, the necessary turnouts, and the several planes, with their fixtures. The report was adopted, and the company, in 1832, commenced on the eastern end, by request of Mr. Girard, which was completed at seven per cent. less cost than the estimate.

It was the cherished idea of Girard to extend the Danville and Pottsville Railroad up the west branch, to Erie, connecting the most distant parts of the State, by rail and navigation. This road passed under several names; it was sometimes called the "Central," and again the "Girard Road." It was the design of the directors, that the eastern division should transport the coal from the Mahanoy basin to Pottsville, and thence by canal to Philadelphia; while the western section should convey the coal from the Shamokin region to Sunbury, and thence, by the Pennsylvania Canal, to Baltimore, and other places, while the entire route should be devoted to passenger travel and lumber traffic.

In November, 1831, Girard and Montgomery died. They were the main pillars in the enterprise, and their deaths exerted a chilling influence on the progress of the road.

From the beginning, Stephen Girard had been one of its warmest supporters, and but for his untimely death, the great undertaking would have been completed much sooner. It is known that his sudden illness prevented his appropriating three hundred thousand dollars towards its completion.

In 1832, a further supplement to the charter was passed, extending the time of completion to April, 1838.

During the Summer of 1832, the eastern section of the road was commenced, in conformity to the desire of Mr. Girard, and more than half of the work on this end was done this year. In his anxiety to push the work vigorously, he ordered from England the iron to plate the rails for the entire road. The eastern end was completed in the beginning of 1834, and was worked for a short time, but owing to the imperfect connection caused by the bad working of the planes, the work was abandoned in a few years.

This year the legislature passed an act, guaranteeing five per cent. interest on three hundred thousand dollars, for twenty-seven years, providing two-thirds of the funds thus obtained, should be applied to the completion of the western section. Bonds were sold at auction, in Philadelphia, for this purpose, and in July, 1834, work was commenced on twenty miles of the western end, between Shamokin and Sunbury, and was graded completely in the early part of the Summer of 1835. Shamokin at this time, and previously, was known as John Boyd's stone-coal quarry. In August, this year, contracts were made for putting down the superstructure, and laying the strap iron on the wooden rails, for thirteen and three-eighth miles, between Sunbury and a point now called Paxinos. This was completed in three months' time. On November 26th, 1835, the opening ceremonies occurred under the charge of the Chief Engineer, Mr. Totten. "Two elegant and commodious passenger cars," just built at Pottsville, for this road, named "*Shamokin*," and "*Mahanoy*," were placed on the track on the bank of the Susquehanna, at Sunbury. Each car contained about thirty passengers inside and outside, drawn by ten mail coach horses. At twelve o'clock, the train started, amid the ringing of bells, and the cheers of hundreds of people, who had assembled to witness this novel spectacle. At two o'clock, the party arrived at Paxinos, the terminus of the completed portion of the road. Here, a large concourse of people from all parts of the Shamokin Valley, had assembled to witness the arrival of the first passenger train from Sunbury.

A sumptuous dinner had been prepared for the visitors, after which a meeting was held, presided over by G. Daniel Levy, the oldest citizen of Sunbury, and the oldest member of the bar attending. Lewis Dewart and Charles Donnell were appointed Vice Presidents; and Peter Lazarus, and Daniel Brautigam, Secretaries; Hugh Bellas, Esq., delivered the address, giving a detailed history of the road, and the bright prospects of its future.

The following toasts were read:

By the President—"The memory of Girard and Montgomery—the founders of our railroad." Drank standing.

By Vice President Dewart—"The President and Managers of the railroad—faithful to their trust—persevering in a good cause."

By Mr. Bellas—"Moncure Robinson, our Chief Engineer, whose science has triumphed over the mountain—whose labors insure success—whose estimates never fail."

By Charles C. Hegins, Esq.—"Local improvements, like the separate cultivation of our intellectual faculties—while they benefit and enrich the part, increase the resources and strength of the whole."

By Col. Paxson—"Our railroads and canals—the pride of our State; the people look with confidence to their completion, guided by the hand of judicious economy."

By Peter Weimer, Esq.—"Hugh Bellas, Esq.—The view he has just afforded of the present work, shows how intimately he has been connected with its origin and completion."

The balance of the road, some six miles in length, leading from Paxinos to Shamokin, was not completed until August, 1838. The particulars of the completion of the road, etc., will be given in another article under the head of "Origin of Shamokin."

ORIGIN OF SHAMOKIN.

The land upon which Shamokin stands, is principally on the Samuel Clark survey. This tract originally comprised about four hundred acres, but it has been divided into smaller tracts. The patent for this land was issued to Samuel Clark, on April 11th, 1776, by John Penn, Jr., and John Penn, the successors of the great and good William Penn, the founder of the State. This transaction occurred about four years after the formation of the County, and about three months prior to the Declaration of Independence. The price per acre was most likely the usual one for proprietary lands of that period, and it is quite probable a British stamp legalized the transaction.

In June, 1776, Samuel Clark sold one-third of this tract to Thomas Lightfoot, and in 1792, the remainder to Francis Johnson. In 1803, Abraham Cherry, and afterwards John Cherry, became owners of the Johnson portion, and Jacob and Mary Tomlinson, of the Lightfoot part. During this year, by agreement, they divided the Clark survey; John Cherry getting two-thirds, or what is now the lower town, and Jacob and Mary Tomlinson one-third, or what is the upper town.

The one-third part, in the course of time, appears to have been sold for the taxes, and finally came into possession of Walter Brady, a former sheriff of Northumberland County. Walter was a fast man of that period, and on his retiring from office, was considerably in debt. The property was put up at sheriff's sale several times, but there were no bidders for the property. It finally was sold August 19th, 1824, on account of a debt of eighty-three dollars and fifty cents, due Michael Zuerne, the grandfather of Mr. Joseph Zuerne, of our town. It was described as a tract of land situate in Shamokin Gap, bounded by lands of Benjamin Campbell, late Benjamin Tomlinson, on which there is a *stone-coal quarry*. A small portion of the land is cleared, on which is erected a small log-dwelling, occupied by the widow of the late William Ducher, deceased. The western line of this track ran from near the Central School-house, south to the Methodist Church, and along the western side of Grant street. The present line between the east and west wards of the borough was the division line.

Jesse Major was the purchaser. Major was a loose character; in fact, an outlaw. He had been accused at different times of robbery, horse-stealing, and counterfeiting, but managed generally to escape punishment. He was a wandering tailor, and was very fleet of foot. Every bad act that occurred in the neighborhood was attributed to him. Tradition says that at the time of sale, Major had just been released from jail, and in passing by, in a joke, made a bid of *twelve dollars*. There being no other bidders, the tract was knocked down to him, amid considerable merriment, as the by-standers supposed he had no money. But to their surprise, he paid down the sum in gold. Coal was known to exist upon this tract for many years previously, but its value as a fuel was not fully known. Major visited his purchases several times, and obtained some samples of stone-coal in the creek, between Clay and Webster streets. It is said he took some of these pieces to a blacksmith at Paxinos, and told him to try them. The smith placed some of the chunks upon the top of the hearth-fire (a charcoal one), but as they commenced to fly in small pieces as they became heated, the coal was pronounced worthless. But Major did not lose confidence in his *stone-coal*, and in his travels over the country exhibited his mineral specimens. His character, however, was so poor that his coal and assertions received but little attention. Major was very axious to obtain a horse, and offered his "kingdom for a horse." Finally, in the Spring of 1826, he stopped one night at the tavern of Joseph Snyder, who then kept a hotel at the "Liberty Pole." Here he exhibited his coal, and offered to trade his tract, now the most beautiful part of Shamokin, to Mr. Snyder for an old grey horse. Mr. Snyder declined the offer, but told Major to go and see John C. Boyd, whom he said was fond of speculations. Major went to Boyd next, and finally made a sale, Mr. Boyd having ascertained that there was coal on the premises. Mr. Boyd paid Major two hundred and thirty dollars for the property, an old horse, valued at about fifty dollars, was part of the payment. The tract contained one hundred and six acres, eighty perches.

He afterward purchased of Jacob Tomlinson his interest in the land for five dollars. This purchase was made just after the passage of the Danville and Pottsville railroad bill.

Coal was known to exist here at a very early date, but its use was not fully understood, and hence but little valued. Mr. John Thompson, an old citizen of Shamokin, near eighty years of age, informed the writer that coal was discovered in the Shamokin region long before it was known in Schuylkill County. He says that the Cherrys, the first settlers, had noticed it, and that Isaac Tomlinson picked up some pieces in Quaker Run, about 1790, and took them to Maiden Creek, Berks County, for a blacksmith to try. In 1810, Mr. Tomlinson erected a blacksmith-shop, and used Shamokin coal.

In 1814, Mr. Thompson, who, then a boy of fifteen years, mined a two-horse load of coal out of the Quaker Run, hauled it to Sunbury, a distance of twenty-five miles, and sold it to a shoemaker for five dollars. He used it for his house. Parties before had purchased Wilkesbarre coal. This was the first Shamokin coal that ever went to market.

Farmers at the upper end of Irish Valley frequently picked up black stones in the creek, and finally traced the place they came from at Shamokin. For some years previously, farmers came here occasionally and got some coal, but little was done until Mr. Boyd acquired possession. In 1828, Mr. Boyd and Ziba Bird built a dam in the Shamokin Creek, near Webster street, and opened a mine, which for many years was known as Boyd's stone-coal quarry. Here they mined several hundred tons of coal out of the bed of the creek. Mr. Ziba Bird was the miner, John Runkle wheeled it out, assisted by Joseph Bird, Esq., who was then a small boy. Casper Reed and Samuel Startzel were hired to haul this coal to Danville in wagons, which took them several weeks. At Danville it was put in arks, and sent down the river to Columbia. This was the first coal sent down the Susquehanna to market from the Shamokin region.

Between 1826 and 1835, the ownership of this tract passed out of Mr. Boyd's hands one or more times. About 1830, it was owned by Jacob Graaff, of Reading, who conceived the idea of laying out a town here, and during that year had a portion surveyed for that purpose, but nothing was done except cutting out a partial path for the surveyors. About 1834, the property again came into the possession of Mr. Boyd.

The borough of Shamokin was laid out March 1st, 1835, by John C. Boyd. Joseph Bird, Esq., now of Northumberland, was present at the laying-out of the place, and gave the writer the following particulars: "During 1832-33, Ziba Bird, my father, was a contractor on the Girard road. In the Spring of 1834, he built a saw-mill at Locust Gap for Burd Patterson, who was one of the leading men of that day. Mr. Bird took a contract to saw two hundred thousand feet of oak rails for the Danville and Pottsville Railroad. He built the saw-mill for eight hundred dollars. He cut, hauled, and sawed for one-half, and thus got out his money. During the Spring of 1835, Mr. Boyd conceived the idea of laying out a town, and, as soon as the weather would admit, he had Ziba Bird to come to the present site of the town and lay it out. Kimber Cleaver was the engineer. Mr. Cleaver had been engaged several years upon the Danville and Pottsville Railroad as an engineer. I helped to carry the chain. We laid out the part included in the Major tract. Remember seeing the roads cut where Graaff had run his street.

"On the very day they commenced laying out the town, March 1st, Mr. Bird had the frame stuff and lumber for a house hauled from the saw-mill, at Locust Gap, already framed. Alexander Caldwell was one of the teamsters. This was the first house built, and is now a part of Weaver's National Hotel. It was a plank house, and as it had been all prepared at Locust Gap, it was soon put up. The building had no stone walls, but was set on posts. The house was commenced on March 1st, and was far enough completed on April 5th, to be used as a dwelling. Mr. Bird then moved in this house and immediately commenced another house, which is now the United States Hotel. When the second building was completed, he moved into it, and then finished the Weaver house by digging a cellar and putting a wall under it. Hots and Rishel were the carpenters."

No further houses were built until 1837. During July, 1835, Mr. Joseph Snyder, who had kept a tavern in Rush township, moved to Shamokin and opened a hotel in the second building erected, and remained there until August, 1837.

The following letter, published in a Philadelphia paper of this date, gives a good picture of the first days of Shamokin, when Mr. Snyder took charge of the *first hotel* of the town:

SHAMOKIN P. O. (PAXINOS), July 9th, 1835.

"I have just returned from a short ride of six miles to the termination of the graded part of the western section of the—allow me to call it 'Girard Railroad'—being accompanied by the assistant engineer, Mr. Totten, to whose polite attentions I am much indebted for much of the pleasure of the trip through the mountains. The road from this point (which is on the Shamokin Creek, thirteen miles east of Sunbury) passes up the creek, principally through an almost uninhabited country—the population at least is very sparse. Some three or four miles up we come into the Shamokin coal region, by the mines of which the country below, as far as Sunbury, is supplied, and from which, when the road is completed, large quantities will be sent to the Susquehanna River for exportation. On arriving at Mr. Boyd's mines (Shamokin), near the termination of the graded part of the road, and amidst the solitary mountains, we were gratified to see a large two-story dwelling-house, a large store, barn, and other out-houses, erected and nearly completed in a neat and handsome style. But if our surprise was great at observing such buildings, in such a place, judge what it must have been when, on our return, we met five or six wagons, loaded with furniture, women, children, cats, dogs, and chickens, and accompanied by cows, calves, sheep, and pigs, wending their way, up the railroad, to these very buildings, where *Daddy* informed us he was about to open a tavern. From whence his guests were to come, I could not, for the life of me, conceive, at least until the road should be completed to his place, and the mines should be worked. The next building erected, I suppose, will be a blacksmith-shop, when the place will have all the attributes of a town in a new country, and will be entitled to a post-office."

From 1803, the Cherry family held possession of the lower part of the town for many years, and one of the family built a log-house which stood on the site where the brick-house of W. and B. F. Lake now stands. In the course of time, this tract came into the possession of McCarty, Davis, Warner, and Jordan, who laid it out as a town about 1835, the same time that Boyd's part was laid out. It was called Groveville, in honor of Miss Grove, whom Mr. McCarty had recently married. The town was laid out under the supervision of David Rockefeller, Esq., of Sunbury, now well advanced in years, and noted as one of the most eminent land surveyors of the day.

Mr. Boyd first named his town "Marion," but a town in the west, of the same name, turning out badly, the name was abandoned, and that of Shamokin substituted. Soon after, the lower town dropped Groveville and adopted Shamokin also. But, notwithstanding the place was named Shamokin, the people did not accept the name for many years afterwards, invariably calling it "Newtown."

Though the road from Paxinos to Sunbury was opened at the close of 1835, it did not seem to have much effect on Shamokin, as no houses seem to have been erected during 1836. The tract between Paxinos and Shamokin was not laid, as the chief engineer, Mr. Robinson, suggested no further work should be done "until some accommodation shall have been obtained for the coal trade at Sunbury. The board will probably deem it expedient to present an application, on this subject, to the next legislature. If an appropriation should be made by that body to effect, at this point, a connection with the Pennsylvania Canal, by means of a guard-lock and basin, there can scarcely be a doubt that in a short time an active trade would exist on this portion of the railroad."

During 1837, several houses were erected. The third house built was a small, one-story frame school-house, on Dewart street. The fourth house was a small frame-kitchen, located where Mr. Bittentender's brick residence now stands. It was occupied by S. S. Bird, Esq. The fifth house put up was that of Joseph Bird, on the north-east corner of Shamokin and Commerce streets, on the ground now occupied by May's three-story block. The Bird house was afterwards moved up Commerce street, and a part of it is now occupied by Mr. William Rote, as a meat-market. The next house erected was by Mr. Benjamin McClow, on Commerce street. During 1838, Houseworth & John erected a store-building, on Shamokin street, on ground now occupied by Morganroth & Co.'s store-building. William Fegely built a residence on Sunbury street, and soon after erected a store-house on Shamokin street.

Abio John, who taught school the previous winter, the first in Shamokin, in the Spring built the frame-house on Sunbury street, now occupied by John Philips, as a hardware-store. Quite a number of houses were put up on Sunbury street, this year. David Foux put up a frame-building where Mr. Marshall's brick residence now stands. About 1850-53, it was occupied by a Mr. Sminkey, who kept a saloon, the first in Shamokin. The foundry, machine-shop and carpenter-shop were erected this year, by Boyd & Bird. S. S. Bird was the contractor of these and many other houses. The railroad company built their office this year, which was on the corner of Shamokin and Independence streets, and is now a part of Tenner's saloon. A small house was put up on site of D. S. Miller's residence, and another building, now occupied by J. F. Eisenhart. George Kreeger put a house on corner of Sunbury and Pearl streets, which has since been remodeled and is now occupied by R. A. Ammerman. Daniel Kreeger built a house on the corner of Commerce and Pearl streets, now occupied by his family. Boyd & Bird put a row of houses on Commerce street; Yoxthelmer built a store-house in the lower town, now occupied by Mr. J. P. Fincher, and the late Jacob Mowry built his residence on Market street. All the houses at the furnace, except the lower row, were put up this year, and a row was put up on Rock street by S. S. Bird, now occupied by William Owen, Sr.

In August, 1837, Mr. Kram took charge of the hotel. From 1836 to 1838, coal was hauled in wagons from the mines, at Shamokin, to Paxinos, where it was unloaded in shutes, dumped in cars and hauled by horse-power to Sunbury, for the local trade. This coal was mined from the flat-vein. In August, 1838, the railroad was completed from Paxinos to Shamokin. When this great work was completed, a great meeting was held at Shamokin, in commemoration of the event. A dinner was prepared for the occasion, in the foundry-building just erected. Mr. Kram, of the hotel, was the caterer, and no doubt the tables groaned with the luxuries of the season. Speeches were made by Mr. Bellas and others, portraying, in glowing colors, the future coal trade of Shamokin and the great prospects of its becoming a great centre of trade. The locomotive, the first one on the road, was the "North Star," built by Eastwick & Harrison, of Philadelphia, Mr. Eastwick acting as engineer on the occasion. The locomotive was a small one, and had been shipped in parts to Sunbury by canal, where it was unloaded and put together by Mr. Eastwick.

During 1838, coal was mined at the following places: At the Gap on the east side by Yoxtheimer; on the west side by Purdy & Co., at Buck Ridge, at the furnace, and the flat-vein back of Rock street.

During 1839, the times were most excellent. A number of mines were opened; several lateral roads were graded, and one or two laid with rails; a large number of houses were built, and there was a great demand for labor. Lots came into demand, and numbers of persons came here and purchased lots for speculation. A new market was erected for the farmers of adjoining townships, and the so-called "Newtown" was the rising town of the day. Additions were made to the United States Hotel and Weaver's Hotel, and Daniel Evert erected a brick-house, the first of this material in Shamokin. It is now occupied by his son, William W. Evert, Esq. Boyd & Bird started up the foundry, making car-wheels and hollow-ware. John Beal was the founder.

During 1840, the town continued to flourish, but a change was evidently approaching. The improvements made and capital expended exceeded the requirements of that day, and a reverse was sure to follow as certainly as in case of the Northern Pacific Railroad. But at this time, the indications to the people of the town and neighborhood seemed favorable still, and its progress for the past few years was looked upon as marvelous.

The *Sunbury American* of September 12th, 1840, in speaking of the town, says, "The Shamokin coal region, connected with Sunbury by a railroad twenty miles in length, which, a few years ago, was a solitary wild, untrodden by the foot of man, save the solitary hunter in pursuit of game, is now teeming with a busy and industrious population. The town of Shamokin, located in the coal region, in a narrow valley, contains about one hundred houses. It has sprung up as if by magic. These improvements which are but a commencement of a series of works upon a large scale now in progress, recent as they are, have already given a new life and impetus to this section of our County."

The same paper, in an editorial on Shamokin, of September 19th, 1840, states that, "We have been informed that this flourishing town, according to the late census, already numbers about five hundred inhabitants. Three years ago, the site of the town was a perfect wilderness. We distinctly remember, two or three years ago, when Coal township was erected, an objection was made *that it contained but seventeen voters.* It will now poll about two hundred votes.

"Notwithstanding the pressure of the times, the town still continues to improve. Two anthracite furnaces are now under way, and will be ready for blast next Spring. With an abundance of coal and iron, in, under and surrounding the town, it must soon become a place of importance."

FIRST TRIP TO SUNBURY.

As before stated, the railroad to Shamokin was completed in August, 1836; and then a great meeting was held at this place, to witness the first trip of a locomotive and passenger train to Sunbury. A number of the friends of the road were present, among whom may be mentioned John C. Boyd, Burd Patterson, Hugh Bellas, and others. After some speeches upon the completion of the great enterprise, and the partaking of a most excellent dinner, prepared by *mine host*, Mr. Kraus, preparations were made to start the first train from the mountains to the Susquehanna. This formal opening of the road brought together at Shamokin the largest crowd that had ever met here, to witness the novel sight. Men, women, and children, from far and near, dressed in their Sunday clothes, assembled on the ground at an early hour, and patiently waited the time the iron horse should start out on his journey. The locomotive used on this occasion was the "North Star," built by Eastwick & Harrison, of Philadelphia, with Mr. Eastwick as engineer. Two passenger cars, named the *Shamokin* and *Mahanoy*, and a few other cars, were attached to the engine on this occasion. Most of the people present had never before seen a railroad or engine, and when the "North Star" commenced blowing off steam, they kept at a respectful distance, viewing the strange creature with awe, as well as curiosity.

How proud that engineer must have felt, seated on his throne, the observed of all observers, when, after sounding the shrill whistle, that echoed for the first time along the mountains, he drew the lever, and slowly, amid the deafening cheers of the crowd, started the first passenger train for Sunbury.

ABOUT THE FIRST LOCOMOTIVES AND ENGINEERS.

The first locomotive placed on the road was the "North Star," in 1838, and a short time afterwards the second one, the "Mountaineer," was added, both being built at the shops of Eastwick & Harrison, Philadelphia. The first engineer was Charles Gill, who had the "North Star," and the second, Lewis Garretson, who had the "Mountaineer." After about five months, these engineers left, when Benjamin Katerman took the "North Star," and George Shipe the "Mountaineer." In a short time Mr. Katerman left, when Mr. Shipe took his engine, and Franklin A. Clark, afterwards somewhat famous for his stories and *hotel-keeping*, took the one vacated by Mr. Shipe.

During the shipping season, these two locomotives made two trips per day to Sunbury, hauling down about forty loaded cars of coal, and bringing back from forty to fifty empty ones. It is related that great trouble was experienced in keeping up steam, and in coming up to Shamokin it frequently happened that all hands were summoned to rob some farmer's fence of dry rails to keep up steam. Another great trouble was the bad condition of the railroad structure. The white oak rails were framed in wooden-ties, and fastened by oaken wedges. On top of these wooden rails were spiked down strap-iron, two-and-one-half inches wide and three-quarters of an inch thick. The engines were too heavy for this structure, and, as a consequence, were frequently off the track. Hours of time, and much patience, were lost in righting up things; but the more the road was used the worse it became, and finally the engines were taken off, and the cars were hauled by horse-power. A caboose was then used for passenger travel, called the *Black Hawk*, which, until within a few years, might be seen at the Shamokin Iron Works, used for the storage of bar-iron.

The first cars put on the road were brought from Girard's Works, and held about two-and-one-half tons. Soon afterwards, Mr. Bittentender built some that held three tons, and finally cars that held four-and-one-half tons.

FIRST OFFICIALS.

Moncure Robinson, for years, was the Chief Engineer of the Danville and Pottsville Railroad. Mr. Totten was his principal Assistant.

Kimber Cleaver, Esq., afterwards the Chief Engineer of the road, commenced as a peg-driver, but soon reached the position of engineer, with charge of a level.

Thomas Sharpe was the first Superintendent. He is represented to have been an able official, but rather passionate. In 1839, he resigned, and went to Richmond, Va., to take charge of a road there. He was succeeded by Samuel R. Wood, who had previously been Warden of the Eastern Penitentiary. He was a Quaker gentleman, of excellent business qualities, but rather self-willed. He continued as Superintendent until the road failed, in 1842, when he was appointed Sequestrator. He acted for the railroad for many years.

Patrick Riley was the Master Mechanic. He and Mr. Sharpe spent a great deal of time in trying to invent a coal-burning engine.

William H. Chessington was one of the first brakesmen and conductors on the coal trains. The trains were made up by coal from Buck Ridge, Shamokin Coal and Iron Company, Yoxtheimer's, Purdy's, and the mines at the flat-vein, called the "Sour Krout vein."

The first coal operators were Brannigan & Cowan, at Buck Ridge; Purdy & Co. and Yoxtheimer, at the Gap; the Shamokin Coal and Iron Company, at the furnace; and William Fegely, at the flat vein.

THE OLD READING ROAD.

The old road that connected Sunbury with Reading, and which had been laid out before the formation of the County, was called by this name. All the emigrants to the Shamokin Valley and adjacent parts, from New Jersey, and the lower counties of our State, traveled over this famous route. It was the outlet by which the farmers hauled their products to the markets of Reading and Easton. Mr. Philip Persing, a resident of our town, and now in his *one-hundredth year*, related to the writer that sixty-six years ago he hauled dried peaches over this road to Easton, and received one dollar and fifty cents per bushel. It was then about one week's work to make the round trip. He described the site now occupied by Shamokin as a very wild one at that time. He said the green briars and laurel along each side of this road about Shamokin, formed an almost impassable thicket, and that rabbits, which were then very plentiful, could hardly penetrate it in places.

The old road is supposed to have been laid out from an Indian trail. In many places this old thoroughfare is still visible. It ran along at the foot of the Big Mountain, in the gap just where the Northern Central Railroad entered the town somewhere near where the stables of the Cameron Colliery stood, and continuing along the base of the mountain just above the Central school-house property, through the property of W. H. Douty, and touched Sunbury street at Seibert's corner. The road then ran eastward until Luke Fidler was reached, it deflected to the right, and nearly opposite the Luke Fidler breaker, it crossed Coal Run and ran over to Springfield, and thence along the Sow's Back to the Cut, and thence towards Mt. Carmel.

Mr. John Thomson says, the first road from Sunbury to Reading was as nearly straight as possible, running over hills and through ravines, having only regard to directness. In the course of time the road was improved; abrupt hills were wound around, and instead of going straight up Sunbury street, the road curved around by Benjamin McClow's house. The Reading road ran to Paxinos and thence to Snufftown, along the farms of David Miller and Solomon Fegely, to Sunbury. At Paxinos, a tavern was kept as far back as 1800, by a man from New Jersey, by the name of Zeitsmith, which was a famous stopping-place for emigrants in those early days. After the Centre turnpike was opened, a great deal of travel that heretofore had gone over the old road, was directed to the new and better route.

The stages ran along the road before the turnpike was made.

INDIANS.

It is not at all likely that any party of Indians ever made a settlement in our vicinity, though the *Delawares* occupied this part of the country. No relics or implements of the red man, as dart-heads, beads, etc., have ever been found around here, which may be regarded as good evidence of their having no permanent settlement in our parts. But several of their paths passed through here. The old Reading road, the first highway through this part of the County, is said to originate from an Indian trail.

Another path passed through the western part of the Shamokin cemetery, and over the high top of the point named Shickelemy Point, to Tulpehocken, and thence to Philadelphia. Mr. Jacob Maury informed the writer that he had frequently noticed this path. It is more than likely that, in his frequent conferences with Penn, *Shickelemy* traveled this route, and from the eminence named after him, took a survey of the wild country then, which now comprises the Shamokin Coal Basin. Little did this noble chief dream that the howling wilderness, that lay spread before him, would some day in

PLATE XIX

STORE & RES OF HARRY DENIUS,
TURBOTVILLE, NORTH^D CO., PA

RES. OF GEORGE W. RYON, ESQ., SHAMOKIN, NORTH^D COUNTY, PA

HAAS & SEILER,
DEALERS IN DRY-GOODS, GROCERIES, FLOUR, FEED &c
COR. SIXTH & SPRUCE ST., SHAMOKIN, NORTH^D CO., PA

RES. OF C. W. WEAVER, M.D. SHAMOKIN, NORTH^D CO., PA

the future he built up a busy mining town, whose suburbs would be studded with collieries mining millions of tons of coal; little did this *Cayuga* Sachem suppose that a village would spring up here to take the name of his beloved home, on the banks of the Susquehanna.

OLD SETTLEMENTS.

Several settlements had been made along the old Reading road prior to the Revolution.

The Cherrys were the first settlers in the Shamokin region, they having come here while Pennsylvania was a colony of Great Britain. These, with other settlers, were chased away several times by the Indians. It is related that the old man Cherry, on one occasion, when being obliged to seek shelter at Fort Augusta, tied the bed-clothing on his cow and fled. The first Cherry lived at the house now known as Lich's. He cleared off a farm at Luke Fidler, another at Springfield, and several others. There were several sons. One, Joseph Cherry, settled on the flat near where the Shamokin brewery now stands. The stones of the chimney and foundation may still be seen. Another one settled on the hill east of Shamokin, and put up a distillery.

A man by the name of Dunkelberger put up a log-house on the spot now occupied by the brick-house of B. F. Lake. This was the first house in the present limits of the borough.

Gotlieb Goss took up two tracts of land between the Big and Little Mountains, the one tract taking in the poor-house farm, J. Zimmerman's farm, and Uniontown and the brewery, and the other the Brush Valley tract. Improvements were made on them, and they were occupied by his two sons, Martin and George Goss. Towards Bear Valley, settlements were made by a man named Maury, and others.

FOURTH OF JULY CELEBRATIONS.

Shamokin has ever been noted as a patriotic town, and from its commencement duly observed the anniversary of Independence. It will not be out of place to mention a few of the celebrations in the early days of our town.

The first celebration was held at the hotel of Dr. Robert Philips, on July 4th, 1839. About a year previous, Dr. Philips, who represented the interests of Purdy & Co., at their mines, built a hotel and office, and what is now known as the Philips' tract, opposite the Cameron Colliery. The hotel stood on a pleasant, green tract, along the public road in the Gap, and was a noted place in those days. The doctor was a very sociable man, and was a great favorite with the people who came to Shamokin. Here our citizens met in 1839, and duly observed the day with speeches, toasts, etc. James Porter, who built and resided in the house now occupied by Jacob Bades, made a cannon out of a gum tree, which answered every purpose. The next year the second celebration was held at the same place.

The third celebration was held in 1842, at the house of Franklin A. Clark, who kept a public house on the corner of Sunbury and Washington streets, afterwards the "Douty House," burnt down in 1872. The Shamokin Grays were present, and a number of military men from other parts of the County.

The following were the officers: President, Chas. Derring; Vice Presidents, Captain W. H. Kase and John Boughner; Secretary, Emanuel Zimmerman.

After the reading of the Declaration of Independence by the secretary, numerous toasts were read, a few of which are given:

By Chas. Derring—"The heroes of the Revolution—May their memory be indelibly stamped on the hearts of the American people." Three cheers.

By Capt. W. H. Kase—"Col. Richard M. Johnson, the next President of the United States." Three cheers and three guns.

By John Boughner—"The heroes of the War of 1812—May their posterity follow their example as patriots and soldiers." Three cheers and three guns.

By Emanuel Zimmerman—"The Day we celebrate." Three cheers and three guns.

By Henry Bird—"Anthony Wayne, the farmer's son of Chester County—May our legislative halls be well supplied with men of his stamp, and our armies with hearts like his." Three cheers.

By Joseph Bird—"Henry Clay, the next President of the United States." Three cheers.

By Joseph Allison, Jr.—"Peace and prosperity."

By E. Zimmerman—"May Democrats once more reign, bring hard currency up with Buchanan, and down with the banks. May the echo Democracy sound throughout the United States." Three cheers and three guns.

By Captain William H. Kase—"Shamokin town—May peace and harmony reign throughout the place, and business of all kinds prosper under the hands of the people." Three cheers.

By Pemberton Bird—"May the next anniversary of our Independence be celebrated without the use of alcohol." Three cheers.

By E. Zimmerman—"The framers of the Declaration of Independence—May their names be held sacred by the American people, and their fame be handed down to posterity, till time shall be no more." Three cheers and four guns.

By Benjamin McClow—"The opposers of Temperance—May they see the errors of their ways, and join in the temperance army heart and hand." Three cheers and six guns.

By F. A. Clark—"The Shamokin Grays—May they ever be ready to protect their rights." Six guns and six cheers.

By Joseph Bird—"Here is to the Temperance cause; hoping the time is not far distant when the glorious day of Independence may be celebrated with the use of cold water." Three cheers and four guns.

By Dr. Philips—"Washington—First in war, first in peace, and first in the hearts of his countrymen." Three cheers and four guns.

By Patrick Loncton—"The fair sex; the life of mankind." Three cheers.

By E. Zimmerman—"David R. Porter—He has been weighed, and found not wanting." Four cheers and four guns.

By J. Cowen—"May the Eagle of Liberty never lose a feather." Three cheers.

By John Eisely—"The Tutor who taught General Washington the alphabet between his knees, when five years old—He rests in peace." Three cheers.

By the Company—"May peace and prosperity attend the host and hostess."

Almost every year, since this date, the Fourth has been properly celebrated by the citizens of Shamokin.

SHAMOKIN COAL AND IRON COMPANY.

This corporation deserves a passing notice, as much of the earlier prosperity of Shamokin, to 1842, was owing to the improvements started up under its auspices.

This company was incorporated in June, 1836, but in November, 1839, the whole of the stock being taken, arrangements were made to mine and transport coal. Several drifts were opened opposite the Furnace, and a lateral road put in to connect with the Danville and Pottsville Railroad. They commenced shipping coal in 1839. They owned fourteen thousand acres of coal and iron land; seven hundred and fifty of which were in Columbia County, the balance near Shamokin. Several of the stockholders obtained a charter in March, 1840, for the manufacture of iron. They at once proceeded to purchase the necessary machinery for the erection of two furnaces. Up to July 1st, 1841, they had shipped three thousand tons of coal, mining about two hundred tons a day during the shipping season. Opposite these drifts they put up a large anthracite furnace, one of the first of the kind erected in the County.

The following description of the furnace is taken from the *North American* of 1842:

"This furnace, erected on the property of the company, at the village of Shamokin, is now in full blast, under the charge of William Frimstone, turning out pig metal of the very best quality. The machinery performs admirably. The forest has given place to the march of civilization, and the wilderness has been made to blossom as the rose. The village of Shamokin now contains more than six hundred inhabitants, nearly three hundred of whom are scholars in the Sunday-school, and it is destined, at no distant period, to become a large and flourishing town. Few places possess greater advantages for prosecuting the coal and iron business. The furnace is thirty-eight feet square, bore built up eleven feet plumb, then battered two-and-one-half inches to the foot to the top of the stack, which is forty-seven and one-half feet high from the commencement of the base. Foundation under the whole, five feet deep and forty-two feet square. Engines, one hundred and eighty horse-power. Ten boilers, each thirty feet long, and thirty inches diameter. Engine-house, sixty by thirty feet. Boiler-house, sixty by forty-five feet. Boiler-stack, seventy feet high. Casting-house, forty-five by forty-eight feet."

On May 24th, 1842, a fire broke out, burning down the casting-house, and part of the boiler-house, and hoisting apparatus. The furnace blew out a few weeks afterwards. A short time after the burning, the company failed, and Benjamin H. Yarnall, of Philadelphia, was appointed assignee. Several parties afterwards attempted to run the furnace, but were unsuccessful, and in 1845 it was sold at sheriff's sale. For several years it remained idle, but was started up again about 1855, and continued running with varied success under different managements until 1872, when it was finally blown out. The furnace and stack are still standing.

SHAMOKIN FROM 1842 TO 1852.

During this period, Shamokin passed through much vicissitude, and reached a very low ebb in her prosperity. The furnace burnt down; the Danville and Pottsville Railroad Company failed, and appointed Samuel R. Wood, Sequestrator. The rolling stock was sold at sheriff's sale. William and Reuben Fegely, who had been engaged in putting in a turning-table, and some lateral roads, and in making some of the principal repairs, were familiar with the workings of the road, and were on terms of intimacy with some of the principal officers. They had come to Shamokin in 1838, and in 1830 erected the store-house now occupied by them, and commenced store-keeping. In 1841, they commenced coal business, by opening the "tape vein," in the Gap, and putting up the improvements. At this time, Purdy & Jordan operated on the west side, and Yoxtheimer & Snyder on the east side. The Fegelys soon became possessed of these openings, also.

In 1842, when the railroad failed, and the engines were taken off, on account of its dilapidated condition, William and Reuben Fegely took charge of the road, put it in repair, and hauled coal to Sunbury by horse-power, which they continued until 1852.

During this time, the Fegely's carried on nearly all the business of the town. They mined and shipped all the coal; they bought and sold the principal part of the goods; they furnished all the provisions, and gave all the employment to labor. During the shipping season, the men worked at the mines, or hauled the coal mined to Sunbury; while during the winter months they were sent in the woods to prepare material for the railroad, or else work on the repairs. Taxes and all debts were paid by orders on their store, and even the salaries of preachers and teachers were paid in this manner. Not a marriage or funeral could take place, not a visit to another town could be made, without consent of "Uncle William." Child-birth was said to be the only condition of humanity not under their control. Candidates for office merely consulted with William and Reuben, and if they consented, the vote of the town was secured; and it is said sermons were shaped to meet their approval. At this time their power over the inhabitants was as great as the Emperor of Russia exercises over his subjects. If a laborer did wrong, he was sent to "Goose Hill," to work on a farm, picking stones, until his offence had been atoned, when he was permitted to work among his fellows again. But it must be said for the Fegelys, that, though they held absolute power over the people, they used it not altogether for their own advantage. Their people were always well supplied with provisions; there were no paupers, and in case of sickness, through the kindness of "Aunt Kitty," no one was allowed to want for what could be procured for their relief. Yes, years hence, when the selfish acts of men, that were noised abroad with great *eclat*, will be forgotten, the kind deeds of this good Samaritan towards the sick and dying will live green in the remembrance of many a relieved one, and the name of "Aunt Kitty" will be called blessed.

During this period, all that had money had moved away, while those who were too poor to leave, worked for the Fegelys. A few of the inventive kind flooded the country with patent-rights, such as new stoves, new plows, new scales, clothes-machines, patent medicines, etc. Nearly every county in the State was favored with some specimen of Shamokin ingenuity.

A large number of the persons who moved away went to Schuylkill County, where they remained until business revived, when they returned, experienced in the working of coal. At this time, all the coal mined was hauled to Sunbury by horse-power, and during the shipping season, about one hundred horses were used for this purpose. It required two days for the round trip. From four to five horses were required to take a train of ten cars. The coal was sold at Sunbury, or to the towns along the Susquehanna, and most generally exchanged for store-goods and provisions, which were brought back by the returning trains.

But this state of affairs could not last forever. The spirit of progress and speculation was abroad, and soon the old inhabitants of Shamokin were to have their dreams broken by the restless spirit of enterprise, armed with capital and labor. Railroads were to be graded and laid with an iron rail, collieries were to be established with coal-breakers, business was to be conducted on the cash system, and a general revolution take place in the method of transacting affairs. But for many years afterwards, there were those who occasionally sighed for the return of the old times, when Uncle William and Uncle Reuben ruled the destinies of Shamokin.

SHAMOKIN FROM 1852.

During the year 1852, William L. Helfenstein and some capitalists, who had previously been developing the coal interests of the Trevorton region, came to Shamokin and commenced improvements on a large scale. They had the charter of the Danville and Pottsville Railroad Company, renewed as the Philadelphia and Sunbury Railroad Company, and commenced at once in grading and putting down an iron track of T rails. They secured a large portion of the coal lands between Trevorton and Mount Carmel, and proceeded to prove coal veins and open drifts. Professor Rogers had just completed his geological survey of the Shamokin coal field, and had made many important developments, showing the importance of this region, which served to attract the attention of capitalists.

Numerous coal companies were formed, as the Big Mountain Improvement Company, the Carbon Run Improvement Company, the Green Ridge Company, etc. William H. Marshall, Esq., who had for some years been engaged with Burd Patterson, the pioneer in all the great coal and iron enterprises in this part of the State, was placed in charge of the coal lands. He proceeded at once to shaft the coal lands, prove the coal veins, open drifts, build breakers, and have laterals graded. He performed an immense amount of work, and was an indispensable agent to those who had invested their money here.

Another important agent in making all these improvements was Kimber Cleaver, the chief engineer. More extended remarks in reference to him will appear elsewhere.

During 1853, the track between Sunbury and Shamokin was relaid with iron rails, and, in 1854, was extended to Mount Carmel. Locomotives were placed on the road by the names of "David Longenecker," "Thomas Baumgardner," "A. R. Fiske," "Lancaster," "Green Ridge," and "Carbon Run." A. R. Fiske, Esq., a most excellent business man, who had previously had charge of the cotton mills at Lancaster, was the first superintendent, and remained in such capacity for some years.

In 1857, Judge Helfenstein resigned the presidency of the road, and was succeeded by James S. Biddle, of Philadelphia. The title of the road was changed to the Shamokin Valley and Pottsville Railroad, by which it was known until about 1862, when it was leased by the Northern Central Railway, for ninety-nine years. Under the present control the railroad has proved a profitable investment, having a heavy tonnage of coal.

The balance of the history of Shamokin will be treated under the heads of topics.

THE OLD FURNACE.

One of the old landmarks of the first history of Shamokin, was the Old Furnace. For the facts connected with this, we are indebted to Mr. Ephraim Mowry, who resided here when the town was started.

The land on the west side of the Gap appears to have been held by Solomon Dunkelberger, which, in the course of time, was sold to Henry Myers, for five hundred dollars. About 1825, Mr. Myers erected a small charcoal furnace on Furnace Run, the site of which might be detected a few years ago. The furnace run on bog ore found in the vicinity, and charcoal prepared on the ground. The furnace was located at the west end of Walnut street, where it crosses the run. It was in operation for some time, but was suspended on account of the difficulty in obtaining limestone.

About this time, considerable quantities of iron ore were hauled to the furnace at Catawissa. So Shamokin commenced the iron manufacture at an early date.

FIRST IMPROVEMENTS.

Before the war of 1812, Abraham Cherry erected a saw-mill in the Gap, just opposite the Cameron breaker, a little below a willow tree yet standing. An old dwelling-house stood near by.

About 1828, Mr. Myers traded this tract to a Mr. Hoots for a farm in Union County. Mr. Hoots furnished a large number of rails and ties from this tract for the railroad when it was constructed. In 1835, Mr. Hoots disposed of this land to J. H. Purdy and Lewis Dewart, who made openings and mined coal for some time.

During 1836, James Porter run this saw-mill. Dr. Robert Philips lived close by, practising medicine and acting as agent for some parties. This year a saw-mill was built on Coal Run, just above Flagherty's ice-house, which was run by Benjamin McClow, as sawyer.

FIRST STORE.

The first store in Shamokin was opened by Jehu John & Co., in what is now the bar-room of Weaver's hotel, in 1838. Their assortment was not extensive.

FIRST SINGING-SCHOOL.

David N. Lake, Esq., now an old and respected citizen of the town, help the first singing-school. He was a popular singer and had a lareg school.

THE FIRST SUNDAY-SCHOOL.

The first Sunday-school in Shamokin was organized in 1839, and was known as the Shamokin Town Union Sunday-school. It was held in the old frame school-house, in Dewart street, until the Central school-house was built, when it met there.

Among the persons who took an active part in its organization, may be named S. S. Bird, William Fegely, Kimber Cleaver, John John, Samuel John, P. Bird, Amos Y. Thomas, and others. Samuel R. Wood took a great interest in the school, and contributed a number of volumes to the library. A few of these books are now in the possession of the writer. The school continued to meet in the Central school-house until the numbers were too great for the room, when the school was moved to the Presbyterian Church, where it continued until 1854. The school, becoming too large to be well managed, was divided into several denominational ones.

THE FIRST RELIGIOUS SERVICES.

The first religious services were held in the old school-house, on Dewart street, in the Spring of 1837, by a Methodist preacher named Brown, who was then on this circuit. He preached an excellent sermon, and had a good attendance. Among the persons present, was John C. Boyd, the founder of the town. After this meeting, a prayer-meeting was formed, and from this sprung the M. E. Church of the town.

THE FIRST TEMPERANCE MEETING.

On March 20th, 1841, the first temperance meeting was held in the Central school-house. A large number was in attendance. Total abstinence was advocated. A large number signed the pledge. The following officers were elected: President, John John; Vice President, P. Bird; Secretary, Dr. W. P. Ireland; Treasurer, Milton Kerr. This organization continued for several years, and exerted a marked influence.

EFFORTS MADE TO EXTEND RAILROAD CONNECTIONS—MEETINGS HELD.

The planes on the Girard portion of the Danville and Pottsville Railroad working badly, led to the general abandonment of this road. The people of Shamokin felt the great necessity of better outlets for their products, and hence made great efforts to connect Shamokin with Pottsville.

To further this purpose, a railroad meeting was held at Shamokin, on November 2d, 1843, which was largely attended.

S. S. Bird acted as chairman, and Kimber Cleaver served as secretary.

On motion, a committee of five, consisting of Samuel John, Dr. Robert Philips, William Fegely, Stephen Bittenbender, and Kimber Cleaver, were appointed, who presented the following report:—

Whereas, a continuous railroad from the city of Philadelphia to the Susquehanna, at Sunbury, being an improvement in which all the citizens of the former place, as well as a great portion of the entire State, are deeply interested, inasmuch as it will form the most direct, expeditious and cheapest traveling and transportation route between Philadelphia and the iron and coal regions, and the lumber and agricultural districts of northern Pennsylvania; and, in conjunction with the Pennsylvania Canal, of the north and west branches of the Susquehanna, the Williamsport and Elmira Railroad, and other improvements, thereby opening a direct communication between Philadelphia, western New York and the lakes; and, *whereas*, the Philadelphia and Reading Railroad is now completed to Pottsville, and from Schuylkill Haven (on the line of the last-named road), the Mine Hill Railroad extending to Minersville; also the western division of the Danville and Pottsville Railroad, extending from Sunbury to Shamokin, a distance of twenty miles, leaving a chasm of but twenty-five miles, from Shamokin to Minersville, or Pottsville, of which there is a probability a road might be constructed without any inclined planes, and of a grade traversable by locomotives; therefore,

Resolved, that a committee be appointed to collect a sufficient sum of money to defray the expenses of making an experimental survey, from Shamokin to Pottsville, or Minersville, so as to avoid the incline planes; and that said committee shall have power to employ an engineer as soon as a sufficient sum is subscribed and paid.

For this purpose, the following committee was appointed: Dr. Robert Philips, Thomas Postley, William Fegely, Dr. John K. Robins, and Hon. Charles G. Donnell.

The action of this meeting met the approval of all parties interested in the Shamokin coal regions. The money was subscribed, and Kimber Cleaver was appointed the engineer. He was assisted by Samuel John, Peter Boughner, and some others, in the work.

Soon after commencing the work, Mr. Cleaver writes to the *Sunbury American*, as follows:

ROHR'S TAVERN, January 17th, 1844.

H. B. MASSER, Esq.

"*Dear Sir*;—I have been engaged for several days, with the assistance of Samuel John, in making an experimental survey for the contemplated railroad from Shamokin to Pottsville. We confidently believe we will be able to cross the Broad Mountain, by means of a small tunnel at a level little higher than the Locust Gap Summit, which is two hundred and forty-five feet lower than Mahanoy Plane. Owing, as yet, to the unfortunate state of the weather, we have been considerably retarded in our progress, and have not made a satisfactory exploration of the south descent of the Broad Mountain, consequently cannot determine at what point of the railroad of the Schuylkill region will be most suitable to connect with.

"KIMBER CLEAVER."

During July, 1844, he completed this survey, and made an exhaustive report, clearly showing the practicability of the route, giving distances, streams, mountains, and all facts connected with the construction of the work. But the work was in advance of the times, and it was reserved for the Reading Railroad, twenty-five years later, to avail themselves of a route so clearly pointed out by this survey.

SECOND RAILROAD MEETING.

On September 28th, 1845, a large meeting was held at Shamokin, to send delegates to the railroad convention, to be held at Danville, on October 29th.

S. S. Bird presided; William Fegely and F. A. Clark assisted; and Samuel John acted as secretary.

On motion, Samuel John addressed the meeting, showing the great advantages that would arise from a direct route from Philadelphia to Erie, and that from the nature of the country, this route would pass through Shamokin.

The following delegates were appointed: Samuel John, Joseph Bird, Daniel Evert, S. Bittenbender, and Joseph Snyder, the first inn-keeper.

The convention was held, but no decided results arose from the meeting.

FIRES.

The first fire in Shamokin occurred at the Shamokin furnace, in May, 1842, burning down the casting-house and other adjacent buildings.

No further fires of any account occurred until May 4th, 1866, when a very destructive one took place. This fire broke out in a frame-building, occupied by Val. Fogely for a store, about two o'clock in the morning, and soon communicated to the adjacent buildings. For a short time, the town seemed in danger of a general conflagration. The Northern Central Railway office, with all its furniture and valuable papers was destroyed, and some five or six houses were consumed. The loss was estimated at thirty thousand dollars, covered by about thirteen thousand dollars insurance.

The next fire occurred in August, 1867, when it broke out at night, in the photograph rooms of C. L. Raker, on Shamokin street, nearly on the same site where the previous fire commenced. Buckets were freely used; a small fire-engine, recently purchased by some citizens, was effectively worked by the Liberty Hose Company, and the fire was put out after several buildings were burned. The water was from the basin of Mr. Bittenbender.

The "great fire," which took place April 15th, 1872, originated in the "Douty House," then kept by Mr. Reese. The "Douty House" and twenty-four other buildings were destroyed, and at one time it seemed that if the entire town might be burned down. Loss, fifty thousand dollars; covered by twenty-five thousand dollars insurance.

The last fire of any note occurred at midnight, on July 4th, 1875. It broke out in a notion-store, kept by W. L. Clark & Co., on Independence street. Ten buildings were destroyed, making a loss of fifty thousand dollars; covered by about twenty thousand dollars insurance. Several incendiary fires occurred in this locality a few weeks after this, but resulted in no great loss.

LITERARY SOCIETIES—DEBATING CLUB.

In 1838, a debating club was started, which was held in the old school-house on Dewart street. It was well attended, and many of the leading questions of that day were earnestly discussed. Among the prominent speakers of the society, were Pemberton Bird, Dr. Philips, James Porter, Jonas Stine, Joseph Bird, Samuel John, Amos Y. Thomas, George Martz, John John, and Ephraim Mowry. This club continued for some years.

SHAMOKIN SENATE.

During the Winter of 1855–'56, Franklin B. Gowen, who was then book-keeper at the Shamokin furnace; A. R. Fiske, Henry Longenecker, Dr. G. S. Robins, Captain Henry Van Gosken, the writer, and others, established a Senate, which met weekly in the Odd Fellows' Hall. It was conducted on the rules observed by the United States Senate, but probably lacked some in the Roman dignity maintained by the latter body. Mr. Gowen represented South Carolina, and was as troublesome in his peculiar views, as John C. Calhoun was in his days of nullification.

Captain Van Gosken acted for Utah, and was importunate in advocating the *peculiar doctrine* of that territory. Kimber Cleaver was for New Jersey, and lost no opportunity to bring forward bills in the interest of the "Native American" party. A. R. Fiske represented the old Bay State in many a long speech upon the floor. W. P. Withington had the honor to speak for Pennsylvania, and the old hall rang with his eloquence. The Senate continued in existence about one year, when it was superseded by the

SHAMOKIN LYCEUM.

This society was established in 1857, and continued in existence some seven or eight years. It was incorporated by the County Court, and numbered among its members the leading citizens of the town. The meetings were held weekly, in Bittenbender's Hall, which had been fitted up expressly for this purpose. The exercises consisted in readings, lectures, and discussions. A large library was secured, and one of the finest mineralogical collections in the interior of the State was formed. The mineral collection was made through the great efforts of Charles W. Peale. He had made a large collection of the coal fossils of our region, which he exchanged with different colleges in the various parts of the United States, for the peculiar minerals of their localities. This society conducted a series of very interesting discussions, on subjects that were before the public at that time, and exerted no little influence in moulding opinions and cultivating a literary taste. The society continued to prosper, and was looked upon by the citizens of the town, as an object of which they had just reason to be proud; but during the last year of the late war, the Rebellion so attracted the attention of the people, that the Lyceum was allowed to pass away. Several efforts were made to revive the society, but they were unsuccessful, and other literary clubs have been started, but they soon ceased to be.

SHAMOKIN LECTURE ASSOCIATION.

During the Autumn of 1873, a number of gentlemen of Shamokin met together, and formed a society of the above name, and procured a charter for the same. For two Winter seasons they carried through a course of lectures, but not being fully sustained by the public, they have been doing nothing of late.

The officers are: President, Charles P. Helfenstein; Secretary, J. J. John; Treasurer, J. S. Huber.

SHAMOKIN GUARDS.

This finely-drilled and well-uniformed company, which now ranks as one of the best disciplined and most throughly drilled companies in the State, was organized at Shamokin, April 30th, 1870. The first officers were: Captain, Alexander Caldwell; 1st Lieutenant, James May; 2d Lieutenant, James A. Shipp.

The company was composed entirely of veterans, who had seen and done full service with Grant and Sherman, and who had a proud military record for reference.

Several changes in the officers occurred. Captain Caldwell, having been appointed Lieutenant-Colonel and Inspecting Officer, on the staff of Major-General McCormick, commanding Eighth Division of National Guard of Pennsylvania, Lieutenant May was made Captain; Lieutenant Shipp, 1st Lieutenant; and Corporal John A. Weaver, 2d Lieutenant.

When the divisions were consolidated, Lieutenant-Colonel Caldwell was elected Colonel of the Seventh Regiment; Captain James May was made Major, on the staff of Major-General Seigfried. The present officers are: Captain, James A. Shipp; 1st Lieutenant, John A. Weaver; 2d Lieutenant, P. H. Haly.

The company now numbers fifty-six men, rank and file. They have secured eight lots, upon which they design erecting an armory, one hundred and twenty by fifty-five feet, and twenty feet high. They are constantly undergoing drill exercises, and are the next thing to perfect in the manual.

This company has quite a record since its organization, but space will merely permit of naming a few of their achievements:

They were the escort of honor at Governor Geary's funeral; they took an active and prompt part in the suppression of the riots at Williamsport and Shenandoah; while at Camp Anthony Wayne they were justly noticed by the leading papers as one of the finest companies of the Commonwealth.

Their position, now, is Company B, Seventh Regiment, National Guard, under Colonel Caldwell.

GEARY BUCKTAILS.

This fine company was organized June 10th, 1870. It is mainly composed of veterans, who have seen service on many a hard-fought battle field. The first officers were as follows: Captain, F. D. Strauser; 1st Lieutenant, C. S. Chamberlain.

The company now numbers forty men, rank and file. They are well drilled, and present a fine appearance when on parade.

Several changes occurred in the officers at different times. The present officers are: Captain, F. D. Strauser; 2d Lieutenant, J. B. Gettis.

They did good service at the Shenandoah riots, and were favorably noticed at Camp Anthony Wayne. They are now Company D, of the Seventh Regiment of National Guard.

FIRST BIRTH.

The first child born in the town of Shamokin, was John Boyd Snyder, in 1835. His father, Joseph Snyder, kept the hotel at the time. In honor of the event, John C. Boyd presented the firstling with a valuable town lot.

FIRST MARRIAGE.

The first marriage occurred in 1838. Joseph Bird, one of the pioneers of the town, married Rebecca, a daughter of Jacob Kram, who succeeded Mr. Snyder at the hotel this year. The bride was presented with a corner lot by Mr. Boyd.

FIRST POST-MASTER.

William Fegely was the first post-master of the town. It was established about 1839, and was kept in the store-room. It was first called Coal Post-office, as the one at Paxinos was called Shamokin. When the latter was named *Paxinos* after a celebrated Indian chief, *Coal* was changed to *Shamokin*. The mail for some years was brought here two or three times a week, and the matter consisted of a few Sunbury papers and an occasional letter.

FIRST EXPRESS OFFICE.

The first express office was opened July, 1861, at the post-office which was then kept in the basement of Bittenbender's Building, by F. P. Stambach, who was then post-master. The business was very small for some years.

FIRST NEWS-OFFICE.

The first news-office was opened by F. P. Stambach, shortly after the breaking out of the Rebellion to supply a growing want. A large number had sent one or more members of their families to the war, and were anxious to obtain the news daily concerning the progress of the war and the particulars of each battle fought. Bird & John, in 1856, had kept magazines for sale at their drug-store.

FIRST BRICK-HOUSE

was put up by Daniel Evert, in 1839. Brick made on the ground where Springfield now stands.

FIRST BANK.

The Shamokin Bank, now Northumberland County National Bank, was established in 1857, but not fully organized until 1858. Particulars given elsewhere.

FIRST NOTARY PUBLIC.

Shortly after the organization of the Shamokin Bank, W. P. Withington was appointed Notary Public. He held his office until 1861, when he was succeeded by F. S. Haas and John Dunkleberger.

FIRST DRUG-STORE.

Dr. Wm. J. Haas, now of Mount Carmel, started the first drug-store, in the building now occupied by Wm. H. Moore as a residence, on Sunbury street, about 1853. His stock was small.

FIRST CHURCH.

The first place erected for public worship, was by the Catholics, in 1839, through the efforts of Riley, Braunigan and some others. Stephen Bittenbender was the builder.

PLATE XX

"EAGLE HOTEL" D. H. GREISBACH, Propr., TURBOTVILLE, NORTHd COUNTY, PENNSa

RES. OF J. B. LEINBACH, LEWIS TP., NORTHUMBERLAND CO., PA.

FIRST SOAP FACTORY.

In 1862, Daniel Evert starts a soap factory.

FIRST TAN-YARD.

About 1864, Daniel Evert and Paul Ammerman start a tan-yard.

FIRST PAVEMENT.

First pavement put down in Shamokin was a brick one, in front of the house of Daniel Evert, about 1855.

FIRST LUMBER-YARD.

Dr. Wm. Atwater, about 1853, started the first lumber-yard in the lower part of the town.

FIRST BRICK.

The first brick made here was by George Swenk, in 1830, at Springfield.

SHAMOKIN CANAL.

In 1857, a charter was procured to construct a canal, between Shamokin and Sunbury. Its advocates contended that every ton of coal brought enough water with it, to float it to market. It is needless to say the work was not prosecuted.

FIRST FREIGHT LINE.

In November, 1865, Musselman established a freight line, between Shamokin and Philadelphia.

FIRE-DAMP.

The first case of explosion by fire-damp in this section, occurred in the slope of D. Webster's colliery, December 28th, 1865. One man killed, and two badly burned.

FIRST OFFICIALS OF SHAMOKIN.

Justice of the Peace, S. S. Bird; Constable, Samuel Eisenhart; Supervisor, David Thomson.

INCOMES REPORTED FOR 1865.

William Fegely,	$19,471
William H. Marshall,	15,785
John B. Douty,	6,000
W. P. Withington,	3,121
Val. Fegely,	2,445
A. R. Fiske,	2,548
S. Bittenbender,	1,941
George W. Snyder,	1,670
H. Van Gosken,	1,490
Daniel Weaver,	1,350

DEER IN THE TOWN.

During the Autumn of 1855, a deer ran through some of the principal streets of the town. It ran over the porch of the United States Hotel, and thence up Commerce street, and the Mount Carmel road. It was shot a short distance out of town.

ARTESIAN WELLS.

During 1855, John Creech, bored Artesian wells for Jacob Mowry, William Fegely, and others.

SKELETON FOUND.

In 1839, while some men were engaged in digging the foundation of the foundry, a skeleton of a man was found, an old pistol, and some ten dollars in silver. The skeleton was supposed to be that of a pedlar from Mahanoy, who had been missing for some years.

CREEK CHANNEL.

Shamokin Creek was turned in a new channel, September 20th, 1872.

HEAVY TAXES.

During the year 1865, every citizen in Shamokin Borough, between the ages of twenty-one and forty-five, was liable to the following poll taxes: Bounty, ten dollars; County, five dollars; Borough, five dollars; total, twenty dollars.

SHAMOKIN AS A BOROUGH.

Shamokin was incorporated as a Borough by the Court of Common Pleas of Northumberland County, November term, 1864.

For several years, previously, a number of the citizens had agitated the subject, but were overruled by some of the "old residents," who desired to let "good enough alone." During the latter part of 1863, a number of articles appeared in the *Shamokin Herald*, that had a marked influence on public opinion. The subject was treated in a ludicrous light, but still so truthfully, that every one felt the force of the remarks. Some became offended, but most of the people were awakened to new interest, and finally succeeded in obtaining a charter.

A special election for borough officers was held December 2d, 1864, and resulted as follows:

Chief Burgess—R. B. Douty. Council—John J. Esher, Daniel Weaver, John Dunkelberger, W. H. Gilger, and Henry Van Gosken. Judge of Election—Stephen A. Harris. Inspectors—J. W. Young, and R. A. Ammerman.

This Council went to work at once, and enacted a large number of ordinances.

At the Spring election, the following officers were elected:

Chief Burgess—R. B. Douty. Council—Daniel Weaver, John Dunkelberger, John J. Esher, William H. Gilger, and G. H. Coder. Constable—Henry Neihoff. School Directors—D. S. Miller, M. Ernes, Pemberton Bird, J. J. John, W. K. Erdman, and F. S. Haas. Auditors—F. A. Clark, and W. P. Withington. Directors of Poor—George W. Rorer and A. A. Heim. Assessor—David Fegely.

The town had so increased in size and population that, in 1871, it was divided into wards, the east and west wards, by an act of Legislature, approved May 19th, 1871. Grant or Ninth street forms the division line.

Since the formation of the borough, the town has shown a wonderful change. Pavements have been put down all along the principal streets; streets have been opened, and put in excellent repair; a fire department has been created, and all the wants and interests of a growing town are attended to by an attentive chief burgess and an excellent council.

The present town authorities are: Chief Burgess—J. H. Zimmerman; Assistant Burgess—Joseph Henninger; Council—Azariah Campbell, Galen F. Holsher, S. Gottschall, J. H. Johnston, Daniel Yost, and John Clifford

POPULATION.

The present population of Shamokin is estimated at eight thousand. At the census of 1870, it contained four thousand three hundred and twenty souls, showing an increase of about one hundred per cent. in five years. During the year 1875, at least one house was put up for every day in the year, and many of them were first-class houses. For the present year, notwithstanding the hard times, about two hundred houses were erected, many of which are first-class brick buildings.

STREET NOMENCLATURE.

The streets of Shamokin are laid out within a few degrees of due north and south. Beginning at the western limit, they occur as follows: First, Second, Third, Fourth, Fifth, Sixth, Market, Seventh, Eighth, Ninth, or Grant, Orange, Marshall, or Liberty, Washington, Rock, Shamokin, Franklin, Pearl, Vine, Cherry, and Lombard, the last street on the east in the borough limits.

The streets running east and west, beginning on the north, are Packer, Cameron, Dewart, Sunbury, Commerce, Independence, Water, Lincoln, Sprizheim, Clay, Webster, Race, Chestnut, Spruce, Pine, Mulberry and Willow.

ADDITIONS.

Within the past few years, several additions of town lots have been made, among which may be named the following: West Shamokin, on the west; Bellas' Addition, on the south; Marshalton, and M. R. R. and M. Co.'s Additions, on the east, and Cameron Addition, on the north. When these are included in the borough limits, its present size will be doubled.

NATIONALITY OF POPULATION.

The population of Shamokin is composed of nearly every nation in Europe, but the leading nationalities are American, Polish, German, Irish, English, Welsh, Scotch, French, Russian, etc. A large portion of these are law-abiding citizens, and a great number of them have homes of their own.

TOWN CLOCK.

During May, 1866, through the exertions and liberality of John B. Douty, one of the most public-spirited men of the town, a town clock was placed in the spire of the Presbyterian church. There are four dials, each five feet in diameter; the pendulum is fourteen feet long, with a sixty-five pound ball attached. It is a great convenience to the town.

FIRST IRON BRIDGE.

In June, 1867, an iron bridge was built across Shamokin Creek, at Market street.'

AID TO CHICAGO AND THE NORTH-WEST.

The citizens of Shamokin, upon learning the great loss sustained by the people of Chicago and the towns of the north-west, called a meeting and appointed committees to solicit contributions for the sufferers. F. W. Pollock, Esq., was appointed treasurer. The total amount contributed by Shamokin and vicinity, was the large sum of two thousand one hundred and forty-seven dollars and eighty cents. Well done!

FIRE-PLUGS.

There are twenty fire-plugs distributed over the more thickly settled parts of the town, the property of the town. The borough officials had designed to put in twelve more in such parts of the town as were not supplied, which would have fully secured all parts of the borough with water in case of fire. An election was held on August 20th, 1876, to decide whether a tax should be levied for this purpose, but evidently through a misunderstanding, was defeated by a large majority.

INDEBTEDNESS OF BOROUGH.

The indebtedness of Shamokin is about thirty-four thousand dollars, a large portion of which is in the shape of bonds, at six and seven per cent. Provision is made to pay off the interest semi-annually, and such portions of the principal, so that the entire debt will be liquidated in thirty years. This restricts the authorities in the works of repairs and improvements, as the taxes levied are inadequate to fully meet all these purposes.

EXPENDITURES.

For the past five years, a great deal of work has been done in opening streets and keeping them in repair. There are but few towns, perhaps, more expensive to keep in order than Shamokin. A number of streets have been filled up to grade at great expense. To put Market street in its present condition, has cost over ten thousand dollars; while at least five thousand dollars has been expended on Independence street.

PAVEMENTS.

All the principal streets are now graded and paved along their entire length, with a few exceptions, which will soon be attended to by the watchful borough fathers.

FIRE DEPARTMENT.

A fire department was established by the Council, with Jacob Mentchler as Marshal.

SHAMOKIN IRON WORKS.

These works were started in 1838, when the railroad was extended to Shamokin.

The machine-shop and car-shop were built by the Danville and Pottsville Railroad Company, for the use of their road. The foundry was erected by John C. Boyd and Ziba Bird, for the purpose of making stoves and hollow-ware. The power was derived from the engine in the machine-shop.

In 1851, Stephen Bittenbender purchased the foundry, and in 1855, the machine-shop and car-shop. He carried on business here about sixteen years, turning out an immense amount of work, and keeping in employ a large number of men. In 1867, he leased the works to Cruikshank & Bro., practical mechanics, who carried on business for some time.

In September, 1870, Cruikshank & Bro. disposed of their lease to Messrs. Mullen & Hufman, of Port Carbon, two most excellent mechanics. Mr. John Mullen had been foundry boss, and Mr. David Hufman boss machinist of the Franklin Iron Works.

In the early part of 1871, this firm built the first steam-engine that was constructed at Shamokin. This fact attracted quite a considerable attention, and a large number of persons visited the shops to witness it. It was a twenty-horse-power engine, used to propel a fan at the Henry Clay Colliery. It worked to perfection, and proved the builders to be master workmen. It was extensively noticed by the local papers, and asserted as the second engine built in Northumberland County.

In the Spring of 1875, Mr. Rittenbender sold these works to Mullen, Hufman & Co. This new firm proceeded to the erection of new buildings, better adapted to the wants of their business, which were completed in November of the same year. The buildings are of brick, and built in the most substantial manner. The foundry is eighty-six by forty-six feet, and twenty-four feet high in the clear. It is supplied with a crane that can lift twenty-five tons. There are two cupolas and two core-ovens here.

The machine-shop is one hundred feet long by forty feet wide, and sixteen feet high in the clear. It is well supplied with all the latest style of machinery required for the business wants of a mining region. Among the new machinery, they have a forty-inch slide-lathe with a twenty-two foot bed, a planer twenty-six by thirty-six, capable of planing a surface twelve feet in length, a radial drill, a heavy double-plated shaping-machine, and the machinery necessary for a first-class shop. As now furnished, they are the finest shops in the County, and among the finest in the State.

During the early part of 1876, one of the partners, Mr. David Hufman, dying, the firm on June 1st, was changed to John Mullen & Co.

A large quantity of excellent work has been recently turned out from these shops. Among other machinery, they have just completed for the Sterling Colliery, one pair of hoisting-engines sixteen by thirty, link-motion, with a capacity of fifty-horse-power each, which are justly regarded as the best hoisting machinery in the region. They also furnished a similar engine and the machinery for this breaker. A considerable amount of machinery for the soft coal regions has been sent out from these works.

The Shamokin Iron Works are well located for business, standing in a V formed by the Northern Central Railway, and the Philadelphia and Reading Railroad.

When running full, they employ one hundred men, but at the present time there are only forty men at work.

The capacity of the shops is one hundred and fifty thousand dollars per annum. Steam-engines and colliery machinery have been their special branches of work; but everything in their line of business can be turned out as they are well supplied with all the necessary fixtures.

ANTHRACITE FOUNDRY AND MACHINE WORKS.

These works were originally started in 1860, by John Shipp, and then known as the Starr Machine Works. They were carried on by Mr. Shipp, until 1871, at which time they were purchased by John Muller, and by him operated until the month of October, 1874, when William Y. Cruikshank purchased and took possession. Recently, Mr. Cruikshank has associated with him, a young man of experience and ability, and the firm is now known as Lloyd & Cruikshank. The business done embraces the manufacture of all kinds of mining machinery, mill-work, etc. Everything, from a grindstone hanging to a steam-engine, is manufactured here in the best possible manner. At present, the works are busily employed on iron work, for the Northumberland County Jail. The shops, when running at full capacity are capable of turning out sixty thousand dollars worth of manufactured goods per annum, and of affording profitable employment to fifty hands. The force now employed is about thirty. The works are complete. The iron is taken in the pig at one end of the shop, and when it emanates from the opposite end, the engine is ready for steam.

INDUSTRIAL IRON WORKS.

These works were first erected in Sunbury. In 1864, William Rennyson, of Pottsville, purchased them, and carried on business there until 1866, when he removed them to Shamokin, and erected them on their present site. In 1868, Mr. Rennyson retired, and they were idle for some time.

In 1869, William Brown, the present proprietor, purchased them, and put them in running order, and has kept them moving to the present time.

The works consist of the following buildings, all frame: Machine-shop, fifty by one hundred and fifty feet; boiler-shop, thirty-six by forty feet; screen-shop, fifty by thirty feet; blacksmith-shop, fifty by forty-five feet; foundry, fifty by fifty feet; erecting-shop, forty by fifty feet..

When these works are running full capacity, they can give employment to one hundred and seventy-five men, but at present time only twenty-five men are employed. The shops are capable of turning out one hundred and seventy-five thousand dollars worth of work per annum.

The principal business of these works is building engines, pumps, boilers, screens, forgings, and all kinds of machinery and repairs for mining regions. The works are properly named the "Industrial," as they furnish all wants of the coal regions. Considerable work is done for Schuylkill and Dauphin Counties, and some screen-work for Baltimore.

The shops are favorably located between two railroads. Mr. Brown is a very enterprising man, who gives great attention to his business, and will doubtless build up a large trade. In his pattern-shop, over the machine-shop, there is an immense collection of patterns. Mr. Brown has built several engines at his works, and has, at the present time, the only boiler-shop in Northumberland County. He does a large amount of work for the collieries of the Miners' Railroad and Mining Company.

SHAMOKIN PLANING-MILL.

This establishment was started in 1874, by George Marshall, the present proprietor. It is favorably located between Independence street and the Northern Central Railway.

The mill is a frame building, three stories high, forty by fifty-four feet in size.

This mill is fitted up with all the latest improved machinery—a large flooring-machine, a pony-planer, etc. The mill is driven by an engine of thirty horse-power. The principal business is planing rough lumber, and making sash, blinds, doors, mouldings, etc. Capacity of mill, forty thousand dollars; number of men employed at present, ten; but can use twenty when running full capacity.

SHAMOKIN MARBLE-YARD.

Established by Boyd & Rumberger, the present proprietors, in 1861.

Principal business is the erection of tombstones, monuments, and cemetery enclosures. Considerable work is sent to the neighboring counties. Yearly business amounts to about five thousand dollars.

LUMBER-YARDS.

George Marshall has on hand three hundred thousand feet. Sales, about one million feet per annum.

Lumber receipts for 1875: Hemlock, six hundred and fifteen thousand one hundred and thirty-six feet; pine, four hundred and seventy-three thousand feet; total, one million, eighty-eight thousand one hundred and thirty-six feet.

R. S. Aucker has on hand about two hundred and fifty-thousand feet. Sales for 1875, amounted to one million three hunded thousand feet of pine and hemlock.

Daniel Yost has on hand about two hundred thousand feet. Sales for 1875, one million feet.

SHAMOKIN WATER COMPANY.

When Shamokin was first laid out, the inhabitants depended on springs, which supplied the people with the very purest kind of water, but as the town enlarged and the mines were extensively worked, some of these springs gave out and wells were sunk as a substitute. Some time previous to 1850, a small reservoir was made near Cameron and Rock streets, supplied with most excellent water from a large spring near by. This water was conducted in wooden pipes to small portions of Shamokin and Sunbury streets. But, as the town extended southward, the water supply depended entirely on wells with an inferior water. In 1865, Stephen Bittenbender, at a cost of eight thousand dollars, put down iron pipes, from a reservoir built by him. This was also supplied by a large spring. These pipes extended as far as Coal Run, on Shamokin street, and down Sunbury street, as far as Orange street. Mr. Bittenbender supplied parties with water, at reasonable rates.

In 1866, the Shamokin Water Company was chartered, with the following commissioners: Stephen Bittenbender, M. Ewes, John Caldwell, R. B. Douty, J. J. John, W. P. Withington, Reuben Fegely, John B. Douty, F. A. Clark, W. H. Marshall, Daniel Weaver, Daniel Evert, W. C. Roth, D. N. Lake, C. P. Helfenstein, and J. J. Esher. The capital stock was one hundred thousand dollars, to be issued in shares of twenty-five dollars.

A meeting of citizens was called by W. H. Marshall, and great efforts were made to organize the company, but they failed.

Nothing further was done until April, 1872, when a number of citizens employed F. J. Anspach to make a survey, and estimate the cost of water works for the borough of Shamokin. On the first of May, Mr. Anspach submitted his report. He recommended the waters of Trout Run, with a reservoir in Shamokin, and steam pumps. He estimated the expense at sixty-six thousand seven hundred and sixty dollars and eighty-seven cents.

The report was so favorably received that some forty thousand dollars of the stock was subscribed at once.

A charter from the court was obtained in July, and the company organized. The Board of Directors chosen were, Isaac May, Sr., John B. Douty, Reuben Fegely, W. H. Marshall, W. R. Kutzner, M. Ewes, C. Groeber, A. A. Heim, and F. J. Anspach. Isaac May was elected President, and W. H. Marshall, Treasurer. Work was commenced at once. The old Fegely Dam, across Trout Run, was rebuilt. Pumping-works were erected opposite Brown's Industrial Iron Works. Two sixty-horse-power engines, manufactured in Shamokin, were erected, with pumps that were to force one thousand gallons per minute. The water was elevated two hundred and twenty-five feet, perpendicularly alongside of Big Mountain. Pipe was laid from the dam to the pumps, a distance of ninety-two thousand feet, with a fall of fifty-four feet. The distributing-pipes through the town, partly iron and partly wood, are ten, eight, six and four inches diameter, as the wants may be.

On December 6th, 1873, the water was let in the pipes. It reached the reservoir in one hour and fifteen minutes, a distance of ninety-five hundred feet. The reservoir, which contained fifteen thousand gallons, was filled in twelve minutes. Everything worked well.

During January, 1874, W. H. Marshall had water introduced in his house—the first one using Trout Run water.

At a meeting of the Company, held in January, 1874, it was ordered to issue Water Bonds, to the amount of twenty thousand dollars, to complete the works.

For the following terse description of the present works, the writer is indebted to R. A. Ammerman, chief engineer, who is fully acquainted with all the improvements that relate to his profession.

The street mains being partly cast-iron and partly wooden pipes, the latter were found to be insufficient to resist the shock and pressure incident to the working of the pumps, frequently bursting and necessitating constant and expensive repairs. The company, in June or July of 1875, decided to abandon the pumps, and extend their line for supply, about three thousand six hundred feet further up the stream—Trout Run—and to an elevation of ninety-two feet above the old dam or reservoir.

The extension to the new dam or reservoir was completed, the water let in and the pumps stopped, on October 25th, 1875.

The main line now consists of seven thousand and sixty-three feet of twelve-inch wooden pipes, and four thousand six hundred and eighty-five feet of cast-iron twelve-inch pipes, to the site of the pumping-works; the water is distributed thence through the several streets of the town in ten-inch, eight-inch, six-inch and four-inch iron and wooden pipes.

The capacity of main supply line to an elevation of sixty feet above the sidewalk at Douty's "Brown-stone Front," is two hundred and ninety-eight thousand gallons for every twenty-four hours, the pressure, at the intersection of Shamokin and Sunbury streets, being forty-five-and-a-half pounds per square inch, while the pressure at points throughout the greater part of town, will reach fifty-eight to sixty pounds per square inch, being equivalent to a supply of over twenty thousand gallons per hour—sufficient to supply a population of over eight thousand persons, with sixty gallons each, for every twenty-four hours; with an adequate supply, at all times, for any emergency that may arise, except during seasons of extreme drought.

The company purpose, at an early day, to enlarge the dam or reservoir, it being entirely too small for the accumulation and storage of a sufficient supply for a long, heavy drain, in case of protracted fires during excessive drought, notwithstanding, two fires on the same night, during the unusually "dry spell" of August, 1876, failed to exhaust the supply."

The present directors are: Holden Chester, President; Reuben Fegely, Vice President; William H. Marshall, Treasurer; Alexander Fulton, A. A. Heim, W. H. Douty, D. Llewellyn, C. Groeber.

SHAMOKIN GAS-LIGHT COMPANY.

This company was organized July 23d, 1874, and chartered by the State in November of the same year. The capital stock of the corporation is twenty-five thousand dollars. The works were constructed by J. D. Patton, Esq., of Trevorton. The gas, which by the way is a very superior article, is produced from crude petroleum in retorts patented by Mr. Patton. It is regarded superior to coal-gas, and is less liable to condense.

Works of a similar character have been erected in Sunbury, Ashland, Shenandoah, and other places, where they give great satisfaction.

Nearly two miles of main-pipe have been laid in the streets of Shamokin, and father extensions are being gradually made.

This gas is now consumed in about one hundred houses, and is being extended to nearly all the new buildings.

The directors and officers are, Charles P. Helfenstein, President; Samuel John, Vice President; George W. Ryon, Treasurer; J. J. John, Secretary; L. B. Morganroth, J. D. Patton.

SHAMOKIN BASIN.

This coal field, nearly all of which is in Northumberland County, is twenty miles long, and about two-and-a-half miles wide. It contains an area of fifty square miles. It is principally drained by the Shamokin Creek, which leaves the coal region at the Shamokin Gap, and empties in the Susquehanna at Sunbury; this basin is bounded on the north by the Big Mountain, and on the south by the Locust Mountain.

There are supposed to be thirteen veins in this basin, the numbers beginning at the bottom. Numbers thirteen, twelve, and fourteen, are red-ash, and numbers ten, nine, and eight, are white-ash. The two principal veins worked in the Shamokin region are eight and nine, called the Twins, or the two parts of the Mammoth vein. They average from eight to nine feet in thickness, of good coal, the best coal mines in the Shamokin Basin.

The outlets for this coal, are the Lehigh Valley Railroad, the Philadelphia and Reading Railroad, and the Northern Central Railway, the two latter having the larger portion of the tonnage.

There are now some thirty collieries in Northumberland County, which are prepared to mine and ship over two million tons of coal per annum. Twenty-six years ago, the entire region, by hard work, were able to put out eleven thousand, nine hundred and thirty tons during the year; now, one of our second-rate collieries will send off that quantity in one month.

All the anthracite coal of America, which now exceeds nineteen million tons annually, comes from a small locality in eastern Pennsylvania, comprised in the six counties of Northumberland, Dauphin, Schuylkill, Luzerne, Columbia, and Carbon. There are no coal-breakers in the world outside of this favored region. If the several coal-basins were brought into one contiguous body, they would form a small territory, a little larger than Northumberland County, twenty-four miles long and twenty miles wide. And when it is remembered that there is but little anthracite coal in the world outside of this small tract, and that one-tenth of the anthracite coal territory, and one-twelfth of the anthracite product is in and from good old Northumberland County, the reader will form some definite order of the great mineral wealth of the Shamokin region.

SHAMOKIN COAL TRADE.

The coal trade of our region commenced in a very humble way. Beginning with 1839, for a number of years it did not average fifteen thousand tons.

During the Summer of 1853, the railroad between Shamokin and Sunbury (then called the Philadelphia and Sunbury Railroad), was relaid with iron rails, and was formally opened, August 25th. The coal shipment this year was a little over fifteen thousand tons, a tonnage that the Cameron Colliery would now send in one month, and regard as a small shipment. The coal was loaded in boats at Sunbury, and consigned to different points along the river. The next year, the road was extended to Mt. Carmel, and some seven or eight collieries sent off sixty-three thousand five hundred tons, about what one ordinary colliery would now do in that time.

A coal-operator of this period, informed the writer that he traveled from Williamsport to Elmira and Buffalo, trying to sell coal, but met with little success, as the people knew little or nothing about this kind of fuel. This led coal men to employ men to travel these regions, and teach the people how to burn anthracite coal.

During the Autumn of 1855, the railroad between Sunbury and Williamsport was opened, and at the New York State Agricultural Fair, held at Elmira, in October, Shamokin was represented by two large masses of anthracite coal, each weighing over a ton. The exhibitors of these were Messrs. Cochran, Rede & Co., of Lancaster Colliery, and Boyd, Rosser & Co., of Luke Fidler Colliery. These specimens attracted a great deal of attention, and a number of speeches were made on the occasion. Among the speakers was Gov. Bigler, who stated, in his remarks, that the first coal from Shamokin to Elmira, direct in cars, had arrived that day, and that he was using a sample of it for a platform. This was considered quite a novelty, and had the effect of drawing the attention of western New York to Shamokin coal.

Doubtless, at this meeting, Mr. Langdon first noticed the fuel, and with the uncommon foresight of a great business man, fully comprehended the situation, and commenced the operations in coal, for which he afterwards became so famous. A few weeks after this, some gentlemen from Elmira came to Shamokin, and offered to buy one hundred thousand tons of coal. Our Shamokin operators were greatly surprised at so large an offer, but readily availed themselves of the opportunity.

The shipments this year increased to one hundred and sixteen thousand one hundred and seventeen tons, and in 1857, reached one hundred and fifty-five thousand eight hundred and six tons, a large proportion of which was handled by Mr. Langdon. At this time, the only money in circulation about Shamokin, was that on Chemung Canal Bank, and for each pay a remittance from Elmira was necessary. Had Mr Langdon then ceased his purchases of Shamokin coal, it would have thrown our collieries out of work and beggared the town. The writer has been particular to show how much our region is indebted to one man alone, whose far-seeing business mind enabled him to dispose of our excellent fuel to mutual advantage; whose wonderful energy and foresight has opened up a great market for Shamokin coal, beginning with Elmira, and pushing the trade northward and westward until it took the Canadas in its circuit, and extended to the towns and cities of the far West, even to Omaha. He soon became interested in mining Shamokin coal, and through his able and experienced superintendent, Alexander Fulton, Esq., the works of J. Langdon & Co. have been extraordinarily successful.

In the course of time, new outlets were opened. The Reading Railroad first connected with the Shamokin region, at Locust Gap, but after some years, extended their track to Shamokin, and thence to Trevorton, and the Susquehanna. Next, the Lehigh Valley Railroad came into our region, connecting at Mt. Carmel. With these new connections, the shipments largely increased, and in 1870, exceeded one million of tons per annum.

A few years ago, the Mineral Railroad and Mining Company took charge of some four collieries in this region, viz.: the Cameron, Luke Fidler, Hickory Swamp, and Hickory Ridge. These collieries are under the efficient superintendence of Holden Chester, Esq., a gentleman of great experience in mining affairs. These collieries are the best equipped of any in the region, with all the most approved machinery. The shipments from these four collieries for 1875, are as follows: Cameron, two hundred and seventy thousand one hundred and ninety-nine dollars and ten cents; Luke Fidler, one hundred and three thousand eight hundred dollars and nineteen cents; Hickory Swamp, seventy thousand five hundred and nineteen dollars and fourteen cents; Hickory Ridge, eighteen thousand nine hundred and forty dollars and two cents; total, four hundred and sixty-three thousand four hundred and sixty dollars and five cents.

This coal is put in the markets of Baltimore, Philadelphia, New York, and Boston, as Cameron coal.

For the year 1875, there was sent from Northumberland County, one million six hundred and twenty-eight thousand six hundred and eighty-three tons of coal. More than one-half of this tonnage passed over the Philadelphia and Reading Railroad.

To mine, prepare, and put in cars for market, this amount of coal, requires the employment of at least five thousand men and boys, at thirty breakers, with one hundred engines, representing at least six thousand five hundred-horse-power, to hoist, pump, and drive the machinery. Add to this the horses and mules employed; the amount of hay and grain consumed by them; the quantity of rails, sheet-iron, spikes, etc., required; the powder and oil consumed, and the millions of feet of timber required, and the reader will form an idea of the immense capital employed in mining the anthracite coal of Northumberland County.

The collieries in the vicinity of Shamokin, pay out, each month, to their men, an average of one hundred thousand dollars per month, when running to their full capacity.

The writer had intended to dwell more extensively on this topic, giving a description of each colliery, but was prevented by his limited space and time in this work.

SHAMOKIN CARRIAGE AND BLACKSMITH-SHOPS.

These shops were established in 1869, by J. H. Zimmerman, to supply a want long felt in Shamokin. He commenced business in a small shop on Market street, between the Northern Central Railway and Philadelphia and Reading Railroad. The size of this building was twenty by thirty feet, and when it was built it stood in the bushes at one end of the town, but now a business portion of Shamokin. When he commenced, he had but one fire, but business so crowded him, that in the course of a few months, he was obliged to enlarge his shop and work with seven fires.

Soon after starting the blacksmith-shop, he opened a carriage works on quite a large scale. Two other buildings were erected for this purpose, and the large mill-property of Reuben Fegely was also occupied for a warehouse. Mr. Zimmerman engaged in the manufacture of all kinds of wagon work, from the heavy wagons for colliery service, to the lightest and finest of carriages. Many of the finest vehicles in Shamokin and vicinity are from these shops.

PLATE XXI

RES. OF GEORGE STOHL,
LEWIS Tᴾ NORTHUMBERLAND COUNTY, PA

RES. OF CHRISTOPHER RAUP,
LEWIS TP. NORTHUMBERLAND CO. PA

While business was good, some twenty-five men were employed; but only eleven are at work at this time.

In March, 1876, J. H. Zimmerman, retired from business, and was succeeded by his son, J. B. Zimmerman, who carries on the shops at the present time.

During the prosperous years, over twenty thousand dollars worth of work was put out per annum, but at this time, the amount will not exceed twelve thousand dollars per year.

PRINCIPAL HOTELS.

Shamokin is well provided with hotels, but there is not a hotel-building in the town adequate to the wants of the place.

The principal hotels are: Weaver's National Hotel, and the United States, on Shamokin street; the City Hotel, on Sunbury street; Market Street Hotel; and the Exchange, on Commerce street.

STORES.

There is not another town in the County that is better furnished with stores than Shamokin. The following are the principal ones: Kutzner's drug and hardware store, carry about forty thousand dollars of stock; C. Gracher & Son, dry goods, about twenty thousand dollars; A. Strouse & Co., dry goods, twenty thousand dollars; L. B. Morganroth & Co., dry goods, about twenty thousand dollars; Leader, Muir & Co., dry goods, about twenty thousand dollars; Fegely & Marty, dry goods, about fifteen thousand dollars.

Besides these, there is a large class of good stores, which carry from six thousand dollars to ten thousand dollars of stock.

SOLDIERS' MONUMENT.

This monument to our fallen heroes, stands on the highest ground of the Shamokin Cemetery. It was erected through the efforts of Lincoln Post, of the Grand Army of the Republic. On May 30th, 1871, it was dedicated with appropriate ceremonies. The monument is a beautiful piece of workmanship, and cost about seven hundred dollars. It is thirteen feet high, and stands fifteen feet above the level of the ground, being surmounted on a mound, two feet high. The base is a solid block of granite from the Gettysburg battle-field, three-and-a-half feet square, weighing three thousand two hundred pounds. The monument is of American marble. Upon the front panel is the inscription:

Erected
Under the Auspices of
Lincoln Post, No. 140,
G. A. R.
May 30th, 1871.

Surmounting the die is a plain shaft, seven feet high, with a raised shield on front, bearing above it the words:

"To Our Fallen Heroes."

The monument makes a fine appearance, and can be seen from nearly all parts of the town.

POOR-HOUSE.

During the Winters of 1857 and 1858, there was but little, if any, work in the Shamokin region, and, as a consequence, about one hundred families were thrown upon the township for support. This was very expensive, and led many of the larger property-owners to devise some plan to lessen the burden of their support. A poor-house in Coal township, which then included Shamokin, was proposed, but it met with serious opposition. The question was then dropped for some time. One evening in the Winter of 1862, Samuel John, John B. Douty, and one or two more, met and prepared a bill for establishing a poor-house. The bill was taken to Harrisburg by Samuel John, and passed in a few weeks afterwards.

In the Spring of 1863, a meeting of citizens was held at the Central school-house, to consider the poor-house question. The question was warmly debated, and finally decided that an election should be held to decide the matter. This was done on June 12th, and carried by a small majority. By this act, William H. Marshall, Joseph Bird and George McEleice were the first Poor Directors.

On March 1, 1864, they purchased from Jacob Maury his farm, about one mile north-west of Shamokin, consisting of forty acres, on which were erected a large brick-house and suitable out-buildings, for eight thousand dollars.

Emmanuel Zimmerman was appointed Warden, who entered upon his duties at once.

During the year ending April 1st, 1876, three hundred families received outside relief, averaging fifteen dollars and sixty-one cents per family; fifty-nine persons were lodged at the poor-house, extending from a few days to a year; three were maintained at the lunatic hospital, and three hundred and sixty-five tramps lodged at the poor-house.

The expenditures for the year were eight thousand four hundred and eighty-eight dollars and fifty-eight cents. The products of the farm amounted to five hundred and sixty-four dollars and sixty-five cents.

The poor officials at the present time, are as follows: Directors—Isaac May, Sr., Dr. D. S. Hollenbach, W. W. Wary; Secretary—J. J. John.

NEWSPAPERS.

During many years, Shamokin had no newspaper, although possessed of a reading population, who largely supported the papers of Sunbury and Milton in advertising and subscriptions. About 1853, when the Philadelphia and Sunbury Railroad commenced operations, there was a general revival of business in the Shamokin region, and, as a consequence, a large number of people from different sections came here. At this time, a newspaper was projected, and some steps were taken in that direction, but nothing was accomplished. No further effort was made until the Summer of 1858, when John Robins, a practical printer, who had published the *Miltonian* for several years, came to Shamokin, and, in July, started a newspaper, called the

SHAMOKIN JOURNAL.

This paper was issued some four or five months, by Mr. Robins, but, owing to the stringency of the times, he was obliged to suspend the enterprise. The office was in what was then well-known as the "*Red House*," which stood on ground north of Tomnoes' saloon, where the Reading Railroad now passes over. Mr. Samuel John purchased the press and material about January 1st, 1859, but did not continue the paper.

SHAMOKIN REGISTER.

The first number of this paper was issued March 8th, 1860, by Samuel John, Esq., editor and proprietor. The *Journal* press and material were used for its issues. The paper was Republican in politics, and took a strong stand in favor of the election of Abraham Lincoln. The *Register*, in the hands of Mr. John, was a good newspaper for that day. On June 6th, 1861, the *Register* passed into the hands of Daniel Bower, who had previously published the *Williamsport Times*. Mr. Bower was a man of considerable ability, and was a ready writer and a fluent speaker, but was not as diligent in business as success required. On April 29th, 1862, he discontinued the *Register*. The press and material passed into the possession of Samuel John, Esq., but no paper was issued, and he finally sold the entire stock to a party of Sunbury, who started up the *Democratic Guard*.

SHAMOKIN HERALD.

The next, and most successful paper in Shamokin, was the *Herald*, which first appeared June 10th, 1862. Daniel Bower, the proprietor, issued shares of stock, and thus obtained means to purchase the complete outfit of a printing establishment for job and newspaper work. The paper was edited by Daniel Bower and J. J. John. Twelve numbers were issued, when Mr. Bower retired from the editorship, and accepted a position as Recruiting Officer at Camp Curtin. After occupying this office a short time, he entered active service as a Lieutenant, and died from wounds received at Chancellorsville. No *Herald* was then issued until December 25th, 1862, when J. Stewart McEwen took charge of the paper, and continued its publication until July 2d, 1863, when he retired, and S. B. Sisty, who had been foreman in the office, took charge, and published one number, which was so intensely *democratic* in politics that the stockholders would not allow him to hold possession of the office. No further number of the paper was put out until July 23d, 1863, when Owen M. Fowler, a young man of great worth, and a most excellent printer, who had just returned from the *three months'* service, took charge of the *Herald*. Mr. Fowler was poor, and labored under great difficulties, but, by untiring industry and close application, he succeeded in building up a newspaper and job establishment, second to none in the County. To this he added a very complete book-bindery. Under Mr. Fowler's charge the *Herald* became an influential paper, Republican in politics, outspoken in its course, but ever dignified in its manner. Unfortunately, the health of Mr. Fowler failed, and in May, 1874, he died after being confined to his bed one week. His last wish was, that the "*Herald* should not miss a number." The paper was then conducted by J. J. John, (who has been the real editor since 1868,) to July 1st, 1874, when the establishment was sold at administrator's sale, to Messrs. Heffelfinger & Cader, who had been in Mr. Fowler's employ for several years. Under the management of these two practical printers, the *Herald* has improved in its appearance, and increased in its circulation. It is regarded as the organ of the coal trade in Northumberland County, and is very attentive in publishing all matters of local interest. It is Republican in politics, and has, for years, taken an active part in support of the men and principles of the party.

SHAMOKIN ADVERTISER.

This, as its name imports, was an advertising sheet, started about January 1st, 1872, by J. L. Gilger & Son, who had just opened a new printing-office, under the control of John A. Gilger, who, for several years previously, had been the foreman of the *Monitor* office at Tamaqua. Some twenty-six numbers of this sheet were issued, and distributed gratuitously, the profits coming from the advertising. The *Advertiser* was then merged into the

SHAMOKIN TIMES.

The first number of the *Times* appeared July 13th, 1872, published by the same firm, with John A. Gilger as local editor. The paper was neutral in politics, if such a thing is possible, and paid great attention to the collection of local news. During the Summer of 1874, Mr. Jonas L. Gilger retired from the paper, and the publishers were then Gilger & Fegely, for a few months, when Mr. Fegely retired. On January 1st, 1875, Mr. D. D. Domer, of Washington City, became associated with the *Times*, as editor. This paper is now published by the Shamokin Times Company, with Mr. Domer as editor and manager. Under the present management, the paper has been enlarged and greatly improved; it is now one of the best papers in the County. Mr. Domer is a good writer, and keeps his columns well filled with news.

FRIENDSHIP HOSE COMPANY.

This company was organized in May, and chartered in November, 1873.

Soon after their organization, they uniformed themselves, and purchased a hose-carriage. They have now five hundred feet of good hose.

During 1875, Mr. Bittenbender having presented the company with several lots, near the corner of Franklin and Spurzheim streets, they erected a fine two-story brick-building, twenty by thirty-five feet, for carriage-house and place of meeting.

The company is prosperous, and numbers at present seventy-five members. They have attended every fire since date of organization.

The officers are: President, John Owen; Vice President, Lewis Spears; Secretaries, H. Rohrheimer, S. Owen; Treasurer, W. R. Kutzner.

CITIZENS' FIRE, HOOK AND LADDER COMPANY.

Organized October 12th, 1875. This organization numbers twenty-two members, fully equipped for service. Meetings held at Liberty Hose House.

Present officers are: Foreman, C. W. Scott; Assistant Foreman, D. B. Felix; Secretary, Theodore Strawser; Treasurer, A. G. Marr.

THE INDEPENDENCE FIRE ASSOCIATION

Was organized August 14th, 1873, with Wesley Van Gosken, as President; and Thomas Tindle, as Secretary. The company was chartered in November of same year.

The present officers are: President, Isaac Goldsmith; Vice President, Wesley Wilson; Secretary, M. L. Strouse; Treasurer, H. H. Keiser.

This company numbers forty-five men, fully equipped for service. Their hose-carriage was built in Shamokin, by Wesley Van Gosken, at a cost of six hundred and seventy-five dollars. It is a very handsome carriage. The company are now building a two-story brick hose-house, the first story of which is now completed. Mr. Jacob Mentchler is the builder. The company has no debt. They have attended all fires. Have five hundred feet of hose.

RESCUE FIRE ENGINE AND HOSE COMPANY.

Organized in March, 1873. The present officers are: President, Frederick Haas; Secretary, Harry Neihoff; Treasurer, Joseph H. Kase.

There are thirty-six members uniformed, and well equipped for service. They have about four hundred feet of hose.

Their meetings are held, and personal property kept at the Friendship Hose Building.

VOLUNTEER FIRE DEPARTMENT,

Consists of the following companies: Friendship, seventy-two members; Rescue, thirty-six members; Independence, forty-five members; total, one hundred and fifty-three members.

This organization was started about a year ago, with Wesley Van Gosken as Chief Engineer. In his last report, he states the personal property of department to consist of the following: Three hose-carriages; thirteen hundred feet antiseptic gum-hose; six hose-pipes; six lanterns; four hundred feet of rope; five carriage-spanners; five speaking-trumpets.

WILLIAM BROWN'S RESIDENCE.

This is the largest private residence in Shamokin, and is, at least, deserving of a passing notice.

The building is fifty-four feet square and five stories high, with a slate-roof. It is a brick structure of a very imposing appearance, situated on the corners of Arch, Lincoln and Market streets. The building contains forty-six rooms, well laid out with halls, closets, etc.

It was erected by a number of lot-owners in 1854, for the purpose of a hotel. In 1858, Mr. Longenecker purchased it, and resided there for several years. Previous to Mr. Longenecker occupying it, it had been used for church fairs, dancing-schools, etc.

A few years ago, Mr. Brown purchased the property and had it finished. The first story is used for store purposes; the second and third stories are used by Mr. Brown for a residence, whilst the fourth and fifth stories are unoccupied.

The following description of this truly elegant place, which is at once a model of convenience and an ornament to the borough, is taken from the *Shamokin Herald*:—

"It is always a pleasure to note improvements in our town, but more especially so when they are of a first-class character, such as we are about to describe. The very large and increasing drug and hardware trade of Major W. R. Kutzner, long since convinced him that he must have more room, and accordingly, early last Fall, he commenced an addition to his building, corner of Sunbury and Shamokin street, to be devoted exclusively to the hardware branch of the business, which heretofore was associated with the drug trade, having drugs on one side of the room and hardware on the other. The new addition corresponds in outward appearance with the old building, is three stories high, press-brick front, and is thirty-two feet wide by ninety-three feet deep, making, with the old building, a frontage of fifty-seven feet, and the largest business house in Shamokin. We enter the main salesroom of the new store through a French plate-glass front, the two large show windows of which are lighted by six glasses, three to each window, each glass being forty-eight inches wide by one hundred and thirty-three long. The sash and doors are grained walnut. The floor of the entrance between the show windows is laid with black and white tiles. Entering we stand in a room twenty-nine feet wide by eighty-nine feet deep in the clear. The first objects that arrest one's attention, are the gracefully poised stairway leading to the second and third floors, the book-keeper's office and the arched entrance to the drug store. The counters (except the tops, which are of oiled ash) and shelving are grained oak. The two front counters contain twelve show-cases each, all with French plate tops set in the counter, and under each is a drawer which may be easily removed with the entire contents of the case. On the right, as you enter, are eight cases with glass doors displaying silver-ware, guns, etc. Under the rear counters are numerous nail-bins, with the respective sizes painted on, and so arranged that the customer can see and examine for himself. The shelves and drawers back of the counters are arranged in the most convenient manner; there are in all two hundred and sixty drawers, each bearing a label of contents. We now enter the book-keeper's office, near the rear end on the right-hand side. It is a cosy, neatly furnished, seven by ten feet room, wainscoted with oiled chestnut, and has a handsome glass front. Here our friend, Mr. A. G. Goodwill presides. He is very proud of his new cage. From this, we enter Major Kutzner's private office, immediately in rear of the book-keeper's. It is ten by twelve and finished and furnished similar to the one we have just described. Back of this office, is a roomy fire and burglar-proof vault. Leaving the offices, we enter through a door in rear end of the salesroom, and on a level with it, into the oil cellar, which is ten by fifteen feet, with floor and sides cemented, sheet-iron roof, and lighted by three sky-lights. The oil is kept in patent cans. This arrangement is a great convenience. Much light is had in the main salesroom from a large sky-light running through the centre of the building. At night, it is lighted by five chandeliers, three in the room proper, and one in each show-window. This room is connected with the drug-store by an arched doorway. We now ascend to the second floor up the handsome stairway, with walnut rail and oiled ash balusters. The second floor is equal in size to the lower room, well-lighted, and largely stocked with wooden and willow-ware, glass, children's carriages, clover and timothy seed, etc. The third-floor room is similar in size and appearance to the one we have just left, and contains a large stock of farming implements, mine supplies, etc. The building is heated by a furnace in the cellar."

SHAMOKIN IN THE WAR.

Shamokin has ever evinced a military spirit, and the part taken by her in the late Rebellion is a proud record of martial deeds. She was represented in a large number of regiments, and on almost every battle-field. Soon after the town was laid out, a military company was formed, known as the Shamokin Grays, numbering about seventy men, rank and file, commanded by Captain Charles Derring, who, after some years, was succeeded by Captain F. A. Clark, and finally by Captain J. L. Gilger, who retained the command until the company disbanded, which was about nine years after its formation. Several battalions was held at Shamokin, during the existence of this company, on which occasions, majors and brigade inspectors appeared in their best regimentals to great advantage. At one of these battalions, held in June, 1846, an effort was made to obtain volunteers for Mexico, which did not result very favorably, as only one soldier stepped out for the Mexican campaign.

SHAMOKIN GUARDS.

During 1854, a new company of the above name was formed, with S. M. Kase, as captain. Captain Kase was soon succeeded by Captain Reeder, who being elected brigadier-general, was followed by Captain Cyrus Strouse, a most excellent soldier. Upon the call for troops, at the breaking out of the Rebellion, the Shamokin Guards nobly responded to the call.

On April 16th, 1861, the citizens of the town held a meeting to assist the "Guard," in filling up their company. Speeches were made by A. R. Fiske, W. P. Withington, and Alexander Caldwell, and measures taken to assist the families as enlisted. The compliment was made up the same evening, numbering one hundred and eight men, rank and file. The following is the muster roll of the National Guard:

Captain, C. Strouse; 1st Lieutenant, William J. Allen; 2d Lieutenant, George B. Cadwallader; Brevet 2d Lieutenant, George Shiff; Orderly Sergeant, John Harris; 2d Sergeant, A. Kreeger; 3d Sergeant, John B. Snyder; 4th Sergeant, Ferd. Rhodes.

Privates—Jacob B. Rhoads, Jacob Meutchler, Israel Stambach, William P. Caldwell, Alexander Caldwell, Henry Startzel, Cyrus Bittenbender, Michael Dooley, Frederick Dipner, Michael Salter, Charles Kreeger, David Shiff, Thomas R. Williams, William Booth, Jacob Getter, William Culp, William Colier, John Colier, Thomas Harris, Henry Holshoe, Patrick Colier, Charles Conrad, Jacob W. Irich, Henry Irich, Hugh Boyd, William Stillwagner, Michael Melsberger, John Meighan, John Hancock, John B. Zuender, Thomas Caldwell, John E. Eisenhart, C. L. V. Haas, John R. Lake, Jacob Dindorf, Peter Wentz, Frank Baronosky, Ephraim Folk, William Shock, John Brennan, Nicholas Curn, James Durms, Jacob Guskey, David Eveland, Wesley Van Gasken, James H. Haas, Guy McCulley, John Weis, Francis Toby, Benjamin Culp, P. P. Dunaren, J. B. Eaton, John Neufer, Charles Brand, H. C. Bolst, D. J. Woodley, John W. Heilner, William Bone, Charles Morganes, Daniel Jones, William Smith, Charles Madon, John Doronis, August Schensil, William B. Osman, Samuel Clouser, Reuben Mullen, Samuel Barnesley, Joel Holshoe, Jacob Peiper, William Farrell, Moses Reed, John Hartline, Benjamin Crist, Jacob Shiel, Jonas Holston, John McCulley, John Lannan, J. M. John, Josiah Roup, George Roup, Michael Regan, James Sterret, Francis Hollister, Michael Dawson, John McManns, George W. Weaver, George Kramer, Jeremiah Maize, George Blankeley, J. W. Philips, John Shillehood, J. Pennypacker, John Vanzant, Daniel Money, Ziba Bird, Thomas R. Jones, G. Klase, and B. F. Lake.

On Sunday morning, the company attended services at the Methodist Church, which was festooned with the stars and stripes, and listened to a patriotic sermon, suitable to the occasion, by Rev. Mr. Dixon. During the evening they attended services at the Presbyterian Church, and were eloquently addressed by Rev. A. D'Huron, the pastor, and the Revs. Wampole, and Swenk, of the Lutheran and United Brethren Churches. On Monday morning, April 22d, they took their departure for Harrisburg. Hundreds of people from the town and the neighboring townships had assembled to witness their departure, and to give them a good-bye. They arrived at Harrisburg the same day, and were at once marched to Camp Curtin, where they were formed in the Eighth regiment, as company A. The next day they were hurried on to Chambersburg, and entered into quarters at Camp Slifer. Their trip from Shamokin all the way to Chambersburg, was a perfect ovation; refreshments were supplied by the people at the different towns, and the greatest enthusiasm prevailed. They were placed under the command of General Robert Patterson. On June 9th, they moved to Camp Emely, about seven miles from Hagerstown. From this point, Colonel Caldwell will take up the narrative, and pursue it through the whole Rebellion. Having been one of that devoted band of veterans that served through the entire war, one of the heroes of the gallant Forty-sixth, that followed the victorious Sherman in his glorious march to the Sea, none are better prepared to relate their martial record. And he has done it well. Not a comrade has been overlooked, not an engagement forgotten, and he "fights his battles o'er," as though they occurred but yesterday.

Soon after their arrival at "Camp Emley," the Eighth regiment, to which the Shamokin Guard (company A) was attached, was ordered to Williamsport, Maryland. Orders were received to have three days' cooked rations in haversacks, and to be prepared for a forward movement. By the time the rations had been stowed away in haversacks, came orders to "strike tents." This order was hailed with delight, for, novices in the art of war, the command was anxious to meet the enemy.

The Eighth regiment was ordered to escort Captain (now Major-General) Doubleday's thirty-pounder battery to Martinsburg, then in possession of our army. The battle of Falling Waters—simply an affair of outposts—had been fought and won; the way had been opened by the advance-guard, so that the work of occupation for the Eighth regiment was only a hard march—no glory, no scars. From Martinsburg, the company—the right of the Eighth—marched to Bunker Hill; from thence to Charlestown, where it remained about ten days. The battle of Bull Run having been fought and lost, and the term of the troops comprising General Patterson's column having nearly expired, the command was withdrawn to Keep Ferry, on the Shenandoah River; thence to Harper's Ferry, and from there, via Baltimore, to Harrisburg, where they were mustered out of the service. By the expiration of the term of service of the three-months' troops, the curtain fell upon the first act of the great drama of war—a war in which the Shamokin Guard acted a prominent part; a war which resulted in the emancipation of a race—the striking off the shackles of four millions of human beings.

The company having returned to their homes, the work of recruiting for "three years or during the war," begun in earnest, as the results of the three-months' campaign had demonstrated that this was to be no ordinary war.

On the 20th of August, 1861, the ranks were nearly full, with the following officers: Captain, Cyrus Strouse; 1st Lieutenant, G. B. Cadwallader; 2d Lieutenant, William P. Caldwell. The company rendezvoused at "Camp Curtin," where, on the 4th day of September, 1861, it was mustered into the service of the United States by Captain D. H. Hastings, United States Army, and assigned to the Forty-sixth regiment, Pennsylvania Volunteers as company K, Colonel Joseph F. Knipe.

Having remained in camp of instruction for about six weeks, the regiment was ordered to Washington; thence to "Camp Kalorama," where it remained a short time, and from there, one stormy Saturday night, marched for Darnestown, western Maryland, where it was assigned to the brigade of General A. S. Williams, of Michigan, Major-General N. P. Banks' division.

The usual routine of duty pertaining to a camp of instruction was here instituted; drills were regularly established; camp and picket duty rigidly enforced, thus to prepare the command for the *serious* work of the impending campaign. (As the Shamokin Guard was now part and parcel of the Forty-Sixth regiment, Pennsylvania Volunteers, with whose history it was identified during the whole struggle, it will not be necessary to mention it as a company, save recording the number of its killed and wounded.) With the exception of an occasional picket *rencontre*, nothing occurred to break the monotony of camp life, until the day of the battle of Balls' Bluff. For several days the air had been thick with rumors of impending battle, but with the "happy-go-lucky" disposition so characteristic of the soldier engaged in the desperate game of war, they were passed by unheeded, until about twilight of that bloody day, when a courier, who had been riding post-haste, brought the news of the disaster to our arms, of the death of the gallant Baker, and the urgent need of assistance. With the exception of the head-quarters, the command was, of course, in ignorance of what was in progress, and when the order came to prepare for a forward movement, long and loud were the shouts that went up—for soldiers soon get tired of camp-life, with its restrictions, and long for a change. The change in this case came, alas, to soon. The distance from Darnestown to Poolesville is about twenty-three miles, and all night long the troops marched steadily forward, and cheerfully, for, as they neared the scene of the disaster, couriers from the front brought the ominous news of defeat, and they longed to wipe out the disgrace. At Poolesville, the command had its first look at the *dark* side of war. Long trains of ambulances, laden with the crushed and broken forms of those who, in the early morning, were all buoyant with life, and the hopes that young life begets were hurrying to the rear, thus confirming the story of defeat. Notwithstanding the cheerless outlook, the men went gallantly forward, no stragglers, all impatient to close with the foe. Bivouacking on the field, near the river, the rain falling in torrents, the wearied troops sought such repose as they could find, and "eagerly awaited the morrow."

After a hurried breakfast, the column was formed, and the roll called. Arms were then stacked, and orders to march waited for. The day was passed in expectation of getting marching orders, varied by watching our skirmishers on the southern bank of the Potomac, engaging the enemy on the battle-field of the day before. At twilight the orders came, the regiment was formed, on the river bank, but the order to cross was countermanded, General McClellan having arrived on the scene. From Ball's Bluff the command was ordered to their old encampments, where they remained until late in the Fall of 1861, when they were ordered to Frederick. Here they remained in camp of instruction until Winter, when they marched to Hancock, on the Potomac, to aid in repelling the threatened invasion by Stonewall Jackson. Jackson having retreated, the command went into Winter-quarters, and in the early Spring marched to Williamsport, crossed the Potomac, and entered on its first *real* campaign in the Shenandoah Valley. The Shamokin Guard, company K, was one of the advance skirmishing companies in the "affair" at Bunker Hill, Va., and entered Winchester on the 11th of March, 1862. Remaining at Winchester a short time, the command was ordered to march to Warrenton, via Berryville and Berry's Ferry, on the Shenandoah. They had proceeded as far as the latter place, when couriers brought the news of Shield's battle at Winchester, and asking assistance. The movement on Warrenton was abandoned, the column was faced toward Winchester, and, after a long night-march, arrived on the field, and took the advance in pursuit of the retreating enemy. In this night-march, the Shamokin Guard were in the extreme advance. The pursuit of Jackson ended at Port Republic. After a week's delay, the command returned to the vicinity of Woodstock, where it remained for several weeks. Jackson, having been reinforced, came down the Luray Valley, and threatened our communication with the rear. The command fell back to Strasburgh, and there awaited developments. Captain Strouse was at the latter place, presiding at a court-martial. The command having received orders to proceed at a forced march to Middletown, passed hurriedly through the town of Strasburgh, and on to Middletown, where, assisted by Woodberry's Battery M, of the First New York Artillery, it repulsed the enemy, who had interposed across its line of march, and pushed on to Winchester, the objective, and took position on the right of the road to Front Royal. Here it bivouacked for the night, the men lying on their arms, thoroughly wearied, trying, in a few fitful hours of repose, to gain strength for the impending conflict. Long before the day had dawned, the reveille was beaten, and the roll called. The wearied men partook of a hurried breakfast. The bright rays of the morning sun dispelled the fog, which had settled over the field, (it had rained the day before,) and out of the dissolving mist came the bright flash of the enemy's guns, posted on a ridge about half a mile away, on the Front Royal road, the hurling of shot and the whistling of shell telling that the *second* battle of Winchester had begun. Battery F, Fourth United States Artillery, commanded by the brave Lieutenant Cushing, afterwards slain at Gettysburg, replied to the enemy, and for a short time the artillery had it all to themselves. This was, however, of short duration, for Jackson, knowing our strength, advanced his infantry, and then came the "tug of war."

Company M occupied the extreme right of the First Brigade. For a while, they acted as skirmishers, but the enemy advancing rapidly, and in force, they were recalled and fought in the *line* during the continuance of the engagement. The men fought splendidly, and soon repulsed the foe. In this contest, the Forty-sixth regiment was pitted against the Twenty-seventh North Carolina, and the numbers of new-made graves, afterward counted on the field of this brief, but desperate struggle, showed how well the regiment could fight, and was an earnest of its future achievements.

As the only object in engaging the overwhelming force of the enemy was, to cover the withdrawal of our large trains, and the enemy, with his superior force, having seriously menaced our flank, thus jeopardizing our line of retreat, the troops were withdrawn in good order, and with little opposition, made good their retrograde movement to the Potomac and across to Williamsport. There was no demoralization, as the humblest private soldier in the command knew that the enemy outnumbered them three to one, but, as this was the test of their bravery, they nobly responded to the orders of their chief. This, their first serious lesson in the art of war, made the men self-reliant, and they never disgraced the record made on their maiden-field. A short halt on the north bank of the river, to repair damages and bring up material; thence across the swollen stream one stormy Saturday night, company K in the advance, as usual, on to Martinsburg, to Winchester, which the enemy had hurriedly evacuated (as a force was coming down on their flank from Fredericksburg and from Romney), thence over the battle-field of the 25th of May, to Front Royal, on the Shenandoah. The usual round of camp and picket duties, and a reconnoissance up the Luray Valley, kept the troops employed for several weeks, when camp was struck, and the line of march taken up for Warrenton, and thence to Culpepper Court House. Major-General John Pope was, about this time, assigned to the command of the "Army of Virginia."

Except a reconnoissance toward Gordonville, nothing occurred to vary the monotony of camp life, until the afternoon of the 8th of August. The enemy having become unusually bold, General Bayard was ordered to push them back with his cavalry. This he accomplished; but when he reached Cedar Run, about nine miles out from Culpepper, he found the enemy strongly posted, and he asked for reinforcements. The First Brigade, to which the Forty-sixth regiment was attached, was at once ordered forward to his support. After a very fatiguing march, they reached the field about six o'clock in the evening. Here they bivouacked for the night.

Strong columns of infantry being pushed forward, developed the fact that the advance guard of Lee's army, under Stonewall Jackson, was in the immediate front. If Lee's advance was to be checked, in order to allow the army of the Potomac time to reach Washington first, here is where it was to be done. All knew that the struggle on the morrow was to be desperate, yet all were cheerful. With the exception of the usual skirmishing for position and to gain time, nothing serious occurred until about three o'clock in the afternoon of the 9th, when the bugles sounded the assembly, the troops "fell in," took arms, and were ready for the fray.

The First Brigade was sent to the *right*, company K occupying the extreme right of the line. The day was extremely hot, and the men suffered considerably. They were formed in the edge of the woods, a wheat-field in their front. Beyond the wheat-field was a dense pine woods, filled with a thick undergrowth. In this woods the enemy was strongly posted, but concealed. On a road running diagonally through the woods was a six-gun battery. This battery the Forty-sixth regiment was ordered to take. With a cheer, their colors well to the front, they advanced in battle-line, cleared the fences, and in one grand, magnificent charge, swept the enemy back to and across the road. But that passage across the wheat-field cost them terribly, and when they reached the battery, finding themselves unsupported and outflanked, they were compelled to relinquish what they had won and retire from the field, which they did in good order. Although the line was broken and the command somewhat scattered, yet there was no panic, the men, after a display of magnificent gallantry, only retiring before an overwhelming force of the enemy. Cedar Mountain has passed into history; all the historians of the war classing it among the most desperately-fought battles of the whole struggle.

Company K received its baptism of fire on the wooded slopes of this new historic mountain. The company went into action with forty-five men and two officers. It came out with no officers and twenty-six men. The action did not last more than two hours, so far as company K and the Forty-sixth regiment was concerned, yet the loss was very heavy. Among the killed, were the gallant Lieutenant William P. Caldwell, who commanded the company; the brave Sergeant James H. Hass; the heroic Corporal Shock; and those true soldiers, Coder, Titsworth, Eurich, Gillinger, Arter, and Werzkowski.

Among the wounded, were 2d Lieutenant Alexander Caldwell, and those brave soldiers, Sergeant Gilger, Corporal Shipp, Corporal McEllen, Sergeant Thomas Caldwell, Corporal J. Weimer Young, and Privates Paul, Sharp, Roth, Bird, Donovan, and Neufer.* Heroes all, they paid with their young lives "their full measure of devotion" to Liberty, having offered themselves a willing sacrifice on the altar of Freedom. As incidents of the battle of "Cedar Mountain," let us quote the opinions of eye-witnesses of the struggle:

"I have witnessed many battles during this war, but I have seen none where the tenacious obstinacy of the American character was so fully displayed," says one correspondent.

Lossing says: "None were more desperately fought during the war. A part of the sanguinary struggle was hand-to-hand, under the dark pall of smoke that obscured the moon."

At the close of the battle, "Banks' Division" was a thing of the past. The flower of the command were either dead or wounded; the shattered remnant sadly buried their comrades, and vowed eternal fealty to the Republic. In this desperate fight, 1st Lieutenant Caldwell was shot dead at the head of his column. 2d Lieutenant Caldwell was wounded through the

PLATE XXII

RES. OF JOHN EYSTER, DISTILLER, DELAWARE TP., NORTH'D CO., PA.

RES. OF JOHN NIGELY, DELAWARE TP., NORTHUMBERLAND CO., PA.

thigh, had five bullets through his coat, and one through his haversack. 1st Sergeant Gilger was wounded through the right arm; he was again wounded at Gettysburg (while on the staff of Brigadier-General Knipe) by a fragment of shell in the same arm, making him a cripple for life. Sergeant James H. Haas was mortally wounded, and lived only long enough to regret that he had no more lives to give to the Union. The brave Gillinger went down, with "three cheers for the Union" on his lips. Corporal Shipp was terribly hurt, his shoulder having been almost shot away. He was captured by the enemy and taken to Staunton, where a *capital* operation was performed upon him. He lived through it; was taken to Libby Prison, and was finally exchanged. Private Roth had five bullets in his person; Private Tharp five; Private Arter, five, and Private Werzkowski five. Had the leaden compliments been more equally distributed, company K would not have suffered so much. The soldiers who were *not* hurt, deserve as much credit as those who *were*, for never in the history of the war did men march more gallantly into the smoke and flame of battle. Reinforcements having arrived, the battle-scarred remnant of Banks' Division marched back to their camp; regiments commanded by captains; companies by non-commissioned officers.

The enemy allowed but little time for rest The result of the fight at Cedar Mountain having demonstrated the fact that Lee's entire army was marching on Washington, Pope's column fell back to the line of the Rappahannock. Company K participated in the series of engagements on the Rappahannock, ending with the second battle of Bull's Run, August 29th, 1862. From Bull's Run to South Mountain, and on to Antietam. At this battle the column to which company K was assigned, fought under the lamented Mansfield, at the famous Dunker Church, one of the key-points of the fight. Here the brave Charles Brandt was killed, and privates Epler and Barinoske wounded, the latter losing his arm. From Antietam to Maryland heights, where the command was reorganized and assigned to the Twelfth Army Corps—Major General Slocum. About two months in camp, doing only the routine duty that pertains to all camps, whether of instruction or of temporary location, thence to Fairfax station, and on to Stafford Court House, where the command went into winter-quarters. In the latter part of April, 1863, the command crossed the Rappahannock at Kelly's ford, and the Rapidanna, at "Germania ford," and marched to Chancellorsville where it participated in the battles of the 1st, 2d, and 3d of May. The engagement having resulted in the defeat of our army, the command was ordered to its old camps at Stafford Court House. The halt here was of short duration, for Lee, encouraged by his success at Chancellorsville, determined to invade Maryland and Pennsylvania. When the invasion had become a fixed fact, the column to which company K was attached, marched by way of Dumfries and the Occoquan, to Fairfax Court House. A halt here for a day, then on to Leesburg, as a corps of observation. A short halt here, only long enough to learn the intention of the enemy, then across the Potomac at Nolan's ferry, thence to the Monocacy and Frederick City, Maryland. The command was halted at Frederick only long enough for the wagons to come up. The advance guard of Lee's army having pushed forward as far as York, the command was ordered to pursue. Forced marches were the order of the day, and with weary limbs, but buoyant spirits, the troops pushed steadily forward, and on the 30th of June, (in the afternoon,) struck a portion of Ewell's column, which was falling back from York, at the village of Littlestown, about ten miles from Gettysburg.

The enemy's force was soon brushed out of the way, and the command bivouacked for the night. Early the next morning, July 1st, the head of column was put in motion, toward Gettysburg. Arrived at the "Two Taverns," about midway between Gettysburg and Littlestown, arms were stacked, and the men ordered to prepare their dinner. As dinner on the march, in close proximity to the enemy, is not usually an elaborate affair, this did not consume much time. While lying along the road, the rebel brigade of General Archer passed to the rear prisoners of war. This was evidence sufficient that the enemy was in force in the front, and soon the heavy boom of artillery, and the smoke rising from the plain below, told in unmistakable terms, that the battle of Gettysburg had begun. Gettysburg! ah, what memories cluster around the name. A battle, whose results not only stayed the tide of invasion, but saved the nation; a battle which was the turning-point of the war, for here perished the flower of the "Army of Northern Virginia."

The position of company K was on the extreme right of the First Brigade, First Division, Twelfth Army Corps. The position was one of great natural strength, being on the slope of a wooded ridge among the rocks. Although assailed by the enemy in heavy force, the line did not waver, but poured a stream of fire into the faces of the foe. To the strong position occupied by the command, can be attributed the fact that company K did not lose a man killed, in all the three days' fight. Toward evening of the second days' battle, the command was withdrawn from their position and sent to reinforce the extreme left. As the enemy had been repulsed, they were not put into action, but were ordered to occupy their first position. During their absence, the enemy had pushed his skirmishers into the position occupied by the Brigade, and had not darkness made his movements very cautious, the result of the battle might have been vastly different. It was only after a severe struggle in the early morning of the 3d, that he was dislodged, and forced to yield the advantages he had gained by their withdrawal. When the grand assault on the centre was made, in the afternoon of the 3d, the command (a thin skirmish-line having been left to occupy the barricades which had been hastily thrown up) was sent to reinforce the Second Corps, and occupied a position to the left of the "cemetery." Their services not having been needed, they remained in this position until the shattered remnant of Longstreet's column, flying from the field, proclaimed that the battle of Gettysburg was fought and won.

The morning of the 4th of July found the command back in their original position. After burying the rebel dead, in their immediate front, a reconnoissance was ordered around and through Gettysburg, company K occupying the right of the line. From Gettysburg back again to Littlestown, through Frederick City, across the South Mountain at Crampton's Pass, over the field of Antietam, when the column closed up on the left of the Army of the Potomac, near St. James' College, in front of Williamsport, Maryland. Lee having effected his retreat across the river at "Falling Waters," and at Williamsport, the command marched to Sandy Hook, opposite Harper's Ferry, where it rested a few days. Thence across the Potomac and Shenandoah Rivers, at Harper's Ferry, through Thoroughfare Gap to Warrenton Junction, and on to Kelly's ford, on the Rappahannock. Here the enemy was found in possession of the south bank of the river. Bivouacked for the night, and in the early morning pushed the enemy from the ford, and crossed to the opposite side. Remained on the southern bank for several days, when they were recalled, and went into camp to rest and refit for the next campaign.

While in camp at Kelly's ford, company K received twenty-five (25) conscripts, which again filled up the ranks pretty well. These conscripts were principally from the vicinity of New Brighton, on the Allegheny River. General Meade having ordered an advance of the whole army, the column was put in motion, and took up position at the Raccoon ford of the Rapidanna River, to the left and in advance of Culpepper Court House. Here it remained until about the 25th day of July, when orders came from the head-quarters of the army, ordering the Twelfth Corps to march to Brandy Station. Of course, the subalterns knew nothing about the movement, but every one supposed that a reconnoissance in force was on foot. But when the command reached Brandy Station, and wagons were ordered to be left behind, they soon ascertained that they were going to reinforce the Army of the Cumberland, via the Baltimore and Ohio Railroad, to Benwood, below Wheeling, across the Ohio, on a pontoon bridge, to the town of Bellair.

The scenery through Western Virginia, was of the grandest description. The transition from the wasted fields of Virginia to the picturesque mountain region, along and over which their route lay, infused new life into the troops, and, though this was no holiday excursion, the spirits of the men *rose* with each new scene, and all was *life* and jollity.

From Bellair to Columbus, from Columbus to Indianapolis, to Jeffersonville, across the Ohio to Louisville, and on to Nashville, Tennessee. The trip across the great States of Ohio and Indiana was a grand ovation; the citizens along the route seeming to vie with each other in their attention to the troops. If there were any in the great crowds which welcomed the men from the Potomac, who would much rather have greeted the "men in gray," they prudently held their peace. The great heart of the people was true to the *cause;* and many encouraging smiles and words of good cheer did the "boys" get from the fair daughters of Ohio and Indiana. The battle of Chickamauga had been fought, and resulted disastrously to our arms—hence the transfer of the Eleventh and Twelfth Corps to the banks of the Tennessee, with General Hooker in command. The Eleventh and Twelfth Corps were consolidated and designated the Twentieth Corps. The rebel General Wheeler, having made a raid into Tennessee, thus threatening our line of communication, the command was hurried forward to War-trace, on the line of the Nashville and Chattanooga Railroad. Here a portion of the command was ordered to Shelbyville, for the purpose of intercepting Wheeler, but he and his rough-riders had retreated and recrossed the Tennessee. From

Shelbyville to Decherd, where the Forty-sixth regiment was stationed during the Winter of 1863. Scouting and picket duty, with occasional incursions into the country, in search of the guerilla bands that infested the strip of territory lying between the Tennessee and the Elk Rivers, made the Winter months pass rapidly. But when the grass began to grow in the Spring, the command was ordered to be in readiness for a forward movement.

General Sherman, having been assigned to the command of the "military division of the Mississippi," after the battle of Chattanooga, had determined on a campaign against Atlanta, the great railroad centre, and one of the chief manufacturing cities of the South. At Atlanta, were cast the shot and shell, and the plating for gunboats, forged for a great portion of the armies and navy of the Confederacy.

The orders were to rendezvous at Chattanooga; therefore, about the 30th of April, the camp was "struck," and the line of march taken up for Chattanooga. Across the Cumberland Mountains, that giant chain which bisects Tennessee, and on to Bridgeport; thence to Shellmound, to Wauhatchie—the scene of Geary's desperate night encounter with Longstreet—round the point of "Lookout," and thence to Chattanooga. From Chattanooga, on the 6th of May, 1864, began the grand campaign which culminated in the capture of Atlanta, that great arsenal of the Southern Confederacy. At a terrible cost, however, for among the gorges of the mountains of northern Georgia sleep in death many of the bravest and best of the young men of the North. The Twelfth Corps was deflected from Dalton, and debouched from Snake Creek Gap on the 13th of May, and took position on the left, closing well in toward the Tilton road, which leads from Dalton to Resaca. The 14th was spent in skirmishing for position, but at nightfall, the Fourth Army Corps, General Howard, having asked for reinforcements, the First division, General A. S. Williams, was hurried to their assistance, and arrived in time to drive back the enemy, who had nearly turned Howard's flank. The fight was short, sharp, and decisive, and the wearied troops bivouacked on the field they had so gallantly won.

About noon of the 15th of May, Sunday, orders came to "fall in." From the ridge, which they had taken the night before, the Forty-sixth marched to an open space on the road. The regiment was formed in columns of divisions, *en masse*, company K, being the right of the First division, and in the extreme advance. They were ordered to charge down the Tilton road, and take a battery, which was annoying our troops, and right gallantly did they respond to the call, taking the charging step as handsomely as if on parade. They had reached an angle in the road, and were pushing forward rapidly, when a fire from the flank caused a change in the order; the column was deployed, front changed, and over a wooded slope the brigade charged, driving the enemy before them in handsome style. All day long the men fought magnificently, and when night hid the combatants, the battle of Resaca had been fought and won by the Nationals.

The wearied soldiers threw themselves upon the ground to seek a few hours of much needed repose. The stars came out in the sky, and shone peacefully upon the soldiers, living and dead, upon friend and foe. With their faces upturned to the sky, lay the broken and bruised forms of hundreds, who, in the flush of young manhood, had that pleasant May afternoon, flung themselves upon the enemy's works. The enemy gave us a parting fusillade about midnight, and then precipitately fled, leaving their dead and many wounded in our hands.

In the battle of Resaca, company K did not suffer much, as the position was on the top of a ridge, and was superior to that of the enemy. The only casualties were several men slightly wounded.

Private Joseph McCarty had a narrow escape, a rifle-ball having passed through his waist-belt, through eight thicknesses of his rubber blanket, and finally, flattening on his coat button. The ball did not penetrate the skin, and he fought all through the engagement. After burying the dead, and caring for the wounded, the command pressed on across the Ostenaula and Coosawattie rivers, in close pursuit of Johnson, and in the afternoon of the —— came upon the enemy in battle array at Cassville. The enemy had intended to give battle, but during the night, fell back across the Etowah, and took position in the wooded country about Allatoona Pass, New Hope Church and Dallas. A short halt was made here, to allow supplies to be brought forward, as well as to allow the men the rest they so much needed; as they had been marching, skirmishing, and fighting continually since the 6th of May. On the 23d, the march was resumed, and in the evening of that day, the command was across the Etowah; the next night they bivouacked at "Burnt Hickory." Early in the morning of the 25th, Williams' division of the now Twentieth Army Corps, marched out in the direction of Dallas, company K, of the Forty-six regiment, in the extreme advance, as skirmishers. The command pushed steadily forward, not meeting with much opposition, when about four o'clock, P. M., an order was received to halt the skirmishers, and retire on the main column. This was done at once, and with company K as rear guard, the column hurriedly retraced its steps. When near the bridge, which spanned Pumpkin-Vine Creek, the order for the retrograde movement was fully explained.

Artillery was planted, covering the bridge, and over it at a run went the gallant fellows, though wearied through the exertions of the morning. While reconnoitering on the western side of the bridge, General Hooker had suddenly come upon the enemy in force, near the New Hope Church. Using his escort, he kept the enemy at bay until General Gray's division could be brought up. They passed the bridge, and engaged the enemy, but finding him in heavy force, they took position until the division of Williams could be brought up. The strange coincidence occurred here which has often occurred in wooded countries, where the opposing commanders are not well informed as to the topography: Johnson was manœuvring for position at the same time that Sherman was making his movement on Dallas, the *objective* of the latter being the Allatoona Pass, a strong defensive position, through which ran the railroad from Chattanooga to Atlanta. The First Division was at once deployed, the Forty-Sixth Regiment going in on the right of the First Brigade. With lines well dressed, and ranks well closed up, the column advanced rapidly, driving the enemy's skirmishers, and soon came upon the main body, strongly entrenched, occupying a strong natural position, with artillery well posted and supported. When well up to the enemy's works, a terrible storm of grape and canister, shell and shrapnel, was poured on the advancing column, which caused them to halt. Again and again the attempt was made to carry the enemy's position, but as often was it repulsed, and when night came the battered column was relieved by fresh troops, and bivouacked a short distance to the rear of the position they had so gallantly maintained during the afternoon. From the position occupied by our troops, it was impossible to bring artillery into action, while the enemy, with his artillery entrenched, and in good positions, opened great gaps in our lines.

By the explosion of a shell in the lines of company K, 2d Lieutenant John W. Phillips was killed, the left side of his head being shot away. 1st Lieutenant Jacob B. Getter was severely wounded in the leg by a grape-shot or a fragment of shell, and Corporal John Raup had both legs carried away by a grape-shot. Always heroic in action, he was doubly a hero in this fight; for though terribly hurt, he urged his comrades to leave him where he fell, and avenge him. Brave fellow; death put an end to his sufferings, and he sleeps side by side with the gallant Lieutenant Phillips, on that Georgia hill-side. Comrades in life, they were not separated in death. Private Elias Maurer was wounded severely; others slightly. The brave Corporal John Medlycott, though suffering from a severe wound in the arm, received at Resaca, came into the fight when the battle was raging the fiercest, and although remonstrated with, and requested to go to the rear, laughingly replied "that he wanted to see what was going on." His own gun having been turned over to the ordnance officer, (as he was unable to carry it,) he took a musket from a rebel prisoner, and used it until the close of the engagement. This is an illustration of *pluck*. After the withdrawal of the command from the front, line was formed and the roll called. After a battle, this is always a sad duty. Familiar forms are missing; comrades who have stood shoulder to shoulder on many hard-fought fields, who have felt that touch of the elbow which has nerved them in many a desperate conflict, are now sleeping the sleep that knows no waking, or are stretched on beds of suffering in the hastily improvised hospitals. As if to wipe out all traces of the conflict, all the blood-stains which crimsoned mother earth, who was about to take back again to her bosom her dead ones, slain in freedom's holy cause, the rain fell steadily during the night succeeding the battle. "New Hope Church" had passed into history; on the wings of the death-angel had passed to the good Father the spirits of patriots, as true as ever died for Liberty.

The battle was not renewed in the morning, though all was in readiness, and the armies, National and Confederate, contented themselves with watching each other. This state of affairs continued for several days, when the Twentieth Corps swung to the left toward the railroad. Communication with the rear having been established, the command again moved forward, skirmishing continually, sometimes far into the night. During this memorable campaign, the men slept on their arms every night, ready for anything that might occur, as the country was mountainous and densely wooded, and the enemy contested every foot of ground.

On the 22d of June, when turning "Kenesaw," and trying to find the left flank of the foe, the First Division of the Twentieth Corps encountered Stewart's Division, of Wood's Corps, on the Powder Springs road, near the Kulp House. The battle was a sharp, and so far as the Nationals were concerned, a decisive one. The enemy left his dead and many of his wounded on the field. The battle of the Kulp House resulted not only in victory to the Union arms, but it compelled the evacuation of Kenesaw and Manetta, and all the country north of the Chattahoochee, and gave us the *railroad.* The railroad was our "cracker line," and as an old war maxim says, that an "army marches on its belly," this was all important. Kulp's farm, or Kulp's house was an easy victory for the National troops, as the enemy came out of his entrenchments, and was the *attacking* party. The Forty-sixth regiment occupied a small elevation in full view of the rebel lines. They supported Woodberry's Battery M, 1st New York Artillery, the guns being placed at intervals in the line, thus allowing the infantry no opportunity of firing. Company K was on the right of the line, connecting with the One Hundred and Fiftieth New York regiment.

The rebels advanced to the attack several times in magnificent order, but were as many times repulsed, and finally withdrew. In this battle, Private William Jones was killed. Two days before June 20th, Private Zancoler was shot dead while in the act of pouring water on Captain Caldwell's hands. Always thoughtful of others, his last act was one of kindness. Peace to his ashes.

From Manetta, across the Chattahoochee, and on to "Peach-tree Creek." Hood, having succeeded Johnson in command of the Confederates, attacked the Twentieth Corps, while making the passage of the Peach-tree Creek, on the 20th of July. He assaulted vigorously, expecting no doubt to catch the command in the "air," but he was sadly mistaken. To quote his own words, he says, "I attacked the enemy while making the passage of Peach-tree Creek, hoping by a vigorous assault to break his lines, separate his columns, and beat him in detail." He also says, that instead of finding the column in the confusion incident to the crossing of a stream, whose banks were as marshy as those of Peach-tree Creek, "I found there, (at the point of attack,) the veteran Twentieth Army Corps from the Potomac."

The battle raged fiercely all that hot July afternoon, and when darkness fell upon the scene, what were not killed or wounded of that arrogant band, who were "going to drive the Yankees into the river," were seeking safety in flight. General Sherman says that it was one of the best contested battles of the war. The enemy was driven behind his inner defenses, and the second day after the battle, Sherman drew his lines of investment around Atlanta. The goal was in sight, but at a fearful cost. At Peach-tree Creek, the Twentieth Corps lost about one thousand six hundred men, killed and wounded. The Forty-sixth regiment suffered very severely. The following were the casualties in company K: 1st Sergeant Alderson, severely wounded; in trying to get to the rear, he was captured by the enemy, and afterwards taken to Andersonville, whence he was finally exchanged, and rejoined his company at Raleigh, North Carolina. Private Brady lost a leg; the gallant Medlycott, before mentioned, was mortally wounded, and died at Nashville soon afterward; Sergeant Joseph Long was killed; Privates Kerlin and Daly were killed; Private Baker killed, and Privates Derk and others, slightly wounded. In battle, the proportion of killed is about one to five wounded; here the conditions were reversed. During the siege of Atlanta, Private William H. Liebig was killed on the advance picket-line, and Private Samuel W. Claybenger wounded by a fragment of shell. In all the operations around Atlanta, company K did its full duty, and was one of the first companies to enter the captured stronghold.

During the occupation of Atlanta, the command indulged in a general rest, making up for its hardships and privations during the campaign which had culminated in the capture of the "gate city" of the South. Company K accompanied Sherman in his magnificent march from "Atlanta to the Sea;" sharing in its fatigues—rejoicing in its brilliant success. In the brilliant and arduous campaign through the Carolinas, it bore its share of duty, always occupying the post of honor, "the right of the regiment." It participated in the battles of Averysboro, March 16th, 1865, and Bentonville, March 19th. In the former battle, Sergeant August Shensel was wounded. The sergeant was always fond of smoking, and if a battle lasted too long to allow him to indulge in his favorite pastime, he would denounce the rebels roundly, and blaze away more energetically than ever. At Averysboro, a bullet struck him in the arm, and he was disabled temporarily. He did not lose his *self-possession* nor his *pipe*, but, shouldering his musket, he marched leisurely to the rear, as though nothing out of the ordinary routine had occurred.

From Bentonville to Goldsboro, where the command refitted. When the head of column marched down the principal street of Goldsboro, in columns of companies, in *semi*-review, to do honor to their chief—the gallant Sherman—one of his staff-officers remarked: "Very dirty, but covered with *glory.*" So far as the *dirt* was concerned, it was literally true; history has taken care of the rest.

A word in passing. Had General Sherman been unsuccessful in his campaign from Atlanta to the Sea, and again, in his Carolina campaign, the military critics—so-called—would have said: "I told you so." Since he was successful, he is the hero of the hour; so prone are we to judge by *results*, rather than by the *possibilities* of results.

The column had reached Goldsboro, after a campaign which has no parallel in modern warfare. The Spring campaign was about to open. Grant against Lee, Sherman against Johnson. The army of the Mississippi knew that Johnson could not successfully fight *them*, having fought him all the way down from his mountain fastnesses in Tennessee and north Georgia, and *successfully* too, but they feared, a long campaign, should Lee elude Grant. Trained to discipline, they patiently awaited developments, and when on the afternoon of the 7th of April, 1865, came the news that Grant has carried the defenses of Richmond, such a shout went up as soldiers only knew how to give.

The next day, April 8th, all the columns were in motion in pursuit of Johnson. At Smithfield, on the Neuse River, on the morning of the 9th of April, came the news that Lee had surrendered the "Army of Northern Virginia" to Grant. Across the Neuse and on to Raleigh. A halt of a few days, and again in pursuit of Johnson, who finally surrendered to his old adversary.

From Raleigh the command marched to Washington, via Richmond, and participated in the grand review at Washington, May 24th, 1865. The war had ended. The *Union* for which they had fought so long and so well was saved. On the 24th of July, 1865, company K of the Forty-sixth regiment Pennsylvania Veteran Volunteers ceased to exist. They had fought the fight of freedom; they had kept the faith, and were hereafter to be enrolled among the patriots who, in all ages have given their lives for enlarged liberties for the people. In a *military* point of view, company K ceased to exist on the 24th of July, 1865; but so long as valor has a worshiper, their deeds will be remembered; so long as patriotism shall be a cardinal virtue in the breasts of American freemen, their names will be enshrined in the hearts of a grateful posterity.

Participants in some of the most desperate struggles of the war, they have written the story of their valor on twenty-six battle-fields. The men of company K have fallen by the river, by the mountain and the sea, but they have not died in vain.

> "On fame's eternal camping-ground
> Their silent tents are spread,
> And glory guards, with solemn round,
> The bivouac of the dead."

It has been truly said, that "the memory of our dead, is their noblest monument." By the Shenandoah's stream, on the sunny slopes of Cedar Mountain, in the green fields of Maryland, in the valley of the Tennessee, by the Allatoona Pass, in the shadow of Kenesaw, and down where the waves of the Savannah meet the sea, are lying the remains of gallant spirits of company K. They shall never be forgotten, so long as any of their comrades are above ground. Peace to their ashes! May the recollection of their deeds be an inspiration, and our thought of them, in the coming years, be that of love, and love for the cause for which they died.

DIED IN HOSPITALS.

Daniel G. Stortzel, William H. Shenker, Peter G. Zimmerman, Samuel Clark, Isaac N. Robinson, John Dunran, Joseph Jaggers, William J. McDowell, Charles W. Mittler, Jacob W. Hesson.

Captain Strouse, having been promoted to major, of the Forty-sixth regiment, 2d Lieutenant Caldwell was promoted to the captaincy of company K. Major Strouse was killed at Chancellorsville. In his fall, the nation lost one of its noblest defenders.

SOLDIERS NOT ENUMERATED IN THE MUSTER-ROLL OF NORTHUMBERLAND COUNTY.

36th Regiment—Company K.

Major, H. C. Harper; Captain, A. R. Fiske; 1st Lieutenant, J. M. John; 2d Lieutenant, J. A. Shiff.

1st Sergeant, E. B. Rhoads; 2d Sergeant, John Harris; 3d Sergeant, Ferd. Rhodes; 4th Sergeant, John McElfee; 5th Sergeant, M. Sholl.

1st Corporal, F. Dubner; 2d Corporal, W. H. Carlisle; 3d Corporal, William Booth; 4th Corporal, John Weis; 5th Corporal, J. M. Best; 6th Corporal, John Hancock; 7th Corporal, David Eveland; 8th Corporal, John Fincher.

Musicians—H. Startzel, John S. Bittenbender.

Privates—Henry Allison, Hiram Bird, William Brown, William H. Bowler, William Buse, G. N. Carlisle, Thomas Curtin, Nicholas Curran, William Curlin, John Clifford, John Curtis, Lewis Chamberlain, Adam Derk, T. S. Dewees, John Dower, M. Dooley, J. B. Eaton, M. Enes, William Eadie, William Early, W. H. Gilger, James I. Getter, Jesse Gensel, A. Helt, Jacob Hess, E. Henninger, William Hume, I. Hower, J. P. M. Haas, Isaac Hause, David Hine, Sol. Hill, Henry Irich, J. J. John, George D. John, Robert Jones, William Kissinger, Joseph Kopp, Isaac Keiser, Frederick Kasemann, John R. Lake, Withington Lake, George Liebig, Charles Liebig, William Liebig, M. McCarty, El. Matthews, George Madara, George W. Miller, Henry Neihoff, John Roach, Jer. Rothermel, John Rupp, Daniel Rupp, Thomas Reese, John E. Reese, Isaac P. Raup, William Stillwagner, Jacob Stillwagner, Edw. Stillwagner, Daniel Stehler, John Strickland, John Sterrett, Jacob Triebley, Samuel Tiley, Jacob Tiley, John Tiley, Francis Tahey, M. Taney, Daniel Unger, John Vauzant, David Weaver, Elias Wagner, William E. Walter, Lucius Wynn.

56th Regiment.—Company C.

William Bean, Francis Dunlavy, Jacob Guskey, Michael Haley, John McDonald, John F. Starbzel, James Sterrett, Frank Startzel, George Weary, Josiah Yohe.

Company D.

C. Alderson, Patrick Burns, George B. Clark, Simon Collier, Jacob Christ, Henry Day, John Downey, John Meighan, Michael McCarty, John McCauley, Mark Moran, George Nolter, Francis Reed, John Reed, M. Schochnerry, James Strauser, Robert Toole, Thomas R. Williams, Stewart Yost.

Company G.

Thomas Clark.

Company K.

Michael Maher.

131st Regiment.—Company C.

Cyrus Bittenbender, Silvorius Bird, John R. Boughner, Samuel Bower, Azariah Campbell, Charles Culp, William Evert, O. M. Fowler, Ephraim Foulke, James D. Harris, Francis Hoover, John Huffman, Jacob Keiser, Daniel Keistmer, George W. Levan, H. W. Moore, Jacob Mowry, A. M. Osmun, Joseph L. Reeder, Henry Shiff, Reamon Stambach, Josiah Strauser, George Weimer.

J. M. John's Company.

J. M. John, William Kute, A. Meighan, P. H. Philips, George Shiff, David Shiff.

In other Companies and Regiments.

William Allen, Daniel Bower, William Ballow, George Fredericks, David Guss, Reuben Kreeger, William Kreeger, William Osmun, Dr. O. Robins, H. A. Shissler, Frank Reed, Godfrey Scheeman, William Worrell, Wesley Van Gosken.

METHODIST EPISCOPAL CHURCH.

The first religious services in Shamokin were conducted by a preacher of the Methodist denomination. During the year 1837, a Rev. Mr. Brown, one of the preachers on the Sunbury circuit, chanced to come to Shamokin. He preached in the old school-house, on Dewart street, to a full house, among whom was John C. Boyd, the founder of the town. A class was soon afterwards formed, by the Rev. Henry G. Dill, with S. S. Bird as leader.

This class was composed of some eight persons, as follows: S. S. Bird and wife, Benjamin McClow and wife, Joseph Bird, Pemberton Bird, and John John and wife.

The next Spring, the class was taken in the Sunbury circuit, and supplied with preaching every two weeks. The meetings were held in the old school-house, until the Central was built, when the meetings were held there. The congregation continued to prosper, and increase in numbers.

The first resident preacher was Rev. B. F. Stevens. He was followed by Rev. J. F. Porter, who was the first preacher in charge of this church. Mr. Porter came in 1863, and remained three years. The church under his charge flourished in numbers. He was greatly beloved by all, and his departure was sincerely regretted. He was succeeded by Rev. F. B. Riddle, one of the most talented clergymen in the Methodist Church. He remained three years, highly appreciated by his congregation, which now had become one of the largest and most influential in the town. He was succeeded by Rev. N. S. Buckingham, in 1869, who also remained three years. Mr. Buckingham was a very popular pastor, and his church flourished under his pastoral care. He was succeeded by Rev. James C. Clark, an able and earnest worker in the church. Mr. Clarke is an excellent business man, and in all the business relations of the church he introduced system, the good effects of which are still felt. The membership was largely increased under his stewardship. He remained until 1875. In his farewell sermon, he reports his labors, stating that he had married forty-nine couples, baptised one hundred and seventy-two persons, attended the funerals of one hundred and thirteen, preached two hundred and eighty-eight regular sermons, made one hundred and sixty-five visits to the sick, and had collected fifteen thousand dollars and twenty-three cents for various purposes. He was succeeded by Rev. W. Lee Spottswood, D.D., the present pastor. Dr. Spottswood is an eminent scholar, and an able divine. His sermons are of a very practical character.

As the congregation increased in numbers, a strong desire was manifested to erect a building for worship. During 1856, at the time the Revs. Tannehill and Colburn were on this part of the circuit, a meeting was called at the Central school-house, to discuss the propriety of building a church. Judge Helfenstein had donated to the society seventeen building lots, with the provision that one-third of the proceeds of the sales should be returned to him. The following members were appointed trustees: P. Bird, George Weaver, John Shipp, F. A. Clark, Benjamin McClow, George H. Coder, David Chidester, Joseph Reeder, and D. S. Miller. At a meeting held December 23d, 1856, H. Van Gosken, Benjamin McClow, and George Weaver were appointed a committee to select a piece of ground on which to build. They decided to take, for a church site, the ground presented to them by Charles P. Helfenstein. P. Bird and John Shipp were named a committee to circulate subscriptions among the citizens. A charter was obtained, and a seal adopted, with the device of an open Bible.

In May, 1859, the work was commenced. The contract was awarded to James L. Gilger. The size of the church erected was sixty by forty feet. It cost twenty-three hundred dollars, without completing the basement. It was dedicated in February, 1860, at which time six hundred and ninety-three dollars and fifty cents were collected; seventeen hundred dollars having been previously collected.

During 1867, a very comfortable parsonage was erected.

The Methodist Church edifice commands a fine site. It is located on Lincoln street, and is very accessible from all parts of the town.

In May, 1866, a bell, weighing eight hundred and thirty-three pounds, which cost four hundred and fifty dollars, was put in the tower, through the exertions of Captain Van Gosken. In October, 1866, the audience-room was re-opened, after undergoing extensive repairs. A collection of twenty-two hundred dollars was made on this occasion. There are nine classes in the church.

The trustees are: D. S. Miller, Isaac May, Sr., John J. Wagner, A. A. Helm, Robert Goodwill, and Withington Lake.

There are three hundred and sixty full members, and seventy probationers; making in all four hundred and thirty members. Valuation of church property, twelve thousand dollars.

METHODIST EPISCOPAL SUNDAY-SCHOOL.

This Sunday-school was started about 1858. Previous, it had been a part of the Union Sunday-school. The first superintendent was Rev. Pemberton Bird. After the erection of the church edifice the school became very large, and was looked upon as a model school. For several years, the school was under the charge of F. A. Clark. At this time, great interest was displayed, and old and young took part in the exercises.

The present superintendent is Mr. R. T. Owen, an experienced teacher, who brings with him in the Sunday-school room the knowledge of governing and teaching, that he acquired in the public schools. The school is regarded as one of the best in the town. Number of scholars, four hundred and thirty-six; number of teachers, fifty; number of volumes in library, eight hundred and fourteen.

PRESBYTERIAN CHURCH.

The first services of the Presbyterian Church were held about 1844, by Rev. James J. Hamilton, in the Central school-house. The method of making this appointment was somewhat novel.

PLATE XXIII

RES. of THOMAS DEARMOND,
DELAWARE TP. NORTHUMBERLAND COUNTY, PA.

RES. & DAIRY FARM of J. HUDSON KASE,
RUSH TP. NORTHUMBERLAND CO. PA

About four o'clock in the afternoon of a certain day, the good people living along Shamokin and Sunbury streets, had their attention attracted by seeing a fine-looking man, on horseback, riding along these streets, saying: "There will be preaching in the school-house this evening." A large number attended who became much interested in Mr. Hamilton, and he was invited to remain and build up a congregation.

Mr. Hamilton went to work in earnest, and after great effort, succeeded, in 1845, in building the church now occupied by this denomination. Mr. Stephen Bittenbender was the builder, but the pews were put in by Jonas L. Gilger. The church was organized April 8th, 1845, by Rev. William R. Smith and Elder John B. Boyd, a committee appointed by the Northumberland Presbytery. This was the second church edifice erected in Shamokin, the Catholic being the first. The following is the first organization: Pastor, Rev. James J. Hamilton; Elders—Solomon Eckert, Daniel Evert, and Alexander Caldwell; Original Members—Solomon Eckert, Daniel Evert, Alexander Caldwell, Jacob Snirk, Mary Ann Runyan, Mary Canterman, Mary Evert, Martha Caldwell, Catharine Caldwell, Sarah Ann Reed, Eva Snirk, Harriet Eckert, Mary Black, Sarah Hamilton, and Elizabeth Reppard.

Mr. Hamilton remained with the congregation until 1850, when he resigned and moved away. The church was then supplied with preachers, for some years, that had charge of Elysbury Church. Rev. David Hill succeeded Mr. Hamilton, who, in turn, was followed by Rev. Mr. Barr.

About 1856, the Rev. P. B. Marr succeeded as pastor, and continued in the work, greatly appreciated by his congregation, until July, 1859, when the Rev. A. D. Hawn, a young man who had just completed his studies, was called to supply the pulpit here, and one or two other points. Here the real history of this church begins. Mr. Hawn was a most untiring worker, and, in the course of a few years, the congregation became the leading church in the town.

During the year 1864, the church building was raised eight feet, and a stone basement placed under it. A spire was erected, and the interior arrangements greatly improved.

In November, 1864, he was installed as the regular pastor. During this time he took great interest in the welfare of the town. He edited the *Herald* for some time, served as president of the school-board, took a great interest in the Lyceum, and identified himself with all the leading movements of the times. In June, 1869, he resigned, after serving eight years as pastor.

Mr. Hawn was succeeded by Rev. J. P. Conkey, one of the ablest preachers that ever resided at Shamokin. Mr. Conkey remained about two years, and was followed by Rev. Mr. Dewing, who remained one year.

In April, 1872, the Rev. S. P. Linn, of Philadelphia, was called to take charge, who remained about two years. After a vacancy of some months, during which time the pulpit was filled by preachers from other churches, the Rev. A. C. Clarke was called, and installed in June, 1874.

Mr. Clarke entered upon his duties under some difficulties of a very discouraging nature, but, by uniform courtesy and a persistent effort to do right, he has succeeded, in a great degree, in building up the broken-down walls. Mr. Clarke is a good speaker, who closely devotes his energies to his great calling. He deserves the success he has achieved.

The church edifice is a neat frame building, located in the central part of the town, on Sunbury street. It will accommodate about four hundred people. The present membership numbers two hundred and ninety. The elders are Alexander Fulton, George H. Liebig, and John James.

PRESBYTERIAN SUNDAY-SCHOOL.

On the dissolution of the Union Sunday-school, in 1854, the Presbyterian Sunday-school was organized. Dr. William Atwater was the first superintendent. A large number of scholars were in attendance from the beginning. It is now one of the best regulated schools in town. The present superintendent is George H. Liebig. Number of scholars, two hundred and twenty-five; teachers, twenty; volumes in library, eight hundred.

PROTESTANT EPISCOPAL CHURCH.

There were several families of this denomination in Shamokin soon after its first settlement, but not remaining long, there were no services until December 11th, 1854, when the Rev. D. Washburn, then of Pottsville, held the first meeting in the Presbyterian Church, and continued occasionally until 1856. But nothing further was done until May 14th, 1865, when the Rev. Rowland H. Brown, rector of the church at Lewisburg, held the services of the Episcopal Church in the Presbyterian Church. On the day following, the clergyman met several gentlemen favorable to the organization of a church in the town. The result of the conference was the determination to begin the enterprise at once. At the request of Rev. Mr. Brown, the Rev. G. W. Shinn, rector of a church in Philadelphia, visited Shamokin on a Sunday in May, and officiated twice. The vestry, which had been previously formed, consisting of Charles P. Helfenstein, R. B. Douty, John H. Dewees, C. P. Boyd, and others, met the next evening, and among other matters, asked the reverend gentleman to assume its rectorship. During the Summer and Autumn, services were occasionally held in the Presbyterian and Welsh churches by Messrs. Brown, Jerome, Shinn, and others.

During the Summer, plans were adopted, and a contract awarded to J. B. Gibson for the erection of a chapel. The original plan contemplated a small building (capable of seating about one hundred and fifty persons) upon lots donated by J. H. Dewees, Esq., but subsequent changes were made, until it was finally concluded to put up a building twenty-eight by seventy-eight feet, with stone basement, on lots given by C. P. Helfenstein.

The corner-stone of the church was laid on November 7th; Revs. Shinn, Brown, Gibson, and Allen present.

At Christmas, a fair was held by the ladies in Rorer's building, which realized about eight hundred dollars for the church.

On January 12th, 1866, the Rev. Mr. Shinn entered upon his duties as rector, and held services in the Central school-house to May 6th.

The structure was rapidly approaching completion, when on the morning of Sunday, April 29th, a furious gale of wind blew it down, with great destruction of material.

On the morning of May 11th, in eight days, the chapel that now stands, was erected from the ruins of the wrecked building, and fifteen persons were confirmed that day by Bishop Vail, of Kansas.

Mr. Shinn was a very active and talented man, and exerted a marked influence over the town. In his report of the first year's work he enumerates the following results: "One year ago there were five communicants, there are now twenty-five; baptism has been administered to eighteen children and two adults; public service has been held one hundred and thirty times; thirty families are connected with the church. The Sunday-school numbers fifty children and seven teachers."

Amount of money expended the first year: Loss by destruction of church, three thousand dollars; erection of chapel, one thousand five hundred dollars; work about the ground, three hundred dollars; organ, ninety dollars; Sunday-school, thirty dollars; salary of rector, eight hundred and ninety-five dollars; salary of sexton, fifty dollars; incidentals, two hundred dollars. Total, six thousand and sixty-five dollars.

February 10th, 1867.—Mr. Shinn resigned his rectorship.

February 17th, 1867.—Rev. I. Newton Spear, of Altoona, officiates, and accepted a call, commencing March 17th. During this Spring, the chapel walls were papered, and the backs of the seats improved. Expense, one hundred and thirty dollars..

June, 1867.—Owing to the depressed condition of the parish finances, application was made to the Diocese for aid, which was granted for 1868,

Mr. Spear, having resigned in 1868, was succeeded by Mr. Rev. J. H. H. Millet, who was succeeded by Rev. F. M. Bird, in 1869; who was followed by Rev. A. H. Boyd, in 1871, who remained about a year.

During 1872.—From this time to 1875, services were frequently held by the rector from the old parrish.

On Thursday, October 28th, 1875, the vestry extended a call to the Rev. Samuel S. Chevers to take the rectorship, and he entered on his duties at once.

During the Summer of 1876, the chapel was enlarged by the addition of twenty-five feet, and the interior was pretty generally remodeled at an expense of about six hundred dollars.

Under the charge of the present rector, Mr. Wright, who is a very active and popular gentleman, the church is increasing in numbers, and it does seem as *if the days of her vicissitudes had passed.*

PROTESTANT EPISCOPAL SUNDAY-SCHOOL.

This school was organized in 1866, by Rev. George W. Shinn, who served as first superintendent.

The present superintendent is W. C. Richardson.

Number of scholars in attendance, fifty; number of teachers, eight.

The school is prosperous.

WELSH BAPTIST CHURCH.

This church was built in 1865, on back end of lots owned by Mrs. Rosser, one of its members. The building is a frame one, located on Rock street,

The congregation commenced with fair prospects and a full congregation of forty members, but at the end of two years, a number of the members leaving Shamokin, the church was suspended.

During 1870, through the efforts of Rev. A. D. Still, a Baptist church and Sunday-school were organized. The church numbered thirty-three members, and continued about fifteen months, when the effort was abandoned.

A Sunday-school was organized in 1870, with John W. Gillespie as superintendent. The school consisted of ten teachers and seventy-five scholars, with one hundred volumes in the library. The school prospered for some time, but eventually followed the fate of the church.

ST. JOHN'S EVANGELICAL CHURCH.

There were members of the Evangelical Association, living at Shamokin, as early as 1842. They had preaching occasionally by ministers from other places, until about 1854, when a regular appointment was made here, which was served with Mahantongo circuit. During this period, services were held in the Central school-house, and sometimes in private houses and awhile in the United Brethren Church. In Spring of 1867, it was formed into a mission with Trevorton, with Rev. C. Gingrich as pastor. He preached every alternate Sabbath. In 1869, Rev. S. S. Chubb, was appointed pastor. During his administration, the church they now occupy was erected. It is a handsome frame structure, on West Sunbury street. The membership increasing considerably, in 1871, it was constituted a mission by itself, and Rev. R. Mott was appointed the first regular pastor, that resided in the place. He had two services each Sabbath, German in the forenoon, and English in the evening. The church debt was paid off, and the society so prospered that in the Spring of 1872, it became a self-supporting station, with a membership of two hundred.

Mr. Mott was succeeded by Rev. B. J. Smoyer, who served the congregation acceptably two years. The church prospered under his labors, numbering some two hundred and fifty-three members on his retirement. He was followed by Rev. W. A. Leopold, the present incumbent, who is filling out his second year. The church, under the able charge of Mr. Leopold, has increased to four hundred and two members, the largest membership in the town except the Catholic Church. Last year, the church edifice was enlarged so as to contain three hundred more. It will now accommodate eight hundred persons. The trustees are: D. C. Smirk, Daniel Rahn, John Wolf, Joseph Kopp, and H. L. Renn. Value of the church property, about seven thousand dollars.

ST. JOHN'S EVANGELICAL SUNDAY-SCHOOL.

This school was started in 1869, and has prospered to a wonderful degree. Number of teachers, forty-two; number of scholars, five hundred and fifty. The pastor is the superintendent. Besides this, the church has three mission schools under its charge, viz.: one at Burnside Colliery, with fifty scholars; one at Big Mountain, with forty scholars, and one at Springfield, with fifty-five scholars.

UNITED BRETHREN IN CHRIST.

The first services of this denomination were held by Rev. Samuel Sides, about 1850. During this year the church was organized, with Rev. Jacob Breuer as pastor. The original trustees were: Jeremiah Zimmerman, S. S. Bird, George Kreiger, H. Hogey. The following are the several pastors that have served this church: Jacob Breuer, James Young, Israel Carpenter, George Hoffman, George Gilbert, P. L. Zimmerman, W. Deitrich, A. F. Yeager, J. Sweak, G. W. Miles Rigor, G. A. Snapp, J. P. Long, G. A. Lee, W. B. Evers, J. F. Mower, J. R. Reitzle, J. D. Killian, Rev. Brinckly, and finally, the present pastor, Rev. W. S. H. Keys, D. D., one of the most able clergymen in the State. Mr. Keys has acquired considerable popularity as a pulpit orator and lecturer, and his discourses draw full houses.

The church is a frame structure, located on Sunbury street, and built in 1851, the third church built in the town. During 1870, the church was enlarged and renovated. It has a capacity for four hundred persons, and is valued at five thousand dollars. The congregation numbers one hundred and sixty-one persons. The present trustees are: Josiah F. Bird, Eph. Weimer, John Rudisill, and Dr. Brown.

UNITED BRETHREN SUNDAY-SCHOOL.

The school was organized in 1863, with Mahlon Sholl as first superintendent. The school commenced with ten teachers and fifty scholars. The school, at the present time, has twenty teachers, one hundred and seventy scholars, and a library of four hundred volumes. The pastor acts as superintendent.

SOCIETY OF FRIENDS.

There is no organization of this persuasion here, but, as several families of the residents incline towards that faith, meetings of this society are occasionally held in the other churches, with a good attendance. An effort was made, at one time, to build a meeting-house, but was finally abandoned.

WELSH CONGREGATIONAL CHURCH.

The members of this denomination held services in Shamokin, for the first time, about 1860; the meetings were held in Odd Fellows' Hall. The first services in Welsh were held by the Calvinistic Methodists, by Rev. John Moser, in 1860. At this time, the Welsh, though composed of Baptists, Congregationalists, and Methodists, all worshiped together in their own language. But, as the congregation increased in numbers, the Congregationalists received several lots on the corner of Spurzheim and Rock streets, and in 1865, erected a small frame church, and had it incorporated as the Welsh Congregational Church of Shamokin, with the following as trustees: John D. Lewis, John W. Thomas, Isaac Thomas, Seth Francis, Evan Lloyd, with Henry C. Harris as pastor. They occupied the building about five years, when they sold the property to the W. B. A., of Northumberland County, who now occupy it as their head-quarters. It is known as "Union Hall."

During 1870, they built a small frame church on Grant street, which they now occupy. Mr. Harris, the first pastor, labored hard for his church. He worked in the mines for his support, and fulfilled his pastoral duties on the Sabbath. He served his congregation about two years. He afterwards joined the Mormons, and now lives at Salt Lake City.

After Mr. Harris, the church had no regular supply until 1875, when the Rev. T. Davis was called to the charge, who now occupies the same, and fills it with great acceptance to his members. He labors zealously for the advancement of his church, which is prospering greatly under his ministration. He has charge of the church at Mt. Carmel, also, devoting alternate Sundays to these churches.

The present trustees are: Richard Griffith, John Philips, D. H. Morgan, Richard Price, and John Orwurth. The membership numbers about fifty. The church will contain one hundred and seventy-five persons.

WELSH CONGREGATIONAL SUNDAY-SCHOOL.

This school was started in 1874, and is now the only Welsh Sunday-school in Shamokin. First superintendent, John W. Thomas; present superintendent, John Orwurth. Number of teachers, nine; number of scholars, seventy-five. No library.

WELSH CALVINISTIC METHODIST CHURCH.

This congregation built a church on Independence street, about 1870, and occupied it a few years, when most of the members moving to other places, the church was abandoned, and the property was sold to Chas. P. Helfenstein. Wm. Thomas, of Minersville, was the last pastor, who died suddenly in 1872.

AMERICAN PRIMITIVE METHODIST CHURCH.

Organized in Shamokin, November 20th, 1871, through the efforts of Rev. Daniel Savage. The meetings of the society were held in the Baptist church, on Rock street.

Names of persons who organized the church: James T. Harris, Thomas Lovel, William Owens, Anthony Smith, Jonathon Tillet, Benjamin Hudson, Ellen Hudson, Lizzie Hudson, Thomas James, Job Lovel, and David Tillet.

The Baptist Church was rented, and used as the place of worship, until August, 1875, when they moved to their own building just erected. This is a two-story frame building, located on West Chestnut street. It is called a mission-house.

The first stationed preacher was Rev. James Millington, who labored some nine months, when he was succeeded by Rev. E. Humphries, who remained here two years. Mr. Humphries was a popular preacher, and labored with great earnestness, in building up his church. He was succeeded by Rev. Francis Gray, who continued until August 20th, 1876, when he resigned, to complete his studies at the seminary. He was followed by Rev. Thomas Philips, the present pastor.

Number of members, sixty.

AMERICAN PRIMITIVE METHODIST SUNDAY-SCHOOL.

Organized in 1871. Number of teachers, twenty; number of scholars, one hundred; Anthony Smith, superintendent.

A temperance society, numbering seventy-five members, is connected with the Sunday-school.

ST. JOHN'S REFORMED CHURCH.

Among the first settlers of Shamokin, were a number of persons who either belonged to the Reformed Church, or leaned towards that faith.

As far as can be ascertained, the first services were held in the Central school-house, about 1850, by the Rev. Mr. Fisher, of Sunbury, who, at different times, held services here. A Rev. Mr. Gingrich, from the Mahanoys, frequently preached also for this people. About 1855, the Rev. Mr. Hoffman, who then had charge of the St. Jacob's and St. Peter's Churches, in Shamokin township, organized the St. John's Church, and served about two years as pastor. The services were held in different places.

Mr. Hoffman was succeeded by Rev. Mr. Rittenhouse, who remained two years, and then resigned and moved away.

The church was without a regular pastor for a year or so, when, in April, 1864, the congregation extended a call to Rev. H. W. W. Hibshman, of Lancaster, Pa., which was accepted, and Mr. H. at once entered his new field of labor. Mr. Hibshman had just completed his theological studies, and commenced his work with great zeal. The real history of this church begins with his ministry here. The services were held, at first, in the United Brethren Church, but soon after, the Reformed and the Lutheran congregations fitted up a room in the Odd Fellows' Hall, and held services there. Mr. H. commenced at once to prepare for building a church, and the beautiful brick edifice, located on Seventh street, was the result of his untiring energy. The congregation was poor, and hence the pastor devised various expedients to raise means to erect a building. Fairs were held; a series of lectures, by eminent Reformed ministers, were given in the Methodist Church, and contributions were solicited far and near. Work was commenced on the new building in 1865, and it was completed in 1867. Daniel Yost was the builder. The church was dedicated May 5th, 1867. The pastor was assisted by Rev. J. H. A. Bomberger, D.D., and others. In 1868, Mr. H. resigned. For a short time, the pulpit was occupied by Rev. Mr. Losch, when the Rev. C. Scheel was called to take the charge, who remained about two years, when the Rev. D. W. Kelley succeeded him. Mr. Kelley remained about four years, serving with great acceptance, when he resigned, to accept a call at Manchester, Md.

In December, 1874, the Rev. Mr. Shoemaker accepted the pastoral call, and is the present pastor. Mr. Shoemaker is doing a good work in building up the congregation.

The membership numbers two hundred and sixty, with accommodation for five hundred.

The present consistory are, Samuel Yost, W. W. Wary, R. S. Aucker, H. Swavely, John Martz and J. K. Haas.

Valuation of church and parsonage, fifteen thousand dollars.

ST. JOHN'S REFORMED SUNDAY-SCHOOL.

For a number of years, the children of the Reformed and Lutheran congregations formed a Union school, with Solomon Weaver as superintendent. The school numbered about one hundred scholars. When the St. John's Church was finished, a Reformed Sunday-school was organized, but was not a full denominational school until the Rev. Mr. Kelley took charge of the congregation, in 1870. The pastor serves as superintendent. The present standing of the school is as follows: Number of teachers, twenty; number of scholars, two hundred and seventy-five; number of volumes in library, five hundred.

TRINITY EVANGELICAL LUTHERAN CHURCH.

The first Lutheran services were held in the Central school-house, about 1840, through the exertions of William Fegely, who was reared in this church. He sent to Sunbury for the Rev. J. P. Shindle, an eminent preacher in the Lutheran Church, to visit Shamokin occasionally, and preach to the people. Mr. Shindle complied with the request, and came frequently here, and held services. He was a popular speaker, and his meetings were largely attended. About this time, the Mormons had been holding a series of meetings here, and had awakened considerable interest in religious matters, and had, in fact, gained several converts. It appeared as though they might gain a strong foothold here, in the absence of other services, and so the good sense of Mr. Fegely led him to procure what he deemed "sound doctrine" for the people.

About 1842, a partial organization of the church was made by the Rev. Mr. Alleman, who had charge of St. Peter's and St. Jacob's Churches, in Shamokin township. He was followed by the Rev. Mr. Willard, who served the congregation for some time. But the real history of the church begins in 1854. On October 11th, of that year, the church was fully organized, with the Rev. C. J. Ehrhart as pastor. He was an active worker, and, under his charge, the congregation prospered. He was a sanguine man, and as Shamokin, at this period, was a very prosperous town, he conceived the plan of establishing a Lutheran college at this point. He talked and worked until he awakened a great interest in his enterprise, and commenced the undertaking, and would have succeeded, had it not been for the jealousy of other towns that were competing for the school. An account of this work will be given elsewhere. Mr. Ehrhart established a select school, which continued for several years, and acquired considerable celebrity. Mr. Ehrhart was succeeded by Rev. J. F. Wampole, October 11th, 1857, who filled the pulpit for eight years. For two years, the services were held in the Presbyterian Church, but in June, 1859, a room in the Odd Fellows' Hall was fitted up with seats and pulpit, and used by them and the German Reform congregation. Mr. Wampole was an active worker, and the church greatly prospered. During the last year of his ministry, he commenced making preparations to erect a church building. He had taken steps to secure the ground, and had adopted plans of building. Mr. Wampole resigned in 1865, and was followed by the Rev. J. B. Keller, who commenced at once to carry out the building already projected. During the Summer, the ground was excavated, and on October 10th, 1865, the corner-stone was laid. On January 20th, 1867, the basement was first used for worship, and on August 11th, 1867, the church was dedicated, and the audience-room was first occupied as a place of worship.

The building was designed by C. S. Wetzell, and erected by Jonas L. Gilger, of Shamokin. The structure is of brick, painted and sanded. It is fifty by seventy-five feet, with a tower at one corner, one hundred and eighteen feet high, containing a superior bell. The basement is twelve feet high, and divided into apartments for Sunday-school and lecture rooms. The audience-chamber is twenty feet high, and will seat over five hundred persons. It is one of the most handsome of our church structures.

In 1869, Mr. Keller resigned, and was succeeded by Rev. J. R. Williams, who remained about two years. He was followed by Rev. S. Domer, a very eminent preacher in the Lutheran Church. The congregation prospered greatly under his charge. In 1873, he resigned, to take charge of the principal Lutheran Church in Washington. The congregation was now without a regular pastor for a short time; but, in December, 1874, the Rev. H. C. Haithcox, of Muncy, was unanimously elected pastor, and fills the position at the present time with great acceptance to his people. Number of members, two hundred and sixty.

The council consists of D. Y. Gilham, J. J. W. Schwartz, Daniel Deibler, John Dunkelberger, Daniel Zuerne, and Reuben Fegely. Valuation of church property, fifteen thousand dollars.

LUTHERAN SUNDAY-SCHOOL.

This school was established soon after the erection of the church, and is now in a flourishing condition. The superintendent is D. Y. Gilham. Number of teachers, thirty-four; number of scholars, four hundred; number of volumes in library, one thousand.

ST. JOSEPH'S CATHOLIC CHURCH, LOCUST GAP.

Before September, 1866, no regular Catholic service was held at Locust Gap. Rev. E. Murray, of Danville, who had charge of the place, lived too far away to pay much attention to this new field of labor. In the month of September, 1866, Rev. Joseph Koch came to Shamokin, with the charge of Locust Gap in his parish. He set to work immediately, and organized the congregation, giving them a regular Sunday attendance. Divine service was held every Sunday in the school-house, and no effort was left untried to improve the moral and spiritual condition of the people.

In May, 1870, a lot having previously been secured from the coal company of the place, Father Koch began the foundation of a church, and under his supervision, the work went on without interruption. The building is two stories high, and forty-five by seventy feet. The basement is ten feet in the clear, and the upper story thirty feet high. The following November, the basement-room was finished, and the congregation and pastor had the satisfaction to leave for good the small and uncomfortable school-house, and hold service for the first time in a large and comfortable basement.

On the 27th of August, 1871, the church, being completed, was dedicated to the service of Almighty God, under the patronage of St. Joseph, by Bishop Shanahan, of Harrisburg.

The cost of the church edifice and furniture amounted to seventy-eight hundred dollars.

There is a small debt, which will be liquidated as soon as the times improve.

The number of communicants exceeds six hundred, and two hundred and twenty children attend Sunday-school.

St. Joseph's Beneficial Society, numbering some sixty members, is connected with the church.

A parochial-school of seventy children is held in the basement of the church.

ST. EDWARD'S CATHOLIC CHURCH.

The first church built in Shamokin, was by the Catholics, in 1839, through the efforts of Brannigan, Riley, and some others, who were prominent men at that time. The builder was Stephen Bittenbender. The first services were held by Bishop Kenrick, October 11th, 1840. Previous to this, through the influence of the pastor of the St. Joseph's Church, of Danville, a few lots were secured for a burial-ground. The church building was erected on the south-west corner of these lots. It was a small frame building, twenty by thirty-two feet, and fourteen feet high, unplastered, and very rude in its finish. For twenty-two years this congregation had no other place of worship, when the priest from Danville visited them, to administer the consolations of religion.

But a better day dawned for these people. In September, 1866, Shamokin was formed into a parish, with Trevorton and Locust Gap attached to it, and Bishop Wood, of Philadelphia, appointed as first resident pastor of the new parish, the then pastor of St. Joseph's Church, of Milton. The new pastor came on a Saturday, to take charge of his new flock, which he found in a very unsettled condition. With a zeal and energy that has ever characterized the man in his commendable work, Father Koch at once applied himself to his new field of labor. On Sunday afternoon, a meeting of the congregation was held, at which it was resolved to buy a suitable property, on Shamokin street, upon which a temporary church should be built, until a better structure could be erected. Consequently, the following day a corner lot was secured, for the sum of thirty-four hundred dollars. In November, a temporary church was put up on the corner lot, and the next Spring it was enlarged, so as to accommodate the large congregation of the borough and vicinity.

In the Spring of 1869, an adjoining lot was purchased for nine hundred dollars, and a handsome pastoral residence, a three-story brick building, erected upon it, at a cost of eighty-five hundred dollars.

The congregation increased so rapidly in a few years, that the temporary church, which was fifty-six feet square, would not contain them all.

Therefore, during the Summer of 1872, the foundations of a new church were laid out and dug, and on 14th of September, of the same year, the Rev. Joseph Koch laid the first stone in the trench. The work was interrupted by the Winter, but was resumed in the Spring of 1873. On the 23d day of May, 1873, the corner-stone was laid by Bishop O'Hara, of Scranton, in the presence of a very large assemblage of people.

A contract for the stone-work was then made, which was an extensive one, as the entire building was to be stone. After working six weeks on the job, the masons abandoned their contract, and the work seemed to be doomed. But such was not the case. There was a man in the pastor, who allowed no difficulties to thwart him from his purpose. Notwithstanding his onerous pastoral duties, he took charge of the whole building, superintended its construction, attended to all the work which was done by the day, and after a struggle and labor of four long months, the walls were up, ready for the roof. The following Christmas day, service was held for the first time in the basement of the new structure. The following year the front was all completed, with the exception of the tower; the scaffolding taken down; the walls pointed with cement; pavement was made around the church; and the basement was plastered and fitted up, making a very large and comfortable room for divine worship.

Some idea of the magnitude of the work can be formed from its dimensions. It fronts on Shamokin street, sixty-four feet, running back on Webster, one hundred and twenty-five feet. The side walls from the pavement, are thirty-six feet high. The entire edifice is built with cut stone—a white mountain sand-stone found upon the mountain, about one mile from Shamokin.

The basement is ten-and-a-half feet, and the main auditorium, forty-two feet in the clear.

The tower from the pavement to the top of the cross, is two hundred feet high. There were over two thousand perch of stone used in the building. It is the largest church edifice, and the highest tower in Northumberland County.

The style of the church is pure Romanesque, and this architecture has been scrupulously carried out in all its details. In the beautiful tower erected, will be placed a chime of four bells, well harmonized, weighing over five thousand pounds. These will speak every day, and on Sundays, will call the faithful to the house of the Lord.

The congregation numbers nearly two thousand souls, being the largest one in this diocese.

ST. EDWARD'S SUNDAY-SCHOOL.

The Sunday-school connected with this church, was organized soon after Father Koch assumed the duties of the parish. It numbers upwards of four hundred children.

CATHOLIC SOCIETIES.

There are three societies connected with the church, under the supervision of the pastor.

St. Patrick's Temperance Society was organized in August, 1867; St. Patrick's Beneficial Society, organized in 1873, and a *German Beneficial Society, started the same year. There is likewise another society, composed of boys, between the ages of twelve and seventeen, called the Cadets of Temperance. All these societies are in a flourishing condition, and will probably number from fifty to sixty for each organization.

ST. EDWARD'S PAROCHIAL SCHOOL.

In order to supply the Catholic children of the congregation with a better religious education, a parochial school was started by Father Koch, in September, 1874. The next year, five Sisters of Charity, from Mount St. Vincent, New York, took charge of the school, and are now conducting it with great success. It contains two hundred and fifty scholars. It is under the direction of the pastor. All branches taught in public and select schools, including music, are taught here. Daily religious instruction is given to the children.

ST. STANISLAUS POLISH CATHOLIC CHURCH.

The Polish portion of St. Edward's congregation becoming so numerous by emigration, that a separation was deemed advisable, so, in 1870, they formed another congregation, called the St. Stanislaus Church.

In 1874, Rev. Joseph Juskienski was sent by Bishop Shanahan, of Harrisburg, as pastor of the church. He bought a pastoral residence, and erected a temporary frame building for a church. Lots were secured, and work commenced in 1875, on the foundation of a stone church. The following is a description of the proposed building: The church is located on the corner of Cherry and Race streets, and will be ninety-three by fifty feet, to be constructed of stone and brick. The stone-wall will be twelve feet high, on which will be a brick one of twenty-five feet. The basement-room will be fifty by sixty-four feet, and ten feet in the clear. The audience-room will be the size of the building, and twenty-five feet high. The tower will be one hundred and twenty-six feet high. The building will cost, when completed, about twenty-five thousand dollars.

The work on the structure has been suspended, after the stone work was completed, owing to the hard times.

On account of some difficulties occurring between the pastor and a portion of his congregation, he resigned in June, 1876, and was succeeded by the Rev. Florian Klonouski, who will commence the work as soon as the times will admit.

Number of communicants, five hundred.

POLISH SUNDAY-SCHOOL.

This school is connected with the St. Stanislaus Church, and numbers one hundred and forty scholars.

ST. STANISLAUS BENEFICIAL SOCIETY.

This organization is connected with the church. It numbers eighty members.

BURIAL GROUNDS.

For many years, Shamokin was without a suitable resting-place for the dead. Its population was principally composed of those who were in the prime of life, and being busily engaged in building up a town, but little attention was given to burial-grounds. But in the course of time, as the town increased in numbers, the want of convenient and suitable places for interment became so pressing, that proper provision for this purpose was finally made.

* St. John's.

PLATE XXIV

RES. OF WM P. DOUGAL, MILTON, NORTHD CO., PA.

RES. OF MISSES S. M. & L. B. CAKE, NORTHUMBERLAND, NORTHD CO, PA.

IRICH'S GRAVE-YARD.

The first grave-yard in the region, was what is now familiarly known as "Irich's Grave-yard," located about one mile east of Shamokin, on the public road, leading to Mount Carmel. It contains about one-half acre of low and wet ground, enclosed by an old fence, and is in a very neglected condition. It is nearly all taken up, but is so overgrown that many of the graves are not to be distinguished. It was laid out a short time after the Revolutionary war, by the Cherrys, the first settlers of this locality, several of whom are interred there. For many years, the people of Shamokin, who did not bury at the "Blue Church," in Shamokin township, or the Catholic grounds, used this as their burial-ground. There has been no interment there for some years.

CATHOLIC GRAVE-YARD.

About 1839, the Catholic population of Shamokin secured about one acre of ground, in the lower part of town, and on it erected a small frame-church, and consecrated a burying-place, exclusively for their denomination.

SHAMOKIN CEMETERY.

During 1859, some of the citizens of Shamokin associated together, under the title of the Shamokin Cemetery Company, and secured a charter from the court. The following managers were then elected: William H. Marshall, William M. Weaver, Rev. C. Rittenhouse, C. P. Helfenstein, Joseph Bird, Solomon Weaver, and P. Bird.

The ground selected, is in the southern part of the borough, and belonged to Messrs. Marshall, Weaver, and Helfenstein, who deeded it to the company, subject to certain provisions and restrictions. The terms of purchase, were arranged by the managers, and a set of by-laws adopted. William H. Marshall subsequently purchased the interests of the other two parties. One-half of the gross receipts belong to him; the other half, after the proper expenses are deducted, is applied to the keeping of the grounds in order, and making the necessary improvements. There are about twenty acres enclosed. The company own a house and lot, occupied by the sexton, valued at fifteen hundred dollars.

Shamokin Cemetery is beautifully located on rising ground, south of Academy Hill, that commands some of the finest views of the surrounding region. Possessed of a dry and gravelly soil, with excellent drainage, it is well adapted to the purpose of a cemetery. Under the skillful engineering of the lamented Cleaver, the grounds are tastefully laid out in blocks and ranges; avenues for carriages have been provided, and footways to every lot in the enclosure. A large number of evergreens were left to shed their purifying influence around, and every effort was made to preserve the natural beauty of the locality.

A number of the lot-owners have tastefully decorated their lots, and erected beautiful tombstones and monuments, in memory of their dead. The first interment in the ground, was a child of Mr. Harmon Snyder.

The present managers are: Alexander Fulton, William H. Marshall, J. J. John, F. S. Haas, R. S. Aucker, R. R. Teitsworth, W. H. M. Oram.

The officers are: President, Alexander Fulton; Secretary, J. J. John; Treasurer, W. H. Marshall; Superintendent, John Geywitz.

ST. EDWARD'S CEMETERY.

As the Catholic grave-yard in the town became filled up, the Rev. Joseph Koch, during the year 1873, secured four acres of ground, about one mile east of the borough, and adjoining the village of Springfield, for a cemetery. He had it enclosed at once, and beautifully laid out for burial purposes. The ground is dry and elevated, and is very pleasantly located. Under the care and good taste of Father Koch, it will soon become one of the most beautiful cemeteries in the region. Quite a large number of interments have already been made here, and many of the lots are tastefully arranged. Several very handsome monuments and tombstones have been erected recently.

YOUNG MEN'S CHRISTIAN ASSOCIATION.

This excellent society was organized December 3d, 1874. The present officers are: President, Joseph Wilson; Secretary, William Keaggy.

Board of Managers: Rev. E. Humphries, S. P. Fink, Philip Thomas, George Dawson, D. C. Smink, and John P. Helfenstein. The monthly meetings are held on the fourth Monday evening of each month. Sunday services are held at their hall, at four P.M. The cottage prayer-meetings are held on each Tuesday evening. The association numbers eighty-eight active members.

The National and State meetings are properly represented by delegates and contributions.

Much of the success of the association is to be attributed to the untiring exertions of Rev. E. Humphries, the first president.

LINCOLN POST, NO. 140, G. A. R.

Was chartered June 17th, 1868.

The following were the charter members: Col. A. Caldwell, H. Boughner, Dr. C. W. Weaver, W. C. Roth, Major James May, John Cruikshank, O. M. Fowler, A. M. Osmun, W. B. Bird, T. C. Boyle, H. W. Morgan, C. F. Reyer, Benton Smith, James A. Shipp, J. B. Getter, and John Boughner.

This post has shown a great deal of energy, and by fairs, and other means, collected considerable sums of money for the objects of their organization. Their principal work was the erection of a monument, in the Shamokin Cemetery.

SANITARY COMMISSION.

Shamokin, all through the war of the Rebellion, took an active part in sending men to the front, and it was quite natural that her citizens would become interested in the great effort made by the United States Sanitary Commission to afford relief to the wounded and dying.

On May 17th, 1864, the first meeting was held at the residence of Mr. F. S. Haas, and was attended by a number of citizens. Rev. J. F. Porter was elected President; J. J. John, Secretary, and Rev. P. Bird, Treasurer.

The following committee was appointed to solicit contributions: Mrs. A. R. Fiske, Miss Kate Nash, Mrs. W. H. Douty, Mrs. F. S. Haas, Mrs. Osmun, Mrs. D. Yost, Mrs. W. P. Withington, Chas. P. Helfenstein, J. J. John, Rev. P. Bird, Rev. A. D. Hawn, Rev. Hilsman, John Caldwell, Jno. H. Gable, R. B. Douty, W. Rhodes, J. Dunkleberger, J. H. Zimmerman, F. S. Haas, J. S. Bittenbender, Geo. Martz.

Large sums of money were collected and forwarded to the great Sanitary Fair, held at Philadelphia. Captain H. Van Gosken and A. M. Eastwick captured a large *Copperhead*, near Shamokin, which they boxed securely, and forwarded to the exhibition. The managers of the fair refused to accept the donation, deeming a copperhead too dangerous a reptile for such an occasion.

CHRISTIAN COMMISSION.

The several churches of Shamokin took an active part in raising funds to aid the United States Christian Commission in its noble work. Collections were made in all the churches in 1865, and large sums of money obtained and forwarded.

SHAMOKIN FEMALE BIBLE SOCIETY.

This society was organized September 17th, 1863, with Miss Kate Nash as secretary.

The first anniversary of this society was held in the Presbyterian Church, by the Rev. I. H. Torrence, the General Agent of the Pennsylvania Bible Society. A collection of fifty-three dollars was taken up. The depository, for some years, was at the millinery store of Mrs. Mary Moore, where English, Welsh, and German Bibles were kept on hand. A number of the ladies visited the houses at the collieries, and took great pains to have the sacred volume introduced in every house. A number of dwellings were found that had no Bibles. The depository at present is at the Northumberland County National Bank.

SCHOOLS.

Shamokin has ever shown a high appreciation for education, and through a long series of years has always stood in the foremost rank for good schools. Shamokin almost dated its history with the building of a school-house.

In 1835, portions of the buildings, now known as the National and United States Hotels, were put up—the first houses in the town of Shamokin. About 1837, four or five more houses were erected, and among the number, to the great credit of the founder of the town, was a *school-house*. This was a small, one-story frame building, located on Dewart street. It was burned down in the great fire that occurred a few years ago. After this house had been in use for school purposes for some years, it was converted into a dwelling, then into a shop, afterward was used as the armory for the Shamokin Guard, and finally was reduced to a stable. What changes!

During the Winters of 1837–38, J. C. Boyd, the founder of the town, and Ziba Bird, his superintendent, who resided here, started a school which was *free to all*. They employed Abia John, now an old citizen of Shamokin township, as teacher, for a term of three months, at the *liberal salary* of eight dollars per month and boarded. What branches he taught, and whether he boarded around among the scholars, we cannot state. The school was small, the furniture rude, but the teaching appears to have been satisfactory. No maps or charts adorned the rough walls; no slated blackboard was in use;

the school-books were not uniform; the master made all the pens, and set all the copies; he acted as janitor, and the desks and seats were of the most primitive kind. Compare this dark, dingy, little room of near forty years ago, with our parlor rooms of the present day, with all the modern equipments and improvements, and note the progress in the educational system. It is a pity that the sketch of this old school-house could not be procured, to contrast with the handsome buildings of the Shamokin schools, illustrated in this book.

The following is the list of pupils of the first school: Hannah Bird, Zilla Bird, David Snyder, Rachael Snyder, Ephraim Philips, Ellen Philips, William W. Weary, Catharine Weary, Perry J. Eaton, Lydia Ann Porter, Elizabeth Porter, Ephraim Mowry, Marie Mowry, Emeline Mowry, and Morgan Mowry.

This was the first school in a region now comprising the six school districts of Shamokin borough, Coal township, Mt. Carmel borough, Mt. Carmel township, Cameron township, and Zerbe township, embracing the wealthiest and most populous portion of Northumberland County. This territory has now about three thousand five hundred scholars in its schools, and school property amounting to over one hundred and fifty thousand dollars.

During the year 1838, the system of public schools was adopted in Coal township by a small majority. Coal township then embraced all the territory above-named. The election was held in Cameron township, which was then a part of Coal township, and the school vote came from the mechanics, who were then working at Shamokin, as the people of Cameron were most bitterly opposed to the Free School System.

The following directors were elected: Sylvanus S. Bird, President; Kimber Cleaver, Secretary; Jehu John, Treasurer; James B. Porter, George Long, David Billman. The last two named were from Cameron township. Nothing was done this year.

In 1839, the School Board consisted of—Sylvanus S. Bird, President; Kimber Cleaver, Secretary; Jehu John, George Long, Wm. Fegely, David Billman.

Samuel John was elected treasurer, and Benj. McClow collector of school-tax.

The school finances of this board were as follows: School-tax levied, two hundred and one dollars and thirty-five cents; State appropriation, six hundred and thirty dollars; total, eight hundred and thirty-one dollars and thirty-five cents.

Mr. McClow, the collector, had a difficult time to collect this tax, especially in Cameron township, where the school system was looked upon as an odious and tyrannical measure. The farmers threatened to shoot him, and all possible obstruction was put in his way, but without avail. Mr. McClow was bound to fulfil his task, and employed the constable to assist him. It is said he traveled over five hundred miles to collect this tax of two hundred and one dollars and thirty-five cents, and received for the same, a little over *five dollars* for his commission. What would our present directors think of such a tax as this, and what would the modern tax-collector say about such a duplicate?

After drawing the appropriation, the board proceeded to divide the district into eight sub-districts:

1. Embraced all the territory between the top of the Little Mountain and the top of the Locust Mountain, from the eastern boundary of the County to the west boundary-line of the tract of John C. Boyd, occupied by David Thompson.

2. Embraced all the territory between the top of the Little Mountain and the top of the Locust Mountain, from the western boundary of No. 1, to the west boundary-line of a certain tract of land lying in Bear Valley, occupied by John Mowry; thence in a direct course to Shamokin Creek, at the Gap in the Little Mountain, including the dwelling of Samuel Eisenhart.

3. Embraced the territory westward of No. 2, between the Shamokin township line, and the top of Locust Mountain, to a line due north, and south twenty rods west of the house occupied by James Rennie, at the large coal mine, (Trevorton).

4. Embraced the territory in the same limits, from the No. 3 division to the western boundary of Coal township.

5. Embraced the country between the top of Locust Mountain and the south boundary of township, from the western limit of township to a line one mile east of George Kramer's.

6. Embraced the territory in the same limits, from eastern line of No. 5 to a line due north and south, dividing the lands of George Derk and Isaac Zeigler, deceased.

7. Embraced the territory by same limits, from eastern line of No. 6 to east end of the farm of John Weikle.

8. Embraced the balance of the township.

The divisions have been given in detail, to show the condition of this part of the County in 1839, and to exhibit how well our first directors planned the good work. All these men are now gone to their reward, but the field first occupied by them, is now dotted with elegant school-houses, and over two thousand scholars are enjoying the benefits thus provided. A large portion of the credit is due to Kimber Cleaver, who was the principal worker.

In reference to building school-houses, the board took the following action:

1. A few scholars—a house may be rented. (Mount Carmel, etc.)
2. A double house needed. (Shamokin and Coal townships.)
3. No house required. (Zerbe township.)
4. No house required.
5. Few scholars—perhaps a house may be rented.
6. Few scholars—perhaps a house may be rented.
7. One school-house needed. (Gowen City, etc.)
8. No inhabitants.

The board proceeded to work in great earnestness. During the Summer of 1839, they commenced putting up a two-story brick building in Shamokin (the eastern part of the present Central school-house), which was completed and occupied about February of next year. It cost six hundred dollars. In No. 5 division, they put up a small frame building, at an expense of ninety-four dollars and eighty-seven cents. This building is still standing near the Weikle stand.

The following teachers were employed in Cameron township: John Fidler was first employed, and taught until his salary amounted to eighteen dollars, when, for some reason, he was succeeded by William Stizes, whose salary amounted to seven dollars and twenty cents. This ends the school system here.

The first teacher employed in the public schools of Shamokin, was John T. Rood, of New York—a very able and successful teacher. He taught in the old frame school-house, but, for some cause, quit after teaching fourteen days. He was followed by Mrs. Mary Shipman, who also only taught a few weeks. The first two teachers who taught any length of time, were Amos Y. and John John, the former still living, an honored and respected citizen of the town, and the oldest teacher in the County.

The leading members in the board at this time, were Kimber Cleaver, afterwards the famous civil engineer, and William Fegely, one of the pioneer coal-operators of the region. Through their labors and foresight, the foundation was well laid. Honor to their memories!

By Act of Assembly, 1840, the district was divided into two districts, known as North Coal and South Coal School Districts. Divisions, numbers one, two, three, and four, were in North Coal District. At an election in South Coal School District, held this year, the school system was rejected, and a long night of ignorance hung over this section for thirty years.

The finances this year, were: School tax levied, three hundred and twenty-seven dollars and eighty cents; State appropriation, one hundred and forty-five dollars; total, four hundred and seventy-two dollars and eighty cents.

About 1852, the Lutheran congregation, of Shamokin, through the efforts of Rev. C. J. Ehrhart, contemplated erecting a Lutheran college. Aided and encouraged by such men as Judge Helfenstein, William Fegely, Kimber Cleaver, Jonas L. Gilger, Joseph Bird, and others, they commenced the project. A corporation was formed, with William Fegely, as president; and Jonas L. Gilger, as treasurer. Bonds were issued, and considerable stock taken, with the expectation that the Lutheran Synod would endorse and assist the movement. But through local jealously of neighboring towns, especially Selinsgrove, this movement was defeated.

Kimber Cleaver was the architect, who took a great interest in the college. A large brick structure was erected, but after putting on the roof, owing to the want of funds, the work was stopped, and it stood in an unfinished condition for many years.

In 1857, while the school board were engaged in putting up the Pearse school-house, Major Bevans, who was then post-master, suggested the idea that this college or academy building, as it was generally termed, should be bought for the use of the public schools. He talked this up for some time, and finally, a meeting of the citizens was held at the Central school-house, to vote on this question, and it was then decided to be useless and visionary.

So the matter rested until July 15th, 1863, when it was resolved by the school board, that the academy building should be purchased for the benefit of the public schools, provided a good title can be obtained.

A committee consisting of W. F. Roth, George McEleice, and Jonas L. Gilger, were appointed to look after it.

At a special meeting of the board, held at the residence of F. S. Haas, the secretary, on March 7th, 1864, at which the following directors were present: Dr. E. S. Robins, J. L. Gilger, W. F. Roth, F. S. Haas, and George McEleice, the following resolutions, on motion of Dr. E. S. Robins, were passed by a vote of four yeas—one member not voting.

Resolved, That the Academy building be purchased at Coroner's sale on the 14th instant.

Resolved, That Jonas L. Gilger and George McEleice be appointed a committee to go to Sunbury, and purchase the said building, if it does not go beyond two thousand nine hundred and fifty dollars."

It was purchased at this price, and the four directors who voted for this measure, will ever be proud of their vote, and the people will hold their names in remembrance.

In 1864, Shamokin was erected into a borough, and became a separate school district in 1865. At this time, the following buildings were on hand: The Academy, with one room finished in the basement; the Central, with four rooms in a dilapidated condition; the Penrose, with two rooms in excellent order; and an old frame building in Newton, with one room. The schools then consisted of one Grammar-school, three intermediate, and four primary-schools.

During 1865, J. J. John was elected district superintendent of the borough schools, which office he continued to hold until June 1st, 1875, a period of ten years. Much work was accomplished in this time, a large portion of which was done so quietly that it was hardly noticed. His efforts were ably sustained by an active and intelligent board of directors, who were ever anxious to improve the conditions of the schools.

In the year 1869, the Shamokin High-school was established, after encountering considerable difficulty. S. J. Barnett, a graduate of Millersville Normal-school, was the first principal. He was a most excellent teacher, and the steady success of the school is in part owing to his successful beginning. Mr. George W. Campbell, the present principal, and a most successful teacher, is zealously building up the school, and it has now quite a local reputation. At the close of the last session, four of the pupils graduated, and had diplomas bestowed upon them. A public school library is being formed, which, in a few years, bids fair to number hundreds of volumes. The creation of a High-school was an important event in the Shamokin schools. Its successful and effective operations for the past seven years, has had a decided influence for good on the other schools, and no true friend of learning would now be willing to see it put away.

There are at present nineteen schools, with twenty-two teachers, and about one thousand three hundred scholars. The schools are divided as follows: One High-school, one Grammar-school, seven secondary schools, and nine primary schools.

A uniform series of school-books has been established, which have been maintained for a number of years. A graded course of instruction has been prepared, which is rigidly adhered to. Promotions in divisions and schools are made at stated intervals by the principal, when the pupils pass a satisfactory examination. The plan has worked most excellently. With the changes made, the improvements adopted, and the course pursued by directors and teachers, it may be safely asserted, that the system of public schools, in the borough of Shamokin, has passed its transition period of experiment. The plan of organization is complete, and needs only to be honestly carried out, to meet the full expectations of its most ardent friends. These schools are now noted for their thoroughness, discipline, and excellent methods of instruction. The primary object of our noble school system, is to make good citizens and useful members to society. The greatness of our State depends, not so much on its rivers, plains, mountains, and valleys—on its bridges, canals, commerce, and navigation—as upon the strong arms, clear heads, and sound hearts of its citizens.

"What constitutes a state?
Not high-raised battlement, nor labored mound,
High wall, or moated gate;
Not cities fair, with spires and turrets crowned;
Not bays and broad-armed ports,
Where, laughing at the storm, rich navies glide.
Not starred and spangled courts,
Where low-bowed baseness wafts perfume to pride—
No! Men—high-minded men—
Men who their duties know,
But know their rights, and, knowing, dare maintain,
Prevent th' long-aimed blow,
And crush the tyrant, when he bursts the chain;
These constitutes a State."

SCHOOL BUILDINGS.

Shamokin has four first-class school buildings, which she justly holds in high estimation, and her citizens lose no opportunity in pointing them out to strangers. As they are illustrated in this work, a brief description of each will be highly proper. The school property is valued at forty thousand dolllars.

ACADEMY BUILDING.

This fine structure is located in the central part of Shamokin, and is well situated for the advanced schools which are kept there. It is a three-story brick building, one hundred feet long and forty feet wide, standing in the center of nine lots, fronting Grant street. It contains six large rooms, forty feet square, and five recitation-rooms. Most of these rooms are furnished with elegant patent furniture; matting on the floors, and handsome paintings and decorations on the walls. There are, perhaps, but few school-rooms in the State that are better fitted up interiorly. The district library is kept in one of the recitation-rooms. The teachers and pupils take great pride in keeping their rooms in order. A janitor has charge of the building and grounds.

CENTRAL SCHOOL-HOUSE.

This is a two-story brick building, fifty-nine by twenty-three feet, fronting on Sunbury street. It contains four rooms, one of which is furnished with patent furniture. The rooms are principally used for primary schools. The grounds contain about three-fourths of an acre, beautifully shaded by pine and other trees. This is an old building, but has been renovated to meet the present work. It makes a plain, but handsome appearance. This, as well as the other building, is in charge of a janitor.

PENROSE SCHOOL-HOUSE.

This is a two-story brick building, twenty-seven by thirty-five feet, with an addition, twenty-four by forty feet, fronting on Franklin street. It contains four first-class school-rooms, and two recitation-rooms, separated from the others by glass partitions. The rooms have high ceilings, and are ventilated by proper air-flues. Two of these rooms are furnished with patent furniture. The system on which these rooms are constructed and fitted up, meets with the approbation of all teachers who have visited them. There are three lots for this building.

STEVENS' SCHOOL-HOUSE.

This is also a two-story brick building, of the same size, and built on the same plan as the Penrose, fronting on Third street. There are three lots enclosed with the building. This house was named in honor of the great "Commoner" who so nobly defended the *free school system* in the days of its peril. Two of the rooms are fitted up with patent desks and seats.

Present officers: J. J. John, president; J. J. W. Schwartz, secretary; Joseph Scott, treasurer; F. S. Haas, R. S. Aucker, Dr. Harpell.

SECRET SOCIETIES.

There is, perhaps, no town in the coal regions, that has a larger number of secret orders than Shamokin. Their membership is composed of many of our best citizens; and the good accomplished by their beneficial systems, will never be all published. Aid in sickness, attendance at funerals, and watchful solicitude for the welfare of the orphan family, are some of the good results of these orders.

SHAMOKIN LODGE, NO. 255, A. Y. M.

The first movement towards opening a Masonic lodge, in Shamokin, was made, January 18th, 1851, when a preliminary meeting was held, in the office of Honell & Helfenstein, at which Wm. Fegely presided, and Kimber Cleaver was elected secretary. It was resolved to start a lodge, and committees were appointed to raise the necessary funds and make provisions for the same.

On September 4th, 1851, the District Deputy Grand Master, George C. Welker, and some members of the Grand Lodge, and Sunbury Lodge, organized the Shamokin Lodge, with the following officers: Wm. H. Marshall, W. M; Kimber Cleaver, S. W; Emanuel Kaufman, J. W; D. N. Lohe, secretary; William Fegely, treasurer.

This lodge commenced under very favorable circumstances, and in the course of a few months, a large number of members were initiated. It is at present in a very prosperous condition, and ranks in its membership, a number of the most influential citizens of the town. There are about seventy-five members at present. The lodge meets in the Odd Fellows' Hall, and holds its meetings monthly, on the Wednesday preceding full moon.

The present officers are: O. C. Kubach, W. M.; W. A. Richardson, S. W.; B. F. Boughner, J. W.; W. H. Gilger, secretary; J. L. Gilger, treasurer.

MT. TABOR LODGE, NO. 125. I. O. OF O. F.

This, the first secret society in Shamokin, and next to the oldest lodge of Odd Fellows in the County, was organized September 5th, 1845.

The charter members were: J. L. Gilger, Peter Boughner, Joseph Zuerue, George Kreeger, and George Shipe.

The first officers were: Jonas L. Gilger, N. G.; P. Boughner, V. G.; Joseph Zuerue, secretary; George Shipe, treasurer.

The lodge was instituted by the aid of the Milton Lodge, which was the first lodge of the order in Northumberland County. The progress of the society was remarkable, and at times, its membership exceeded two hundred. Five new lodges were created from this parent, viz.: Numidia, Snydertown, Elysburg, Mt. Carmel, and Shamokin lodges. The first place of meeting was in the garret of a frame building, that stood on the corner of Sunbury and Rock streets, afterwards known as the "Douty House," where they continued to meet some five years.

Feeling the want of proper accommodations, during the year 1850, they secured some lots on Sunbury street, and erected on it a two-story brick building, known as the Odd Fellows' Hall. The corner-stone was laid July 4th, 1850, at which time a great display was made. A number of lodges from this and adjoining counties participated. The address was delivered by the Rev. Mr. Dinger, a Reformed clergyman, who occasionally officiated here.

On July 4th, 1851, dedicated the Hall. On July 4th, 1866, held a grand parade, which was participated in by a number of lodges from other places.

The membership, at present, numbers about one hundred, with a healthy balance in the treasury.

The meetings are on each Saturday evening, in their Hall. The present officers are: William Gillespie, N. G.; W. Malick, V. G.; Enoch P. Jones, secretary; Jacob Mentchler, treasurer.

SHAMOKIN LODGE, NO. 664. I. O. OF O. F.

This lodge, which was an off-shoot of Mt. Tabor Lodge, was organized April 19th, 1869.

The charter members were: George Shipe, George Scott, Francis Hoover, William Rote, E. S. Shipe, John W. Hegins, Jacob Kramer, W. B. Eadie, W. H. Shipe, Luther Gable, A. A. Heim, Robert Goodwill, Samuel Yost.

The first officers were: George Shipe, N. G.; John K. Erdman, V. G.; William H. Shipe, R. S.; Francis Hoover, Asst. R. S.; Samuel Yost, treasurer.

Meetings on each Monday evening, in May's building. The society numbers eighty-three members, with a good condition of its finances.

The present officers are: William Krouse, N. G.; F. W. Rhoads, V. G.; Francis Hoover, R. S.; William F. Smith, Asst. R. S.; William Rote, treasurer.

SHAMOKIN LODGE, NO. 156, K. OF P.

This order was organized June 9th, 1869. The charter members were: W. H. Musselman, A. J. Medler, Jeremiah Drew, J. A. Weaver, Jos. Wolf, Reuben Kline, Thomas M. Helm, John Jones, and John Kline.

The first officers were: W. H. Musselman, P. C.; Reuben Kline, G. C.; John Jones, V. C.; Jeremiah Drew, F. S.; Thos. M. Helm, R. S.

The present officers are: Wm. Caldwell, P. C.; Joseph Shivelhard, G. C.; Michael Moll, V. C.; Gabriel Warz, M. of F.; W. H. Musselman, M. of E.; Jeremiah Drew, K. of R. and S.

This society numbers seventy-five members, and is in a prosperous state. It meets in Helfenstein's Hall, on Thursday evenings. It is a beneficial society.

SHAMOKIN LODGE, NO. 90.—AMERICAN PROTESTANT ASSOCIATION.

The first officers were: D. S. Miller, W. M.; James Fullmer, W. D. M.; Jno. K. Slesser, R. S.; John Berdouier, F. S.; Joseph Henninger, treasurer.

The present officers are: Elias Culp, W. M.; Henry Startzel, W. D. M.; Isaac Smirk, R. S.; Frank Price, F. S.

This lodge was very prosperous for some months after its formation, but some divisions, in its membership, has reduced its numbers. There are at present, forty members, and the lodge appears to be on the increase again. The meetings are held in Helfenstein's Hall, on Friday evenings.

SHAMOKIN LODGE OF D. O. H., NO. 115.

This order was started in Shamokin, July 13th, 1865. The charter members were: N. Deitman, Christian Lawrence, Henry Bach, John Geyrioty, and John Myers.

The first officers were: Henry Bach, N. G.; Christian Lawrence, V. G.; N. Deitman, secretary; Sol. Fegely, treasurer.

The present officials are: Fred. Petermann, N. G.; John Conder, V. G.; Joseph Conrad, secretary; Martin Hoffmann, treasurer.

This lodge has thirty-three members. It meets weekly, in Miller's Hall, on Thursday evening. It is a beneficial order, similar to the Odd Fellows in its workings, and nearly all its members are Germans. The exercises are conducted in the German language.

SHICKALAMY TRIBE, NO. 148, IMPROVED ORDER OF RED MEN,

Was organized at Shamokin, on the 15th day of March, A. D. 1870.

Its place of meeting is in the third-story of May's building, corner of Shamokin and Commerce streets.

First officers installed were the following: Sachem, John Kemp; Senior Sagamore, A. F. Elms; Junior Sagamore, Isaac A. Kerlin; Prophet, Samuel Hirsh; Chief of Records, W. F. Smith; Keeper of Wampum, Isaac Smirk.

Its membership numbers seventy-five, in good standing.

The objects of the order are freedom, friendship, and charity.

The present officers of the tribe are: Sachem, C. W. Scout; Senior Sagamore, B. F. Gillham; Junior Sagamore, R. T. Gillham; Prophet, John Hancock; Chief of Records, R. T. Owen; Keeper of Wampum, W. F. Smith.

SHAMOKIN COUNCIL, NO. 71, O. U. A. M.

Organized in 1865. Present officers: C., W. Linderman; V. C., J. J. Hoffman; secretary, Jeremiah Dreis; treasurer, Simeon Hoffman.

This order has fifty-six members, and meets at Haas & Seiler's Hall, on Wednesday evenings.

WASHINGTON CAMP, NO. 30, P. O. S. OF A.

Organized in November, 1869. The present officers are: P. P., Daniel Carl; P., P. R. Mentchler; V. P., Henry Walp; Secretary, W. F. Harpel; Treasurer, Jeremiah Helt.

There are eighty members. Meetings on Monday evening, in Odd Fellows' Hall.

WASHINGTON CAMP, NO. 149, P. O. S. OF A.

Organized in August, 1874. Present officers: P. P., H. R. Rupert; P., A. J. Campbell; V. P., S. A. Smith; Secretary, A. E. Zuerne; Treasurer, D. Y. Gillham.

There are fifty-nine members. Meets on Tuesday evenings, in Helfenstein's Hall.

KNIGHTS OF THE MYSTIC CHAIN.

Cœur de Lion Castle, No. 31.—This order was organized July 5th, 1872. It numbers one hundred and fifteen members. The meetings are on Monday evenings, in Haas & Seiler's Hall.

The present officers are: S. K. C., Edward Yoder; S. K. V. C., Jonas Trego; S. K. F. L., Alexander Ross; R. S., J. P. Boyd; F. S., Thomas M. Dilly; Treasurer, William F. Lake.

SHAMOKIN MARBLE-WORKS.

These works were established in 1871, by Boyd & Rumberger, the present proprietors.

Their business is principally confined to this and neighboring counties, and is chiefly building tombstones and monuments, constructing cemetery enclosures and building work.

Annual trade, about five thousand dollars.

MERCANTILE APPRAISEMENT FOR SHAMOKIN, 1876.

Number of stores, eighty-seven; lumber-yards, three; coal-yards, two; licensed houses, thirty-five; billiard tables, one.

INTERMENTS IN SHAMOKIN CEMETERY FOR 1875.

Adults, and children over two years, forty-two; children under two years, eighty-nine; total, one hundred and thirty-one.

NORTHUMBERLAND COUNTY NATIONAL BANK, OF SHAMOKIN.

This is the oldest banking institution in Shamokin, and after passing through a great many vicissitudes in its early days, it has, through the able management of late years, become noted as one of the soundest institutions in the County. It is located in a fine building, in the central part of the town, and is under the charge of a very efficient president and other officials.

PLATE XXV

RES. OF REV. M. J. CAROTHERS, 2D & MARKET ST, MILTON, NORTHD COUNTY, PA

HOMESTEAD OF DAVID MARR, DECEASED, PRESENT RESIDENCE OF THE FAMILY, MILTON, NORTHD CO, PA.

The first movement toward establishing a bank in Shamokin, was made on January 31st, 1855, when a number of citizens met at the National Hotel, and discussed the propriety of starting such an institution. The meeting was followed by others, and finally, a bill was prepared, which passed the legislature in April, 1857, through the efforts of J. H. Zimmerman, our member then, and others. The authorized capital was one hundred and fifty thousand dollars.

On June 8th, 1857, the commissioners met at Shamokin. The following commissioners were present: John Taggart, William L. Dewart, Josiah Reed, John P. Pursel, Daniel Evert, S. M. Kase, Joseph Bird, W. H. Muench, John B. Douty, F. A. Clark, Solomon Marts, Casper Schall, Henry Van Gasken, Jonas L. Gilger, Elias Eisenhart, A. R. Fiske, W. P. Withington, W. H. Marshall, D. J. Lewis, and Stephen Bittenbender.

John Taggart was elected president of the meeting, and W. P. Withington, secretary. A number of committees were appointed to secure subscriptions to the stock. After the County and town had been pretty thoroughly canvassed, a second meeting was called, and it was found that only one hundred and twenty shares of stock had been subscribed. A different course then, unfortunately, was pursued. The institution was passed over to a party from Buffalo, consisting of Thayer, Robinson, Street, and others, who were interested in new banks at Warren, Crawford County, Tioga, and other places, loosely instituted for speculation.

They took one thousand five hundred and twenty shares, paying seven thousand dollars in gold and twenty-eight thousand dollars in notes on these doubtful banks. J. H. Robinson was elected cashier. Great dissatisfaction soon prevailed with the management, and in the Spring of 1858, a committee appointed by the legislature examined its condition, and made a very damaging report.

In August, 1858, this party was gotten rid of, and a new organization was effected, consisting of well-known and responsible citizens, as follows: Directors, Joseph Bird, William M. Weaver, Elias Eisenhart, William H. Marshall, George Schall, Felix Maurer, William Deffen, Elisha John, William T. Grant, Horatio Wolverton, William Elliott, and Joseph Hoover. J. H. Zimmerman was elected president, Samuel John, cashier, and Charles W. Peale, teller.

Things now assumed a better shape, but, owing to the dullness of the times, the officials had a severe struggle to regain the confidence that had been lost through the mismanagement of adventurers.

At the close of 1858, J. H. Zimmerman resigned, and Felix Maurer was elected president. The bank was located in Bittenbender's Building, on Shamokin street. To show the condition of the bank at that time, their statement for December, 1858, is given:

Bills receivable, $60,906.41; stock owned by bank, $9,750.00; specie in vault, $8,121.16; due by other banks, $2,527.68; notes of other solvent banks, $2,210.00; bank property, $2,168.00; due by city bankers, $2,442.15; total, $88,125.40. Notes in circulation, $16,000; due depositors, $9,707; due other banks, $313.56; total, $26,020.56.

During the early part of 1859, another committee was ordered to examine the condition of this bank.

In August, same year, strong efforts were made by some of the stockholders, to have the institution moved to Sunbury, on account of their being so little business in Shamokin.

In November, 1859, Samuel John, resigned as cashier, when the following changes were made: F. W. Pollock, of Lewisburg, was elected president; and Charles W. Peale, cashier.

The prospects of the institution soon became more encouraging. The bills of the bank, which previously had no circulation out of the neighborhood, and sometimes difficult to pass at home, now were looked upon as something like money. Confidence became established, and the bank stock commenced to advanced.

In 1861, Bicknell's Reporter speaks decidedly in favor of the bank, and gives great credit to the good management of its officers. This year, the bank issued one and two dollars bills.

In January, 1863, C. W. Peale resigned as cashier, and was succeeded by Thomas C. Trotter, of Philadelphia, who served until December 15th, when he resigned, and Thomas D. Grant, of Sunbury, was appointed. About this time, the name was changed from the "Shamokin Bank," to "Northumberland County Bank." The old red Shamokin bills were called in, and new ones of a different color circulated.

On February 1st, 1865, it became a National Bank.

During August, this year, one hundred and twenty thousand dollars of the old issue of their notes were burned in Mr. Bittenbender's work-house, superintended by S. Bittenbender, V. Fegely, P. Bird, and F. A. Clark.

About April 1st, 1865, Thomas D. Grant resigned as cashier, and was succeeded by T. G. Boyle.

During the Spring of 1868, a lot was secured on the corner of Sunbury and Washington streets, and preparations were made at once to erect a banking-house, suitable to the wants of such a well-conducted and substantial institution. The building was completed and occupied about February 1st, 1869.

The edifice is of brick, and three-stories high, with a very imposing front. The building is thirty feet front, and seventy-five deep. It costs ten thousand dollars. The banking-room and the directors'-room, are very comfortable and neatly fitted up for the business. The bank is provided with a large and first-class safe. The remainder of the building is occupied by a family. Mr. Daniel Yost was the builder.

In June, 1869, Mr. F. S. Haas, was elected cashier, which position he ably fills at the present time.

When Mr. Pollock took charge of the bank, in 1859, the amount due depositors, was about two thousand dollars; now it exceeds three hundred thousand dollars. At that time, shares were valued at little over five dollars; now shares are quoted at one dollar and ten cents. The present capital of the bank, is sixty-seven thousand dollars. The officers are: President, F. W. Pollock; Cashier, F. S. Haas; Teller, Samuel J. Haas.

THE SHAMOKIN BANKING COMPANY

Was chartered May 24th, 1871.

Incorporators.—Conrad Graeber, Alfred J. Medlar, George W. Ryan, Charles F. Rahn, George McEleice, Levi Huber; George W. Ryan, president; Conrad Graber, vice-president; Ivanhoe S. Huber, cashier.

Business was commenced September 4th, 1871. Authorized capital, one hundred thousand dollars; paid up, fifty thousand dollars. The Bank is chartered by the State, and does the usual banking business, receiving deposits, discounting paper, etc. Exchanges on most places in Europe bought and sold.

The original Board of Directors were: G. W. Ryan, Conrad Graeber, Samuel John, W. H. Marshall, C. P. Helfenstein, A. A. Hein, and G. McEleice, of Shamokin; Levi Huber, A. J. Medlar, Charles F. Rahn, and Jacob Huntziger, of Pottsville.

The present officers are: Conrad Graeber, president; A. A. Hein, vice-president; Ivanhoe S. Huber, cashier; D. W. Hein, teller, and George W. Ryan, solicitor. Place of business on Sunbury street, near the corner of Sunbury and Washington streets. Average deposits, about two hundred thousand dollars.

THE MINERS' TRUST AND SAFE DEPOSIT COMPANY

Was incorporated in the year 1871, by the following gentlemen as incorporators: A. Robinson, Isaac May, Henry Gayterman, A. Langdon, Alex. Fulton, and A. G. Marr. The original incorporators became, and continue, to be the Board of Directors. A. Robinson was chosen first president; Isaac May, vice-president; A. G. Marr, cashier; Wellington Lake, teller. The banking-house of A. G. and J. C. Marr was merged into and formed the nucleus of the company as now organized. The business done is that of general banking, receiving deposits, discounting, etc.

The present officers are: Isaac May, president; A. Langdon, vice-president; A. G. Marr, cashier, and Wellington Lake, teller.

The banking-house is a very neat building, situated on the corner of Sunbury and Rock streets, and appears to have been designed for the purpose implied in its name—the safe and trusty keeping of the deposits of its customers.

MINERS' SAVING FUND ASSOCIATION.

This was the first building association in Shamokin. It was organized through the efforts of R. B. Douty, O. M. Fowler, and a few others, who were convinced, that through such means, a large number of workingmen would be able to build up homes for themselves. And, perhaps, it is safe to say, that no other one influence contributed so much towards building up Shamokin, and making its citizens interested in its welfare, than this society. The association was organized August 14th, 1865.

The first officers were: President, R. B. Douty; Secretary, O. M. Fowler; Treasurer, W. H. Douty.

In September, 1873, the secretary reports that, after eight years, with ninety-six payments, made on eight hundred and eighty-six original shares, there are one hundred and twenty-five yet to cancel.

In March, 1870, a second series was issued, of which seven hundred and fifty-eight shares were taken. The remaining shares of the first series were all cancelled on September 1st, 1876, and only about one hundred shares of the second series are still outstanding. It is estimated that all these will be cancelled in two years, and the business of the association closed. A move had been made to issue another series, but the times were not favorable. The monthly meetings are on the third Monday of each month, in the Liberty Hose Building.

The present officers are: President, J. H. Zimmerman; Secretary, Alex. Caldwell; W. H. Douty.

WEST WARD BUILDING AND LOAN ASSOCIATION.

This association was organized December 23d, 1878. About five hundred shares were represented.

Officers elected: President, J. H. Zimmerman; Secretary, W. Lake; Treasurer, John Dunkleberger.

Stated monthly meetings of stockholders are held on the first Tuesday after the third Saturday of each month. Directors' meeting is held on the Tuesday night following the meeting.

The society is in a prosperous condition—fifteen hundred shares were taken out. There are about eight hundred five shares at the present time.

The present officers are: President, R. S. Aucker; Secretary, W. H. Shipe; Treasurer, R. G. Eisenhart.

The meetings are held in Haas & Seiler's Hall, on Spruce street.

---

*TREVORTON.

The town of Trevorton is pleasantly located, in a narrow valley, on a tributary of the Mahanoy Creek, just outside of the coal basin, in the northern part of Zerbe township; connected with Shamokin on the east, and the Susquehanna River on the west, by a branch of the Philadelphia and Reading Railroad. It is eight miles from Shamokin and twelve miles from the river.

It takes its name from John B. Trevor, who was one of the members of the Shamokin and Mahanoy Improvement Company, the party that bought the bonds, developed the mines, and constructed a railroad to the Susquehanna River.

Howell, Helfenstein & Co.—who were the Improvement Company—having purchased the tract, erected an office in the Spring of 1850, and secured the services of Kimber Cleaver, who proceeded at once to lay out the town. At this time, there was only one house on the site of the town—an old log one—occupied by George Holshue and family, consisting of eight persons. This house was located at the west end of the town, but has long since given way to the march of improvement. About a mile up the "Gap," on the coal lands, was another rude house, occupied by James Rennie, a Scotchman, who still resides at Trevorton, well advanced in years. He may justly be regarded as the patriarch of the town. For many years, he was the sole occupant of the coal tracts of Zerbe, holding possession for various owners. He had made some coal openings, and, during the winter months, with pick, shovel, and wheelbarrow, supplied the farmers of the neighborhood with coal. He still resides here, well-advanced in years, being some eighty-eight years of age.

On May 28th, 1850, there was held the great sale of town lots at Trevorton. Immense preparations had been made for this event, and on the day of sale, people from all parts of Northumberland, and several sections of adjoining counties, were on the new town site, with a view of making purchases. A meeting was organized, and some speeches were made, when Judge Jordan threw off his coat, and broke the first ground. In the hole made, there was deposited a bottle of Susquehanna water, a lump of coal from Zerbe Gap, and a lump of iron ore from the adjacent mountain. Then, after an address by Mr. Bellas, Judge Helfenstein came forward, and published the bans, as follows: "I publish the bans between Zerbe Gap and the Susquehanna River; if any one know just cause or impediment, why the two should not be joined together by a railroad, on the *first of November, next*, let him declare it now, or ever hereafter hold his peace." This announcement was received with great applause. A collation was then eaten by the audience, at which Mr. Rennie occupied the seat of honor; after which the sale of lots commenced. The bidding was spirited, and a large number of lots were sold; the price ranging from twenty-five to one hundred dollars. Liberal provisions were made for churches; a railroad to the Susquehanna River had been placed under contract; possessed of most excellent water, and superior drainage, with wide streets, and delightful scenery, it seemed to offer superior inducements for a large town.

The lots were sold in such a manner, that the laborers could buy, without money, and pay a portion of their wages each month. By these means, the town improved rapidly for the next few months. On the first day of May, the town site was a perfect wilderness, with one log house on the site; at the end of October, there were nearly one hundred houses erected. The company had opened a large store, and made every preparation for business. In their anxiety to send some Trevorton coal to market, they hauled two or three boat-loads of coal to Sunbury, in the Autumn of same year, and had it shipped to New York by canal.

Things went on prosperously until December 6th, 1851, when the company suspended, and all work was stopped for nearly two years.

In the Fall of 1853, a New York company took hold of the concern, and pushed things forward with great vigor. They erected a saw-mill, built a large breaker, in 1854, and in January, 1855, completed the railroad to the river, and erected a splendid bridge, three thousand six hundred feet long, across to Port Trevorton, where wharves were constructed, and the coal was dumped in boats. As soon as the shipment of coal commenced, the progress of the town became very great. Every house was crowded with tenants. This party continued at work until the Fall of 1857, when they were obliged to suspend. After a few months, a company from New York took possession, and continued work about a year, when it was turned over to another party, with George Mowton as superintendent, who pushed things forward with great vigor for some years.

Things thus continued until the Philadelphia and Reading Railroad Company purchased the railroad from Trevorton to the Susquehanna River, and acquired an interest in the Trevorton coal lands. They commenced opening a railroad between Shamokin and Trevorton, which was completed in July, 1869. Z. P. Boyer & Co. were the first shippers of coal over this road.

There are two collieries at Trevorton, operated by the Philadelphia and Reading Coal and Iron Company. The shipments are not extensive. The population at the present time is about one thousand four hundred, though in its most prosperous days it exceeded two thousand six hundred.

FIRST POST-MASTER.

Dr. William Atwater was appointed post-master of the village, on December 21st, 1850. He was afterwards a citizen of Shamokin for many years.

THE FIRST WEDDING.

On Tuesday, December 24th, 1850, Mr. Michael Chappell was married to Miss Rebecca, daughter of James Rennie, Esq., the pioneer of Trevorton. In honor of the event, the following presents were bestowed: The wife—the best dress in Company's store; the husband—a town lot.

THE FIRST CHILD.

John B. Knopp was the first child born in the town, and, according to custom, received a present of a town lot.

THE FIRST HOTEL.

The "Trevorton House" was the first hotel opened in Trevorton. It was opened by Henry B. Weaver, the present landlord. In 1850, Mr. Weaver was keeping a hotel in Danville, but was induced by Mr. Boyd and others, to open a public house in the new town just laid out. Mr. Weaver had prepared the collation at the founding of the town, and had made some purchases of lots on this occasion. Urged by the proprietors, he put up a building for a hotel, and on August 28th, 1850, moved into it, which was yet minus windows and doors. At this time, there were some five or six houses erected. Mr. Weaver still keeps the house, which is a credit to the place.

FIRST FOURTH OF JULY CELEBRATION.

The first celebration was held July 4th, 1851. Mr. Weaver prepared a breakfast on the top of the Little Mountain, which was partaken of by a number of persons, including the Danville Band, who were on their way to Trevorton. An oration was delivered by Robert C. Helfenstein, Esq., and during the evening there was a splendid display of fireworks.

---

* The History of Shamokin, Trevorton and Mount Carmel has been prepared by Dr. J. J. John, of Shamokin, a long resident of that place. Its history is a part of his own experience in the battle of life he has so successfully fought.

FIRST CHURCH.

The first church erected was the Methodist, put up in 1856. The first services were held in a frame carpenter-shop.

FIRST PHYSICIAN.

The first physician was a gentleman by the name of Holmes, who remained a short time.

FIRST JUSTICE.

David Dumbach was the first justice of the peace.

ST. PATRICK'S CHURCH (CATHOLIC).

As soon as work in the coal mines was started at Trevorton, a number of Irish Catholic families, together with a few Germans, were found in this new place, attended by Rev. Michael Sherridan, pastor of St. Joseph's congregation, at Danville. The first catholic service was held in the house of Mr. Compton, and the first baptism and marriage are recorded in the church-book, October 1st, 1854. In 1857, Rev. George Gostenschnig, an Austrian priest, the well-known "Father George" throughout the whole County, took up a collection for the building of a church. He continued in his collections till May, 1859, when the contract for the stone-work was signed, and the work commenced. The church is built of mountain white sand-stone, thirty-five by sixty-five feet; walls, twenty feet high. The following September, the church was under roof, and on the 19th of the month, the plastering was given out. In May, 1860, the building was completed, and on the 20th of the month was dedicated by Bishop Newman, of Philadelphia. But it was not allotted to "Father George" the crowning event of his untiring work. In making preparations for its dedication, he overheated himself, and died on May 18th, at Milton, where he was buried on the 21st. The church, however, was dedicated on the appointed day, in the presence of a large concourse of mourning people of all denominations.

Rev. E. Stenzel was soon appointed pastor, and was succeeded by Rev. M. Multberger, in 1861, who was succeeded by Rev. E. Murray, in 1862. In November, 1863, Rev. Joseph Koch was appointed pastor of St. Joseph's Church, at Milton, with the charge of St. Patrick's, Trevorton. Since that date, the Catholic congregation has been attended by him without interruption. Under his able pastorate, the debts of the church have been paid, the building has been enlarged, the interior has been painted and handsomely frescoed, a stone-wall has been erected in front of the cemetery, east of the church, and a good substantial fence put all around the two blocks which form the Catholic Church property. Under the charge of so energetic a man as Father Koch, no church property is allowed to suffer for want of attention.

The frequent and continued suspension in the coal trade, particularly affected the Catholics, whose support depended on this kind of business. The most of the old Irish settlers left for Shamokin, where they could improve their condition, so that the congregation at this writing is almost exclusively German.

The church numbers two hundred and fifty communicants. Divine service is held every Sunday in the year, either by Father Koch, or his assistant.

ST. PATRICK'S SUNDAY-SCHOOL.

This school has been established for several years, and numbers something over one hundred scholars. It is under the control of the pastor.

ST. PATRICK'S BENEFICIAL SOCIETY.

This society numbers over forty members, and is in a prosperous condition.

METHODIST EPISCOPAL CHURCH, OF TREVORTON.

There were quite a number of Methodist families at Trevorton, soon after it started. The society was organized in 1854. The first pastor was the Rev. Mr. Russ. The congregation put up a brick building, in 1856, but being too small, and not well adapted to church purposes, it was sold to the School Board, and a frame building, better adapted to the wants of the people, erected in 1858. The church will accommodate four hundred and fifty.

The congregation has been greatly reduced during the past year, owing to the large number of removals to other places.

The membership numbers about one hundred. The present pastor is the Rev. John W. Feight.

METHODIST SUNDAY-SCHOOL.

This school was started in 1858. A. A. Heim, now of Shamokin, was the first superintendent; the present superintendent is John Cooper.

Number of scholars, one hundred; number of teachers, fifteen; number of volumes in library, three hundred and fifty.

BAPTIST CHURCH.

This is a fine stone structure, located on Coal street. It was commenced in 1860, and dedicated in 1861. Mr. Mowton, the superintendent of the Trevorton Company at that time, took an active part in its erection. The congregation soon dwindled down to a small number, owing to many of the members moving away, and the building was finally leased to the Evangelical Society, who occupy it at the present time.

TREVORTON EVANGELICAL CHURCH.

This society was started about 1856. Their services were held in a school-house for some years. During 1860, a frame church was erected on Coal street, but only the basement was completed. It will seat about two hundred.

The society has rented the Baptist Church for five years, and worship there. The present membership is seventy.

The pastors are Revs. B. F. Miller and I. H. Shirer. The trustees are: Joseph Kline, Daniel Smith, David Feister, L. L. Conrad, and Joel Derk.

EVANGELICAL SUNDAY-SCHOOL.

School was started in 1866. Number of scholars, one hundred; number of teachers, fourteen; number of volumes in library, one hundred and fifty.

LUTHERAN CHURCH.

The Lutheran Church is a plain frame building, located on Market street. It was erected about 1858. The congregation numbers about fifty persons.

LUTHERAN SUNDAY-SCHOOL.

The Lutheran school was organized in 1875. The present superintendent is B. F. Miller. Number of scholars, seventy-five; number of teachers, eight; number of volumes in library, sixty-seven.

POWDER-MILLS IN VICINITY.

Maurer & Co. have two mills, with a capacity of eighteen thousand kegs per year; Beury & Co. have one mill, with a capacity of nine thousand kegs per year; A. S. Speece has one mill, with a capacity of nine thousand kegs per year; Bruce & Weaver have one mill, with a capacity of nine thousand kegs per year. Sales of powder made in Northumberland and Schuylkill Counties, and the soft-coal region.

FLOURING-MILL.

A. S. Speece has a merchant flouring-mill, water-power, with the capacity of one hundred bushels of grain per day.

VINEGAR FACTORY.

Mr. D. C. Brymire has a vinegar factory. He manufactures over two hundred barrels of vinegar per annum.

LIME-KILNS.

H. J. Renn has four lime-kilns at Trevorton, at which he burns large quantities of lime for the surrounding country.

LODGES.

There are four lodges of secret societies in Trevorton. They are Knights of Pythias, Odd Fellows, Red Men, and American Mechanics.

STORES AND HOTELS.

There are four dry goods and grocery-stores, one shoe-store, two tin and stove-stores.

There are five hotels, the principal ones being the Trevorton House, the Grant Hotel, and the Franklin House.

PUBLIC SCHOOLS.

There are two good brick school buildings, one located on Shamokin street, the other on Market street. There are six schools, divided as follows: One high-school, one grammar-school, two secondary-schools, and two primary-schools.

Miss May Hay, a most-excellent and experienced teacher, is the Principal. The schools are well graded, and in a very satisfactory condition.

The first school-house was a small one-story building. In 1857, the Board secured the services of Miss Hay, of Pottsville, who first graded the schools. Some years ago, the Methodist Church was purchased for a school-house, and now has two schools. In 1872, the fine two-story brick building on Shamokin street was erected, containing four rooms, well ventilated, heated by a furnace, and furnished with patent desks.

JAMES RENNIE, ESQ.

The most interesting personage at Trevorton is its pioneer settler, James Rennie, an old gentleman of great intelligence. Upon being questioned by the writer, recently, in regard to his nationality, he replied: "I am neither a Scotchman, or Englishman, or Welshman, nor an Irishman, but was born in Great Britain for all that. I was born at Berwick-on-Tweed, a small island of seven miles, which is regarded as neutral ground."

Mr. Rennie was born in 1788, and is consequently in his eighty-ninth year. He came to America in 1830, and first settled at Pottsville, but soon moved to Sunbury, where he became acquainted with Mr. Bellas. About 1828, a man by the name of Weise, son of the miner who made the first coal openings at Mauch Chunk, was employed by Burd Patterson, Hugh Bellas, and others, to make some developments of the coal veins at Zerbe Gap. Weise proceeded to uncover the veins instead of driving a drift. His work was not satisfactory to his employers, and they at last got rid of him. He was a terrible swearer, and was looked upon with fear.

Mr. Rennie took charge of the place about 1833. He built the house he now occupies, about one mile south of Trevorton. His duties were to develop the coal lands, and hold possession of them. During the Winter months, he sold considerable coal to the farmers, who came far and near to what was then called Rennie's mines. He had no neighbors within one mile, and no place of business nearer than Sunbury, which was twelve miles off. Mrs. Rennie says, sometimes she did not see a woman's face from Christmas to the 4th of July.

Mr. Rennie opened the first drift, and for years was the sole miner of the region. There were plenty of deer and foxes in the woods, but no wolves. Samuel Sleuker lived in a log-house—where the Grand Hotel now stands—a small orchard was on the premises.

Mr. Rennie was well represented in the late Rebellion. His five daughters had five sons in the war. He had eleven grandsons in the Union army. He is a patriotic old gentleman, and loves his adopted country.

Mr. Rennie says, that coal was discovered at Zerbe Gap by being exposed by the water. He is a practical miner, having commenced mining when ten years of age, and continued to work in the mines until he was sixty-nine. Mrs. Rennie is eighty years of age. Both of them enjoy excellent health. He has a good library of English and Scotch works, and for forty years he has spent his evenings in reading his favorite authors, among which is Robert Burns. Mr. Rennie is a good talker, possesses excellent sense, is well read, is fond of a joke, and is very hospitable. For years, his home was head-quarters for all who visited the region. Professor Roberts, in making his geological survey, stopped with him, and Mr. Patrick Daly, one of his valuable assistants, ever regarded it a home.

Mr. Rennie is now in the employ of the Philadelphia & Reading Coal and and Iron Company.

*MOUNT CARMEL.

The borough of Mount Carmel possesses a very fine location, being situated on an elevated plain, between Red Ridge and Locust Mountain. The health of the place is excellent. It has good drainage, and is plentifully supplied with the purest of water. There is not a town in Northumberland County that has a better site. Its railroad communications are good. The Lehigh Valley, the Philadelphia and Reading Railroad, and the Northern Central Railway, connect with the town, and offer excellent facilities for freight and travel.

It is somewhat singular that a place so favorably located, so closely connected with the cities of Philadelphia and New York, and possessed of such beautiful scenery, should not become a favorite Summer resort. The pure water, the bracing air, and the mountain landscape should be great attractions to the residents of crowded cities.

The first settler in the vicinity of Mount Carmel, of which there is any record, is a Brooks Wilkerson, who made pots, somewhere near where Graham's tavern now stands, in 1809.

The first house erected in Mount Carmel, was by Richard Yarnall, about 1812. He erected a log hotel on the site of the present "Deffen House," on the corner of Third and Oak streets. He kept tavern here for four years, when he moved near Bear Gap. Thomas Osman succeeded him, and kept the house for several years. In 1831, the house was taken by Felix Lerch, and kept by him until 1838, when he was followed by Solomon Fegely, who kept it several years. Paul Roth succeeded Fegely, and kept the place for several years. When Roth left, the tavern was abandoned for some time; but in 1846, when the steam saw-mill was erected, the hotel was opened by a Mr. Perkins. In the Spring of 1849, Felix Lerch, again took the stand, and kept it until 1854, when he was succeeded by his son, William H. Lerch.

The town was laid out in 1853, by Charles Hegins, F. W. Hughes, W. L. Dewart, and others, and in 1863, was created a borough. The town derives its name from the post-office here named, with this scriptural title. The present population is about two thousand.

FIRST MARRIAGE.

The first marriage in the town, was that of Charles Culp to Elizabeth Lerch, daughter of Felix Lerch. A lot was presented to the bride.

FIRST BIRTH.

The first child born in the town was Sarah Culp.

FIRST SCHOOL TEACHER.

John T. Mervine was the first teacher in the town.

FIRST MECHANICS.

First shoemaker, Isaac Hollister; first tin-shop, Benjamin Fegely; first blacksmith, Isaac Miller; first carpenter, John H. Yarnell.

FIRST STORES.

Dr. William J. Haas started the first drug-store; David J. Lewis started the first dry goods store; William H. Lerch started the first shoe and clothing-store; Henry Trugellar started the first hardware-store.

FIRST HOUSE.

The first house was erected by D. J. Lewis.

PROFESSIONAL.

First physician, Dr. William J. Haas; first dentist, George Mears.

FIRST POST-MASTER.

Paul Roth was appointed the first post-master, in 1846, when the Bradford's steam saw-mill started.

FIRST SHIPPER OF COAL.

D. J. Lewis was the first shipper of coal by railroad; the shipment was made from Green Ridge Colliery.

FIRST BOROUGH OFFICERS.

Chief Burgess, Dr. William J. Haas; Council—John H. Yarnell, William Biles, A. F. Stecker, J. L. Stine, and Obed Kerr; Constable, George A. Keeler; Justice of Peace, Felix Lerch.

THE PIONEER CITIZEN.

Mr. Jesse Yarnell is the oldest citizen. He is a son of Richard Yarnell. He states that years ago he found many Indian relics around Mt. Carmel, such as dart-heads, etc.

An Indian trail leading from Mahanoy to Catawissa, passes through Mt. Carmel, and Mr. Yarnell was familiar with its course.

THE OLD TAVERN STAND.

This was located on the Centre turnpike, a short distance north of the Northern Central Railway. It was erected by a Mr. Louison, previous to the Revolution. It was an old log structure, and was last kept by Jesse Yarnell.

* The History of Shamokin, Trevorton, and Mount Carmel, has been prepared by Dr. J. J. John, of Shamokin, a long resident of that place. His history is a part of his own experience in the battle of life he has so successfully fought.

"RIVERSIDE NURSERY," DAVID CLIFFE, PROP.
DEALER IN ALL KINDS OF NURSERY STOCK, RIVERSIDE, NORTH'D COUNTY, PA.

RES. OF JOHN KNOUF, MILTON, NORTHUMBERLAND COUNTY, PA.

Years ago, it was kept by a man by the name of Kunkle, and after that by one named Riffert. During this time, numerous robberies were committed in the vicinity, and it was supposed this old building was their headquarters.

HOTELS.

The three principal hotels of the place, are the Mt. Carmel House, the National, and the Diffen House.

MERCANTILE APPRAISEMENT.

By the last appraisement made, Mt. Carmel has twenty-six stores, and eight licensed places.

PRESENT BOROUGH OFFICIALS.

Chief Burgess, Geo. E. Moser; Council—H. T. John, Rudolph Herb, B. Harvey, John Stine, Chas. Whitman, and David Camp.

PUBLIC SCHOOLS.

There are two school buildings—one brick and one frame. The brick building is two-stories high, and containes four rooms, furnished with patent desks. The rooms are heated by a furnace. It was erected at a cost of four thousand dollars.

There is one high-school, one grammar, one secondary, and three primary schools.

For the past two years, they have been under the charge of Prof. Jno. E. Ross, during which time they have been brought up to a high degree of excellence. During 1875, the average attendance was three hundred and fifty, out of four hundred admitted.

CHURCHES.

The first religious services were held in the school-house, about 1853, by the Rev. Mr. Fisher, of Sunbury. The first church erected was the Methodist, in 1854, through the efforts of Rev. F. B. Riddle, then of Shamokin.

ST. MARY'S CATHOLIC CHURCH.

The Catholics of Mt. Carmel were served by Rev. Mr. Sherridan, pastor of St. Joseph's Church, Ashland. In 1868, the new diocese of Harrisburg was formed, with Bishop Shanahan as its first bishop. The County of Northumberland was included in the division, and Mt. Carmel was added to the Shamokin parish. The first Catholic service was held by Rev. Joseph Koch, in August, of this year, in the Beaver Dale school-house. He kept charge of the Catholics until the following October, when they were placed under the pastorate of Rev. Daniel J. McDermott, appointed to Centralia. Early in 1869, Mr. McDermott having organized the new congregation, began the building of a church in the borough of Mt. Carmel, and on the 1st of November following, had it completed and dedicated, by Bishop Shanahan.

The church is a frame structure, gothic style, forty-two feet front, by forty-four feet deep, and one story high.

During the same month, Mr. McDermott resigned this mission, and it was again transferred to Shamokin parish. Rev. Joseph Koch took charge of it, and with the aid of his assistant, attended to it regularly every Sunday until October, 1871, when it was placed under the charge of Rev. E. T. Field, successor of Mr. McDermott, at Centralia.

The congregation numbers about four hundred communicants. The church is entirely free from debt.

ST. MARY'S SUNDAY-SCHOOL.

This school was organized about the same time as the church. It averages about one hundred and fifty scholars.

ST. MARY'S BENEFICIAL SOCIETY.

Organized by Rev. Joseph Koch, in 1870. There are upwards of fifty members. The society is in a flourishing condition.

POLISH CATHOLIC CHURCH.

A Polish congregation has been recently formed, under the charge of the Polish priest of Shamokin. They have divine service regularly on every Sunday. There are about two hundred and fifty communicants. They worship at present in St. Mary's Church, but purpose building as soon as the times will admit.

POLISH BENEFICIAL SOCIETY.

There is also a Polish Beneficial Society connected with the church, which numbers upwards of seventy members.

ST. PAUL'S CHURCH OF THE EVANGELICAL ASSOCIATION.

This church was erected in the Fall of 1871. The first services were held that Winter, by Rev. Thomas Bowman, presiding elder of Pottsville district.

It was organized into a mission in 1872, with the Rev. James Bowman as missionary.

The present pastors are Rev. L. N. Worman and N. B. Sheik. The church is a brick structure, forty by sixty feet. The audience-room is not yet completed, but the services are held in the lecture-room. The church numbers sixty members.

ST. PAUL'S EVANGELICAL SUNDAY-SCHOOL.

The school was organized in April, 1872, by the Rev. James Bowman, the first missionary, who was the first superintendent. The present superintendent is L. N. Worman. Number of scholars, one hundred and forty; number of teachers, twenty-five.

Have no library, but use papers, etc.

LUTHERAN CHURCH.

The Lutheran congregation was organized in 1860, and during same year, obtained a charter. The first pastor was Rev. Mr. Heisler. He was succeeded by Rev. J. F. Wampole, who attended this charge for many years.

The church edifice was dedicated July 20th, 1867. It is a neat, plain frame building, located on Mount Carmel street. The present pastor is Rev. J. A. Adams, who preaches here every two weeks. The membership numbers about fifty.

LUTHERAN SUNDAY-SCHOOL.

Was organized soon after the congregation was formed. Number of scholars, eighty; number of teachers, ten; number of volumes in library, three hundred.

PRIMITIVE METHODIST CHURCH.

This congregation worshiped in a frame church located on Market street. Membership about fifty. They have a Sunday-school.

UNITED BRETHREN CHURCH,

Located just outside the borough limits. Rev. I. P. Sanders is the pastor. Membership about fifty. There is a Sunday-school connected with the church.

WELSH BAPTIST CHURCH.

The church edifice of this denomination, is located on Market street. It was erected in 1871. The membership was not obtained.

METHODIST EPISCOPAL CHURCH.

About 1856, Rev. Mr. Rothrock preached in the public school-house. This was the first Methodist service in Mt. Carmel. At this time, a class was formed, and preaching in the school-house was had occasionally.

While Rev. F. B. Riddle was stationed at Shamokin, in 1858, and was engaged in collecting for the church of that place, he met Mr. Auspach, in Philadelphia, and solicited him for a contribution. Mr. Auspach, being concerned in Mt. Carmel lots, replied that if a Methodist Church should be built in Mt. Carmel, he would subscribe two hundred and fifty dollars.

Mr. Riddle at once drew up a subscription, and Mr. Auspach gave two hundred and fifty dollars. This accounts for the commencement of the church edifice. The work once started, went on apace. The following lots were given: Frank Hughes gave two lots; John Hughes gave one lot; General Bickel gave two lots.

The following building committee were appointed: Daniel Heiser, A. F. Slecker, Joseph Ramsey, John Yarnell, and Daniel Heiser.

Trustees: Daniel Heiser, Peter Yocum, and S. K. Gilger.

A brick building, thirty-five by forty-five feet, was erected at a cost of one thousand five hundred dollars. It will seat three hundred and fifty persons.

The present pastor is N. W. Colburn. The membership is about seventy-one members.

METHODIST SUNDAY-SCHOOL.

This school was started soon after the erection of the church. It is in a prosperous condition.

The present superintendent is Frederick Gross. Number of scholars, one hundred and thirty-five; number of teachers, twenty-three; number of volumes in library, five hundred and sixty.

BURNSIDE POST, NO. 92, G. A. R.

This is probably the strongest and most active post in Northumberland County. They have accomplished a great deal of good since their organization. Worthy comrades have been relieved, soldiers' orphans have been sent to proper schools provided for this purpose, and a large amount of charity has been bestowed.

The present officers are: P. C., D. J. Lewis; Senior V. C., A. Ayres; Junior V. C., D. Delcamp; Q. M., J. Gould; Adjutant, Dr. F. M. Thomas; Relief Committee, William Sigfried, A. Ayres, and Joseph Delcamp.

During the present year, they have completed a handsome hall, which was appropriately dedicated. The audience-room is thirty by fifty feet, exclusive of a stage, twenty by forty feet, and will comfortably seat five hundred persons. They have established a reading-room.

MT. CARMEL LODGE, NO. 181, K. OF P.

The present officers of this lodge are: P. C., John Helurich; C. C., Thomas Wardrop; V. C., John Lawson; P., George Scott; M. of E., Joseph Blouch; M. of F., Isaac Keiser.

The lodge is in a flourishing condition.

MT. CARMEL LODGE, NO. 378, A. Y. M.

This lodge was instituted a number of years ago, and comprises in its membership many of the leading citizens of Mt. Carmel. It numbers about fifty members. The meetings are held on the first Tuesday evening of each month before full moon.

The present officials are: W. M., H. T. John; S. W., William Philips; J. W., J. H. Smith; Secretary, Joseph Gould; Treasurer, Morgan Davis.

MT. CARMEL LODGE, NO. 630, I. O. O. F.

A flourishing lodge, with a number of most excellent members. The present officials are: N. G., W. W. Watkins; V. G., John Powell; Secretary, F. Gross.

MT. CARMEL SAVINGS BANK.

Organized and opened, July, 1872. The banking-room is in Deffen's Building. The bank is under the control of solid business men, and is in an excellent condition. The amount of deposits averages sixty thousand dollars.

The present directors are: Amos Vastine, president; S. A. Bergstresser, vice-president; H. D. Rothermel, cashier; A. M. Montelius, secretary; Robert Davidson, Joseph Reeder, Simon Vought, Joseph Deffen, Henry Walter.

CENTENNIAL BUILDING AND LOAN ASSOCIATION.

Organized and chartered by the State, October 14th, 1875. The society is prosperous, having one thousand and seventy-six shares sold.

The officers are: President, S. A. Bergstresser; Secretary, M. K. Watkins; Treasurer, Joseph Deffen.

MT. CARMEL BUILDING AND LOAN ASSOCIATION.

This association was organized in 1869. Number of shares sold, nine hundred and ninety-two. About three hundred free shares on hand yet.

The officers are: President, S. D. Allen; Secretary, George E. Moser; Treasurer, S. A. Bergstresser.

SCREEN, BOLT AND CAR-SHOPS.

These works were started by Greenwood & Co., who carried on business for six or seven years. In March, 1876, they were succeeded by P. W. Hoffman & Co., the present proprietors.

The principal business of these shops is the manufacture of screens and the building of drift-cars. There are six men employed. A five-horse engine furnishes the power. The shops are well supplied with all the requisite machinery for their business.

MT. CARMEL SHOVEL-WORKS.

These works were started some years ago, and have changed hands several times. The present proprietor is George E. Moser. He is prepared to do a large business, but at the present time, owing to the dullness of the coal trade, the works are not doing a very extensive business.

VALUATION OF REAL ESTATE AND PERSONAL PROPERTY IN SHAMOKIN, IN 1874.

East Ward—Real estate, two hundred and ninety-four thousand two hundred and fifteen dollars; personal, four thousand three hundred and thirty-five dollars; total, two hundred and ninety-eight thousand five hundred and fifty dollars. West Ward—Real estate, one hundred and ninety-five thousand four hundred and eighty-four dollars; personal, one thousand five hundred and forty-six dollars; total, one hundred and ninety-seven thousand and thirty dollars.

REAL ESTATE NOT VALUED.

Church property, seventy-five thousand dollars; school property, thirty-five thousand dollars; cemetery property, five thousand dollars; total, one hundred and fifteen thousand dollars.

YEARLY INCOMES OF MT. CARMEL, 1865.

John Hough,	$21,118
M. Donohoe,	17,094
George Schall,	18,814
William Starr,	4,084
Jonathan Hoover,	2,021
David Heiser,	1,600
I. A. Montelius,	1,175

PRINCIPAL HOTELS.

Mt. Carmel House, Deffen House, and National Hotel.

MERCANTILE APPRAISEMENT FOR 1876.

Sixteen stores and six licensed houses.

COLLIERIES.

There are five collieries in the vicinity of Mt. Carmel, the principal shipments of which are over the Reading and Lehigh Valley Railroads.

MILTON BOROUGH.

Twelve miles above the confluence of the west and north branches, and lying on the eastern bank of the former, is the present borough of Milton. Limestone Run flows to the westward, directly through the lower portion of the town, and enters the west branch, opposite two islands of considerable size and great fertility. These islands divide the river into three channels, and the general course of the main stream, at this point, is nearly south.

The West Branch Canal passes through the town, as does also the Philadelphia and Reading, and the Philadelphia and Erie Railroads.

By the course of the latter, the distance is about two hundred and seventy-five miles to the city of Erie, the only port which Pennsylvania holds upon the great lakes of the north-west.

This is the Milton of to-day: a healthy, flourishing, industrious borough of four thousand inhabitants. But a century ago, it was not Milton; the name had never been spoken or thought of, in connection with the log buildings—too few to be even called a hamlet—which stood on the leafy bank of Limestone Run.

We really have no knowledge of the events which occurred there, or in its immediate vicinity, until after the year 1770; but, notwithstanding the lack of historical data up to this period, it can hardly be true, as one chronicler has it, that "In 1772, the place where Milton now stands, was covered by a dense forest, and no sound was heard save that of the wild beast or bird, or of the Indian, as he roamed over the grounds in search of prey," for it appears that in that year, Marcus Hulings had built a log-house, and opened it as a tavern, near the head of Limestone Run, and that Marcus Hulings, Jr., a son, or, perhaps a nephew of the former, had established a blacksmith-shop further up the river, probably about the present intersection of Broadway and Front streets. And a little later, George McCandlish opened another tavern on what was afterwards the Hepburn farm (now within the borough limits,) which, in 1776, had grown to such importance, that on the 8th of July, in that year, an election was held there, for the choice of delegates to the Pennsylvania Constitutional Convention. These facts seem to indicate quite conclusively, that there must have been a considerable number of settlers in the vicinity, at least as early as 1772;

for public-houses and blacksmith-shops must have had *white* support, and would not have been established for the accommodation of wild Indian hunters.

The business of inn-keeping was evidently quite prosperous there, or else the Hulings were especially inclined toward that calling—or, perhaps, both—for in the next year, on the fourth Tuesday in August, the Court of General Sessions granted Marcus Hulings, Jr.—the blacksmith—"a license to keep a public house, he giving bond, etc., agreeable to the laws of the Province," which latter condition shows that inn-keepers, even in those times, were compelled to conduct their establishments in a lawful and orderly manner. But taverns alone, be they ever so orderly, will not promote immigration, nor bring prosperity to any but their proprietors; and so, while Freeland's mills were bringing steady accessions of settlers to this neighborhood, no progress was made at Limestone Run, and no step was taken in the direction of prosperity, until Andrew Straub came there, late in the year 1779. He was from the county of Lancaster, and, besides being a man of sobriety and enterprise, he was a capable mill-wright and miller—two callings most necessary to the well-being of new settlements. When he arrived, he found no buildings standing there. The houses and shops of the Hulings, as well as another strong log-house, which had been built after theirs, had all been burned, at the capture of Fort Freeland, in July; but there was a new log-house then in process of erection, ("logged up to the square,") on the lot, now corner of Water street and Broadway. This building stood until it was burned in the fire of May 4th, 1876. Andrew Straub at once set about building a house for his family. It was a log structure, and stood on or near the site now occupied by the Milton National Bank. This, however, was intended only as a temporary shelter, and soon thereafter he built a larger house, with stable in connection—in the German way—on the west side of the present Filbert street. There he lived until 1793, when he removed to his new house, on the rear side of his farm—near the property now owned by Isaac Marsh, at the east end of Centre street—and there he remained till the time of his death, August, 1806. Meanwhile, about 1792, he had planned and prepared to build a mill to grind corn and wheat, for the subsistence of the settlers. He had dug a race-way from the easterly bend of Limestone Run to the river. The mill was to stand on the river bank, on or near the line between his own lands and those of James Black, right by the ruins of Hulings' blacksmith-shop, and where the engine-house now is. But, just then, there occurred an event which changed all his plans, and probably, to some extent, the future of the town; and it was in this way that it happened: Limestone Run, which then furnished all the mill driving-power which the settlement had, or could seem to hope for, came down in a westerly course, to the point where Mr. Straub had planned to divert the water, by means of his race, to his mill-wheels, and thence to empty it into the river. From that bend, it took a more south-westerly course, till it came within a hundred yards of the west branch; but there, again, it capriciously turned towards the south, and, after a devious course in that direction for about two miles, it fell into Housel's Run, only a short distance above its mouth. Now, at the point where it approached within a hundred yards of the river, there was a low neck of ground, which, at high-water, was sometimes submerged, and which was, at all times, rather damp for cultivation. So the plowman, with an eye to better drainage, had thrown the furrows *from* the lowest part, leaving a deep depression there. And the result was, that when, in a high Summer freshet, Limestone Run was swollen far beyond its ordinary bounds, the waters went tearing through the accidental furrow, and made it a permanent channel, closing forever the lower part of the stream to its junction with Housel's Run.

Here was a new aspect of affairs; and Andrew Straub was not slow to profit by it. The flood had opened a new channel, and had, in a single day, made a better mill-site at the lower bend, than he had been able, with all his toil, to make at the upper one. So, without any vain regrets, he closed the head-race, on which he had spent so much labor, and in a few months he had built, near to where the present stone bridge is, a log-mill, with wheel out-side, and one run of stones, which gave the settlement its first real start on the road to importance, and which also gave to the town its name. For when the mill was completed, and in operation, the settlers of the surrounding country, glad to abandon the long route to the mill at Warrior Run, flocked in to Andrew Straub's, and called it "Mill-town," which afterwards was shortened and euphonized to

THE NAME MILTON,

At the suggestion of Mr. Straub's surveyor, when in the next year he laid out that portion of the town south of Broadway.

Andrew Straub had, in partnership with a man named Yentzler, bought these lands from the insolvent estate of Colonel Francis, and afterwards, Yentzler becoming involved, his interest was purchased by Straub, who thus became sole owner.

Settlers from New Jersey and the eastern counties of Pennsylvania, came steadily in, and Straub's mill became so filled with work, that, in 1794, he erected a new frame building, with three run of stones, and when all was ready, the water was turned from the wheel of the old log mill, into that of the new one, and the grinding continued without interruption.

After the flood upon Limestone Run had cut the new channel from the bend to the river, it became necessary that a bridge should be built across it, to preserve communication between the upper and lower portions of the town; so two stone abutments were built, with short wing-walls, and a wooden bridge, eighteen feet in length, was thrown across them. Against these abutments and wing-walls, the earth was embanked, and the road-way (now Front street) passed over it. It was a narrow, low, and rather insignificant bridge, but it answered the purposes of travel very well, for more than fifteen years.

It became so much decayed in 1810, that it was replaced by a new stone bridge, with three small arches, built by Peter Swartz.

LAYING OUT THE TOWN.

In 1793, Andrew Straub laid out, from the lands which Yentzler and himself had purchased from the estate of Colonel Francis, all that area embraced between Broadway and Ferry Lane, and it was called the town of Milton. But, two years later, when James Black, Esq., of Sunbury, laid out his land from Broadway northward to Locust street, August 11th, 1795, the two plots of Black and Straub became known as Upper and Lower Milton, respectively.

From the time of the completion of the mill, the bridging of Limestone Run, and the laying out of Lower Milton, the young town enjoyed for several years a growth, and an increase of importance which were very gratifying. Settlers—mostly of the better-class—came in rapidly, from the eastern counties, and from New Jersey. Dr. Daniel Faulkner was one of these. He was

THE FIRST PHYSICIAN

who established in Milton. Another accession was Bethuel Vincent, who had been captured by the British and Indians, at Freeland's fort. After his return from captivity, he was not slow to perceive that the importance of the settlements on Warrior Run had declined, and that Milton must far surpass them. So he lost no time in transferring his family and all his interests to the new town, and there, for many years, he lived one of her most prominent and respected citizens. William and Thomas Pollock, Robert Taggart, John Chestnut, John Tietsworth, James Latimore, Samuel Hepburn, and John Dixon, are found among many other well-remembered names, as residents of Milton previous to 1795.

THE SECOND PHYSICIAN

Was Dr. James Dougal, who left Ireland under proscription, and located here in 1795, but did not bring his family from the old country till 1798.

THE FIRST LAWYER,

Daniel Smith, established in Milton as early as 1793. He was most eminent in his profession, and famed for his powers of oratory. Samuel Hepburn, another excellent lawyer, came but very little later.

As regards religious worship, the Methodists were the pioneers. They had held occasional services in private houses in Milton, and the immediate neighborhood since 1788. The Episcopalians were worshiping in their own log church in Morris Lane, in 1795.

THE FIRST TANNERY

Was established in 1795, by John Armstrong, from Montgomery County. It stood near Straub's mill, and on or very near the site of the present tanning establishment of William H. Reber.

Nor was the school question neglected by these enlightened settlers, for on the 3d day of July, 1795, Andrew Straub, for the consideration of five shillings, and other good causes thereunto him moving, conveyed to Robert Taggart, Daniel Faulkner, John Tietsworth, James Latimore, Samuel Hepburn, and John Dixon, as trustees, "two certain lots of ground in Milton, the one being a triangle-cornered lot, and situate on the south side of Market street, and the other situate on the north side of said street, and adjoining a lot of William Boland. The one for the sole and proper use of a school and school-house to be erected thereon, for the general good and benefit of the said town. The other for the sale and proper use and benefit of the English Presbyterian congregation of said town and its vicinity."

The school lot was the triangular one upon the south side of the street.

The inhabitants of the town were thoroughly awake to the necessity of establishing a school for the training and education of their children. They had had some desultory teaching there, to be sure, but it was unsatisfactory, and the sentiment seemed nearly unanimous, that an established school, and a regularly employed teacher were necessary; and so a meeting was called and duly organized, at which it was voted to build a school-house upon the lot which Andrew Straub had donated to them, and three persons were chosen to superintend its erection. A subscription being circulated for the purpose, ninety-three persons—presumably heads of families—responded, in sums varying from two pounds, five shillings, down to one shilling and two pence. The result was, that a log building was at once commenced, and late in the year 1790, it was completed, under the supervision of James Faulkner, John Cochran, and George Calhoun.

It was called the Milton English School, and the first teacher was James McQuinn.

All went satisfactory for three or four years; but in 1799, the question of a division of the school, and the building of a second school-house was agitated, and after several meetings being held in reference to the subject, it was decided to divide, and to build another house. The work proceeded, and the edifice was finished in 1802. It was a frame building, and stood on the south side of Broadway, upon the site of the present brick school-house.

THE FIRST STONE HOUSE

In Milton was built in 1796, by Peter Swartz, stone-mason, for James Black, Esq., on his land on Water street, just north of Broadway. Before this, all buildings had been of wood—either log or frame—and this one was looked upon as a very superior structure. When Mr. Black's financial troubles came, the house and land fell into the possession of William and Thomas Pollock, and is now owned by ex-Governor James Pollock, who is making elegant and extensive repairs upon it. The character of the old mansion may be judged from the fact that, on May 4th, 1876, when (in its eighteenth year) it was damaged by the fire at the corner of Water street and Broadway, the insurance upon it (exclusive of furniture) was three thousand dollars.

THE SECOND STONE HOUSE

Was that of Dr. James Dougal, also built by Peter Swartz, in 1803. It is still occupied by Dr. James Dougal, the son of the first proprietor. It is a large, solid, quadrangular house, and certainly does not seem to have lived out half its days.

The same, or the following year, Swartz built a third house, of the same material, for John Hetherington, in the lower part of the town.

THE FIRST BRICK BUILDING

In Milton, was a one-and-a-half story dwelling-house, built in 1802, for Miss Ellen Sanderson, who afterwards became Mrs. David Ireland. The house stood on the north side of Market street, directly east of, and adjoining the residence of George Corry, deceased.

FIRE APPARATUS.

At the commencement of the year 1798, so many buildings had been erected, that the thoughts of the people began to turn towards the possibility of disastrous fires, and the necessity for some means of prevention and extinguishment. The citizens met for the consideration of the question, and the following is a transcript of the record of their proceedings:

"Friday Evening, January 19th, 1798.

"A meeting was holden at the house of John Chapman, in the town of Milton, by a number of the inhabitants of said town, and after having come to order, a motion was made for some method to be fallen upon to procure ladders, hooks, etc., for the purpose of preventing and extinguishing fire in the town of Milton.

"Agreed unanimously that it was necessary to have six ladders, and six poles with hooks.

"Agreed that after they are obtained, they shall be deposited in the following places and manner, to wit: One pair of ladders and hooks at Samuel Hepburn's; one pair of each at James McNight's house; and one pair of each at Peter Egner's.

"Agreed that the money for defraying the expenses of said ladders and hooks, shall be raised by a tax, and that a committee be appointed to levy and collect the same, and likewise to procure and deposit the same, in the places and manner aforementioned, the committee to consist of three persons, to wit: Samuel Hepburn, John Chestnut, and Moses Teas, who were then unanimously chosen.

"Agreed that the ladders and hooks be kept for the *sole* purpose of preventing and extinguishing fires, and that any person taking them for any other use, shall forfeit and pay the sum of four dollars, which is to be appropriated to the Use of the Society."

Milton, in the year 1805, contained more than five hundred inhabitants. There was no census made, but the oldest and best informed residents—basing their judgment on the school-lists of that day, and other data—are confident that the number mentioned above, is considerably too low.

The shape of the settled parts of the town was—as one of the principal citizens expresses it—that of a pair of saddle-bags, there being two clusters of dwellings, one below the stone bridge, in the present locality of Mahoning and adjacent streets, and the other on Broadway and northward from thence, while the string of shops and business places, on Front street, and contiguous to the river, connecting the upper and the lower settlements, completed the fancied resemblance to the saddle-bags.

Milton was then a very important depot of agricultural products, which were brought there from the teeming country which surrounded it—Paradise, Pleasant Valley, Chillisquaque, Buffalo, Sugar Valley, and White Deer—and of course a prosperous merchandise trade, an exchange of commodities, was the result. In the frozen months, this traffic passed to and fro, between Milton and Philadelphia, on wagons or sleds, over the hills by the way of Reading, the trip occupying three weeks. In the months of navigation, the route over land was discontinued, and the business was done by boats on the river via Columbia.

The principal general merchants were then William and Thomas Pollock, James Moody, Charles Comly and his brother, James and Ezekiel* Sanderson, and Seth Iredell. The stores were mostly on Front street, but the storage warehouses (for grain, etc.,) were upon the river bank.

All those merchants, with, perhaps, the exception of Mr. Moody, made modest fortunes in their vocations. The owners of boats, too, often realized as much of profit as did the merchants, and they were a class whose well-being was closely linked with that of the town.

THE FIRST BUTCHER

In Milton, and the only one at this time, was Michael Gower. There were four blacksmiths, of whom Jerome Egler was one, and two cabinet-makers on the main street—James McCord and one Moody. Philip Goodman, from Berks County, was a weaver and a maker of weaver's reeds. A Mr. Kirk, a Scotchman, was also a weaver. Both had shops on Front street, and near them was the store and workroom of Shunk, a German hatter.

About that time, was started the carding-mill of Henry Follmer. It stood on Limestone Run, a short distance out of town, on premises now owned by H. P. Follmer. McGowan's sickle and carding-mill, at Front street, was built a few years later.

On a back lane, now known as Elm street, stood two distilleries, owned by Moses Teas and Samuel Teas, with a large storage-building belonging to each; and near them, Armstrong's tannery was doing a small business in the tanning of slaughter-hides; while only a few yards away, Straub's frame mill—now thirteen years old—still kept chattering away, in the production of honest wealth.

THE FIRST COOPER-SHOP,

And the only one in Milton, at that time, was that of Isaac Osburn, who made both flour and whisky-barrels. Some of the people complained of the din which he made by his hoop-driving, and certainly it was far more noisy than the clack of the flour-mill.

There were other callings, which clearly suggested luxury, young as the settlement was: Nancy Reese—afterwards the wife of Bethuel Vincent—kept a millinery establishment on Front street, in partnership with her sister, Hannah. While, as regards men's wear, James Hutchinson† was prepared to furnish it, from his genteel tailor-shop, on the same street. There were several boot and shoemakers, and, among the chief of these, was Christian Wood, whose residence and shop were on the main street. Sometimes, at his establishment, even in that frugal day, the price of a pair of warranted calf boots with high legs, and tops of red leather, cost the extravagant figure of sixteen dollars!

* After the death of Ezekiel, which occurred about this time, his brother, William, took his place in the business.

† It was this James Hutchinson who, on a trip to Jersey Shore, recognized in the fair Esther McDowell, the young impostor, in male attire, who had previously, in Milton, worked for him as journeyman tailor.

David Rittenhouse was located on Front street, as a clock and watch-maker—or, rather, repairer; and Philip Housel was engaged in the same business. Each of these gentlemen annexed to his ordinary trade-title the more sounding one of silversmith, and each, at a later day, received the additional dignity of Justice of the Peace.

But the trade of *inn-keeper* seems to have had the most numerous following: Hugh Montgomery had built and kept a public-house, on the spot now occupied by the dwelling of Mr. Isaac Brown, on Front street. But Montgomery had died in 1802, and the house was then kept by John Brady.

David Derrickson added to his vocation of auctioneer, that of inn-keeper, and his tavern was on the east side of Front street, just below, and adjoining the present premises of Gutlob Brown. (That hotel was afterwards carried away by the great Limestone Run flood, in 1817, and was then owned by a Mr. Hill.)

Bethuel Vincent's inn was at the corner of Front street and Broadway, and was, at this time, probably the most frequented of any, except John Brady's.

Christian Holler was inn-keeper, sadler, and cavalry officer. His inn was on Front street, below the bridge, the spot now occupied by the premises of P. H. Schreyer.

Joseph Hammond's tavern was in the upper portion of the town, and was a great deal frequented by those whose fancy ran in the direction of fine horses.

Gower's inn was in the lower town, on a site which would now be described as the north-east corner of Front and Lower Market streets. Gower was a German, and an enthusiastic lover of good, solid German amusements. His house was the head-quarters of dancing parties, and many were the festive nights spent by the young people there. These occasions sometimes provoked the ill-will of those whom circumstances compelled to be absent, and who were occasionally known to attempt annoyance of the parties within, by lowering live geese down the capacious chimney, and many other similar tricks, partaking somewhat of the malicious. But the appearance of the old soldier-landlord, with a "Queen's arm" in his hand, and threatenings and slaughter upon his tongue, always caused the outsiders to cease their annoyances, and beat a retreat.

While speaking of the graceful science, it would be unpardonable to omit a mention of Robert Patterson. He was the dancing-master *par excellence* of the lower West Branch Valley. It was not alone at Milton, but at Northumberland, and Lewisburg, and Muncy, that he was known, and patronized, and *feared!* for at that day, and in that neighborhood, none dare assert their claims to polite recognition, unless their patent of gentility bore the terpsichorean stamp of Robert Patterson, dancing-master.

Mrs. Patterson was a lady of many graces, physical and mental; and it is very probable that much of the popularity of the husband was reflected from the beauty and accomplishments of the wife.

THE RELIGIOUS WORSHIP,

At this time, was rather meagre. In the log school-house, in Lower Market street, the Rev. John Bryson preached to the Presbyterians every fourth Sabbath, and the Reformed Church people held occasional services there, when preachers of their persuasion happened in the neighborhood. The Methodists, too, worshiped there with considerable regularity. There was not a single Baptist person in the town, for nearly twenty years after this.

The Catholics held no services in Milton, but they met for worship from time to time at various houses in the immediate neighborhood.

The Episcopalians had a regular place of meeting, a log church-building, in Morris Lane, Upper Milton, where the Rev. Mr. Depuey ministered to their spiritual needs.

The school-houses were the log building of 1796, on Lower Market street, and the frame of 1802, on Broadway. In these, in the year 1805, the youth of the town were taught and flogged by teachers John L. Finney and Joseph Kerr; the former being the better skilled in the language, but the latter showing far more proficiency in the use of the rod. He (Kerr) was, on this account, a good deal unpopular with his scholars, and, to some extent, with their parents, also. Miss Owens, the daughter of an Episcopalian clergyman, had charge of the female school.

THE FIRST POST-OFFICE

Had been established the previous year, with Bethuel Vincent as post-master. The office was at Bethuel's tavern, Front street and Broadway. A young man named Moore was the carrier, in the employ of James Cummins, mail contractor.

There were no telegraphs, railways, nor steamers then. The European mails came and went in *fast* packet ships, consuming only from thirty to sixty days in crossing the ocean. The time from Philadelphia to Milton, was three days, and the mail service was weekly, arriving from the east, on Saturdays, and all their news and correspondence passed through this slender and infrequent service.

But it answered its purpose well enough; and who can say, that at the present day, the coming of the morning train, as it thunders up with fresh newspapers, telling us the doings of the previous evening in Paris and Vienna, arouses more of interest than did the coming of young Robert Moore, the mail messenger on horseback, of a Saturday morning, seventy years ago, bringing the Wednesday's *Gazette*, with latest European advices, announcing the battles of Ulm and Austerlitz, only sixty-five days after their occurrence.

Andrew Straub, the original proprietor of the lower town, was still living, as was also, Mr. Daniel Smith, though both died in the succeeding year.

Mr. Straub's enterprise had given the settlement its first impetus, and Mr. Smith had done great honor both to himself and to Milton, by the fame which he achieved as a lawyer and an orator. At the bar of Northumberland, none surpassed him in legal ability, while in oratory, he stood pre-eminent.

Few, if any, now live, who heard his funeral oration and eulogy, pronounced at Sunbury, in 1799, on the occasion of the obsequies of George Washington. But as long as any of those hearers did live, their old eyes would fill, and their voices grow tremulous, when they told how he stood that day, in the old Lutheran Church, with Revolutionary heroes all around him, and citizens crowding seats and aisles to their utmost; and how men, and women, and veterans, held their breath, that not one silver word might be lost; and how the whole auditory were moved to tears, as he told them, in strains of marvelous eloquence and pathos, of the virtues and deeds, and death, of the Father of his Country.

That day established his fame, and brought him clients and honors without stint. But it was not long that he staid to enjoy them. Even then the shadows were lengthening for him, and during the next year, 1806, both Daniel Smith and Andrew Straub, passed away.

The only physician then in town, was Dr. James Dougal, and this position he held for about seventeen years, from the time of Dr. Faulkner's departure in 1798, till Dr. Piper's coming, about 1815. His practice was very large. It not only embraced Milton, but extended over nearly all of the County above the north branch, and an equally large territory on the west side of the river. His visits were made on horseback, carrying his medicines with him in saddle-bags, and making up his own prescriptions. To reach his patients at White Deer, Buffalo, Sugar Valley, and other points west of the river, he crossed on the old ferry at the Murr farm, a short distance above the town, or at George Hoffman's, below the island, when that ferry was established, somewhat later.

Horseback traveling was not confined to physicians, however. It was the usual means of travel for all. Of wheeled vehicles, there were but four then in Milton—a gig, owned by James Sanderson; a nondescript, belonging to Dr. Dougal (a rude, home-made affair, probably similar to the "buckboard"), while Daniel Pollock and William Pollock each owned a lumbering two-horse carriage. These last-mentioned were considered very luxurious establishments, and were, upon extraordinary occasions, lent by their proprietors to favored friends.

As for stage-coaches, there were none entering Milton until 1809, when James Cummins established

THE FIRST MAIL-COACH

between Williamsport and Northumberland, making the trip in one day. Its stopping place in Milton was Eckert's hotel, on Front street. Robert Moore, the former mail messenger, having faithfully served Mr. Cummins in that capacity, had been promoted to the office of driver, and we may imagine the pride with which he first reined up his horses in full view of Post-master Vincent, who had always been his friend and patron.

THE INCORPORATION OF MILTON AS A BOROUGH

Dates February 26th, 1817. The first officers elected were: Chief Burgess, Arthur McGowan; Assistant Burgess, Robert McGuigan; Town Council—Christopher Woods, president; Samuel Hepburn, Daniel Scudder, Joseph Rhoads, George Eckert, Daniel R. Bright, Thomas Conly; Supervisors of Roads, John Jones, David Derrickson; Town Clerk, John Titsworth; High Constable, James Sharp.

The population of the borough at the time of its erection, is not exactly known. Three years later (1820), it was one thousand and fifteen, which makes it probable that, at this time, it varied but little from nine hundred.

The town had improved, and grown steadily in importance during the twelve years preceding its incorporation. Many of the new buildings had been erected of brick, and there had also been a few of stone, one of the principal of the latter class being the new residence of Bethuel Vincent, on Front street, just below his former tavern-stand, and this ranked among the chief residences of the town. David Rittenhouse had, in the preceding year (1816), built the large brick-house on Front street, now known as the United States Hotel. He first intended it as a dwelling-house, but afterwards rented it to Lemuel B. Stoughton, who opened it as a public house, and advertised it in the *Miltonian* as follows: "*Spread-Eagle Tavern* (first below where Bethuel Vincent formerly kept)—*L. B. Stoughton* respectfully informs travelers and others, that he has rented that spacious, airy and convenient three-story brick-house of *David Rittenhouse, Esq.*, where he keeps a public house of entertainment, for the accommodation of travelers and others. No possible exertion will be spared to render general satisfaction."

The mention of this house recalls to mind the enterprise of Elisha Babbitt and Isaac Straub, who, looking at the unusual height (three stories) to which Mr. Rittenhouse had reared his dwelling, fancied that it was lofty enough for a *shot-tower!* and that it might be profitably used as such; and when Lemuel Stoughton opened it as a public-house, the way seemed clear to the prosecution of this project. So they took a third story room, and, from its window poured melted lead, through a sieve, into a large tub of water, which stood directly underneath. But the experiment was not successful, and they found that the height of *three stories* was far too little to cause the lead to assume the necessary globular form in its descent. The failure, however, was not a disastrous one; in fact, it cost them nothing more than a little good-natured ridicule.

George Eckert's mill was one of the recent erections which dignified the new borough. After the death of Andrew Straub, his executors had sold the mill property, on Limestone Run, to James Moody, who, in turn, sold to Eckert; and he, in 1816, demolished the old frame mill, which had done such good service to Straub and to the settlement, for nearly a quarter of a century, and, in its place, built the fine new stone mill, which has now been in constant operation—it may almost be said, by night and day—for sixty years, and it was an establishment most creditable to the new borough.

An institution conferring still greater dignity, was the

NORTHUMBERLAND UNION AND COLUMBIA BANK,

Which had commenced business, two years before, under a State charter, and was now "in full tide of successful experiment," paying semi-annual dividends of four per cent., under the management of Seth Iredell, as president, and W. Cox Ellis, as cashier. Their banking-rooms were in a wooden building, which stood on Front street, on the site now occupied by Huff's Hotel. The bank was *the* feature, the accomplished fact, which, more than any other, tended to mark the borough of Milton as a place of consequence—to remove all suspicion of rusticity, and to stamp indelibly upon it the character of a *town*.

A new and very substantial wooden building had been erected on Limestone Run, west of Front street, by Arthur McGowan, as a carding-mill and sickle manufactory. About this time, D. R. Bright added to his inn-keeping and general merchandising, an extensive iron-mongery, with drugs and medicines, paints and hardware.

David Rittenhouse had purchased the Sunbury Brush Manufactory, and removed the business to Milton, and nearly all the trades and vocations had received such augmentations and accessions, as might be expected in the natural course of the town's growth. Among them was the first public bakery, which was advertised by its proprietor, as follows:

"BAKE-HOUSE IN MILTON.

"*Lila Hudman*, just from Philadelphia, has the pleasure of informing the citizens of the Borough of Milton and vicinity, that he will commence the *Baking Business*, after the first of June, in the house lately occupied by Mr. Clinton, in Market street. Such of the inhabitants as become regular customers, will be served with fresh bread, Hot Rolls, Twist, etc., every morning in Philadelphia fashion.

"Beer and Cyder will be kept constantly on hand.

"N. B.—Tavern keepers and ferrymen may be supplied with every kind of bread or cakes, which will always be kept on hand.

MILTON, May 24th, 1817."

The above appeared in the *Miltonian*, which was the first newspaper published in Milton, having been started in the previous September, by General Henry Frick. It is still in existence, and will be further mentioned in another place. The increase of the business of the borough, in one respect, however, was by many, regarded with other feelings than those of gratification. That is, in the matter of the production and consumption of spirituous liquor, for John A. Schneider had added a new distillery, making the third in Milton, while the number of taverns had grown to twelve, or about one, to every seventy-five of the population, large and small. Ten years later, the public houses numbered seventeen, with five distilleries.

When the borough was incorporated, its principal lawyers were Samuel Hepburn and Abem Marr. Daniel Scudder and Joseph B. Anthony were admitted to the bar in the following November. Mr. Scudder married Grace, the daughter of Daniel Smith, and he became almost as eminent in the profession as was his father-in-law. He afterwards moved to Lock Haven, and died there. Mr. Marr removed to Danville shortly after.

The only physicians were Drs. Dougal and Piper. There was one *James Steward*, who pretentiously advertised in the *Miltonian*, announcing himself as "a successful physician and surgeon," as well as a professed "botanist," and after enumerating twenty-five diseases, which he could invariably cure, wound up *poetically* in this wise:

"The public I have notified,
That I in Milton now reside."

"The healing art I do profess,
Like many others in this place."

"I practise physic and surgery both,
From east to west, from north to south."

"Two thousand, thousand miles I've rode,
To find my patients on the road."

With much more of the same kind, showing plainly that there were ignorant pretenders and quacks sixty years ago, as well as now. It was but a little later, that this same William Steward was advertised and denounced as a *swindler*, in the same journal.

Dr. Piper afterwards removed from Milton to Turbutville, and Dr. James Dougal was killed by a fall of his horse, near where the Paradise churches now stand. His death occurred July 18th, 1818. For twenty years, he had practised very extensively, not only in Milton, but over a large section of country on both sides of the river. Many of his students afterwards became eminent physicians.

RELIGIOUS WORSHIP

Was held by the Episcopalians, Presbyterians, Methodists, Lutherans, Catholics, and the German Reformed. The two last named, and the Methodists, had no regular pastor. The Lutherans were under charge of Rev. Philip Repass; the Presbyterians under Rev. Thomas Hood; while the Episcopalian rector was Rev. Abijah Hopkins.

In that year occurred the destructive flood on Limestone Run, which not only swept away the Front street bridge, built seven years before, but did great injury to the street itself, and also to private property. It was a memorable event, on account of the severe loss which it occasioned to the borough and the County, as well as to individuals. How the disaster was regarded at the time, is shown by the following mention in the columns of the *Miltonian* of August 16th, 1817:

"*Awful Calamity.*—The fine, industrious, and very thriving town of Milton was visited, on Saturday last, by an awful calamity. From Friday evening till Saturday, at four P. M., the rain poured forth in continual torrents, and the small streams emptying into Limestone Run, which enters the river through the town, increased with so much rapidity, that the inhabitants were compelled to guard against it, and, if possible, to impede the force of that destructive element; but though every effort of human industry was used, it was still unavailing. The stone bridge on the main street was undermined and almost entirely razed to the foundation, which filled up the channel, and opened a new one on the opposite side. The water continued to come with an increased force and rapidity, undermining some houses, and sweeping the lots on which they stood to a level with the water. The houses swept away are: the inn of Mr. Hill, occupied by George Nagle, and dwelling and store-house of Arthur McGowan, and a small saddler's-shop, occupied by Mr. Merkle; the store-house of D. R. Bright, and the foundation of part of his inn, tenanted by H. Wolfinger; the store-house of Mr. Moses Teas. By the activity of the inhabitants the moveable property was saved from destruction. One corner of Mr. George Eckert's superb stone mill was partially undermined, but, we are happy to state, this valuable edifice, so necessary to the community at large, is now under repair.

"Mr. McGowan's carding-machines were also saved, together with the building in which they stood, and we rejoice to think that they can be put in operation in a short time. This building stands upon the edge of the run. Mr. Samuel Teas' distillery sustained considerable injury, as did also the buildings attached to the distillery of Mr. John A. Schuckler. A substantial bridge is now erecting over the run, on the old foot-bridge, to pass by Mr. Moses Teas', Mr. Eckert's, and the saw-mill, and then into the main street by Dr. Dougal's. The persons at work at this bridge proceed with a celerity and industry highly creditable, and we think the bridge will be passable by Monday next. Added to this calamity, we will have to regret the great impediment to travelers, as it will probably be eighteen months before we can possibly have the new bridge in the main street, together with all the other repairs necessary."

The bridge that was destroyed had been of stone, with arches, but it was decided to replace it by a wooden bridge, resting on stone abutments, and such a one was built and completed in the succeeding year, by James Moore, Sr., as contractor. The borough received aid from the legislature, in addition to the sum received from the County, towards the cost of rebuilding. This structure did good service to the public for thirty years, when, becoming so much decayed as to be judged unsafe, the wooden portions were rebuilt by Neil Kleckner, in 1847 or 1848, the old abutments being used in the rebuilding.

In 1869, this was demolished, and replaced by a double-arched bridge of stone. The old one had existed long enough—the wooden portion was again decayed and unsafe, and the abutments themselves, were considered unfit to place a new bridge upon. So it was thought expedient to build anew, from the foundation. A higher, wider and more commodious bridge, in every particular, was wanted, and was decided on. The cost was ten thousand five hundred dollars. The County paid seven thousand dollars, with the condition that the borough of Milton should furnish the remaining three thousand five hundred dollars; should cause the work to be done in a substantial manner, and guarantee it to stand for five years from time of completion. David Starick was the builder. It has stood safely through the five years of guaranty, and will stand for a great many years to come, unless old Limestone Run should unexpectedly become even more ungovernable than it was on the ninth of August, fifty-nine years ago.

THE HARMONY CHURCH.

This old landmark was built by a union of the Lutheran, Presbyterian and German Reformed congregations. It stood in the south-eastern corner of the Presbyterian burying-ground, at the upper end of Mahoning street.

It was built of brick, and, in that day, was considered a splendid structure. It was commenced October 5th, 1817, but (probably from the lack of funds) was not completed until the Spring of 1819. The event of its consecration was a very impressive one. Divine services upon that occasion, were held in both the English and German languages, and occupied two days—the 23d and 24th of May.

The "union" appears to have still labored under pecuniary difficulties, in the way of paying for the church, for we find, on June 10th, 1822, announced the first of a series of Lottery Drawings, for the benefit of Harmony Church, with Joseph D. Biles and Adam Follmer, as managers. These drawings continued for a number of months, and it is presumable that they resulted favorably to the fiscal condition of the "union."

During the succeeding Summer, the building was struck by lightning, and considerably, though not seriously, damaged in its interior.

By those who recollect the time, it is represented that there was but a solitary flash, and that from a cloud not much larger than a man's hand—in fact so insignificant as to appear almost like a thunderbolt from a clear sky; but probably some allowance should be made for the power of *imagination*, especially when operating through an interval of more than fifty years.

It was occupied in common, as a place of worship, until 1832, when the Presbyterians withdrew. The Lutherans followed in 1850, and the Reformed congregation remained alone until 1866, when they demolished the old building, to use the material contained in it, in the erection of their new church. A severe blow to the importance of the town was the failure of the Northumberland Union and Columbia Bank. After a five years' existence, and just as the citizens had come to regard it as one of the permanent institutions of the place. This occurred in 1820, and the charter was declared [illegible]d in 1823.

THE POPULATION IN 1830

Was one thousand three hundred and fifty-two. A part of this accession was, of course, due to the building of the West Branch Canal, which, after several years of labor, had been completed to Muncy Dam in October, 1828. Freight boats had commenced running upon it in 1829, and the people now looked for a new departure towards prosperity. It is questionable whether, as regards Milton, or Muncy, or other towns similarly situated, the canal ever realized the citizens' anticipations in that direction, though it certainly changed the methods of their trade, to some extent, though Arks and Durham boats continued to navigate the river, after the advent of the canal. Mr. John L. Watson recollects that he made trips with them, certainly as late as 1834.

But the Philadelphia grain and produce market was generally preferred to that of Baltimore, and thus the canal received the preference.

It was certainly a long step towards encouraging the establishment of manufactories, requiring heavy freighting; and it, without doubt, went far to induce Major Joseph Rhoads to build, in the year 1830, at Milton,

THE FIRST IRON FOUNDRY ON THE WEST BRANCH.

It was considered a novel enterprise, as well as one of doubtful success, and was visited out of curiosity by people from Williamsport, and other places in the valley. It was located on Upper Front street, and Major Rhoads manufactured there mill-gearings, stoves, wool carding machines, and farming implements, and these, together with the brass-working, and copper-smithing, which he had started three years before, made a most successful business.

THE FIRST BRIDGE ACROSS THE RIVER,

At Milton, was commenced in 1830, and completed in 1833. It was built by a bridge company, incorporated by the legislature, and composed of stockholders in Milton and vicinity. The bridge was built across the channels of the river, at the islands just below the mouth of Limestone Run. It consisted of three sections: First, that from the left bank of the river, across the east channel, to the first island; second, the section crossing the centre channel, between the two islands; and third, that crossing the right hand channel, from the western island, to the Union County shore. It was a truss-bridge, with double tracks. The contract for building was awarded to Abraham and Isaac Straub, the price being twenty-two thousand dollars. This price was understood to be wholly unremunerative to the Messrs. Straub, but they took the contract, and carried it successfully through, being influenced by consideration of the great advantage which would accrue to their lumber and grist-mills, which they had built on the island in 1824. By damming the outer channels, they had secured in the centre a head and fall of four feet, and this, upon their re-action wheels, (the first of the kind ever used in the United States,) gave a water-power sufficient for their operations. So, as their mill business was a prosperous one, they were willing, for the sake of securing a good and permanent communication with the island, to build the bridge at the price named, but which afterwards proved insufficient to cover their money outlay.

The mills were operated successfully, until the building of the Lewisburg dam, which injured them so much, by backing the water and ice upon them, that, in 1840, they were removed to Muddy Run, a mile and a half above Milton. In 1846, an interest in them was sold to Moses Chamberlin, and, in 1852, the remaining interest was purchased by Daniel Bisel; and, after passing through various other hands, was burnt in 1874, as mentioned in the account of the "Boonville flour-mills," in Turbut township.

In connection with the building of this bridge, and before its completion, there occurred an incident, which, at the time, created great excitement along the river, and which is now well remembered by many of the older inhabitants of the valley. It was

THE RESCUE OF JOSEPH BAILEY.

Late in the afternoon of the 4th day of February, 1832, Mr. Joseph Bailey, of Jersey Shore, went down to the river side, to secure a flat-boat, which he had moored at the lower end of the island, opposite the town. The water in the stream was rising, and the ice was becoming loose and detached, notwithstanding that the weather was cold. Stepping on board the flat, and having his attention diverted for a moment, he was dismayed, on looking up, to find himself not only loose from the shore, and in the current of the river, but that his boat was so fastened to, and encumbered with the masses of floating ice, as to be entirely unmanageable. He had neither oar nor paddle, and, indeed, if he had, they would have been useless. He was in the swiftest part of the stream, and whirling along, sometimes broadside to the current, and sometimes stern foremost. But his shouts were heard on shore, and his neighbors were not slow in showing their will to help him. They mounted their horses, and armed with coils of rope, rode on to Linden, to head him off, and, as they believed, to rescue him there. But they had miscalculated their strength and skill, for they failed to reach him, and so the swift waters hurried him on.

At Jaysburg, they repeated the the trial, but only succeeded in cheering him by their shouts and assurances of eventual rescue.

Again at Williamsport, he went careering past, wedged and helpless in the crowded masses of ice, and again they found themselves powerless to do more than to renew the promise to stand by and not desert him. But night had now closed in, and there could be no hope of rescue till daylight should come, and by that time were would he be? They could not keep him in sight during the hours of darkness, and it must surely be a night of danger and of suffering—both bodily and mental—to him. There was no bridge across the river at any point nearer than Milton, but the very fact of its distance was an encouraging one, for it was so far away, that he might not reach it until after daylight, and *if* he could safely pass the Muncy dam, and survive all the perils of the ice and the flood, and the cold, and *if* the friendly light would come before he reached the Milton bridge, they would certainly save him there. So the mounted messengers went on, carrying the warning to Muncy and Milton, and he was unwillingly left to the mercies of the night and the river.

The current was very rapid, and swept him on, till soon he was nearing the dam at Muncy. We may imagine, but we can never know, his anxiety as he approached it, his thankfulness, when he found himself safely past, nor the eagerness of his gaze, as he looked in vain to the eastward, over the Muncy hills, for the first streakings of the February dawn. He was moving on as rapidly as ever, hour after hour passed, it was but a few miles more to the bridge, and the night seemed interminable.

It became evident that he must pass Milton in the darkness, and could now only look for his friends to save him at Lewisburg or Northumberland. He knew they would be there, if they failed at Milton. They would have stood by him to the Chesapeake, if need be!

Suddenly he felt himself moving slower, and soon he was stationary grinding among the loose ice, against the head of Tyler's (now Fisher's) Island, a short distance above Dewart.

In good earnest he set himself at work, with what means he had, to get in and secure his flat to the island, but, after two or three hours of vain labor, he found his boat and himself moving into the current, and again carried irresistibly down the stream. But it was morning now, and the hard labor which he had had, in endeavoring to land the boat, had moved his blood, and driven away the chill and numbness, so that when he approached the unfinished bridge, and saw the preparations made for his succor, he felt confident that his dangerous journey was nearly at an end.

The rescuers, when they saw he would pass in the eastern channel, had gathered upon that section of the bridge with ropes securely looped, and cast over the side—which was very conveniently done, as the bridge had not yet been weather-boarded. They feared, however, that he would be too much benumbed with cold to secure himself in the loops, or that he might lose his hold and drop in the river, after his boat had passed from under him. As he came to the upper side of the bridge, General Henry Frick threw him a thick cloak, and General Hammond, an overcoat, so that if he failed to catch the ropes, he might, at least, have a covering for his chilled limbs. But coat and cloak struck the water, and were carried away in an instant. He did not need them, however, for, as he came near the loop, he stood up, grasped it firmly, and, in a few moments, was standing on the floor of the bridge safe and sound, and, it must be said, but little injured by his Winter-night's voyage down the west branch!

His boat was caught at Lewisburg, and was purchased by Mr. Daniel Caldwell, who used it as a ferry-boat between Watsontown and White Deer mills.

THE FIRST STEAM FLOUR-MILL

Was built in 1832, by Fleming W. Pollock.

The Straub mill, and its successor, the "Eckert," had enjoyed a monopoly in their line for forty years, but now the other portion of the town, although it possessed no *water* power, invoked the aid of *steam*, and this Pollock mill was put in motion on upper Front street, opposite the Rhoads foundry.

Its builder, Mr. Pollock, is now a resident of Shamokin, and president of a bank there, but the solid old stone-mill—now owned by Mr. Bickel—is still running as glibly as ever, on the site where he started it, *forty-four years ago.*

Of Benevolent, Bible, Missionary, and Tract Societies, there were not less than seven then in existence in Milton, and in 1831, there was organized the "Milton Temperance Society," and, for years later, the "Reformed Temperance Society,"—probably, in view of the great increase of distilleries and taverns.

During the decade which ended in the year 1840, the population of Milton had increased but one hundred and fifty-six souls. The reasons for these unsatisfactory figures, cannot be absolutely given, but perhaps it is safe to infer that the canal had its effect on the town, just *as*, in later days, we have seen railroads operate unfavorably towards many places, which are not actually terminal points. At all events, Milton no longer seemed to enjoy that preference—it might almost be said monopoly—in trade, which she had twelve and fifteen years earlier, when the stable accommodations, below the Front street bridge and on Mahoning street, amounting to more than two hundred feet, side by side measurement, often fell far short of the demand, by farmers, and others, entering town from a distance, for disposition of their grain and produce.

Trade and methods of transportation had changed, not only in the matter of freight, but of passenger traffic—freight boats had taken precedence of arks and Durhams, and the packets offered better inducements to travellers, than had ever been offered by Hulings' or Cummins' stage-coaches. These, and the succeeding years, were the palmy days of canal boating, when the packets were commanded by such royal souls as Captains John M. Huff, and David Blair, who secured a degree of personal popularity and esteem, which is never attained by *railway* officials in the hurry-scurrying of their profession at the present day.

THE FIRST STEAM SAW-MILL

On the west branch, was built by Dr. William McCleery, at Milton, in the year 1842. It was driven by a twenty-five horse-power engine, sawing capacity about two thousand five hundred feet per day, of twelve hours. The saws were two "Mulays." None of the slabs, edgings, etc., were utilized, by being worked into lath, pickets, and shingles, as the machines for their manufacture were unknown at that day.

The *best* white pine and oak timber could then be bought at two to two-and-a-half cents per cubic foot, the sawed lumber selling at six to eight dollars per thousand feet.

This modest mill (situated on the east side of the canal just above Locust street,) was the pioneer, in the vast lumber-cutting industry, which *made* the city of Williamsport, as well as many other places of lesser importance, on the Susquehanna and its tributaries.

THE GREAT FLOOD OF 1847,

On the west branch, made comparatively little havoc at Milton. The principal damage was done to the Milton bridge, of which the middle section, that between the islands, was carried away. The bridge company set about re-building it at once, and the work was done by Thomas Murdock and brother.

During the time between the destruction and the re-opening of this section, a ferry, from island to island, was operated by Jacob Wheeland, in the employ and interest of the company.

THE FIRST TELEGRAPH

Connection with Milton was made in 1850. The office was in the store of William F. Nagle, at the corner of Broadway and Upper Front street, and Russell Wingate was the first operator.

It was continued at Nagle's store for some years, and from there was removed to the *Miltonian* building, which then stood on the spot now occupied by J. F. Ganger & Son's store, on Front street. One of the next operators after Wingate, if not his *immediate* successor, was L. M. Morton, Esq., the present editor of the *Miltonian*, at which printing office is, to-day, the only telegraph in the borough, except those at the railway depots.

The population, in 1850, was one thousand six hundred and forty-nine, a still smaller increase than that from 1830 to 1840. It was not flattering, but there was hope of recovering, as soon as railway trains should supersede the canal boats, and this was close at hand.

PLATE XXVII

RESIDENCE & FERRY OF CAPT. JOHN BLY,
WATSONTOWN, NORTHUMBERLAND COUNTY, PENNA.

RESIDENCE & BUSINESS BLOCK OF O. C. HOGUE,
WATSONTOWN, NORTHUMBERLAND COUNTY, PENNSYLVANIA

RESIDENCE OF SAMUEL CALDWELL,
WATSONTOWN, NORTHUMBERLAND CO., PA.

HARDWARE STORE,
of
I. N. MESSINGER,
MAIN ST. WATSONTOWN, PA.

THE FIRST RAILWAY

Communication with Milton (the Catawissa) was opened in 1852, *eastward;* that is, Milton was the western, or northern terminus, so that passengers coming from the east, and bound for Williamsport, could go, *by rail,* only as far as Milton.

Three years later, (1855,) that section of the Sunbury road, between Milton and Williamsport, was opened, but still that portion between Milton and Sunbury was not completed; so that passengers from Reading or Philadelphia, for Williamsport, could reach Milton by the Catawissa, but must there change to the other road to reach Williamsport.

Downward from Milton, the railway was opened to Sunbury in December, 1855, but it was not until 1858, that the continuous line was completed to Harrisburg, and then, and not before, could passengers by rail from Harrisburg, reach Williamsport and Ehnira, via Sunbury and Milton, without change of cars. But even the coming of the iron-horse only raised the population of the borough to one thousand seven hundred and two in 1860, an increase of but fifty-three in ten years.

When, in 1854, during its construction, the Sunbury and Erie Railroad had appropriated to its use the bed of the old Northumberland and Muncy road, northward from Milton, it became obligatory on the company to furnish the County another road for that which had been taken. In this, as in most similar cases, the ideas of the citizens were diverse as to which route should be adopted. One party wished it to be by Water street, and thence northward, and another by way of Upper Front street, and thence to Watsontown. Either route would cut the farm of Mr. David Marr, and he, favoring Upper Front street, offered *free* right of way by that route, while he demanded three thousand dollars damages if the Water street route was adopted. The decision of the question virtually lay with Robert H. Faries, Esq., Chief Engineer of the Railroad, and, for more than six months, both parties paid assiduous and persistent court to him whenever he came to Milton. The *free right of way,* offered by Marr, caused him to favor Upper Front street, and that route would surely have been obtained, but that the old Episcopal burying-ground laid directly in the way, and the law forbade disturbing it without consent of the proprietors.

This consent was *positively refused.* Some said that the machinations of the Water street party induced the refusal, but, however this might be, it turned the route *from* Upper Front street. David Marr received his three thousand dollars, and the highway passed through Water street, on to Watsontown and Muncy.

Immediately after the route was fixed through Water street, Dr. Wm. McCleery laid out his addition to the town as follows: North boundary, Church lane; south boundary, Locust street; east boundary, West Branch Canal; west boundary, the river, containing thirty-two acres, and subdivided into one hundred and one lots.

A short time prior to this (July, 1853) Mr. J. J. Reimensnyder had laid out the addition called "Shakespeare," viz.: North boundary, land of Philip Follmer; east boundary, land of Samuel T. Brown; south boundary, land of ——— Teas; west boundary, Sodom public road, containing seven acres, eighty-five perches.

ADDITION OF WILLIAM T. NAGLE,

Laid out in 1855, extending eastward from the borough limit to the "old Follmer farm," and northward from Broadway to Helnen's addition. Area, thirty acres.

J. B. DAVIS' ADDITION,

Laid out in 1856. Boundaries: North, Ferry lane; east, West Branch Canal; south, street crossing at Nail Works; west, the river; containing thirty acres.

LAWSON & SCHREYER'S ADDITION

Was laid out in 1864, and contains forty acres. It is bounded as follows: On the north, by Washingtonville road; on the east, by land of John Houtz; on the south, by Limestone Run; on the west, by borough limit.

MOSES CHAMBERLAIN'S ADDITION

Was laid out October 28th, 1867, and contains twenty-six acres. West boundary, the river; east boundary, canal and basin; south boundary, Locust street; north boundary, other lands of M. Chamberlain.

WILLIAM HEINEN'S ADDITION

Contains about fifty acres, and extends eastward from the borough line to Fifth street, and from Locust street northward. It was laid out in 1872, and twenty-three dwellings have already been built upon it. These last three additions are, chronologically, out of place here, but are inserted with the others, for obvious reasons.

OPENING OF CENTRE STREET.

As late as the year 1860, Milton still preserved, in a great measure, its original shape, that is to say, there were *two* towns, one below Limestone Run, and the other on and above Broadway; while between these there was no settlement worthy of mention, except the connecting line of business places and residences on Front street. The project of filling up this vacant space, by the opening of a new, wide street, from Front street eastward, across the canal, had been entertained for two or three years by a number of prominent citizens. The principal obstacle was the Methodist Church building, which stood directly in their route, but this they succeeded in purchasing in 1859, and the way then being clear, they opened their thoroughfare (Centre street) in 1860. It is wide, and well graded—in fact, one of the best streets of the town. Upon it stands the fine edifice of the the Baptist Church, the Centre school-house, and a large number of most desirable residences. Its opening has proved a great benefit, by gradually building up the vacant spaces between the solid extremities of the borough.

WAR ATTITUDE, 1861.

From the first call for troops, made by President Lincoln, in 1861, until the final suppression of the Southern Rebellion, Milton nobly sustained a character for patriotism, second to no community *in the Keystone State.* What more than *that* need be said? The names of those who went to the battle-field will be found in another part of this work, with the roster and muster-roll of the County. Many names are of those who returned, and are now peacefully and honorably engaged in the pursuits of civil life. But many, too, are of those who returned not, but who still lie far off on the Southern fields on which they fell.

THE GREAT FLOOD OF 1865.

On the 17th of March of that year, commenced a flood, unprecedented for the height of the water, and the amount of damage done, not only at Milton, but at all other points along the river. The following account of the havoc at Milton, is from the *Miltonian,* of March 20th, 1865:

"On Wednesday of last week, the river commenced to make a gradual swell, which slowly continued on Thursday, through the effects of rain and melting snow among the hills, until Friday, when the rise became more rapid, fast filling the river-bank full. But still it rose and rose, higher and higher, not caring for any former precedent as to height, until, Saturday morning, it had risen to such a depth that Front street, in some places, contained over six feet of water. On Saturday morning, the good news came that the water was falling. This glad news was welcomed by one and all. Each then wore a cheerful face. It was Noah's dove returning to the ark!

"It was a sad sight to see such a destruction of property—bridges, houses, household furniture, stables, fences, etc., came floating down the river in confused masses.

"On Friday it was perceptible, to each one's eye, that the Milton bridge could not much longer withstand the pressure brought against it by the accumulating logs and debris of all kinds. The western portion was swept away some time on Friday night. The eastern portion, or that nearest to town, left about three o'clock Friday afternoon. Many aching hearts witnessed the grand scene! Just previous to starting, her creaking timbers made loud throes of agony. By the bridge breaking in two, and swinging round towards either bank, she floated grandly down the river, never to return. The middle bridge—that between the two islands—was swept from the piers about the same time, but, lodging against trees, moved only a few rods down the river.

"To enumerate and individualize the losses experienced by different ones in this locality, would be impossible in a newspaper article. The families on the river-bank, in the upper portion of the borough, as well as the lower, were compelled to forsake their homes, without much loss, however. Many of those in the lower part of the town, took refuge in the German Reformed Church, reminding one of those sad, rebellious times, when refugees are driven from their homes—while others were provided for in other ways.

"There is but little injury done in the upper portion of the town, as the water had little or no current. In the lower portion, however, where the current was swift and strong, it washed out streets and did great damage.

"Mr. John Datesman, of West Milton, is a heavy loser in grain, which became wet, and may nearly all be destroyed by not being made dry. We are informed that about two thousand bushels had to be taken from his warehouse, and through the kindness of friends and neighbors, was hauled to the different barns in the country to dry. It is stated that, while the goods were being removed from his store, some rascal robbed his till of all the money it contained. Such a man will steal from the devil, when he can.

"John Halter, on Mrs. Marr's farm, had his house swept away and his furniture all lost. He also lost two crops of tobacco, leaving him penniless. Mrs. Marr also lost tobacco to the amount of a thousand dollars and over. But there is loss, more or less, by each family residing along the river, and we cannot now enumerate. Farms lying along the river were swept of all fencing, which proves a very heavy loss.

"Our citizens all, no doubt, feel thankful that Milton escaped with such a slight loss. Many in other towns lost their all. Lock Haven was entirely overflown, the water being from five to six feet in depth in the highest part of the town. Williamsport fared but little better. At Muncy, the canal is much damaged—the towing-path having been entirely torn away in some places, and in others, the canal filled up even with the banks. The aqueduct, at the mouth of Muncy Creek, was swept away, and the piers much injured. The steam saw-mill of Courson & Fox, at the mouth of Muncy Creek, was moved from its foundation, and swung across the bank of the canal, separating in the middle. These gentlemen also lost a considerable quantity of lumber—their loss is estimated at from ten to twelve thousand dollars The Muncy bridge suffered materially. One span is entirely gone, and several others had the lower timbers carried away."

The rebuilding of the bridge was now the serious question. The disaster had been so great that the stock of the company was nearly extinguished. It was declared to be depreciated *four-fifths*, which left a total of only about five thousand dollars in existence, while sixty thousand more than this sum was necessary for rebuilding. The old stockholders were unwilling to pay the assessment of eighty per cent., and there seemed to be no new takers of stock. The prospect for a new bridge seemed gloomy enough, and, indeed, it could not have been accomplished—perhaps for years—but for the unwearying and persistent exertions of Colonel Thomas Swenk, and a few other individuals, who were determined that Milton should suffer no such blow as the permanent loss of her bridge. At last, the company was rehabilitated, and the contract for the new bridge was given to Benjamin Griffey, who employed David Starick to build the necessary stone-work. The entire cost of the structure was sixty-five thousand dollars. During the construction, a ferry, to partially fill the place of the bridge, was run across at the lower end of the islands.

The Catawissa Railroad northward from Milton, was completed through to Williamsport, in 1871. The entire road is now leased to the Philadelphia and Reading Railroad Company, and bears the name of the latter corporation. Thus Milton has the advantage of two lines of railway in each direction—northward to Williamsport and eastward to Philadelphia. She has also a stage-line still left—running daily between the borough and Lewisburg, Union County.

The old "Eagle Hotel," on Front street, a building part frame and part log, which, sixty years ago, was occupied by the Northumberland, Union and Columbia Bank, and which later, at various times, was kept as the "Spread Eagle Tavern," and as the "Eagle Hotel," by Lemuel H. Stoughton, Captain John M. Huff, and others, was, in 1871, demolished by the latter gentleman, and he erected in its place a fine three-story house, and named it for himself, "Huff's Hotel." Since his death, which occurred soon after, his widow has continued it as a public house, under the same name.

THE FIRE OF DECEMBER 12TH, 1875.

At eight o'clock in the evening of Sunday, December 12th, 1875, Mr. Henry Huth, proprietor of the Riverside Hotel, on Front street, discovered heavy volumes of smoke, issuing from the rear basement of his house.

He at once gave the alarm of fire, and then, with the assistance of Mr. J. G. Kurtz, entered the room, with buckets of water, to find the location of the fire, and to extinguish it, if possible. But the dense smoke made it impossible to remain inside for more than a single moment. In a very short time, the two hand-engines were on the spot, and each had a stream into the burning basement—one from the front, and the other from the rear. The house was kept closed as tightly as practicable to smother the fire, or at least, to retard its progress until help could arrive from Lewisburg and Watsontown. Dispatches had been sent to those towns for aid, but, as it was Sunday evening, there was no locomotive under steam at either place. Permission, however, was received from the superintendent of the railroad, and they were then fired up as quickly as possible.

Meanwhile, although the hand-engines had done their best, the fire was steadily gaining on them, rising from floor to floor, till, at half-past ten, it burst furiously from the roof. Just then, the steam fire-engine, from Watsontown, arrived, and, a little later, the "William Cameron" steamer, of Lewisburg, came in. It was but a few moments until each engine was playing two heavy streams upon the fire. The companies worked most manfully, but the fire had too much headway, and had eaten through the walls of the "Riverside," into the adjoining building, and, spreading with great rapidity, it consumed everything in its course, and was only subdued when it had reached the building of George J. Piper, on the north, and that of W. H. Phillips, on the south. The loss was estimated at one hundred thousand dollars. Thirteen places of business were burned, including some of the best buildings in the town of Milton.

The origin of the conflagration was unknown, as there had been no fire for two days in the room where it was first discovered. The warmest gratitude was manifested by the citizens of Milton towards the Lewisburg and Watsontown firemen, for their prompt and manly aid in saving the town.

BURNING OF THE OLDEST HOUSE.

At two o'clock in the morning of the 4th of May, in the present year, (1876,) there occurred, at the north-east corner of Broadway and Water streets, a fire, which, though not a very destructive one, as regards the amount of property consumed, yet should receive more than a passing notice, because it destroyed the oldest building in the town—the old log house, which, when Andrew Straub came to Limestone Run, in 1779, he found, not yet roofed, only "logged up to the square," and *the only building of any kind in the place.* This house, when burned, was ninety-seven years old, more than fifteen years older than Governor Pollock's old stone mansion, which stood adjoining, and which was unroofed and badly damaged by the same fire.

The old house and a small building on the same lot, and both consumed, were the property of Dr. Waldron, who had no insurance. The Pollock house was insured for three thousand dollars.

At the census of 1870, the borough contained a population of one thousand nine hundred and nine, but as fully three-sevenths of the population of the *town* live outside the limits of the *borough*, and as the growth, since 1870, has been very good, it is confidently believed that four thousand is very nearly the correct figure for this year of 1876.

There are, in the town, five hotels, ten groceries, two hardware, three drug, and six dry goods stores; four merchant tailors, three watchmakers, three saddlers and harness-makers, three dentists, one printing and two express offices, besides the numerous small dealers and shops, which are not easy to enumerate, but which are in the usual proportion found in similar towns.

ATTORNEYS AND COUNSELORS AT LAW.

The members of the legal profession in Milton are: John F. Wolfinger, William C. Lawson, John Porter,* Franklin Bound, C. W. Tharp, J. Woods Brown, Peter L. Hackenburg, John McCleery, Thomas Swenk, Jr., Edmond Davis.

THE PHYSICIANS

Are Dr. James S. Dougal, Dr. David Waldron, Dr. U. Q. Davis, Dr. T. R. Hull, Dr. Charles H. Dougal, Dr. James P. McCleery, Dr. J. H. Miles.

Dr. James S. Dougal is not now in practice, being in the eighty-third year of his age. In 1798, at the age of four years, he was brought by his mother from Ireland, across the ocean, to join his father, Dr. James Dougal, who had settled in Milton three years before.

In the war of 1812, he volunteered for the army, and served, for a considerable time, at Marcus Hook. His medical education, he received from his father, and succeeded to his large practice, at his death, in 1818. His professional life has been a long, a busy, and an honorable one. May his remaining years be painless and serene!

The physicians of the Homœopathic School, are: Dr. J. A. Osborn and Dr. J. R. Ely.

THE MILTON FIRE DEPARTMENT.

The apparatus for extinguishment of fire, consists of a "Silsby" steam fire engine, a hook and ladder truck, and two suction hand-engines.

The hook and ladder company, when full, numbers forty members, and is called the "Fisher Hook and Ladder Company, No. 1., of Milton." D. K. Fisher, foreman. Their organization is independent, and only under control of the borough authorities when on duty at fires.

*Died July 4th, 1876.

The steamer, named the "Miltonian," is located on Front street, just above bridge. The company in charge of it, consists of about seventy-five members, under Franklin Hoy, foreman. The two hand-engines lie in the engine-house on Front street, opposite Broadway. But they have no companies, and are now for use, only in case of accident to the steamer. The Chief Engineer, in charge of all, is Charles McGee.

Milton has had, during the past seventy years, three fire-engines, other than those in its present department. The old hooks and ladders were procured in 1798, and eight years after Andrew Straub left, by will, one hundred dollars, towards a fire-engine, and this sum being supplemented by the citizens, an engine was purchased in Philadelphia, for the use of Milton. It was named the "Pat Lyon" in honor of its maker, who was reckoned among the best of that day. It is still in existence, and is now the private property of Mr. Louis Hilgert. He has placed it in thorough repair, and it is said to throw as strong a stream as it did in its youth, sixty years ago.

The "Enterprise," a rotary engine, came next. It was located on the river bank at Lower Market street. In 1840, it became a tender or supply machine for the "Harmony" engine, (not a suction,) which was purchased at or about that time. Of the apparatus now in use, the hand-engines were purchased, one in 1861, the other in 1870. The steamer and the hook and ladder truck were both procured in the present year, 1876.

The employment of a

POLICE FORCE

Commenced May 30th, 1874. It consists of only two patrolmen, whose duties *cease at midnight*. Thus much for the good morals of Milton.

MILTON LODGE, NO. 256, A. Y. M.

Constituted, 1851. Names of charter members: Amos Witter, John M. Huff, John F. Caslow, Joseph Eckbert, James Sheter, Christopher Steine, A. F. Ludwig, John N. Oyster, John Frick, Samuel Logan, David H. Watson, Allen Schreyer, James R. Caldwell. Wardens—John M. Huff and J. F. Caslow. Place of meeting, Masonic Hall, Goodlander's block.

THE OLD LODGE, NO. 144, A. Y. M.,

Was organized in Milton, about 1815. The members were: General Robert Hammond, General Henry Frick, Hon. John Montgomery, William Cox Ellis, Esq., Colonel Robert McGuigan, Dr. James S. Dougal, of which, only Dr. Dougal survives.

This lodge disintegrated in 1828, and working tools removed to Lewisburg.

MUTUAL LODGE, NO. 84, I. O. O. F.,

Meets Saturday evenings, at Academy of Music.

PILGRIMS' ENCAMPMENT, NO. 160, I. O. O. F.,

Also meets at Academy of Music.

KNIGHTS OF PYTHIAS,

Meets in Haag's building, second floor.

PATRIOTIC SONS OF AMERICA.

Place of meeting, Hackenburg's block.

ORDER OF AMERICAN MECHANICS,

Meets in Swartz's block.

JUNIOR ORDER OF AMERICAN MECHANICS,

Meets in Swartz's block.

THE MILTON SILVER CORNET BAND AND THE MILTON INDEPENDENT BAND,

Have lately been organized, and bid fair to attain excellence.

THE MILTON ACADEMY OF MUSIC.

Is a three-story brick building, one hundred and forty feet in depth, with a frontage of fifty-four feet, situated on Water street, a short distance above Broadway.

The lower story is sixteen feet, and the audience-hall, twenty-seven feet in height. In the first story are two stores, each twenty by fifty-four feet; one occupied as a grocery and seed-store, and the other as a drug-store. In the rear of these is a room, fifty-four by eighty-six feet, fitted up for a market-house, and most suitable for the purpose. In this, festivals and similar gatherings are held. It has side and rear entrances for rapid egress.

The main entrance is on Water street, and the hall is reached by a stairway ten feet in width. At head of stairway, on each side, are suites of offices, two rooms each, also ticket-office, while immediately above these is a hall, fifty-four feet in length, used by the Independent Order of Odd Fellows. The audience-hall will comfortably seat seven hundred and fifty persons. The large stage has every appliance for theatrical performances, for which, as well as for lectures, the hall is chiefly used. The entire building is supplied with gas. The hall is lighted from the ceiling by two large reflectors of forty-eight burners.

The frescoing, and all the decorations and appointments, are first-class in every particular.

The building was erected by J. Woods Brown, John McCleery, Samuel T. Brown, and Jacob F. Ganger. It was commenced in the Spring of 1870, and formally opened on the 13th of the succeeding December. Entire cost, twenty-eight thousand dollars.

MILTON GAS COMPANY

Was incorporated in 1856. The first officers were: W. C. Lawson, president; Thomas S. Mackey, secretary and superintendent; and William F. Nagle, treasurer.

The works are located on Filbert street, at Limestone Run. They were built, in 1860-61, by William Helm, of Philadelphia, as contractor, at a cost of about twenty-two thousand dollars.

The gas is manufactured from Clarion and Westmoreland counties bituminous coal, and is furnished at four dollars per thousand feet. Before the present year, the price was five dollars per thousand. The mains extend to Chamberlain's addition, on the north, and to Lower Market street, on the south.

In April, 1876, W. C. Lawson, Esq., having resigned the presidency, Mr. W. A. Schreyer was chosen his successor. The secretary is J. Woods Brown, Esq., and W. P. Hull is the treasurer. The company pays a semi-annual dividend of five per cent.

Milton has no water-works nor public parks.

MILTON CAR-WORKS,

Murray, Dougal & Co., proprietors. The enterprise was started in February, 1864, for the manufacture of agricultural implements, which was soon after changed to the manufacture of railway-cars, and the new firm of Murray, Dougal & Co. was organized, the partners being S. W. Murray, W. P. Dougal, J. S. Stoughton, John McCleery, and S. H. Pollock. In November, 1865, the firm was re-organized under the same style and name, but with only Murray, Dougal, McCormick and McCleery, as partners. It continued, without change, till the retirement of Mr. McCleery, in 1874, the three remaining partners continuing the business and firm name. Other branches have since been added, as the manufacture of mine-cars, oil-tanks, steam-boilers, bridge-bolts and castings, bill lumber, etc. The buildings consist of machine-shop, iron-foundry, brass-foundry, smith-shop, erecting-shop, paint-shop, two repair-shops, boiler-shop, planing-mill, wareroom, saw-mill, and office, and they occupy about six acres of ground. At full capacity, the works employ about four hundred and fifty men.

THE MILTON IRON COMPANY.

W. A. Schreyer, president; P. C. Johnson, secretary and treasurer; John Jenkins, superintendent. Stock owned by citizens of Milton and vicinity.

The works were established in 1872. They embrace the mill buildings, three double dwelling-houses and office, covering six acres of ground, about half-a-mile from the centre of town, and adjoining the West Branch Canal and the Philadelphia and Erie and Philadelphia and Reading Railroads, thus giving excellent facilities for transportation. They manufacture merchant bar-iron, the annual product of which is fifteen hundred tons. The engine is of one hundred and forty horse-power. There are one heating and six puddling furnaces. Hands employed, thirty-five.

MILTON NAIL WORKS.

Established in 1875, by C. A. Goodcharles & Co. They manufacture muck-bar and nails. Run nineteen machines, and employ about seventy hands. Mill located at junction of the Reading and Philadelphia & Erie Railroads, about half a mile from centre of town.

IRON FOUNDRY OF BICKEL & BAILEY.

This is the business established by Joseph Rhoads in 1830, which has been before mentioned. After Major Rhoads, it passed through several hands to those of the present proprietors, who run it on general foundry and machine work, and the manufacture of farming implements.

IRON FOUNDRY AND MACHINE SHOP

Of Lawson & Company, consisting of foundry-building, machine-shop, pattern-shop, and warerooms, is situated on both sides of Upper Front street, below the old Rhoads foundry. They manufacture all kinds of mill-gearing, reapers and mowers, and other agricultural implements. These works were established by John Patton, about 1838. They have passed successively through the ownership of White & Marvine, and White, Marvine & Lawson, till the coming in of the present firm. They employ eleven hands.

FOUNDRY AND MACHINE SHOP

Of J. M. Sussman. It is located on Upper Front street, nearly opposite the McCleery saw-mills. Is run in the manufacture of engines, lathes, drills, and mill-gearing. Was established in 1843, by the present owner, who has carried it on constantly till the present time. When busy, there are eight hands employed.

STEAM SAW-MILLS

Of McCleery, Newhard & Co. This business was established by Dr. William McCleery, in 1842, and has been mentioned as the first steam saw-mill ever built on the west branch. The old original mill was kept in operation until 1857, when a new firm was organized, the partners being Moses Chamberlain, William McCleery, John Runkle, and Charles Newhard, who erected a larger mill, above the old one, and on the opposite side of the canal. Its power was forty-horse, and cutting capacity eight thousand feet per day. Lath, shingle, and picket-machines, were operated for utilizing the offal.

This mill was destroyed in the Spring of 1864, but in October of the same year, a larger and better mill had been completed, and is now still in operation by the firm, consisting of William P. McCleery, Charles Newhard, and John W. Clinger. The mill runs a circular and a Mulay saw, and its cutting capacity is fifteen thousand feet per day, and, in addition to this, it manufactures eight hundred thousand laths, five hundred thousand pickets, and six hundred thousand shingles, annually. Besides the lumber saws, it operates a planer, re-saw, and flooring-machine. Number of hands employed, twenty.

MILTON SAW AND PLANING-MILL,

Situated on the east side of Upper Front street, and joining the West Branch Canal, is owned and operated by D. Clinger, and is believed to be the oldest planing-mill in northern Pennsylvania. It was built in 1855, by Balliet, Billmyer & Goodlander; it is eighty by eighty-six feet, two stories high, and propelled by a forty-horse engine; has dry-kilns attached, capable of drying twenty-five thousand feet at once. The mill was purchased by the present proprietor in 1867. When running to capacity, it employs forty men.

THE EXCELSIOR PLANING-MILLS

of Knouf & Co., is situated at Centre street, and the Philadelphia and Erie Railroad. They manufacture flooring, siding, doors, frames, sash, and shutters. Use thirty horse-power, and employ twenty-three hands. The main building is eighty by eighty feet, and the dry-kiln, forty by sixteen feet.

The first firm was Knouf, Crist, & Co., who built the mills in 1873, commencing on the 17th of March, and completing them ready for work on the 5th of May, of that year.

KEG AND STAVE-FACTORY

of Shimer & Co. This commenced work in Milton in 1872, working the offal of an oak bill-mill, located in Union County. That mill was removed to Milton in 1873, and the two were run in connection.

In May, 1875, a machine-shop was added. They manufacture oak bill-lumber, boxes, cloth-boards, staves, nail-kegs, and wood-working machinery. Value of productions, in 1875, thirty-five thousand dollars.

CARRIAGE MANUFACTORY

of Seydell & Tilden. It is situated at the corner of Upper Front and Upper Market streets. They manufacture carriages, spring-wagons, and sleighs. They employ eleven hands. Carriage works on this site, were started by Robert and Duncan Patterson many years ago, but were burned about 1845. Since then, the business has passed through several firms before the present one.

THE OLD "ECKERT" FLOUR-MILL,

Built by George Eckert, in 1816. Mr. Eckert died January 25th, 1850, after which it was rented for two years by George Baker, who, in December, 1851, (before the expiration of his rental) purchased the mill, and has owned it till the present time. He does custom work, wholly, has four run of burrs, and a capacity of fifty barrels per day.

THE "POLLOCK" FLOURING-MILL

On Upper Front street, opposite the Rhoads foundry, has already been mentioned as having been built in 1832, by F. W. Pollock, Esq. It is now owned and run by Elias Bickel, has forty-five-horse-power, and a capacity of thirty to forty bushels per hour. Annual business, thirty-five thousand dollars. Custom and merchant work.

TANNERY OF W. H. REBER,

Is located on Elm street near Mahoning. The tanning business was started here in a small way, before the present century, by John Armstrong, from Montgomery County. By him it was sold to William Jordan, who, in turn sold to Abraham Straub, about 1818. Twelve years later, Straub sold to Samuel T. Brown, and from him, it was purchased, in 1863, by William H. Reber, a practical tanner from Berks County. The tannery was burned, October 7th, 1867. The present one was immediately commenced upon the ruins, and in the following December it was completed, and business resumed. The work is principally sole-leather, of oak and hemlock tannage. Annual production, twenty-two thousand sides. Hands employed twenty-one. Tannery building, one hundred by seventy-three feet, two-story.

FLY-NET FACTORY, OF B. F. WILSON.

This business was commenced, in a small way, in 1856, by Robert Wilson, who was the inventor of the machinery used in the manufacture. The business increased steadily, and on January 1st, 1860, he removed to the second-story of Goodlander's block, where it remained until 1871, when it was removed to its present location; the new building is on Lower Front street, near Philadelphia and Reading Railroad depot.

THE MILTON NATIONAL BANK.

The germ from which this institution sprung, was the *Milton Savings Bank*, incorporated in 1855, and organized in 1856, with a capital of only twenty-five thousand dollars. James Pollock was president, and Robert M. Frick, cashier.

In 1857, Mr. Pollock resigned the presidency, and W. C. Lawson was elected to fill his place.

March 8th, 1862, it was made a bank of issue, the capital increased to fifty thousand dollars, and the name changed to *The Milton Bank;* Mr. Lawson and Mr. Frick, respectively, retaining the offices of president and cashier.

On the 17th of January, 1865, having complied with the requirements of the National Banking Law, it became the Milton National Bank, with a capital increased to one hundred thousand dollars, and with W. C. Lawson and Robert M. Frick still as president and cashier.

The banking-rooms were first in the Cadwallader Building, adjoining the Bethuel Vincent corner. Its present quarters are in one of the brick dwelling-houses, purchased by the bank from the estate of William H. Sanderson. The residence of the cashier occupies the remainder of the property.

FIRST NATIONAL BANK OF MILTON, PA.

This institution commenced business, under the National Banking Law, February 13th, 1864—J. Woods Brown, president, and Samuel D. Jordan, cashier. In 1875, Mr. Jordan died, when the teller, Mr. John M. Caldwell, was promoted to be cashier.

The institution does a general banking business, and makes collections at accessible points. The present president is J. Woods Brown, and the cashier is John M. Caldwell. Capital, one hundred thousand dollars.

Its first place of business was in a brick building owned by the Sanderson estate, on the site now occupied by the law office of Lawson & Brown. Two years later, it was removed to Haag's Block, and it remained there six years. At the end of that time, banking-rooms were rented for a term of twenty-five years, in the block of Mr. Henry Huth, on Front street. There it continued business until the block was destroyed in the great fire of December 12th, 1875. The safes and other property were got out, with but very trifling loss, and removed to premises on the opposite side of Front street, owned by Mrs. Frymire, and occupied by D. W. Angell, who vacated to accommodate the bank.

Here it did business until July 12th, 1876, when it was moved to the new banking-house which had been built on land purchased from Mr. Huth; being the same spot which it occupied at the time of the fire.

The cost of land and building was seven thousand dollars. The new banking-house is twenty by forty-five feet—two stories, each fourteen feet high. The material is brick, with eighteen-inch walls, iron beams and girders, brick-arched ceilings, heavily covered with cement, iron stairway, corrugated iron doors and shutters, and metallic roof; making it, as nearly as practicable, fire-proof. Its interior finish is of walnut, with solid furniture of the same material. The "Valentine & Butler" vaults, with chronometer locks, afford as much security against burglars, as steel, chilled-iron, and ingenious mechanism can give.

THE MILTONIAN.

Soon after the expiration of the first decade of the present century, the citizens of Milton began to think that their population, and their importance, entitled them to a local newspaper—one which might reflect their own views and feelings, untrammeled by the opinions and prejudices of the older towns. The *Freiheitsvogel*, of Sunbury, had died several years before, and the *Republican Argus*, of Northumberland, was already in the throes of dissolution. The *Northumberland Gazette*, the *Northwestern Post*, and the *Sunbury Times*, still came up regularly by mail, but Milton needed a journal of her own; and so General Henry Frick, one of her principal citizens, bought presses and type, and all the expensive necessities of a newspaper, and on Saturday, September 21st, 1816, he issued the first number of the *Miltonian*, from his office of publication, at the corner of Broadway and Water streets.

It was the pioneer, as it is now the sole survivor of journalism in Milton. There is pride in the term pioneer, and there is inexpressible melancholy in that of last survivor; but neither pride nor melancholy seem to have sown the seeds of decay in the *Miltonian*, for now, in the sixtieth year of its existence, it is as fresh and vigorous as ever. It has lived under the administrations of fifteen Presidents, and has noticed fourteen of them in obituary. At the time of its birth, George the Fourth had not yet come to the throne of England, and the great Napoleon had been but a few months on St. Helena. So we find among the foreign news in that first issue, as follows: "*Bonaparte.*—We have a roundabout West India account that Bonaparte had escaped from St. Helena on the 22d of June. Particulars are not given, but the report is said to have been believed at Barbadoes." Also, an item referring to a recent ball given by the Prince Regent (afterwards George Fourth), on which occasion the Princess Charlotte had interdicted the wearing of any stuffs not of British manufacture. (It would be well if Americans to-day would emulate that royal economy and patriotism). There is no marriage recorded in the first number, but there is an announcement of death, as follows: "Died, on Tuesday last, in this place, after a short illness, Mr. Edmund Hogan, a respectable inhabitant."

Abner Cox advertises in it a general assortment of dry goods, boots, shoes, china, glass and crockery-ware, Montezuma salt, and, also, old rye whisky, by the barrel or gallon. And Henry Follmer returns his sincere thanks to the public for their encouragement to his wool-carding factory, and he reminds them that flax-seed will be taken, at Milton prices, in payment of debts due him.

It publishes *Grotigan's Philadelphia Prices Current*, of date September 9th, 1816, as follows:

Wheat, per bushel,	$1.25
Rye, per bushel,	1.25
Barley, per bushel,	1.00
Oats, per bushel,	.50
Superfine wheat flour, per barrel,	9.50
Rye flour, per barrel,	6.50
Rye whiskey, per gallon,	.50
Butter, per pound,	.16
Spanish dollars (premium),	.10
American dollars (premium),	.08
Gold dollars (premium),	.08
Western notes (discount),	.12

It carries a disproof of the popular belief, that in the olden times "the office sought the man and not the man the office," for we find John Wheatley, George Leshar, Jacob Markley, and Jacob Urban, advertising themselves as candidates for the office of County Commissioner, and asking the votes of their fellow-citizens. That candidates and voters were as bibulously inclined, and also that liquor bills were as difficult of collection then as now, seems apparent from the following, which is found among the advertisements.

"CAUTION TO INN-KEEPERS.

"As an election is drawing nigh, and as Samuel Maus, Esq., among other candidates for the office of Commissioner, may be riding through the County, canvassing for votes, all inn-keepers should be cautious in trusting him beyond the amount of twenty shillings, as they will perceive, by the following transcript from the Magistrate's docket, that they cannot recover any sum beyond the amount. (Signed) VALENTINE SMITH."

(Then follows the transcript above mentioned, showing that Esquire Maus had, in a certain action, pleaded the "Bar Act," as against Smith, and thereby brought him to grief, in the sum of three dollars and forty-four cents, Valentine being himself an inn-keeper, and having incautiously trusted the defendant with that amount for certain gill-glasses, in excess of the twenty shillings allowed by law.)

For ten years and seven months, the *Miltonian* continued under the proprietorship and management of General Frick, but during the thirteen succeeding years he had associated with him, in its publication, at different times, Montgomery Sweeny, Robert Bennett, John W. Correy, and John H. Brown.

This latter-named gentleman assumed the entire management of the paper on June 3d, 1840, when General Frick permanently retired. Mr. Brown continued alone till January 1st, 1842, and was then succeeded by John Frick and E. B. Hunter. On May 5th, 1843, Hunter retired, and from then until 1854, the paper was successively under control of John Frick, Robert M. Frick, and Henry Frick, Jr., sons of the founder.

On January 1st, of that year, it was purchased by John Robins. Three years later, viz: January 1st, 1857, it passed from the hands of Mr. Robins into those of Robert M. and Jacob Frick.

The next year, 1858, it was purchased by L. H. Funk, who published it alone for five years.

In 1863, L. M. Morton purchased a half-interest, and the publishing firm-name became Funk & Morton. In 1867, Mr. Funk died, and his interest in the paper was sold to Hon. Franklin Bound. In 1869, Mr. Bound sold his interest to William M. Mervine, and the firm was then Morton & Mervine.

The next year, a one-third interest was sold to Rev. D. C. John, and the paper was then, for five years, published by Morton, Mervine & Co.

In March, 1875, the paper was sold to P. L. Hackenburg, Esq. At the end of nine months, however, he sold it to L. M. Morton, Esq., who is still editor, proprietor, and publisher.

All things terrestial must have an end, and so will the *Miltonian*; but now, after outliving all local contemporaries, it seems so well and firmly established, that it is not unlikely to live to announce the festivities of the next centennial.

THE STATES ADVOCATE

Was first printed in Milton, February 26th, 1826, by William Tweed and E. H. Kincaid. On April 13th, 1829, Mr. Kincaid withdrew. August 15th, 1833, the firm became Tweed & Kelchner. November 13th, 1834, Tweed withdrew, and, after four years more, Kelchner removed the paper to Lewisburg, Union County, November 1st, 1838.

THE WEST BRANCH FARMER AND TRUE DEMOCRAT

Was started by Montgomery Sweeny, a former partner with General Frick, in the *Miltonian*.

Its first issue was September 3d, 1834, and it expired after about three years.

THE NORTHUMBRIAN

Was very short-lived. It first appeared in November, 1837. Mr. A. Kerr was its proprietor and publisher.

THE MILTON LEDGER.

This newspaper was commenced in 1838, and existed for a little more than six years. It was founded by McGee & Wilson, and its subsequent publishers were: McGee & Collings, H. L. Dieffenbach, John M. Porter, and Brewer & Armstrong. Its last publisher was a gentleman named Frank. The paper was suspended in 1844.

THE ADVOCATE AND DAY SPRING.

First publication in Autumn of 1844, by Rev. W. H. T. Barnes, who afterwards died in the Mexican war. The paper was devoted to temperance, and existed some two years.

On April 17th, 1852, was issued the first number of

THE MILTON DEMOCRAT,

by John R. Eck, Esq. It died a natural death in 1859.

THE NORTHUMBERLAND COUNTY HERALD

Was started as a temperance journal in 1868. It was neutral in politics, and was published by Rev. E. W. Kirby and J. W. Speddy, Esq. It was continued about a year.

PUBLIC SCHOOLS.

The gentlemen composing the present board of Milton School Directors, are: Thomas R. Hull, president; William H. Gotwald, secretary and district superintendent; Leonard C. Beddleman, Hugh D. Barr, Samuel H. Tilden, Leander M. Morton; Robert M. Frick, Treasurer.

The number of schools is nine, with an average attendance of about four hundred and fifty scholars in the aggregate. The schools are creditable, but neither they nor the school buildings are what they should be in the town which once boasted a Kirkpatrick, and which, to-day, swells with just pride at the mention of him and his peerless academy.

No fault, however, can attach to the district superintendent or to the directors, who, each and all, take a deep interest in the welfare of the schools, and in every effort towards their advancement.

The Centre school-house is of brick, respectable in size and most other respects; but of some of the others, particularly that on Broadway, there can hardly be as much said.

The high-school is ably conducted, and its pupils acquire all the necessary qualifications for freshmen. Its principal is a graduate, and receives eighty dollars per month. The other teachers' salaries are from thirty-five dollars upwards. The free school terms amount to eight months of the year, and this is supplemented about two months by subscription.

Of the Milton schools, in olden time, there were some which deserve mention. The earliest of these was that taught by Joseph D. Biles, who announced his capacity to teach "reading, writing, arithmetic, English grammar, geography, book-keeping (Italian form), mensuration, surveying, navigation, algebra, natural and moral philosophy, and the Latin and Greek languages." This school was commenced in 1815, in the old frame school-house on Broadway, and was called the "Milton academy," whereof the trustees were: David Rittenhouse, John Chestnut, and Bethuel Vincent.

This was, doubtless, a good school, but it languished and soon expired, probably for lack of support. And Mr. Biles, after keeping a book-store in Milton for a few years, removed to Reading, and became there a lawyer of some note.

The Kirkpatrick School.—But the "school of schools" was the second, the *real* Milton Academy—"Kirk's school," as it was admiringly called. The project was initiated in 1822, by Rev. George Junkin. The school was opened in a room which had been a printing-office, in a building standing on the spot now occupied by the residence of Dr. James P. McCleery. This was used for some time, before the low, square, hip-roofed Academy was built, on the rise of the hill upon the north side of Broadway. Its cost did not reach four hundred dollars, which was made up by stock subscriptions, in twenty-five dollar shares, placed among ten or twelve citizens of the town. Mr. Junkin had, from the first, thought of his friend, the Rev. David Kirkpatrick, intending to persuade him to assume charge of this school. He was a graduate of the University of Dublin, Ireland, and, coming to this country, had commenced teaching in a small way in Oxford, Pennsylvania. Mr. Junkin's persuasions prevailed, and Mr. Kirkpatrick left Oxford, to take charge of the Academy in Milton. But so high did he stand in Oxford, that several who were students there, followed him, to continue their studies, in the Academy.

His career was more than a success. It was a triumph! During the eleven years that he remained, his students numbered four hundred, very many of whom attained *distinguished* positions, and very few, if any, remained in mediocrity. One hundred and fifty of them are still living, and, among these, are Representatives and Senators in Congress, lawyers of the highest repute, and more than one who has been Governor of Pennsylvania. It is believed that in all the State, there has never been a school of similar size and pretension, which turns out such a bright galaxy. But, in 1834, he embraced what seemed an advantageous opportunity, and removed to Indiana County and the glory of the old academy went with him. The school lived on, an ordinary existence, under charge of Rev. Mr. Ferguson and others, until 1854, and then it was discontinued.

From that time, the old house remained vacant till about 1872, when it was purchased, to be used as a *storage-house* to a carriage manufactory. It was like planting cabbages in the Roman Forum.

The Reunion.—At Milton, on the 14th of July, 1874, there gathered, from near and from far off, fifty-seven of the one hundred and fifty surviving scholars of Kirkpatrick. They had come to look again at the old academy, and to revive memories of their youthful tribulations and triumphs within its walls. There were those present who had followed him from Oxford, and many who had been his pupils half a century before.

There were some to whose eyes the old house had not become unfamiliar—some who had seen it nearly every day for years; but to those who had *not* seen it since their school-days, the feeling could not have been other than that of deep disappointment, as they looked upon it in its dinginess and dilapidation; with even these, intensified by the addition of a pair of decaying wooden wings. They mustered inside the old school-room, as they had done so many years before, but it was only a short session, for dinner awaited them at the Riverside Hotel. The appetites, at least, were as keen as of old, and the exercises *there* were most agreeable.

Thence they adjourned to the Academy of Music, and listened to eloquent words from Governor James Pollock, and others of their own number, and though those words brought frequent tears, and though chords were touched that sometimes thrilled to their hearts' cores, they felt that they had done well in coming there. It was an occasion which they will never forget, and one which will long be remembered by the citizens of Milton.

The Lancasterian School System was one under which pupils were, for superior scholarship and good conduct, appointed to be ushers and monitors over their fellows; and as these positions could only be kept by a continuance of that relative superiority through which they were obtained—a superiority which those under them were always striving to extinguish—it was claimed that the extraordinary spirit of emulation thus engendered, must produce the best possible results to the school.

On that system, the Lancasterian School of Milton was commenced in 1830, in a long one-story brick building, standing where the Centre school-house now is. The enterprise was inaugurated by a stock company, as is shown by the fact that Mr. C. C. Straub has in his possession some of the stock certificates, which he recently discovered among the papers of his deceased father.

A Mr. Wright, of Philadelphia, was the first teacher, and was eminently fitted for the position. Under him, the scholars attained excellent proficiency, but with his successor, Mr. Charles Guenther, the results were not so satisfactory, and it was not very long before the project was abandoned.

The Prospect Hill School, a private subscription enterprise, was commenced about 1847. The house was erected in a square, containing five town lots, at the corner of Upper Market and Second streets—a beautiful high swell of ground, called "Prospect Hill," or, sometimes, "Academy Hill." It was not a very fine or commodious building, but it answered all the purposes of the school until 1859, when it was demolished.

The New Milton Academy was built upon the same spot, by subscribers, citizens of Milton, at a cost of six thousand dollars. It was a handsome two-story brick structure, with symmetrical towers rising from the two front angles. The grounds were neatly enclosed, and well kept, and the entire establishment and surroundings were very attractive to the eye.

The first principal was Rev. William T. Wylie, pastor of the Reformed Presbyterian Church. He was excellent, both as pastor and as teacher, and Milton well appreciated him. He is now laboring in Chambersburg, Pa.

After five or six years, the interest in the Academy seems to have waned, for, about 1865, the stockholders sold land and building to Colonel —— Wright, of Rochester New York, but it was with the condition that the property should never be used for other than educational purposes.

Colonel Wright, however, was not fortunate in his undertaking and investment, for, about two years later, the fire destroyed all his fine buildings, and left but a blackened waste of his beautiful grounds, and this was the end of Milton's third academy. It is to be hoped that it may be rebuilt, but as yet no movement has been made in that direction.

CHURCHES, ETC.

The Episcopal Church is the oldest in Milton, and dates back more than eighty years. The families composing it, at the commencement of the century, were those of Marr, Hull, McCurley, Hepburn, Rittenhouse, Smith, Stadden, Seydell, Covert, and Webb. Their first house of worship was a log-building, which stood on Church lane, (where it now corners with Lincoln street,) upon a lot donated for church and burial purposes, by Joseph Marr, August 18th, 1794, to Matthias Webb, Samuel Stadden, and John Covert, as trustees for the church.

The Rev. Caleb Hopkins was the first who preached to the congregation, but was not their rector. The first rector was Rev. Depuey; the next, Rev. Eldred; and the third was Rev. Abijah Hopkins, who remained up to about 1820. From that time, for about twenty-five years, they had neither rector nor services, and the members mostly united with other churches. About 1845, or a little later, worship was resumed, and the question of building a new church edifice was soon after earnestly agitated by the Rev. B. Wistar

Morris, now Bishop of Washington Territory, who had then just assumed the rectorship. There were but few communicants at that time, and it was only by the most strenuous and persevering efforts of Mr. Morris that the church was built. Mr. Rolland McCurley, who is still living in Union County, gave the lot of ground, and, after years of effort, the corner-stone was laid by Bishop Potter, July 17th, 1849. It was completed without further delay—a substantial and commodious brick edifice, which still remains their place of worship. They are now again without a rector, and their numbers are not large.

The First Presbyterian Church, of Milton, was organized by the Presbytery of Northumberland, December 3d, 1811.

Prior to the organization—from about 1803 to 1810, the Rev. John Bryson, pastor at Warrior Run and at Chillisquaque, preached in the log school-house, on Lower Market street, in Milton, on every fourth Sabbath, and during the latter part of that time, on alternate Sabbaths.

Their first regular pastor was the Rev. Thomas Hood, who was installed, October 7th, 1812, and, under his ministry, the congregation worshiped in the Episcopal Church edifice, in Morris lane, or Church lane, until 1819, when they removed to the Harmony Church, on Mahoning street, and this they occupied alternately with the German Reformed and Lutheran congregations until 1832. Then, on account of pecuniary embarrassments, they left the Union, and obtained the use of the Baptist Church, until 1838. Then, for two years, they worshiped in Shiloh Church, until the dedication of the new brick church building, which they had erected on Water street. This was on July 29th, 1838. In this edifice they worshiped through the pastorates of Rev. James Williamson, installed November 27th, 1838, and Rev. David Longmore, D.D., installed November 17th, 1840.

On December 14th, 1854, the Rev. James C. Watson, D.D., was installed as their pastor, and his ministry has continued until the present time.

In May, 1856, their church building was removed, and a new edifice commenced upon the same site. It was completed in 1857, and dedicated on the the 16th day of August of that year. It is a substantial brick building, and is still used as their place of worship.

Methodist Episcopal Church.—As early as the year 1788, worship was held, at irregular intervals, by the Methodist residents of Milton and vicinity. These meetings were held, sometimes at one, and sometimes at another, of the citizens' houses, and at such times as a preacher could be secured for the day or evening, that is, whenever a minister of their persuasion came in their vicinity from other localities.

In this manner they continued until the building of the log school-house in Lower Market street, in 1796, after which that building was used for their meetings, but they still had no regular pastor.

It is a matter greatly to be regretted, that there are no accessible data by which the correct time of organization can be given, nor the names and dates of service of the different ministers. Some time after the commencement of the century, a small log church was built opposite the old school-house on Market street, and in this they held their worship, under the ministrations of a large number of different pastors, until 1835, when their new church building, on the east side of the canal, was completed and occupied. This edifice stood on a spot which fell directly in the middle of Centre street, when that thoroughfare came to be laid out, and so, as the most satisfactory way out of the difficulty, the projectors of the street purchased and removed the church in 1850, and the congregation then built and removed to the new church building in Upper Front street, which has been their place of worship till the present time. Their pastor is now the Rev. A. D. Yocum. The membership is three hundred, which is also about the average attendance at their excellent Sabbath-school.

Lutheran Church.—The Lutheran and Reformed churches of Milton, being union congregations for many years, the history of one is, to a certain extent, that of both. From 1796 to 1807, the Lutherans of Milton were supplied with preaching by traveling ministers. Services were held in the old log school-house, in Lower Market street. About 1807, a small one-story log building on south side of Mahoning street, was purchased by the congregation. It stood on land now owned by Baltzer Critzer. Here preaching and German day-school were regularly held. The Revs. Oyer, Stock, and Engle, were the first preachers. After them, in 1811, came the Rev. Philip Repass, as pastor. The old "Harmony Church," at the eastern end of Mahoning street, became their place of worship, in union with the Presbyterians and German Reformed people. It was dedicated May 23d and 24th, 1819. The church was now organized, under Mr. Repass, as pastor; Philip H. Schreyer, as elder; and John Hill, as deacon.

The successors of Mr. Repass, till 1850, were Rev. Frederick Wange, Rev. —— Garman, Rev. Charles P. Miller, John G. Auspach, Charles F. Stoever, Eli Swarts, and Frederic Ruthrauff. The Lutherans, having sold their interest in the Harmony Church to the Reformed congregation, built for their own use, in 1850, a new two-story brick church building—naming it *Trinity Church*. It stood near the western end of Mahoning street. The pastors who preached in this church, were Rev. F. Ruthrauff, John J. Reimsnyder, C. C. Culler, T. Titus, and P. Sprecher.

In 1861, their present large and beautiful church edifice, situated on the north-east corner of Second and Mahoning streets, was completed, and dedicated to God's worship.

The pastors who have successively ministered in this church, are Revs. George Parson, N. Graves, A. Burnman, and the present pastor, Rev. W. H. Gotwald.

Reformed Church.—As early as can now be ascertained, this congregation was first regularly organized on the 25th of April, 1819—the first election for church officers resulting in the choice of Christian Markle, as elder, and Joseph Rhoads, as deacon. The few Reformed families living in and around Milton, had been more or less frequently supplied with preaching by Reformed clergymen, who came this way, as early as 1805—first in the log-school-house, on Lower Market street, and, later, in a small log building in Mahoning street.

In 1817, the Reformed people united with the Lutheran and Presbyterian congregations in erecting a church edifice, on the hill at the east end of Mahoning street, to be known as the "Harmony Church," (completed 1819) in which this congregation worshiped until that building was remodeled, in 1866. The church edifice now occupied, is a commodious brick building, on Upper Front street, and was erected in 1867. Following is a list of all the ministers who have served since the organization: Rev. Justus Henry Fries, 1812-23; Rev. Samuel Gutelius, 1824-27; Rev. Henry Wagner, 1827-35; Rev. Daniel Gring, 1835-46. Rev. Ephraim Kieffer became Mr. Gring's colleague, to preach in the English language, in 1840, and continued until 1844. Rev. Henry Harbaugh then associated himself with Mr. Gring, preaching in English, until 1846, after which, Mr. Gring having resigned, he served the congregation as pastor until 1849. Rev. E. M. Long served 1845-52; Rev. A. G. Dole, 1853-65; Rev. Samuel H. Reid, 1866-73. The present pastor, Rev. F. F. Balmer, assumed charge in 1873.

The congregation has a communicant membership of two hundred and twenty-five, and has connected with it a flourishing Sabbath-school.

The Milton Baptist Church.—The Rev. Eugenio Kincaid has, during all his life, been eminently a soldier of the Cross. Early in the year 1826, he came into the valley of the Susquehanna—a Christian knight-errant—in search of the neglected and destitute, and reaching Milton, and finding that one solitary individual, a woman, stood alone in all that town as the representative of the Baptist persuasion, he resolved to plant the standard there, and to give stated preachings, for he knew where two or three were gathered together in the earnest desire to serve under the Divine Commander, that He would come down in their midst, and that His panoply would cover them.

These stated preachings very soon produced their effect, for around this nucleus there collected a little band, which, on the 25th of August, in the same year, was recognized as the Milton Baptist Church, regularly constituted. There were nine members, viz.: Eugenio and Emily Kincaid, Nathan and Martha Delany, William and Catharine Thomas, Susannah Thomas, Sarah Watts, and Harriet Geddes. On Sabbath morning, the 10th of the following September, immediately after morning service, occurred their first baptism. A great concourse of people thronged the river bank, and the scene was a most impressive one. Now the church prospered apace, continuing under the ministration of Mr. Kincaid, until his appointment as missionary to Burmah, in 1830, when his place was filled by Rev. George Higgins. He was an itinerant, but made the Milton Church his centre of labor, and his home. During the five years of his charge, fifty-one were received into the fellowship of the church. In August, 1832, James Moore, Sr., and William Thomas, were ordained deacons, and in March, 1833, their first Sabbath-school was commenced.

The exact date of the erection of their first meeting-house is not known. It was commenced, however, not far from 1830, but was not entirely finished for some years. Deacon James Moore, Sr., gave the lot. The church stood on the spot where Daniel Kramer's house now stands, in Filbert street. It was then called Church Alley. After Mr. Higgins, came Rev. S. B. Brown, who remained till 1837, and added fifteen to the church in baptism. Following him was Rev. D. C. Wait, till 1839, during which time twenty-nine were received. His successor was Rev. C. A. Hewitt, whose pastorate continued till 1845, and was a most successful one. The Rev. J. E. Bradley, and theological students Kelly, Hay, and Chroshan, supplied the pulpit up to 1852, when Rev. Howard Malcolm held charge for about four years. For the succeeding ten years, preaching was supplied, principally, by Professor Curtis, and by various students of the Lewisburg University. Then, in 1864, came Rev. J. A. Kirkpatrick, followed successively by Rev. James Parker, Rev. T. E. Clapp, and Rev. W. B. Thomas, until 1868, when their new place of worship was completed. It is a handsome brick structure, standing on Centre street and Elm, at the south-east corner. In December, 1868, Rev. A. C. Wheat assumed charge, and remained untill 1870. The present pastor is Rev. J. Green Miles, whose ministry commenced in 1871. The membership is one hundred. The Rev. Mr. Kincaid, their present pastor, still lives at a very advanced age, in Girard, Kansas. Three times he went as missionary to the kingdom of Burmah, freely braving the terrors of that climate, in the hope of saving souls. His life has been truly a noble one.

Reformed Presbyterian Church.—The organization of this church was effected in 1831. Their first church edifice was a frame building, near the present site of the Philadelphia and Erie Railroad depot. Their first pastor was Rev. William Wilson, whose ministration continued until 1836, when he was succeeded by Rev. John McKinley, of Philadelphia, who, at the end of three years, was in turn succeeded by Rev. J. A. Crawford. His ministry extended over a period of six years. The fourth pastorate was that of Rev. Matthew Smith, which continued but little more than a year. Their fifth (and last regular) pastor was Rev. William T. Wylie, a man eminent in every Christian grace and virtue, who remained with them eleven years—(1854 till June, 1865). He is now laboring in Chambersburg, Pa. Since his time, the pulpit has been supplied by the Second Reformed Presbytery of Philadelphia.

In 1854, during Mr. Wiley's ministry, their old church building and land were sold to the railroad company, and they removed to their new brick edifice, which had just been completed, on Walnut street, between Upper Front and Water streets, and which is their present house of worship. The cost of this church building was about nine thousand dollars. They are wholly free from debt, and prosperous.

St. Joseph's Catholic Church.—This church, in Milton, was founded in 1837. The first entry in the baptismal register is of date, November 5th, in that year, and is signed by Rev. Edward Maginnis, the first priest in charge. The names of his successors are not all known, but among them were Revs. Daniel Sheridan, Basil, Sharb, and George Gostenhuigg; the latter of whom died on the second day of May, 1860, and now lies interred in the yard of their church on Walnut street, east of the Philadelphia and Erie Railroad. This church is a brick structure, and was built in 1844. It was their first (and has been their only) regular place of worship in Milton. Rev. Louis Grotemeyer is the present pastor.

The Zion African M. E. Church.—The date of its organization, as a church, is not exactly known. The congregation worshiped, for some years, in the frame school-house on Broadway, and in the year 1849, they purchased that building, and removed it eastwardly to a point near the top of the hill, upon the same street, (its present location,) and with some repairs it became their church edifice, which they have occupied for worship until the present time. Their pastor is now Rev. James Henry, who, in 1875, succeeded Rev. T. N. Allen. Before Mr. Allen, the Rev. James Barnes had preached for two years. Of the names of their earlier pastors, there is no record. The number of communicants is at present twenty-seven.

Milton Mission of the Evangelical Association.—This mission was founded in the year 1866. The first missionary was the Rev. S. Dane, who labored on the mission for two years. In the Spring of 1869, the Rev. J. M. Pines became pastor of the congregation. During his pastorate they had no regular place of worship, and he found it very difficult to build up the society. The next Spring, he was succeeded by Rev. A. H. Irvine, who aided the society in the purchase of a house and lot on Lower Market street. The building was fitted up, and used as a place of worship during the pastorate of Mr. Irvine. His successor, in 1873, was the Rev. H. B. Hertzler, during whose ministry the house was removed, and the lot cleared for the building of a new church edifice. After this removal, the congregation held their meetings in a school-house in Lower Market street.

The Rev. A. W. Schenberger became pastor in the Spring of 1874, and it was chiefly due to his unwearying labors, aided by those of Rev. M. J. Carothers, Presiding Elder of the Lewisburg District, that the new church building was carried to completion. Its size is seventy-four by fifty feet, and the total cost was four thousand two hundred and seventy-two dollars and ten cents. It was dedicated to Almighty God, by Bishop Dubs, of Cleveland, Ohio, January 31st, 1875. Rev. Mr. Schenberger is still their pastor. The membership numbers eighty-four, and they have a large Sabbath-school.

The Christian Association.—At the time of its commencement, in 1871, it was called the *Young People's Prayer Meeting.*—Its object was, and is, the dissemination of religious knowledge and ideas, with meetings for prayer, and religious interchange. After an existence of five years, they adopted, in March, 1876, their present name and designation. Their meetings are held at the various churches, in rotation. Contributions for necessary expenses, are received by the executive committee, but are not solicited in public at the meetings.

The President of the Association is W. P. Wheeland; Vice President, William D. Snyder; Secretary, J. F. Wolfinger; Treasurer, John M. Caldwell; Librarian, George T. Gauby.

THE CEMETERIES OF MILTON.

The first place where interments were made by the inhabitants of Milton, was a ground situated south of Ferry lane, and about midway between Front street and the river. Its use dates back beyond 1790. The name of the first interment is not known. The bodies have all been removed years ago, and no trace of its ancient character is now visible.

The German Reformed Burying-ground directly north of the Presbyterian, was donated by Andrew Straub, on March 11th, 1793. In that year, his son John Straub was buried there, and that was the first interment. His remains have recently been removed to Harmony Cemetery, by his nephew, C. C. Straub Esq., president of that association.

Very few interments are made there now, and it is going into disuse.

Episcopal Burying-ground.—On August 18th, 1794, Joseph Murr gave a lot of ground in Church Lane, adjoining Upper Milton, to Matthias Webb, Samuel Stadden, and John Covert, trustees of the Episcopal congregation, for burial and church purposes.

This ground was principally used by members of the congregation, but it has been abandoned for many years, and most of the dead removed to the cemeteries.

Methodist Graveyard.—A year or two later, ground for a burial place and church was given to the Methodist congregation by Andrew Straub. It was situated on the north side of Lower Market street, just north of the present school-house. It has been many years since any interments were made there, and all the remains have been transferred to other grounds.

It is now in disuse, and a lumber yard occupies its site.

The Old Presbyterian Graveyard was donated to that society by Daniel Scudder, Esq., about 1820. Very few burials are now made there, and many of those buried in earlier times, have been removed.

The Milton Cemetery Association was incorporated in 1853. Their grounds contain ten acres, beautifully located on a high swell of land, just outside the eastern limits of the borough, and beyond the Philadelphia and Erie Railroad. They are enclosed by a handsome paling fence, and are tastefully laid out with avenues and walks. Much pains has been taken to beautify this last resting-place, by the planting of trees, shrubbery, and flowers, and many handsome and expensive monuments have been reared by sorrowing friends.

The cemetery is a beautiful one, and most creditable to the citizens of Milton.

The Harmony Cemetery Association was incorporated in 1860, Abraham Straub was the first president, and was succeeded, in 1864, by C. C. Straub, who still holds the office.

The first interment was that of a child of William Derrickson, which was buried there, even before the laying out was completed.

The cemetery is a tract of ten acres, lying on a beautiful southerly slope, bounded by the borough limits on the west, and by a public road on the east.

The grounds are laid off in sections, fronting south-westerly, and thence running to the rear line upon the crest of the acclivity. Avenues run entirely around the enclosure, and divide the sections from each other. Foot-walks are laid between the avenues, and give access to all the burial lots.

The plan and the embellishments are in the true spirit of the modern idea—that the home of the departed should be made attractive to the eye, and freed from the gloom, with which our forefathers were too apt to invest it. No "naked rows of graves, and melancholy ranks of monuments" are here,

PROPERTY OF JOSEPH EMRICK, LOWER AUGUSTA TP., NORTH'D CO., PA.

RES. & MILL OF JOHN SHIPMAN, HUGHES STATION, NORTH'D CO., PA.

but flowers are springing upon the green sod, and the willow trails its long pendants over the pure white marble. The larch, the ash, and the maple, wave their graceful branches above the mounds; the walks are bordered with shrubbery, and a living hedge of honey-locust encloses the whole.

"Peace to the dust, that in silence reposes
Beneath the deep shade of the cypress and yew;
May Spring deck the spot with her earliest roses,
And Heaven wash their leaves with its holiest dew."

The Catholic Cemetery is about two miles east of the town. Its area is about five acres, enclosed by a substantial brick-wall. Within the enclosure is an old brick building, which was formerly their church. It is now in decay. The interments are very numerous.

These are the cemeteries of Milton, but her dead are not *all here*.

There is another, and a wider burial-place—stretching from the locust-fringed Potomac to the sand beaches of the Gulf—and all over that broad ground, all along the slopes of Virginia, and on the ridges of Georgia and Tennessee, her soldier sons are sleeping in unmarked graves; and there they will slumber on till the reveille of the archangel awakens them.

NORTHUMBERLAND BOROUGH.

THE FIRST SETTLER.

The first settler on the site of Northumberland was Robert Martin, who was originally from New Jersey. He first settled at Wyoming under the Pennsylvania title, but, being unable to live there in peace, removed to Northumberland. He erected a house and kept tavern here, as early as 1760. His house, at that time, and a number of years subsequent, was the only one to be seen about Northumberland Point, or even on the other side, except at Fort Augusta.

After Penn's purchase of land from the Indians, in 1768, Martin's tavern was thronged with numerous speculators, pioneers, surveyors, and adventurers, who came to view and settle upon the lands of the west branch. Mr. Martin was the father of the wife of Captain Grant, who had command of a fort on the frontier during the Revolutionary war, and Martin himself became a noted character, for he was a member of the Pennsylvania Provincial Conference, in 1776, and a member of the State Convention, that formed the State Constitution, and also a member of the State Legislature of 1778-79.

The following statements are taken from an old deed, now in the possession of Mr. Priestly, of the borough of Northumberland:

"The Town of Northumberland is laid out upon four tracts of land, two of three hundred acres each, and two of five hundred acres each, in the forks of the north-east and west branches of the Susquehanna River, called Sarah's Delight, Essex, Nottingham, and Townside.

"Sarah's Delight—Patent July 7th, 1770. The Proprietaries to Sarah London, enrolled at Philadelphia in Patent Book A., volume II, page 360, 1771, April 23d. Deed. John London and Sarah, his wife, to William Espy, recorded at Sunbury, in book C, page 239.

"1771, April 23d. Deed. William Espy to John London, recorded at Sunbury in book C, page 238.

"1772. London and Patterson lay out the town called Northumberland.

"1775, March 20th. Deed. John London to Reuben Haines, recorded at Sunbury, in book C, page 240.

"Essex—1772, London and Batterson lay out the *old* town of Northumberland.

"1775, Jan. 7th. Patent to Esther Patterson, the wife of William Patterson, enrolled in the Patent Book A. A., volume 15, page 57.

"1775, April 6th. Deed. William Patterson and Sarah, his wife, to Reuben Haines, recorded at Sunbury, in book A., page 248.

"Nottingham—1772, Sept. 14th. Patent to Richard Peters for five hundred acres along the north-east branch, enrolled in Patent Book A. A., volume 13, page 256.

"Townside—1772, September 16th. Patent to Richard Peters, for 500 acres along the west branch, enrolled in same book, page 259.

"1773, December 17th. Deed. Richard Peters to Reuben Haines, for the above mentioned tracts, recorded in Philadelphia, Deed Book I, volume 13, page 126."

The title to these four tracts being thus in Reuben Haines, he enlarged the town plot, and recorded a general plan of London and Patterson's town, with his own additions, at Sunbury, in book B, page 273, April 24th, 1781, which was afterwards recorded by John Boyd, May 10th, 1808, in book C, pages 367 and 368.

Reuben Haines died, and devised his estate by will, proved at Philadelphia, to his four children, Caspar Wistar Haines, Josiah Haines, Reuben Haines, and Catharine Haines. Reuben Haines, Jr., died, and devised his estate to his two brothers and sister, who make partition; and Caspar W. Haines, and Catharine Haines convey, among other things in partition, the unsold lots in the town of Northumberland, by deed, dated March 24th, 1785, recorded at Sunbury, in book G, page 481, to Reuben Haines.

At first the progress of the town was slow, as all its inhabitants, during the Revolution, to escape being murdered by a cruel enemy, were obliged to flee and seek refuge in Fort Augusta. It was not until 1784, or 1785, that Northumberland was re-occupied, and in 1796, it numbered nearly one hundred houses. In 1847, it contained about one hundred and sixty. The country expands behind the town in a semi-circular form, rising in gentle swells towards Montour's Ridge, which crosses between the two rivers at a distance of about three miles. Opposite the town, in the north branch, is a long and beautiful island, called Bird's Island, which is connected with the main land, on both sides, by two railroad bridges. In 1814, there was a highway bridge built, in two parts, one of which was on each side of the island. It was built by a joint stock company, and cost ninety thousand dollars, of which the State subscribed fifty thousand. The part on the east side, however, was washed away in March, 1875. Another bridge crosses the west branch at its mouth. At the southern end of this latter bridge, rises the steep and precipitous sand-stone of "Blue Hill," from which a magnificent prospect is enjoyed of the valleys of both rivers. The town is well laid out with spacious streets, and to those who love quiet, is a pleasant spot to reside.

INDEPENDENCE AT NORTHUMBERLAND.

In 1776, the question of Independence or no Independence became so warm at Northumberland, that it was decided to have a discussion on the subject. A scaffold was erected near where the market house used to stand, and the discussion took place. Colonels Cooke and Hunter took the stand on the side of liberty and independence, and Dr. Plunkett and Charles Cooke took the side of loyalty. Considerable warmth was manifested on both sides.

FIRST IRON FOUNDRY.

The first iron foundry in the Shamokin region was established in Northumberland, in 1827–28. An ingenious workman from New York, named David Rogers, came to the place, bringing with him a quantity of patent scale-beams, of which he was the inventor, or owned the right for this portion of the State. Mr. Shannon assisted him in erecting a small foundry in which to cast the necessary irons. As he succeeded very well, it was his intention, in conjunction with Mr. Shannon, to enlarge the business and make other and larger castings. Owing to cruel and wicked tricks played on him, Rogers became deranged, and the business was discontinued, Mr. Shannon not being acquainted with the same.

JOHNNY MASON'S LEANING HOUSE.

Opposite the borough of Northumberland rises a high promontory, called "Blue Hill," on the top of which, many years ago, a very odd building was erected by an eccentric old bachelor, by the name of Johnny Mason.

This curious structure, the emanation of an eccentric mind, was located leaningly, at an angle, probably of thirty degrees, apparently, over a frightful precipice of upwards of five hundred perpendicular feet in heighth, perhaps the greatest natural perpendicular heighth in Pennsylvania. The west branch winds gracefully around the angle of Blue Hill at this point, and when visitors stood upon the still further projecting portico, nothing but the blue bosom of the river was visible below. Thirty years ago, it was a great place of resort for the young people of Sunbury, Northumberland and Lewisburg, and even later, it has been an attractive place for pic-nic purposes, the beautiful scenery, as well as the romance with which it was surrounded, through the mysterious old man who dwelt there, making it such. Few persons visited the place who did not inscribe their names somewhere upon the building, and in the last days of the existence of the old fabric, but little room was left for names. About ten years ago, some years after this place became a railroad centre, this curious structure was destroyed by a number of railroad attachees, strangers, who were led to the spot through curiosity, and conceiving the mischievous idea of its destruction by throwing it over the precipice, they loosened it from its moorings, and in a few moments the air was filled with the detached parts of the old house, hallowed by time and the associations of early youth. Nothing but the iron fastenings remain. The citizens of Northumberland offered a reward, but the culprits remain undiscovered.

Mason was born at Philadelphia, in 1768, and died on his Long Reach farm, near Newberry, Lycoming County, in 1849, aged upwards of eighty years, and his remains lie buried under a chestnut tree, near where his Blue Hill leaning summer-house used to stand.

THE FIRST FRUIT TREES

Planted in Northumberland were brought from Lancaster, Pa., about the year 1771, by William Hoffman. One of these trees, called the "Centennial Pear Tree," is still standing in the yard of what is now known as the Burr House, and still bears fine pears.

THE FIRST WELL

In the borough, was dug by Mr. Hoffman, and is still in use on the premises of the Burr House. It has never been known to become dry.

THE FIRST BIRTH

Of a white child, on the west side of the Susquehanna, occurred in Northumberland, about the year 1772, and the subject was Elizabeth, daughter of William Hoffman.

BOROUGH CHARTER.

The Act of Assembly, erecting the town of Northumberland into a borough, was signed by Ner Middleswarth, Speaker of the House, and by Daniel Sturgeon, Speaker of the Senate, and was approved April 14th, 1828, by J. Andrew Shultze, Governor of Pennsylvania. It contains forty-eight sections. Section thirty-eight is as follows:

"*Section* 38. And be it further enacted by the authority aforesaid, That the town of Northumberland, in the County of Northumberland, comprising the original plan of said town, and so much of the adjacent land as is embraced in the following bounds, to wit: Beginning at the point at the junction of the north-east and west branches of the Susquehanna River; thence up the north-east branch of the same, the courses and distances thereof, four hundred and sixty-eight perches, to a stone at low-water mark; thence by land of Joseph Nourse, north forty-two degrees, west one hundred and ten perches, to the road leading from Northumberland to Danville; thence along said road, thirty-nine degrees east, thirty-six perches, to a small bridge; thence by land of Joseph Nourse, north fifty-one degrees, west one hundred and fifty perches, to a pine in a line of John Lighow; thence by land of Lighow and Cowden, south seventy-six degrees, west one hundred and seventy-four perches, to a stone heap in a line of Philip Frick; thence by the same, south thirty-nine degrees, west sixteen perches, to a stone heap; thence north fifty-one degrees, west sixteen perches, to a post; thence by land of Teas and Eckard, south thirty-nine degrees, west two hundred and twenty-nine perches, to a road; thence by land of William A. Lloyd, south fifty-one degrees, east sixteen perches, to a street marked Eighth street, in the town of Northumberland; thence along the said street, south thirty-nine degrees, west ninety-four perches, to another street in the town of Northumberland, marked in the plan thereof by the name of 'West Way;' thence along said street, south fifty-one degrees, east seven perches to a post; thence by land of William A. Lloyd, south thirty-nine degrees, west eighty-eight perches, to low-water mark on the west branch of the Susquehanna River; thence down the courses and distances of the same, two hundred and ninety-three perches, to the place of beginning, be, and the same is hereby erected into a borough, which shall be called the borough of Northumberland."

FIRST TELEGRAPH.

The first telegraph office in Northumberland was established by the Susquehanna River and North and West Branch Telegraph Company, in 1851, A. C. Goell, president; George M. Leslie, secretary; T. O. Van Allen, treasurer.

Miss Agnes Forsyth, now Rev. Mrs. Isaac Cornelison, was the first operator. Miss Forsyth was succeeded as operator by her sister, Mary Alice Forsyth. The third operator was Miss Harriet Wenk. The present operator is Mr. J. J. Howell, who took charge in May, 1871.

The total receipts of this office, for the year ending June 30th, 1876, were four hundred and thirty-nine dollars and seventy-eight cents, of which five dollars and sixty cents were from other lines. The total number of messages sent was one thousand three hundred and twenty-four, of which thirty-six were half rate, and forty-seven dead head.

EDUCATIONAL.

The borough of Northumberland can boast of one of the finest school buildings in the State. It is a brick structure, two stories high, and sixty-five by one hundred feet. It is located on Second street, in the eastern part of town; was erected in 1872, and cost, with the furnishings, and ground on which it stands, about twenty-seven thousand dollars. The present superintendent is Prof. William M. Beal, and the corps of teachers numbers ten. There is no regularly organized high-school, but this want is supplied by a higher department, in which some of the higher branches are taught.

The State School Law was adopted by the borough shortly after its passage, in 1834. In 1871, the schools were graded, and the erection of the new building, in 1872, marked an era of improvement. Previous to this time, the place had but three small one-and-a-half story buildings. In 1875, the schools enrolled about six hundred and thirty pupils. The following gentlemen constitute the present Board of Education: William H. Leighow, president; Daniel Sterner, secretary; J. O. Tracy, William Elliott, Jacob Paul, and John Scholvin.

The Presbyterian Church in Northumberland was established about the year 1789, and the first preacher of this denomination was Rev. Morrison. It is also supposed that he was the first English preacher who ever held service here.

About this time, a church edifice was erected, which was a log structure, and stood on the corner of King street and Church alley. In 1841, it was superseded by a brick building, upon the same site. Its dimensions were forty by sixty feet, and cost about four thousand dollars. It is now used as a town hall.

The First Presbyterian Church of the borough was organized in 1838, with twenty-seven members. The first pastor was John Patton. A Sunday-school was organized at the same time.

In 1844, a church edifice was built at a cost of about six thousand five hundred dollars. In September, 1870, the two Presbyterian churches united, and the union is now known as the First Presbyterian Church of Northumberland. The membership is about one hundred and seventy-five. There is also connected with the church a large and flourishing Sunday-school.

The Unitarian Church was organized in 1790, by Dr. Joseph Priestley, who was the first pastor. He was succeeded by Rev. Robert Christy. Until 1825, the church held services in the houses of other denomination, and in 1826 erected a brick church edifice at a cost of about one thousand dollars. The present membership is about forty, and Rev. H. D. Catlin is the present pastor. There is connected with the church a flourishing Sunday-school of about one hundred members. The library contains about six hundred volumes.

Lutheran Church.—About the year 1817, a Lutheran church edifice was erected in Northumberland, on the corner of Queen and Third streets. Quite a number of years previous, a church organization was effected. The first pastor was Rev. J. P. Shindel, who had his residence at Sunbury, and also supplied a church at that place.

In 1847, the church building was remodeled. The present church membership is about one hundred and forty-three.

Methodist Episcopal Church.—The first church edifice of this denomination here, was a frame structure, built about the year 1820, at a cost of about two thousand dollars. It stood on Third street, between King and Orange. The present house of worship is a brick building, and was erected in 1856, and cost, including the lot on which it stands, about seven thousand dollars. The present pastor is Rev. George Warren. The present membership is something over three hundred.

The Sunday-school was organized in 1828, and now enrolls upwards of two hundred members. L. M. Morgan is the superintendent, there are about five hundred volumes in the library.

Baptist Church.—The Baptist Church was organized in 1841. Rev. D. C. Wait was one of the first preachers of this persuasion. The following gentlemen, among others, have served this church as pastors: Rev. C. A. Hewitt, Rev. Mr. Davidson, and Rev. John S. Miller.

The first church building was erected in 1842, on the corner of Second and Queen streets. It was a small brick structure, costing about one thousand five hundred dollars. In 1870, it was taken down, and the present beautiful brick-house of worship erected on the same site. When completed, it is estimated that its cost will be about nine thousand dollars. The church membership is about seventy, and the Sunday-school enrolls some fifty. The present pastor is Rev. David Williams.

St. Mark's Episcopal Church.—This church was organized in 1847, and the corner-stone of the church edifice was laid on the 20th of October, of the same year. The building is a frame structure, and stands on the corner of Second and Queen streets. It was enlarged in 1875, at a cost of four thousand dollars. Its original cost was about five hundred dollars.

The first rector was Rev. B. Wistar Morris, now Bishop of Oregon. The next rector was Rev. William B. Musgrave. After he ceased to officiate, a period of some twenty years followed, in which services were held from time to time by Rectors Lewis W. Gibson and Charles H. Van Dyne, and others, of St. Matthew's Church, Sunbury.

The next regular rector was Rev. William Moore. The last rector was Rev. Charles G. Adams, who served but a short time. The society at present (July 1876) has no rector. The membership numbers forty-six. The Sunday-school was organized at the same time with the church, and now numbers some seventy. The superintendent is J. O. Tracy.

First National Bank.—This Bank was organized September 20th, 1864, with a capital of one hundred thousand dollars. A. E. Kapp, president, and J. H. Jenkins, cashier. The Board of Directors consisted of A. E. Kapp, John McFarland, D. M. Brautigam, A. H. Stone, John Taggart, D. G. Driesbach, W. Leighou, John Youngman, Benjamin Hummel, Isaac Bidelspach, J. B. Smith, D. G. Voris and Washington Lee, Jr.

They first occupied as their place of business, a room in the present residence of Joseph Bird, on King street, which was formerly occupied by the old Bank of Northumberland.

The present officers are: J. W. Cake, president, and Fred. Burkenbine, cashier. The present directors are: J. W. Cake, A. H. Stone, W. T. Forsyth, S. A. Burkenbine, D. G. Driesbach, John Martin, S. R. Yearrick. The present bank building was erected in 1868, and occupies the south-east corner of King and Water streets.

Northumberland Iron and Nail Works.—This manufacturing establishment was erected in 1867, by Messrs. Van Allen & Co. The mill and factory building is three hundred and five feet long, and sixty-five feet wide. The foundry, machine-shop and keg-factory, eighty feet long and thirty-four feet wide.

The establishment contains seven single puddling-furnaces, one heating-furnace, one train of rolls, twenty-one nail machines, with other necessary machinery for the manufacture of nails.

The product of these works is nails, nail-plate, muck and scrap-bars, and some sizes of bar-iron. The annual capacity is five thousand tons of muck-bar, and fifty thousand kegs of nails. A coal yard and store is also connected with the establishment. It gives employment to about one hundred and forty hands. The proprietors are T. O. Van Allen and G. M. Leslie.

Lumber Interests.—Quite an extensive establishment for the manufacture of lumber, is located here under the firm of Chamberlain, Frick & Co. The mill was built in 1866, and is fifty by one hundred feet. It has an annual capacity of bill lumber of about five million feet. It is located on the south-west corner of West Way and Sixth streets. The property of the firm is estimated at about forty thousand dollars.

The borough has also a large flouring-mill, built by D. A. Finney in 1874, at a cost of about nine thousand dollars. It has a capacity of some twenty barrels per day.

The machine-shop of A. H. Stone is also an industry of considerable importance.

Hotels.—Northumberland is well supplied with hotels, of which the following are the principal ones. The Van Kirk House, on the north-west corner of Second and Queen streets. Charles F. Hess, proprietor.

The Burr House, on King street, between Second and Third. Jacob Hunsecker, proprietor. The Eckert House, on Duke street opposite the depot. George E. Eckert, proprietor. Washington House, on the north-east corner of King and Railroad. J. F. Stamm, proprietor.

WATSONTOWN BOROUGH.

If we stand upon the high ground, which rises abruptly to the eastward of Liberty street, in Watsontown, we see at once the whole of the borough. Its length is unusually great, in proportion to the breadth, for the space between the river and the acclivity is but narrow, and therefore the increase of the town must be made longitudinally.

The chimneys of the manufactories, and the spires of the four churches, stand out as prominent objects, and then the lower buildings, and the trees, and the water, till the picture. The Philadelphia and Erie Railroad, and the West Branch Canal traverse the town lengthwise, and the river, sweeping down from Muncy, passes in front and then trends away to the south-east.

It is sixteen miles hence to Northumberland, the venerable town to which, from this part of the County, all highways lead—just as it was once said that all roads lead to Rome. The roofs of the village of Dewart can be seen to the northward, and the spires of Milton are visible four miles down the river. The ground upon which Watsontown stands, was, on February 3d, 1769, granted by the Province of Pennsylvania, to Lieutenants Housegger and Hunsicker, in payment for military services; the former owning below, and the latter above, the present line of Front street, which line formed the boundary between their respective grants. A few years later, these grants—having in the mean time passed through several hands—were purchased by John Watson, Sr. He laid out the road or lane, running straight back from the river, on the Hunsicker and Housegger line. It is now named Front street, but for many years it was called Main, until that name was, very properly transferred to the long, principal street of the present town, which crosses Front at nearly a right angle, and runs upward a course nearly thirty-three degrees west. This laying out was made in 1794, and Mr. Watson sold small lots of land to several purchasers, among them being James Watson, (not, however, a relative of the proprietor) who, upon his lot, on the north side of the (then) Main street, commenced a business which is, and has ever been, the curse of all communities, new and old, and yet, one which seems always the first thought of in new settlements, particularly—a shop for the sale of whisky. His establishment was a shanty built of slabs, and altogether a very disreputable place, frequented by the lowest class of boatmen and others, and from this slab-built hovel, the entire neighborhood soon gained the undesirable appellation of "Slabtown."

Mr. John Watson was very naturally incensed at this, and repenting of having sold any lots at all, he now tried to re-purchase them, and was in several cases successful, but not, however, in that of James Watson. After this he sold no more, and at his death his lands, embracing about one thousand and fifty acres, were divided between his three sons; David receiving a tract lying on the river and below Main (now Front) street; John a similar tract *above* the same street; and George's portion, consisting of the higher lands, to the eastward of, and adjoining those of both his brothers, David and John. David was the merchant of the family. He established trade in a small way in Slabtown as early as 1794, and continued in it, experiencing the prosperity and increase which usually attend honest and well-conducted enterprise, until 1839, a period of forty-five years. His son, John L. Watson, Esq., now seventy-six years of age, and one of the oldest and most respected citizens of Milton, remained with his father continuously (except absences at school) for twenty-seven years, and well recollects many of the incidents of his successful career. Among these, it is noteworthy that he (David) "ran the river" with his arks and Durham boats, carrying produce to the lower markets without accident or loss, for *thirty-nine years*; and when, in 1833, an ark of his, carrying eleven hundred bushels of wheat and some barrels of whisky, was sunk in the river, (the wheat being a total loss and the whisky mostly saved), he very philosophically said it was but a just toll paid to the river highway, which, for nearly forty years, had served him gratuitously and well, and then he abandoned it forever.

His place of business was first a log store-house fronting the river, on the lower side of Main (Front) street. Contiguous to and below that, he soon built the warehouse, which the increase in his business rendered necessary, and in these modest structures, he bought and sold, and bartered with profit, up to the fortieth year of the present century.

It seems proper to make this much mention of his private affairs, because, at that time, he and his business were all there was of Watsontown, or rather, Watsonburg, for this latter was the name which first obtained, after the opprobrious one of "Slabtown" had passed into disuse. The place had really but very little history for many years. John Watson, the brother of David, prosperous too, but not prominent, living on the spot, and in the stone-house where his father—the proprietor of all—had lived. George, dwelling back in the higher lands, a farmer, but quite as independent as either; and James Watson, notwithstanding, the anathema of the elder John, still holding his own—though not in that slab castle which had brought such scandal on the neighbors—five or six dwellings in all, while up the river, were the farms of Rev. Mr. Hogue, Major Wilson, William Irvin, Samuel, and John Brown, Robert Craig, and still further up, the Kerrigan and Murray farms, all of which, and several others, laid between the tract of John Watson and the Muncy Hills.

As early as 1822, a mail for Sugar Valley and other westerly points, began to pass through Watsonburg, and across the river, by the ferry which Daniel Caldwell had established about the first year of the century. It was a weekly mail, carried on horseback, by Samuel McKee. Mr. Caldwell was the father of the route, for he had procured its establishment under the administration of James Monroe.

But Watsontown had no post-office until 1830. David Watson was the first post-master, as was entirely proper, for there was no other person in the place who was in all respects eligible.

A SECOND STORE

Was opened in 1827, by Thomas Arbuckle, in a building owned by James Watson, and which was on Front street, near where Mr. Kirk's mansion now is. This store did not continue long. Mr. Arbuckle removed to Union County, where he still lives at a very advanced age.

THE WEST BRANCH CANAL

Was finished as far up as Muncy Dam, in October, 1828, but there was really no business done on it until 1830. From that time on, David Watson and others, sent their grain and produce down, and received goods up by canal, instead of river as before; but this change produced no marked effect in growth, or prosperity to Watsontown.

THE SUNBURY AND ERIE RAILROAD

Was approaching completion, in 1854, and then the question—and a vital one it was for Watsontown—arose where the depot should be located. The officers of the company were in favor of a point below the mouth of Warrior Run, and it would doubtless have been placed there, but that John L. Watson, and E. L. Piper—the son, and the son-in-law, respectively, of David Watson—promptly made a free gift to the company, of land for a depot, also, a never-failing spring, near, and much higher than their track, for a water-station, and over six hundred dollars in cash. These inducements decided the question in favor of the donors. The depot and water-station were located on David Watson's land. The next year, the railroad went into operation, and the future of the town was secure.

In 1857, just after the opening of the railroad, Moses Chamberlain built his lumber mill, which was the commencement of the business now carried on by Cook & Pardee. At that time, the entire settlement consisted of not more than twelve buildings, the stone-house of John Watson, at the river bank, foot of Front street; the brick-dwelling, store and warehouse on the river, below Front street; and another brick-house higher up, on the south side of the street; these last four being owned by David Watson. The tavern house of James Watson, on the north side of Front, near Main street and the frame-house of Joseph Hogue, just west of the tavern on the south-east corner of Front and Main streets, was the store of E. L. Piper, (now the stand of Goodman & Brother,) to which he had removed the business of his father-in-law, David Watson, and which was also the post-office. Directly opposite this, on the north-west corner of Front and Main, stood Conner's tavern, which had been built the previous year on the spot before occupied by George Fox's blacksmith-shop. Above this, upon the Main street, there was but a single building, a very small one-story frame, built by E. L. Piper, for the Misses Campbell, two elderly and needy maiden sisters, who had been in his employ. (This is now standing below and adjoining Minerva Hall.) Below Front street on Main, there was but a single house, that of Thomas Barr, built in 1851. These were the insignificant proportions of Watsontown, in 1857. David Watson had died the previous year, and now when his brother John followed him to the grave, E. L. Piper, who had bought his lands, laid them out in lots and offered many inducements to such as would purchase with a view to settlement, and yet it was not until after 1861, that there was much increase. In that year, when Joseph Everett built his brick-house on what is now Liberty street, it was the only building east of the railroad track; while upon Main, above Second, there were as yet but two houses, one occupied by Joseph Bly, and the other by Zachariah Yeagel. But from that time, the town's growth commenced and continued with such rapidity, that in six years it had reached a stage of importance which warranted its

ORGANIZATION AS A BOROUGH.

The incorporation was made November 4th, 1867, and the first election held November 16th, 1867. It resulted in the choice of the following officers: Burgess, Joseph Hollopeter; Council—Thomas Carl, Frederick S. Whitman, C. O. Bachman, John Bly, D. C. Hogue; High Constable, Eli Loehner; School Directors—J. Y. Ellis, William Cooner, H. K. Whitman, James Ott, H. W. Kriner, Thomas Barr; Justice of the Peace, John Orr; Overseers of the Poor—Peter Shenffler, Robert Johnson.

The borough limits include an area one mile-and-three-quarters in length, and more than half-a-mile in width. The population, in 1870, was one thousand one hundred and eighty-one. It is now probably fully two thousand. It has three public houses, eight general stores, one dry goods-store, three hardware-stores, two drug-stores, two boot and shoe-stores, two saddlery-stores, and harness-makers, and the usual variety and number of small dealers and shops, found in similar towns.

The Attorneys and Counselors at Law are three in number, viz.: A. J. Guffy, Oscar Foust, and W. Field Shay.

There are five *Physicians*: Drs. H. D. Hunter, J. Rhoads, Joseph Hunter, J. I. Leiser, and J. A. McClure, one of whom (Dr. Hunter) was the *first medical practitioner* who established in Watsontown. Before his coming, patients in the town and its vicinity had been attended by physicians from Milton, and from Union County.

The Watsontown Record newspaper was first published in April, 1869, by a joint stock company, with Oscar Foust, Esq., as editor. On the 27th of June, 1871, the office was purchased by John J. Auten & Co., (J. J. Auten and H. F. Algert,) and was conducted under that firm name for four years. In 1875, Algert sold his interest to Auten, who has since edited and published the paper alone. The *Record* has a circulation of nearly eight hundred, and is, financially, quite prosperous.

Minerva Hall is a handsome frame building, at the south-east corner of Second and Main streets. Erected in 1869, by the "Minerva Association." Its size is sixty by ninety feet, and two stories in height. The street floor is occupied by the post-office, and two stores. The entire second floor is embraced in the audience-room, which is reached by a broad stairway, affording ample facility of egress, in case of fire. It is handsomely frescoed; has a good stage, and all the appointments necessary for a place of public entertainment.

Watsontown Lodge, No. 401, *A. Y. M.*, constituted in 1868. Past Masters—Joseph Hollopeter, Isaac N. Messinger, Isaac Vincent, Joseph H. Wagner, Jacob M. Follmer, Oscar Foust, William M. Wagner, S. G. M. Hollopeter. Place of assembly, Masonic Hall, Miller's building, corner Fourth and Main streets.

Warrior Run Chapter, No. 246, *H. R. A.*, constituted June, 1874. Past High Priests, Robert M. Claxton, Jr., Oscar Foust. Assembles at Masonic Hall, Main and Fourth streets.

Watsontown Lodge, No. 619, *I. O. of O. F.*, meets in hall over the shop and ware-rooms of the Watsontown Boot and Shoe Manufacturing Company.

Patriotic Order Sons of America; Wawenoc Tribe, No. 153, *I. O. of Red Men; Order of United American Mechanics; Junior Order United American Mechanics.* These four last-named societies meet weekly in Hogue's Hall, Main street.

Knights of Pythias meet in Shay's Hall, Main street.

Watsontown Silver Cornet Band, organized in December, 1872, consists of fourteen members. Uniform, cadet gray, trimmed with scarlet; gray cap, with scarlet and white plume. Their performances are held in very high estimation by the towns-people.

The Fire Department.—Until 1873, the borough was entirely without a fire-engine. Some years before, several ladders, fire-hooks, poles, etc., had been procured, but they were entirely too heavy for any force which the town could furnish, and so they were never used. But, in the Spring of that year, the borough decided to, and did, purchase a hand-engine and hose-carriage, and a company was at once raised to operate them. It was organized June 11th, 1873, and was called the "Hope Hose Fire Company, No. 1." Very soon after, a second company was started, and named the "Eureka Fire Company." The Hope Hose Company had charge of the hose-carriage, and the hand-engine was given to the Eurekas.

The "Hope" soon became ambitious of independent organization, and the *ownership* of a hook-and-ladder truck, with first-class appointments. Receiving the hearty co-operation and assistance of the citizens, they were enabled, on the 1st of July, 1875, to dedicate to the service of the towns-people, an apparatus, which is said to be one of the most perfect of its kind.

Though an independent company, it is, when on duty, under orders of the Chief of the Fire Department.

There has been erected, especially for its use, a fine frame building, twenty by forty-five feet, with tower and fire-alarm, and with a well-furnished meeting-room on the second story.

The company is incorporated, and numbers thirty-six men, fully equipped. They have figured prominently at fires in Milton and Williamsport.

In June, 1874, the borough authorities purchased a new No. 3 "Silsby" steamer, with two hose-carriages and one thousand feet of hose. To have in charge and to operate this apparatus, the "West Branch Steam Fire Company" was raised. Their number was about one hundred, among them being many business men of the place. The engine-house is on East Fifth street, and there lies the engine and paraphernalia, *nunquam non paratus.*

Happily, there have been no great conflagrations in this borough, but many of the best citizens of Milton say that *their* town was saved from destruction by the prompt and generous succor rendered by the firemen of Watsontown and Lewisburg, on the night of December 12th, 1875.

Watsontown has neither gas nor water-works, but its manufacturing industries are very considerable, and chief among them is the business of the

Watsontown Lumber Company.—These mills were commenced in 1866, and completed in April, 1867, by Ario Pardee, of Hazleton, Pennsylvania, at a cost of one hundred thousand dollars. Since May of the latter year, they have been operated by the above-named company, composed of A. Pardee, A. T. Goodman, John H. Goodman, and John Bly. The stock of logs is furnished from Mr. Pardee's timber lands on White Deer Creek, and on the tributaries of the west branch, in the counties of Clinton, Elk, Clearfield, and Cameron. These lands aggregate one hundred and fifty thousand acres, and are believed to be sufficient to keep the mills fully supplied for thirty years.

These mills are singularly well located. The river, which brings them their stock, is within a cable's length; and then the canal and the railway track both pass so near, that the manufactured lumber is shipped upon cars or boats without extra handling. The upper mill, or "jack-mill," as it is called, takes the logs from the river, carries them high over the canal, and transfers them to the log-pool, or basin, from whence, in due course, they are drawn up into the saw-mill, and cut into merchantable lumber. The "jacking" of the logs from the river into the company's basin, although so ingenious and admirable an operation, would be very difficult of written explanation; but the process, as well as the arrangement for securing logs in the river, are both so perfect that, in nine years' business, and during the floods, which, in that time, have created such havoc among lumbermen, this company have never, to their knowledge, lost a single log.

During the process of transfer from the river to the pool, all such logs as are in part defective, are separated from the others, leaving only the perfectly sound ones to be floated to the gangs. Of the defective logs, the sound portions are cut into shingles, and the mill for this purpose has a capacity of twenty-five thousand shingles per day. The main mill has four gangs and three Mulay saws, all driven by an engine of one hundred and twenty horse-power, supplied with steam by twelve boilers, each thirty-two feet in length. Fuel for these boiler-furnaces, is furnished by the saw-dust alone. The capacity of the saw-mill is one hundred thousand feet per day. Of the slabs, the best parts are manufactured into fence-palings, and the inferior portions into laths. Twelve thousand finished palings, and twenty-five thousand laths are turned out daily. Below the saw-mill is the company's planing-mill, producing matched flooring, siding, and dressed lumber, principally for the lower river and seaboard markets.

These mills are mentioned the more minutely, partly because they are among the very best in Pennsylvania, and, more particularly, because the establishment of Mr. Pardee's enterprises (of which this is the principal one,) in Watsontown, was really the commencement and chief cause of the prosperity and growth of the place.

Lumber-mills of Cook & Pardee.—The commencement of this business in Watsontown, was made by Moses Chamberlain, of Milton, and William H. Follmer, who, in 1857, built their first mill, on the West Branch Canal, and (then) entirely above the settlement. The next year, an interest in the concern was purchased by Joseph Hollopeter, and, in 1859, Chamberlain left it. The mill was destroyed by fire November 3d, 1860. On the re-building of the establishment, in 1861, Chamberlain returned to the firm, and its style became Follmer, Hollopeter and Chamberlain. In 1863, Hollopeter retired, leaving the business to Chamberlain and Follmer, from whom, in 1865, it was purchased by Cook, Hollopeter & Co., this firm being composed of Robert G. Cook, Joseph Hollopeter, Enoch Everett, and Enos Everett. In 1867, Hollopeter, and the two Everetts sold out to Ario Pardee, and this constituted the present firm of Cook & Pardee. The production is about thirty thousand feet per day—nearly all bill lumber. They run one circular, and two Mulay saws. Number of hands employed, about thirty. Belonging to the establishment is a factory for the manufacture of match-sticks, employing a number of men, but this is not now in steady operation.

Watsontown Planing-mill Company.—Their works occupy the space from Sixth to Seventh streets, on the Philadelphia and Erie Railroad. They commenced work on May 1st, 1876. The manufacture is, flooring, siding, mouldings, surfaced work, sashes, doors, frames, and every kind of work usually done by such establishments. Hands employed, thirty-five. The company is made up of J. H. Wagner, J. W. Muffly, William Huckenburg, and F. B. Wagner. This business is a continuation of that done by the old mill of Wagner, Starr & Co., built by them in the Spring of 1868, on the canal, between Second and Third streets, and which did an annual business of eighty thousand to one hundred thousand dollars, up to the time of its destruction by fire, September 22d, 1875. The loss by that disaster was twenty-five thousand dollars above insurance.

The Watsontown Steam Flour-mill, is located on the line of the Philadelphia and Erie Railroad, at Eighth street, and was built in 1868, by John McFarland, who is still its proprietor. The mill is fifty by sixty feet, with engine-house attached, and also a storage-house, thirty by forty-six feet. The engine is of sixty-horse-power. There are four setts of burrs, doing merchant work to the amount of one hundred and sixty thousand dollars annually.

The Watsontown Tannery, situated in the north-easterly portion of the town near the railroad track, was built in 1867, by William M. Wagner and Joseph Hollopeter. In 1869, it was purchased by Messrs. George Burns and Samuel Caldwell, Mr. Wagner however, retaining an interest. The present owners are Samuel Caldwell, George Burns, Samuel Miller and William M. Wagner. The yearly tannage has reached ten thousand sides, but at present the establishment is not in operation.

Watsontown Car-works.—These are extensive buildings recently erected by Ario Pardee, and others, with view to the manufacture of railway and mine cars, but thus far they have stood unemployed, and it is now improbable that they will ever be devoted to the business for which they were intended. The shops stand on the line of the railroad in the upper part of the town.

Watsontown Boot and Shoe Manufacturing Company.—Isaac Vincent, president; Samuel Miller, treasurer; F. H. Miller, secretary; O. S. Lawrence, superintendent. The enterprise was inaugurated in 1869, and the factory building, fifty-five feet front by eighty-five feet in depth, three stories high, was erected on Main street above Second. The company employs forty hands in the manufacture of work for men's wear, of which their annual production is to the amount of fifty thousand dollars. In the third story over the company's work, and warerooms, is a hall used for the meetings of the lodge of the I. O. of O. F.

The Ferry from Watsontown to White Deer Mills, was started by Daniel Caldwell, about the year 1800. His house stood on the west bank of the river, and there he lived and plied his ferry during a period of more than half the years of man's life—allotment. His boats were propelled across the stream at low water, by "setting poles" of which one end was set upon the river bottom and the other placed against the shoulder of the ferryman; but at high stages when the poles would not touch the bottom, large oars or "sweeps" were used, and if the booming current carried the boat far below its proper landing place, then when they reached the still water near the shore the oarsman must head her up stream, and pull patiently till the lost ground was regained. But when Mr. Caldwell died, on the 18th day of December, 1836, and when soon after, the ferry franchise was purchased by Henry High, he determined to abandon the old method and adopt the more modern one of attaching the boat to a cable stretched from shore to shore, by which plan not only is the drifting avoided but the current itself is made to propel the boat across. So a manilla rope one-and-three-quarters inches in diameter was purchased and placed in position, but the experiment was not successful, for wet weather produced an irresistable contraction, which neither the cable nor the shore fastenings could withstand; and again, the dry heat of summer lengthened it till it sometimes nearly reached the surface of the water. The raftsmen, too, passing down the river were prone to do malicious injury to the cable when it came within their reach.

These objections were so great that it was abandoned in a few months, and sweeps and setting-poles came in use again. In 1854, High sold to a stock company, composed of John Bly, John L. Watson, and others, who revived the project of the cable, but this time it was a *metallic* one, which they purchased of John A. Roebling, of Trenton, New Jersey, the engineer of the Niagara suspension bridge. This proved successful, and it is still in use.

After several changes of ownership, the ferry became, in 1873, the property of Captain John Bly, who is still sole proprietor, and who says that since the wire cable was put in position in 1854, it has safely crossed more than ***eighty million*** feet of logs from the western to the eastern side of the river.

The ferry is but an humble enterprise, yet it has been, and is, a very material convenience to the people of the two counties. The citizen, in his daily avocations; the traveller on his journeys; merry pleasure parties and sad mourning processions, all have safely crossed over it, while clergymen and physicians, on their errands of spiritual and corporeal ministration, have passed to and fro without money or price for three-quarters of a century.

The Watsontown Bank, chartered by the State of Pennsylvania, March 27th, 1872; commenced business January 2nd, 1873; A. Pardee, president; De La Green, cashier. The cash capital paid in was twenty-seven thousand six hundred and seventy dollars, which, on September 2nd, 1873, had been increased to one hundred thousand dollars, and on July 2nd, 1874, to one hundred and twenty thousand dollars. On May 1st, 1874, Mr. De La Green resigned, and R. R. Claxton, Jr., the present cashier, was elected in his place. The directors meet weekly and exercise a personal supervision over all the bank's affairs. The stockholders are individually liable to the creditors of the bank in double the amount of their stock, and an approved bond of forty thousand dollars is required from the cashier. The surplus fund is at present six thousand six hundred dollars.

PUBLIC SCHOOLS.

The only school building standing within the limits of Watsontown, when it was organized as a borough, in 1867, was the brick-house known as the academy, standing on First street, a short distance up the rising ground to the eastward of Liberty street.

A year later, in the fall of 1868, a second one was built by contract, on Ash street above Seventh. It is of brick, and its size is thirty by fifty feet.

In addition to the two houses above mentioned, a part of the Methodist Church is occupied by the select grammar-school. The number of schools is six, to which the attendance, last winter (1875 and 1876) was four hundred and twenty-seven scholars. Within the past year, three town lots have been purchased, upon which, it is intended to build a school-house of sufficient capacity to accommodate all the schools of the borough.

The present school board is, Daniel C. Hogue, president; Isaac Vincent, secretary; William M. Wagner, treasurer; Oscar Faust, S. M. Miller, Samuel DeArmond.

CHURCHES, ETC.

First Presbyterian, of Watsontown. Presbyterian worship had been held in the Baptist house, for a considerable time prior to June 1st, 1872, at which time their church organization was first effected, with William B. Bryson, Dr. Joseph H. Hunter and Samuel W. Riddle as ruling elders, and Samuel Caldwell, Philip Shay and James L. Schooley as trustees. After this, their meetings were continued in the Baptist Church until April 1873, when they were transferred to the Methodist house of worship, and there they were held for nearly two years. Meanwhile, the erection of an edifice of their own had been decided on, the lot purchased and the building commenced. It was so far completed, in January 1875, that the chapel wing was then dedicated, and services regularly held there. The church is a fine large brick building, with slated roofs and spire, standing on the north-west corner of Main and Fourth streets. Its cost was ten thousand dollars.

Preaching was had by supply, until the installation of their first regular and present pastor, Rev. George Elliott, who also has in charge, the Warrior Run and McEwensville Churches. The Sabbath-school attendance is an average of about one hundred.

Evangelical Lutheran.—Prior to 1866, the Lutherans of Watsontown and vicinity, had neither regular place of worship, nor church organization. They had held services in the academy building, from time to time, principally conducted by Rev. George Parsons, pastor of the Milton charge.

In the Spring of that year, an organization was reached, and officers elected, as follows: Trustees and Elders—Christian Gosh, and Silas Rambach; Deacons—A. T. Goodman, S. M. Miller; Treasurer, S. Rambach; Secretary, A. R. Latshaw.

The number of members was forty-six. Rev. Mr. Parsons continued as supply pastor.

Looking towards the erection of a church building, a consultation was held with the officers of the German Reformed Church, and an agreement made on July 14th, 1866, for the building of a house of worship, by the two congregations, in Union. Two lots were purchased, and the corner-stone laid, July 15th, 1866, with appropriate services, by Rev. Jacob Albert. The church was dedicated, May 12th, 1867, the Rev. Joshua Evans, of Lewisburg, and Rev. George Parsons, of Milton, being the officiating clergymen.

The first regular pastor was Rev. T. C. Bilheimer, who assumed charge in the Fall of 1867, and continued one year. His successors were: Rev. Charles Albert (supply,) Rev. —— Lentz (supply,) Rev. J. R. Keller, Rev. P. S. Mack, and Rev. S. P. Orwig, the present pastor, who took charge October 1st, 1873. From forty-six members, in 1866, the number has increased to two hundred and twenty. A Sabbath-school was commenced in July, 1874, and now has an attendance of two hundred and fifty, including teachers. Their house is a good brick structure, thirty-seven by fifty feet in size, with commodious basement for use of Sabbath-school. It is called "St. Bartholomew's Church," and stands on Main street, at its north-west corner with Fourth.

The Reformed Church was organized in 1865, by Rev. S. H. Reed, of Milton, who preached a short time as a supply. In 1866, the church was connected with the Paradise charge, and Rev. Henry Masser, became their first pastor. He was succeeded, in 1873, by Rev. J. K. Millett, who still labors with them. Two years after the organization, they united with the Lutherans for building purposes, and erected a substantial brick edifice ("St. Bartholomew's Church,) in which both congregations still worship. The reformed people have also a Sabbath-school, with a goodly attendance.

The Watsontown Baptist Church.—This is the old Union Baptist Church, of Delaware Run, under a change of name, which was made by unanimous consent, November 17th, 1860. Their meetings, however, were continued in the old edifice for several years after.

On July 2d, 1869, a building committee, of which Joseph Everitt was chairman, was appointed to collect funds for the building of a new meeting-house, and to prosecute its erection, which they did with so much vigor, that the new building, at the corner of Fourth and Main streets, was dedicated February 26th, 1871, the morning sermon being preached by Elder T. O. Lincoln, D.D., and that of the evening, by Elder G. J. Brensinger, of Sunbury, which were so effectual, that seven hundred and seventy-five dollars and fifty cents was received in collections towards freeing the church of the debt which lay upon it, a small portion of which yet remains. From 1866 to 1868, preaching was supplied principally by Elder J. S. Hudson. In June, 1868, Elder A. C. Wheat, M.D., was elected pastor, and served from November 7th, in that year, until April 1st, 1872. Elder A. H. Emmons followed him, September 1st, 1872, and remained three years, when he was called to Lima, New York.

For a few months, the church was without a preacher, but on January 15th, 1876, Elder P. T. Warren, of Maryland, assumed the pastorate, and is still in charge. The membership is at present one hundred and five.

The Methodist Episcopal Church, of Watsontown, was organized in 1862, by Rev. Franklin Gearhart, preacher in charge of Milton circuit, in 1862; the membership being fourteen.

In 1863, and 1864, and 1865, the appointment was connected with Milton circuit, under preachers Gearhart, Swallow, Haughwout, Church, and Shoemaker. In 1866, it was with Chillisquaque circuit, preachers King and Chilcoat. In 1867, and thereafter, until 1874, it was Watsontown circuit, with preachers Wilson, Reese, Cleese, Gearhart, Comp, Olewine, Burnley, and Pemberton; the Rev. John W. Olewine being its pastor in 1873. In 1874, Watsontown was made a station, and Rev. John A. Woodcock was appointed the pastor, which he continued to be until 1876, when Rev. Andrew W. Gibson, the present pastor, assumed charge.

During the pastorate of Rev. John W. Olewine, and through his earnest efforts, a church building was commenced, and so far completed, in 1872, that on the 10th of November, of that year, the basement-story was dedicated by Bishop Bowman. It is a good brick building, forty-five by seventy feet, standing on Third street, east of Main.

Previous to the building of this edifice, services had been held in the Academy.

The church membership is about two hundred. Their Sabbath-school attendance is over two hundred scholars.

The Young Men's Christian Association had its origin in the deep religious fervor engendered in its members during a week of prayer, in Watsontown.

They at once proceeded to organization, which was effected in the first days of January, 1876. Their officers are: President, S. A. Speddy; Vice President, William Bedford; Secretary, G. A. Lippincott; Treasurer, Oliver Leiser; Corresponding Secretary, C. C. Follmer.

They meet for prayer and religious advancement at the building association room, Miller's building, on Friday evenings, and in the different churches on Sabbath evenings.

The Watsontown Cemetery Association was incorporated November 5th, 1868. The officers elected were: President, George Burns; Secretary, A. B. Latshaw; Treasurer, Silas Rambach; Managers—Joseph Hollopeter, F. S. Whitman, A. B. Latshaw, Peter Schaeffer, Silas Rambach, D. S. Kramer.

The ground is a tract of eight acres, lying in the form of an almost perfect rhomboid, upon the hill, on the north side of First street, above the Academy. It is enclosed by a paling fence, and the main entrance is on First street. By the plan, it is divided into twelve blocks, but of these only eight are actually laid out.

A main avenue passes longitudinally through the centre, and is ornamented with circular mounds, planted with firs and *arbor vitæ*. Other avenues divide the blocks, and pass entirely around the margin of the ground. The lots, within the blocks, are divided by foot paths, and a considerable number of shade trees have been planted. The first interment there was that of Mrs. Joseph Everitt, and the second was of Mrs. George Burns; while among the first transfers from the old burying ground were those of the remains of deceased members of the Watson family, made by their surviving kinsman, John L. Watson, Esq., of Milton. The subsequent burials have been quite numerous, and there are many handsome monuments erected.

The old Presbyterian Burial Ground at Watsontown, dates back a full century. For, in an old log church that stood there, services were held by Rev. P. V. Fithian, on the 16th of July 1775. The exact date of the first interment is not known. The oldest legible inscription, is one "sacred to the memory of Jenny, wife of John Wilson, who died March 6th, 1787." Her husband survived her twenty-six years (February 15th, 1813,) and, during that time, married again. His second wife also lies beside him. An old but luxuriant mulberry tree is growing over their graves, and an ancient, crumbling wall, of rough stones, imperfectly encloses them. A similar rough, dilapidated wall surrounds the graves of the Ferrin family, who lived in Delaware township, above Watsontown. These have no inscriptions, and even the stones are hardly visible. There is a very plain inscription upon the headstone of Daniel Stocks, who died April 16th, 1844, aged 71 years. David Bly, father of Captain John Bly, was interred there April 25th, 1827, but there is no lettering, and the grave is hardly recognizable. A very small stone, bearing the almost illegible letters "J. H." marks the last resting place of Jane Huff, the daughter of Charles Huff of Union County, who was himself buried there in the year 1863. His, was the last interment; and so, after ninety years of use, the old ground was abandoned, and most of the remains were taken away.—It is a green nook, almost surrounded by the water of the Lumber Company's basins, and deeply shaded by old locust, oak, and walnut trees.

McEWENSVILLE BOROUGH.

The first settler within the territorial limits, at present embraced in the borough of McEwensville, was John Quigley, who came there about 1805, and built a log house on the spot where now stands the dwelling of John P. Beard, on Main street, nearly opposite the Reformed Church. Here he commenced the trade of plough-maker and carpenter, at which he was reasonably prosperous, for there was a good demand for work in his calling, among the Montgomerys, the Vincents, and other substantial farmers at Paradise, Warrior Run, and other parts of old Turbut township. In this way, he continued until 1812, when he moved up the river, after selling his property and his business to a Mr. Stalnaker, who kept up the trade till the time of his death, in June, 1813. After Quigley came, other settlers followed, and among them was Alexander McEwen, an unmarried Scotch weaver, who arrived in 1800, and first lived at the house of Thomas Wallace, a farmer of the vicinity, and who afterwards, during the thirty years of his residence, became a man of so much note, that the village (when it grew to be one) received his name.

Three years after his coming, the last war with England was declared, and then, as he had, or claimed to have had some experience in military matters, he obtained the endorsements of Dr. James Dougal and General Giffin, and having, by these, secured a Captain's commission, he entered the army under General Scott, and was present at Lundy's lane. At that, or another engagement occurring near that time, he was made prisoner, and remained in the hands of the enemy until the close of the war.

When John Quigley built his house on what is now the main street of the borough, and when McEwen came there, a weaver, a magnificent pine forest covered more than the entire site of McEwensville, but it was particularly heavy where Rev. George Elliott's residence now is, and also at Peter Jones' blacksmith-shop, near where the Covenanters built their place of worship. From this, not only did the "Pines" Church receive its appellation, but the entire locality became known as *Pine Grove*, a name which clung to it for years, even after the Post-office Department had set the seal of official recognition upon the name which the town now bears.

While Captain McEwen remained a prisoner of war in Canada, it would seem that he found some means of adding to his wealth, for, although in 1812, he had left Pine Grove with very little of this world's goods, yet, on his return there, in 1815, he at once opened a general store on the main thoroughfare, and became apparently prosperous. On June 11th, 1818, he announced himself a candidate for the office of Sheriff, and added to the announcement the following *Nota Bene*: "It is the usual manner of electioneering for the above office, to apply personally to the elector. This, in my opinion, is insulting to the elector, and mean in the candidate. Of course I will not adopt it. I hope my not doing so will not be considered as any disrespect to my fellow-citizens." Surely it seems as if his theory of candidacy was the correct one, but the voters of Northumberland County evidently liked the solicitation, or what accompanied it, and did *not* think the custom more honored in the breach than in the observance, for, notwithstanding the honorable course pursued by the Captain, they refused to elect him Sheriff.

The year before Captain McEwen established the first store, at Pine Grove, William Moritz had opened *the first public house* in a log building which he built upon the spot where is now the furniture manufactory of McLain & Brother, near the south end of the town.

In 1816, Isaac Baker also built upon the highway, and opened a tavern, which, two years later, he sold to a young man, twenty-six years of age, who had been a miller, at George Eckert's, in Milton, as well as at the Hower mill, on Warrior Run, and who, having taken unto himself a wife on the 15th day of September, in that year, at once occupied his newly-purchased house, and commenced business as an inn-keeper. That young man was Henry Reader, now the venerable ex-sheriff of Northumberland County, who, at the age of eighty-four years, is still living in the same house to which he took his bride on that Autumn evening, fifty-eight years ago.

The mania for tavern-keeping, which seems always to rage with peculiar violence in embryo towns, now showed itself in Pine Grove. In 1820, when there were not, within the present borough lines, more than seven houses, all told—two of which were taverns—Captain McEwen's ambition moved him to become an inn-keeper, too; so he built the third hotel, which, with himself as landlord, became, in a short time, the principal hostelry of the place. It still stands there, upon the main street, directly opposite the head of the Watsontown road. Upon its weather-beaten sign (perhaps the same which its ancient military landlord placed there) is a painted picture, labelled as representing "*General George Washington*." Its present host, Mr. H. J. Reader, nephew of the ex-sheriff, is the senior publican of the County, having been in the profession continuously for thirty-seven years.

McEwen, though an uneducated man, seems to have been well thought of by many of the best people of that day, who often called at his inn and bestowed their patronage.

Long before there was a post-office there, the mail-coach, passing up and down the Northumberland road, made his house its stopping-place, and thus materially enhanced its consideration. It was there, in 1825, at a military dinner, that the town first received its name. The event was then considered an important one, and was mentioned at length in the newspapers of the day. Early in that year, Adam Surver had laid out, and offered for sale, a considerable number of "village lots," on the road which is now the main street. Probably his sales were very meagre, but they drew public attention to the place, as will be seen.

Camp Calhoun and the Christening of the Town.—On the 25th of October, 1825, a military encampment, of the Independent Battalion of Volunteers, was pitched at "Camp Calhoun," a short distance from Pine Grove. *Lieutenant-Colonel James S. Dougal* commanded, and his Majors were: *Robert H. Hammond* and *John Montgomery*. The battalion was composed of "the Northumberland Troop of Horse, Captain Anthony Armstrong; Milton

Guards, Captain Henry Frick; Warrior Run Infantry, Captain Wm. Fulkerson; Lewisburg Guards, Captain Jackson McFadden; Union Guards, Captain James Finney, and the Lafayette Artillerists, Captain John Ludwig." The reviewing officer was *Brigadier-General Adam Light.*

In reference to a portion of the ceremonies, the following is found in the *Miltonian* of November 5th, 1825: "After the review of the Independent Battalion of Volunteers, on the 28th of October, Captain Alexander McEwen invited Brigadier-General Light and his staff, the field-officers of the battalion, and several respectable citizens, then on a visit to the camp, to partake of a dinner with him. After much conversation, it was observed that a new town was about to be laid out in the vicinity of the camp-ground, and the inquiry arose, what was the town to be named? No one could tell. But we think the following sentiment, given as a volunteer toast, by General Light, will be sufficiently indicative of what it ought to be called. The toast was loudly and most heartily applauded by the company.

"By Brigadier-General Light—'*Camp Calhoun*—May we shortly have the satisfaction of *seeing* a new and flourishing village, situate in the immediate vicinity of Camp Calhoun, and may it be appropriately named *McEwensville!*'

"By Captain Frick—'The town plot just laid out by Adam Server—let the blank be filled with *McEwensville*, and may the town increase with the exactness, neatness and rapidity of Camp Calhoun, and vie with her more flourishing neighbors, *Milton* and *Pennsborough!*'

"We have long been persuaded that a town ought to be laid out in the neighborhood of Captain McEwen's. The people in that vicinity might easily have a post-office established there, which they would find very advantageous."

It was prophetic. The newly laid-out town did receive the name in honor of the Captain. The establishment of a post-office followed, and the *first postmaster* was Alexander McEwen.

On the tenth day of December, 1827, John L. Watson moved from Watsontown to McEwensville, and built the brick residence and store now occupied by General Armstrong, and also the warehouse just above there. His firm was Watson & Vincent, and they did a very heavy business in the purchase of produce, and sale of general merchandise. Mr. Watson lived in the town until 1840, when he removed to Danville.

A similar business was soon after commenced by William Hayes and Robert H. McCormick, their style being Hayes & McCormick. They occupied a large store, on the west side of the main street, and directly opposite McEwen's hotel. In the rear, upon the Watsontown road, was their warehouse.

Not only did the business of these firms prove profitable to themselves, but, for many succeeding years, the town experienced a rapid growth, and an importance in the trade of the surrounding country, equalled by no other business point between Northumberland and Muncy (Milton alone excepted).

In this year, too, (1827,) the first daily mail-coach commenced running through the place, and this, of course, added considerably to its activity. The proprietors were Joseph Hall and James Huling, and this was the completing link in the daily mail service between Harrisburg and Williamsport.

In 1833, McEwensville received a new dignity, in the election of Henry Reader to the office of Sheriff of Northumberland County. This he held until 1836, and, in his absence during that time, at the county seat, the business of his tavern was managed by his brother, Michael, who died in the present year, at Turbutville.

About this time, the affairs of Captain McEwen became seriously involved, and the sale of his establishment became a necessity. It was purchased by several of the citizens, in shares of one hundred dollars each. After McEwen left the house, it was rented to John Eguer, and afterwards to Mr. Eckbert, who, at one time, kept the "Spread Eagle Tavern," at Milton. These rentals covered about three years.

The Shedden School.—In 1842, Rev. S. S. Shedden, a Presbyterian clergyman, who had been a pupil of Kirkpatrick, at Milton, opened a subscription school, in the upper story of the foundry building, now occupied by Samuel Gray. Later, it was moved to the north wing, and lower floor, of the same building. This school, under charge of Mr. Shedden, continued for about ten years. It stood very high in public estimation, and its success, as an educator, was most distinguished. It is doubtful whether—with the single exception of the famous Milton Academy, under Kirkpatrick—it has ever known any superiors, or even equals, among the schools of Northumberland County. In the list of its students, are found many who have attained distinction; not only in Pennsylvania, but in other and distant States.

The writer recollects, a few months ago, meeting a gentleman, a prominent citizen of Kansas, who had been one of its first pupils. He spoke with evident pride and affection of the school, and his old preceptor, and, as he recurred to those years of his boyhood with the natural and justifiable tenderness which we all feel in such retrospect, it seemed to him that in all Pennsylvania there never was another such a teacher as Mr. Shedden, nor such an *alma mater* as the old "Foundry School," at McEwensville.

"Tina," or "Teeny" Robinson, was the widow of William Robinson, who had lived three miles northward from McEwensville, and, at his death, she removed into the southern part of the village, where she turned many an honest penny, by the sale of beer, cakes, and "kickshaws." The pupils of the Shedden school regarded her modest shop as almost an institution of their own, and her relations to them were much the same as those which the famous "Benny Havens" bore for so many years to the cadets at West Point. As long as they live, they will never forget the delicious sweetness of her cakes, nor the unrivalled sparkle of her beer.

The McEwensville Academy.—After the closing of the Shedden school, the project of an academy was conceived by a few of the citizens of the town, and they acted so promptly upon the conception, that, late in 1852, a commodious brick building (owned by private stockholders) was completed, at the north end of McEwensville, and opened as a classical-school, under charge of C. L. Rynearson, (one of Dr. Shedden's pupils,) as principal. Under his administration, the school received a good patronage, and achieved an enviable reputation. At the end of eight years, he was succeeded by Rev. J. P. Hudson. After him, the Academy was successively in charge of the following gentlemen, as principals: Nelson Wagener, Julius Reimensnyder, Allen Albert, George Horner, and John Showers.

In 1869, when it became apparent that the public schools of the town needed, and must have, increased room, it was proposed to purchase the Academy building for the purpose. It had never brought much pecuniary gain to the stockholders, and, indeed, the enterprise had not been commenced in any such expectation. What they had at heart, was that advancement to the village and its vicinity, which was sure to result from the better and higher education of their rising youth; and if this result could be assured, and the continuance of the school's high standing be guaranteed, they were not unwilling to make the proposed sale. So, in 1869, their building was purchased for the use and occupancy of the graded public schools, and, after an honorable existence of seventeen years, the McEwensville Academy ceased to exist as a private institution.

The year before the building of the Academy, 1851, there was opened *the first telegraphic communication* between McEwensville and the great outside world. The first office was in the store of Hayes & McCormick, and it was operated by Henry K. Culp, one of their clerks. It was afterwards moved to Wenck's drug-store; but in 1862, the line was withdrawn from McEwensville, and its towns-people, if they wished for the accommodation of the wire, could find it no nearer than at Watsontown.

The organization of the borough was made November 11th, 1857. The first burgess was John F. Deutler. It was about the time that the opening of the Sunbury and Erie Railroad had begun to attract trade to the towns upon its route, but it had the contrary effect upon McEwensville, and from that time the town deteriorated in importance. It has not now one tenth of the trade that it had thirty years ago. It has neither railway, canal, telegraph, gas, nor water-works, place of amusement, Masonic or other secret organizations, lawyers nor fire department. It has one public house, three general stores and one drug store. The population in 1860, was three hundred and ninety-one, and in 1870, three hundred forty-two, a decrease of forty nine souls in ten years.

The first resident physician was a Doctor Hazleton, who established there more than thirty years ago. He was very popular with the people, but died before he had practiced many years. The next was Dr. R. H. Watson, a son of John Watson, of Watsontown, and cousin of John L. Watson, Esq., of Milton. Later came Dr. J. H. Grier, who removed to Jamestown, Lycoming County, and now resides there.

After Dr. Grier, the next was Dr. George Bons, who was succeeded by Dr. Henry Life, the present physician of the borough.

The manufacturing interests of McEwensville are neither numerous nor important.

Foundry and plough-shop, Main street, Samuel Gray, proprietor. The principal work done is the manufacture of ploughs and other agricultural implements.

RES. & STORE OF CAROLINE DALIUS,
DEALER IN SEWING MACHINES & MUSICAL INSTRUMENTS, SUNBURY.

RES OF HON. J. J. JOHN & JAS MAY,
SHAMOKIN ST. SHAMOKIN NORTHUMBERLAND CO. PA.

RES. OF T. H. PURDY, SUNBURY, PENNA

Carriage-shops of Mauser & Brother.—These were first put in operation by William Hood, April 4th, 1839. His business at first was small, not reaching more than five thousand dollars per year, but increased afterwards to twenty thousand dollars. On the 1st of April, 1870, he sold out to Mauser & Co., who are still the proprietors, employing twelve men, and producing annually, work to the amount of fifteen thousand dollars.

Furniture Manufactory of McLain & Brother.—Have twelve-horse-power engine, and employ three hands, in the manufacture of bedsteads, tables, chairs, and all the articles usually made in similar establishments. Their father, Mr. Charles McLain, formerly carried on the cabinet-making business in the same place, but sold out some years ago and removed to Turbutville.

The Public Schools.—The first school-house within the bounds, or in the vicinity of the present town of McEwensville, was a log building, standing in a pine grove on, or very near, the spot now occupied by the stable of Rev. George Elliott. This was probably before the commencement of the century. It was afterwards moved to a point further south, upon the "Potash road" leading to Turbutville, and was finally destroyed by fire, but the date of this cannot be ascertained.

The second, was of brick, and built by subscription, on a lot donated by Adam Sarver. This was also burned, and another brick structure erected on the same site. This last is the school-house now standing, adjoining the Lutheran Church, on Church street.

The usual course of study was pursued, and the common branches alone were taught, until the purchase of the academy building in 1869.

On the closing of the private academy, and the transfer of the house to the use of the public schools, they were graded, and in the higher one, the academy standard was maintained.

The teachers of this high school are graduates, and receive a salary of seventy-five dollars per month.

The names of those teachers following Mr. Showers, are: Willard Shaffer, W. M. Boal, and William F. Derr, the present principal. Regular instructions are given in algebra, geometry, natural philosophy, physiology, and the languages, in addition to the ordinary branches. The schools are free for five months in the year, as directed by law, and are supported by subscription for five months more. The present board is composed of William F. Kreich, president; G. W. Armstrong, secretary; Henry Life, treasurer; Alem Mauser, William C. Montgomery, H. K. Culp.

The Old "Pines" Church, of the Covenanters, or Associate Reformed denomination, although it was not strictly within the area of the town, yet, from its proximity and intimate associations, seems proper to be mentioned in this connection.

On June 5th, 1810, Alexander Guffy sold to trustees for the church, three-quarters of an acre of ground, "in the forks of the road leading to Milton and to Daniel Vincent's mill," at the rate of thirty dollars per acre, agreeing, also, to give them the right of passage to and from his spring, for "five shillings, and other valuable considerations." (He, however, afterwards dug a well upon the three-fourths of an acre, and this the trustees accepted in lieu of the right to the spring,) and upon this spot of ground the old log church was built.

The first pastor was Rev. George Junkin; after him came Revs. William Wilson, McKinley, and others, under whose ministrations the congregation worshiped in it for more than forty years. It really owed its existence to a dissatisfaction which had sprung up in the Presbyterian Church in Milton, by which the Pollocks, father and uncle of Governor James Pollock, transferred their favor and material support to the church of the Pines, and members of that family continued to attend service there until its dismemberment, about 1854, when the congregation scattered to other churches, and the ground was purchased and the building demolished by Rev. Simon Boyer.

Presbyterian Church.—This organization, called then the Bethel Church, was formed in April, 1842. Its constituent members were those who, in the previous year, had withdrawn, in consequence of an irreconcilable disagreement, from the Warrior Run Church, under the ministry of the Rev. Mr. Bryson. The passions which caused and resulted from that rupture, were exceedingly strong at the time, and, indeed, it can hardly be said with truth, that even now, after a lapse of thirty-five years, they are entirely allayed.

Upon the separation, they at once arranged to worship in the "Peniel," or "Pines" Church, which belonged to the Associate Reformed Congregation. In the fall of 1842, they completed and occupied the brick edifice in which they still worship, on Church street.

Their pastor, from the time of the secession, was the Rev. J. P. Hudson, who labored with them for about twenty years, up to the Fall of 1861. He is still living in Williamsport.

The next regular pastor was Rev. Frederic Kolb, who ministered to them from May 21st, 1866, until February, 1873. In July, same year, he was succeeded by Rev. George Elliott, their present pastor, who also has charge of the churches at Warrior Run and at Watsontown.

Reformed Church.—This congregation crystalized in 1840. The first pastor was Rev. Henry Wengandt, who remained until 1866. The next was Rev. Henry Mosser, who, in 1873, was succeeded by Rev. J. K. Millet, the present shepherd.

For the first two years after the organization, they worshiped in the school-house, but, in 1842, united with the Lutherans, for building purposes, and erected a union church-house, during that year. In this, they worshiped until 1874, when their present brick edifice was built and occupied. It is located on Main street and the Turbutville road. They have a large Sabbath-school in connection.

Evangelical Lutheran Church.—On the 1st day of June, 1842, this congregation was organized, under the pastoral care of Rev. C. F. Stoever.

The corner-stone for a church was laid on the 5th day of May, 1842, upon ground donated to them by Henry Reader. The building was consecrated to the service of Almighty God, October 9th, 1842. It was a union church, built jointly by the Lutheran and Reformed congregations of the place. The Lutheran Church Council, at this time, was composed of Elders Solomon Truckenmiller and David Gold, and Deacons Henry Hartranft and George Hittle.

On the 1st of April, 1846, the pastorate was assumed by Rev. S. R. Boyer, and it was not until 1863, that the Rev. A. R. Horne succeeded him. Mr. Horne resigned in 1865, after which the congregation was long without a pastor, and, during that time, the pulpit was occasionally supplied by Mr. Griffith, a theological student.

The charge was taken December 27th, 1865, by Rev. E. J. Wolf, who continued as pastor until March, 1869, when he was succeeded by Rev. G. Sill, who left in June, 1870.

The present pastor, Rev. U. Myers, entered the charge January 1st, 1871. During his pastorate, the Lutherans purchased the half-interest of the Reformed congregation, and became sole owners of the church.

Extensive revivals have been experienced in the last few years, and the congregation is goodly in numbers.

Baptist Church.—In the Spring of 1842, James Moore, Sr., Joseph Meixell, and E. W. McCarty, purchased a suitable lot of ground in McEwensville, and also made a further contribution towards the erection of a church-building upon it, for the use of the Baptist worshipers of the town and vicinity, these contributions being increased by the citizens. The brick church—their present house of worship—was completed and dedicated during the same year.

By the action of a council, convened at McEwensville, February 19th, 1853—of which Rev. Dr. Malcolm, was moderator, and J. P. Tustin, clerk—this church was duly organized. The constituent members were:—E. W. McCarty, James M. McCarty, Joseph O. McCarty, John Young, Leah McCarty, Rebecca V. McCarty, Mary Guffy, Martha E. Marshall, and, Sarah W. Parker.

The church was first supplied with preaching by Rev. Robert Lowry, and after him, successively, by Brothers Frear, Jones, Furman, Conard, Hutton, Rush, King, Hutson, Young, Patton, Waltz, Lloyd, Davis, Copeland, and Nichols, down to the present time.

Prayer-meetings, and Sabbath-school, have been sustained a portion of the time.

Methodist Church.—This organization has been in existence many years, but its date is not precisely known. Preaching was first had in the school-house, and afterwards in the academy. The church was built in 1867. It is a neat and convenient frame-building, on the main street, east side, and a short distance north of Potash street. It was built during the pastorate of Rev. William Wilson, and its cost was one thousand four hundred and fifty dollars. The present pastor is Rev. Mr. Vrooman, of Montandon. The church is not in a flourishing condition.

The Presbyterian Burial-ground.—This is a ground of moderate size, near the academy building. In it lie the remains of many of the old inhabitants who, in their day, were prominent in affairs both secular and ecclesiastical.

Not the least among them was the Rev. John Bryson, the veteran Presbyterian clergyman, who was here laid to rest, after having lived almost a century in piety and usefulness.

The Lutheran and Reformed Burial-place is a ground of some eight or ten acres in extent, lying a short distance out of the town, across Warrior Run bridge, on the road to Muncy. It is a neatly laid-out enclosure, but of recent origin.

Any narrative of events in McEwensville would be incomplete if it omitted a mention of two old men who are now living there, within a few rods of each other, upon the main street. They are eighty-four years of age, with but a single day of difference between them. The elder, Henry Reader, was born in Montgomery County, August 12th, 1792, and the very next day, August 13th, Andrew Guffy was born in Northumberland County.

Mr. Reader's parents came to this County when he was two years old. He lived with his father upon several different farms in Turbut township, and was, on April 1st, 1813, apprenticed to Stalnaker, the plow-maker and carpenter, in McEwensville. This apprenticeship lasted but two months, for Stalnaker died in the following June, and young Reader went to work as a miller at Hower's mill; but, in 1818, he bought the Baker tavern-house, before mentioned. He was married September 15th, 1818. From 1833 to 1836, he was Sheriff of Northumberland County, and from 1839 to 1842, he held the position of Canal Supervisor. His life has always been a busy one, and now, at eighty-four, he is as active as many a man twenty years less in age.

In Andrew Guffy's childhood, his father lived on a farm south of Pine Grove, and was the owner of much of the land on which the town now stands. Mr. Guffy well recollects assisting his father to clear some of this land more than seventy years ago, and before the road to Muncy passed through it. He was married to Eliza Armstrong, by Rev. John Bryson, January 4th, 1821. In 1826, he received the appointment of Justice of the Peace, and held that office for nineteen years. Through his official and private life, he has always held the esteem and respect of his fellow-citizens.

He and his old friend have had a long march, but they are nearing its inevitable end, and the route does not seem to have been, to them, a very thorny one.

TURBUTVILLE BOROUGH.

The settlement, which is now Turbutville, was commenced in the way in which such beginnings are usually made, that is, by the establishment of a *tavern*. It was opened in 1825, upon the north-west side of the road which is now the principal street of the town, and at a point a little to the northward of Paradise street. Philip Reifsnyder was the landlord—or rather his wife Fanny* was the landlady, who supervised the cooking and attended at the bar, while Philip plied his trade of blacksmith, at a shop which he had erected hard by. Where there was a tavern and a blacksmith-shop too—a double nucleus—should there not be a town? The people of the surrounding country answered this affirmatively, and out of respect to the proprietor of *two* initial institutions, the bar and the anvil, they called the settlement for Philip, *Snydertown*, playfully dropping the first syllable of his name, for the sake of euphony as well as friendly familiarity.

The widow McCarty was not long behind Reifsnyder. She soon opened the second inn, on the opposite side of the road, and a short distance south of the present hotel of F. Keller.

A third public house followed about 1833. This was at the place now occupied by Keller, and was opened by Samuel Burrows, a son-in-law of Rev. John Bryson. He also, in company with Mr. Bryson's son John, started *the first store*, and their firm was Burrows & Bryson. This store was directly opposite Burrows' (now Keller's) tavern.

Burrows & Bryson afterwards sold out to Amos Bisel, who, some years after, disposed of the business and removed to Jersey Shore, where he died.

Among the proprietors of the store, after Amos Bisel, were Michael Reader and his son Isaac. Michael was also proprietor of the Burrows' tavern for some years.

The next store was that of Dr. Piper, who had removed to Turbutville from Milton, and commenced merchandising not long after Burrows & Bryson.

* This lady died in 1872, when over ninety years of age, at the house of a relative, one mile from Seneca Falls, New York.

The settlement went on, and made some increase in population, but, in connection with its very slow growth, there scarcely occurred (with the exception of the building of the churches, and the burning of one or more) any events more noticeable than the ordinary incidents of every day life—openings of stores, taverns, or workshops, or changes in the ownership of them.

The inauguration of canals, railways, and public works, are events which mark eras in the lives of adjacent communities, and which excite jealousy and rivalry and intrigue, in the attempts of men and of towns, to secure the advantages which are known to follow in their train; but no canal or railroad ever came near Turbutville; no telegraph, not even a stage-line of any importance—no connecting with any of the more populous places—and no stream flows past it to furnish power for the wheels of industry.

And so it existed, a quiet, healthy, Christian village, but one which made scarcely perceptible progress in population or importance. Its old name, Snydertown, was used to designate it so late as the year 1850.

Its erection as a borough, was accomplished in 1859, and the first meeting of its Town Council was held February 8th, in that year. The president of that council was S. A. Savidge, and its secretary, William B. Schyler. The name, Turbutville, was given in honor of the old township of Turbut.

The next year after the incorporation, (1860,) the population was three hundred and eighty, and in 1870 it had increased to four hundred and seventeen—a gain of thirty-seven souls, which, although by no means a brilliant showing, was, at least, better than to have *lost* that number, which McEwensville did (and more) during that same decade.

On the 31st of March, 1871, there occurred a destruction of property, by fire, which, in the annals of Turbutville, seems very considerable. The buildings consumed were two dwelling-houses, a large store-house, and a warehouse, being the property of Mrs. Kuable and Daniel Smith. The only fire apparatus in the borough is a small hand-engine, out of repair, and worthless; but if it was a Silsby steamer, it would still be powerless to extinguish a fire of any magnitude occurring in Turbutville, as there is no supply of water for such a purpose. The buildings destroyed in the fire of 1871, have been rebuilt.

There are, in Turbutville, two hotels, five general stores, two stove and hardware-stores, one drug-store, and two saddlery and harness-shops.

The one attorney of the town is S. A. Savidge, Esq. The physicians are: Dr. E. H. Horner, Dr. Andrew Tenbrook, Dr. N. C. Giddings, and Dr. P. A. Seel.

Independent Order of Odd Fellows, No. 645.—This organization has recently purchased a commodious two-story brick building, on Main street, and in this their meetings are held.

Mail-stage.—Turbutville is still the head-quarters of a mail-stage—a short, cross-route, between Watsontown and Exchange, Montour County. It runs daily, viz.: in the morning to Exchange, and return to Turbutville; and in the afternoon to Watsontown, and return to Turbutville, where it stops over night—the proprietor resides here.

The manufacturing industries of the town are neither numerous nor extensive.

The Tannery of J. & H. Hertwick is the only one in Turbutville, and its business is small.

The Foundry of Philip Steinruck, and the *Machine-shop of F. Gardner* are both in one building, (owned by George Wykoff,) and, in connection, they turn out plough and other castings, and do something in the manufacture and repair of mowing and reaping-machines, and other agricultural implements.

Carriage Shops are carried on in a small way, by H. Bittner, and also by Thomas Ritter.

Public Schools.—Turbutville has but two public schools—the common and the higher English. They are both taught in the brick school-building, on Paradise street. The free term covers about five months in the year, viz: From the middle of October till about the first of April, with a week's vacation at the holidays. The subscription terms are before and after harvest, making about four months additional. The teachers' salaries are thirty and fifty dollars per month. The present board of directors is as follows: President, Nathan Wetzel; Secretary, E. H. Horner; Treasurer, George P. Kump; P. L. Dieffenbacher, J. F. Wampole, and D. H. Driesbach.

The Reformed Church.—This organization was made about 1823. Rev. Samuel Gutelius was their first pastor.

Soon after, a small church building was erected in union with the Lutherans. Rev. Henry Wagner, succeeded Mr. Gutelius, and then came in succession, Rev. Daniel Gring, George Wolff, and Mr. Kelly. During the pastorate of Mr. Wolff, the Turbutville and River Churches were taken from the Paradise charge. After the retirement of Rev. Mr. Kelly from this church, they were without a regular pastor until the assumption of the charge by Rev. Tillman Derr, the present minister.

After worshiping in the old Union Church for more than thirty years, the question of retirement from the union was agitated by the Lutherans, (1855 to 1859,) resulting in the withdrawal of their consistory and part of their congregation, and in their building a new edifice, but leaving a portion of the congregation, (which afterwards became the New-school Lutherans,) still in the union. A new union building was soon commenced, on the land adjoining the old one, but before it was completed, it took fire, and was burned down, destroying the old church building with it. This ended the union, and each congregation, (*i. e.*, the Reformed, and the New-school Lutheran,) then built a new brick church for their respective sole use, upon the ground which they had held as a union. The edifice built at that time is still the place of worship of the Reformed congregation.

The Lutheran Church was organized in 1823, and soon after, a small meeting-house was built, in union with the Reformed congregation. About the year 1850, they withdrew from the union, and built for themselves a new and commodious brick building, which they still occupy. Their first pastor was the Rev. Jacob Repass, who assisted at the dedication of the Union Church, at Paradise, in 1824, (Mr. David Eschbach recollects seeing him there on that occasion, more than half a century ago.) He was succeeded by Rev. Mr. Miller. It is regretted that the chain cannot be made complete by giving the names of all, from Mr. Miller down. Their present pastor is Rev. Jacob F. Wampole.

New-school Lutheran Church.—This church first had existence at the time of the consistory, and part of the Lutheran congregation withdrew from the union with the Reformed Church, the portion remaining assuming the name of "New School." Not long after that withdrawal, the union commenced building a new edifice, which, however, was burned before completion. This disaster caused a dissolution of the union and the erection of two new church buildings, one by the New-school Lutherans, and the other by the Reformed, both edifices standing on the ground which had been held by the union. In the building of this house, pecuniary assistance was kindly offered by their friends of the Reformed Church. Their present pastor is Rev. U. Myers.

The Baptist Church, of Turbutville, is an offshoot from the "Derry Baptist Church," which was organized in Derry township, Montour County, July 1st, 1846.

On December 7th, 1867, that church voted to build a place of worship in Turbutville, and in due time they proceeded with the work, so that it was dedicated, September 12th, 1869. During the process of construction, the congregation held services in the school-house, until August, 1869, when they were enabled to meet in the basement of the new building, though that was before its dedication.

The church, during the time of its existence, has received many into its fellowship, of whom some have removed to the west, and to other sections, and have united with churches there. The pastor is Rev. Henry C. Munro who has labored in the churches at Derry and Turbutville during the past twelve years.

Places of Interment.—There are two within the town boundaries, viz.: the graveyard of the Reformed and New-school Lutherans, contiguous to their church, in which but few burials are now made, and that of the original Lutherans, which last, is wholly in disuse.

The Turbutville Cemetery is an enclosed ground of five-and-one-tenth acres, well situated on the main road, to the north-east of the town, and just outside the limits. It was incorporated in 1867, the owners and managers being Samuel Leinbach and B. H. Barto. It is divided by the usual avenues and foot-paths, and is laid off into four hundred and eighty lots, of which seventeen are reserved for the free burial of the poor.

The first interment within it, was the wife of Daniel Menges; the next, Mrs. William Levan; and the third was William Deutler.

The plank-walk from the town is extended as far as the cemetery. Thrifty maples are growing along its front, and a considerable number of evergreen-trees have been planted within the enclosure. It is the intention to intersperse these with ornamental, deciduous trees, which will add greatly to its beauty.

SNYDERTOWN.

This town derives its name from the venerable Jacob Snyder, who, soon after the war of the Revolution, cut a road through the wilderness, and settled, with a large family, about one-half mile above the present site of the town that, in its name, honors the memory of the hardy old pioneer.

Some difficulty has been experienced in establishing the date of Mr. Snyder's advent into this section, his grandson, Barton Boughner, from whom the information is derived, maintaining that the first improvement was made by his grandfather about 1807 or 1808. The burden of testimony would establish about the date given above. The Lewis family, and some others, had settled, previous to the close of the war, above Snydertown, and the safe presumption would be, that this location, which was peculiarly eligible, was not left until twenty-five or thirty years afterwards. Again, Mr. Snyder's attention was directed, very soon after his settlement, to the building up of improvements of a public character, and it is found that, within a short time after his settlement, he erected, on Shamokin Creek, near his residence, a saw and grist-mill, a distillery, and linseed-oil factory. These properties were not assessed as late as 1786, and, as it is not probable that the lynx-eyed revenue officials would overlook such valuable acquisitions to their assessment-book, the presumption again would be, that they were not built until about 1790. Mr. Snyder took up a large tract of land in the vicinity of Snydertown, and set to work making a home in the wilds. The improvements built by him, have long since gone to decay. His son Jacob, a few years afterwards—probably about 1807—built a saw and grist-mill, near the site of the town, on the realty now owned and occupied by Jesse Gener.

Mr. Snyder was a public-spirited citizen, and early selected the spot where now stands the flourishing little town, and gave grounds for a church, school-house, and cemetery. On this ground a log-house was erected, which, for many years, served for school-house and church. This house was raised, and in its stead the frame building, now standing, near the Methodist Church, was built by Barton Boughner. This house served all denominations for a sanctuary, and, until the completion of the Methodist Chapel, was the only one in the place. This chapel was erected, about 1860, by the Methodists.

Godfrey Rockefeller was another early settler here, having moved in a few years after Mr. Snyder, and located near his place. Mr. Rockefeller's son is still living in Sunbury, who, at the age of eighty-six, guides the compass and chain as unerringly as when a youth of twenty. His grandson, the Hon. Mr. Rockefeller, occupies the position of President Judge of the Northumberland County Court. Edward Colket built the first log-house in Snydertown, where now lives Jackson Barriger. Peter Rockefeller opened a hotel about 1810, where William Farrow now dispenses good cheer to those who are ahungered or athirst; Mr. Rockefeller undoubtedly had a good stand for his business. At that time, mills were scarce—farmers came a long distance to get their grain ground; and, in those days, farmers were proverbially dry, and the liquor, then manufactured, having none of the poisonous properties which now make it as destructive to human nature as powder and lead, Mr. Rockefeller found abundant patronage.

James Alexander, another early settler in Snydertown, opened the first store, about 1812. The house built and occupied by him, was burned in 1870, and the more portentous edifice of Pencil Brothers erected in its place. A store, established near the railroad by Mr. Startzel, and still owned by him with the Pencil Brothers, forms the only trading-places in Snydertown. There are now in town one blacksmith-shop, one shoe-shop and one coach-maker's-shop. A large brick school-house has been erected in the past twelve years, which furnishes, in the second-story, a room for the society of Odd Fellows. This society is the oldest in the neighborhood, and for many years held its meetings at private houses, and wherever a suitable room, sufficiently retired, could be obtained.

Just west of the town, on the road leading to Sunbury, stands the German Reform and Lutheran Church. Many years ago, these societies, who generally, in the County, are united in the erection of their houses of worship, assembled in a small frame-house, then standing in one corner of their cemetry, opposite the present imposing structure. This house becoming too small, in 1869, they unitedly built the brick church, which, in architectural design and finish does credit to any locality. Their cemetery is tastefully laid out, occupying a sloping location, near the church.

Snydertown is now in tri-daily communication with the outside world, by means of the Shamokin branch of the Northern Central Railroad. In May, 1872, upon petition of its citizens, the territory for some miles around was erected into a borough, since which time the place has steadily improved; roads have been built, and well-cared for.

ELYSBURG.

The location of Elysburg is peculiarly charming. After crossing over mountains and through vales, from the summit of a high hill, the view suddenly is arrested by a beautiful scene, spread out like a panorama, at the foot of the hill. Fifteen miles from the river, among mountains that offer but little attraction to the traveler, and, doubtless, much less to the husbandman, is situated the little hamlet, which, in earlier days, was christened Elysburg. The valley has the appearance of a huge basin, with a spout on one side, surrounded by hills which rear themselves like huge walls, to guard the peaceful homes clustered at their base. Fields, waving with grain, dot the hills; farms, fringed with the dark-green foliage of the forest, form the filling-in to the background of a picture seldom seen and enjoyed from one point of observation. The town itself is beautifully situated, and has been built up by a people of cultivated taste. The houses are fine architectural specimens, and everything within and about indicates comfort and abundance. The surroundings and interior of the place all tend to impress one with the feeling that an earthly Eden, where the fell destroyer, Satan, has not yet come, has been reached. This delusion deepens when the entire absence of the blighting stain, left by whisky, is observed.

The lands on which the town now stands were originally improved by a family named Campbell, some time before the Revolution, who were extensive landed proprietors in the County. The farms on which the town was built, were owned by Mr. Ely and Mr. Campbell. Mr. Ely built a house here in 1810 or 1811, which is still standing, in good state of preservation, on the farm then owned by him. Mr. Benjamin Campbell built where Mrs. Gulick now lives, about the same time. On this spot the ancestors of Mr. Campbell resided anterior to the Revolutionary war, from whence they were driven by the Indians, but subsequently returned. The plan of the town was originally conceived about 1825, by Mr. Elisha Barton and Davy Dodge.

The first store in the place was started by John Irvin, about 1815. He kept in the building now occupied by Mrs. Noble. His assortment was generally exchanged for such barter as the people could gather. Mr Irvin dropped from view after a few years, and his place was filled by Messrs. Fisher & Higgins, emigrants from New Jersey. Fisher soon returned to Jersey, and Mr. Higgins passed on into the future, to exchange his experience in this world for the uncertainties of the next.

The town now boasts of three stores, all selling general merchandise of all kinds, except, liquid lightning. A tannery was started near the site of the town, about 1830, by Mr. Barton. This tannery has not been operated for forty years. The tannery was built on the lot now occupied by Charles Tietsworth. Mr. Hull started a tannery about 1836, about one-half mile from the town, where now stands the extensive establishment operated by William and Francis Persil. Schools had been established and sustained here before the close of the seventeenth century. As early as 1810, Mrs. Reeder, and some others still living, attended school where the brick school-house now stands. Now a fine public school-building and an academy grace the town. About 1840, the Methodist Society erected the first church-building in Elysburg. Since that, the Presbyterians have erected a new brick edifice. Religious meetings were held in the neighborhood many years before, in school-houses or any other place open to religious assemblages. The Methodist Society now numbers not less than one hundred members. The Presbyterian about fifty, each ably supported by regular pastors.

A foundry was started about 1860, that does sufficient business to supply the demands for their products.

The town now contains about forty residences—not a shabby-appearing house in its limits—and a population of about two hundred; a post-office, but no hotel. Its location is about fourteen miles from Sunbury; nine miles from Shamokin, on Little Shamokin Creek, one-and-half miles from its confluence with the Big Shamokin. Two blacksmith-shops and two wheelwright-shops.

GEORGETOWN.

This town is beautifully situated on the left bank of the Susquehanna River, seventeen miles south of Sunbury, and thirty-eight north from Harrisburg. The view from this place borders on the romantic. Spreading out in front with a width of nearly one mile is the Susquehanna, dotted with islets, once the abode of the aborigines of the country. Back, rise the hills, running with a gradual ascent from the river bank to an elevation of some hundred feet, just rapid enough to form good drainage. The site was selected for a town by John George Brosius, and under his direction laid out by William Gray, D.S., in 1798, thus ranking next to Sunbury in age as a town. The land was patented to Thomas McKee, by the Penn Government, in 1767. It was sold by order of the Court of Northumberland County, September 27th, 1773, to William Dunbar, and by him sold the same day to Sebastian Brosius, who, by will dated 1789, devised the same to his son John George Brosius, the originator of the town. The house built by Mr. Brosius is still standing, and now occupied by Tobias Long. Mr. Brosius erected a grist-mill on Stone Valley Creek, near his residence, the first in this section. This mill, although built about 1777, is still standing.

The first settlers of Georgetown and vicinity were Germans, and the population of the day is largely made up of their descendants, who cling to the customs and language of their Faderland with wonderful tenacity, and evince a fondness for home and its associations that it would be well if Americans generally would imitate. Daniel Bothamel emigrated here prior to 1795, and after some years opened a hotel in the same building, now occupied by his grandson, who keeps the house known as the Railroad Hotel. The first house erected on the site of Georgetown was built by John Borell, on the site now occupied by Esquire Bubb's office. The first store at which the people could secure their favorite weed and rum, was started by George Brosius about 1810, in a house then standing where Mr. Spotts now lives. There are now in the place three hotels, two stores, one saw-mill, and one tin-shop, and a post-office. The Philadelphia & Erie Railroad passes through the town, but thus far no station has been built. The original schools of this section were somewhat primitive in character, and supported entirely by subscription. The opposition to the free-school system was very strong, and for many years the large mass of the people fought resolutely against the obnoxious innovation—as they viewed it—and at each successive election voted *no schools*, but better counsels, or strategy rather, at last prevailed, and a board of school directors were elected, who at once attempted to set the wheel of progress in motion by passing a resolution looking to an early opening of the schools, upon the free system. David Seiler, B. M. Bubb, Adam Lenker, Franklin Markley, and S. B. Heigh constituted the first board chosen in 1865. The opposition was still strong, and it was only by almost superhuman exertions that the efforts of the faithful few were at last crowned with success. In January, 1866, the last objection had been successfully met, and the schools were started with a good corps of teachers. The German Reform and Lutheran Church was organized about 1846, from the old Stone Valley Church—a house erected and pastor employed. This is the only church edifice in Georgetown. The place was once the site of a prosperous Indian village, and many relics are every year exhumed in excavating for wells and cellars. The savages held on to the town with great tenacity, and many years elapsed, and many white scalps of its early settlers dangled from the belts of the white man's foe, before the territory was secured for the peaceful occupation of our ancestors.

SOUTH DANVILLE.

This place is located on the north branch of the river Susquehanna, immediately opposite Danville, known the world over as the *great iron mart*, with which city, the town is connected by a bridge over the river. The land on which the town is located, belonged originally to the heirs of Harmon Gearhart, and was laid out in 1870, by W. F. Gearhart. The first house built in the new town, was by Andrew Druffner. The first store in South Danville, was started by A. J. Lober. The town is regularly laid out, and occupies a high and healthy location, overlooking its more portentious neighbor across the river. The place now contains forty to forty-five residences, one brick school-house and one hotel. The Danville, Hazleton and Wilkesbarre Railroad passes through the town, affording daily communication with Sunbury, and markets east. The bridge across the river here, has had its share of mishaps. On the 17th of March, 1875, the water raised to an unprecedented heighth, owing to an ice-gorge formed below, and backed the water up to a level with the bridge, and carried away the entire structure. A new bridge was built at once, having been completed within four months from time of commencement, by the Smith Bridge Company, of Toledo, Ohio, at an expense of forty thousand dollars.

In Rush township, and but a few rods from the line of South Danville corporation, stands the flouring-mill of H. B. Crane. This mill was completed in the Fall of 1875, and is complete in all parts. The cost was about twelve thousand dollars. A coal-yard, operated and owned by W. D. Woodrow, is located near the mill. One of the institutions of South Danville,

Dr C. I. KRICEBAUM.

RES. OF O. H. OSTRANDER, RIVERSIDE, NORTHD CO., PA.

that should not be passed by, is the file-cutting manufactory of Mr. Rosenstein. In this establishment, one of the happiest and merriest Teutons in the Commonwealth, will, in the short space of fifteen minutes, with a small chisel and large hammer, renovate an old file, and make it equal to the best. His files have well earned for him a wide reputation.

HERNDON.

This town is of recent origin, having been laid out about the time of the completion of the Philadelphia and Erie Railroad. The land was owned by George Seiler, who early saw the advantage of position, and as soon as the railroad became a fixed fact, he laid out the town, and sold the plot to the railroad company. The place now contains one licensed hotel, one temperance house, and two stores. The post-office was christened Herndon, in honor of the brave Captain Herndon, who, as master of an Aspinwall steamship, lost his life in an effort to save his ship, off Hatteras Shoals. The location is pleasant and healthy.

PAXINOS.

This place, for a century, had been in the enjoyment of a Rip Van Winkle state of lethargy which promised to be perpetual, and it doubtless would have slumbered undisturbed for all time, if the quick eye of its present proprietor had not discovered in its central location, its eligibility, the nucleus for a settlement and prospective business centre. In the Summer of 1874, Dr. Mifflin, son-in-law of Jacob Leiscaring, commenced the improvements, by erecting tenement-houses, shops, and finally a three-story brick hotel, which would do credit to any locality. This improvement necessitated an expenditure that the appearance of the place would scarcely justify at that time, but the good judgment of the ruling spirit has been well attested by the experience of the present. As before stated, the location is central; roads from all important points near converging, and drawing through here a vast amount of travel. The only communication with the extensive coal regions of Shamokin, from the west, is by road through Paxinos. These coal regions afford a market for the products of the farms and gardens, along the Susquehanna and its tributaries, scarcely equaled by the large marts of Philadelphia and suburbs. The scenery around the town is somewhat grand. Lofty hills rear their heads on all sides, as if contending in majesty with the clouds. These hills are peculiar in that they all have the appearance of individuality, shooting up prominently in isolated peaks, but all connected in one continuous range, which encircle the little basin where the town is located, and are designated as Shamokin Hills.

The improvements of the place consist of a blacksmith-shop, wheelwright-shop, shoemaker-shop, store, hay-scales, and last, but not least, the hotel. This last is worthy of more than passing notice. The location as described is somewhat isolated, and would seem, to the eye of the stranger, to be too much outside of the world to justify the erection of such an edifice as now graces the town. It was built by its present proprietor, of material found in the immediate locality. The brick were manufactured from clay dug from the flats, where a bed six feet in depth, of finest brick-clay, is found. The finishing is all of native timber, cut from the hills adjoining. The external and internal arrangements of the house are complete.

Limestone was discovered in excavating for the foundation of the hotel, which will be opened and burned for agricultural purposes, for which there is a large demand. For the origin of the name and first settlements, see Annals of Shamokin township.

RIVERSIDE.

Riverside, situate on the south bank of the north-east branch of the Susquehanna River, and opposite Danville, was laid out in 1869, and incorporated into a borough by an Act of Assembly, May, 1871. The contour of the land is gently sloping towards the river, soil fertile, water good, location desirable, and scenery attractive. The site of the town embraces about three hundred acres of land, originally taken up and surveyed, under patents to Elijah Weed, Isaac Craig, and others, as early as 1769, and at that period formed a part of Berks County. In 1868, one hundred and thirty acres of the above area was purchased from William Hancock by Thomas Beaver, Daniel Morgan, B. G. Welch, and J. H. Torrence, and by them divided up into town lots.

The idea of founding a town so near to Danville, was considered by the Solons of the neighborhood as an impracticable scheme, but, contrary to such expectations, two-thirds of all the lots were sold within two years, at prices varying from sixty to one hundred and fifty dollars for each lot, on the plan of ten per cent., cash down, and balance in thirty-six monthly instalments, at six per cent. interest. The first house erected on the town site was built by William Spotts, in May, 1869, and occupied by him shortly afterwards.

During this year, a number of houses were put up and occupied by their owners. In the year 1870, some twenty or more cottage-houses were erected and occupied. At this time, the need of better school accommodations being apparent, a few enterprising citizens advanced the means for the construction of a large and substantial two-story brick building, costing four thousand six hundred dollars, and rented the same to the school district, until such time as they would be able to purchase it.

There still being an active demand for town lots, William Faux, an adjoining land-owner, made an addition of thirty-two acres to the original plat, and disposed of the same in blocks and sections, in a few months realizing a handsome profit.

In the Fall of the year 1870, B. G. Welch, and others, purchased the adjoining farms of C. P. Gearhart and F. G. Van Nostrun, laying on the south side of the public road leading to Sunbury, containing about one hundred and forty acres, which were subsequently laid out to conform to the general plan of Riverside; and, about the same time, Daniel Leiby laid out an addition of twelve acres, on the west side of the town, making the entire area, embraced within the limits of the town, nearly three hundred and fifteen acres. In the year 1871, the town was incorporated into a borough. A post-office was established here by the department at Washington, and many new buildings were erected. At this time an effort was made, by the friends of the Methodist congregation, who were holding their meetings in the school-house, to secure means for the building of a chapel. In the earlier part of the following year, a sufficient sum had been raised, and work was commenced. The corner-stone was laid in June, 1872, with appropriate ceremonies, and the chapel dedicated to the service of God in December, of the same year. This denomination has accomplished a great deal of good in the community, many new members having been received into the church since its erection. Rev. Alfred B. Bowman was the first pastor, who was succeeded by Rev. James T. Wilson, the present incumbent.

During this year (1872), a bridge and boiler manufactory was built by the National Iron Company, of Danville, and leased to William H. Law, a master mechanic and bridge-builder. This manufactory has turned out many excellent wrought-iron bridges, which are now spanning streams in Lehigh, Northumberland, Schuylkill, and other counties of the Commonwealth.

Among other branches of business carried on in the place, may be mentioned Keim's brick manufactory, the Riverside Dairy Company, and Cliffe's green-house and nursery.

About the time the town was laid out, David Cliffe, an experienced florist and landscape gardener, settled here, starting a nursery on a small scale, gradually enlarging his business operations, until the name of Cliffe, as connected with the growing of flowers, plants, and trees, has become quite familiar to the country around.

Beautifully located on the high ground, in the south-east part of the borough, is the Mount Vernon Cemetery, and near which still stands what is known as the "Old Gearhart Church."

The school district, in 1873, obtained an act from the legislature, authorizing the issue of six thousand dollars, in six per cent. bonds, to purchase the building rented for school purposes, and to buy additional ground.

The present indebtedness of the district does not exceed three thousand four hundred dollars.

Owing to the financial panic of this year, business in every branch of trade became depressed, and has so continued for the past three years.

The growth of the new town has been retarded, and with the exception of a few cottage residences of the better class, but few notable improvements have been made.

At this time (1876), there are within the borough limits seventy buildings, five of which are brick.

The assessable value of town property is one hundred and three thousand dollars, and the population of the place, four hundred.

The people of Riverside have evinced commendable taste in the building of their houses and fences, in the planting of many trees, and in the general adornment of their grounds. In fact, no town of equal age within the Commonwealth can boast of better or more substantial improvements.

Intelligence, sobriety, and industry, characterize the citizens of the place.

PERSONAL SKETCHES

—OF—

PROMINENT MEN OF NORTHUMBERLAND CO.

HON. SAMUEL J. PACKER.

This great and good man, now deceased, was born in Bald Eagle Valley, Centre County, Pa., March 23d, 1799.

When a young man he learned the printer's trade, in Bellefonte, Centre County, and in 1820, came to Sunbury and established a paper called the "*Public Enquirer,*" which, however, he conducted for a brief period only. While engaged on this paper, he read law under the instruction of Hugh Bellas, Esq., and was admitted to the bar, in Sunbury August 23d, 1823, to which profession he devoted his life.

In 1830, he was elected to the Senate of Pennsylvania, where he served four years, and died in the Autumn, after the expiration of his term of office.

While in the Senate, he took a very active interest in the Internal Improvement system of the State, which was then in its infancy, and secured the passage of the act that afterwards resulted in the construction of what was then called the Danville and Pottsville, but now the Shamokin Valley and Pottsville Railroad.

As Chairman of a Select Committee, appointed by the Senate, he also prepared and made to that body the earliest Legislative Report regarding the Anthracite and Bituminous Coal Fields of the State. For the first extensive investigation of these interests, and the inauguration of important measures, which have since led to the development of these leading industries of the Commonwealth, Mr. Packer will ever be held in grateful remembrance.

He possessed great force of character and a remarkably cheerful, social disposition, and was admirably calculated to make friends, among whom was the Hon. Simon Cameron, who was very warmly attached to him. He was also endowed with great tact and energy, and became a very active and influential politician. He was a leading spirit in the initiatory steps of the campaign in which the Hon. Joseph Ritner was elected Governor of Pennsylvania, and it was understood that, had he lived, he would have been made Secretary of State under that administration. His life, however, so full of promise, was brought to an untimely close on October 20th, 1834, at the age of thirty-five.

Mr. Packer's wife was Miss Rachel Black, by whom he had a family of two sons and two daughters, the latter deceased. The youngest daughter, Mary, became Rev. Mrs. F. B. Riddel, of Huntingdon County, Pa. The second son, Samuel J. Packer, Jr., is the Cashier of the First National Bank of Sunbury. The oldest child,

HON. JOHN B. PACKER,

of Sunbury, was born in this borough, March 21st, 1824. When a child he attended school in Harrisburg, at the time his father was a member of the Legislature. After his father's death, which occurred when young Packer was in his eleventh year, he was, for some four years, a student at the old Sunbury Academy; first, under the tuition of Calo Pelton, and subsequently, that of F. M. Lebbrun; both gentlemen of high reputation as educators.

At the age of fifteen, he entered a corps of engineers where he was employed for nearly three years; first, on the Wiconisco Canal, and afterwards on the State's exploration of the route between Harrisburg and Pittsburg, on which is now constructed the Pennsylvania Railroad.

He then began the study of law in the office of Ebenezer Greenough, Esq., of Sunbury, and was admitted to the bar on August 6th, 1844. He at once entered on the practice of his profession in Sunbury.

In 1845, he was appointed Deputy Attorney General for Northumberland County, and served about three years.

In the Autumn of 1849, he was elected, on the Democratic ticket from Northumberland County, to the House of Representatives of the Pennsylvania Legislature, and was re-elected in 1850. At this time, Mr. Packer was the youngest member in that body. During the first session he served on the Judiciary Committee, and also upon the Committee on Internal Improvements. An important measure before the Legislature at this time, and one which created great interest throughout the Commonwealth, was the proposed amendment to the State Constitution, which provided that the judges should be elected by a direct vote of the people.

This amendment, Mr Packer supported in a vigorous, pointed and masterly argument, which at once established his reputation as a sound legislator and an able debater. His speech was very extensively copied by the press of the Commonwealth, and used in the campaign in support of the principle of an elective judiciary.

In the second session, (1851), Mr. Packer was made Chairman of the Committee on Estates and Escheats, and also served as a member of the Committee on Corporations.

The measure, however, which was of the greatest local interest to Northumberland County, and in which Mr. Packer took a leading part, was the passage of an act incorporating the Susquehanna Railroad Company, with authority to construct a railroad from the northern terminus of the York and Cumberland Railroad to Sunbury; also, with authority to construct branches to Williamsport and Wilkesbarre.

Prior to this, Philadelphia had looked with a jealous eye upon any improvement which would be likely to divert the trade of the Susquehanna Valley towards Baltimore, and up to that time, through her large delegation in the Legislature, had successfully resisted all attempts to secure a charter for the construction of a railroad or other improvement in that direction.

After a severe struggle, however, which lasted until the close of the session, the act authorizing the incorporation of the company just named, was finally passed, and in a short time thereafter, the company was organized, the route selected, and the work put under contract. The organization was effected by the election of William F. Packer,—subsequently Governor of Pennsylvania—president; John B. Packer, Simon Cameron, George F. Miller, Joseph H. Priestly, and Eli Slifer, directors, residing in the State of Pennsylvania, who were associated in the direction with a number of gentlemen from the city of Baltimore.

Upon the completion of this public thoroughfare, it was consolidated, under authority granted by the Legislatures of the States of Maryland and Pennsylvania, with the York and Cumberland, the York and Maryland, and the Baltimore and Susquehanna Railroads, under the title of the Northern Central Railway, forming a continuous line of railroad from the city of Baltimore to the borough of Sunbury, a distance of one hundred and thirty-eight miles.

During the construction of this work, and for some time after the consolidation, Mr. Packer was one of the Directors of the road, and from the commencement of the enterprise he has been the attorney of the company. Indeed, for a period of some ten years, he devoted much of his time to this undertaking, and it is largely owing to his energy and able management that its success became assured.

In 1857, Mr. Packer was elected President of the Bank of Northumberland, then located in Northumberland borough, but now known as the First National Bank of Sunbury, and still remains the head of this institution. It may be added that he succeeded his father-in-law, William Cameron, Esq., who was for several years the leading officer of the old bank.

Mr. Packer has not, however, on account of his connection with the bank, omitted his attention to his professional duties, but has prosecuted the same with great diligence and signal success. He has been engaged, on one side or the other, in all the leading causes tried in Northumberland County, as well as in many of the more important cases

Respectfully Yours
A. S. Cummings
Respectfully Yours
Yours Truly
Jeremiah Snyder

in some of the adjoining counties. Among these, were a number of very important railroad cases, and also a number of suits involving the original land titles of the Commonwealth, many of which have now become the leading ones in this branch of the law in the State.

Up to about the year 1856, Mr. Packer had acted with what was known as the Democratic party. He had, however, always been a firm advocate of a tariff for the protection of American industry, and the position upon this point assumed by many leading Democrats who began to control the policy of that party, did not coincide with Mr. Packer's views of political policy.

In 1852, he opposed the nomination of Mr. Buchanan for the Presidency, and subsequently, in 1856, when Mr. Buchanan was the Democratic candidate for the Presidency, Mr. Packer took a decided stand with the Republican party, in whose platform the protective system formed an important plank. Since then he has been prominently identified with this party.

During the late protracted struggle of the Union for existence, he stood boldly forth in the cause of the Government, and most efficiently supported the Administration in its efforts to subdue the Rebellion and maintain "*the Union, one and inseparable!*"

In the Autumn of 1868, Mr. Packer was elected on the Republican ticket, from the Fourteenth Congressional District of Pennsylvania, and has since then represented this district in the Lower House of the National Legislature, having been re-elected in 1870, 1872, and 1874.

At the time of his first three elections, this district was composed of the counties of Union, Snyder, Dauphin, Northumberland, and Juniata, the first three being Republican, and the last two Democratic.

When last elected, in 1874, the district comprised the counties of Northumberland, Lebanon, and Dauphin; the first being Democratic, and the last two Republican.

At each of these elections his native county—Northumberland—although usually pretty strongly Democratic, gave him a majority; and at the last canvass, in 1874, he carried that county by a majority of about six hundred; thus receiving a large majority in every county of his district.

During his eight years of Congressional service, Mr. Packer has taken a very active part in all the most important measures that have been before that body.

In the Forty-first Congress, commencing March 4th, 1869, he served on the "Committee on Banking and Currency." Among other important matters, this committee was charged with the investigation of the "Gold Panic," or the proceedings of "Black Friday," and made the memorable examination and report that exposed the fraud resorted to by Fisk, Gould & Co., to enrich themselves at the expense of the public.

It was also during this session that the original limitation on the amount of currency, as fixed by the original "Banking Act," was extended by a bill reported from this committee, which found in Mr. Packer an able supporter.

His effort, also, at the time of the pendency of the bill for the re-adjustment of the tariff, was an earnest protest against any reduction of the duty upon iron, and a masterly defense of the policy of protection to American industries.

In the Forty-second Congress Mr. Packer was Chairman of the Committee on "Railways and Canals," to which were referred many important measures affecting the internal improvements of the country, and particularly those proposed to be constructed in the Territories of the United States.

In the Forty-third Congress he served as Chairman of the Committee on "Post-Offices and Post-Roads." The duties of this committee were very arduous and responsible, being charged, as they were, with the legislation relating to the management of the entire Postal System of the United States, which has grown into proportions so gigantic as to be truly astonishing. One of the leading questions before this committee was the restoration of the Franking Privilege in its application to the distribution of public documents, by which provision such Congressional documents would be transmitted to the people free of postage; also, in its application to the free transmission of newspapers in the County where published.

As chairman of this committee, Mr. Packer reported a bill securing the free transmission of newspapers through the mails, in the county wherein published, and after very considerable effort, succeeded in effecting its passage, by virtue of which this privilege has been since enjoyed.

Among other measures reported by this committee was one to prevent what is known as "Straw-bidding." This was an act of very great importance, and was designed to protect the Government against the fraudulent devices resorted to by mail-contractors to extort from the Postal Service Department exorbitant pay for carrying the mails.

In the Forty-fourth Congress Mr. Packer served as a member of the Committee on "Foreign Affairs."

On the 7th of October, 1876, he was, for the fifth time, unanimously nominated for Congress by the Republican Conference of the Fourteenth Congressional District, but declined the nomination, "out of a regard for the rights of the other portions of the district;" whereupon the conference adopted the following resolution:—

"*Resolved*, That the Republicans of the Fourteenth Congressional District have watched the course of their distinguished representative in Congress, Hon. John B. Packer, with great interest, and they cordially approve and endorse it. His record throughout has been pure and stainless, his advocacy and support of Republican principles has been consistent and efficient, and his whole public service has been honorable to himself, and reflects credit on the constituency whom he has represented. They yield to his desire to retire from public service with sincere regret, and assure him of their undiminished respect and confidence."

In declining this honor, and that, too, in a district where a nomination is equivalent to an election, Mr. Packer exhibited a magnanimity and self-forgetfulness that command alike the fullest confidence and the highest admiration; and by this course he has set an example of self-sacrifice and unswerving adhesion to the right, which is in happy keeping with that high-toned honor for which he has ever been distinguished. His public career has been an exceptionably creditable one. In his eight years' service in the National Assembly, there has never been a suspension of his integrity; while the ability and fidelity with which he has represented the various interests of his country, have placed him in the front rank of American patriots.

His courteous dignity, urbane bearing and generous sympathies, moreover, characterize him as a gentleman of great moral worth.

On May 22d, 1851, Mr. Packer was united in marriage with Miss Mary M., daughter of William Cameron, Esq., of Lewisburg, Pa., and niece of the Hon. Simon Cameron, of Harrisburg. This union has been blessed with a family of two sons and four daughters—one daughter deceased. The oldest son, William C. Packer, studied law with his father, and was admitted to practice in Sunbury, on the 5th of November, 1872, and has before him a future full with promise.

DAVID ROCKEFELLER, Esq.

This widely-known and useful citizen of Sunbury was born in Northumberland County, on the 6th of September, 1802.

In the early part of his manhood he was engaged in the mercantile business, but in 1820 entered the field as a surveyor, which occupation he followed up to the time of his decease. His services in this department were sought after in the trial of nearly every important ejectment case tried within the last thirty years or more in Northern Pennsylvania. Evidences of his efficient labor may be found in Berks, Lebanon, Schuylkill, Dauphin, Northumberland, Columbia, Montour, Lycoming, Clinton, Centre, Cameron, Bradford, Potter, Elk, Tioga, and other counties of this State.

In this important profession he won a reputation far and near, and became one of the most distinguished Surveyors in the Commonwealth. He had been preceded in this vocation by his uncle, Jacob Rockefeller. He filled the position of County Surveyor for many years, and was practically filling it at the time of his death.

His last service was for Mr. John Haas, of Upper Augusta Township.

He possessed a most remarkable memory, which enabled him to give, with perfect accuracy and without reference to his notes, the minute details of surveys made more than a quarter of a century ago.

During his long and active life he filled many prominent official positions. For a period of twenty years he occupied the office of Deputy Sheriff; a part of the time under Henry Reader, of McEwensville.

In 1848 he was appointed Register and Recorder of this county by Governor Johnson. He was a candidate for the same position afterwards, but was beaten by a small majority.

He was also appointed Notary Public by Governor Curtin, and subsequently by Governors Geary and Hartranft, and was filling the position when he died.

For several days previous to his demise he had been feeling somewhat ill, but notwithstanding this indisposition, still adhered to his usual work of surveying. This exertion, and the oppressive heat, overcame him, and he was subsequently found prostrated on the porch of his office, with an attack of paralysis. He lingered in this paralyzed condition for eight days, when he passed suddenly away, on the morning of the 22d of August, 1876, at the age of seventy-three years, eleven months and sixteen days.

Mr. Rockefeller was a man of a remarkably social disposition, and very popular among his many acquaintances. He possessed a constitution of more than ordinary vigor, and applied himself with indefatigable industry to his profession; and his death is especially regretted by those whose honest title to lands is still in dispute.

In his family and social relations he was kind, affectionate, and genial. He had every opportunity to become one of the wealthiest citizens in the northern part of the State, but he abhorred covetousness, and his easy and generous disposition caused him to be the friend and counselor of all who called upon him for aid.

Mr. Rockefeller had a family of five sons, one of whom, at the time of his premature decease, possessed a rapidly-growing reputation in the legal profession. The only surviving members of his family, are his widow, Mrs. Catherine Rockefeller, and his oldest son, the

HON. WILLIAM M. ROCKEFELLER,

of Sunbury. He was born in that place, August 18, 1830. His education was obtained at the Sunbury Academy, and during his vacations or absences from the same he was variously employed in working on a farm, teaching school, and in the capacity of clerk in the store of Ira T. Clement, then, as now, one of the leading business men of the place.

In 1847 he commenced reading law under the tuition of the Hon. J. B. Packer, of Sunbury, but upon the election of this gentleman to the Legislature, young Rockefeller repaired to the office of Judge Jordan, with whom he completed his legal studies, and was admitted to the bar in 1850.

He began the practice of his profession in Minersville, Schuylkill County, but in about a year returned to his native town, where he has since resided.

In early life he entered the field of politics, and was a prominent member of the Democratic party. In the Gubernatorial campaign of 1851, he was Secretary of the Bigler Club, of Schuylkill county, and in 1852 was President of the Pierce and King Club, of Northumberland County. He also held, for several years, the office of Chief Burgess of the Borough of Sunbury. In 1871 he was elected to the office he now holds, of President Judge of the Eighth Judicial District—one of the largest in the State. Although this district was, at the time, strongly Democratic, Judge Rockefeller carried it by a Republican majority of over fifteen hundred.

The *Legal Intelligencer*, at the time of his election, remarked, that "Our State Reports, from 1. Casey to 14 P. F. Smith, show that he has been counsel in the most important cases from his district." An innate fondness for legal studies has, for some years past, inclined him to give to the same his almost exclusive devotion.

The Judge is married and has three children.

SIMON P. WOLVERTON.

The gentleman whose name forms the caption of this biographical sketch, is a leading member of the Sunbury bar. He is the second child, in a family of two sons and three daughters, of Joseph Wolverton, Esq., now residing in Lawrence County, Pa., and was born in Northumberland County, January 28th, 1837.

Up to the age of seventeen he worked on a farm, enjoying such educational facilities as the common schools of that day presented. He there spent a couple of years in the Danville Academy, under the tuition of Prof. J. E. Bradley, employing his winters, however, in teaching; but while so doing, keeping up with his classes in the academic studies.

At the age of nineteen he repaired to Lewisburg University, and entered the Freshman class in its third term, and having finished the Sophomore year, left the University with a view of studying law. He was actuated to this step by the fact that he was dependent upon his own resources, and, at that time, felt compelled to forego the advantages that would accrue from a completion of his collegiate course. To replenish his already depleted purse, he took charge of a school in Danville, but after teaching six months, although he was then quite deeply in debt, came to the determination to struggle through college, and trust to his after efforts for the payment of his creditors.

Accordingly, in September, 1858, he returned to the University at Lewisburg, and by extra energy and application, completed the studies of the Junior and Senior years in the time of one year, and in 1860 graduated, wearing the honors of his class in a Latin salutatory. At this time, he was six hundred dollars in debt, all of which he subsequently liquidated by teaching.

In September of this year, he came to Sunbury and became principal of what was known as the Sunbury Academy, which position he held until April, 1862. Upon taking charge of the school, he also began the study of law under the instruction of H. J. Wolverton, a relative. Upon the death of the latter, Mr. Wolverton entered the office of Judge Alexander Jordan, with whom he finished his legal preparation, and was admitted to the Bar in Sunbury, in April, 1862, when he immediately opened an office and began practice.

Soon after his admission to the Bar, he was employed in an important criminal case which brought Mr. Wolverton into notice as a promising young lawyer of fine ability. Since that time, he has been employed in almost every case of importance tried in the County.

The disaster to the Union arms at Fredericksburg and Chancellorsville, in the late Civil war, emboldened the Southern army to attempt for a second time, an invasion of the North, and accordingly, a proclamation was issued by the President, calling for one hundred thousand men. On the 26th of June, 1863, Governor Curtin called for sixty thousand men for State service for ninety days. Under this call, twenty-eight regiments were organized. A company was raised in Sunbury by Captain S. P. Wolverton, letter F, and joined the Thirty-sixth Regiment at Harrisburg, under Colonel H. C. Alleman. It was mustered in July 4th, 1863, and discharged August 11th, 1863. During the time of their service, Captain Wolverton and his men were constantly on duty. Although the campaigns of these emergency companies were bloodless, their prompt response to the call of the country gave sure guarantee of their readiness for duty, and of their patriotism.

In September of the previous year, Captain Wolverton also recruited Company E of the Eighteenth Regiment, for the emergency service upon Stewart's invasion of Pennsylvania. The company was held in service, however, only a few days.

In 1867, Mr. Wolverton received the appointment as Attorney for the Philadelphia and Reading Railroad Company. About the same time, he was also appointed Attorney for the Danville, Hazleton, and Wilkesbarre Railroad Company, and has since been counselor for both organizations. He was also the prime mover for obtaining the charter of the last named road, and was one of its first Directors.

Mr. Wolverton is endowed with almost unlimited powers of endurance, and while in college disciplined himself to work from fifteen to eighteen hours out of the twenty-four, allowing himself an average of not more than six hours for sleep. This he then felt necessitated to do on account of his straitened pecuniary circumstances, and the same habit of close application to duty still obtains. When not absent from home on professional business, he may be found in his office at seven o'clock in the morning; and he not unfrequently remains there till near midnight. Perhaps no man in the State performs so much severe, professional labor, and is at the same time so regular in his habits.

Such steady application and unremitting toil, however, must, sooner or later, tell upon the strongest constitution, and the fear is entertained by the friends of Mr. Wolverton that his unusually arduous and useful life may be unduly shortened by the burdens he is now carrying.

Mr. Wolverton early realized the fact that the highest success in any avocation is attendant only upon a singleness of aim, coupled with persevering toil. As, therefore, it was his greatest ambition to excell in the practice of the law, he has applied all his energies in that direction; and, although he has been often solicited to become a candidate at different times for various positions of public trust and honor, he has declined to do so, and has held himself aloof from all active participation in politics, and made his profession his specialty.

As might be expected, his career has been crowned with most signal success, and the legal eminence to which, when a youth, he so ambitiously aspired, has been happily reached.

In this brief sketch of the life of this gentleman, is presented a most striking example of what can be accomplished by a resolute determination and persevering effort;—an example well worthy of imitation by all young men whose ambition prompts them to aspire to a high place in some noble calling. "*Perseverantia omnia vincit.*"

Socially, Mr. Wolverton is a man of genial manners and of obliging spirit, and combines all the elements of a thorough gentleman.

He married Miss Elizabeth D. Hendricks, daughter of Benjamin Hendricks, of Sunbury, and has a family of two daughters.

HON. T. H. PURDY.

The subject of this sketch was born in Purdytown, Wayne County, Pennsylvania, June 20th, 1831. His father, Harvey Purdy, was a native of the same place, and was a farmer and lumberman by occupation. His mother was Ruth Clark, of Clarksgreen, Luzerne County, Pennsylvania. His ancestors on his father's side were among the settlers of Wayne County, previous to the Wyoming massacre. His great-grandfather, Rev. William Purdy, was the founder of what is known as the Abington Baptist Association. His grand-father on his mother's side was Rev. William Clark, a native of New England.

Mr. Purdy's boyhood and early youth were spent in the lumber woods and on the farm, and his facilities for education were those of the winter common school. After his father's death, which occurred when young Purdy was seventeen years of age, he carried on the lumber and farm business for some two years, during which period he spent a short time at the Madison Academy, in Luzerne County, and also taught a school during one winter.

When about twenty years of age, he became assistant instructor in the Madison Academy, where he spent two years as teacher and student. At the expiration of this time, the principal of the academy, Professor H. D. Walker, was elected principal of the academy connected with the University of Lewisburg, and urged Mr. Purdy to accompany him to that place, which he did, and became a teacher in the academy there, and at the same time entered as a student, the freshmen's class of the university, where, at about the age of twenty-seven, he completed his course.

About a year later, he was induced by the stockholders of the *Union Argus*, at Lewisburg, to assume the editorial management of that paper, and, at the expiration of two years, he had bought up all the stock and owned the establishment. He then sold the same, and continued the study of law in the office of Judge Joseph C. Bucher, of Lewisburg, with whom he had commenced reading a year previous.

On the 8th of March, 1861, by the urgent solicitation of a number of the citizens of Northumberland County, he came to Sunbury, and started the *Northumberland County Democrat*, beginning with only three hundred subscribers.

In the Autumn of 1864, Mr. Purdy was elected to the House of Representatives of the Pennsylvania Legislature, and re-elected in 1865.

In 1867, he sold the *Democrat* to Messrs. Eichholtz and Day, the paper at that time having a circulation of two thousand nine hundred. He then finished his law studies with Judge Alexander Jordan, of Sunbury, and was admitted to the bar here in 1868. Previous to this, Mr. Purdy had been, from time to time, purchasing various tracts of land adjoining the borough of Sunbury on the east, which are now laid out into lots, and constitute what is known as Purdytown. The lots have been nearly all disposed of, and are already covered with dwellings, stores, shops, etc., forming quite a pleasant little village.

In 1866, he purchased a beautiful knoll of some two acres, in the vicinity, which he beautified with trees, shrubs, flowers, and walks, and upon which, in 1872, he erected his present palatial residence, a view of which will be found among the illustrations of this work.

In 1870, Mr. Purdy was connected with S. P. Wolverton, Esq., in obtaining the charter for the Sunbury Gas Works, and the establishment of the same, which works are principally owned by those gentlemen.

In 1872, he delivered, by appointment, the historical oration at the centennial celebration of Sunbury, in that year. It was a carefully prepared and very valuable production.

In April, 1870, Mr. Purdy, in company with Dr. H. Long, of Sunbury, and J. B. Ewing, Esq., of Harrisburg, purchased a large tract of land lying between the Pennsylvania Steel Works and the Lochiel Iron Works, below Harrisburg, which land has been laid out into a town called Ewington, and thirty-two thousand dollars' worth of lots were sold between April 10th and September 1st, 1870. A large number of buildings also have been erected thereon.

On December 10th, 1861, Mr. Purdy was married to Miss Mary E., daughter of Dr. Robert E. James, of Northampton County, Pennsylvania. This union has been blessed with the birth of three sons and one daughter, one of the former deceased.

Mr. Purdy is a gentleman of superior mental organization, clear judgment, great caution, and of unusually fine business abilities. What, perhaps, is most noticeable in his character is his remarkably quiet, unassuming disposition, and his candid, unimpassioned manner of dealing with things. With these elements are united a power of reading human nature, which is developed far above the average. He belongs to the solid, conservative class of men, and is held in high esteem by the community.

In politics he is a Democrat, to which party he has ever maintained an unswerving fidelity. In religious views he is a Baptist, and has been for many years the leading member of this denomination in Sunbury.

Mr. Purdy possesses also a large amount of genial humor, coupled with æsthetic literary abilities of a high order, as is illustrated in his historical oration at the Sunbury centennial, on July 4th, 1872. He has also in preparation a poetical volume on science and religion, some of the advance pages of which the biographer has been privileged to examine, and from which, had he permission, he would gladly make some extracts. In all that constitutes the essentials of true poetry, the work will compare favorably with the productions of our best authors.

THE CAKE FAMILY.

JOHN CAKE, Sr.

This gentleman was a native of Scotland, and when quite a young man was brought to America, sometime previous to the Revolution. His wife was Jane Cummin, also born in Scotland, who was likewise brought to this country prior to the great American struggle, and at the age of twelve, was at Valley Forge at the time that General Washington was there encamped.

Mr. and Mrs. Cake had but one child,

JOHN CAKE, Jr.,

who was born in Chester County, Pa., and was brought to Northumberland, this county, when a child, where he grew up to manhood, and married Miss Sarah McCord, a native of Easton, Pa., who came with her father's family to Northumberland when she was quite young.

Mr. Cake was a cooper by trade, and for many years carried on the business in Northumberland quite extensively, frequently having in his employ at one time, as many as thirty-five or forty workmen. His wife's father, Mr. Joseph McCord, was a carpenter and builder, which business he followed in Northumberland to a good old age.

Mr. and Mrs. Cake died in Northumberland, the former at the age of seventy-eight, and the latter in 1873, in her eighty-fifth year.

Mr. Cake had a family of six sons and four daughters, as follows:

Colonel J. W. Cake, of Sunbury; Mrs. Mary Ann (John) Harlan, now a widow, and residing in Tamaqua, Schuylkill County, Pa.; Sarah M. Cake, Isaac M. Cake, Lucetta R. Cake, and George Cake, all residents of Northumberland, Pa.; General Henry L. Cake, of Philadelphia. In addition to these, were Alphæus and Sarah, both of whom died in infancy.

GENERAL HENRY L. CAKE,

the youngest son, served four years in the late war, going out as colonel of the Twenty-fifth Pennsylvania Volunteer Infantry, for the three months' service, under Generals Stone and Patterson. He subsequently organized the Ninety-sixth Pennsylvania Volunteer Infantry, at Pottsville, and served as its colonel for nearly three years, and during most of the time was commander of a brigade; his last engagement being the famous battle of "Antietam," in which he led the terrible charge at "South Mountain."

COLONEL JOSEPH WARREN CAKE.

This gentleman is the eldest son of John Cake, Jr., just noticed. He was born in Northumberland, Pennsylvania, on the 25th of November, 1811. Being the son of a pioneer, he was cradled in the wilderness, and reared amid surroundings the humble nature of which the youth of the present day can form no adequate conception. His opportunities for learning were simply those of the pioneer common school, supplemented by a few years' attendance upon what was then known as the Northumberland Academy, presided over by the late Judge Robert Grier. The studies pursued here at that time were simply the common English branches, with the exception of a small class just beginning Latin. Mr. Cake, however, subsequently prosecuted his studies by himself, and acquired quite a considerable knowledge of the Natural Sciences, and also some acquaintance with the Latin and Greek classics. By extensive reading and close observation, moreover, he has accumulated a large fund of general information. He is one of those practical, self-made men, who are of far more value to a community than the erudite theorist, who, however well versed in the lore of books, is unable to utilize his learning in its application to the matter-of-fact affairs of life.

When about eighteen years of age, he went to Harrisburg, where, under the direction of Andrew Keefer—brother-in-law to General Cameron—he learned the business of ornamental painting, an occupation for which he early developed a special talent. His progress was very rapid. In the brief period of six months he had acquired such proficiency in the art that he was promoted to the position of foreman in the establishment, and supplanted a man who had been imported from Philadelphia to fill this place.

Between two and three years were devoted to this trade, and although he might have taken a front rank as an artist, he nevertheless made choice of the law as his profession, and at the age of twenty-one began the study under William McClure, of Harrisburg, with whom he remained about a year and a half. He then repaired to Muncy, and, spending about the same time, finished off in the office of the late William Cox Ellis.

Early in 1837, he was admitted to the bar in Williamsport, Lycoming County, Pa. In May, of the same year, he located in Harrisburg, and, with a few books, began the practice of his profession, in which he continued for ten years. During this time he met with very encouraging success, and realized from his practice a handsome income.

On the 1st of August, 1839, Mr. Cake was united in marriage with Miss Julia Adam, a daughter of John Adam, of North Canaan, Connecticut. Miss Adam's grandfather was also John Adam, Sr., and his grandmother, an only child of a Mr. John Forbes, in whose life may be mentioned the following interesting reminiscence:

Early in the settlement of Connecticut, a Mr. Livingston, a very wealthy Scotch-Irish immigrant, became the owner of quite a large section of land in the vicinity of North Canaan, in that State. He employed a poor blacksmith by the name of John Forbes to make for him a trip-hammer, the price of which was to be some sixteen dollars. When Mr. Forbes had manufactured the hammer, Mr. Livingston, instead of paying him the sixteen dollars, gave him a title to a large hill near by, at the same time assuring him that it contained vast quantities of iron ore, and advising him to build a furnace and "try out" the iron. Mr. Forbes informed Mr. Livingston that he had no means with which to erect a furnace, upon which Mr. Livingston offered to furnish the money for that purpose, and to wait for his pay till Mr. Forbes could make it out of the iron, at fifteen cents on the dollar of the sales.

Mr. Forbes and his wife were greatly disappointed in not receiving the cash for the hammer. They knew very little about this speculation in iron ore, and, at that time, cared less. Mr. Forbes had but little faith in the project, but his wife finally advised him to accept, and rather spitefully added, that "If the thing failed, and Mr. Livingston should lose his investment, he could blame nobody but himself!"

The furnace was built and paid for, and the proceeds from the sales of the iron made Mr. Forbes independently wealthy. He had a daughter—an only child—who, as just stated, became the wife of John Adam, Sr., and grandmother of Mrs. Colonel J. W. Cake.

Mr. Adam had two daughters and four sons. Lucy Adam became Mrs. Judge Walker, of Lenox, Massachusetts; the other daughter married a Mr. John Beckley, of North Canaan, Connecticut.

The sons were Samuel, Leonard, John, and William, of whom William is the only one surviving, and resides in North Canaan.

John Adam, the third son, was father of Mrs. Colonel Cake, and his wife was Miss Amy Brown, a relative of the immortal Ossawatomie Brown.

Colonel Cake has had a family of three daughters and two sons, as follows:

Alice E. Cake, married James G. Lowery, of Elmira, New York, and now resides in Pottsville, Pennsylvania.

Joseph Warren Cake, Jr., a member of the Pottsville bar.

John Adam Cake, a member of the Sunbury bar, and also president of the Augusta Bank.

Amy Brown Cake, married Joseph Samson Adam, an iron dealer and chemist, of North Canaan, Connecticut.

Edith Brown Cake died in infancy.

JOHN ADAM CAKE

was born in Harrisburg, August 25th, 1846. His education was obtained in the academy at Pottsville, Pa.; the Russell Military Academy, of New Haven, Conn., and Yale and Princeton Colleges. After being employed, for something over a year, as assistant cashier, under his father, in the office of the Philadelphia Coal Company, he commenced reading law with Hon. Benjamin H. Brewster, at that time Attorney-General of Pennsylvania. In the Fall of 1868, he came to Sunbury, finished his law studies under Judge Wm. M. Rockefeller, and was admitted to the bar in March, 1870. In 1872, he received the nomination of the working men of Northumberland County, as a candidate to the Constitutional Convention. In the Spring of 1873, he was elected president of the Augusta Bank of Sunbury. He also served two terms as a member of the town council, being elected as an independent candidate.

In February, 1868, Mr. Cake was married to Miss Minnie E. McCullough, of Shippensburg, Cumberland County, Pa. He has a family of six children—three deceased.

In 1842, Colonel Cake conducted a suit in the United States Court, in Philadelphia, under the Fugitive Slave Law Act, which resulted quite complimentary to him.

Three male slaves had made their escape from Harford County, Md., the property of John and George Hall; and, while passing through Perry County, Pa., when near the Juniata River, they were rescued by the enraged populace, and their pursuers, the Halls, were thrown into the canal—horse, buggy, and all. The Halls applied for redress to Colonel Cake, who, under the law as it at that time existed, brought suit against the leaders of the mob, which came to trial, as just stated. The case was argued before Judge Baldwin. Colonel Cake, and Ovid F. Johnson, the Attorney-General of the State, being associated together in the prosecution, and Wm. M. Meredith and Henry M. Watts, for the defense.

There being two cases, Mr. Johnson conducted the first, and Colonel Cake the second. As a compliment to the masterly effort of Mr Cake, on this occasion, may be quoted the brief, but significant charge of Judge Baldwin. Drawing his watch from his pocket, Judge Baldwin said:

"Gentlemen of the Jury: I am obliged to go to Trenton to hold court, and the boat will start * * * minutes; therefore, I have no time to make a lengthy charge to you. But Mr. Cake has explained this case in a remarkably clear and candid manner. You *will pay attention to what he has said.*"

The jury returned an immediate verdict for the prosecution.

In the Autumn of 1846, was organized the Farmer's Bank of Schuylkill County, at Schuylkill Haven, Pa., of which institution Mr. Cake was made the cashier, and in the Spring of 1847, he moved his family to this place. In 1850, it was determined, by the board of directors, to move the bank to Pottsville, which was done early in 1851, when Mr. Cake changed his residence accordingly. The charter of this bank ran for a period of twenty-five years, beginning in 1845, so that in 1870, its affairs were wound up and the institution ceased to be. During its whole existence, Colonel Cake was identified with it, either as president or cashier.

For most of the time during this period, Mr. Cake was also engaged in business projects in Sunbury, having, in 1858, purchased what was known as the old "Scott Farm," and in 1859, the old "Hunter Farm," and shortly afterwards, the "Bayers," "Bright," and "Haas" properties, making, in all, upwards of four hundred acres.

At this time, these pieces of real estate presented a most uninviting, dilapidated appearance. The "Scott" farm, especially, was in a very neglected condition, and was purchased for sixty-eight dollars per acre. It contained one hundred and sixty-seven acres. The "Hunter" farm, of one hundred and six acres, was bought about one year later, for one hundred and fifty dollars per acre.

When Colonel Cake made the purchase of these lands, it was more with a view of holding them as an estate, than with the expectation of any very near speculation in them. His business sagacity, however, assured him that the time would eventually come when these acres would acquire a value far greater than the nominal amount at which they were then purchased. His chief object, however, as just stated was to obtain a piece of "*terra firma*," upon which he could settle down secure against the manifold contingencies that necessarily attach to all business transactions.

The site of his present residence is one upon which his eye had long rested, with a conviction that it might be made a most delightful home, and the wisdom of his purchase of the same, together with the other adjoining properties, has been fully demonstrated.

At this time, the Sunbury and Erie Railroad—now the Philadelphia and Erie—was constructed only to Lock Haven, and Mr. Cake clearly foresaw that when this thoroughfare should be completed to Erie, it would cause an instantaneous rise in the value of property in Sunbury and vicinity. Hence to locate just at this particular point, there was presented to him the two-fold inducement of securing a beautiful home, and of getting into his possession a property which would eventually become very valuable. The realization, however, of this latter feature, came much sooner than he had allowed himself to expect.

In September, 1863, this plateau of four hundred acres was laid out into town lots, and now forms what is known as

CAKE'S ADDITION TO SUNBURY.

It extends from the old borough line on the South to the North Branch of the Susquehanna on the north, a distance of more than half a mile; and from the main river on the west to the Catawissa road on the east, a distance of about a mile. The tract forms a part of the "Manor of Pomfret."

Since the last-named date, Colonel Cake has sold off lots to the amount of one hundred and fifty thousand dollars, having disposed of about one-third of the original area.

This addition is familiarly known as

CAKETOWN,

the streets of which are very wide, and cross each other at right angles. In selecting the names for certain streets, Colonel Cake conceived the unique yet appropriate idea of christening them with the *pre-nomina* of his children.

While carrying on these operations here, Mr. Cake had his home in Pottsville, and from 1858 to 1867, he was in frequent passage between that point and Sunbury, doing business as a banker in the former, and as the projector of a new town in the vicinity of the latter place.

In April, 1867, he received the appointment of Collector in the United States Custom House, Philadelphia, and was there till May, 1869. The duties of this position he "discharged with great ability and fidelity, and to the entire satisfaction of the government."

Since the last-named date, he has made his home alternately in Pottsville and Sunbury, having a fine residence (besides other houses) in both of these localities. His Sunbury residence, erected in 1862, a view of which will be found among the illustrations of the Northumberland County History, is most beautifully located on the east bank of the Susquehanna River, a few rods below the junction of the north and west branches of that noble stream. Just across the river, on the west side, tower the mountain-like bluffs of Snyder County, clad in their drapery of evergreen, presenting a scene of beauty on which the eye may always rest without weariness or satiety.

The country, too, for miles around, is of the most picturesque character. From a hill on the Catawissa road on the east, is presented a view of superlative beauty. From this point, facing the west, may be seen the neat borough of Northumberland, lying on the right at a distance of two miles up the river, on a point of land formed by the confluence of its two branches; while on the side opposite to the town, looms up the historic promontory of "Blue Hill," to a perpendicular height of perhaps five hundred feet from the water's edge. Immediately in front lies the level tract of land of four hundred acres, which now constitutes "Cake's Addition to Sunbury," beautifully laid out into spacious lots, with wide streets, many of which are already lined with shade-trees.

Here, too, are located the extensive shops of the Philadelphia and Erie Railroad Company, from which there arises the city-like din of industry, said shops being the headquarters of over four hundred employees. On the left hand, reposes the old borough of Sunbury, nestled under its century of trees, and washed on the south by a placid lakelet, formed by the waters of the Shamokin dam.

The two boroughs are thus hemmed in by the mountain ridges that skirt the river, and for miles, both up and down the stream, there is presented to the eye a grand panoramic view of hill and valley, bluff and river, town and country, with all their characteristic points of beauty, the whole forming a scene of surpassing loveliness.

Indeed, some who have traveled in the east, and have looked upon the finest Indian scenery, unhesitatingly declare that they have seen *nothing that will equal, in beauty and grandeur, the surroundings of the borough of Sunbury!*

But, aside from the exquisite loveliness of the location, this point presents some of the finest facilities for manufactures to be found in the country. It is a natural centre, with water-power sufficient to run the mills of a continent, while inexhaustible supplies of coal underlie the surface of the country for leagues around. From this point, also, radiate five lines of railroads, which put it in immediate communication with all points of the compass. The educational facilities of the place, moreover, are fast taking rank among the first in the Commonwealth, while for healthfulness, the location cannot be surpassed.

From its combination of all these important features,—a combination so seldom found, and yet so essential to business success and comfort,—Sunbury presents one of the most inviting points, to enterprising and wealthy capitalists, to be found in the country, and it is surprising that a greater number of such men have not, before this time, been attracted here. Colonel Cake, however, is one of a few who have taken advantage of the superior natural advantages of the place.

A bridge has been projected by Mr. Cake, to be thrown across the Susquehanna at the foot of Packer street, thus effecting a direct business connection between Northumberland and Snyder counties, and attracting a portion of the trade of Snyder and Union counties to that part of Sunbury which he has so much improved. It is estimated that the cost of this structure will be some sixty thousand dollars, of which Mr. Cake has subscribed twenty-five thousand.

At the risk of a little repetition, we subjoin the following description of Sunbury and vicinity, from the pen of Hon. Truman H. Purdy, of this place; it being an extract from his historical oration at the Centennial Celebration of Sunbury, July 4th, 1872:

"The same causes which made Sunbury an important Indian town, make it an important American city. It is a railroad and commercial centre—a city in its infancy, surrounded by all the elements of wealth, and by nature's richest scenery. To be convinced of this, go to the grave of John Mason, upon Blue hill, or up to the old prospect chestnut, upon Catawissa road, and feast your eye upon the unmatched beauty of the scene. From out the misty distance come the creeping trains upon six lines of rail. The old canals unite their waters with the gentleness of age. The mighty rocks rise up as sentinels on either side. Two growing towns lift up their spires, and from their stacks send up the smoky ensign of a nation's toil. View next the green-clad islands which seem to rise and slumber in the silvery sheen below, laved with the rippling waters from these mingling Susquehannas, coming, as they do, from Wyalusing and Wyoming, on the north, to join the mists of Clearfield and the silvery fountains of Emporium. What more could nature add, unless it were the broad, blue mirror of Shamokin Dam?

"These are stately Susquehannas, joining waters for the bay,
And on either side are towering mountain summits, grim and grey.
'Tis a masterpiece of nature, picture-like from nature's hands,
And amidst it, in its beauty, our old Indian city stands—
Queen of all these rolling rivers, rich in history sublime,
Crowned with glories undiminished, from the unremembered time;
Stored with relics rare and olden, relics which no charm outvies,
Reaching, with their shadowy fingers, back to sacred memories.
What the marvel that such beauty breathes upon the heart a spell?
What the wonder that such grandeur wakens enterprise as well?
Why should nature not combine, linked with art's enchanting chain,
Giving impulse to our labor, health and brilliancy to brain?
Yes, from out this regal city, sitting on its wave-washed throne,
Towers a standard for the people, for us all to gaze upon;
'Tis the standard of improvement, 'tis by freedom's toil upheld,
And the furnace-blast shall fan it, and out of nature's field
Shall come the coal and lumber, and the iron from earth's breast,
To reward us for our labor—and our sons may tell the rest,
When the moss-grown clock of ages shall have tolled for you and me,
And have measured off the summers of another century."

HON. ALEXANDER JORDAN.

If genuine yet modest worth entitles any one to a place among these biographical sketches, no one is more worthy of this honor than the gentleman whose name forms the caption of this article.

He was born in Jaysburg, Lycoming County, Pa., May 10th, 1798. He is the second son, and third child, in a family of three sons and four daughters. His father was Samuel Jordan, and his mother Rosanna McClester, both natives of Pennsylvania. In 1802, the family moved to Milton, where the parents died, at an advanced age.

When a lad of about fourteen years of age, young Jordan had a military experience of a few weeks, serving in the militia, in the war of 1812, in the capacity of deputy commissary.

After a three years' clerkship in a store in Milton, he repaired to Sunbury, where he became clerk in the office of Mr. Hugh Bellas, at that time Prothonotary of Northumberland County, and also an attorney at law.

Although possessing a natural bias towards mechanical and artistic pursuits, Mr. Jordan conceived the idea of making the law his profession, and began the study of the same under the direction of Mr. Bellas. As his duties in the Prothonotary's office required all his attention during the day, the young law student was limited to the night time for his study. As evidence, however, of the diligence with which he applied himself, it may be remarked that even under such disadvantages, he exceeded even the present demands for admission to the bar.

After the resignation of Mr. Bellas, Mr. Jordan continued to serve as clerk under the successive Prothonotaries, Dr. Geo. W. Brown, and Andrew Albright.

In 1820, he was admitted to the bar, and most successfully practiced his profession in Union, Northumberland, and Montour counties. The bar of Northumberland County, at this time, was composed of some of the most distinguished lawyers of the State—Hall, Bradford, Bellas, Greenough, Hepburn, and Marr; all belonged to a high order of acquirement and ability.

In 1850, Mr. Jordan was elected President Judge of the Eighth Judicial District, without opposition. At the close of his first term, of ten years, at the earnest solicitation of his friends, he became a candidate for re-election, and obtained a handsome majority over his opponent. He was likewise solicited, near the close of his second term, to accept a nomination for a third term, but he declined on the score of feeble health.

Judge Jordan has been twice married; first, on May 11th, 1820, to Miss Mary, daughter of Daniel Hurley; and a second time on October 13th, 1858, to Miss Hannah, daughter of David Rittenhouse, a lineal descendant of the celebrated Natural Philosopher, David Rittenhouse, of Philadelphia.

In August, 1832, he was ordained an elder in the Presbyterian Church, which position he still honors.

For nearly forty years he served as superintendent of the Sunday-school. In politics, he has always been a Democrat, and his first vote was cast for Governor Findlay, of Pennsylvania.

The Judge is now in his seventy-ninth year, and as a professional man, a citizen and a Christian gentleman, enjoys the profound regard of all who know him. In his historical oration at the Centennial Celebration of Sunbury, on July 4th, 1872, Truman H. Purdy, Esq., pays Judge Jordan the following merited compliment; and, speaking of the lawyers of olden time, and then, referring to the subject of this sketch, Mr. Purdy says:

"Has not he whose well-remembered voice has dignified this day, made this end of a century upon the bench as grand in justice and as eloquent in law, as did the twelve who bore commissions from their sovereign Lord? We miss him from the bench, but share the greetings of his social life—a life well spent, adorned with toil, replete with honor, full of victory."

"A great red sun is gliding down the West,
The shadows lengthen, be his evening blest,
And may God stay the hour which sinks him into rest."

THE DEWART FAMILY.

This family is of Irish extraction, and has been identified with the interests of Sunbury from its settlement.

WILLIAM DEWART

was born in Ireland, in 1740, and emigrated to America in 1765. For a number of months he worked in Chester County, Pennsylvania, at four or five dollars per month, for the payment of his passage-money. He subsequently came to Sunbury, and, in 1775, opened the first store in the town. The building was a log structure, and stood on Chestnut street, between Second street and Centre alley, on the site of the present residence of Miss Ann Hillinguan. He afterwards purchased a lot on north side of Market street, where he erected a store and residence. He died in Sunbury in 1814.

HON. LEWIS DEWART,

son of William Dewart, was born in Sunbury, in November, 1781. At that time the place was little more than a military post in the wilderness. For many years he was assistant in his father's store.

In 1815, he was elected to the House of Representatives of the Pennsylvania Legislature, where he served for several years. He was also subsequently elected to the State Senate.

From 1831 to 1836, he was Representative in Congress. He was then returned to the Pennsylvania Legislature, where he was made Speaker of the House of Representatives, which position he held for the years 1837 and 1838.

With Stephen Girard, of Philadelphia, and General Daniel Montgomery, of Danville, Mr. Dewart was a prime mover in the enterprise of what was then known as the Danville and Pottsville Railroad. He was also a member of the first board of directors of the same.

In 1840, he retired from active business, and led a private life until April 26th, 1852, when he died at his residence in Sunbury, at the advanced age of seventy-one. His remains rest in the only vault, in the old Sunbury burying-ground. In politics, Mr. Dewart was a Democrat, and a very warm friend of General Jackson. He possessed a fine personal appearance, was honorable in his dealings, and popular among the people. His wife was Elizabeth Liggett, of Chester County, Pa. He had but one child—

HON. WILLIAM L. DEWART,

who was born in Sunbury, June 21st, 1820. Much of his boyhood was passed away from the place of his nativity. His early education was largely obtained at Harrisburg, whither his father took him, and where he remained during a number of sessions of the Legislature, of which his father was at that time a member. He took his preparatory collegiate course at Dickinson College, Carlisle, Pa., and then entered the Sophomore class, in Princeton, N. J., in 1836, where he finished his education, in 1839. He then read law with Hon. Charles G. Donnel, of Sunbury, and was admitted to the bar in 1843, and for several years was in partnership with Captain Charles J. Bruner, of Sunbury. In 1850, his father's health failing, Major Dewart relinquished the practice of law, and devoted himself to the supervision of his father's business.

Major Dewart's wife was Miss Rosetta Van Horn, of Williamsport, to whom he was married on June 21st, 1848. He has had three sons and two daughters, one of each now deceased.

In 1853, he took a trip to Europe with his family, where he spent about a year in traveling through England, Scotland, Ireland, France, Germany, Italy, Switzerland, and other interesting localities.

Among the public positions which Major Dewart has filled, may be mentioned that of delegate to the National Democratic Convention, at Baltimore, in 1852; also, to the Cincinnati Convention, in 1856, and to the Douglas Convention, in 1860. He was also an elector upon the Douglas ticket, from Pennsylvania, in the presidential canvass of 1860.

In 1856, Mr. Dewart was elected to Congress, and served four years.

Since 1860, the Major has withdrawn from public service, and has been devoting his attention to his private business.

He is a portly gentleman, of fine appearance, and of genial disposition, and is a very influential member of society.

It is a coincidence, quite striking, that Mr. Espy Van Horn, Major Dewart's wife's father, was the direct predecessor, in Congress, of Major Dewart's father; and also, that Mr. William Wilson, stepfather of Mrs. Dewart, was her father's predecessor in the same house.

GEORGE HILL.

The gentleman whose name we have placed at the head of this biographical sketch, has been for quite a number of years a prominent member of the Sunbury bar. He is the youngest son of Daniel Hill, a highly respectable farmer, who, a half-century since, died in Lycoming County, Pennsylvania.

In this county, the subject of this notice was born on the 3d of August, 1821. He was left fatherless at the age of six, and two years later, started out to earn his own living, his mother having no means with which to provide for her family of two sons and a daughter. His early history is that of a fatherless boy, struggling to make something of himself amid the difficulties that gather around childhood and poverty. For a number of years he was employed at such farm labor as he could perform, attending school in the winter months, during which time he worked for his board.

As further illustrative of the pecuniary straits through which he was compelled to pass, it may be mentioned that, when about twenty-one years of age, having just completed a three years' apprenticeship at coach-making, in McEwensville, he started on foot for New Berlin, to secure a position as journeyman in his trade. The Susquehanna was reached, and young Hill, with a bundle of clothes thrown over his back, presented himself before the toll-collector of the bridge at Milton, for passage. "*Two cents*" toll was demanded—but not even as much as *one* cent could be found either in bundle or pockets of this young pedestrian. After some little parleying, and a "promise to pay as soon as he could earn the money," the gate-keeper, seeing that the youth had an honest face, permitted him to pass. In due time the "two cents" toll was paid, and the bridge company suffered no loss on account of the leniency of their toll-collector.

HON. SOLOMON MALICK.

This gentleman is a descendant, of the third generation, from David Malick, one of the early settlers of Lower Augusta Township, Northumberland County, Pennsylvania. This ancestor had his residence near a spring, at that time somewhat noted, upon what is now known as the old Renner farm. It was situated upon the well-known Indian trail that radiated from Fort Augusta, southward. The old gentleman entered some twelve hundred acres of land in the township just named. Here he spent his life and raised a large family of children, and to each son and daughter he gave a farm. One of his sons was David Malick, Jr., and father of the subject of this sketch. He was twice married, his first wife being a Miss —— Herb, by whom he had two sons and four daughters. His second companion was Miss Catharine, daughter of George Miller, of Upper Mahanoy Township, this County. By this marriage he had three sons and two daughters, one of the former of whom is now the Hon. Solomon Malick, of Sunbury. He was born in Lower Augusta, June 15th, 1831, and was only two years old when his father died. His mother, under the will of his grandfather, David Malick, was secured in the use of the farm of her husband, and the appliances thereof, until the youngest child was fifteen years of age.

Young Malick worked on this farm till he was eighteen years old. He then spent some two years in the cabinet-maker's business. Possessing fine talent for vocal music, he early turned his attention to the same, and received instruction in singing from William Youngman, a brother of the editor of the *Sunbury Gazette*. His advancement was rapid, and he soon became distinguished as a singing-master, and for quite a number of years taught music and gave public concerts with most gratifying success. By this means he obtained funds to aid him in securing an education. Mr. Malick subsequently received instruction in thorough bass from Charles S. Nydegger, and also became the author of some choice musical compositions, some of which were published.

At the age of twenty, he repaired to Selinsgrove, where, for a time, he was under the tuition of Dr. J. C. Fisher. This was followed by a four years' term of classical and scientific instruction in the Freeburg Academy, under the efficient care of Professor Jacob S. Whitman, who was subsequently Professor of the Sciences in the State Farm School in Centre County.

We next find Mr. Malick principal of the Selinsgrove High-school, and at the same time reading law with George Hill, Esq., now of Sunbury. On February 23d, 1858, he was admitted to the bar, having passed a highly creditable examination before Judge Wilson and a committee composed of Hon. Isaac Slenker, Absalom Swineford, and Colonel A. C. Simpson.

After a short legal partnership with Colonel Simpson, Mr. Malick accepted a co-principalship in the Freeburg Academy, with Revs. C. S. Weber, and J. K. Millett, which continued for several years.

Early in 1858, he married Miss Mary Ann Roush, daughter of Andrew Roush, of Freeburg. His family consists of four sons and one daughter.

In the Spring of 1861, he came to Sunbury, where he has since been engaged in the practice of his profession, during which time he has been connected with many leading cases, among them four murder trials, and also the well known Mahanoy robbery trial, which involved some of the Mollie McGuires, and created intense interest throughout the community.

In 1866, he was made County Attorney, and in 1867 was re-appointed by the Commissioners to the same position. Of this re-appointment, the *Sunbury Gazette*, a paper politically opposed to Mr. Malick, says:

"The re-appointment of Solomon Malick, Esq., as attorney for this county, by the Commissioners, is a sufficient endorsement of the faithful manner in which he performed his trust. In the discharge of his duties, it was frequently incumbent upon him to give advice involving questions of considerable pecuniary interest to the county, and, as we have learned, in all instances, his advice resulted to the advantage of the tax-payers. For such service he deserved a re-appointment. We are willing to give proper credit to one who, although a political opponent, has, nevertheless, made an efficient and trustworthy officer."

Mr. Malick, also, efficiently served the people as District Attorney for three years, after which term he declined a re-election.

Early in 1872, he was elected Chief Burgess of Sunbury, and, at the same time, to the town council, composed almost entirely of new members. With this event, dawned a new and important era for Sunbury. Various public improvements, long badly needed, were now begun.

Under the efficient administration of the Chief Burgess, supported by a council of progressive ideas, the borough was, for the first time, lighted with gas. Market square, which, from time immemorial, had been a deserted-looking spot, and an eye-sore to every person endowed with even a medium amount of æsthetic taste and public spirit, was enclosed with a neat iron fence, and transformed from its former desolated condition into a park of beauty. The fence was erected by George Rohrbach & Son, at a cost of four thousand two hundred dollars, and is a credit to the Sunbury manufacturer. Other improvements followed.

Within this year, Chestnut street was graded its whole length; Second street, over a mile; also, Parker, Spruce, and Pine streets, and a portion of Front. Various ponds were filled up, bridge-crossings erected, and pavements laid. A fine town-clock, of the Howard manufacture, was also placed in the court house tower. A plate on the same bears the following inscription:

"Chief Burgess, Solomon Malick. Committee—Wm. L. Dewart, Wm. H. Miller. Projector, H. B. Masser."

In 1873, Mr. Malick was re-elected. The *Sunbury Gazette* thus supported him: "We regard our present Chief Burgess as the most efficient our borough has ever had, while the council have zealously backed him in the works of improvement."

In 1874, Mr. Malick was elected Chief Burgess for the third time. During his three years' administration, very great changes were wrought in the public appearance of the town, and for many of the improvements the people are indebted to the high-toned enterprise, progressive spirit, and genuine grit of this gentleman.

Mr. Malick is a gentleman of commanding personal appearance, fine social qualities, and of unswerving devotion to what he believed to be duty.

—

L. H. KASE.

The history of the subject of this notice, involves the oft-repeated tale of a young man struggling, through discouragements and poverty, to elevate himself to the legitimate honors and rewards of a professional career.

He is the second son and third child in a family of eight, and was born in Northumberland County, Pa., February 10th, 1834. He passed the first nineteen years of his life on a farm and in a tannery, receiving only a meagre common-school education. Being desirous, however, to make the law his profession, and receiving no aid from his father, he was thrown entirely upon his own resources in obtaining the means to qualify himself for the same. Accordingly, he engaged for a time, respectively, as store-clerk in the patent-right trade, and in the fire insurance business; and, indeed, in any work that would enable him to earn an honest dollar. He was prompt, industrious, and frugal.

When about twenty-two years of age, he entered Elysburg Academy, this County, where he remained about two years, industriously employing his vacations in earning his means of subsistence. He also, for several years, taught school during the Winter season. Upon the opening of the late war, he served one year in company H, Ninety-third Pennsylvania Volunteer Infantry, going out, in August, 1861, as first lieutenant of the Baldy Guards, of Danville, Pa. For most of the time, however, he acted as adjutant of his regiment. In 1862, he resigned his position, and came to Sunbury, where he read law with Simon P. Wolverton, Esq., till 1865, serving for some eighteen months of the meantime as Deputy Prothonotary. In March, 1865, he was admitted to the bar, and has since devoted himself exclusively to his profession, having refused to comply with various solicitations of his friends to allow himself to become a candidate for office. In this course, he has exhibited a sound judgment, for it is a principle to which there are but very few exceptions, that no man can properly and thoroughly do more than one thing at a time. His decision and action in this regard, have been well rewarded by the position he now occupies, as a solid and influential member of the Sunbury bar.

On March 28th, 1865, Mr. Kase married Miss Susan A. Covin, of Sunbury. He has had a family of two sons and three daughters, one of each now deceased.

HON. GEORGE W. ZIEGLER.

The subject of this biographical sketch is a native of Gettysburg, Pennsylvania, and was born May 24th, 1816.

He is the third child in a family of eight—six sons and two daughters—of whom, one of each have died. His father, George Ziegler, was also a native of Gettysburg, and was a hatter by trade. He possessed a finely balanced mind, combined with good, sound common sense. For a number of years he filled official positions in Adams County, under the appointment of the Governor of the Commonwealth, among which may be mentioned those of Register, Recorder, and Prothonotary. His mother was Gertrude Elizabeth Chritzman, who was born in Germany, and was brought to America when quite young.

His grandfather, Emanuel Ziegler, lived to be nearly one hundred years old, being about ninety-eight at the time of his death. It is also a remarkable fact that his grandfather's brothers and sisters lived to be upwards of ninety. His father died at the age of sixty-three, and his mother would have been seventy-four, on the day she was buried.

When about seventeen years of age, young Ziegler was apprenticed to the printer's trade, under Jacob Lefever, of Gettysburg, where he remained nearly three years. While thus employed, he improved his spare time in study, and took a course in the Greek and Latin classics, reciting in the evening to one of the professors in the Pennsylvania College, in Gettysburg. He had previously enjoyed only the meagre advantages of the old-time subscription school.

From Gettysburg, Mr. Ziegler repaired to Butler, Pennsylvania, where he was employed for about three years in the printing establishment of his brother, Jacob Ziegler. While here, he read law under the instruction of Samuel A. Purviance, then of Butler, but now of Pittsburg, and was admitted to the bar in Butler, in 1840.

He then opened an office in Kittanning, Pennsylvania, where he was engaged in his profession for about three years. After this he removed to Brookville, Jefferson County, and there resided for a period of fifteen years. He here enjoyed a very extensive and successful practice, but, owing to ill health, was compelled to seek some other locality. Accordingly, he left Brookville, though at a time when his business was in its zenith of prosperity, and located in Selinsgrove. In less than two years afterwards, however, he came to Sunbury, where he has since resided. This was in October, 1864.

In the Autumn of 1854, Mr. Ziegler was elected to the House of Representatives of the Pennsylvania Legislature, and re-elected in 1855. This was the district at that time composed of the counties of Jefferson, Armstrong, and Clarion.

In the Fall of 1861, he was again sent to the Legislature, from the district comprising Jefferson, Elk, Cameron, and Clearfield counties.

In 1870, he was a candidate for nomination for President Judge for Northumberland County, on the Democratic ticket, and carried the county by two hundred and sixty-one majority over all competitors, but lost the nomination by frauds perpetrated in some of the townships.

Mr. Ziegler has made his profession a specialty, and has enjoyed a very successful legal practice, especially on the criminal docket. He possesses a great amount of genial humor, is a fine public speaker, and is highly esteemed for his urbane and gentlemanly bearing. For many years he has been a leading member of the Presbyterian denomination.

IRA T. CLEMENT.

The subject of this biographical notice is a native of the State of New Jersey, and was born on January 11th, 1813. He is the posthumous son of Thornton Clement a soldier in the war of 1812.

When he was about three years old, his mother located in Northumberland County; and at the early age of four, he was indentured to a farmer, the articles of apprenticeship being expressed in the usual quaint style of old-fashioned times. The articles specified among other things, that he was to serve his master faithfully until the age of eighteen, and that during the many years of his indenture, he should receive "four quarter years of schooling!" It will be seen from this, that Mr. Clement's educational advantages were exceedingly meagre.

Young Clement's tastes, however, did not lie in the pursuit of agriculture, but rather in that of the mechanic. He accordingly devoted the three remaining years of his minority to learn the carpenter's trade.

He subsequently, in 1838, accompanied a corps of engineers in the survey of the Sunbury and Erie—now the Philadelphia and Erie Railroad. The country through which passes this public thoroughfare, though now dotted over with cities, towns, and villages, was then an almost unbroken wilderness.

In the Autumn of 1842, he embarked in the mercantile business in Sunbury, and in 1845 he erected a saw-mill, and a number of years later, a planing-mill.

In May, 1876, Mr. Clement received the contract for the erection of the Northumberland County Prison, which building is now in process of construction.

For many years he has been the leading business man of the borough, and has taken a very prominent part in the building up of the place. He possesses business talent of a superior order, an indomitable energy, and unimpeachable moral integrity.

In 1830, Mr. Clement married Miss Sarah, daughter of David Martz, of Northumberland County, and has a family of three sons and nine daughters, of whom two sons and five daughters are deceased.

In politics, Mr. Clement was formerly an *old line*, but is now a Republican.

A. N. BRICE, Esq.

Before entering upon a sketch of the life of this gentleman, we will briefly notice his ancestry.

His paternal grand-parents were natives of Ireland, and immigrated to this country about the beginning of the present century. They resided, for a while, in Washington City, D. C., but subsequently removed to Southwark, Philadelphia.

Upon the breaking out of the war of 1812, the father, Thomas Brice, and grandfather of the subject of this notice, entered the service of his adopted country and was killed.

His widow, then left with five small children, engaged as nurse and doctress in attendance upon the sick and wounded soldiers who were brought to the upper end of the city. She gained a fine reputation as a female physician, was very efficient in her profession, and became very popular on account of her ministrations of kindness to the suffering. She subsequently married Andrew Nebinger, who had also served in the war with Great Britain, and was wounded in the same.

By him she had three sons and two daughters, one of each now deceased. The three sons became members of the medical profession, in Philadelphia. The surviving daughter is married, and also resides in Philadelphia. Both parents lived to an advanced age, and died some fifteen years since.

THOMAS BRICE, Jr.,

father of A. N. Brice, was born in Washington City, D. C., in the year 1808.

Under the then dormant and backward condition of popular education, his acquirements, in this direction, were obtained principally at odd intervals and at night-schools. At an early age he was bound out by his mother to learn the shoemaker's trade, at which he served seven years.

Inspired, however, by a restless desire to travel, after finishing his trade, he left home and started out to seek his fortune, wending his way to New York; and, finally, at a somewhat advanced age, settled in the Keystone State, in Lewisburg, Union County.

His wife was Mary Wenck, whose mother was a native of Holland. The latter having some difficulty of a domestic nature, resulting from the conduct of a step-mother, resolved to make her way to America, which had been represented to her as an "asylum of the oppressed and down-trodden," and where poor boys and girls could rise to position and affluence by their own exertions. Accordingly, near the close of the last century, she embarked on a vessel, at the age of but seventeen, without friends or money, and, after a three months' ride on the surging billows of the Atlantic, arrived at Philadelphia, a stranger in a strange land.

Mr. and Mrs. Thomas Brice, had two sons and six daughters, one of each now deceased. Of this family, the oldest child is A. N. Brice, Esq., of Sunbury. He was born in Lewisburg, Pennsylvania, February 2d, 1840. When he was about eleven years of age, his father met with a financial reverse which materially interfered with the education of his children. Young Brice, therefore, was compelled to "shift for himself," and for several years hired out at such labor as he could perform, engaging principally on a farm, and in a tannery. He subsequently served an apprenticeship to the printer's trade in the office of the *Sunbury Gazette*, and then became foreman on the *Northumberland County Democrat*. While thus acting as foreman, he commenced reading law under Judge Jordan, with whom he remained two years.

In the Summer of 1862, he assisted in recruiting company C, One Hundred and Thirty-first Pennsylvania Volunteer Infantry, in which he was made first lieutenant, and served about nine months, during which time he participated in the engagements of Antietam, Fredericksburg, Burnside's "Muddy March," and of Chancellorsville. He subsequently re-enlisted in a six months' Independent Cavalry company, and was in the service before Gettysburg. He again enlisted in company H, Fifth Pennsylvania Cavalry, and performed arduous service under Generals Krautz, McKenzie, and Sheridan. In a cavalry fight, while on special duty, with a detachment of men, on the Darbytown road, near Richmond, on the 14th of December, 1864, he was captured by General Longstreet's command, but escaped. In his flight, however, he was slightly wounded in the right side by a musket-ball, and his clothes were riddled by three other balls.

He was also in the battle of Five Forks, Dinwiddie Court House, South Side Railroad, and at the surrender of Lee, at Appomattox, on the 9th of April, 1865.

On July 31st, 1862, he married Miss Rebecca Friling, by whom he has had two sons and a daughter.

After the close of the war, he engaged, for a few years, in various departments of the mercantile business. In January, 1869, he was admitted to the bar, and has since been engaged in his profession in Sunbury.

In October, 1870, he was elected Justice of the Peace, and re-elected in 1875. Among other positions which he has held, may be mentioned that of Overseer of the Poor, Assessor, and also a member of the Town Council.

On May 30th, 1875, Decoration Day, Mr. Brice delivered an oration, giving the military record of Sunbury and vicinity. It was a fine production, and prepared at a cost of months of time and labor. The minuteness of its detail rendered it very valuable, and it will be found, in substance, in the foregoing History of Northumberland County.

The oration closes with the following beautiful tribute:

"And now we go forth in the performance of the solemn duty of the day. Thoughtfully let us move among the mounds of the dead. The humblest of these men were martyrs in the cause of their country. They sleep their last sleep. They are not moved by the tread of friend or foe. Their quiet is undisturbed by our song and muffled strains of music. We will some day rest with them, and the country we served side by side will be left to our children and to strangers. In the language of the great Lincoln, as he stood by the dead on the field of Gettysburg: "It is for us to be here dedicated to the great task remaining before us, that from these honored dead we take increased devotion to that cause for which they gave the full measure of devotion; that we here highly resolve that these dead shall not have died in vain; that this nation, under God, shall have a new birth of freedom, and that government of the people, by the people, and for the people, shall not perish from the earth."

Squire Brice is a gentleman of genial and obliging manners, an industrious worker, and public-spirited citizen. In politics he is a Republican, and is the Chairman of the Republican County Committee.

L. T. ROHRBACH.

The gentleman whose name stands at the caption of this biographical notice, is now serving his second term as Prothonotary and Clerk of the Criminal Courts of Northumberland County.

He is the fourth son, and sixth child, in a family of nine,—six sons and three daughters,—of whom there survive four of the former and two of the latter.

His father is George Rohrbach, a well-known business man and highly respected citizen of Sunbury, who has, for many years, been engaged in the foundry trade.

Prothonotary Rohrbach was born in Upper Augusta township, this county, on the 22d day of January, 1840. His facilities for acquiring an education were, to a great degree, those of his own making.

Having obtained some rudimentary knowledge in the common schools of Sunbury, he spent a year in Pennsylvania College, at Gettysburg, when he returned to the former place, and was employed as teacher for some two or three years. He subsequently spent a year in what was known as the Missionary Institute, in Selinsgrove, under the tuition of Professor Bourne.

Returning to Sunbury, he resumed the work of teaching, and at the same time commenced the reading of law in the office of Hon. Wolverton. Upon Mr. Wolverton's death, Mr. Rohrbach placed himself under the instruction of Wm. M. Rockefeller, with whom he finished his legal studies, and was admitted to the bar, in Sunbury, on March 10th, 1863.

Upon the breaking out of the late Civil war, Mr. Rohrbach enlisted in the three months' service, in Company F, of the Eleventh Pennsylvania Volunteer Infantry, under the command of Captain Charles J. Bruner, of Sunbury.

Subsequent to serving out his enlistment, he was appointed clerk in the Disbursing Office of the Government, at Harrisburg, under the control of Major R. I. Dodge, of the United States Army, where he remained for upwards of two years.

He then returned to Sunbury, and began the practise of law, in the office of Mr. Rockefeller, which arrangement continued for some four years, till 1871, when Mr. Rockefeller was elected Judge of this Judicial District.

Upon this event, Mr. Rohrbach formed a legal partnership with George W. Ziegler, of Sunbury, but on December 2d, 1872, the partnership was dissolved, Mr. Rohrbach having been in the Fall of this year, nominated by the Republican party, and elected to the office of Prothonotary and Clerk of the Criminal Courts of this county. In the Autumn of 1875, he was honored by a re-election to the same important office.

On the 21st of December, 1860, Mr. Rohrbach was married to Miss Jennie C., daughter of John Haas, Esq., of Sunbury. This union has been blessed with the birth of three sons, the eldest now deceased.

DAVID C. DESSINGER.

This gentleman is the present popular Treasurer of Northumberland County.

He was born in Schaefferstown, Lebanon County, Pa., on March 5th, 1840, and was the youngest son in a family of eleven children—eight sons and three daughters—of John Dessinger and Catharine Conner, both natives of Pennsylvania.

His parents were poor, and having a large family to provide for, were able to give their children but very meagre opportunities for acquiring an education, and some eight months inside of a common country school-house would comprise all the privileges in this respect enjoyed by the subject of this sketch.

When about eleven years of age—at which time his mother died—he was apprenticed to the tailor's trade, where he remained five years.

At the age of sixteen he went to Lebanon, the county seat of his native county, and hired out for four years to the stone cutter's trade. Just before the expiration of this time, the late Civil war broke out, and young Dessinger enlisted for the three months' service, in company E, Fourteenth Regiment, Pennsylvania Volunteer Infantry. At the expiration of this time he returned to Schaefferstown, and with Captain John S. Long, recruited company F, which was joined to the Ninety-third Pennsylvania Volunteer Infantry, at Camp Coleman, at Lebanon. Of this company, Mr. Long was made captain, and Mr. Dessinger, 1st lieutenant. Their first engagement was at the battle of Williamsburg, Va., upon which occasion the command of the company fell upon Lieutenant Dessinger, in the absence of the captain. The next engagement was the battle of Fair Oaks, in which company F, in connection with company A, of the Ninety-third, and several other companies, served as the advance picket guard. These companies were surrounded by the enemy on the first day's fight, and were in great danger of being captured, but were saved from this fate by the remarkable presence of mind and heroic daring of Lieutenant Dessinger, who in the wild panic that prevailed, drew his revolver, and with wonderful coolness and in commanding military style, ordered the terror stricken men into line, and, losing no time, led the flight, and at night, arrived safe at the rifle pits, with more than a regiment of men.

For this gallant and meritorious exploit, Lieutenant Dessinger received the highest compliments from General Peck.

After the seven days' fight, that resulted in the defeat of the Union forces, at Harrison's Landing, Mr. Dessinger, on account of sickness, was taken to the hospital in Washington, and three weeks passing without much progress towards his recovery, he resigned his position and returned to his home in Lebanon, where he assisted in recruiting a company for the emergency service.

After a year spent in Lebanon, in the book and stationery business, he went West, and was engaged at his trade for a period of about six months, in each of the cities of Fort Wayne and Chicago, and was present at the Chicago Convention which nominated General McClellan for the Presidency, in the Summer of 1864. He then returned to his native State and followed his trade for a number of years.

On the 24th of September, 1865, he came to Sunbury and opened the first marble-shop in the place.

On April 10th, 1866, Mr. Dessinger was married to Miss Fannie, daughter of Ira T. Clement, of Sunbury, and has had a family of four sons and one daughter, two of the former being now deceased.

In April, 1867 or '68, he formed a partnership with Philip H. Moore, in the mercantile business. In ——, Mr Ira T. Clement bought out Mr. Moore's interest in the store, and Messrs. Dessinger and Clement still continue to conduct the business in partnership.

In 1871, Mr. Dessinger, in company with Mr. P. H. Moore, erected the fine hotel, on Third street, called the Clement House, and which was named in honor of Hon. Ira T. Clement. In the same year, also, these gentlemen put up the imposing structure on the corner of Market and Third, known as Moore and Dessinger's block. It forms the finest business block in the borough, and is a highly creditable monument to the public spirit and enterprise of its builders. Mr. Dessinger has also erected a row of houses—eight in number—on the east side of Third street, above the depot, which is known as "Dessinger's Row."

For a number of years, he has been prominently connected with three building associations, in Sunbury, having been the heaviest stockholder in the same, and has devoted his special attention to the interests of these institutions, and to them he very largely attributes his pecuniary success.

In 1872, Mr. Dessinger was brought forward as a candidate for nomination for the Legislature, and came within two votes of securing said nomination, which nomination would have been regarded as about equivalent to an election.

In 1873, Mr. Dessinger erected his present beautiful residence, on Chestnut street, which is a model of convenience and beauty.

In the Fall of 1875, he was elected Treasurer of Northumberland County, by the handsome majority of eight hundred and fifty-seven, carrying the borough of Sunbury by one hundred and twenty-seven majority, which latter was a greater vote than was ever before given to any democratic nominee. The duties of this responsible position he is discharging with a strict integrity and an impartial obedience to the requirements of the law.

Great credit is due Mr. Dessinger, not only for his efficiency as a public officer, but also for the persevering public spirit and enterprise which he has exhibited in all that conduces to the welfare and building up of the borough.

Mr. Dessinger's father is still living in Campbellstown, Lebanon County, at the advanced age of eighty-six.

THE SHIPMAN FAMILY.

Representatives of this family have been residents of Northumberland County from a very early day. They seem to have emigrated from the State of New Jersey, where lived

WILLIAM SHIPMAN,

whose wife was Catharine Campbell, both of Sussex, now Warren County. This William Shipman had a son,

JOHN SHIPMAN,

who married a Mary McKinney, who was a daughter of Abraham McKinney and Abigail Lennison, of Virginia, though both originally from New Jersey. John Shipman settled in Northumberland County in May, 1798. The McKinney family were here some time before.

JUDGE ABRAHAM SHIPMAN,

a son of John Shipman, was born in Lower Augusta, March 6th, 1810. When a young man, he served as orderly sergeant, for a period of nine years, in a volunteer militia company, called the "Jackson Rifles," and commanded by Captain John Weiser. Said company was recruited in Sunbury and Lower Augusta.

Mr. Shipman studied surveying under David Andrews, and entered upon the profession in March, 1830, his first work being performed for Colonel John Snyder, of this County.

In connection with David Rockefeller, now deceased, and whose biography appears among these sketches, he has been for many years engaged in all the important land cases in northern Pennsylvania. He married Elizabeth Youtzheimer, of this County, February 14th, 1837, and has had a family of seven sons and four daughters. One son died in infancy, and another, Mark, served in the late war, and died about four years after his return home.

For some ten years, Mr. Shipman was one of the Associate Judges of Northumberland County. For a considerable time, also, he served as County Surveyor. He is now Justice of the Peace of Lower Augusta. In 1854, he engaged extensively in the milling business, but lost largely by the failure of the Trevorton Coal Company.

Judge Shipman is a man of remarkably robust constitution, and a very industrious worker. His opportunities for becoming wealthy have been very considerable, but his benevolent disposition has prompted him to bestow manifold favors upon his friends, such as going bail, loaning money, etc., by means of which he has lost largely. The Judge is still actively engaged in his profession of surveying, and of his presence the old land marks of this and adjoining counties will for many years to come bear witness; while his professional acts and deeds will be rehearsed in courts of justice, long after he shall have passed away from the scenes of his active and useful life.

LEMUEL SHIPMAN.

This gentleman is the eldest child of Abraham Shipman, just noticed. He was born in Northumberland County, December 15th, 1838. When a boy, he was employed in the saw and grist-mill of his father, and his education was confined to the Winter attendance of a common country school, supplemented by a short course in the academy, in New Berlin, under the supervision of Professor Hendricks.

On September 27th, 1860, he married Miss Maria, daughter of William Bloom, of Lower Augusta township. The ancestors of this family were residents of this County from a very early day, and some of them were remarkable for their longevity—Mrs. Bloom's grandmother having died a few years since, at the advanced age of ninety-four. Mr. Shipman has had four sons and two daughters, one of each now deceased.

In the Autumn of 1862, he enlisted in company D, Third Pennsylvania Artillery (152d in line), in which he made eighth sergeant, but was subsequently promoted respectively, to first sergeant, second lieutenant, and first lieutenant.

Shortly after his promotion to lieutenant, he was presented, by his company, with a sword, sash, belt, and revolver, bearing the following inscription:

"*From the Enlisted*
Men of his Company.
To Lieut. L. Shipman."

Upon the reception of which, Mr. Shipman responded, in substance, as follows:

"That, in accepting these emblems of authority, as a token of your appreciation, I shall the more highly prize them, as I have so lately been one among you; and, in my promotion, I shall still cherish in grateful remembrance the many happy hours we have spent together, as comrades. Yet, in the discharge of my duty, I shall be as rigid and faithful as in my former position. And when duty and country call for the unsheathing of this sword, I can assure you that it shall never be returned in dishonor. And, when victory shall perch upon our banners, and our country shall have been restored to peace and prosperity, and we shall have been disbanded, and returned to our homes, these emblems will be to me a priceless memento, not only of the struggles through which we have passed, but also of the patriotism and valor of the noble men of this company."

Upon the illness of the Captain, in the early part of 1865, the command of the company fell upon Lieut. Shipman, which position he filled through his term of service. In this capacity, he made a most efficient and popular officer, to which fact the men under his command bear ample testimony, of whom upwards of thirty reside in this County. The company had the reputation of being among the best drilled ones in the service. It was selected by General Butler, as guard of the head-quarters of his department, and was retained by General Ord, who succeeded General Butler, until after the fall of Richmond.

After the capture of Jeff. Davis, this company returned to Fortress Monroe, the head-quarters of the regiment, and Mr. Shipman performed the notable service of conducting Jeff. Davis from the boat to his prison-cell in the Fort. Two other distinguished prisoners accompanied Davis—Clement C. Clay, Jr., of Huntsville, Ala., and John Mitchell, the Irish patriot.

Mr. Shipman also delivered to Mr. Davis his first rations in his prison. They consisted of bread and coffee. Mr. Shipman was in the service for upwards of three years, but was never off of duty on account of sickness.

In making up the company's rolls, he was assisted by Dr. F. M. Thomas, of Mt. Carmel, who was quartermaster's sergeant and company's clerk. He was mustered out of service in Philadelphia, November 9th, 1865; and, after his return to his home, in Lower Augusta, was engaged for some seven years in the mercantile trade. For some eight successive years he filled the position of Auditor of his township.

He has always taken a live and active part in educational affairs, and has been a leader in advancing the school interests of his neighborhood. He is the present Secretary of the Board of School Directors of Upper Augusta.

In the Fall of 1873, he was elected to the offices of Register of Wills, Recorder of Deeds, and Clerk of the Orphans' Court for Northumberland County, and led his ticket by upwards of two hundred votes.

In April, 1874, he moved to Sunbury, and now owns and occupies the late residence of the Hon. Truman H. Purdy.

In the Autumn of 1876, he was re-nominated on the Democratic ticket, for his present county office, a nomination which is regarded as almost equivalent to an election. Out of one hundred and twelve delegates, he received one hundred and three votes on the first ballot.

Mr. Shipman possesses great energy and activity, is firm in his convictions, and very persevering in his undertakings. As an officer, he is faithful in duty, and as a citizen, social and popular.

GEORGE W. STRINE.

This gentleman is the present Sheriff of Northumberland County. He is the fifth son, and eighth child, of a family of nine, of Matthias Strine and Catharine Welshans, both natives of York County, Pa., and was born in Union County, Pa., March 15th, 1818. In the following April, the family moved to Milton, Northumberland County, where the parents spent the remainder of their life.

From the age of fourteen to twenty-six he was engaged in boating on the Pennsylvania canal. On October 14th, 1841, he was married to Miss Mary Burman, of Milton, daughter of Frederick Burman, of that place. Mr. Strine has had a family of two sons and three daughters—one of each deceased.

In 1844, he engaged in boat building, in Milton, which business he followed some thirty years.

In the Autumn of 1875, he was elected, on the Democratic ticket, to the office of Sheriff of this County, which position he is filling with ability. He is also assisted in this office by his son, Melancthon Strine, as Deputy-sheriff.

Though, himself, deprived of any more extended advantages for learning, than those afforded by the early common schools of the County, Mr. Strine has ever been an earnest advocate of popular education, and for a period of six years was a member of the Milton Board of Education, and contributed not a little to the advancement of the educational interests in that place. For some thirty-five years, both he and his companion have been connected with the Lutheran denomination, in which church he has for many years held responsible, official positions, among them, that of deacon and elder. He has also been an active worker in the Sunday-school, serving for upwards of a quarter of a century, as superintendent.

He is a gentleman of pleasant address, liberal views, and of great kindness of heart, and is held in high esteem, both in the church and community.

His first Deputy is

J. HAMMOND McCORMICK,

who is a grandson of Seth McCormick, one of the first settlers of Lycoming County, Pa., and a great maternal grandson of Matthew Brown, one of the framers of the first Constitution of this Commonwealth.

He was born in Lycoming County, February 3d, 1811. At the age of eleven, he was left fatherless, and, being the eldest in a family of five children, was compelled, not only to earn his own living, but also to contribute to the support of his widowed mother, and her family. The early-day common school supplied all his privileges for learning. After arriving at his majority, he learned the harness-maker's trade, which he followed for some forty years, and has accumulated a comfortable competence.

He polled his first vote for General Jackson, and has voted for every Democratic president since. He has always been a warm and earnest advocate of an "undivided union," and, during the late National struggle, he contributed of his influence and money, as much as any man of his means, to put down the "unholy rebellion."

Mr. McCormick is a decidedly positive man, plain in his manners, and very outspoken and independent—so much so, that he has never been popular with the masses, but he has held, by appointment, various responsible and honorable positions in the community.

On January 1st, 1876, he was appointed Deputy-sheriff of Northumberland County, and is filling the position with great credit, alike to himself and to the public.

He has a wife, five daughters, and a son, and resides in Milton.

HON. JEREMIAH SNYDER.

It is a well-known fact in the history of President Andrew Johnson that he reached his young manhood before he could read or write, and that he received instruction in these elementary branches from his faithful wife, who, true to the noble instincts of her sex, gladly embraced an opportunity to assist a companion less favored than herself. It is to be supposed, however, that while aiding her husband in this particular, she little dreamed that she was *teaching a President!*

The history of the subject of this sketch contains an incident that furnishes a striking parallel to a portion of the experience of the illustrious statesman. Mr. Snyder was nearly *twenty years of age before he could read or write.* This fact is a sufficient commentary upon the meagreness of his early educational facilities.

He is the oldest son and second child in a family of ten children of George A. Snyder and Catharine Schoch, and was born in what was then Union, but now Snyder County, Pennsylvania, June 18th, 1831. The first twenty years of his life were passed partly on the farm and partly in the saw and grist-mill of his father. He then began to attend a common school during the Summer months, and worked in the mill during the Winter.

He had now arrived at an age when he felt most keenly the need of an education. He, therefore, applied himself with great diligence both in and out of school. Frequently he would be found with a book in his hand, while superintending the running of the mill, a circumstance that greatly amused many of his associates equally as ignorant as himself, and of which some of them were greatly disposed to make no little sport.

"O wad some power the giftie gie us,
To see oursel's as ithers see us;
It wad frae mony a blunder free us,
And foolish notion."

Nothing daunted, however, by these derisive taunts, and the oft-repeated slur that he was "*a big boy getting larning out of a book,*" young Snyder stuck to his studies with a perseverance that meant nothing but victory, and in a short time became qualified to impart instruction to others in the common English branches, and taught school for a few winters in the vicinity of his home, and also, for a short time, in New Berlin. While thus engaged in teaching, he began the study of law by himself, bending all his energies in that direction, and improving all his spare time therein. During this time he received occasional instruction from Isaac Slenker, Esq.

When about twenty-five years of age, he entered the law-office of Charles Hower, Esq., in Selinsgrove, where he finished his preparation for his profession, and in March, 1861, was admitted to the bar in Middleburg, Snyder County. In the previous Summer, Mr. Snyder had served as a delegate of the Democratic party to the Charleston Convention.

When, in April, 1861, the call was issued by President Lincoln for seventy-five thousand volunteers to aid in quelling the Southern Rebellion, Mr. Snyder offered himself for the service of his country, and was the first man who enlisted from Snyder County. He was elected corporal in company G, of the Fourth Pennsylvania Volunteer Infantry. After the three months' service, he was honorably discharged, and returned to his home in Middleburg. In June, 1862, he recruited company F, of the One Hundred and Thirty-first Pennsylvania Volunteer Infantry, and although he was the unanimous choice of the company, yet, owing to political influences, he yielded the honor to George W. Ryan, of Snyder County, who obtained the position. Mr. Snyder was then elected lieutenant of the company. Unfriendly political influences, however, were still brought to bear against him, and he resigned his position at Hagerstown, Maryland, and returned home.

In the Winter of 1863, he removed to Shamokin, where he entered upon the practice of his chosen profession, but, in the following April, came to Sunbury, where, both as a lawyer and a citizen, he has won a very favorable reputation.

In the Fall of 1865, he was elected District Attorney, and re-elected in 1868, serving in all six years. The duties of this responsible office Mr. Snyder discharged with credit, alike to himself and to his constituents.

In August, 1866, he was a delegate from the Fourteenth Congressional District of Pennsylvania to the Union Convention in Philadelphia. In 1873, he was elected Justice of the Peace, and still occupies the position.

In the Fall of 1876, Mr. Snyder was elected by the Democratic party of Northumberland County as Representative in the Lower House of the Pennsylvania Legislature.

Mr. Snyder is a man of plain, unassuming manners, but of very genial nature, and by his gentlemanly bearing has made friends of many who differ from him on political issues.

On April 24th, 1862, he was married to Miss Harriet Smith, daughter of Henry A. Smith, of Middleburg, Snyder County, Pennsylvania. To the frugality and other noble qualities of this estimable lady, he is indebted in no small measure for his various successes.

A. S. CUMMINGS, M. D.

The subject of this biographical sketch is a son of John Cummings and Catharine Swineford, both natives of Pennsylvania. He is the youngest in a family of seven sons and six daughters, and was born in Union County, Pennsylvania, January 3d, 1817.

His early educational advantages were those of the common school of that day, which was little short of a burlesque on the improved organizations of the present time. He possessed, however, a great thirst for knowledge, and made the best of the meagre facilities that he had, and diligently improved what spare time could be obtained from his work on his father's farm. When about twenty years of age, he entered Pennsylvania College, at Gettysburg, in which he acquired a liberal knowledge of Latin, Greek, and all the English branches. His means not being sufficient to support his growing ambition for an education, he was then compelled to leave and seek further support, and, therefore, at the time, was unable to take a full course, which he was seeking and trying to obtain. However, in another sense, he did not leave; he left college, it is true, but never left off studying, and so great was the progress in his acquisitions in a knowledge of the few branches in which he was lacking, for the want of money, when he left, that in a very short time afterwards, upon examination, he was advised to go back and take his diploma.

At this point in the history of this young man, being so absorbed in business and a preparation to attend medical lectures, he was in no little trouble in deciding as to what he should do. Upon reflection, however, he concluded, if he had no ability, he could never make his mark with it, and that by hard study and perseverance, if he had the ability, he would run the risk of his mark without one, and the consequence was he never went back, and to-day stands in history where the reader of this sketch now sees him—1837. After leaving school, he immediately entered upon the study of medicine in Lewistown, Mifflin County, Pennsylvania, under the direction of Dr. Joseph B. Ard. He attended lectures at the Pennsylvania Medical College, Philadelphia, and subsequently at Jefferson Medical College, in the same city, and from the latter institution graduated in 1842. To accomplish this extended course of education, young Cummings surmounted many difficulties and passed through severe struggles. The young people of the present day, surrounded, as they are, with all the conveniences, comforts, and even luxuries, that modern science and civilization have brought into being, can but poorly appreciate the trials and privations of their fathers in their start in the world.

The early life of the subject of this sketch was one of hardship and self-denial. His father, having a large family to care for, could give him but little assistance, and young Cummings was compelled to borrow money to enable him to prosecute his studies, and when he had finished his course, he found himself from fifteen hundred to two thousand dollars worse off than nothing. This, however, was only a financial view. In a disciplined intellect and well-stored mind he had obtained a capital that was not to be estimated in dollars and cents. Years before he realized the fact that a good education was the best fortune that a young man could seek, even as it is the best legacy that a parent can leave his children.

This he had now obtained, and at once entered into a partnership practice with his former preceptor, Dr. Ard, of Lewistown, which arrangement continued three years. This was followed by an independent practice of about four years in the same place.

But even after his settlement in his profession, he was the subject of the same hardships as before. For the first two years of his practice, all the property he had was a horse and saddle, and those not paid for. With a heavy load of debt pressing upon him; with such temptations to resist as are incident to almost any man of his age; and when, at every turn, confronted by the tempter to join in the allurements and fascinations of society, and, in many instances, would demoralize, ruin, and take from a beginner a hard and well-earned professional reputation, he pressed onward, for the sake of saving and making, and the accumulation of that knowledge and the name he and his friends can now enjoy.

In this way he struggled, and with an energy worthy the imitation of the proudest intellect, until he competed with success, side by side, with his preceptor, Dr. Ard, and Drs. Culbertson, World, Hoover, and Vanvalzah, and in a very short time made a good living, and paid his debts.

On February 20th, 1849, he married Miss Louisa E., daughter of Peter Richter, Esq., of Selinsgrove, Pennsylvania. This union has been honored with two sons and two daughters—the former deceased, the latter of whom have received a good education. The older, Lizzie K., graduated at Oakland Female Institute, at Norristown, near Philadelphia; the younger, Nellie M., at the University Female Institute, at Lewisburg, June 27th, 1878.

In 1852, Dr. Cummings moved to Selinsgrove, Snyder County, and surrendered his office and practice in Lewistown to his brother, Dr. S. S. Cummings, also a graduate from Jefferson Medical College, Philadelphia. Whilst here, for several years, the doctor paid very little attention to his profession, on account of his health, being almost irrecoverably broken down by a laborious practice, from which his brother had now relieved him, and from which, in order to realize the hope of recovery, he was advised, for the present, to divert his attention, and, as a specialty, make use of such means as he and his friends, in consultation, and in their judgment, might think would restore his health, and enable him again to resume the duties of his calling. For this purpose, after, as he thought, he had exhausted his own skill, he went to Philadelphia, to consult and get the opinions and prescriptions of all the most eminent authors upon the science of medicine, and more particularly of that branch relating to hepatization and enlargement of the liver, the result, as it turned out to be in the case of Dr. Cummings, of a very violent and protracted attack of congestive fever.

After giving a fair trial of the remedies prescribed by all the scientists in the city and elsewhere, and no manifestation of permanent, nor even of temporary relief, he again fell back upon the resources of his own skill, and prescribed for himself, as a last resort, the use of the Bedford water—a place he visited for three consecutive seasons; and from that day to this, any one, to see him now, would conclude that he never had an hour's sickness in his life. To this and traveling through all the Western States and Territories, from 1856 to the breaking out of our late Civil War in 1861, Dr. Cummings attributes his entire recovery and his present state of good health.

After the recovery and enjoyment of his good health for a few years, he again resumed the responsibilities and arduous duties of his profession, and continued in it until some time in the Fall of 1872, when he was elected President of the Augusta Bank, located in Cake's Addition to Sunbury, and in November following moved to that place.

After organization and several meetings of the Board of Directors, and discovering the irregularity with which he conceived the business of the bank was proposed to be transacted, Dr. Cummings resigned, and came to Sunbury and took a place in the front rank of the medical profession in that town. In February, 1875, with great reluctance on his part, but by the persuasion of his friends, at an annual meeting of the Board of Directors of the Sunbury Fire Insurance Company, allowed himself to be elected president of that institution, in which capacity he remained for nearly three months, and upon an investigation of the standing of the company, the liabilities and amount of assets to meet them, he discovered that the company was insolvent, and as our State Insurance Commissioner said, "a fraud;" he again resigned this position, in connection with the Hon. A. Jordan, then acting with the doctor as vice-president.

In the late war, he was surgeon in charge of the United States hospital at Harrisburg. The doctor and his family are all connected with the Presbyterian denomination.

This sketch of the life of Dr. Cummings is presented to the young people of Northumberland County as an example, which, for industry, self-reliance, perseverance, and Christian integrity, is well worthy of emulation.

JACOB SHIPMAN.

The subject of this notice was born in Northumberland County, July 27th, 1833. His parents were John B. Shipman and Keziah Reeder. His grandfather, Jacob Shipman, emigrated from New Jersey, and settled in this County at a very early date. His maternal ancestors were natives of Germany.

His father—a resident of Limestone Valley—was a prominent member of the Methodist Episcopal Church, being a class leader and exhorter, and was a very zealous, active Christian worker. He organized a number of Sunday-schools in his neighborhood, and was instrumental in the accomplishment of great good. He is held in grateful remembrance by many whose characters attest the moulding power of his consistent, Christian example.

In the Spring of 1838, he left this County, and located in Louisa County, Iowa, where, on the tenth of the following December, he passed away to his reward.

At the age of sixteen, young Shipman was apprenticed to the printer's trade, in the office of the *Sunbury American*, where he remained till he was twenty-one. For two or three years he served as foreman in the office of the *Miltonian*. While here he learned the art of telegraphy, and was subsequently employed for about two years in the Milton office of the Catawissa Railroad, as assistant agent and operator.

In March, 1859, he came to Sunbury as clerk and operator, in the ticket office of the Northern Central Railway. In 1868, he was appointed joint Ticket Agent at this place, of the Philadelphia and Erie and Northern Central Railways, and still occupies the position, being one of the most reliable agents on the line.

About 1863, he also served for about a year, as clerk in what is now the First National Bank, of Sunbury.

In the Autumn of 1866, he began the business of Life Insurance, to which, in the following Summer, he added that of Fire Insurance. Under his enterprising management, the business of both of these departments has grown to handsome proportions.

On September 1st, 1857, Mr. Shipman was married to Miss Catharine M., daughter of John S. and Julia Peterman, of Milton. He has had four sons and as many daughters, of whom two of each have died.

For upwards of eight years, he was a Director of the "Sunbury Mutual Savings Fund and Building Association," which started business in September, 1867.

Of the *Fort Augusta* Building and Loan Association, which was incorporated in March, 1860, he was one of the organizers, and has since been, a Director, and the Secretary.

He was also one of the organization members of the "Accommodation Savings Fund and Loan Association"—incorporated in November, 1870—and has, from that time, been a Director, and the Secretary. For a period of six years likewise, he served as Clerk of the borough of Sunbury.

In politics, Mr. Shipman is a Republican, and, in religious views, a Lutheran. For a number of years he has been Sunday-school Librarian, and to his active and efficient interest, is largely due the excellent system of library management in that school.

Mr. Shipman is a gentleman of retiring manners, and is rather inclined to be reticent, but possesses a very obliging, accommodating spirit. His active public enterprise, and high-toned integrity, moreover, have rendered him a very useful and highly-respected member of the community.

S. B. BOYER.

The subject of this biographical narrative, is one of the most energetic and wide-awake Attorneys at the Sunbury bar. His parents were John Boyer, of Berks County, and Elizabeth Bixler, of Schuylkill County, Pa. The former died in January, 1876. The family consisted of five sons and six daughters—one of each now dead—of whom the subject is the eldest son. He was born in Northumberland County, January 4th, 1829, and up to the age of sixteen, was reared upon a farm. At this time, his father engaged in the mercantile business, and young Boyer was sent to Philadelphia to purchase a stock of goods, and then was employed as store-clerk until he was twenty-one. From this time up to the age of twenty-seven, he worked at the carpenter's trade.

On August 25th, 1850, he was married to Miss Esther Haupt, daughter of Benjamin Haupt, of this County.

Mr. Boyer has had two children, a son and a daughter. The son, Francis, a promising lad of nine years, met a melancholy death by drowning, on the 10th of February, 1864. He was skating on the Sunbury Canal, and the ice broke and he fell through.

In 1851, Mr. Boyer was elected Justice of the Peace of Cameron township, and served five years.

At the age of twenty-seven, Mr. Boyer commenced reading law in the office of Horatio J. Wolverton, and was admitted to the bar, in Sunbury, August 5th, 1858, and subsequently, in the counties of Snyder, Union, Lycoming, Columbia, Schuylkill, Dauphin, Clinton, Allegheny, Montour, Chester, and Philadelphia.

While engaged in his law studies, he was elected Coroner of Northumberland County, and held the position three years.

Mr. Boyer was elected Chief Burgess of the borough of Sunbury, and was three times re-elected, holding the position four years.

Under his administration, various important improvements in the town were put under way, among which may be mentioned, the grading of certain sidewalks, and the laying of the first pavements. He made a very energetic and efficient Chief Burgess.

Mr. Boyer has for some time been prominently connected with various benevolent organizations. He is a leading member of the I. O. O. F., of Sunbury, and for six years held the position of District Deputy Grand Master of Northumberland County, and for four years was District Deputy Grand Patriarch. He was also for a year District Deputy Grand Chancellor in the Knights of Pythias.

He is, likewise, a prominent member of the Masonic Fraternity, being now Master Mason of the Shamokin Lodge, No. 255. In 1875, he was elected Grand Warden of the Grand Lodge of I. O. O. F., of Pennsylvania, and in 1876, was made Deputy Grand Master of the Grand Lodge of the State.

Mr. Boyer's legal practice has been a gratifying success. He never enjoyed the advantages of a collegiate, or even academic course. His fine natural abilities, however, coupled with his great energy and close application, have placed him in the front rank of the profession.

On October 5th, 1860, he was admitted to practice in the Supreme Court of the Commonwealth; and shortly afterwards in the District and Circuit Courts of the United States, of the Eastern and Western Districts of Pennsylvania.

Mr. Boyd is a gentleman of fine social qualities, and is an influential member of the community.

DR. R. H. AWL.

This gentleman has been a member of the medical profession for a period of nearly forty years. He was born in Northumberland County, December 27th, 1819, and is the son of Samuel Awl, Esq., and Mary Maclay, who had a family of five sons and five daughters, of whom the subject of this notice is the youngest child. His father was born in Dauphin County, in 1773, and died in Upper Augusta, in 1842, at the age of sixty-eight. He was, for many years, Justice of the Peace of old Augusta township, and also filled some county offices.

His wife was the daughter of Wm. Maclay, who was the first Register and Recorder and Clerk of the Orphans' Court for Northumberland County. He was an old surveyor, and was extensively engaged in that work in the State at a very early day. From 1789 to 1791, he was also United States Senator from Pennsylvania, and his brother, Samuel Maclay, occupied the same position from 1803 to 1808. He had previously, in 1794, been the first Representative in Congress from Northumberland and Dauphin counties.

The Maclay family were of Irish extraction; and at an early day, in that country, bore a title—"*The Baron Fingle.*" The following statement briefly indicates their genealogy:

CHARLES MACLAY,

by his first wife, had three sons—*Owen*, *Charles*, and *Henry*—all officers in King James, Army before the battle of the Boyne, in which engagement Henry was killed.

The second wife of Charles, Sr., was a Scotch lady, by the name of Hawthorn, by whom he had a son,

JOHN,

who also became the father of three children—*Charles*, *John*, and a daughter.

The sons emigrated to the United States, and settled near Shippensburg, Franklin County, Pa., where they both died, Charles leaving five children—*John*, *William*, *Charles*, *Samuel*, and *Eleanor*.

The second son, William Maclay, was, as before stated, the maternal grandfather of Dr. R. H. Awl. William Maclay's wife, or the maternal grandmother of Dr. Awl, was Mary Harris, a daughter of John Harris, Jr., who assisted in laying out the city of Harrisburg. This John Harris married a Miss Elizabeth McClure, said to be one of the loveliest women of her day. It may here be added, that a sister of this John Harris, (daughter of John Harris, Sr., an English immigrant, in the settlement of William Penn, and Assistant Surveyor, in the laying out of the city of Philadelphia,) became the wife of Dr. William Plunket, a high-toned gentleman of the old school, and a near relative of W. C. Plunket, Lord High Chancellor of Ireland. Previous to the removal of the Pennsylvania Capitol from Lancaster to Harrisburg, John Harris, Jr., donated to the Commonwealth four acres of the plot of ground on which is now located the State Capitol.

The name, moreover, of John Harris, Sr., has passed into history, as that of the one who emancipated the first slave on the American Continent. This was done as a reward to the negro who was instrumental in rescuing him from being burned by the Indians. This occurred at Harrisburg, in 1720, and the name of the slave was Hercules.

Dr. R. H. Awl's privileges in the educational line were simply those of the early-day common school. He read medicine under the instruction of Dr. John W. Peal, of Sunbury, and attended lectures in the Pennsylvania Medical College, in Philadelphia, from which institution he graduated in the Spring of 1842. He began practice in Gratztown, Dauphin County, Pa., spending some two years there, and about the same time in Halifax.

He then removed to Ohio, and located in Columbus, but was soon appointed assistant physician in the Ohio Lunatic Asylum, in that city, which position he occupied for nearly three years.

In the Spring of 1849, he returned to Sunbury, which has since been his residence. In the years 1864 and 1865, he served the people of Northumberland, in the capacity of County Treasurer.

The Doctor has enjoyed a long and successful practice, and is the oldest physician in the borough. For a number of years past his more active practice has been interrupted by feeble health, very greatly to the regret of his numerous patrons.

Dr. Awl is a gentleman of pleasing address, fine social qualities and strong convictions, and occupies a prominent place among the substantial and much respected citizens of Sunbury.

Dr. Awl's oldest brother, Dr. William M. Awl, has been for many years a very prominent physician in Ohio. He was the founder, and, for nearly twenty years, the Superintendent of the State Lunatic Asylum, at Columbus. He was also the first President of the United States Medical Society for the Treatment of the Insane. He is now in his seventy-eighth year, and has retired from professional service. To him, also, is due the credit of initiating the movement for the erections of asylums for the Idiotic in the United States. In his whole life work, the Doctor has been a genuine Philanthropist.

Dr. Awl is also the author of a "Chronological Chart," with tables, showing the genealogy of the race, and the ages of the prominent Bible characters from Adam to Moses. It is the result of a number of years of patient research, and is designed for the use of Sunday-schools and Bible students. It is accompanied by an explanatory key, and is a very valuable contribution to religious literature.

EMANUEL WILVERT.

The present editor and proprietor of the *Sunbury American* was born in Dauphin County, Pennsylvania, March 24th, 1830. His boyhood up to the age of fifteen was passed upon a farm. In the Spring of 1844, the family came to Sunbury, and on August 15th, 1845, he entered, as an apprentice, the office of the *American*, then conducted by Messrs. H. B. Masser and Joseph Eisely, where he served for a period of five years and six months.

After a year or more spent in the book office of Messrs. King & Baird, of Philadelphia, in 1851 he became foreman in the office of the *Pottsville Emporium*, conducted by Hon. S. N. Palmer, where he remained till the Fall of 1852. He subsequently entered a corps of civil engineers on the Northern Central Railway under Hon. Kimber Cleaver, and remained with them till the road was completed, and was then employed for a year-and-a-half as brakesman on a coal train. He soon afterwards was appointed foreman in the office of the *Sunbury American*.

On the 24th of September, 1864, he became a partner with Mr. Masser in the establishment, and upon the retirement of Mr. Masser on January 1st, 1869, Mr. Wilvert became sole proprietor and conductor. Mr. Wilvert has since greatly enlarged the establishment by the addition of steam and power-presses, and other important materials.

Since Mr. Wilvert assumed charge of the *American*, he has been an earnest, active, Republican politician. For nine successive years he held the position of Chairman of the Republican County Convention. He is a gentleman of genial and obliging spirit, but a bold and out-spoken writer, and has ever pursued a fearless and independent course. Not even the oft-repeated threats of assassination at the hands of the "Mollie Maguires" could deter him from waging a long and relentless war upon that infamous organization. The influence of the *American* in this direction was materially felt throughout this County, and, by the copying of its articles into other papers, in many of the adjoining counties.

As a political journal it has had not a little to do in the reduction, from time to time, of the Democratic majorities in Northumberland County, as may be instanced in the campaign of 1871, when Judge Rockefeller was elected on the Republican ticket by upwards of fifteen hundred majority.

As an illustration of Mr. Wilvert's genuine Republican grit, it may be mentioned that, in the summer of 1863, he discharged the only compositor in his office for refusing to place the name of Lincoln at the head of the columns of the *Americaner*, of which Mr. Wilvert was at the time the foreman. This determined stand won him great favor from all loyal citizens.

Mr. Wilvert's public spirit and enterprise have placed him in prominent connection with all the public improvements of Sunbury since he entered upon active life.

J. E. EICHHOLTZ.

The subject of this notice is the editor and proprietor of the *Northumberland County Democrat*. He was born in Lebanon, Pa., November 11th, 1836, and was educated at Lancaster. From 1854 to 1858, he served an apprenticeship to the printer's trade, in Mifflintown and Lewisburg, and was employed as foreman in the printing offices in Lancaster city, from the latter date to the year 1865, when he took charge of the *Lewisburg* (Pa.) *Argus*, changing its name to "*Journal*." After a brief editorship there, he was called to the editorial chair of the *Pottsville Standard*, which was under the proprietorship of Messrs. Barclay Brothers. About a year later, Mr. T. H. Purdy, the proprietor of the *Northumberland County Democrat*, wrote to Mr. Eichholtz, (the latter having served Mr. Purdy for some time, while he was editing the *Lewisburg Argus*, aforesaid,) and offered him the *Democrat*. Mr. Eichholtz accepted, purchased the *Democrat*, and has since presided over its columns. He has had several partners during his residence in Sunbury, but is now the sole proprietor of the establishment. He has had various "ups and downs," financially and otherwise, but his untiring energy and perseverance have carried him victoriously through all difficulties, and to-day he is a permanent institution in Sunbury. He has made the *Democrat* a power in the County, and edits it with a sharp and vigorous pen. He is also the proprietor of the *Sunbury Daily*, the only daily paper in the County.

Mr. Eichholtz is a gentleman of fine social qualities, very positive in his convictions, and ranks among the leading editors in northern Pennsylvania.

THOMAS M. PURSEL, Esq.

The subject of this notice is a descendant of Peter Pursel, a native of New Jersey and who, at a very early day, came to Pennsylvania, and settled in Columbia County, and in 1824, removed to Northumberland County, and settled on Bird's Island, at the junction of the north and west branches of the Susquehanna River. There was but one house on the island, and this Mr. Pursel occupied for a time, but subsequently settled on what was then known as the Maclay Mill property, east of the borough of Sunbury, now owned by John S. Haas.

The old gentleman was well and favorably known throughout the County, and reared a family of twelve children, of whom the subject of this sketch was the fourth son and eleventh child.

Thomas M. Pursel was born on Bird's Island, September 11th, 1825.

When an infant of between three and four years of age, he was initiated into public service in this wise: His father had a contract for the construction of a section of the North Branch Canal, above Northumberland, which ran through what was known as the old Nurse Farm, and young Pursel—then at the age just named—was employed as "*Jigger Boss*," the duty of which position was to carry the whisky to the men engaged upon the work.

"Then whisky made by *honest* men,
Was drunk by men *upright*."

In the discharge of this business, Thomas was as faithful as any employee in the enterprise, and even at that tender age, developed those elements of thoughtfulness and promptness which have characterized him as a business man. When a young man he was engaged, for a number of years, as Captain of a boat on the Pennsylvania Canal.

On July 24th, 1856, he married Miss Emily M., daughter of George Zimmerman, of Sunbury, by whom he had a son and two daughters, the son now deceased.

In 1868, he was appointed, and served for about a year, under the administration of President Johnson, as Weighmaster in the United States Custom House, in Philadelphia.

In 1871, he was elected Justice of the Peace, in Sunbury, for a period of five years, and in the discharge of the duties of this responsible position, he has been prompt and impartial.

'Squire Pursel is one of those plain-spoken, solid men, who form the valued portion of a community.

Other members of this family have also been prominently connected with the affairs of the County. John P. Pursel, brother of the subject of this notice, was "Register and Recorder and Clerk of the Orphans' Court," for a period of six years, and was succeeded by another brother, C. Boyd Pursel, who served three years. The latter died at the expiration of his term.

JOSEPH G. DURHAM.

This gentleman is a descendant from ancestors who were participants in the hardships and dangers of the Revolutionary war. His paternal grandmother, Mrs. Margaret Durham, had a hair-breadth escape from death in this wise: Sometime in the Autumn of 1778, Mrs. Durham and a Mrs. McKnight, with small children in their arms, and mounted on horseback, with a number of men on foot, started from Freeland's Fort to go to Northumberland. One mile below the mouth of Warrior Run, they were surprised and fired upon by a party of Indians. Mrs. McKnight's horse suddenly wheeled and galloped back. She came very near losing her child, but caught it by the foot, and held it firmly, dangling by her side, till the frightened animal brought her to the fort. Mrs. Durham's infant was shot in her arms, and she fell from her horse, and was taken prisoner and scalped by the Indians, and left for dead. She was found, and taken by her brother down the river in a canoe to Fort Augusta. Her wounds were dressed by Dr. Plunket, and as she had received no other injury than the loss of a portion of her scalp, she recovered. Her husband was taken prisoner by the Indians, and carried to Canada, where he remained several years, but at the close of the war was exchanged and returned home, to the great joy of his wife, both of whom, in the meantime, had supposed each other to be dead.

After this re-union, Mrs. Durham became the mother of five children, and lived to a good old age. One of her sons, James Durham, born in this County, in 1784, became the father of the subject of this sketch.

This last-named gentleman was born in Northumberland County, Pa., November 20th, 1813. The first twenty years of his life were spent upon a farm. He then learned the carpenter's trade, which he followed for several years. After this, he settled upon a farm in Delaware township, where he remained till the Summer of 1876, when he removed to Watsontown, his present residence.

On June 9th, 1840, he married Miss Margaret, daughter of James Lowry, of this County.

Out of a family of four sons and two daughters, one daughter died in infancy, and the eldest son, James L. Durham, enlisted in company B, One Hundred and Thirty-first Pennsylvania Volunteer Infantry, was wounded at the first battle before Fredericksburg, December 13th, 1862, and died in the Georgetown College Hospital, on the 31st of the same month, in the nineteenth year of his age. He was a young man of promise, and was contemplating a collegiate course, with a view to enter the ministry. It may be said of him, as of thousands of others, "*He fought and died for his country.*"

In 1872, Mr. Durham was elected Commissioner of Northumberland County, which, considering the fact that he was a Republican, and the County strongly Democratic, was a high compliment to a meritorious man. In 1875, he was re-elected to the same responsible office. He is a gentleman of modest manners, genial nature, and solid worth.

For considerably upwards of a quarter of a century, both he and his companion have been connected with the Presbyterian Church, in which he now holds the office of Elder.

HARRISON HENRIE.

This gentleman is one of the present Commissioners of Northumberland County. He was born in Shamokin township, January 29th, 1832. When he was only five years of age, his mother was left a widow with a family of six children to care for. Just before his death, her husband had purchased a little farm, upon which, at the time of his decease, rested a considerable debt. At that time the law was less merciful in its protection of the widow than now, and Mrs. Henrie was compelled to part with all her property, and was left destitute. The family were scattered, and the children found homes among strangers. The educational advantages of the subject of this sketch were, consequently, very meagre. No one will care for an orphan boy, as will his father.

From the tender age of six years, up to his manhood, young Henrie was kept at work almost without intermission. Whatever, therefore, he may be to-day, has been the result of his own determined effort, and in this he is an imitable example of a self-made man.

When about fourteen years old, he repaired to Schuylkill County, and entered upon an apprenticeship to the bricklaying trade, which he followed for some twenty-five years. In 1853, he located in Shamokin, where he has since resided.

On January 26th, 1857, he married Miss Mary Jane Bird, daughter of Ziba Bird, of Montour County, Pa., and has had a family of five sons and four daughters, two of the former, and one of the latter, deceased.

For a time, Mr. Henrie was engaged in the grocery business, in Shamokin, but discontinued it, as the confinement in the store interfered with his health.

Among the positions of public trust which Mr. Henrie has been called upon to fill in the community, may be mentioned that of Assessor and Collector of Shamokin borough.

In the Autumn of 1874, he was elected to fill a vacancy in the Board of County Commissioners, caused by a change in the State Constitution, and in 1875, was re-elected for a period of three years.

Mr. Henrie is a man of practical common sense, clear in his judgment, conservative in his views, and popular in his County, as may be inferred from the fact that in both of his elections for Commissioner, he received a larger vote than any other candidate before the people.

In politics, Mr. Henrie is a Democrat; in religious views, a Methodist.

D. S. REITZ.

Mr. Reitz was born in Northumberland County, Pa., October 18th, 1840. He is the youngest son of Jonathan Reitz, also a native of this County, who is now in the seventy-third year of his age.

At the age of eighteen, young Reitz learned the shoemaker's trade, and worked at this business for some eleven years, in the vicinity of the house of his childhood.

On March 19th, 1865, he married Miss Sarah Peifer, daughter of George Peifer, of this County, and has had a family of four sons and two daughters, one of the former having died in infancy.

For a number of years he was engaged in the mercantile business, at Dornsife Station, at which place he was also post-master for some seven years. After leaving the store he purchased a grist-mill, which he ran for some five years, when he took in his brother, Henry Reitz, as a partner, who subsequently became sole owner of the establishment.

In the Autumn of 1873, Mr. Reitz was elected a Commissioner of Northumberland County, and, serving two years, was re-elected in the Fall of 1875, for a term of three years. This position is one of the most responsible of the County offices, and subjects the occupant to his full share of censure, and entitles him to a corresponding degree of credit for duties faithfully discharged.

Mr. Reitz is a man who thinks for himself, and will favor only those measures which, in his judgment, the welfare of the people demands.

In April, 1876, he removed to Shamokin, and has erected a fine business house, which is a credit to the place. He is highly esteemed as a sober and industrious citizen.

On the 10th of May, 1876, Mr. Reitz was called to mourn the loss of his wife by death, under peculiarly trying circumstances. The day previous to this sad event, Mrs. Reitz had been visiting her parents, in Little Mahanoy, and returned to Shamokin in the evening, and retired at her accustomed hour in apparently good health. On the following morning she was found dead in her bed, with her youngest child still sleeping in her arms. She had evidently died without a struggle. An inquest was held by Coroner Taylor, the jury rendering a verdict of death from heart disease. The attending physician was Dr. Weaver.

At the time of her death, Mr. Reitz was in Sunbury, attending to the duties of his official position; when a telegram announced to him the startling intelligence, the stricken husband hastened home to pay the last sad tribute of devotion to all that death had left of her who was the solace of his sorrows and the comfort of his home

Her remains were taken to Baker's Station, on Tuesday evening, and the funeral took place on the following Thursday, from the residence of her father.

J. K. DAVIS, Jr.

The subject of this brief notice, is a rising young lawyer of Sunbury. He is the eldest son of of James K. Davis, a retired business man, and much esteemed citizen of Selinsgrove, Pa. The old gentleman has also been, for some years, a Director of the First National Bank, of that place, and also of Sunbury.

Young Davis was born in Selinsgrove, October 14th, 1842. At the age of eighteen, he entered Allegheny College, at Meadville, Pa., from which institution he graduated in 1865. He then came to Sunbury, and read law under the instruction of the Hon. John B. Packer, and was admitted to the bar in August, 1867. In January, following, he was also admitted to practice in the Supreme Court of the Commonwealth, in Philadelphia. In 1869, he was honored by his "*Alma Mater*" with the degree of "Master of Arts." From 1867 to 1873, Mr. Davis was entrusted with the management of the legal business of his preceptor, the Hon. John B. Packer, while the latter was a Representative in Congress. In this position, Mr. Davis acquitted himself with creditable efficiency.

In 1873, he visited South and Central America, with the expedition to make examinations and surveys for the proposed route for the Inter-oceanic Canal, between the Atlantic and Pacific Oceans

In 1874, he returned home, making a tour of various Southern States, and in August, 1875, became Managing Clerk in the law-office of S. P. Wolverton, Esq., which position he is now filling.

Mr. Davis possesses legal abilities of a high order, coupled with great energy and business tact. He is a man of positive views, plain and outspoken, but combines all the elements of a thorough gentleman.

JACOB MOWRY.

The five original citizens of Shamokin were, Ziba Bird, Joseph Snyder, Dr. Robert Philips, James Porter, and Jacob Mowry. Mr. Mowry, the last survivor of this number, was born near Danville, about 1802, and died at his residence, in Shamokin, April 9th, 1875, aged 73 years. In the Spring of 1836, Mr. Mowry, who had for some time previously been engaged on the Girard Road, in various capacities, came to Shamokin. The abovenamed parties were his only neighbors, with the exception of John Thomson, who lived at Springfield, and Peter Wary, who lived in what is now West Shamokin. Mr. Mowry's first place of residence was a small house, now covered up by the refuse from the Cameron Colliery. In the Spring of 1837, he removed to another log house near the spot where the brick house of B. F. Lake now stands.

Mr. Mowry was a man of wonderful energy and his success in driving work on the Girard Road attracted the attention of Burd Patterson and John C. Boyd, who induced him to locate here when the town started, feeling certain he would be a valuable man in developing the resources of our region, which were then only partially known. For several years he was busily engaged by the land proprietors in opening mines. He opened the first drifts at Buck Ridge, now Big Mountain, and also those for the Shamokin Coal and Iron Company, opposite the old furnace. He likewise made some openings for Mr. Dewart at what is now the Cameron Colliery. Mr. Mowry may justly be regarded as the pioneer "boss miner" of the region.

In the Spring of 1838, he built the house he lived in at the time of his death. Some years later he purchased some land on Gass Hill, and made the substantial improvements there that are now known as the "Poor House Property." Upon disposing of this property, he took charge of the United States Hotel, of which he was proprietor, and kept it about two years. Mr. Mowry was possessed of excellent judgment and was regarded as an excellent citizen. He was plain and simple in his habits, and deprecated all ostentation. He was the last link of those who might be termed the pioneers.

JOHN B. DOUTY.

Mr. Douty, one of the oldest and most substantial citizens of Shamokin, was born near Lambertville, New Jersey, May 5th, 1812, and died November 18th, 1873, aged sixty-one years.

About 1822, the Douty family moved to Rush township, Northumberland County, but in 1826, moved to Pottsville, when it was just emerging from a wilderness. Mr. Douty's father commenced boating on the Schuylkill Canal this year, being the owner of five boats. Mr. Douty, who was then only a boy, had charge of one of them. He was one of the earliest boatmen of the Schuylkill Navigation. He continued in this business for some years with considerable success

In 1842, he quitted the canal, and entered the coal business at the East Delaware Mines, mining coal by contract for some years, when he went to the West Delaware Mines, and continued there until about 1851, when the company failed. By this failure, Mr. Douty lost all he had acquired by years of toil. But with an undaunted will and valuable experience, he came to Shamokin, in 1852, and commenced in a small way at the "Gap," where the Cameron Colliery is now located, as one of the firm of Kase, Douty & Reed. At this early day in the coal trade of the Shamokin region, when all the coal was hauled to Sunbury by horse-power, but little was done or made.

In October, 1856, Shraf & Black having failed, Mr. Douty, as one of the firm of Bird, Douty & John, took charge of the Big Mountain Colliery, and under his care and labor it became one of the principal collieries of the region. In 1857, Mr. J. J. John, retired from the firm, and in 1859, Mr. Douty withdrew to start another colliery—the Henry Clay—the coal of which under his supervision has justly acquired a celebrity wherever anthracite is used. Mr. Douty, by energy, tact, and the favorable times, acquired a handsome competence here. Some years afterward, he started the Ready Colliery, and worked it for several years.

In 1872, he became connected with the Benjamin Franklin Colliery, under the firm of Douty & Baumgardner.

For over twenty years, Mr. Douty has been largely connected with the coal trade of this region, as one of the most enterprising and successful coal operators.

He made good use of his wealth in putting up substantial buildings that are an ornament to the town. He was a public spirited man, who was closely identified with every movement that looked towards the welfare and improvement of his adopted town. For religious and charitable objects he contributed largely.

Mr. Douty was a man of positive convictions—of strong likes and dislikes, and perhaps of eccentricities, but possessed a kind heart and an honest purpose. He was deservedly well esteemed by the working class, and his name and many good acts will long be remembered by them.

KIMBER CLEAVER.

The subject of this sketch was born at Roaring Creek, in Columbia County, on the 17th day of October, in the year 1814. He was the son of Joseph Cleaver, an industrious and respectable farmer of that region, a member of the Society of Friends.

During his minority he enjoyed but a few of the facilities for improving his mind that are enjoyed by the youth of the present time. Reared in a township that even at this day is not noted for its intelligence, and before the great common school system was established, he had but little opportunity to culture a mind which Nature had so profusely gifted with the choicest of talents. His education consisted of a few months of imperfect instruction during the Winter season, at an ordinary country school, where he was taught to read, to write, and to cipher in the elementary rules. His insatiable thirst for knowledge was but poorly slaked by his teacher, who was only able to afford him shallow and turbid draughts from the Pierian spring. But he had an instructor in misfortune. His early trials and struggles, his hopes, disappointments and afflictions constituted an ordeal through which he passed triumphantly, and finally developed the mind of the man, whose character we now so much esteem. Mr. Cleaver in his conversation and letters, frequently alluded to these, which he pleasantly designated his sweet uses of adversity. Afflicted during his youthful days with that painful affection, known as white-swelling, and not possessed of a robust constitution, his boyhood hours were somewhat exempted from the cares and labors of farming, which he industriously applied to study. The invalid student, under the most unfavorable circumstances, began the Herculean task of self-improvement. Having access to but few books, which he carefully gleaned of all their treasures, his mind though depressed by acute bodily suffering, was ever active, and naturally turned on its favorite bent of study—Mechanics. One of the first efforts of his genius, whilst yet a boy, and confined to a bed of sickness, was the construction of a clock, which served his father's family as a time-piece for many years. This he executed by means of a jack-knife alone.

When Mr. Cleaver had his health partially restored, he taught school for some time, and here no doubt, while pursuing this avocation, which has been the stepping-stone of so many of our American youths, his mind underwent that discipline, which peculiarly fitted it for the profession he afterward pursued. Mr. Cleaver, being a natural mechanic and mathematician, had a strong inclination for civil engineering, and when the first improvement for the Middle Coal Field—the noble project of constructing the Danville and Pottsville Railroad was put into operation, he entered the Corps of Engineers as a peg driver. He was gradually promoted from one station to another until 1835, when he began as an engineer for that road. Upon this work he continued until 1836, when he removed to Pottsville and became connected with the Mt. Carbon Railroad. From this period until 1844 his time was variously divided on labors in this and Schuylkill County. During these years, Mr. Cleaver, at much personal cost and labor, made most of the surveys, from which he afterwards constructed his great map of the Middle Coal Fields of Pennsylvania. This work was of eminent service to capitalists, who have since become interested in our rich mineral regions, and rendered Mr. Cleaver one of the most useful and indispensable of men. The coal formation of Mt. Carmel, Coal, and Zerbe townships, so accurately represented on the county map, is from the work of Mr. Cleaver.

During this time he located a route for a railroad from Shamokin to Danville, and also one from Shamokin to Pottsville, without inclined planes.

From 1844 to 1850 he resided in Pottsville, and devoted most of his time to professional labors in that county.

In 1850 he removed to Shamokin, where, in connection with Mr. H. Marshall, he has been connected with all the improvements that have metamorphosed our regions. He was Chief Engineer at Trevorton in locating and building its railroads to the Susquehanna, when that town emerged from a wilderness; and when Shamokin had finally awakened from an incubus of years, he was appointed principal engineer of the Philadelphia & Sunbury Railroad, of the collieries, and of lateral roads. Here he labored faithfully for years, and added many improvements to his genius.

In 1858, he was called to Schuylkill County to make some surveys in the mines at Glen Carbon. Being much exposed to dampness, and sometimes in water up to his knees, of an icy temperature, he contracted a sickness, of which he died on the 10th of October, 1858, at Pottsville.

The announcement of his death created a pang of sorrow throughout the community in which he moved, and even in wider circles where his name had become familiar. His decease was kindly noticed in the public prints of the day, and the different associations with which he was connected passed resolutions, showing that they had lost more than an ordinary member.

Having given a hasty outline of Mr. Cleaver's life, the sketch will be concluded with a brief review of him, first as an *inventor*, second as a *politician*, and lastly as *a man*.

Mr. Cleaver was a natural genius, but like Fitch and most inventors, his inventions never repaid him, but rather kept him poor.

Mr. Cleaver invented a draughting instrument, known as *Cleaver's Improved Protractor*. The United States Government, appreciating the value of this instrument, kept the manufacturer, W. J. Young, of Philadelphia, for some time employed in making them for the government service.

Mr. Cleaver gave much study to the subject of electricity, with the view of introducing it as an agent in the propagation of news. He is entitled to the distinguished honor of having first conceived and suggested the idea of a sub-marine telegraph, and from his description of the apparatus, we are justified in the opinion, that he was not then aware of the Morse telegraph, which was invented in 1837 and not put in practical operation until 1844. The following article from the pen of Mr. Cleaver, in 1841, under the signature of *Cosmopolite*, and published in a Harrisburg paper, will show that much credit for this great American invention is due to him.

"Mr. Editor.—*Dear Sir:* I believe the time has now arrived, when the postulatum will be admitted, that the more intelligent the people are, and the better the facilities are for conveying that intelligence from State to State, and from nation to nation, the sooner will all distrusts and *jealousy* subside, and the human family be united in one harmonious whole. I admit 'the age of *steam*' affords facilities for conveying intelligence very rapidly, and the broad Atlantic is traversed as a mill-pond, and Europe is brought to be our next-door neighbor; but if we can employ a messenger more expeditious, and equally truthful, then it is certainly our duty, as peace-makers, to do so. I mean electricity, which, of all material agents that we are acquainted with, is the most fleet. Perhaps my readers will entertain some doubt as to the possibility of constructing an electric telegraph across the broad Atlantic; but only tell a Yankee boy that the project is impossible, and he will be sure to try it. Neither do I view it as a thing impossible, and will therefore briefly describe the plan, as follows: Manufacture a number of copper wires, equal in number to the letters in the alphabet, and long enough to reach from the Capitol, at Washington, to St. James' Palace, each wire being separately covered with silk, or some other non-conductor, then all being collectively covered with a strong, water-proof covering, which would form a string of perhaps five inches in diameter; then assemble a sufficient number of water-crafts, and extend the string across the Atlantic, and at intervals, say every two or three miles, fasten a weight, sufficient to sink the string, and at a given signal leave it down, retaining one end on shore at Washington, and one in England, and arrange the wires at both ends on a table, each wire pointing to a letter of the alphabet, somewhat after the fashion of the keys of a piano-forte, and so constructed, that when a current of electric fluid is communicated to either wire at one end of this string, it will produce an effect perceptible to one of the senses at the other end. Then, if any boundary or commercial treaties are to be negotiated, let the ministers of State be seated on a 'glass stool,' at this alphabetical musical table, and with an electricising-machine supply the negotiators with the fluid; then, when he 'strikes the lyre' in truth, 'the nations would be as entranced.' Or, if a speech delivered in Congress is to be reported, let the reporters in the same way send it thrilling across the waters. It would be like uniting to the lightning's flash the thunder of our Republican eloquence, and 'earth's loveliest bounds, and ocean's wildest shore,' would be made vocal with the shouts of liberty.

Yours, &c.,

Pottsville, Pa. COSMOPOLITE."

Mr. Cleaver invented a very ingenious car-box; the spiral shute, for breakers; the coal hammers, to take the place of rolls, in the preparation of coal; a cast-iron lock; and a new mode of framing, in place of mortise and tenon.

Mr. Cleaver had contemplated publishing a small work on the "Geology of the Coal Regions," which doubtless would have been of great interest.

As a politician, Mr. Cleaver did not belong to the modern class. He was no office-seeker, but preferred the quiet walks of private life.

He became connected with the Native American party, which started in 1844, and soon became one of the leaders. He was frequently nominated for office—positions which he never sought. In 1852, his party nominated him for Governor; in 1853, for Surveyor-General; in 1854, he was the American candidate for Congress in the Eleventh District; and in 1855 he was nominated for Canal Commissioner. For each of these offices he received a highly complimentary vote. In 1856, his name was placed on the Fillmore electoral ticket.

In private life he was universally esteemed. Possessed of strict integrity, and habits of industry, he won the good opinions of all. He was emphatically more than a common man, and his death left a void in social and scientific circles not easily filled.

"Patriot, yet friend to truth; of soul sincere,
In action faithful, and in honor clear,
Who broke no promise, served no private end,
Who sought no title, and who lost no friend."

GENERAL DANIEL BRODHEAD.

One important feature of the Illustrated History of Northumberland County, will be the sketches of the lives and services of the prominent men, both dead and living. Their lives and acts enter into and form an essential part of the history of their times. Without the lessons to be drawn from their self-denial and patriotism, the past would be but an imperfect guide for the future. One of the most notable men of Revolutionary times was Daniel Brodhead. General Brodhead was not a native of this County, nor did he spend much of his time while a soldier here; but the services rendered by him were so conspicuously productive of good to the people, and his magnanimous treatment of his enemies, was so marked in contrast with that of many others, and withal, the course pursued by him was so effectual in the accomplishment of the purposes of his campaign on the Susquehanna, that every fact and incident in the life of this truly great man is published.

In writing of the Revolutionary war, an author says: "The conflict was with the tomahawk and scalping knife, united to the arms of scientific warfare; and to defend the country against the ravages of such a war, required men of iron nerve, determined will and no ordinary character;" and that "the skill, bravery and consummate judgment of able officers, and experienced frontier soldiers saved the West from the diabolical system of subjugation, meditated by the British Ministry."

Looking back to that period, one is forced to conclude, that its actors, having achieved entire and glorious success, were so contented with their triumph, and happy in its enjoyment, that they failed to give just deference to any such thought, as that the generations unborn, still more contented and happy, would yearn to know and be instructed in all the details of the war, as well as those general operations, which usually are matters of History, as those other oftimes more deeply interesting occurrences, which individual biography, can only furnish. Hence, the difficulty, at the end of a hundred years, in furnishing anything like a fair or just sketch of the lives of most of the members of the Revolutionary Army. All that can be now done, is to gather together scattered statements, found here and there, in publications issued from time to time, having other main objects in view, and thus scantily supplied, what a little more personal ambition, in such individuals, would have given to their posterity in the shape of a perfect record. The following memoir, briefly prepared, of one of the men of much prominence in our early history, but like most others of that period, without any specially prepared biography, published at the time, when all could have been accurately delineated, is appropriately inserted here, inasmuch as at a time of most urgent necessity, his services were devoted to the protection of Muncy, and the region round about.

In the Historical Collections of Pennsylvania, by Day, page 452, it is said: "Shortly after the Big Runaway (so it was called,) Colonel Brodhead was ordered up with a force of 100 or 150 men, to rebuild Fort Muncy, and guard the settlers while gathering their crops, which service he performed."

The Pennsylvania Archives, second series, vol. 3, page 215, contains a "Memorial of the Inhabitants of Muncy, dated June 10th, 1778, to the Hon. the Supreme Executive Council of the State of Pennsylvania, which after stating their calamitous situation, proceeds to say: "That upon being informed of the melancholy event of the 20th of June last, at Wyoming, the few militia which were stationed at the little stands throughout the county, were called into the town of Sunbury, which so much alarmed the country, that every inhabitant, without exception, were flying from the county, when they were informed that Colonel Brodhead, at the head of the 8th Pennsylvania Regiment, who was with General M'Intosh on his march to the westward, at his own particular instance, had obtained a permit from the General to come from Carlisle, to their relief. This account gave new life to the sinking spirits of such of the inhabitants as had not gone too far with their families to return, and induced your petitioners once more to attempt a stand, but are at the same time under the greatest apprehensions of danger, when they are informed by the Colonel that he has no orders to stay amongst them." They, therefore, pray that an application be made to Congress for an order "to continue Colonel Brodhead's Regiment, or some other Continental troops amongst them."

The following incidents in the life of Colonel, more generally known as General Daniel Brodhead, are all that we have been able to collect at the present time. His ancestors were settled in Yorkshire, England, and after the Restoration, one of them also named Daniel, a captain of Musketeers, was sent with Colonel Nicolls, to New York, in 1664; and after the surrender by the Dutch, was appointed by Gov. N., in 1665, to the chief command of the militia at Esopus (now Kingston,) in Ulster County, on the Hudson River. He was married in England to Ann Tye, by whom he had three sons. Richard, his third son, had a son Daniel, who was born in Ulster County, N. Y., in 1693, and married in Pennsylvania in 1737, and settled near Easton. He had several children, one of whom was Daniel Brodhead, the subject of this memoir. General Daniel Brodhead, was married to Elizabeth Depuy, daughter of Samuel Depuy, residing near the Delaware, about five miles east of Stroudsburg, and one of the early settlers, a substantial farmer, noted for his hospitality. By her he had one child only, named Ann Garton, who married Jasper Heiner, of Reading, Pa., and their children were Elizabeth, intermarried with Captain Silas Webb, of Brooklyn, N. Y.; Margaret, with John Faulk, of Kittanning, Pa.; Daniel, who died unmarried, and Rebecca Justina, intermarried with Samuel Johnson, of Newton, N. J. This last daughter, after the death of her husband, removed with her children, to Muncy, Lycoming County, where she resided until her death, in 1802, and where her surviving children now live. The following is an extract from the General's will, dated August 8th, 1800. "I give to my granddaughter, Rebecca J. Johnson (late Rebecca Heiner,) my miniature picture set in gold." This little souvenir is now held by her only surviving son, Hon. Henry Johnson, and is by him considered of inestimable value. It is the penciling of the best painters of that time, and looks as fresh as if just from the easel. It represents the General as he was in military costume of the year 1776, and it was painted just after his entering the Revolutionary Army.

The earliest mention of him is found in the Colonial Records, when under date of December 25th (year not stated,) it is recorded: "Accounts from Easton of the whole country up the river being deserted, from that to Brodhead's, who, with his sons and others, defended himself stoutly, till the Indians retired." This settlement of Brodhead's, was probably not far from the mouth of the creek which bears his name, or it might have been near the site of Stroudsburg. One of the sons who defended themselves so gallantly, was no doubt the same who was afterwards distinguished in the Revolution, and in the subsequent Indian wars as General Brodhead. He had command at Fort Pitt, about the year 1780; and previous to that, had charge of a garrison on the West Branch. He was particularly distinguished for his intrepidity and success in heading small parties of frontier men against the Indians." (His. Col. p. 475.)

On the 15th of July, 1774, a provincial meeting of Deputies, chosen by the several counties in Pennsylvania, was commenced in Philadelphia. Daniel Brodhead, being elected and representing the county of Berks, he having removed to Reading. The sixteen resolves, finally adopted unanimously by this body, could have no other tendency than to hasten a final separation from Great Britain. The last resolution, instructed their Representatives in the Assembly, "who are to meet next week," to appoint "members to attend a Congress of Deputies from the several colonies, at such time and place as may be agreed on, to effect one general plan of conduct."

In 1775, on the 10th of May, Congress proceeded to the organization of an army, placing General Washington at its head. The Assembly of Pennsylvania, immediately took measures to raise forty-three hundred men apportioned to that province; made appropriation for their support, and the purchase of saltpetre. It authorized the enlistment of a battalion of eight companies for the Continental service, under Colonel John Bull, and fifteen hundred men for the defense of the province, until January, 1778, forming two battalions of Riflemen, under Colonel Mills, and Lieutenant Colonels Ennion Williams, and Daniel Brodhead, and one battalion of Infantry under Colonel Samuel Atlee.—(His. Col. p. 35, 36.)

In 1776, he was in the battle of Long Island with his Pennsylvania Riflemen, in the report of which, it is stated, this regiment rendered distinguished service.

During the Revolutionary war, a garrison was maintained in the Fort at Pittsburg, which served to guard not only the settlement, but was also used as a central post, from which offensive expeditions could be set to attack the Indians on the northwest of the Ohio.

It has been stated, in the introductory portion of this article, that in 1778, he rebuilt and occupied Fort Muncy, having been authorized by his General to do so, on his urgent solicitation, and the favor with which he was received by the inhabitants is manifested by their memorial of June 10th, in that year.

The following letter, will show in what estimation he was held by the Father of his Country, and is given in full, as it supplies the date of his appointment to the command of the Western Department.

HEADQUARTERS, MIDDLE BROOK, 5th March, 1779.

"SIR:—Brigadier General McIntosh having requested from Congress leave to retire from the command to the westward, they have, by a resolve of the 20th of February, granted his request, and directed me to appoint an officer to succeed him. From my opinion of your abilities, your former acquaintance with the back country, and the knowledge you must have acquired upon this last tour of duty, I have appointed you to the command in preference to a stranger, as he would not have time to gain the necessary information between that of his assuming the command and the commencement of operations.

"As soon as Congress had vested me with the superintendence of affairs to the westward, I gave General McIntosh orders to make the preparations and inquiries contained in my letters of the 31st January, and 15th February last. Copies of these letters he will deliver to you, and will inform you how far he hath proceeded in the several matters recommended to him, and will likewise communicate to you what measures he may have taken and what orders may have been given towards the completion of the remainder.

"You will observe by my letter of the 15th February, that I have directed the Commissary General, to endeavor to form his magazines by the 1st of May, by which time I hope the other preparations will be in sufficient forwardness to move. To induce you to exert yourself to the utmost to be ready by the above time, I need only make use of my argument, which is, that the success of the intended expedition does not depend upon the progress of one body of men, but upon the co-operation of several, anyone of which failing in point of time, may occasion the failure of the whole. The establishment of adequate magazines, and the preparation of a sufficient number of Boats, of the kind that may be deemed most proper, are what ought principally to engage your attention, should the inquiries concerning the Country, the waters, the distances, etc., be not so complete as might be wished, we might yet proceed; but without the others we must be entirely at a stand.

"I had desired General McIntosh to come down after he had put the matters recommended to him in a proper train, and to bring down a list of such stores and other necessaries as might be wanting for the expedition. But I do not see how there will be a possibility of your doing this. Had General McIntosh have come down, you would have been fully competent to carrying on the preparations, but if you quit the post, I apprehend there will be no officer left of sufficient weight and ability. This is an opinion which I would wish you to keep to yourself, because it might give offence to officers in all other respects very worthy of the station they fill. I must therefore desire you to remain at Fort Pitt, and you shall be from time to time fully informed of everything necessary for your Government.

"I have desired Gen. McIntosh, in case you should be absent, to send to you by a special messenger wherever you may be, and I must desire you to return to Fort Pitt with the utmost expedition, as you will, notwithstanding every exertion, find the time which you have for the execution of the Business fall short for its completion.

I am Sir,

Your most ob't and h'ble serv't,

GEO. WASHINGTON."

Col. Brodhead.

Shortly after this, at a conference of the Delaware Indian Chiefs the following complimentary communication, was made to Col. Brodhead, as found among his military papers:

FORT PITT, April 9th, 1779.

"The Delawares at a conference say:

"Of our ancestors, the good men of our nation, we have now handed you down the name, as we look upon you, to be an upright man. You are henceforth called by us the Delaware nation, the Great Moon, that is, in Delaware, Maghingua Keeshock. Hereafter our Great Grandchildren, yet unborn, when they come to the years of understanding, shall know that your name is handed down, as their Grand Father. All the speeches you now hand to the nations must be signed with your present name Maghingua Keeshock, and all the nations will address you by that name.

"There was four great good Kings of our nation. One of the names you have. Tamenend is another. We have yet two to bestow.

"Our ancestors in former times, they were of a good disposition, and are the cause of our now being as one Man. And now place you in the same light with us. Now hereafter perhaps those of our nation yet unborn are to know that that was the name of their ancestor."

After the reception of this title, all the titles and speeches of Col. Brodhead to and from the Indians, were addressed to him, and signed by this name. A letter book kept by him, contains many very interesting and remarkable communications, thus addressed or signed, and all ought to be published in some enduring form. We can give but one at this time, as it acknowledges the honor conferred by the Delawares.

"Col. Brodhead, or Maghingua Keeshock to the Chiefs of Hurons at Coshocking.

Brothers, the Hurons:

"I am much rejoiced to hear from my friends at Coshocking, that you are on the road to take me by the hand at Fort Pitt, and you may expect a hearty welcome. I send you this speech to inform you that what I told you before is true, and that you shall be well treated.

"Brothers, when you see me, you will see your countrymen and not a stranger that makes fair speeches from his, for which his heart must tell him he is a liar. No, you will see a man well known to your Nephews, the Delawares, and whom they have honored with a great name.

"Brothers, I wish you may be strong on your journey, and make no delay on the road. I know you have a great way to travel and I send you this string to wipe off your sweat.

MAGHINGUA KEESHOCK."

On the 22d of July, 1779, Col. Brodhead effected a treaty of peace and friendship, which is headed thus:

"Articles of Agreement and Confederation made and entered into by Daniel Brodhead, Esq., Colonel Commanding the Western Department, for and in behalf of the United States of North America, of the one part, and the Raven, Chief Warrior, and Shaweeshaw or Peewee Bird, Ochaulatoch or Red Parrot, Oolseuanegh or you say for nothing, Tockquaskeeh or Turpin and Shawillice, Chiefs and Warriors of the Cherokee nation."

In this treaty, there is a provision, that if found conducive to the interest of both parties a state should be formed, to include other tribes, whereof the Delaware Nation shall be the head, and have a representation in Congress.

The incursions of the Indians becoming very frequent, and those outrages so alarming, it was determined to carry into the country occupied by them, the same system of destructive warfare, with which they visited the settlements. For this purpose an adequate force was provided, under the immediate command of Gen. Brodhead. The troops proceeded up the Allegheny River, and at Brady's Bend a battle was fought, and the Indians were routed, many were killed on the banks of the river and in the stream.

In Alman's American Remembrance, will be found the official report of Brodhead's expedition up the Allegheny in 1779.

An expedition was made above the Conewango, and the Indians scattered, their cabins and corn burnt and destroyed. The Indians were thus quieted for some time, but spies were kept out to watch their motions and guard against sudden attacks, on the settlements.

In 1780, an expedition was set on foot to proceed against and destroy the Indian towns on the Coshocton, a branch of the Muskingum River. Wheeling was the place of rendezvous, and the command conferred upon Col. Brodhead. As part of its operations, it is related, that "it was secretly and actively pushed forward, till they surrounded one of their towns, before the enemy were apprised of their danger. Every man, woman and child were made prisoners, without the firing of a gun." The prisoners were taken to Fort Pitt and after some time exchanged for an equal number of captives held by the Indians.

"About six miles below Warren, near the mouth of Brokenstraw Creek, in Warren County, is the town of Cornplanter. On the flats below the village, once stood an Indian village, called Buckaloon, which was destroyed by a Detachment under Col. Brodhead from Pittsburg in 1781. It required a siege of some days to drive out the Indians, who retreated to the hills." (His. Col. p. 653.)

Washington, in a letter dated April, 1779, directed Col. Brodhead to make preparations for a Winter expedition against Detroit, but January 4th, 1780, he again wrote to him countermanding the order, in consequence of the operations against South Carolina, and his ability to reinforce Fort Pitt in case of a disaster. By another letter dated February 4th, 1780, he again declined a compliance with Col. Brodhead's renewed solicitation for a detachment to enable him to march to the reduction of Detroit; on the ground, that his "regular troops would all be needed to co-operate with our French Allies, and that militia too capricious to attempt anything with them which depend upon more than a very short time to accomplish the object." On the 18th of October, 1780, he again writes from "Camp near Passaic Falls." "The smallness of your force will not admit of an expedition of any consequence, had you magazines. You must therefore, of necessity, confine yourself to partisan strokes, which I wish to see encouraged." This letter also states that, "the State of Virginia are very desirous of an expedition against Detroit, and would make great exertions to carry it into execution." For reasons above given the project was abandoned.

At the close of 1781, Gen. Brodhead was transferred to other duties, and his further military acts cannot now be traced. The army was reorganized, probably from expiration of service, for in 1783, his signature as made to the organization articles of The Society of the Cincinnati, is "Daniel Brodhead, Col. 1st Pennsylvania Regiment," and Samuel Brady's, who served under him at Fort Pitt, appears as Captain 3d Pennsylvania Regiment.

This Society, July 4th, 1791, appointed a committee of three—Thomas L. Moore, Francis Johnson and Daniel Brodhead—to take proper measures for obtaining an Act of Incorporation, which was subsequently obtained. The original formation of this celebrated Society, was made on the 10th of May, 1783, at "Cantonment of the American, on Hudson River," by the general officers of the army, Major-General Baron de Steuben presiding.

On the 3d of November, 1789, he was elected by the Supreme Executive Council of Pennsylvania, Thomas Mifflin President thereof, to the office of Surveyor-General of the Commonwealth. This office he held for several successive terms, and most all of the loosed surveys in Wyoming will be returned to him as such.

He was married a second time, and Mrs. Rebecca Mifflin, the widow of General Samuel Mifflin, was his second wife; but there was no issue by this marriage.

Her death occurred at Milford, (then) Wayne County, November 15th, 1809, at the age of about seventy-three years. In 1871, his remains were removed from the old graveyard to the beautiful new cemetery there, and a monument to his memory as a soldier and civilian, erected by his surviving descendants and connections, who are numerous and scattered throughout Pennsylvania and other States.

COL. THOMAS HARTLEY.

Among the many heroes of the Revolutionary times, there are none who deserve to be more gratefully remembered by the people of the Susquehanna Valley, than he whose name heads this sketch. After the big runaway, the settlers manifested great reluctance at returning, until Col. Hartley took charge of the defenses of the frontier. His disposition of troops was effectual.

He planned, and effectually carried out an expedition, the purpose of which was to carry the war into the enemy's country, destroy their towns and places of rendezvous. An extract from his report to Congress, given below, furnishes the soldiers of the present with a clear perception of the trials of the troops of the Revolution.

Col. Hartley was born in Berks County, September 7th, 1748. He studied law, and commenced practice in York. At the breaking out of the war, he entered the army, and soon became distinguished. He was a member of Congress from 1788 to 1800, and held various offices within the Commonwealth. He died, December 21st, 1800, aged fifty-two years.

JUDGE THOMAS COOPER.

There are few people living in Northumberland County, who have not heard of Judge Thomas Cooper, and something of his trial, before the Senate of Pennsylvania, sitting as a court of impeachment, for sundry offenses, committed, or alleged to have been committed, against the dignity of the Commonwealth, while Judge of Northumberland Court. Some of those charges, as judged by the light afforded by the experience of the past fifteen or twenty years, appear exceedingly trivial, and to-day, with the rulings of a Busteed or Durant before us, they would not be noticed. Mr. Cooper appeared well able to manage his own case, and, in his reply, takes up the charges in detail, answering them fully. The various counts in the arraignment have been resurrected, and are herewith published in full:

First charge.—That he has in many instances fined, and even immured in prison, men of respectability, for no other fault than a mere whisper.

Second charge.—He has imprisoned a respectable citizen, for wearing a hat in conformity to a religious habit. The much injured citizen, in this case, was John Hanna, who was at one time Commissioner of Lycoming County. Public sentiment of to-day, would acquit Judge Cooper on this charge.

Third charge.—He has, after passing sentence on a felon, from mere hearsay, called him from prison, and pronounced a second sentence, increasing the penalty.

Fourth charge.—He has, unauthorized, decided important points in a cause in which he was interested in a pecuniary view.

This is effectually disposed of by Judge Cooper, whose statements are substantiated by William Montgomery, one of the Associate Justices of the Court at that time.

Fifth charge.—He has set aside the verdict of a jury, in an intemperate and passionate manner, and declared that he would do the same in every successive verdict, in the same cause, unless it corresponded with his opinion.

Sixth charge.—He has frequently brow-beaten counsel and witnesses, to the great injury of parties concerned.

Seventh charge.—He has appeared in Court, armed with weapons, calculated to awe the peaceful citizen.

Eighth charge.—He has often refused to hear persons in their own defense.

Ninth charge.—He has issued a proclamation against horse-racing, and afterwards, by the solicitation of his friends, ordered a suppression of the proclamation, and told them that no legal notice should be taken of the concern.

Tenth charge.—He has fined and imprisoned a constable for neglecting to execute a process, which was issued contrary to the constitution and laws of the country, as afterwards determined by the Supreme Court of the Commonwealth. This is the whole ground of offending on the part of Judge Cooper. It would probably be difficult to find so much ridiculous nonsense wrapped up in a few words, as is embodied in the ten charges against Judge Cooper. His answers are full, and must have been sufficient in the minds of an unbiased Court, to acquit him of any wrong intent. William Montgomery, associate with Judge Cooper, closes an able defense of his superior, in these words:

"I must say on the whole, that although sometimes one or more of the assistants have differed in opinion with the Judge, he has either submitted cheerfully to their opinion, or, when having a majority, the opinions of others of the judges has been treated with decorum and decency, and when he differed in opinion with any of the gentlemen of the bar, he has left them freely to take their exceptions. As to an improper brow-beating of counsel, witnesses, or parties, I do not recollect of being a witness to it.

Signed,

February 12th, 1811. WILLIAM MONTGOMERY."

Charge second was a strong point against his honor in the Democratic days of 1810. A correspondent arraigns him in the following strong language: "He has signalized his career by a regulation, than which a more tyrannical one never was made by the Ottoman prince, or Asiatic despot; it is pulling off the hat upon entering court." John Hanna, the offended citizen, who was imprisoned as charged in second count, publishes, over his own signature, his views:

"The judge and the nose-biting doctor, may combine to buy plantations, drink Maderia, and carve turkies, but they had better not combine to publish for truth what every one knows to be false. If it be right for Judge Cooper to fine and imprison me for wearing my own hat, let us see the law and constitution to justify it.

Northumberland, 26th of February, 1811. JOHN HANNA."

The committee of the Senate to which was referred the case of Mr. Cooper with the evidence, sum up the case and report as follows: "Your committee for the premises, are of the opinion that the official conduct of President Judge Cooper, has been arbitrary, unjust and precipitate, contrary to sound policy, and dangerous to the pure administration of justice. They therefore submit the following resolution: *Resolved,* That a committee be appointed to draught an address to the Governor for the removal of Thomas Cooper Esquire from the office of President Judge of the courts in the eighth judicial district of Pennsylvania." In accordance with above resolution, Judge Cooper was removed by Governor Snyder. Mr. Cooper was a man of letters, and of attainments well qualified to creditably fill any station in life. His overbearing temper, the unrestraining of which involved him in this disgrace was probably the only cause of complaint. The liberty-loving Democracy of the Susquehanna, could not brook such arrogance from an aristocratic Englishman and his judicial decapitation followed.

The following testimonial as to his worth and attainments, written fifty years after his removal from office, probably unveils the whole secret of his persecutions, in the claim that he lived in advance of the age. Had Judge Cooper presided on the bench of Northumberland in the last three decades of the nineteenth century instead of the first, the same characteristics which marked him as a tyrant then, would enlist in his behalf the encomiums of all law-abiding citizens of his judicial district. Mr. Pearce in his admirable history of Luzerne County says. Thomas Cooper succeeded Jacob Rush as President Judge of this district in August term 1806. Mr. Cooper was born in England and came to Northumberland County, soon after Dr. Priestley. He practiced law in Luzerne County before his appointment as judge. He was a man of learning and of sprightly imagination. He was in advance of the age in which he lived, in his knowledge of mineralogy and geology. He carried with him a hammer and acids and was testing the qualities of different specimens, and was believed, by some persons, to be impaired in intellect on that account. He was the firm friend of freedom, and his bold pen caused his imprisonment under the Alien and Sedition law. After his release, Governor McKean appointed him one of the commissioners to carry out the Compromise Law of 1799, and to his energetic action were doubtless due the quiet and harmony, that speedily ensued in the long troubled and unhappy valley of Wyoming. He was impeached and wrote a pamphlet in his defense, which perfectly demolished the whimsical book that was offered in evidence against him at his trial. He died in South Carolina in 1839, greatly respected as a gentleman and scholar.

JOHN BOURNE.

This gentleman is the present Chief Burgess of the borough of Sunbury. He was born in Germantown, Pa., June 10th, 1822. He was left fatherless at the age of seven. When about sixteen, he was apprenticed to the machinist's trade, for which he possessed a special talent.

In 1842, the family located in Sunbury, and young Bourne found employment at his trade in the machine-shops of the Danville and Reading Railroad Company, until 1850. He then returned to Sunbury, and superintended the erection of the foundry and machine-shops of E. Y. Bright, and filled the position of foreman in the same, till 1853. From this time, until 1857, he had charge of the steamboat Susquehanna, that plied on the river, between Northumberland and the Shamokin Dam. He there became engineer upon what was then known as the Philadelphia and Sunbury Railroad, between the latter place and Mt. Carmel. Upon the completion of the Northern Central Railway, in 1858, he engaged with that company, and ran the first passenger train between Williamsport and Lock Haven, and was retained on the same road after it had passed into the hands of the Sunbury and Erie Company. In the Spring of 1863, he returned to the employ of the Northern Central Railway Company, and remained in the same until 1874. He won the reputation of being one of the most reliable and safest engineers on the line, and during an experience of some twenty years as engineer, there occurred no serious injury to any passenger or employee.

In March, 1848, he married Miss Charlotte, daughter of Daniel Baldy, of Sunbury. His family consists of four sons and three daughters.

Mr. Bourne was educated in the Henry Clay school of politicians, and is a staunch member of the Republican party. In February, 1875, he was placed in the responsible position he now occupies as Chief Burgess, and is filling the same with honor.

For many years, also, he has been an influential member of the Town Council. Mr. Bourne is a man of strong convictions and of strict integrity; speaks what he means, and does not hesitate, when necessary, to give expression to his opinions.

REV. JOHN J. REIMENSNYDER, A. M.

This gentleman was born in Augusta County, Va., June 2d, 1812, and was educated in the schools of the South. He received the degree of A. M., from Roanoke College, Va., and, at the age of twenty, was ordained as a minister of the Lutheran Church, and continued such for a period of twenty-two years.

In 1851, he came to Pennsylvania, and was pastor of the Lutheran congregation, in Milton, till April 1st, 1854, when he resigned on account of a severe affection of the throat.

On June 1st, 1854, he was elected the first County School Superintendent of Northumberland County, and in 1857, was honored with a re-election and an increase of salary.

These two terms of service embraced six years.

In 1860 and 1862, he received the nomination for Congress from the Democratic County Conventions, but each time conceded the same to one of the adjoining counties of the district.

In 1863, he was elected Prothonotary of Northumberland County, and served two terms—six years in all.

He subsequently turned his attention to the law, and was for a time under the instruction of the Hon. Alexander Jordan, before whom he was examined for admission to the bar, on March 14th, 1876. Of his preparation for this position, Judge Jordan asserts that Mr. Reimensnyder passed the most brilliant examination of any candidate for the bar, that he ever had before him during his experience of twenty years on the bench. Though somewhat late in life, Mr. Reimensnyder, nevertheless, has entered upon the profession of the law with the decided advantages of a liberal culture, and an extended literary experience, which, coupled with a thorough legal preparation are promising omens of his professional success.

When Mr. Reimensnyder first entered on the duties of County School Superintendent, he had much to contend with that is not experienced by school officers of the present day. But, undaunted by opposition, he addressed himself to his work in good earnest. He held institutes in the principal towns, delivered educational addresses in various parts of the County, and stirred up the people by articles in the county papers, and also in the *Pennsylvania School Journal,* some of which were necessarily of a controversial nature.

On May 3d, 1838, Mr. Reimensnyder married Miss Susan M. Brynn, of Augusta County, Va., and has a family of eight children. The oldest son, Cornelius, is an Attorney in Toledo, Ohio. Junius B., is a Lutheran pastor, in Savannah, Georgia; and John Milton is pastor of the Lutheran Society, in Lewistown, Pa. The fourth son, George B. Reimensnyder, was Deputy Prothonotary for his father during the latter's second term. In April, 1871, he entered the Recorder's office as Clerk, and in December, 1872, was promoted to Deputy Recorder, and held the office till April 1st, 1876, when he resigned for the purpose of completing his studies for admission to the bar, for which he will be well fitted by his long experience in those county offices, as well as by his acknowledged talent for the profession.

The youngest son, Millard Fillmore, is in the Drug business in Coatesville, Pa.

PROF. WM. M. BOAL.

This young gentleman is the present Superintendent of the Public Schools, of Northumberland, Pa. He was born in Centre County, this State, July 25th, 1848. When he was eight years of age, his father's family moved from Pennsylvania to Johnson County, Iowa, where they still reside.

In 1863, young Boal returned to Pennsylvania, spent a couple of years at the Academy, in Milton, and about a year at the Bloomsburg Normal School, after which he entered Lafayette College, at Easton, Pa. He was not able, however, on account of pecuniary considerations, to complete the college course, having been, since the age of fifteen, dependent upon his own efforts for support.

Accordingly, in 1872, he entered the teacher's profession, taking charge, for a year, of the District Normal School, in Columbia County. This was followed by a two years' principalship of the Academy, at McEwensville.

In the Spring of 1875, Prof. Boal was brought forward by his friends, as candidate for County School Superintendent, and though his name was urgently pressed, the Professor modestly declined the proffered compliment.

In the Autumn of the same year, he became the Superintendent of the Public Schools of Sunbury, and in the Summer of 1876, was called to the position which he now occupies in Northumberland. Of this change, the *Northumberland County Democrat*, published at Sunbury, very appropriately says:

"We very much regret that he is going to leave us. He has been with us but one year, and in that short time our schools have attained a much higher grade than at any time in the past. His strict discipline, always administered with the utmost impartiality, and his thorough methods of instruction, have gained for him many warm friends among those of our community who appreciate education and are capable of judging and appreciating the merits of a teacher. He is a christian gentleman and a thorough classical scholar. We congratulate the Board of Directors for their eminently wise selection, and the citizens of Northumberland for having a Board of Directors who seek to serve so well the interests of their constituents."

DANIEL M. SCHWARTZ.

The subject of this notice is the Clerk of Commissioners of Northumberland County, Pa.

He was born in this County, on the 24th day of July, 1830. He was reared upon a farm, and enjoyed only the limited facilities of the ordinary Winter term of the early-day common-school. By improving such advantages as he had, however, he fitted himself to teach, and, at the age of sixteen, taught a Winter school, in the vicinity of his home. For quite a number of years subsequent, he employed his Winters in the same manner, teaching in Schuylkill, Montour, Dauphin, and Northumberland Counties.

Being of a mathematical turn of mind, he turned his attention to surveying, in which he was more or less engaged for some twelve years.

In 1858, he was elected Justice of the Peace, of Jordan township, has been re-elected each term since, and still holds the position, which fact is a gratifying testimonial to his popularity, as public magistrate.

On November 12th, 1854, he was married to Miss Susanna Coleman, daughter of Solomon Coleman, of Schuylkill County, Pa. His family consists of two daughters.

In 1872, he was appointed Clerk to the Board of Commissioners, of Northumberland County, and held the office one year, when he was succeeded by an occupant of a different political complexion.

In 1875, he was again appointed to the position which he now occupies.

'Squire Schwartz is a genial, accommodating gentleman, and a good citizen.

PROF. SAUL SHIPMAN.

This gentleman was born in Northumberland County, Pa., January 4th, 1844. Reared to labor from his early boyhood, he had but few educational advantages.

In August, 1862, when about eighteen years of age, and weighing only one hundred and three-and-a-half pounds, he entered the army as a volunteer for nine months' service. After his discharge, at the end of this term, being in too delicate health for hard labor, he took a preparatory collegiate course, in Freeburg Academy, under the instruction of Professor Wm. H. Dill, but his limited means prevented him from going further.

In 1864, he commenced his pedagogical career—in which he has become very prominent—by taking charge of a public school in his own district.

In 1869, he was elected County School Superintendent of Northumberland County, and re-elected in 1872, serving six years in all. In this position he made a very efficient officer. Characterized as a hard worker, he followed up what he undertook with an energy and perseverance worthy of imitation. Punctual in all his appointments, he allowed nothing to interrupt their fulfillment, but frequently walked miles to fulfil engagements. He has the reputation of having been the most efficient examining officer that ever filled the position of School Superintendent of this County; also, the credit of having held the best series of Institutes ever held in the County.

By his thorough course he greatly elevated the grade of certificates. In the Summer of 1870, he conducted a Normal School at Shamokin—the first movement of the kind in this section of the country—which proved a gratifying success.

The annual reports prepared by him are concise, pithy, suggestive, and out-spoken documents, and form a valuable contribution to the county school literature.

Under his administration, all the so-called non-accepting districts wheeled into the educational ranks, and some of them now have excellent schools.

Mr. Shipman is an independent thinker, and very positive in his opinions and actions, and too conscientious to be justly called a time-server.

HENRY E. DAVIS.

This enterprising young gentleman is a brother of J. K. Davis, Jr., just noticed, and second son of James K. Davis, of Selinsgrove. He was born in that place, June 7th, 1845, and educated in the Selinsgrove Missionary Institute.

At the age of twenty he began a business career, to which he has since devoted himself. His first experience was a two years' clerkship in a store in his native town. This was followed by a position as salesman in the New York Branch Empire Mercantile House, in Meadville.

In 1867, he entered the First National Bank, of Sunbury, where, for some two years, he served in the capacity of clerk. At the expiration of this time, he was compelled to relinquish this position on account of ill health.

In 1871, he became the representative of Hall Brothers & Company, sole sale-agents of the Mineral Railroad and Mining Company, and also of the Lykens' Valley Coal Company, which position he still occupies.

On October 13th, 1869, he was married to Miss Haas, daughter of Henry Haas, Esq., proprietor of the Central Hotel, in Sunbury. This public house is one of the best conducted and popular hotels in the State, and its proprietor is one of Sunbury's most worthy and highly esteemed citizens. Mr. Davis has a family of two daughters.

In 1876, he was a delegate to the Democratic State Convention, at Lancaster, and in the Autumn of the same year was nominated by the Democratic party of Northumberland County for the State Senate. He possesses fine natural abilities, and has already taken a prominent position among the sterling business men of the place. He is also a polished gentleman.

J. J. JOHN.

Born at Catawissa, Columbia County, Pennsylvania, October 13th, 1820. His father died a short time before his birth, hence he was born an orphan. His parents and relatives for generations back were connected with the Society of Friends. His mother is a Hicks, and closely connected with Elias and Edward Hicks, eminent members and preachers in this Society, and regarded as the founders of the branch known as "Hicksites." His ancestors came from Bucks and Chester counties. The Johns emigrated from Pembrokeshire, Wales, a short time after the first arrival of William Penn, and settled in Chester County.

The subject of this sketch was educated in the public schools, and completed his education at the academies of Coatesville, Chester County, and McEwensville, Northumberland County. During this period, the Summer months were occupied in working on a farm. He read medicine with Dr. Joseph C. Robins, and graduated at the Pennsylvania Medical College in 1853. After practising some months with his preceptor, he married Miss Elizabeth Krick, of Shamokin township, and moved to Shamokin. Here he became connected with the engineer corps under Kimber Cleaver, and remained until the Northern Central Railway was completed. He then became connected with Dr. G. S. Robins in the practice of medicine, and continued in this pursuit about a year. But the pursuit of medicine not being congenial to his nature, he abandoned it, and, with Joseph Bird, started a drug and variety store, under the firm of Bird & John. In 1856, he became interested in the coal business, under the name of Bird, Douty & John. They leased the Big Mountain Colliery, and commenced mining and shipping on a large scale for that day. During the panic of 1857, Mr. John retired from the drug and coal business. He had been a School Director for several years. He resigned this position to take one of the schools. Here as a teacher, he labored for some five years, most unceasingly, and acquired quite a reputation as an educator. All the text-books of the day were consulted, eminent teachers were interviewed, institutes were attended and no opportunity was lost that would improve him for the vocation that was as dear to him as his life. Whatever detraction may have assailed him, his zeal, capacity and fitness as a teacher have never been doubted. His health failing, he resigned his school in 1863, and took charge of the books of the Shamokin Furnace, a position that for some years had been filled by Franklin B. Gowen, now President of the Philadelphia and Reading Railroad. He remained here about two years, when he took charge of the books of Buck Ridge Colliery, and remained here about ten years. In 1874, he was nominated by the Republican party for the Legislature, and was elected by a majority of twenty-three in a county that gives from five hundred to seven hundred Democratic majority. His election was made by his home vote, his townsmen voting for him without regard to party.

Mr. John has recently opened a coal and insurance office, to which he intends devoting his attention. He has been a School Director for thirteen years, and from the organization of the borough to June 1st, 1876, has acted as District Superintendent. During his term great changes have been effected. The school term has been increased, schools have been graded, text-books made uniform, and school buildings erected that are a credit to the State. In all these movements he took an active part. His devotion to the public schools continued unabated, and if he has made a record on no other point, he has here, of which he justly feels proud. He is a strong advocate of compulsory education, and loses no opportunity to advocate its claims.

Through the request of Superintendent Wickersham, he was placed on the Committee of Education, a position for which he was exceedingly well fitted. Here he labored most faithfully. Last Winter he prepared a bill on compulsory education, and read it in place. Notwithstanding the majority of the House was opposed to the measure, he had it carried through his committee, reported to the House, passed first reading, and partly put through second reading, when its consideration was postponed on account of the lateness of the session. He is sanguine of final success, and purposes to renew the effort this Winter as a citizen.

Mr. John has been connected with the Shamokin *Herald*, since 1868, as coal editor, and has given the subject of coal statistics considerable attention. His tables are now regarded as authority at the State Department.

Mr. John is a plain, unassuming gentleman, who does not court notoriety. He is decided in his convictions, and would rather sacrifice his popularity than do violence to his sense of duty. He desires to do right, and, when convinced of his course, no threats or inducements will cause him to change. He is a man of strong likes and dislikes—true to his friends, but not unjust to his enemies.

ERRATUM.

GEORGE HILL.*

The gentleman whose name we have placed at the head of this biographical sketch, has been, for quite a number of years, a prominent member of the Sunbury bar. He is the youngest son of Daniel Hill, a highly-respectable farmer, who, a half-century since, died in Lycoming County, Pennsylvania.

In this County, the subject of this notice was born on the 3d of August, 1821. He was left fatherless at the age of six, and two years later, started out to earn his own living, his mother having no means with which to provide for her family of two sons and a daughter. His early history is that of a fatherless boy, struggling to make something of himself amid the manifold difficulties that gather around childhood and poverty. For a number of years he was employed at such farm labor as he could perform, attending school in the Winter months, during which time he worked for his board.

As further illustrative of the pecuniary straits through which he was compelled to pass, it may be mentioned that, when about twenty-one years of age, having just completed a three years' apprenticeship at coach-making in McEwensville, he started on foot for New Berlin, to secure a position as journeyman in his trade. The Susquehanna was reached, and young Hill, with a bundle of clothes thrown over his back, presented himself before the toll-collector of the bridge, at Milton, for passage. "*Two cents*" toll was demanded—but not even so much as one cent could be found either in bundle or pockets of this young pedestrian. After some little parleying, and a "promise to pay as soon as he could earn the money," the gate-keeper, seeing that the youth had an honest face, permitted him to pass. In due time the "two cents" toll was paid, and the bridge company suffered no loss on account of the leniency of their toll-collector.

After working two years in New Berlin, Mr. Hill taught school for a couple of Winters in Union County, and attended a select school in McEwensville during the Summer seasons, taught by Rev. Samuel S. Shedden. In 1845, he began the study of law under Governor James Pollock, of Milton, and finished in the office of A. Swineford, of New Berlin, Union County. During this time he was also engaged in teaching school, to obtain the means of prosecuting his studies. In May, 1848 he was admitted to the bar in New Berlin, and, spending a year more in teaching, located in Selinsgrove in the following Spring, where he practiced his profession for nine years.

During his residence here, Mr. Hill took a lively interest in the schools of the place, being for the greater part of the time a member of the Board of Education. In 1850, he was elected District Attorney in what was then Union, now Snyder County, and served three years. This was the first election for this office in the State, the position having been previously filled by appointment. In the Spring of 1858, he came to Sunbury, where he has since been engaged in the practice of his profession.

Mr. Hill belongs to the class of self-made men, among whom his faithful application to business entitle him to a front rank. One trait in his character, which stands out in prominent relief, is the caution with which he forms his opinions, and his firmness in the same. He will follow his convictions of right, regardless of all criticism. He possesses also the happy faculty of being very stern or very kind, just as occasion demands—a combination too rarely found.

To a clear head, sound judgment, strict integrity, and an indomitable perseverance, he superadds all the elements of a thorough gentleman. These qualities have long rendered him a safe counselor and an able attorney.

In politics, Mr. Hill was formerly a Whig, but is now a Democrat. He is, however, highly conservative in his views. He has made his profession his specialty, and has taken comparatively but little active interest in political affairs. He holds his religious connection with the Reformed Church, in which he has been for many years a leading member and an elder.

Mr. Hill has been twice married—first in Selinsgrove, on December 23th, 1848, to Miss Martha Bichlar, daughter of Samuel Bichlar, of Catawissa. Mrs. Hill became the mother of seven sons and two daughters, two of the former, and one of the latter, deceased. She died June 2d, 1870. Mr. Hill's present companion was Miss Sue E. Kirlin, daughter of A. J. Kirlin, of Middletown, Dauphin County, Pennsylvania, and the marriage occurred on June 6th, 1871.

* The Biographical Sketch of George Hill, part of which will be found on page 1[illegible], has been misplaced through mistake. We append the following complete.

www.ingramcontent.com/pod-product-compliance
Lightning Source LLC
Chambersburg PA
CBHW021834230426
43669CB00008B/962

* 9 7 8 3 3 3 7 3 7 2 9 6 5 *